Communications in Computer and Information Science 2405

Rationale

The CCIS series is devoted to the publication of proceedings of computer science conferences. Its aim is to efficiently disseminate original research results in informatics in printed and electronic form. While the focus is on publication of peer-reviewed full papers presenting mature work, inclusion of reviewed short papers reporting on work in progress is welcome, too. Besides globally relevant meetings with internationally representative program committees guaranteeing a strict peer-reviewing and paper selection process, conferences run by societies or of high regional or national relevance are also considered for publication.

Topics

The topical scope of CCIS spans the entire spectrum of informatics ranging from foundational topics in the theory of computing to information and communications science and technology and a broad variety of interdisciplinary application fields.

Information for Volume Editors and Authors

Publication in CCIS is free of charge. No royalties are paid, however, we offer registered conference participants temporary free access to the online version of the conference proceedings on SpringerLink (http://link.springer.com) by means of an http referrer from the conference website and/or a number of complimentary printed copies, as specified in the official acceptance email of the event.

CCIS proceedings can be published in time for distribution at conferences or as post-proceedings, and delivered in the form of printed books and/or electronically as USBs and/or e-content licenses for accessing proceedings at SpringerLink. Furthermore, CCIS proceedings are included in the CCIS electronic book series hosted in the SpringerLink digital library at http://link.springer.com/bookseries/7899. Conferences publishing in CCIS are allowed to use our online conference service (Meteor) for managing the whole proceedings lifecycle (from submission and reviewing to preparing for publication) free of charge.

Publication process

The language of publication is exclusively English. Authors publishing in CCIS have to sign the Springer CCIS copyright transfer form, however, they are free to use their material published in CCIS for substantially changed, more elaborate subsequent publications elsewhere. For the preparation of the camera-ready papers/files, authors have to strictly adhere to the Springer CCIS Authors' Instructions and are strongly encouraged to use the CCIS LaTeX style files or templates.

Abstracting/Indexing

CCIS is abstracted/indexed in DBLP, Google Scholar, EI-Compendex, Mathematical Reviews, SCImago, Scopus. CCIS volumes are also submitted for the inclusion in ISI Proceedings.

How to start

To start the evaluation of your proposal for inclusion in the CCIS series, please send an e-mail to ccis@springer.com

Marcin Paprzycki · Ankush Ghosh · Sanjoy Das
Editors

Advanced Communication and Intelligent Systems

Third International Conference, ICACIS 2024
New Delhi, India, May 16–17, 2024
Revised Selected Papers, Part I

Springer

Editors
Marcin Paprzycki
Systems Research Institute
Warsaw, Poland

Ankush Ghosh
Chandigarh University
Mohali, Punjab, India

Sanjoy Das
Indira Gandhi National Tribal University
Imphal, Madhya Pradesh, India

ISSN 1865-0929 ISSN 1865-0937 (electronic)
Communications in Computer and Information Science
ISBN 978-3-032-30989-1 ISBN 978-3-032-30990-7 (eBook)
https://doi.org/10.1007/978-3-032-30990-7

This Springer imprint is published by the registered company Springer Nature Switzerland AG
The registered company address is: Gewerbestrasse 11, 6330 Cham, Switzerland

Preface

This volume is a curated collection of exceptional papers from the 3rd International Conference on Advanced Communication and Intelligent Systems (ICACIS 2024), co-hosted by Jawaharlal Nehru University, New Delhi, India, Warsaw Management University, Poland, and ADSRS Education and Research Foundation, India. Held on May 16–17, 2024, at Jawaharlal Nehru University, New Delhi, India, the conference garnered an extraordinary response, attracting 1046 submissions globally. Rigorous single-blind peer reviews, averaging three per paper, culminated in an acceptance rate of approximately 20%. The selected papers, now published in this book, encapsulate the latest advancements in communication and intelligent systems.

The compendium delves into a spectrum of topics, including Wireless Communication, Artificial Intelligence, Machine Learning, Robotics, Automation, Data Science, IoT, and Smart Applications. It amalgamates both singular and interdisciplinary studies, offering a comprehensive overview of cutting-edge developments. This publication serves as an invaluable resource for academics and industry professionals alike.

We extend our heartfelt gratitude to all contributors whose submissions upheld the high standard of ICACIS 2024. The editors are indebted to each author and reviewer for their pivotal roles. The International Program Committee, session chairs, and Special Sessions Organizers were instrumental in enriching the conference with diverse papers and fostering engaging dialogues.

It is our aspiration that this compilation will enlighten and inspire professors, researchers, and graduate students across Computer Science Engineering, Electronics and Communication Engineering, and related fields, encompassing AI and IoT applications. We eagerly anticipate your participation in future ICACIS endeavors.

Marcin Paprzycki
Ankush Ghosh
Sanjoy Das

Organization

Organizing Committee

Chief Patron

Santishree Dhulipudi Pandit	Jawaharlal Nehru University, India

Patron

Satish Chandra Garkoti	Jawaharlal Nehru University, India

Co-patron

Zahid Raza	Jawaharlal Nehru University, India

General Chair

Marcin Paprzycki	Systems Research Institute, Polish Academy of Sciences, Poland

General Co-chair

Sanjoy Das	Indira Gandhi National Tribal University, Regional Campus Manipur, India

Organizing Chair

Buddha Singh	Jawaharlal Nehru University, India

Organizing Co-chair

Saurabh Kumar Sharma	Jawaharlal Nehru University, India

Technical Chairs

Ankush Ghosh	Chandigarh University, India
D. K. Lobiyal	Jawaharlal Nehru University, India
Satish Chand	Jawaharlal Nehru University, India

Publication Chairs

Monica Bianchini	University of Siena, Italy
Abhay Kumar Singh	Indian Institute of Technology Dhanbad, India
Pallavi Somvanshi	Jawaharlal Nehru University, India
Sushil Kumar	Jawaharlal Nehru University, India
Kunwer Singh Mathur	Jawaharlal Nehru University, India
Haider Raza	University of Essex, UK
Karan Singh	Jawaharlal Nehru University, India
Manish Gupta	University of Adelaide, Australia
Rajesh Kumar	Pennsylvania, USA
Priya Gupta	Jawaharlal Nehru University, India

Publicity Chairs

Prashant R. Nair	Amrita Vishwa Vidyapeetham, India
Mukesh Kumar Khandelwal	University of Delhi South Campus, India
Jyoti Singh Kirar	Jawaharlal Nehru University, India
Gajendra Pratap Singh	Jawaharlal Nehru University, India
Monika Jangra	Shri Vishwakarma Skill University, India
Rakesh Kumar Saroj	Jawaharlal Nehru University, India

Conference Chair

Rabindra Nath Shaw	Chandigarh University, India

Advisory Committee

Bimal K. Bose	University of Tennessee, USA
Muhammad H. Rashid	University of West Florida, USA
Muhammet Koksal	Haliç University, Turkey
Nasrudin Bin Abd Rahim	University of Malaysia, Malaysia
Hamid Ali Abed Al-Asadi	University of Basra, Iraq
Tarek Bouktir	University Ferhat Abbas of Setif, Algeria
Subramaniam Ganesan	Oakland University, USA
Claudio Moraga Roco	European Centre for Soft Computing, Spain
Suganthan P. N.	Nanyang Technological University, Singapore
Sanjib Kumar Panda	National University of Singapore, Singapore
Ralph Kennel	Technical University of Munich, Germany
Udaya Madawala	University of Auckland, New Zealand
Dylan Lu	University of Sydney, Australia
Yeap Peik Foong	Multimedia University, Malaysia
Terence Karran	University of Lincoln, UK
B. Chitti Babu	University of Nottingham Malaysia, Malaysia
Jyh-Horng Chou	Feng Chia University, Taiwan
Yurii Boreisha	Minnesota State University, USA
Herbert H.-C. Iu	University of Western Australia, Australia

Contents

AI/ML

About the Editors

Prof. Marcin Paprzycki received the MS degree from Adam Mickiewicz University, Poznań, Poland, the PhD degree from Southern Methodist University, Dallas, Texas, and the doctor of science degree from the Bulgarian Academy of Sciences, Sofia, Bulgaria. He is an associate professor with the Systems Research Institute, Polish Academy of Sciences. He is a senior member of the ACM, a senior fulbright lecturer, and an IEEE Computer Society distinguished visitor. He has contributed to more than 500 publications and was invited to the program committees of more than 800 international conferences.

Prof. Ankush Ghosh is Senior member of IEEE, Fellow of IETE has received his Ph.D. (Engg.) degree from Jadavpur University, India in 2010. He was a research fellow of the Advanced Technology Cell- DRDO, Govt. of India. He was awarded National Scholarship by HRD, Govt. of India. He has outstanding research experiences and published 6 edited books; 4 from Springer & 2 from Elsevier; 3 National & 8 International patents and more than 120 research papers indexed in Scopus/Web of Science. He is serving as an editorial board member of several international journals including Chief Editor. He has more than 15 years of experience in teaching, research as well as industry. His UG and PG teaching assignments include Microprocessor and microcontroller, AI, IOT, Embedded and real time systems etc. He has delivered Keynote/Invited lecture in a number of international seminar/conferences, refreshers courses, and FDPs. He has guided a large number of M.Tech and Ph.D. students. Dr. Ghosh is an active member of IEEE and organized a number Seminars and workshops in association with IEEE. He is an editor & organizing committee member of the Conference series GUCON, ICCCA, ICEEE, ICACIT. He is a He is a Start-up India Mentor and Global Startup Advisor of Wadhwani NEN. He has reviewed and mentored more than 50 start-ups. He has received award for contributing in Innovate India programme from AICTE- DST, Govt. of India in 2019 and 2020. He has received an appreciation award from AICTE, DST, TI, IIMB, NSRCEL, and myGOV for fostering students to strengthen the ecosystem bridging Government, Academia, and Industry in the year 2021.

Prof. Sanjoy Das is currently working as Professor, Department of Computer Science, Indira Gandhi National Tribal University (A Central Government University), Amarkantak, M.P. (Manipur Campus), India. He received his Ph.D. in Computer Science from Jawaharlal Nehru University, New Delhi, India. Before joining IGNTU, he has worked as Associate Professor, School of Computing Science and Engineering, Galgotias University, India, July 2012 to September 2017, and also, as Assistant Professor G. B. Pant Engineering College, Uttarakhand, and Assam University, Silchar, from 2001 to 2008. His current research interest includes Mobile Ad hoc Networks and Vehicular Ad hoc Networks, Distributed Systems, Data Mining. He has published numerous papers in international journals and conferences including IEEE and Springer.

AI/ML

Enhancing Classification of Leukemia Diagnosis with Transfer Learning Models

Hemant Tharwani(✉) and Anil Mokhade

Department of Computer Science and Engineering Department, Visvesaraya National Institute of Technology, Nagpur, Maharashtra, India
hemant.th99@gmail.com

Abstract. In the category of most widely spread blood cancer is B-ALL (B-cell acute lymphoblastic leukemia). For its diagnosis, the patient must go through tests that may have side effects or are too expensive. Apart from human error, the analysis of images by the lab hematologist has disadvantages. With the advancement in computation and AI techniques, we aim to solve this problem using deep learning techniques. We used two Transfer Learning CNN techniques, Xception and MobileNetV2, to compare and ensure the compatibility of such models so an application (mobile or web-based) can be designed for use in the medical field. Both MobileNetV2 and Xception architectures were successful in accurately classifying leukemia subtypes, achieving test accuracies of up to 100% and 99.67%, respectively. Model training is conducted using optimized hyperparameters, including a batch size of 32, learning rate of 0.0001, and 20 epochs, facilitating efficient convergence and model generalization. Since the dataset obtained contains other characteristics (erythrocytes or plasma) irrelevant to the study, a segmentation method was used to segment the area necessary for research and fine-tune the model. By using the Mean shift clustering algorithm, we could get segmented images that remove the unnecessary components by doing an analysis & comparison of two models (Xception, MobileNetv2) followed by adding a mask. The model concluded that Deep Learning Techniques are a reliable tool and should be used by clinical specialists or hematologists to make decisions in blood cancer cases to minimize the need for biopsy or other acute tests and decrease the diagnosis time for finding the B-ALL stage. Leveraging state-of-the-art transfer learning architectures, including MobileNetV2 and Xception, we conduct a comprehensive analysis to optimize model performance and efficiency.

Keywords: Acute Lymphoblastic Leukemia · Deep Learning · Convolutional Neural Network · Segmentation · Xception · MobileNetV2 · Transfer Learning

1 Introduction

In medical science, the role of deep learning and artificial intelligence plays a significant role in the detection of acute diseases which was not possible before. It has totally changed the diagnosis method and reduced the time duration for the effective treatment of the patients. Acute Lymphoblastic Leukemia (b-ALL) is one of the widespread blood

M. Paprzycki et al. (Eds.): ICACIS 2024, CCIS 2405, pp. 3–17, 2027.
https://doi.org/10.1007/978-3-032-30990-7_1

cancer in children and adults [15]. Manual diagnosis has risks of bleeding, trauma to neighboring structures, anxiety, or shock to the patients are some of the side effects. [1] It is most common in children and is also called acute childhood leukemia. Approximately 6,000 cases of this disease are diagnosed annually in the United States alone. It is the most frequent cause of cancer death before 20 years of age [10]. If not treated timely, it can take life in months [2, 3]. Thus, early diagnosis is critical for treatment. This study conducts not only binary but also multi-class classification of subtypes of lymphoblastic cells which is categorized into three stages. Sometimes, hematogenous or Benign B-ALL are mistaken for cancerous cells because of their similar appearance & cellular diversity [4]. Thus, it is hard for hematologists to differentiate between hematogenous and malignant lymphoblasts when examined through a microscope [4]. Thus, creating such a model which is trained on previous studies and can predict the results will be very much helpful for earlier treatment of acute disease.

This study suggests a new way to diagnose and classify B-ALL using a deep learning approach. We introduce a fine-tuned CNN model so it can be used to make web or mobile applications that can be used further in a laboratory environment.

In this chapter we did intensive study on mobileNetV2 and Xception transfer learning models for leukemia classification. We processed the inputs in depth using some steps such as segmentation and augmentation methods to make them more suitable for training models. Additionally, we had to customize these transfer learning model architectures to match with the details of Leukaemia classification. We wanted to create strong models that could differentiate between various subtypes of leukaemia accurately through thorough experiments and evaluations thus improving diagnosis results as well as care for patients. We therefore took a big leap in fighting against cancer by integrating current technology into our systems which can be used for early detection and treatment strategies against different types of this disease.

2 Methodology

In the pursuit of developing accurate classifiers for leukemia detection, one of the key considerations was the choice of neural network architecture [7]. While convolutional neural networks (CNNs) have shown promise in image classification tasks [6], our preliminary experiments revealed a significant challenge inherent in training CNNs from scratch, the vanishing gradient problem. The vanishing gradient problem occurs when gradients propagated backward through the network during training diminish in magnitude as they pass through multiple layers. This phenomenon often leads to slow convergence and suboptimal performance, particularly in deep architectures.

To mitigate the impact of the vanishing gradient problem and expedite the model training process, we opted to leverage transfer learning models instead of creating CNNs from scratch. Transfer learning involves utilizing pre-trained models trained on large-scale datasets, such as ImageNet, and fine-tuning them on smaller, domain-specific datasets. By leveraging the knowledge encoded in these pre-trained models, we aimed to overcome the challenges associated with training deep architectures from scratch while still benefiting from their powerful feature extraction capabilities.

The method we're suggesting involves using two Transfer Learning CNN deep-learning models to diagnose blood cancer automatically. These methods, MobileNetV2 and Xception, are designed to be efficient and practical for this task.

Dataset Collection: In our research, we use a dataset sourced from the Kaggle website, an online platform dedicated to data science. Kaggle provides access to medical imaging data for research and analysis. This dataset comprises 2990 microscopic blood images from patients suspected of having B-ALL (B-cell acute lymphoblastic leukemia). Expert hematologists and highly skilled laboratory personnel prepared and stained these blood samples. The dataset is divided into two major classes: benign and malignant Table 1. The first class, gentle, contains images of hematogones. These do not require chemotherapy and typically resolve on their own. Fig [1] gives the chart view of the dataset and its subclasses.

The second class, malignant, is further divided into three subtypes of malignant lymphoblasts, all related to B-ALL. **Malignant** (which includes different subtypes like Early Pre-b, Pre-b, and Pro-b) each representing distinct stages of leukemia progression. These subtypes represent various stages of leukemia development. We meticulously shuffled the data for our research to ensure unbiased and random distribution. These images were procured by a Zeiss camera which is a standard in labs.

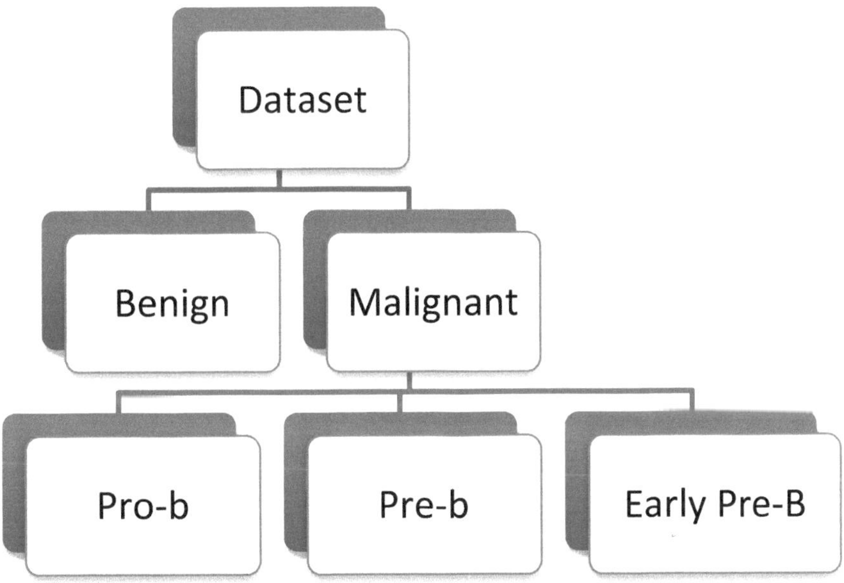

Fig. 1. Dataset Classification into sub-classes

1. **Data Preprocessing:** The process of preprocessing in ML-based models has a significant impact on the performance. Preprocessing involves various techniques that help get the input data ready. In this study, we incorporated three stages of data preprocessing.

Table 1. The local dataset of B-ALL and its subclass

Type	Classes	Samples	Image Dimension
Benign	Hematogones	394	1024X768
Malignant	Early Pre-B ALL Pre-B ALL Pro-B ALL	985 954 657 2990	1024X768 1024X768 1024X768

2. **Preparation:** We processed the dataset images originally in PNG or JPG formats. To do this, we converted these images into numeric arrays that represent pixels within the images. The inputs must have a specific size in the pre-trained network used in the research. In many transfer learning architectures, the dimensions of the input used is 224x224, and most research in medical field also use this dimension[15]. Therefore, for our research, we transformed the size of input images to meet this standard size of 224x224.
3. **Segmentation:** We aim to focus on parts of the images important for our machine-learning model. So, we remove irrelevant elements that could introduce noise and alter the learning process. We used a unique method and Mean-Shift [13] to separate blast cells from other components like erythrocytes and plasma. We achieved blast cell segmentation in Fig. 1 by employing a technique that depends on color intervals and color thresholding[11] (Fig. 2).

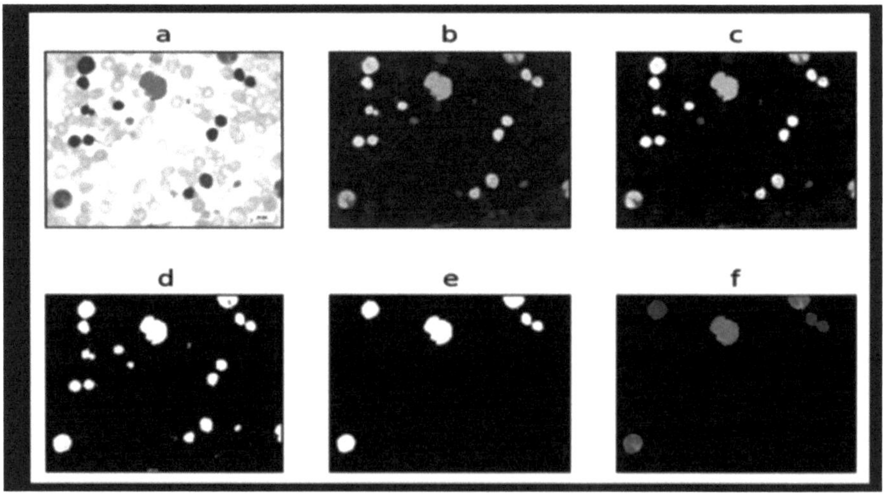

Fig. 2. Segmentation stages: a) RGB color space, b) LAB color space c) Mean-shift clustering d) Binary thresholding e) Cleaning methods & Mask generation f) applied the mask on the RGB original image

4. **Augmentation, Rescaling & Categorization:** Data augmentation is a crucial technique in machine learning, and it involves making modifications to the images to

enhance the count of training examples while retaining their meaningful and inherent information [11]. We introduced two types of transformations, i.e. vertical flipping and horizontal flipping. It involves flipping the images vertically and horizontally, simulating variations occurring in real-world data [12]. We also applied a technique called "pixel intensity normalization" that brought the values of the images into a standard interval, which ranges from 0 to 1[15]. After segmentation, rescaling & categorization, the research data underwent splitting (Table 2).

Table 2. Division of dataset samples into training, test and validation sets.

	Training Dataset	Testing Dataset	Validation Dataset	Data
Percentage(%) No. of paired samples	85 4843	5 299	10 539	100 5681

The dataset used Table 2 in this research comprises samples collected for the purpose of leukemia classification. The dataset is divided into three subsets: training, testing, and validation datasets, with corresponding percentages indicating the proportion of each subset relative to the total dataset size. The dataset includes a total of 5,843 paired samples, where each sample consists of medical imaging data and its corresponding leukemia subtype label.

Training Dataset: This subset comprises 85% of the total dataset, consisting of 4,843 paired samples. The training dataset is utilized for model training, where deep learning algorithms learn to extract relevant features from medical imaging data and classify leukemia subtypes based on these features.

Testing Dataset: The testing dataset accounts for 5% of the total dataset, containing 299 paired samples. This subset serves as an independent evaluation set to assess the generalization performance of the trained models. The models are evaluated on the testing dataset to determine their classification accuracy and performance metrics.

Validation Dataset: The validation dataset constitutes 10% of the total dataset, containing 539 paired samples. This subset is used for model validation and hyperparameter tuning, ensuring that the trained models generalize well to unseen data and optimizing model performance.

5. **Ethical Considerations:** We followed strict ethical rules to protect patient privacy and data confidentiality during the research process. We used datasets that didn't reveal anyone's identity. We follow well-known ethical guidelines like the Declaration of Helsinki [8] to ensure the study was conducted ethically.

3 Experimental Setup, Modelling and Analysis

3.1 Experimental Setup

This section offers detailed insights into the dataset, the experiments conducted, the process of training the model, and the validation of the model's performance.

- We took the Batch Size as 32 i.e one epoch consists of 32 training examples.
- We set 20 epochs for the training of the data.
- Learning rate is 0.0001 which gives the best result after fine tuning.
- Adam optimizer is used for training purpose. Categorical Cross entropy as loss function.
- On the validation set, we save the model when it achieves highest frequency.
- All the experiments were carried out using Google Colab, a platform for running Python code, along with the TensorFlow machine learning library

These hyperparameters were determined through a systematic exploration of different configurations, taking into account factors such as model convergence, classification accuracy, and computational efficiency.

The choice of a batch size of 32 strikes a balance between stochasticity and computational efficiency, enabling efficient gradient updates while maintaining diversity in the mini-batch samples. A learning rate of 0.0001 was found to facilitate stable training and prevent overshooting during optimization. We opted for 20 epochs to allow sufficient time for the models to converge to a stable solution without risking overfitting.

Additionally, we employed the Adam optimizer due to its effectiveness in optimizing deep neural networks and its adaptive learning rate mechanism, which adjusts the learning rates for different parameters dynamically based on the gradients' magnitude. Categorical cross-entropy was chosen as the loss function, suitable for multi-class classification tasks, as it penalizes the divergence between the predicted probability distributions and the true labels.

By fine-tuning these hyperparameters, we aimed to ensure that our models were trained under optimal conditions, maximizing their potential for accurate leukemia classification.

3.2 Proposed Models

Convolutional Neural Network Structure: One of the primary characteristics we looked for in our model was their efficiency and consumption of fewer computational resources. To achieve this, we considered two models: Xception and MobileNetV2.

3.2.1 Xception

It is a better version of traditional convolutional neural network (CNN) architectures because it uses depthwise separable convolutions in its novel convolutional block structure. The architecture called Xception was proposed for image classification tasks and has demonstrated excellent results on ImageNet benchmarks. It combines separable convolutions, global average pooling as well as fully connected layers (Fig. 3).

Xception (Functional)

- This is the base Xception model, which typically consists of convolutional and pooling layers. It's designed for deep learning tasks involving image classification and other computer vision tasks.

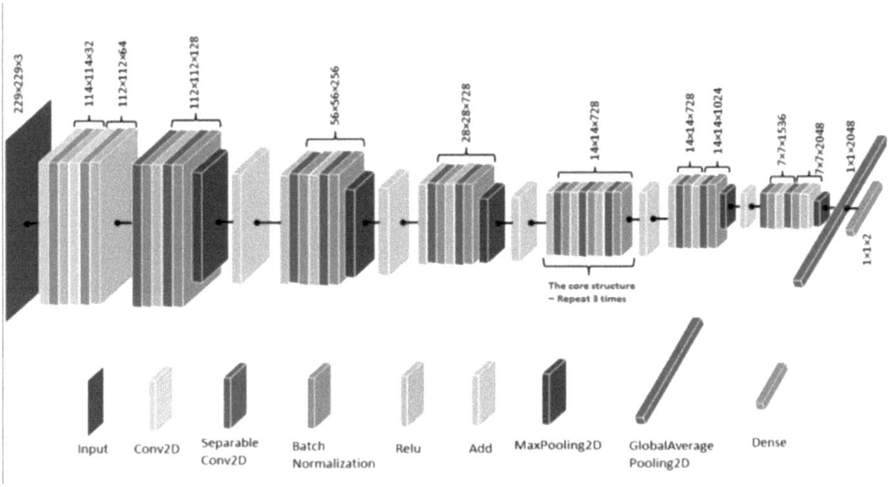

Fig. 3. This modified Xception model consists of several layers:

Table 3. Modified Xception Architecture for classification of B-ALL

Layer Type	Output Shape	Parameter
Xception (functional)	(None, 7, 7, 2048)	20861480
(GlobalAveragePooling2D)	(None, 2048)	0
Dense_1	(None, 128)	262272
Dropout-5(Dropout)	(None, 128)	0
Dense-2	(None, 4)	516

- Output Shape: (None, 7, 7, 2048): This indicates that the output of the Xception model is a 4D tensor with a shape of (batch_size, height, width, channels), where None represents a variable batch size, and the height and width are 7x7 pixels with 2048 channels.

GlobalAveragePooling2D

- This layer performs global average pooling on the feature maps produced by the Xception model.
- Global average pooling reduces each feature map to a single value by taking the average of all values in the feature map.
- This operation results in a fixed-length vector regardless of the input image size.
- The output shape after this layer is (None, 2048), indicating a vector with 2048 elements
- Output Shape: (None, 2048): After global average pooling, the spatial dimensions are collapsed, resulting in a 1D tensor with 2048 elements.

Dense_1

- This is a fully connected (dense) layer with 128 units.
- It takes the output of the global average pooling layer as input.
- The number of parameters in this layer is 262,272, which is calculated based on the number of input units (2048) multiplied by the number of output units (128), plus biases

Dropout-5 (Dropout)

- Dropout is a regularization technique used to prevent overfitting in neural networks.
- In this case, it randomly sets a fraction of input units to zero during training to prevent them from co-adapting.
- The dropout rate is not explicitly mentioned here, but it's common to see rates like 0.5 or 0.3.
- The output shape remains the same as the input shape (None, 128).

Dense-2

- This is the final fully connected layer with 4 units, which corresponds to the number of classes in the classification task.
- It takes the output of the Dropout layer as input.
- The number of parameters in this layer is 516, calculated similarly to Dense_1.

Parameter Count

- The Xception model contributes 20,861,480 parameters.
- The first dense layer contributes 262,272 parameters.
- The second dense layer contributes 516 parameters.
- Dropout layers typically don't contribute parameters since they are used only during training for regularization.

3.2.2 MobileNetV2

MobileNetV2 is the latest version in MobileNet series which is a family of neural network architecture. MobileNetV2, like its predecessors, is an efficient model that takes limited computational resources and is suitable for applications like IoT, mobile devices and real-time applications (Fig. 4).

The architecture of the MobileNetV2 model used for leukemia classification is outlined in Table 4. This model comprises several layers designed to extract features from input images and make predictions about their leukemia subtype.

The MobileNetV2 architecture begins with a base model trained on the ImageNet dataset, which is a large-scale dataset comprising millions of images across thousands of classes. This pre-trained base model serves as a feature extractor, capturing high-level features from the input images.

The GlobalAveragePooling2D layer reduces the spatial dimensions of the feature maps produced by the base model, resulting in a fixed-length vector representation for each image. This vector contains abstracted features that are then passed through a series of fully connected layers for classification.

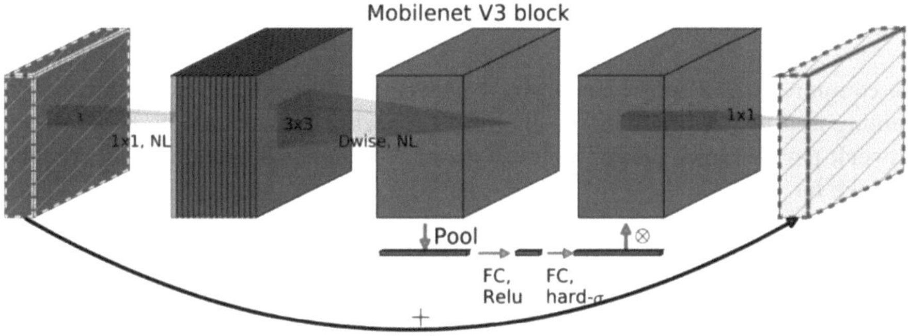

Fig. 4. MobileNet V2

Table 4. Modified MobileNetV2 Architecture for classification of B-ALL

Layer Type	Output Shape	Parameter
MobileNetV2(functional)	(None, 7, 7, 2048)	2422468
(GlobalAveragePooling2D)	(None, 2048)	0
Dense_1	(None, 128)	163968
Dropout-5(Dropout)	(None, 128)	0
Dense-2	(None, 4)	516

The Dense_1 layer consists of 128 units, facilitating the transformation of the feature vector into a lower-dimensional space while preserving important discriminative information. Dropout regularization is applied to the output of this layer to prevent overfitting by randomly deactivating a fraction of units during training.

Finally, the Dense-2 layer comprises four units, corresponding to the four leukemia subtypes targeted for classification. This layer produces probability distributions over the classes using the softmax activation function, enabling the model to make predictions about the input images' leukemia subtype. MobileNetV2 architecture leverages transfer learning to harness knowledge from the pre-trained base model while incorporating additional layers tailored to the specific requirements of the leukemia classification task.

3.2.3 Metric Evaluation

Metric Evaluation: In this study, we focused on three key metrics: Specificity, recall and accuracy. These metrics determine how well the model performs in its task [5]. Below are the parameters to calculate these metrics:

$$\textbf{Accuracy} = (\mathrm{TP} + \mathrm{TN})/(\mathrm{TP} + \mathrm{TN} + \mathrm{FP} + \mathrm{FN})$$

$$\textbf{Specificity} = \mathrm{TN}/(\mathrm{TN} + \mathrm{FP})$$

$$\textbf{Recall} = \mathrm{TP}/(\mathrm{TP} + \mathrm{FN})$$

4 Results and Discussion

We compare two different pre-trained networks to see which works best on the training and test datasets. After fine-tuning specific parameters, we evaluate the network performance using the test dataset. We aim to select the most effective network for the task.

In Fig. 5, we present the learning curve of our selected model during the training phase, depicting the model's performance on both the training and validation datasets as a function of the number of epochs. Our proposed model exhibits a notable trend: as the number of epochs increases, the model demonstrates a reduction in error and an improvement in accuracy when presented with new validation data. **Both the models used in this study did a great job of classifying blood cell images.** Table 4 presents the performance metrics of the Xception and MobileNetV2 models trained for leukemia classification using the optimized hyperparameters described in the Experimental Setup section. Both models were trained for 20 epochs with a batch size of 32 and a learning rate of 0.0001. The validation accuracy, training accuracy, and test accuracy were computed to evaluate the models' performance.

The Xception model achieved remarkable results across all metrics, with a validation accuracy of 98.89%, training accuracy of 99.75%, and perfect test accuracy of 100%. These results demonstrate the effectiveness of the Xception architecture in accurately classifying leukemia samples.

Similarly, the MobileNetV2 model also performed admirably, achieving a validation accuracy of 97.77%, training accuracy of 99.88%, and test accuracy of 99.67%. Although slightly lower than the Xception model, these results underscore the robustness and generalization capability of the MobileNetV2 architecture for leukemia classification tasks.

The results show that the blood cancer detection system effectively classifies blood cell images [9]. **The high accuracy, strong recall, and precision values demonstrate the model's ability to distinguish between cancerous and normal blood cells.**

Table 5. Performance of Transfer Learning Model

Feature Extractor	Epochs	Batch Size	Learning Rate	Validation Accuracy	Training Accuracy	Test Accuracy
Xception	20	32	0.0001	98.89	99.75	100
MobileNetV2	20	32	0.0001	97.77	99.88	99.67

From Fig. 5 we conclude the following below points:

1. Training and Validation Loss:
   - The left graph shows the **training loss** (red line) and **validation loss** (green line) over **epochs** (x-axis).
   - As the number of epochs increases, both training and validation loss decrease.

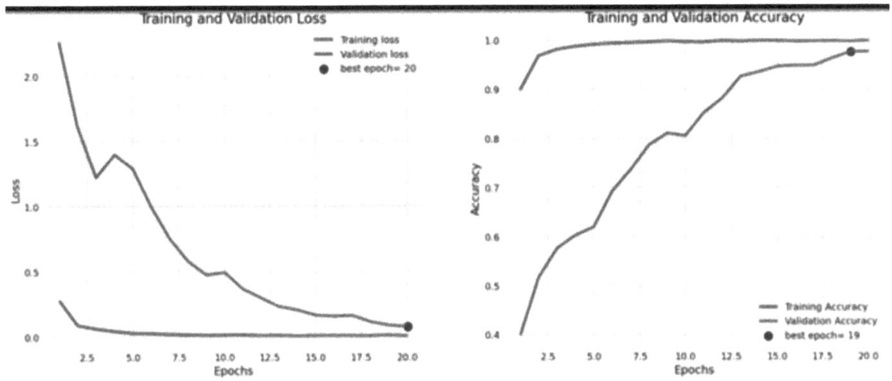

Fig. 5. Xception after training. We sec after 20 Epochs the model converged with training accuracy and loss of 100% and 0.0023, respectively.

- The best epoch, where both losses are minimized, is indicated by a blue dot at epoch 8.

2. Training and Validation Accuracy:

- The right graph displays **training accuracy** (red line) and **validation accuracy** (green line) over epochs.
- Training accuracy increases significantly with epochs.
- Validation accuracy also improves but at a slower rate.
- The best epoch for accuracy, marked by a blue dot, is at epoch 6.

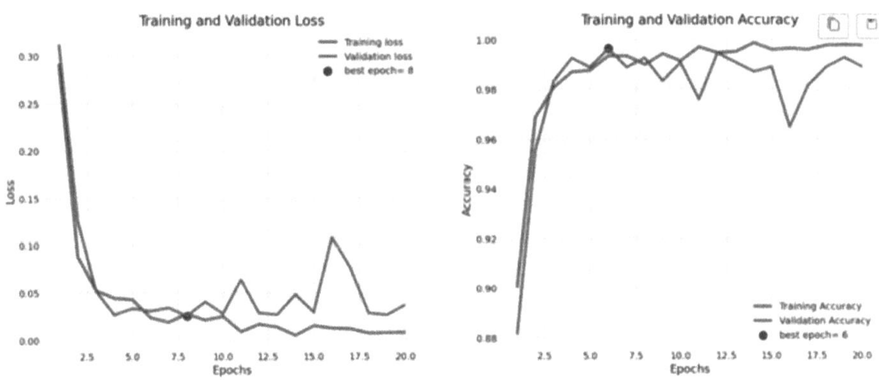

Fig. 6. MobileNetV2 after learning. We see after 20 Epochs the model converged with training accuracy and loss of 99.67% and 0.02 respectively.

From Fig. 6 we conclude the following below points:

3. Training and Validation Loss:

- The left graph shows the **training loss** (green line) and **validation loss** (red line) over **epochs** (x-axis).
- As the number of epochs increases, both training and validation loss decrease.
- The best epoch, where both losses are minimized, is indicated by a blue dot at epoch 20.

4. Training and Validation Accuracy:

- The right graph displays **training accuracy** (green line) and **validation accuracy** (red line) over epochs.
- Training accuracy increases significantly with epochs.
- Validation accuracy also improves but at a slower rate.
- The best epoch for accuracy, marked by a blue dot, is at epoch 19.

Efficient Model Selection

Selecting an appropriate model architecture is crucial for achieving optimal performance in tasks such as leukemia classification. In our research, we conducted a thorough analysis to identify the most efficient model architecture for this specific task. Leveraging insights gained from experimentation and evaluation, we arrived at a decision to employ transfer learning models, namely MobileNetV2 and Xception, for our leukemia classification task.

Our choice of transfer learning models was driven by several factors, prominently including the consideration of computational efficiency and performance. As demonstrated by the results presented in Table 5, both MobileNetV2 and Xception architectures exhibit remarkable efficiency in terms of model size, parameter count, and computational resources required for training and inference.

The MobileNetV2 architecture, with a total parameter count of 2,422,468, offers a lightweight yet powerful solution for feature extraction and classification. Its streamlined design, characterized by depth-wise separable convolutions, enables efficient utilization of resources without compromising performance. Additionally, the utilization of a GlobalAveragePooling2D layer further reduces the model's complexity by generating fixed-length feature vectors, facilitating efficient training and inference.

Similarly, the Xception architecture, with a parameter count of 20,861,480, showcases exceptional performance while maintaining computational efficiency. By leveraging depth-wise separable convolutions and the inception module architecture, Xception achieves superior feature extraction capabilities with a relatively modest parameter count. The incorporation of a GlobalAveragePooling2D layer further enhances computational efficiency by condensing feature maps into compact representations suitable for classification.

Through rigorous experimentation and analysis, we observed that both MobileNetV2 and Xception models offer a compelling balance between computational efficiency and classification performance for leukemia classification. Their ability to efficiently extract discriminative features from input images while maintaining high accuracy underscores their suitability for real-world applications where computational resources are often limited.

Efficient Model Selection: After training with the training dataset and testing on the test dataset after 20 epochs Figs. 5 and 6, the metrics of pre-trained models were obtained under the same scenerio. Table 3 displays the evaluation of the training and test datasets

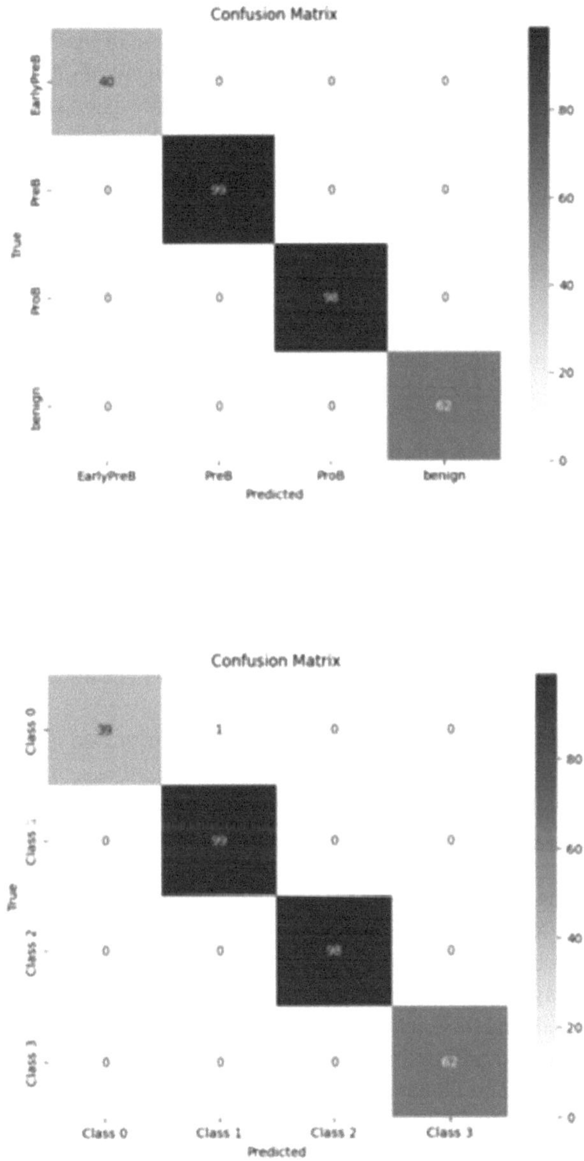

Fig. 7. A) Confusion Matrix Xception B) Confusion Matrix MobileNetV2

for the two pre-trained models. Given that Xception has the highest efficiency, we can use it to make a web-based application for use in the medical field.

Confusion Matrix: Fig. 6 Shows the confusion matrix for the selected model Xception. It summarizes the model's predictions and how they compare to the actual outcomes [14].

The confusion matrix, a fundamental tool for evaluating classification models, provides insights into the performance of the Xception and MobileNetV2 models in distinguishing between leukemia subtypes. In Fig. 6A In the case of the Xception model, the confusion matrix clearly identifies each class, demonstrating its ability to accurately classify leukemia subtypes, including Early Pre-b, with high precision and recall. Figure 6B MobileNetV2 model, a notable observation emerges: the model struggles to correctly classify samples belonging to the Early Pre-b subtype. But still the overall accuracy is close to the Xception Model (Fig. 7).

5 Conclusion

In our research, we've used advanced deep learning models called MobileNetV2 and Xception to detect and classify blood cancer, specifically leukemia. Our experiments showed that these models are really good at identifying different types of leukemia from medical images

Our research represents a significant contribution to the field of medical imaging and cancer diagnosis in several key aspects. using transfer learning models like MobileNetV2 and Xception has helped us overcome the difficulties of training deep neural networks from scratch. This method not only solves the issue of vanishing gradients but also speeds up the model development process, allowing for quicker iterations and experimentation.

We carefully adjusted the settings for training the MobileNetV2 and Xception models. By fine-tuning parameters like batch size (which is set to 32), learning rate (at 0.0001), and training for 20 epochs, we've achieved better accuracy in classifying data while keeping computational demands low

By integrating these models into our system, we've improved accuracy and gained valuable insights into different leukemia subtypes. This advancement has significant implications for healthcare, especially in blood cancer diagnosis. Automated analysis of medical images using these models can revolutionize cancer detection and treatment. With further validation, these algorithms could provide accurate diagnoses from small blood samples, ultimately benefiting patients. These models performed exceptionally well, with the Xception model achieving a perfect test accuracy of 100%, closely followed by the MobileNetV2 model at 99.67%.

The proposed system offers numerous advantages, including improved accuracy, detailed insights, adaptability, and enhanced patient outcomes. Harnessing the capabilities of Xception and addressing the limitations of the earlier system represents a significant step forward in detecting and classifying blood cancer. The results of this research open up new possibilities for improving healthcare, especially for patients with blood cancer, by using advanced technology to analyze medical images automatically. These algorithms have shown that they can detect blood cancer from a tiny sample of a patient's blood. When tested on datasets available to the public, this new model proved to be more accurate than the previously used methods.

References

1. Malempati, S., Joshi, S., Lai, S., Braner, D.A., Tegtmeyer, K.: Bone marrow aspiration and biopsy. N Engl J Med. **361**(15), 28 (2009)
2. Hunger, S.P., Mulligans, C.G.: Acute lymphoblastic leukemia in children. N Engl J Med. **373**(16), 1541–1552 (2015)
3. Behrendt, H., et al.: The significance of an isolated central nervous system relapse, occurring as first relapse in children with acute lymphoblastic leukemia. Cancer. **63**(10), 2066–2072 (1989)
4. Haworth, C., Heppleston, A.D., Jones, P.M., Campbell, R.H., Evans, D.I., Palmer, M.K.: Routine bone marrow examination in the management of acute lymphoblastic leukemia of childhood. J. Clin. Pathol. **34**(5), 483–485 (1981)
5. Shen, D., Wu, G., Suk, H.I.: Deep learning in medical image analysis. Annu. Rev. Biomed. Eng. **19**, 221–248 (2017)
6. Gupta, A., Sharma, P.: A review of machine learning techniques being used for blood cancer detection. Ann. Rom. Soc. Cell Biol. **25**(4), 7796–7811 (2021)
7. Ghaderzadeh, M., Asadi, F., Jafari, R., Bashash, D., Abolghasemi, H., Aria, M.: Deep convolutional neural network–based computer-aided detection system for COVID 19 using multiple lung scans: design and implementation study. J Med Internet Res. **23**, e27468 (2021)
8. World Medical Association: World medical association declaration of Helsinki: ethical principles for medical research involving human subjects. Jama. **310**(20), 2191–2194 (2013)
9. Tan, M., Le, Q.: Efficientnet: Rethinking model scaling for convolutional neural networks. In: Proceedings of the 36th International Conference on Machine Learning (ICML), pp. 6105–6114. PMLR (2019)
10. Campo, E., et al.: In: Swerdlow, S.H. (ed.) WHO Classification of Tumours of Haematopoietic and Lymphoid Tissues, vol. 2, p. 439. International agency for research on cancer, Lyon, France (2008)
11. Ayan, E., Ünver, H.M.: Data augmentation importance for classification of skin lesions via deep learning. In: 2018 Electric Electronics, Computer Science, Biomedical Engineerings, pp. 1–4. IEEE (2018)
12. Cano, E., Mendoza-Avilés, J., Areiza, M., Guerra, N., Mendoza-Valdés, J.L., Rovetto, C.A.: Multi skin lesions classification using fine-tuning and data-augmentation applying NASNet. PeerJ Comput. Sci. **7**, e371 (2021)
13. Bai, P.R., Liu, Q.Y., Li, L., Teng, S.H., Li, J., Cao, M.Y.: A novel region-based level set method initialized with mean shift clustering for automated medical image segmentation. Comput. Biol. Med. **43**(11), 1827–1832 (2013)
14. Beauxis-Aussalet, E., Hardman, L.: Visualization of confusion matrix for non-expert users. In: IEEE Conference on Visual Analytics Science and Technology (VAST)-Poster Proceedings, pp. 1–2 (2014)
15. Yeung, D.T.O., Osborn, M.P., White, D.L.: B-cell acute lymphoblastic leukaemia: Recent discoveries in molecular pathology their prognostic significance and a review of the current classification. Br. J. Haematol. **197**(1), 13–27 (2022)

Automatic Sleep Apnea Detection System Using ECG Signals

Md Shamshad Alam, Mohd Hasan(✉), and Omar Farooq

Department of Electronics Engineering, Z.H College of Engineering and Technology, Aligarh Muslim University, Aligarh, India 202002
mohd.hasan@amu.ac.in, omarfarooq@zhcet.ac.in

Abstract. Sleep apnea is a significant sleep disorder that causes frequent breathing interruptions during sleep, leading to reduced blood oxygen levels. Monitoring this condition is difficult and expensive and requires a sleep expert to inspect the long-duration data collected during sleep. Therefore, the primary objective of this work is to develop an automatic, more precise, and efficient sleep apnea detection system using ECG signals. In this study, four simple features are extracted and a robust machine-learning classifiers are employed to enhance detection accuracy. Our research includes both subject-specific and subject-independent results using the leave-one-out method. Evaluation of this work is based on utilizing ECG signals from the openly available St. Vincent's sleep apnea UCDDB database. Our approach outperforms recent works, with the best model achieving 97.52% accuracy using Ensemble (Bagged Trees), which is better than other studies by 2.42%, 8.62%, and 5.5%.

Keywords: Electrocardiogram (ECG) · Energy · Mobility · Kurtosis · skewness · UCDDB database

1 Introduction

Sleep apnea (SA) is a harmful respiratory disorder characterized by recurring breathing pauses of approximately 10-20 seconds during the sleep cycle. It may occur numerous times throughout the night and is caused by two main factors. The first cause is the collapse of soft tissues in the airway, particularly the throat area. The second cause is related to the brain's role in controlling the muscles responsible for maintaining an open airway. As a consequence of these interruptions, the level of oxygen supplied to the lungs decreases. This reduction in oxygen levels triggers the body's natural response to awaken from deep sleep, prompting the person to partially wake up to reopen their airway and resume normal breathing.

It affects around 15% of men and 5% of women [1]. The disorder is associated with a high risk of various health problems. In its initial stage, individuals with sleep apnea often experience poor sleep quality, leading to daytime sleepiness and fatigue, mood changes, and irregular heart rate, whereas prolonged exposure to these conditions can result in severe complications, including cardiovascular events, cognitive decline,

M. Paprzycki et al. (Eds.): ICACIS 2024, CCIS 2405, pp. 18–27, 2027.
https://doi.org/10.1007/978-3-032-30990-7_2

stroke, and even mortality [2]. The American Association of Sleep Medicine (AASM) finds SA as one of the top 10% of high-risk disorders leading to mortality [3]. Although treatments are available for Sleep apnea, still it remains undiagnosed and untreated in approximately 90% of affected individuals [1].

Cardiorespiratory polysomnography (PSG) is a standard method for diagnosing sleep apnea, involving monitoring various physiological parameters during sleep. However, manual analysis of PSG data is costly, laborious, and prone to human error. Automated methods employing machine learning and artificial intelligence are being explored to enhance accuracy and efficiency in diagnosing sleep apnea. Several research studies have focused on creating automated apnea detection, utilizing a variety of bio-signals, including EEG, ECG, EOG, and EMG [4]. Among these signals, ECG signals play a crucial role in identifying sleep apnea by monitoring heart rate variations, respiratory patterns, and arrhythmias during sleep.

In the past decade, researchers have introduced various methods to effectively identify and classify apnea and non-apnea events in patients using ECG signals. Bahrami et al. [5] evaluated deep-learning models for sleep apnea detection from single-lead ECG signals, with the hybrid CNN and LSTM network achieving an accuracy of 80.67%, sensitivity of 75.04%, and specificity of 84.13%. Nguyen et al. [6] proposed a method of feature extraction using a single-lead ECG and a Convolutional Neural Network (CNN) model, achieving the highest classification accuracy of 91.13%. Asghar et al. [7] combined a Convolutional Neural Network (CNN) and a Long Short-Term Memory (LSTM) recurrent network for automatic feature extraction. The results demonstrate an accuracy of 93.70%, a sensitivity of 90.69%, and a specificity of 95.82%. However, implementing deep learning algorithms on FPGA devices increases circuit complexity and power consumption. Feng et al. [8] introduced a detection model based on frequential stacked sparse auto-encoder (FSSAE) and time-dependent cost-sensitive (TDCS) classification, achieving accuracy, sensitivity, and specificity scores of 85.1%, 86.2%, and 84.4% respectively.

A. H. Khandoker et al. [9] utilized support vector machines (SVMs) to automatically detect obstructive sleep apnea syndrome (OSAS) types from nocturnal electrocardiogram (ECG) recordings. They trained SVMs with features extracted from wavelet decomposed signals related to heart rate variability (HRV) and ECG-derived respiration (EDR) from 83 training sets, including 65 Apnea and 18 Normal subjects. In independent testing on 42 subjects, the SVMs accurately identified 24 out of 26 cases, achieving an overall accuracy of 92.85%. Xie et al. [10] demonstrated the effectiveness of combining electrocardiograph (ECG) and peripheral oxygen saturation (SpO2) signals with machine learning algorithms, achieving a high accuracy of approximately 82%. Mostafa et al. [11] proposed a Deep Belief Network (DBN) approach based on the Spo2 signal. The results demonstrate an accuracy of 85.26% for the UCD database. Li et al. [12] leveraged deep neural networks and Hidden Markov Models (HMM) for OSA detection with an overall classification accuracy of approximately 85% with a sensitivity of up to 88.9%. Gupta et al. [13] proposed an automatic method utilizing EEG signals, achieving a peak classification accuracy of 95.10% with a sensitivity rate of 93.20% and a specificity rate of 96.80%. Bhattacharjee et al. [21] investigated Rician model parameters and statistical measures for multi-band EEG, achieving a K-nearest neighbor (KNN) classifier accuracy of 91.02%, with high sensitivity and specificity. Alam et al. [15] proposed a sleep apnea detector with low-complexity features and a Linear SVM classifier, achieving an accuracy of 94.81% with high sensitivity and specificity.

Various machine learning (ML) models, such as Convolutional Neural Networks (CNN) [16], Support Vector Machines (SVM) [17], K-Nearest Neighbours (KNN) [18], Artificial Neural Networks (ANN) [19], and Long Short-Term Memory (LSTM) [20], have been employed to preprocess medical data for sleep apnea detection by incorporating additional biomedical signals like EEG, SpO2, and EMG.

Prior research mainly focused on categorizing individuals as either apnea or non-apnea patients, while our proposed methodology addresses the specific detection of apnea and non-apnea events within apnea patients. The primary objective of this study is to develop a more accurate and efficient sleep apnea detection system optimized for ECG signals. We utilize four low-complexity features along with a robust machine-learning classifier to enhance the system's detection accuracy. Moreover, our study presents subject-specific and subject-independent results using the leave-one-out method. For this work, we have utilized the publicly available sleep apnea UCDDB database [9].

2 Overview of the Proposed Work

The block diagram in Fig. 1, illustrates the proposed methodology, which demonstrates the software simulation of an accurate efficient apnea detection design. The main objective of this research is to develop a software model for an efficient sleep apnea detection system using ECG signals with improved accuracy. Initially, the process begins by creating a software-based model and testing it using simulation techniques. This approach allows for iteration and optimization of the model efficiently in a software environment before moving to hardware implementation. The complete software simulation process consists of the following sequential steps: pre-processing, feature extraction, and classification. ECG data samples, which are shown in Fig. 2, are collected and pre-processed for the specific application. Subsequently, this processed data is then divided into training, validation, and testing sets.

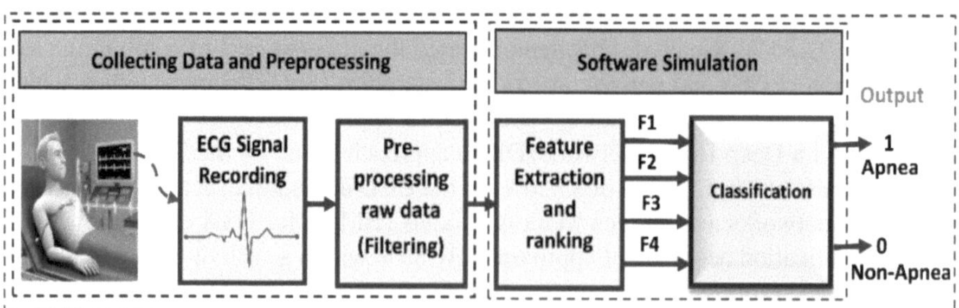

Fig. 1. Block diagram of the proposed work

All the simulation steps of this work are performed using MATLAB R2021a. A comprehensive explanation of all the steps involved in the software simulation process is outlined below:

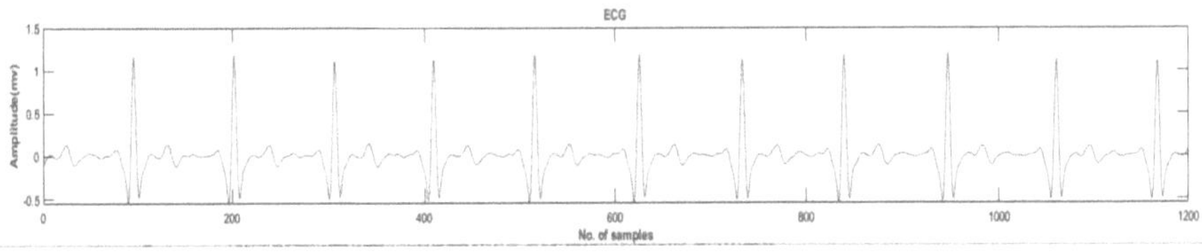

Fig. 2. Samples of ECG signals

2.1 Preprocessing

The preprocessing of ECG signals involves the removal of artifacts, which refers to undesired signals or disturbances that can interfere with the accuracy of ECG data analysis. These artifacts commonly originate from eyeball movements, eye blinks, sweating, and body movements. A Butterworth band pass filter is specifically employed at the input of the ECG signal to exclusively address this artifact. This technique eliminates these artifacts and streamlines the feature extraction and classification process.

2.2 Feature Extraction

Features play an important role in classification, as they capture the essential characteristics of an ECG signal, facilitating the identification of both apnea and non-apnea events. The processing of large volumes of ECG data poses a significant challenge in the field, necessitating the application of feature extraction techniques to reduce dimensionality and alleviate the computational load on the classifier. Frames of 10-second duration are considered to extract features from the pre-processed ECG signals. The four simplest and lowest complexity features, energy, mobility, kurtosis, and skewness are considered for the classification of apnea and non-apnea events. These features are computed from ECG signal (x_i) of 10 seconds duration as per the equations mentioned in Eqs 1, 2, 3 and 4 respectively:

$$Energy = \sum_{i=1}^{N} x_i^2 \tag{1}$$

$$Mobility = \sqrt{\frac{Var(x_i - x_{i-1})}{Var(x_i)}} \tag{2}$$

$$Kurtosis = \frac{\left(\frac{1}{N}\sum_{i=1}^{N}(x_i - x_{mean})^4\right)}{\left(\frac{1}{N}\sum_{i=1}^{N}(x_i - x_{mean})^2\right)^2} \tag{3}$$

$$Skewness = \frac{\left(\frac{1}{N}\sum_{i=1}^{N}(x_i - x_{mean})^3\right)}{\left(\sqrt{\frac{1}{N}\sum_{i=1}^{N}(x_i - x_{mean})^2}\right)^3} \quad (4)$$

Where $'x_i'$ represents a sample value obtained from the dataset, 'N' signifies the total number of samples present in a frame, while x_{mean} represents the average value (dc value) of the signals. Since ECG signals represent the heart rate variations and the respiratory patterns, so statistical features of these ECG signals offer valuable information about the sleeping state. The computation of various statistical features yields significant information, enabling precise differences between apneic and normal conditions. The energy feature of ECG signals reflects the overall power or magnitude of the signal across different frequency bands. During apnea, a decrease in the overall energy or power of the ECG signal, particularly in higher frequency bands, is often observed. Mobility, another feature, quantifies signal variation over time, with lower mobility in apnea events due to altered signal activity. Kurtosis measures the peak of the dataset, indicating patterns or abnormalities in ECG signals, while skewness assesses distribution asymmetry, aiding in identifying abnormal patterns in ECG segments. These statistical features are crucial for accurately distinguishing between apneic and normal conditions in ECG analysis.

2.3 Classification

In this study, we selected six efficient machine learning classifiers to differentiate apnea from non-apnea incidents. The classifiers used were Ensemble (Bagged Trees), Ensemble (Subspace Discriminant), Linear SVM, SVM (Medium Gaussian), Weighted K-nearest Neighbor, and Artificial Neural Network (ANN). Out of these, Ensemble (Bagged Trees), demonstrated the best performance in terms of accuracy, sensitivity, and specificity. Ensemble-bagged decision trees combine several decision trees that learn from different parts of the data to make better predictions together. This method is particularly effective for detecting sleep apnea, as it can manage high-dimensional and noisy ECG data, making the model more robust against individual variability in sleep apnea manifestations. In this research, we used 80% of the collected data for the training phase and the remaining 20% for testing, across each subject. The testing involved classifying the ECG data feature set into two categories: apnea and non-apnea. We implemented a 5-fold cross-validation method to validate the effectiveness of our proposed approach. This involved calculating the accuracy, sensitivity, and specificity for a specific subject and also estimating the average accuracy across subjects using the leave-one-out technique.

3 Result and Discussion

3.1 Database Description

The proposed apnea detector uses the publicly accessible PhysioNET UCDDB database [22]. This database contains recordings from two ECG channels, specifically C3-A2 and C4-A1, with a consideration of their time-averaged values. A sampling frequency of

Table 1. Subjects details of all 25-subjects of UCDDB Database

S.No.	Subject ID	Height (cm)	Weight (kg)	Gender	PSG Start Time	PSG AHI	BMI	Age	Epworth Sleepiness Score	Study Duration (hr)	Sleep Efficiency (%)	No of data blocks in EDF	No. of frames
1	UCDDB002	172	100.3	M	0:11:04	23	33.9	54	16	6.2	84	22470	358
2	UCDDB003	179	107.0	M	23:07:50	51	31.8	44	19	6.9	81	26478	788
3	UCDDB005	176	100.4	M	23:48:42	11	32.4	52	13	7.4	89	24798	758
4	UCDDB006	185	103.5	M	23:57:14	10	30.2	45	9	6.8	90	24267	214
5	UCDDB007	183	84.0	M	23:30:12	12	25.1	47	15	6.8	90	24405	216
6	UCDDB008	145	59.2	F	23:30:44	25	28.1	53	8	7.7	82	23004	140
7	UCDDB009	180	101.5	M	23:35:12	13	31.3	52	19	7.7	90	27759	189
8	UCDDB010	174	115.9	M	22:47:22	41	38.3	61	9	7.5	80	27713	480
9	UCDDB011	188	101	M	22:47:38	28	28.6	51	10	7.5	90	27030	88
10	UCDDB012	171	59.2	F	23:43:21	8	20.2	56	6	6.8	85	25941	166
11	UCDDB013	153	80	F	23:44:00	16	34.2	62	10	6.8	84	23733	162
12	UCDDB014	172	90	M	23:06:45	19	30.4	46	11	6.4	79	24339	194
13	UCDDB017	176	117	M	23:10:45	12	37.8	53	8	7.3	87	23648	184
14	UCDDB018	171	77	M	23:49:07	23	26.3	57	9	7.4	87	24863	184
15	UCDDB019	178	97.8	M	23:30:33	16	30.9	49	10	6.9	90	25578	184
16	UCDDB020	179	108.8	M	23:08:05	33	33.9	46	12	7.6	82	25575	184
17	UCDDB021	161	87	F	22:52:05	13	33.6	53	9	6.6	88	27409	184
18	UCDDB022	165	89	F	22:55:51	32	32.7	64	14	7.2	87	25850	424
19	UCDDB024	179	99.2	M	23:55:55	33	33.8	54	13	7.6	77	23640	184
20	UCDDB025	174	128.6	M	0:25:57	42	42.5	54	24	5.9	77	21350	1576
21	UCDDB026	175	87	M	22:58:13	41	28.4	49	10	7.9	87	25160	142
22	UCDDB027	182	93	M	22:56:30	55	28.1	45	10	7.4	86	26791	910
23	UCDDB028	172	88.9	M	0:29:08	46	30.1	50	13	6	68	21660	662

Table 2. Subjects specific performance using different classifiers

	Subject_3			Subject_11			Subject_20			Subject_24			Subject_26		
Classifiers	Acc.	Sens.	Spec.	Acc.	Sens.	Spec.	Acc.	Sens.	Spec.	Acc.	Sens.	Spec.	Acc.	Sens.	Spec.
Ensemble (Bagged Trees)	99.4	99.2	99.5	100	100	100	96.5	96	97	96.2	97.4	94.9	95.5	99.2	91.7
Linear SVM	99.5	97.3	99.5	97.7	95.5	100	94.9	93.9	96	93.6	99	88.2	91.9	86.8	95
Ensemble (subspace discriminant)	98.9	99	99.7	100	100	100	93.4	93.9	92.9	96.7	100	93.3	91.7	97.5	86
SVM (Medium Gaussian)	99.2	99	99.5	98.9	97.7	100	94.9	92.9	97	96.2	97.9	94.4	94.2	96.7	91.7
Weighted KNN	99.2	98.7	99.7	100	100	100	93.9	92.9	94.9	94.4	94.4	94.4	92.6	95.9	89.3
ANN	99	97.3	99.5	100	100	100	97	97.1	97	87.4	99.5	75.4	85.1	97.5	72.7

128 Hz is employed. Regardless of the type of apnea, our proposed method effectively distinguishes between apnea and non-apnea events. This UCDDB database contains recordings of a total of 25 subjects. Complete description of all 25-subjects of this database is shown in Table 1. For this study, five subjects identified by their subject

Table 3. Average performance of all five subjects using different classifiers.

S.No.	Classifiers	Accuracy (%)	Sensitivity (%)	Specificity (%)
1.	Ensemble (Bagged Trees)	97.52	98.36	96.62
2.	Linear SVM	95.52	94.5	95.74
3.	Ensemble (subspace discriminant)	96.14	98.08	94.38
4.	SVM (Medium Gaussian)	96.68	96.84	96.52
5.	Weighted KNN	96.02	96.38	95.66
6.	ANN	93.70	98.28	88.92

Table 4. Comparison based on different cross-validation methods

S.No.	Cross-Validation	Sensitivity (%)				Specificity (%)				Accuracy (%)			
		Saha et al. [14]	Bhatt et al. [21]	Gupta et al. [13]	Proposed	Saha et al. [14]	Bhatt et al. [21]	Guptaet al [13].	Proposed	Saha et al. [14]	Bhatt et al. [21]	Gupta et al. [13]	Proposed
1.	2-fold	86.99	89.46	91.40	98.30	88.67	89.40	96.20	96.56	87.44	89.37	94.16	97.5
2.	5-fold	86.67	89.90	93.20	98.36	91.27	93.75	96.80	96.62	88.84	91.59	95.10	97.52
3.	10-fold	86.22	90.84	93.20	98.40	91.25	93.69	96.80	96.60	88.90	92.02	95.10	97.55

IDs as UCDDDB003, 011, 020, 024, and 026, which are frequently cited in existing literature [13, 14, 21], were selected. These particular subjects were chosen due to their significant variations in AHI. The analysis involves a consistent number of apnea and non-apnea segments, with each segment lasting 10 seconds.

3.2 Simulation Results

We employed MATLAB R2021a to simulate the proposed architecture. The performance assessment of our sleep apnea classification system involves computing three standard metrics for each subject: accuracy, sensitivity, and specificity utilizing Eqs 5,6 and 7 respectively.

$$Accuracy = \frac{TP + TN}{TP + TN + FP + FN} \tag{5}$$

$$Sensitivity = \frac{TP}{TP + FN} \tag{6}$$

$$Specificity = \frac{TN}{TN + FP} \tag{7}$$

To evaluate the performance of the apnea classification system, a confusion matrix was generated, enabling the classification of data into true positives (TP), false positives (FP), true negatives (TN), and false negatives (FN). Different classifiers, including the Ensemble classifier, K-nearest neighbor, Support Vector Machine (SVM), and the

Artificial Neural Network (ANN), were utilized to obtain classification results. Subject-specific values of accuracy, sensitivity, and specificity were calculated individually for all five subjects using various classifiers within a 5-fold cross-validation scheme, as detailed in Table 2. The summary of the average accuracy, sensitivity, and specificity across all five patients using different classifiers is represented in Table 3.

The data presented in Table 2. highlights that the Ensemble (Bagged Trees) classifier exhibited superior performance in terms of accuracy, sensitivity, and specificity when compared to other classifiers. Consequently, the results from this classifier were used to compare our findings with those of other studies [13, 14, 21], as previously published and summarized in Table 5. All the studies included in the comparison table utilized the same database. In [13, 14], apnea detection relied on a sub-frame-based feature extraction technique, which incorporated Rician model parameters and statistical features into the feature vector. Conversely, [21] employed interband energy ratios as features. The total number of frames used in these studies matches that of the proposed method.

Table 4. presents a comparison of mean results across different cross-validation schemes: 2-fold, 5-fold, and 10-fold. This illustrates the consistency of results across various cross-validation methods.

Furthermore, to gain a comprehensive understanding of the proposed method, we compute the subject-independent average accuracy using a leave-one-out scheme. For each subject, four out of the five subject features are used as the training set, and testing is conducted on the fifth feature set. This process is repeated for each subject, and the resulting five accuracies are averaged to determine the average subject-independent accuracy, which stands at 82.7%. This subject-independent accuracy provides valuable insights into the effectiveness of our proposed method.

4 Conclusion

In this study, we have developed an efficient sleep apnea detection system for ECG signals using four low-complexity features and a machine learning classifier through software simulation. Our proposed method gives better results compared to recently published works. The best-performing model achieves an accuracy of 97.52% using Ensemble (Bagged Trees), surpassing the accuracy reported in [13] by 2.42%, [14] by 8.62% and [21] by 5.5%. In this work, the Ranking of features provides valuable insights into the effectiveness of each feature in detecting apnea and non-apnea events. Additionally, we have computed both subject-specific and subject-independent accuracies, making our method suitable for automatic sleep apnea detection with potential clinical applications.

5 Future Work

In this chapter, we have proposed the best software model for automatic sleep apnea detection using ECG signals, with better accuracy, sensitivity, and specificity compared to previous published works. In future work, we will develop a hardware model of this software using FPGA. During the development of this hardware model, special attention will be given to ensuring that it is energy-efficient and cost-effective so that it can be easily assembled with battery-operated wearable devices in the future, and the cost of these wearable devices remains minimal. Keeping this purpose in mind, we have selected low complexity features while developing the software model so that the hardware model can be easily created in the future. Additionally, we will apply two efficient techniques, pipelining, and progressive bit sizing, to reduce hardware resource usage and power consumption. Pipelining will reduce hardware latency, while progressive bit sizing will optimize resource utilization, making our proposed model cost-effective and energy-efficient. We will thoroughly test this hardware model initially and strive to ensure that its accuracy is approximately the same as the software model. Once the hardware model is developed, we will explore using deep learning concepts for classification instead of machine learning in future iterations to further enhance its accuracy and create a highly accurate sleep apnea detector.

Table 5. Comparison of the proposed work with prior research

S.No	Subject ID	Sensitivity (%)				Specificity (%)				Accuracy (%)			
		Saha et al. [14]	Bhatt et al. [21]	Gupta et al. [13]	Proposed	Saha et al. [14]	Bhatt et al. [21]	Gupta et al. [13]	Proposed	Saha et al. [14]	Bhatt et al. [21]	Gupta et al. [13]	Proposed
1.	UCDDB003	87.56	81.22	97.50	99.2	88.58	87.31	99.22	99.5	88.07	84.26	98.40	99.4
2.	UCDDB011	88.64	86.36	93.61	100	97.73	84.09	100	100	93.18	85.23	96.60	100
3.	UCDDB020	96.97	86.87	87.96	96	97.98	95.96	95.56	97	97.47	91.41	91.40	96.5
4.	UCDDB024	92.82	91.28	90.04	97.4	93.33	93.85	77.20	94.9	93.08	92.56	93.60	96.2
5.	UCDDB026	85.95	85.95	95.08	99.2	92.56	90.08	75.83	91.7	89.26	88.02	95.50	95.5
	Average	90.38	86.33	92.83	98.36	94.03	90.25	97.56	96.62	92.21	88.29	95.10	97.52

Disclosure of Interests. The authors have no competing interests to declare that are relevant to the content of this article.

References

1. Peppard, P.E., Young, T., Barnet, J.H., Palta, M., Hagen, E.W., Hla, K.M.: Increased prevalence of sleep-disordered breathing in adults. Am. J. Epidemiol. **177**(9), 1006–1014 (2013)
2. Yaggi, H.K., Concato, J., Kernan, W.N., Lichtman, J.H., Brass, L.M., Mohsenin, V.: Obstructive sleep apnea as a risk factor for stroke and death. N. Engl. J. Med. **353**(19), 2034–2041 (2005)
3. https://aasm.org/
4. Young, T., Evans, L., Finn, L., Palta, M.: Estimation of the clinically diagnosed proportion of sleep apnea syndrome in middle-aged men and women. Sleep. **20**(9), 705–706 (1997)
5. Bahrami, M., Forouzanfar, M.: Sleep apnea detection from single-lead ECG: a comprehensive analysis of machine learning and deep learning algorithms. IEEE Trans. Instrum. Meas. **71**, 1–11 (2022). https://doi.org/10.1109/TIM.2022.3151947
6. Nguyen, T., Le, H.-K., Pham, H.-H., Do, C.: A novel deep learning-based approach for sleep apnea detection using single-lead ECG signals. In: 2022 Asia-Pacific Signal and Information Processing Association Annual Summit and Conference (APSIPA ASC), pp. 2046–2052, Chiang Mai, Thailand (2022). https://doi.org/10.23919/APSIPAASC55919.2022.9979890

7. Asghar, Z., Beheshti, H., Asl, B.M.: Detection of sleep apnea using deep neural networks and single-lead ECG signals. Biomed. Signal Process. Control. **71**(Part A), 103125 (2022. Online. Available:). https://doi.org/10.1016/j.bspc.2021.103125
8. Feng, K., Qin, H., Wu, S., Pan, W., Liu, G.: A Sleep apnea detection method based on unsupervised feature learning and single-lead electrocardiogram. IEEE Trans. Instrum. Meas. **70**, 1–12 (2021). https://doi.org/10.1109/TIM.2020.3017246
9. Khandoker, A.H., Palaniswami, M., Karmakar, C.: Support vector machines for automated recognition of obstructive sleep apnea syndrome from ECG recordings. IEEE Trans. Inf. Technol. Biomed. **13**, 37–48 (2008). https://doi.org/10.1109/TITB.2008.2008233
10. Xie, B., Minn, H.: Real-time sleep apnea detection by classifier combination. IEEE Trans. Inf. Technol. Biomed. **16**(3), 469–477 (2012). https://doi.org/10.1109/TITB.2012.2188299
11. Mostafa, S.S., Mendonca, F., Morgado-Dias, F., Ravelo-Garcia, A.: SpO2 based sleep apnea detection using deep learning. In: Proceedings of the 2017 IEEE 21st International Conference on Intelligent Engineering Systems (INES), pp. 91–96, Larnaca, Cyprus (2017). https://doi.org/10.1109/INES.2017.8124771
12. Li, K., Pan, W., Li, Y., Jiang, Q., Liu, G.: A method to detect sleep apnea based on deep neural network and hidden Markov model using single-lead ECG signal. Neurocomputing. **294**, 94–101 (2018. Online. Available). https://doi.org/10.1016/j.neucom.2018.03.011
13. Gupta, R., Zaidi, T.F., Farooq, O.: Automatic detection of sleep apnea using sub-band features from EEG signals. In: 2020 3rd International Conference on Signal Processing and Information Security (ICSPIS), pp. 1–4. IEEE (2020). https://doi.org/10.1109/ICSPIS51252.2020.9340133
14. Saha, S., Bhattacharjee, A., Fattah, S.A.: Automatic detection of sleep apnea events based on inter-band energy ratio obtained from multi-band EEG signal. Healthc. Technol. Lett. **6**(3), 82–86 (2019)
15. Alam, M.S., Siddiqui, Y., Hasan, M., Farooq, O., Himeur, Y.: Energy-efficient FPGA based sleep apnea detection using EEG signals. IEEE Access. **12**, 40182–40195. https://doi.org/10.1109/ACCESS.2024.3374223
16. Almuhammadi, W.S., Aboalayon, K.A., Faezipour, M.: Efficient obstructive sleep apnea classification based on EEG signals. In: 2015 IEEE Long Island Systems, Applications and Technology Conference (LISAT), pp. 1–6. IEEE (2015)
17. Imaduddin, S., Haadi, A., Kumar, A., Alam, M.S.: Power-efficient FPGA implementation of SVM for sleep apnea detection. In: 2023 9th International Conference on Signal Processing and Communication (ICSC), pp. 757–762, NOIDA, India (2023). https://doi.org/10.1109/ICSC60394.2023.10441455
18. Chakraborty, A., et.al. (2022). A Comparative Study of Myocardial Infarction Detection from ECG Data Using Machine Learning, Advanced Computing and Intelligent Technologies. Lecture Notes in Networks and Systems, vol 218. Springer, Singapore. https://doi.org/10.1007/978-981-16-2164-2_21
19. Yılmaz, B., Asyalı, M.H., Arıkan, E., Yetkin, S., Özgen, F.: Sleep stage and obstructive apneaic epoch classification using single-lead ECG. Biomed. Eng. Online. **9**(1), 1–14 (2010)
20. Várady, P., Micsik, T., Benedek, S., Benyó, Z.: A novel method for the detection of apnea and hypopnea events in respiration signals. IEEE Trans. Biomed. Eng. **49**(9), 936–942 (2002)
21. Bhattacharjee, A., Saha, S., Fattah, S.A., Zhu, W., Ahmad, M.O.: Sleep apnea detection based on rician modeling of feature variation in multiband EEG signal. IEEE J. Biomed. Health Inform. **23**(3), 1066–1074 (2019)
22. St. Vincent's university hospital/university college Dublin 2007 sleep apnea database. https://physionet.org/content/ucddb/1.0.0/

AI-Enhanced State-of-the-Art Techniques for Land Cover Classification Using Optical and Synthetic Aperture Radar Data Fusion

Vikas Kumar Tiwari[1,2](✉), Raman Chadha[1], and Rajeev Tiwari[3]

[1] Chandigarh University, Mohali, Punjab, India
vikastiwari87@gmail.com
[2] IILM University, Greater Noida, UP, India
[3] School of Artificial Intelligence, Bennett University, Greater Noida, Uttar Pradesh, India
errajeev.tiwari@gmail.com

Abstract. This chapter presents a comparative study on novel methods for land cover classification that leverages a gradient-based fusion and classification technique, integrating Synthetic Aperture Radar (SAR) and optical image data. Unlike existing methods, this approach aims to delineate land cover boundaries and edges more effectively. By combining multiple information sources, including RGB, HSV, or other color spaces, into a single multi-image color component, we exploit their complementary properties to enhance classification accuracy. The integration of SAR and optical data through multi-image color components provides flexibility in classification tailored to specific data characteristics and requirements. This approach enables more precise categorization and differentiation of various land cover types, facilitating improved remote sensing, feature extraction, and data interpretation. The methods adaptability enhances choices for environmental monitoring, land management, disaster assessment, and urban development. Key applications include optimizing resource allocation, assessing environmental impact, and informing land use planning. Overall, this innovative approach offers significant potential for advancing land cover classification capabilities and enhancing decision-making processes in various domains.

Keywords: Land cover classification · Optical and SAR data fusion · based approach · Remote sensing · Environmental monitoring

1 Introduction

The incorporation of data from multiple sources into a single multimodal dataset has gained significant attention in the field of remote sensing, particularly for interpreting satellite imagery using advanced image fusion techniques. Combining optical and Synthetic Aperture Radar (SAR) satellite images has emerged as a crucial application, leveraging their complementary strengths for improved image interpretation and classification [1]. While optical data captures information in the visible and near-infrared spectrum, SAR data provides valuable insights into ground object properties, regardless

M. Paprzycki et al. (Eds.): ICACIS 2024, CCIS 2405, pp. 28–45, 2027.
https://doi.org/10.1007/978-3-032-30990-7_3

of weather conditions [2]. Recent advancements, such as the availability of Sentinel 1A and Sentinel 2B satellite data, have spurred extensive research into integrating optical and SAR images to enhance interpretation and categorization [3, 4]. In the realm of image fusion algorithms, various methods have been explored, including gradient-based approaches, to improve the quality and detail of fused images. Techniques such as multi-scale transformations and gradient regularization have shown promise in enhancing image contrast and extracting meaningful features [5]. Additionally, innovative methods combining total variation minimization and gradient transfer have been developed to sharpen infrared images, while entropy-based fusion techniques have been employed to merge infrared and visible images effectively [6]. Despite these advancements, current image fusion techniques face limitations in accurately extracting spatial information and features from two-dimensional images. While these methods have demonstrated success in picture fusion, there remains a critical need for further advancements, particularly in leveraging AI techniques to overcome existing limitations and enhance the accuracy and efficiency of image fusion processes [7, 8]. Integrating AI algorithms could potentially revolutionize image fusion by enabling more robust spatial information extraction and feature enhancement, paving the way for more sophisticated and accurate remote sensing applications [3] (Fig. 1).

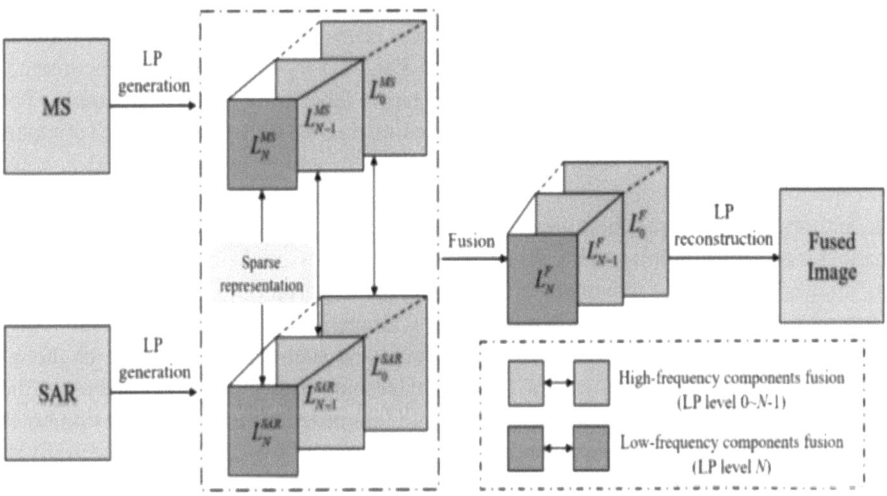

Fig. 1. SAR image Fusion Based. [5]

2 Related Work

In their study, [9] introduced a novel approach for high-resolution remote sensing using Synthetic Aperture Radar (SAR) images, which is not affected by weather conditions. Traditionally, SAR ship image classification relied on manual feature extraction, leading to subjective results highly dependent on image resolution. However, recent advancements in deep learning, particularly convolutional neural networks (CNNs), have shown promise in automating feature extraction and classification tasks, improving precision and normalization capabilities. Despite the effectiveness of deep learning approaches, SAR images often lack labeled data, posing challenges for supervised learning methods. As a result, deep neural networks may not achieve optimal performance due to limited training data. To address this limitation, the authors proposed a semi-supervised machine learning approach for SAR image classification. This method allows the classification model to be trained using both labeled and unlabeled data, leveraging the available information more effectively. Furthermore, the authors introduced a novel symmetric function for unsupervised label computation, which represents a significant improvement over traditional unsupervised data augmentation method. By incorporating this function into the classification model, the proposed method achieved notable enhancements in accuracy compared to standard unsupervised data augmentation techniques. The effectiveness of the proposed approach was demonstrated through experiments conducted on the OpenSARShip dataset, highlighting its potential for improving SAR image classification accuracy and robustness.

[10] introduced a novel approach utilizing the 2D-VMD (2-dimensional variational modes decomposition) technique for target classification in Synthetic Aperture Radar (SAR) imagery. By applying 2D-VMD to SAR images, the authors were able to extract multiscale components that capture the time-frequency characteristics of targets. These components serve as a sparse representation of both the original images and their 2D-VMD decompositions. The classification process relies on analyzing the reconstruction errors generated by different classes of targets. Each class produces distinct reconstruction errors, allowing for the inference of the target label for a given test sample. The proposed method effectiveness was evaluated using the MSTAR dataset, which contains SAR images with varying conditions such as different setups, depression angles, noise corruption, and partial occlusion. Through experimentation with the MSTAR dataset, the authors demonstrated the efficacy and robustness of their approach for SAR Automatic Target Recognition (ATR). Janarthanan [11] addressed the challenge of classifying images from remote sensing by emphasizing the importance of training samples and learning techniques in interpreting multispectral images. With the increasing availability of high-dimensional multispectral data, preprocessing such data has become challenging. Previous studies have shown that traditional learning strategies struggle to handle the complexity of such data. To address this, the authors proposed a method that combines various deep learning algorithms, including weight vector (WV) AdaBoost and ADAM, to mitigate overfitting and achieve high classification accuracy. The proposed method was applied to a database of remotely sensed images, demonstrating significant improvements in classification accuracy. By leveraging deep learning models such as VGG16 and Inception v3, along with optimization techniques, the classification accuracy was enhanced by 96.08%. This approach highlights the effectiveness of incorporating artificial intelligence (AI) techniques in handling the challenges posed by high-dimensional multispectral data in remote sensing applications.

Hu et al. (2022) developed a method for classifying individuals into groups based on their shared assumptions. By leveraging a global dictionary constructed from training samples across all classes, the authors reconstructed test examples or determined the target class based on the reconstruction error for each class. In scenarios with small datasets, their collective representation approach outperformed sparse representation methods. Given the scarcity of training samples for SAR target recognition, collaborative representation becomes crucial. Experiments conducted using the MSTAR dataset demonstrated the effectiveness of the proposed method compared to established classifiers. Despite limited training samples and sensitivity to changes in configuration and depression angle, the proposed method performed well in the SAR target recognition setting.

Examples related to AI:

- In AI-based facial recognition systems, individuals are classified based on shared facial features and characteristics.
- Natural language processing (NLP) models classify text documents into categories based on shared linguistic patterns and assumptions.
- Machine learning algorithms classify images into different classes based on shared visual features and attributes.

Strimaitis [13] conducted research focused on classifying Lithuanian text data to assign multiple classes to each data item, aiding in textual analysis. Their study introduces a novel hybrid method for multilabel text data classification, aiming to enhance the efficiency of standard classification algorithms using similarity metrics results. Financial news from Lithuania was used to collect multilabel text data, categorized into ten classes by experts. Various machine learning methods were employed and compared, including decision trees and support vector machines, with k-nearest neighbors, multinomial Bayes, and linear discriminant analyses. Additionally, metrics such as cosine distance and the dice coefficient were utilized to draw comparisons between methods. Among these, cosine similarity distance and multinomial Bayes classification emerged as the most effective. The proposed method integrates insights from both approaches, resulting in improved global accuracy [11].

Few examples related to [12] are

- Speech Recognition: AI-powered speech recognition systems, such as Google's Assistant and Apple's Siri, can transcribe spoken language into text, enabling users to interact with devices through voice commands.
- Autonomous Vehicles: AI technologies, including machine learning algorithms and computer vision, play a crucial role to automatically decide vehicles driving decisions, and navigate safely.
- Recommendation Systems: AI-based recommendation systems, used by platforms like Netflix and Amazon, analyze user preferences and behavior to recommend personalized content, products, or services.
- Natural Language Processing (NLP): NLP techniques, such as text summarization, sentiment analysis, and machine translation, enable computers to understand, interpret, and generate human language, facilitating communication and information retrieval tasks.
- Healthcare Diagnostics: AI-powered diagnostic systems leverage medical imaging data, patient records, and clinical data to assist healthcare professionals in diagnosing diseases, predicting patient outcomes, and recommending personalized treatment plans.

- Fraud Detection: AI algorithms are employed by financial institutions to detect fraudulent activities by analyzing patterns, anomalies, and trends in transaction data, helping to prevent financial fraud and protect consumers.

[14] Introduce an innovative AI-driven approach to tackle nonlinear optimization problems by transforming them into convex ones, streamlining their complexity. Traditional kernel-based learning methods often face challenges in tasks like classification, regression, and clustering. However, recent advancements in semi-supervised deep learning show promise, particularly in image processing applications with limited labeled data and abundant unlabeled data. These AI algorithms operate under the assumption of identical distributions between labeled and unlabeled data, significantly influencing their output quality. Yet, challenges arise when unlabeled data contains unclassified information, degrading system performance, especially in scenarios like synthetic aperture radar (SAR) image identification. To overcome this challenge, the proposed AI-driven approach integrates threshold filtering in semi-supervised modeling settings to mitigate the adverse effects of unlabeled data on model performance. By leveraging two distinct sets of data and filtering out unnecessary unlabeled samples during training, the method achieves enhanced classification performance. Experimental evaluations on the dataset of MSTAR, demonstrate the superiority of the proposed AI approach over existing semi-supervised classification algorithms, particularly in scenarios where a significant portion of the raw data does not conform to predefined categories. Evaluation metrics, including false alarm (FA) and target miss (TM) rates, further validate the method's effectiveness in reducing erroneous conclusions and improving classification accuracy. These advancements highlight the potential of AI-driven techniques in addressing complex optimization problems and enhancing system performance across diverse applications.

[15] have emerged as prominent contributors in the domain of deep learning (DL), particularly in leveraging convolutional neural network (CNN) architectures to automate the matching process of Synthetic Aperture Radar (SAR) images. Despite DL's vast potential, SAR imagery remains underutilized due to the challenges associated with adapting Visual Geometry Group (VGG) algorithms trained on multispectral datasets to SAR image recognition tasks, which lack expert knowledge of SAR-specific features. This research addresses the challenges by proposing a novel methodology for SAR image matching, considering factors such as SAR variable range imaginary data throughout the similar process. Even with these challenges, the results exhibit the robustness of the proposed registration procedure, facilitated by descriptors that preserve feature localization information. Furthermore, the proposed methodology outperforms traditional correlation approaches or descriptors like ORB when scaled, yielding competitive results compared to state-of-the-art techniques. The developed methodology represents a comprehensive solution for matching SAR images, even in the absence of precise matching parameters computation. The incorporation of AI-driven CNN architectures enhances the efficiency and accuracy of the matching process, paving the way for broader applications of SAR imagery in various domains. This advancement underscores the potential of AI-driven techniques in addressing complex image recognition tasks, particularly in domains with unique imaging characteristics such as SAR imagery (Table 1).

Table 1. Comparative Aanalysis of Different Algorithm

Paper No.	Algorithms/Techniques	Year	Contribution	Advantages	Future Goals
[44]	SSDD and HRSID	2022	High detection accuracy and outstanding detection effect provided by the two-stage target detection algorithm	Utilization of Focus, C3, and CBL structures for feature extraction	Further research on improving detection algorithms and exploring new feature extraction techniques
[45]	Gaussian process classification algorithm	2022	Frequent employment of SAR imaging in the mining industry	Recent studies focusing on the Gaussian process	Continued research on optimizing the Gaussian process for SAR imaging applications
[46]	Adaptive truncation statistical	2022	Great computational complexity and lengthy program execution	Focus on edge texture information in SAR ship image processing	Efforts to reduce computational complexity and enhance efficiency of SAR image processing algorithms
[47]	CNN (DnCNN)	2021	Synthetic speckle generation and fusion of multiple time periods	Benefits and drawbacks of different image processing techniques	Further exploration of image fusion methods and optimization of CNN architectures for SAR image denoising
[48]	Convolutional neural network AlexNet model	2021	Utilization of AlexNet model's network capabilities for SAR image processing	Potential application of YOLO paradigm for future oil leak detection in the ocean	Research on enhancing deep learning models for SAR image analysis and detection tasks

(*continued*)

Table 1. (*continued*)

Paper No.	Algorithms/Techniques	Year	Contribution	Advantages	Future Goals
[49]	MSTAR	2021	Importance of researching cutting-edge SARATR systems	Demonstrated performance advantages of recognition and classification methods	Focus on improving SARATR systems and exploring new applications in target recognition
[50]	MSTAR	2021	great performance advantages over state-of-the-art approaches	Addressing recognition issues under standard operating conditions (SOC) and exploring solutions for EOC nuisance cases	Further optimization of SAR target recognition algorithms and methods
[51]	HOG	2021	Advantages of HOG and reliability of deep neural networks	Experimental findings presented in Sect. 4	Exploration of future research directions and applications of HOG in combination with deep learning techniques

3 Multi Image Colour Component Classification for Sar and Optical Data

Optical data and Synthetic Aperture Radar data are the types of remote sensing data that are useful in many scenarios. Optical data is obtained by recording the reflected visible and near-infrared light from the Earth's surface, whereas SAR data is obtained by producing radar signals and watching their reflection [14]. SAR and optical data classification can be done in a variety of ways, each with its own advantages.

The following are some of the most often used classification approaches for each type:

Classification of SAR Data:

- Single-Look Intensity (SLI): Using an intensity value analysis of SAR images, this approach classifies different land cover or land use types. The statistical characteristics of the radar backscattering signal, such as amplitude and texture, are used to distinguish between classes [15].
- Polarimetric SAR (PolSAR): Based on the polarimetric parameters that are analysed, classification can be achieved. PolSAR data is gathered using a variety of polarisation channels. This approach considers all of the polarimetric data that is available, including the coherency matrix's elements and other decomposition methods (such Freeman-Durden, Cloude-Pottier, or H/A/) [16].
- Interferometric SAR (InSAR): Data needed by InSAR can be obtained by analysing the phase differences between two or more SAR images [19]. One of the categorization techniques for InSAR data is the identification of surface deformations, such as elevation changes or land subsidence.

Classification of Optical Data

- Spectral Reflectance: Because optical data is composed of several spectral bands, classification can be achieved by looking at reflectance values at different wavelengths. This approach makes use of spectral characteristics to differentiate between various land cover and land use classes.
- Vegetation Indices: A variety of indices can be generated from optical data, the most widely used being the Enhanced Vegetation Health Index (EVI) and the Normalized Normalized Index of Vegetation Health (NDVI) [20]. Since these indications provide information about the current state of the vegetation, they can be utilised to categorise it.
- Object-Based Classification: Using the spatial and spectral characteristics of the areas and objects, respectively, the optical data are classified into meaningful objects or regions. Subsequently, the objects are classified into different land cover or land use categories based on their attributes, including shape, size, texture, and context.

It should be noted that the categorization methods outlined above are not limited to SAR or optical data; rather, they can be applied to both kinds of data, but certain modifications are necessary to take into consideration the unique properties of each type. It's critical to remember this [21]. Moreover, more advanced techniques such as machine learning and deep learning algorithms can be used for categorization. These techniques can be used to SAR and optical sensor data.

4 Color Components from Multiple Images Using Sar and Optical Data

Multi-image color elements play a vital role in the analysis of SAR and Optical data. SAR captures surface characteristics like smoothness and moisture content, while optical data captures spectral properties. Integrating SAR and optical data enhances analysis due to their complementary information. This fusion technique involves creating composite images by combining data from multiple SAR or optical images. These composite images provide richer and more detailed information, facilitating better analysis. AI-driven approaches can further enhance the extraction of meaningful insights from SAR and optical data by leveraging advanced algorithms for image processing and feature extraction [22] (Fig. 2).

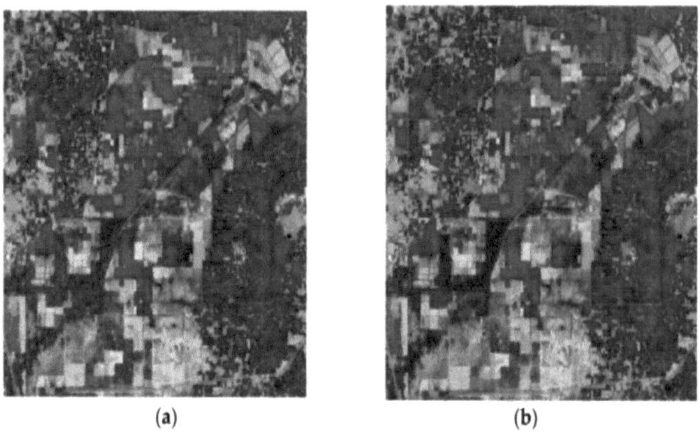

Fig. 2. Multi-Image Color elements data of SAR and Optical image [4]

This approach overcomes limitations of single-channel SAR data by generating composite images that provide a more comprehensive view of the region of interest. Similarly, in optical data, merging images from various wavelengths produces multi-image color components, enabling extraction of valuable information for land cover classification, vegetation health assessment, and water quality evaluation. Integrating optical and SAR data through multi-image color components synergistically combines the strengths of both sensing modalities, such as SAR's cloud-penetration capability and optical data's high-resolution imaging. This comprehensive dataset enables researchers to gain deeper insights into Earth's surface dynamics and facilitates improved decision-making in agriculture, environmental monitoring, and disaster management. AI-driven techniques can further enhance the analysis of multi-image color components by leveraging advanced algorithms for image processing and data fusion, ultimately leading to more accurate and actionable insights.

The actions that follow are those that can be taken in order to identify SAR and optical data utilising multi-image colour components:

- Data Acquisition: Obtain both SAR and optical imagery for the study area. SAR data can be acquired from satellite sensors such as Sentinel-1 or RADARSAT, while optical data can be obtained from sensors like Landsat or Sentinel-2.
- Preprocessing: Preprocess both SAR and optical data to remove noise, correct geometric distortions, and align the images spatially [27]. This step ensures that both datasets are in a consistent format and spatial reference system.

- Feature Extraction: Extract relevant features from the SAR and optical data. For SAR data, common features include backscatter intensity, texture measures (e.g., entropy or standard deviation), and polarimetric parameters (Mechanisms of coherence and scattering, for instance [28]. Common methods for analysing optical data include the use of green/red or red/near-infrared band ratios and spectral indices like the Normalised variations Vegetation index or the Enhanced Vegetation Index.
- Dimensionality Reduction: To alleviate the "curse of dimensionality" and boost classification accuracy, It is suggested that the feature space dimensions be reduced. In order to keep only the most crucial features, Methods such as PCA (principal component analysis) and t-SNE (The stochastic Neighbour Embedding) can be used for this purpose [29].
- Training Data Preparation: Prepare a labeled training dataset by manually delineating regions of interest (ROIs) corresponding to different land cover classes in the study area. The training data should include a representative sample of each class in order to train the classification model effectively.
- Model Training: Train a classification model using the prepared training dataset and the reduced feature space [30]. Classification can be accomplished using a wide variety of machine learning methods, including, but not limited to, neural networks based on convolution, randomly generated forest designs, or Support Vector Machines.
- Classification: Apply the trained model to classify the remaining pixels in the study area. The model assigns a class label to each pixel based on its feature values.
- Post-processing: Perform post-processing steps to refine the classification results. Techniques such as majority filtering, morphological operations [31], or contextual smoothing can be applied to reduce misclassifications and improve the accuracy of the final classification map (Fig. 3).

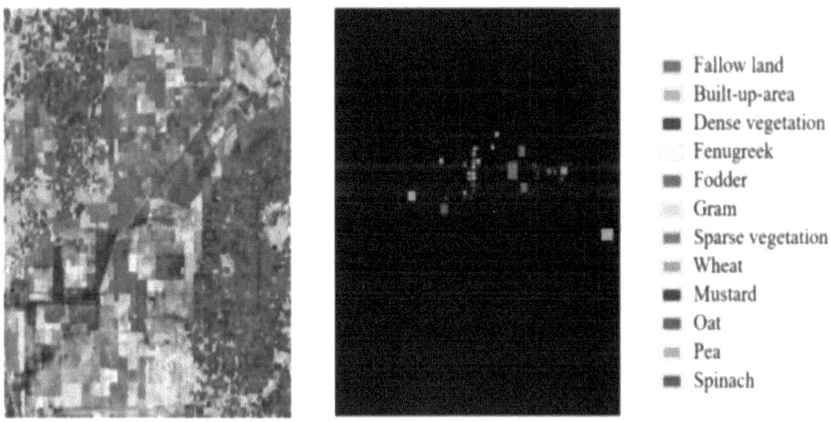

(a) (b)

Fig. 3. Multi-Image Color Components [4]

It is crucial to remember that depending on the software and program environment used for the categorization process, the specific implementation elements may change. Additionally, the accuracy of the chosen classification method, the suitability of a chosen features, & the quality of data itself all play a role in the classification's success [32].

5 Boosting Classifier

A. A machine learning method called a Stochastic Gradient Boosting Classifiers combines the ideas of gradient boosting & stochastic gradient descent into a single framework [33]. Another name for this approach is Gradient Boosting with Stochastic Gradient Descent. It is a powerful method that is utilised for classification jobs as part of an ensemble. The method of machine learning known as gradient boosting works by first constructing an ensemble of less accurate prediction models, which are typically decision trees, and then combining the results of these models to arrive at a single conclusion [34]. It accomplishes this goal by adding new models to the ensemble in an iterative manner, with each new model making an effort to rectify the errors caused by the models that came before it. An optimisation approach known as stochastic gradient descent, or SGD, is frequently utilised in the training of machine learning models. It does this by considering very small steps in the direction of the steepest possible decline of the loss function [35]. This is achieved by reducing the likelihood of the model memorizing the training data. The Stochastic Gradient Boosting Classifier is a powerful and flexible approach for classification tasks that utilises the benefits of gradient boosting and stochastic gradient descent to generate accurate and robust models. In general, the Stochastic Gradient Boosting Classifier is a powerful and flexible technique for classification tasks [36] (Fig. 4).

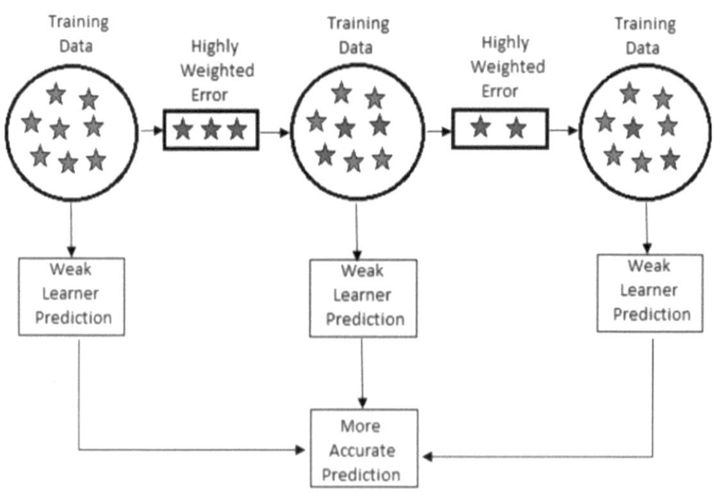

Fig. 4. gradient boosting [34]

B. Extreme Gradient Boosting Classifier

Extreme Gradient Boosting, or XGBoost for short, is a powerful machine learning strategy that belongs to the family of gradient boosting techniques [37]. It is well-known for its effectiveness, scalability, and excellent performance in a wide variety of predictive modeling tasks, including classification, regression, and ranking problem sets [38]. Python, R, Java, and C++ are just some of the computer languages that have been used to create working versions of XGBoost. There are particular libraries, such as 'xgboost' in Python and 'xgboost' in R, which provide straightforward user interfaces for the purpose of training and utilisingXGBoost models. Overall, XGBoost is a versatile and highly effective technique for classification tasks, noted for its performance, scalability, and adaptability [39]. In particular, it is known for its capacity to handle large amounts of data (Fig. 5):

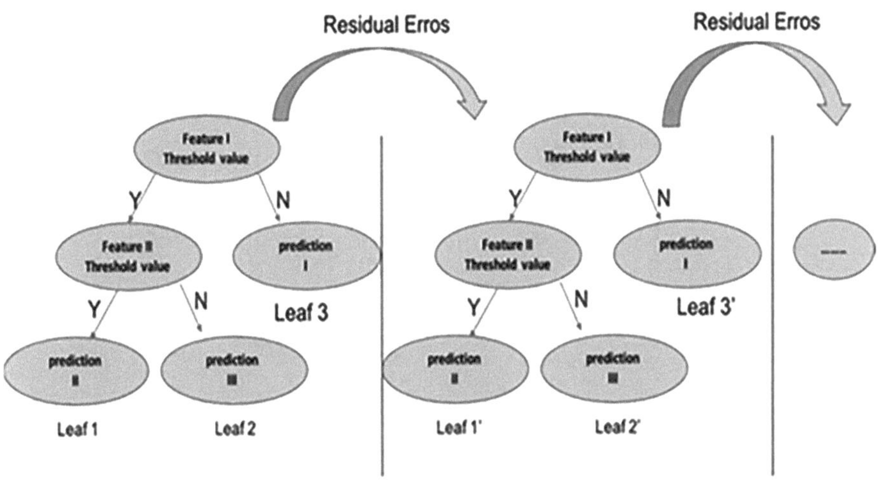

Fig. 5. Extreme Gradient Boosting Classifier [37]

- Regularization:Regularization methods like L1 and L2 regularization are built into XGBoost to combat overfitting and boost the model's transferability.
- Tree pruning, a technique utilized by XGBoost, aims to simplify individual decision trees and prevent overfitting. By eliminating redundant branches and nodes, pruning enhances model interpretability and efficiency [40].
- XGBoost's in-built features allow it to deal with missing values in the dataset. It learns how to deal with missing data during training by allocating them to the correct branches of the decision trees.
- Parallel Processing: XGBoost supports parallel processing, which enables faster model training and prediction, especially when dealing with large datasets [41].
- Each feature in the dataset is assigned a score called "feature importance," which XGBoost then uses to rank their significance. This is helpful for selecting features and figuring out what's really behind the predictions [42].

- Flexibility: XGBoost allows customization of various parameters, such as the learning rate, number of trees, maximum depth of trees, and regularization terms, giving the user more control over the model's behavior [43].
- Wide Range of Applications:XGBoost has been effectively implemented in a number of fields, including economics, medicine, NLP, CV, and more.

C. In the area of machine learning, a Gradient Descent Classifier has a widely used method for solving classification issues. It belongs to the optimisation algorithm family and finds use in many different areas, including computer vision, NLP, and recommendation systems, among others. The stochastic gradient descent (SGD) technique is one of the variants of the gradient descent algorithm [44]. It involves randomly sampling a portion of the training data, also referred to as a mini-batch, in order to compute the gradient and update the parameters. SGD is not just computationally efficient but also capable of more successfully managing large-scale datasets. In a nutshell, the Gradient Descent Classifier is an iterative optimization technique that modifies the parameters of a classifier in order to achieve the best possible results by reducing the value of a cost function. It has been shown to be an effective method that can also be used in a variety of contexts for addressing classification issues in machine learning [45] (Fig. 6).

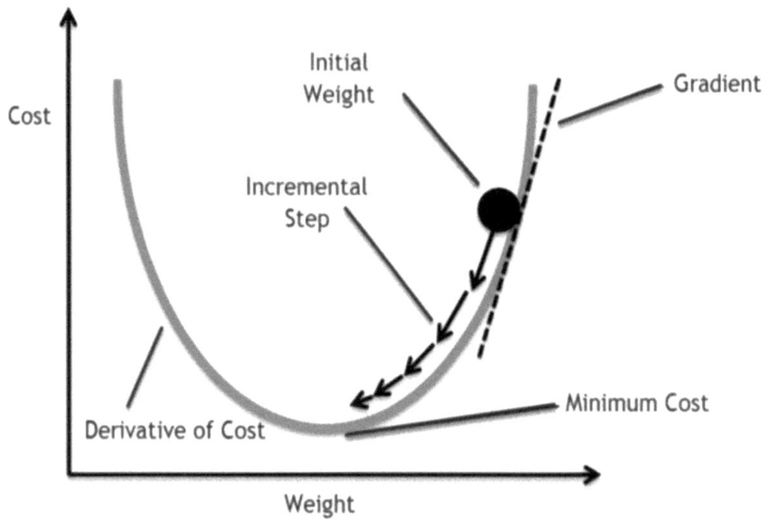

Fig. 6. Stochastic gradient descent classifier [42]

6 Conclusion and Future Scope

In conclusion, multi-image color component classification of SAR and optical data holds significant promise for advancing remote sensing applications across various domains. By combining the supplementary capabilities of SAR and optical data and analyzing their color components, researchers and analysts can extract valuable information about Earth's surface and its dynamics. This approach enables more accurate classification of land cover types, improved detection of changes over time, and better understanding of environmental phenomena such as vegetation health and surface characteristics. The integration of SAR and optical image data through multi-image color elements offers synergistic benefits, allowing for more comprehensive and insightful analysis compared to using either data source in isolation. Furthermore, the future scope of this technique is promising, with opportunities for further innovation and advancement. Future research could focus on developing more advanced AI techniques to enhance the analysis of multi-image color components, as well as integrating SAR and optical data with other remote sensing modalities for even more comprehensive insights. Moreover, there is potential for the development of novel applications in fields such as precision agriculture, environmental monitoring, and disaster management, leveraging the capabilities of multi-image color component classification to address complex challenges and inform decision-making processes. Overall, multi-image color component classification of SAR and optical data represents a powerful tool for advancing remote sensing capabilities and unlocking new insights into Earth's surface and its dynamics, with broad implications for research, industry, and society. Remote sensing applications can leverage multi-image color component classification of SAR and optical data, enhancing classification accuracy and providing valuable insights. By combining SAR and optical data and analyzing their color components, we can extract richer information about Earth's surface characteristics. SAR data captures backscattered electromagnetic waves, while optical data records light reflectance across different spectral bands. Their interdependent characteristics facilitate a more thorough comprehension of the environment.

Multi-image color components, derived from various images in RGB, HSV, or other color spaces, offer insights into texture, vegetation, and surface properties. Integrating SAR and optical data through these color components enables more effective categorization and enriches classification algorithms. SAR data excels in distinguishing metropolitan areas, water bodies, and vegetation, while optical data provides detailed spectral information about objects [52].

Advanced AI techniques can enhance the analysis of multi-image color components, enabling more accurate classification and feature extraction. By combining structural and spectral information from SAR and optical data, classification algorithms can improve accuracy and effectively discriminate between different land cover types. In addition, SAR data is particularly useful in cloudy or atmospherically disturbed environments, where it can penetrate vegetation and clouds to reveal buried structures. Optical data complements SAR by providing comprehensive surface features. Analyzing multi-image color components allows for versatile feature extraction, with the ability to highlight or conceal important details based on the selected color spaces and components. This adaptability enables classification tailored to specific applications and data characteristics. In summary, utilizing SAR and optical data classification based on multi-image color components improves remote sensing applications, thereby enhancing environmental monitoring, land management, disaster assessment, and decision-making processes in urban development. AI-driven techniques play a crucial role in optimizing these processes and extracting valuable insights from complex datasets [53]. In addition to current applications, there are several promising future directions for the utilization of multi-image color component classification of SAR and optical data in remote sensing. One potential area of growth is the development of more advanced AI techniques to further enhance the analysis of these data sources. Deep learning algorithms, for example, could be trained to automatically extract features from multi-image color components, improving classification accuracy and efficiency. Another future direction is the integration of SAR and optical data with other remote sensing modalities, such as LiDAR or hyperspectral imaging. By combining multiple data sources, researchers can obtain a more comprehensive understanding of Earth's surface and its dynamics, leading to new insights and applications. Furthermore, there is potential for the development of novel applications in fields such as precision agriculture, environmental monitoring, and disaster management. For example, multi-image color component classification could be used to detect changes in land cover over time, monitor crop health, or assess the impact of natural disasters on urban areas. Additionally, as remote sensing technology continues to advance, there may be opportunities to collect higher spatial and temporal resolution data, allowing for more detailed and frequent monitoring of Earth's surface. This could enable more accurate and timely decision-making in various domains, from urban planning to natural resource management.

Overall, the future scope of multi-image color component classification of SAR and optical data in remote sensing is promising, with potential applications across a wide range of fields and opportunities for continued innovation and advancement.

References

1. Ma, Q.: Improving SAR target recognition performance using multiple preprocessing techniques. Comput. Intell. Neurosci. **2021**, 6572362 (2021). https://doi.org/10.1155/2021/6572362
2. Albinet, C., Borderies, P., Gastellu-Etchegorry, J.P.: Characterization of maritime pine forests with combination of simulated P-band SAR data and hyperspectral data. Int. J. Antennas Propag. **2012**, 409512 (2012). https://doi.org/10.1155/2012/409512
3. Ji, X., Sun, Y.: SAR Image target recognition based on monogenic signal and sparse representation. Wirel. Commun. Mob. Comput. **2021**, 6630865 (2021). https://doi.org/10.1155/2021/6630865
4. Shakya, A., Biswas, M., Pal, M.: Fusion and classification of SAR and optical data using multi-image color components with differential gradients. Remote Sens. **15**(1), 274 (2023). https://doi.org/10.3390/rs15010274
5. Zhang, H., Shen, H., Yuan, Q., Guan, X.: Multispectral and SAR image fusion based on laplacian pyramid and sparse representation. Remote Sens. **14**(4), 870 (2022). https://doi.org/10.3390/rs14040870
6. Chandrakala, D., Sumathi, S.: Application of artificial bee colony optimization algorithm for image classification using color and texture feature similarity fusion. ISRN Artif. Intell. **2012**, 1–10 (2012). https://doi.org/10.5402/2012/426957
7. Alsamhi, S.H., et al.: Multi-drone edge intelligence and SAR smart wearable devices for emergency communication. Wirel. Commun. Mob. Comput. **2021**, 6710074 (2021). https://doi.org/10.1155/2021/6710074
8. Zhang, X., Fan, W., Xi, J., He, L.: 14-Bit Fully differential SAR ADC with PGA used in readout circuit of CMOS image sensor. J. Sensors. **2021**, 6651642 (2021). https://doi.org/10.1155/2021/6651642

9. Li, Y., Zhang, S., Li, X., Ye, F.: Remote sensing image classification with few labeled data using semisupervised learning. Wirel. Commun. Mob. Comput. **2023**, 7724264 (2023). https://doi.org/10.1155/2023/7724264
10. Weng, W.: Multitask sparse representation of two-dimensional variational mode decomposition components for SAR target recognition. Sci. Program. **2023**, 8846287 (2023). https://doi.org/10.1155/2023/8846287
11. Janarthanan, S., Ganesh Kumar, T., Janakiraman, S., Dhanaraj, R.K., Shah, M.A.: An Efficient multispectral image classification and optimization using remote sensing data. J. Sensors. **2022**, 2004716 (2022). https://doi.org/10.1155/2022/2004716
12. Strimaitis, R., Stefanovic, P., Ramanauskaite, S., Slotkiene, A.: A Combined approach for multi-label text data classification. Comput. Intell. Neurosci. **2022**, 3369703 (2022). https://doi.org/10.1155/2022/3369703
13. Hu, J.: Automatic target recognition of SAR images using collaborative representation. Comput. Intell. Neurosci. **2022**, 3100028 (2022). https://doi.org/10.1155/2022/3100028
14. Chopra, P., et al.: Automated registration of multiangle SAR images using artificial intelligence. Mob. Inf. Syst. **2022**, 4545139 (2022). https://doi.org/10.1155/2022/4545139
15. Elwan, M., Amein, A.S., Mousa, A., Ahmed, A.M., Bouallegue, B., Eltanany, A.S.: SAR Image matching based on local feature detection and description using convolutional neural network. Secur. Commun. Networks. **2022**, 5669069 (2022). https://doi.org/10.1155/2022/5669069
16. Huang, B., Li, Z., Yang, C., Sun, F., Song, Y.: Single satellite optical imagery dehazing using SAR image prior based on conditional generative adversarial networks. In: Proc. 2020 IEEE Winter Conference on Applications of Computer Vision WACV 2020, pp. 1795–1802 (2020). https://doi.org/10.1109/WACV45572.2020.9093471
17. Knott, P., Bertuch, T., Wilden, H., Peters, O., Brenner, A.R., Walterscheid, I.: SAR Experiments using a conformal antenna array radar demonstrator. Int. J. Antennas Propag. **2012**, 142542 (2012). https://doi.org/10.1155/2012/142542
18. Margarit, G., Mallorqui, J.J.: Scattering-based model of the SAR signatures of complex targets for classification applications. Int. J. Navig. Obs. **2008**, 1–11 (2008). https://doi.org/10.1155/2008/426267
19. Wang, W., Zhang, C., Tian, J., Ou, J., Li, J.: A SAR Image target recognition approach via novel SSF-net models. Comput. Intell. Neurosci. **2020**, 8859172 (2020). https://doi.org/10.1155/2020/8859172
20. Ding, H., Lin, A.K.L.: Feature extraction based on non-subsampled shearlet transform (NSST) with application to SAR image data. Math. Probl. Eng. **2020**, 8885887 (2020). https://doi.org/10.1155/2020/8885887
21. Ke, Q., Zeng-Guo, S., Liu, Y., Wei, W., Wozniak, M., Scherer, R.: High-resolution SAR image despeckling based on nonlocal means filter and modified AA model. Secur. Commun. Networks. **2020**, 8889317 (2020). https://doi.org/10.1155/2020/8889317
22. Wang, P., Zhang, X., Hao, Y.: A Method combining CNN and ELM for feature extraction and classification of SAR image. J. Sensors. **2019**, 6134610 (2019). https://doi.org/10.1155/2019/6134610
23. Liu, Z., Blasch, E., Bhatnagar, G., John, V., Wu, W., Blum, R.S.: Fusing synergistic information from multi-sensor images: an overview from implementation to performance assessment. Inf. Fusion. **42**, 127–145 (2018). https://doi.org/10.1016/j.inffus.2017.10.010
24. Li, M.Q., Xu, L.P., Xu, N., Huang, T., Yan, B.: SAR Image segmentation based on improved grey wolf optimization algorithm and fuzzy C-means. Math. Probl. Eng. **2018**, 4576015 (2018). https://doi.org/10.1155/2018/4576015
25. Ezquerro, P., Guardiola-Albert, C., Herrera, G., Fernández-Merodo, J.A., Béjar-Pizarro, M., Bonì, R.: Groundwater and subsidence modeling combining geological and multi-satellite

SAR data over the alto guadalentín aquifer (SE Spain). Geofluids. **2017**, 1359325 (2017). https://doi.org/10.1155/2017/1359325
26. Gao, F., Yue, Z., Wang, J., Sun, J., Yang, E., Zhou, H.: A Novel active semisupervised convolutional neural network algorithm for SAR image recognition. Comput. Intell. Neurosci. **2017**, 3105053 (2017). https://doi.org/10.1155/2017/3105053
27. Hansch, R., Ley, A., Hellwich, O.: Correct and still wrong: The relationship between sampling strategies and the estimation of the generalization error. Int. Geosci. Remote Sens. Symp. **2017**, 3672–3675 (2017). https://doi.org/10.1109/IGARSS.2017.8127795
28. Lee, J.G., Lee, J.H.: SAR reduction using integration of PIFA and AMC structure for penta-band mobile terminals. Int. J. Antennas Propag. **2017**, 6196721 (2017). https://doi.org/10.1155/2017/6196721
29. Zhang, F., Sha, M., Wang, G., Li, Z., Shao, Y.: Urban aerodynamic roughness length mapping using multitemporal SAR data. Adv. Meteorol. **2017**, 1–14 (2017)
30. Han, R., Liu, P., Wang, H., Yang, L., Zhang, H., Ma, C.: An Improved Urban mapping strategy based on collaborative processing of optical and SAR remotely sensed data. Math. Probl. Eng. **2017**, 9361592 (2017). https://doi.org/10.1155/2017/9361592
31. Bucciarelli, M., Pastina, D., Cristallini, D., Sedehi, M., Lombardo, P.: Integration of frequency domain wideband antenna nulling and wavenumber domain image formation for multi-channel SAR. Int. J. Antennas Propag. **2016**, 2834904 (2016). https://doi.org/10.1155/2016/2834904
32. Zhang, S., Wang, S., Chen, B.: Modified hybrid freeman/eigenvalue decomposition for polarimetric SAR data. J. Sensors. **2015**, 168720 (2015). https://doi.org/10.1155/2015/168720
33. Lin, C., Wang, B., Zhao, X., Pang, M.: Optimizing kernel PCA using sparse representation-based classifier for mstar SAR image target recognition. Math. Probl. Eng. **2013**, 847062 (2013). https://doi.org/10.1155/2013/847062
34. Zhang, X., Liu, Z., Liu, S., Li, G.: Time-frequency feature extraction of HRRP using AGR and NMF for SAR ATR. J. Electr. Comput. Eng. **2015**, 478971 (2015). https://doi.org/10.1155/2015/478971
35. Lv, Q., Dou, Y., Niu, X., Xu, J., Xu, J., Xia, F.: Urban land use and land cover classification using remotely sensed sar data through deep belief networks. J. Sensors. **2015**, 538063 (2015). https://doi.org/10.1155/2015/538063
36. Lin, Y., Fan, Y., Jiang, C., Wang, Z., Shao, W.: MIMO SAR using orthogonal coding: design, performance analysis, and verifications. Int. J. Antennas Propag. **2015**, 629506 (2015). https://doi.org/10.1155/2015/629506
37. Deng, B., Wang, H.Q., Qin, Y.L., Zhu, S., Li, X.: Rotating parabolic-reflector antenna target in SAR data: model, characteristics, and parameter estimation. Int. J. Antennas Propag. **2013**, 583865 (2013). https://doi.org/10.1155/2013/583865
38. Luo, X., Deng, Y., Wang, R., Guo, L., Wang, M.: Correction of channel imbalance for MIMO SAR using stepped-frequency chirps. Int. J. Antennas Propag. **2014**, 161294 (2014). https://doi.org/10.1155/2014/161294
39. Wei, L., Balz, T., Liao, M., Zhang, L.: TerraSAR-X StripMap data interpretation of complex urban scenarios with 3D SAR tomography. J. Sensors. **2014**, 386753 (2014). https://doi.org/10.1155/2014/386753
40. Jiang, H., Song, H., Guo, L., Wang, W.: Special MISO-SAR and MIMO-sar modes for bidirectional imaging. Int. J. Antennas Propag. **2014**, 320384 (2014). https://doi.org/10.1155/2014/320384
41. Zhang, H., Ni, W., Yan, W., Bian, H., Wu, J.: Fast SAR image change detection using bayesian approach based difference image and modified statistical region merging. Sci. World J. **2014**, 862875 (2014). https://doi.org/10.1155/2014/862875
42. Zhang, J., Luo, T., Gao, G., Lian, L.: Junction point detection algorithm for SAR image. Int. J. Antennas Propag. **2013**(3), 357379 (2013). https://doi.org/10.1155/2013/357379

43. Tang, F., Bermak, A., Amira, A., Amor Benammar, M., He, D., Zhao, X.: Two-step single slope/SAR ADC with error correction for CMOS image sensor. Sci. World J. **2014**, 861278 (2014). https://doi.org/10.1155/2014/861278
44. Gao, G., Shi, G., Zou, H., Zhou, S.: Characterizing the statistical properties of SAR clutter by using an empirical distribution. Int. J. Antennas Propag. **2013**, 109145 (2013). https://doi.org/10.1155/2013/109145
45. Lu, Y., Gao, Q., Sun, D., Zhang, D.: SAR image despeckling with adaptive multiscale products based on directionlet transform. Math. Probl. Eng. **2013**(2), 197159 (2013). https://doi.org/10.1155/2013/197159
46. Wang, H., Zhang, S.: A Robust and lightweight detector for ship target with complex background in SAR image. J. Sensors. **2022**, 8199418 (2022). https://doi.org/10.1155/2022/8199418
47. Yang, N., Zhang, Y.: A Gaussian process classification and target recognition algorithm for SAR images. Sci. Program. **2022**, 9212856 (2022). https://doi.org/10.1155/2022/9212856
48. Li, H., Duan, X.L.: SAR Ship image speckle noise suppression algorithm based on adaptive bilateral filter. Wirel. Commun. Mob. Comput. **2022**, 9392648 (2022). https://doi.org/10.1155/2022/9392648
49. Fracastoro, G., Magli, E., Poggi, G., Scarpa, G., Valsesia, D., Verdoliva, L.: Deep learning methods for synthetic aperture radar image despeckling: an overview of trends and perspectives. IEEE Geosci. Remote Sens. Mag. **9**(2), 29–51 (2021). https://doi.org/10.1109/MGRS.2021.3070956
50. Wang, X., et al.: Detection of oil spill using SAR imagery based on alexNet model. Comput. Intell. Neurosci. **2021**, 4812979 (2021). https://doi.org/10.1155/2021/4812979
51. Chen, X., Wang, X., Chen, Y., Wang, H.: A Novel SAR image target recognition algorithm under big data analysis. Wirel. Commun. Mob. Comput. **2021**, 4556157 (2021). https://doi.org/10.1155/2021/4556157
52. Shan, C., Li, M., Chen, Z., Han, L.: Region matching of SAR images using blocks for target recognition. Comput. Intell. Neurosci. **2021**, 5410440 (2021). https://doi.org/10.1155/2021/5410440
53. Nguyen-Quoc, H., Hoang, V.T.: A Revisit histogram of oriented descriptor for facial color image classification based on fusion of color information. J. Sensors. **2021**, 6296505 (2021). https://doi.org/10.1155/2021/6296505

Comparative Analysis of Advancements in Precision Farming Using AI and Deep Learning

Mohit(✉), Swastik Sindhani, and Vibha Nehra

Amity University, Noida, Uttar Pradesh, India
{mohit3,swastik.sindhani}@s.amity.edu, vnehra@amity.edu

Abstract. In countries including India, agriculture plays a vital role in sustaining daily life and the economy. India's economic well-being is heavily reliant on agriculture, which also plays a crucial role in ensuring food security by supplying a significant portion of the nation's consumer goods. However, contemporary challenges are making it increasingly difficult for farmers to meet the growing demand for crops. Unpredictable and unnatural climatic changes not only reduce agricultural yields but also hinder farmers' ability to forecast future crop production accurately. To address these challenges, leveraging technology can empower farmers to produce more crops of superior quality.

Advancements in cutting-edge technologies, such as Wireless Sensor Networks (WSN), Unmanned Aerial Vehicles (UAVs), Artificial Intelligence (AI), Machine Learning (ML), Deep Learning (DL), and the Internet of Things (IoT), are transforming agriculture and enabling sustainable solutions to meet future food demands. This paper presents a comprehensive overview of the current contributions of Deep Learning (DL) and IoT in the domain of precision agriculture and a comparative study about the different Al and Deep learning techniques. It delves into studies related to IoT applications in agriculture, including innovative techniques like plant monitoring and crop recommendation, weed detection, and yield prediction, which are at the forefront of modern crop production methods. The study aims to provide guidance to new and existing farmers, assisting them in making informed decisions about their crop choices based on the nutrients present in the soil. Additionally, the paper proposes YOLOv8 Machine Learning model for precision farming specifically for weed detection and outlines the methodology that YOLOv8 follows.

Keywords: Agriculture · Machine Learning techniques · Weed Detection · Yield Forecast · Performance Evaluation

1 Introduction

For a very long time, farmland has been the primary source of food for meeting people's necessities. Agriculture is the backbone of the country because it contributes to ensuring food security for the entire population and because it is constantly essential to a nation's

M. Paprzycki et al. (Eds.): ICACIS 2024, CCIS 2405, pp. 46–64, 2027.
https://doi.org/10.1007/978-3-032-30990-7_4

economic system. Nearly 75% of people worldwide make their living from agriculture. It is one of the primary sources that heavily influence how an economy is structured and run. Because of the population boom and the resulting need to increase agricultural production, more needs to be done to improve agriculture's position. Farmers are looking for practical ways to increase crop yield while spending less money and using their resources more efficiently. By enabling smart technology to be used in agriculture, this aids farmers in making better decisions and increasing yields. Traditionally, farmers engage in naive monitoring and produce harvests without the use of chemicals to preserve a range of plants and living things. Crop yield, however, depends on several variables, including the weather and soil conditions, crop, usage of fertilizer, and the seed variety. One technique to predict the harvest is to use the most recent technological developments, such as machine learning. Every industry, including agriculture, has been greatly impacted by the quick development of machine learning. Most people can benefit from cutting-edge technologies. IoTs have just begun to have a big impact in everyday life, broadening our sensory capabilities, granting us the power to shape our surroundings. IoTs are used in both diagnosis and control, particularly in the agricultural and environmental domains. A prominent trend in smart farming is the use of remote sensing to make it simpler to extract information essential for data-driven decisions. Installing a Wireless Sensor Network (WSN) in the field has boosted farmers' efficacy and efficiency in this optimization of agriculture. Factors influencing crop growth and yield can be tracked and managed with the use of WSN. WSN are additionally useful for controlling equipment, identifying the most suitable farmer for a particular environment, determine when to harvest, and more. The main problem with conventional farming includes detection of pests and diseases, forecasting yield, making predictions about sowing, weeds, soil nutrients, fertilizer, irrigation, monitoring, maintenance, and climate. The development of a robust crop may be impacted by farmers' usual methods of farming. The main causes of the crop being harmed before cultivation include weeds, pests/insects, and diseases. About 40% of global crop losses in recent years have been attributed to pest damage from weeds and insects, and this percentage is predicted to rise in the years to come. Farmers use pesticide spraying on the entire field to solve this issue. In above form of pest management, a lot of pesticides are employed, but if these chemicals are used irresponsibly, they can be costly, toxic for people and the environment, and have a lot of bad impacts, including decreased productivity and effects on crops, soil, and environmental health. As technology advances, precision farming is an innovative approach to pest management that is gaining popularity. Sensors are used to administer the accurate amount of pesticides. As a result, production can be increased while using less pesticide. The lack of knowledge and technology and its improper application, as well as the employment of some antiquated techniques, can result in less production. The farmer's traditional forecast will be unsuccessful and cause further problems. Numerous obstacles must be overcome during the agriculture sector's life cycle, including climatic variations, soil management, weed and pest control, irrigation management, water scarcity, and many others. The structure of the paper and sections have been detailed in Fig. 1.

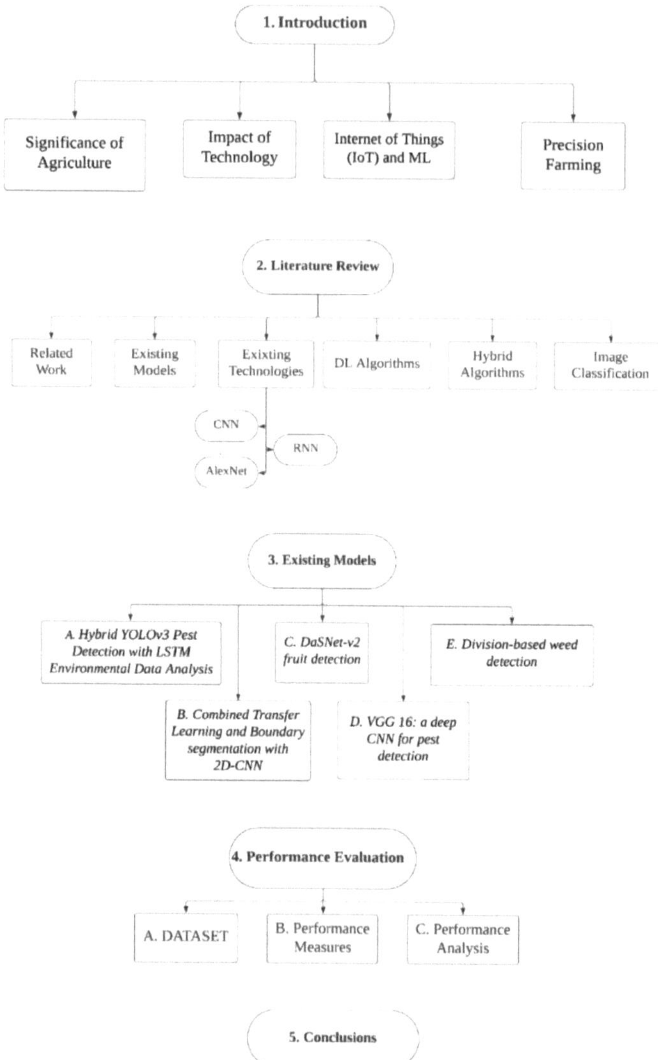

Fig. 1. Structure of the Review Paper and the sections classification

2 Literature Review

The advancements in plant monitoring and precision farming that have significantly contributed to the finest possible models for enhanced agriculture that are intended to increase agricultural monitoring, production forecasting, and weed detection for more accuracy, adaptability, and efficiency are explained in this section.

Nipuna Chamara et al. [1] introduced the different types of Sensors, Sensing platforms, and main control boards that are used to measure different parameters and proposed some future directions in Ag-IoT. In a similar vein, Muhammad Shoaib Farooq et al. [2] talk about the design, platform, and topology of agricultural networks that enable farmers to increase crop productivity and provide connectivity to the IoT backbone. Furthermore, offers a thorough synopsis of recent and ongoing developments in IoT agricultural applications and many innovative technologies. K. Lova Raju and V. Vijayaraghavan [3] discussed embedded technology such as the Raspberry Pi interacting with several sensors and models being utilized to control pests, create intelligent seeds, track crop production, keep an eye on weed identification, manage water, other techniques to improve the outcome of production in agriculture. Automation of the controllers like Arduino, Node MCU, and Raspberry Pi using wireless technologies like WiFi, Zigbee, Z-Wave, and GSM improves crop yield through accurate monitoring and identification of crops damaged by disease. Achilles D. Boursianis et al. [4] examined the enabling techniques used with IoT, explained them in depth, and did an analysis of their key uses and advantages. The ARETHOU5A project framework is briefly explained as an application case for combining cutting-edge technologies. A concise overview of the suggested remedies for agro-industrial and environmental issues was offered by Jesús Martín Talavera et al. [5]. Future methods to fully embrace cloud services and other forms of connectivity for a smart IoT environment were also offered. The tools and constraints of several Deep Learning algorithms, such as backpropagation and feedforward neural networks, CNN, RNN, and GAN, were mentioned by Nanyang Zhu et al. [6]. Bring attention to the value and significance of frameworks like TensorFlow and Caffe. Future Opportunities and Scope for DL Applications are mentioned, Guoyu Lu et al. [7] mentioned how NLP for agricultural issues can be used by AGI to revolutionise agriculture. Additionally, how AGI addresses issues like climate change, food security, and rural development while also offering farmers insightful guidance. AGI can be used to automate farms and can be utilised in computational breeding to create new crop varieties. Gives a thorough overview of the various soil, crop, and weed management algorithms and approaches, including their advantages and disadvantages. Eli-Chukwu et al. [8] also noted the difficulties in implementing AI, such as the need for big data, the method of implementation, the high cost of data, and flexibility. Future technologies were featured, like RAS. Robin Sharma [9] outlined the applications for several agricultural expert systems, including AGREX, TEAPEST, JAFexpert, and others, and explained several AI technologies. Kirtan Jha et al. [10] proposed the idea of training the model so that it can recognise plants or flowers when any image is supplied to it in the future. Due to its simplicity, which only requires 3 into 3 convolutional layers stacked on top of one another in increasing depth, VGG16 is utilised to train the model. Using max pooling, volume size can be reduced. The next layer is a softmax classifier, which is followed by two fully connected layers with 4096 nodes each. Future uses for enhanced agriculture are suggested, including robots and thermal imaging utilising drones. Listed the many AI techniques utilised, along with the outcomes and restrictions. In another study, deep learning-based computer vision has been widely addressed in relation to seven various application areas, including yield estimation, weed management, soil analysis, irrigation management, plant health analysis, and seed quality analysis. Robotic harvesting, knowledge of genetic resources and artificial intelligence, and other practical applications could be extremely important for the future of agriculture. V.G. Dhanya et al. [11] outlined the issues, including the use of vast processing power and data-driven algorithms and the potential solutions might be the adoption of cloud-based systems with characteristics like auto-scaling, load balancing, simplified maintenance, and high availability. The four phases involved in data classification and image recognition are briefly discussed by Padmesh Tripathi et al. [12]. Data collection and preparation comes first. Next, neural networks are trained using methods like AlexNet, K-means feature learning, FCNN, etc. Then, model testing comes next. Finally, results analysis. Andreas Kamilaris et al. [13] listed and provided a brief explanation of the study's performance metrics. Additionally, ran a comparative analysis using various methods and discussed some advanced Deep Learning models, such as CNN + HistNN using RGB histograms, Modified Inception-ResNet CNN, etc. Yuzhen Lu et al. [14] pointed out the applications of GAN in precision farming such as Weed Control, Plant health, fruit detection, etc. and challenges associated with GANs such as Training Instability, Performance Evaluation, High-quality image generation. For predicting crop productivity and drought, an intelligent system combining a wrapper feature selection approach with PART classification technique is proposed by Nermeen Gamal Rezk et al. [15]. The gathered environmental indicator data is evaluated/analyzed using the Wrapper technique to determine which indicators are best helpful for challenges related to agricultural production and drought. The PART method is used to construct the drought and crop productivity predictor. F-Score is 93.40%, and accuracy is 93.42%. The use of time-series analysis to forecast future values based on previously observed values is taken into consideration for future improvement. TensorFlow is the next most popular deep learning technique, and MATLAB is also frequently used, Chengjuan Ren et al. [16]. T. Saranya et al. [17] provide a thorough analysis of IoT and deep learning for precision agriculture, use of DL in various agricultural fields, including the detection of soil nutrients and yield prediction, insect, disease, and weed detection, design of the IoT architecture for smart agriculture, classification and variety of sensors, and the use of sensors in precision agriculture, as well as the recent use of UAV for precision. The study also proposed plant pest detection. Transfer learning is one of the booming techniques in artificial intelligence. In deep learning, transfer learning refers to employing a model that has previously been trained on a different task. Utilizes one of the greatest vision architectures, VGG 16, especially for picture categorization. It has several layers and is a standard deep convolutional neural network (CNN) architecture. The VGG16 model obtains a top-5 test accuracy of roughly 92.7% in ImageNet. There are almost 14 million photos in the ImageNet collection, which may be divided into nearly 1000 categories. It also received great marks out of all the models that were submitted to ILSVRC-2014. Since additional layers necessitate additional weight factors, the VGG model is more complex and has challenges with vanishing gradients. The bootstrap approach is the study's focus, which combines an enhanced new fully connected layer with a customised VGG 16 model. The creation of the suggested framework involves three steps. The first phase involves preprocessing the pest image, the second involves freezing and unfreezing the VGG 16 model, and the third involves creating an ideal fully connected layer with a hyper-parameter Adam optimizer. Jirapond Muangprathub et al. [18] proposed use of WSNs for crop irrigation. Created and put into use a system to regulate environmental elements in crop fields. The three parts of the system were mobile, web, and hardware applications. The first section dealt with the design and implementation of control boxes. This control box had hardware and an electronic control system to link to sensors and collect data on crops. The control box was designed for real-world testing. The implemented design was networked and collected Internet of Things data from any location. A web-based application was developed and utilized as the second component to edit crop data and field information details. And the third component involved using a mobile application to control crop irrigation. R. Bhargava Rama Gowd et al. [19] developed a system that makes use of machine learning techniques and methodologies including Random Forests Regressor and Linear Regression. The final crop forecasting model in this case was the Random Forest Regressor, which was utilised under the requirement of 100% accuracy. It also suggests which fertilisers should be used based on the pH value that the user enters in the front end. Also noted were the data set, which was taken from Kaggle, and the system requirements. Additionally, the accuracy of the system is increased by examining several ML techniques. Future research to increase the accuracy of harvest prediction is also recommended, including the use of pH sensors, ambient sensors, and soil moisture monitors. Alexandros Oikonomidis et al. [20] indicates that processing numerous arrays in nonlinear modules is insufficient to prevent overfitting and improve model performance. Large training dataset limitations are overcome through data augmentation and transfer learning, and future research should focus on how to optimise the labelling and hyperparameter tuning processes. Ruchi Dhall et al. [21] addresses the duty cycling issue, presented a upgraded duty cycling effective path planning algorithm regarding precision agricultural system basis on the Internet of Things. IDC is based on base station residual energy metrics for energy-efficient data aggregation. Two residual energy thresholds are used in the proposed IDC. With the use of the earlier DC and NDC algorithms, the suggested IDC's performance is assessed and studied. Use cases for smart agriculture that have been presented by Anusuya Arumugam [22] that include crop monitoring, field scanning, yield survey, yield assessment, equal crop supply and demand, multidimensional analysis of crops, meteorological circumstances, and economic situations, etc. Additionally, deep learning model performance metrics such as training duration, FPR, sensitivity, specificity, accuracy, etc. Additionally, the Kappa value for several models was illustrated. In order to estimate wheat and barley yield, Petteri Nevavuori et al. [23] describe a training paradigm for a CNN-based deep learning network. The CNN regularisation scheme and the training algorithm's hyperparameters were both optimised. RGB photos appeared to perform better on CNN architecture than NDVI images. And used mean absolute error to assess CNN's performance. M. Dian Bah et al. [24] suggested utilising convolutional neural networks (CNNs) and a line identification algorithm on high-resolution UAV photos to create a system for classification that was vision-based for weed detection. Three phases are involved in this: the first is the removal of soil and residues. The second phase then employs the Houge Transform to find crop lines. Lastly, use a convolutional neural network to distinguish between crops and weeds. To identify plant illnesses, Konstantinos P. Ferentinos [25] created a convolutional neural network model and fed it simple photos of leaves. To construct an early warning tool for real-time cultivation, several pre-trained models were trained, and the best ones from those were chosen. The Gaussian radial basis function surpasses all other activation functions in the quick and easy Extreme Learning Machine used by Suchithra and Pai

[26] to categorise and forecast soil nutrients. For the purpose of predicting wheat and corn yields using remotely sensed multi-spectral, multi-temporal data, Qiao et al. [27] suggested a hybrid DL-based model called SSTNN. A hybrid DL technique of LSTM and 1D-CNN was put forth by Jeong et al. [28] for use two months prior to the pixel-level yield prediction of rice crops. In a growing soyabean field, WorldView-3 (WV) and PlanetScope (PS) raw satellite pictures were used to create a DL 2D, 3D Residual based CNN model and ResNet architecture by Sagan et al. [29]. For regional-scale forecasts of soil organic carbon, Yang et al. [30] developed a CNN model with ten years' worth of phenology data, and it was also compared to RF. According to research by Akash Anand et al. [31], adversarial networks are produced by an unsupervised machine learning algorithm. The goal is to create a huge volume of image dataset. A convolutional neural network (CNN) has been built, and multi–CNN Conv2D has been utilised to identify soil images using picture-based surface analysis, among a range of deep learning algorithms. Megha Sharma et al. [32] present an open-source technology-based smart system to predict irrigation requirements of a field by sensing external parameters like obstacle detection or intruder alert using an infrared sensor, as well as ground parameters like soil moisture and environmental conditions like temperature and humidity. The algorithm on which the suggested system is built also incorporates sensed data in addition to the aforementioned factors. The recent advances in precision farming (elaborated in Table 1) are encouraging, but there is still plenty of room for research. Comprehensive assessments of existing algorithms that highlight their advantages and disadvantages are urgently needed. To ensure more precise and effective smart farming, these analyses are essential for developing and improving these approaches.

Table 1. Summary of Current Related work on Precision Farming

Ref.	Year	Contribution and Focus
[1]	2022	Types of Sensors, Sensing Platforms and Main Control boards
[2]	2019	Agricultural network architecture, platform and topology
[3]	2020	Mentioned embedded technologies
[4]	2022	Explained ARETHOU5A project framework
[5]	2017	Overview of remedies for agro-industrial and environmental issues
[6]	2018	Mentioned the tools and constraints of DL algorithms.
[7]	2023	Mentioned NLP for agricultural issues, AGI for climate change, food security.
[8]	2019	Difficulties in AI implementation. Future technology like RAS were featured
[9]	2021	Outlined the applications of expert systems like AGREX, TEAPEST, JAF expert.
[10]	2019	Lists the AI techniques utilized, outcomes and restrictions. Proposed a model training to recognize Plants and Flower.
[11]	2022	Discussing issues and the potential solutions.

(continued)

Table 1. (*continued*)

Ref.	Year	Contribution and Focus
[12]	2022	Briefly discusses the four phases in data classification and image recognition
[13]	2018	Listed and provided an explanation of the Study's performance metrices.
[14]	2022	Applications of GAN in precision farming.
[15]	2021	Proposed a wrapper feature selection approach, PART.
[16]	2019	Discusses a smart system to predict the disease in Tomato and Potato.
[17]	2020	Lists different algorithms and frameworks used for classification.
[18]	2023	Discussed transfer learning and proposes a model, VGG16inImageNet.
[19]	2019	Proposed use of WSN.
[20]	2023	Developed a system for crop forecasting using ML techniques.
[21]	2023	Discusses challenges and the potential solutions for model performance.
[22]	2018	Addresses the duty cycling issue. Proposed a modified duty cycling path.
[23]	2023	Use cases for smart agriculture and DL model performance metrices.
[24]	2019	Describes a training paradigm for CNN based DL network.
[25]	2019	Proposes using CNN and Line identification algorithm.
[26]	2018	Created a CNN model to identify plant disease.
[27]	2020	Explains Extreme Learning Machines to categorise and forecasts oil nutrients.
[28, 29]	20212022	Proposes a Hybrid DL-based model/techniques, SSTNN and LSTM+1D-CNN.
[30]	2021	DL 2D, 3D Residual based CNN model and ResNet architecture.
[31]	2021	CNN model with ten years' worth of phenology data.
[32]	2023	Creation of huge dataset, use of CNN Conv2D
[33]	2023	Proposes an open-source tech-based smart system for irrigation.

3 Existing Deep Learning Models for Precise Farming

3.1 Hybrid YOLOv3 Pest Detection with LSTM Environmental Data Analysis

In order to detect pests and analyse environmental data, YOLO and LSTM networks can offer a complete solution that not only keeps track of past environmental circumstances but also recognises pests in real-time. Chen et al. [33] created a method that combines environmental sensors and IoT to examine the environmental impacts of pest life cycles. This lets farmers to be aware of Tessaratoma papillosa growth in real time, thereby assisting them in managing pest growth. Long short-term memory (LSTM) was used for environmental data analysis while You Only Look Once (YOLOv3) was used for pest identification and categorization.

3.2 Combined Transfer Learning and Boundary Segmentation with 2D-CNN

An efficient system for plant disease detection can be produced by combining boundary segmentation, inductive transfer learning, and 2D-CNN (2D Convolutional Neural Network). On a sizable dataset of common images, a pre-trained 2D-CNN model is being trained. Annotated dataset is used for boundary segmentation. Integration of segmentation and transfer learning. By optimising inductive transfer learning for disease detection on coconut trees, Tetila et al. [34] created an end-to-end deep learning system. To detect coconut sickness, 2D-CNN is trained and segmented to find aberrant boundaries.

3.3 DaSNet-v2 Fruit Detection

It is critical to accurately identify fruits while plants are still growing using image and computer vision since it is an essential step toward automating processes like harvesting. Since deep learning-based methodologies are more suited than traditional computer vision techniques for managing substantial amounts of data unpredictability, they hold great promise in challenging industries like agriculture. Deep learning-based approaches have emerged as the most cutting-edge solutions for many image segmentation and classification problems. Afonso et al. [35] proposed the DaSNet-v2 deep neural network for fruit identification, instance segmentation on fruits, and semantic segmentation on branches. By using this system, which was developed and tested in an apple orchard, robotic apple harvesting is now possible using optical detection.

3.4 Division-Based Weed Detection

Precision agriculture uses division-based weed detection as a tool to locate and control weeds in crop fields. It is advantageous because it enables more focused and effective weed management. On beet, spinach, and bean, Bah et al. [24] suggested a division-based weed detection method. This can be applied to a UAV to precisely spray herbicides and combines line detection with CNN for weed detection.

There are three steps to it:

Step 1: Get rid of dirt and undesirable objects.
Step 2: Detect crop lines.
Step 3: Classify crops and weeds on CNN.

3.5 VGG 16: A Deep CNN for Pest Detection

One of the top vision architectures, especially for image classification, is VGG 16. It has many layers and is a typical deep convolutional neural network (CNN) design. The VGG16 model hits approximately 92.7% of the top-5 test accuracy in ImageNet. About 14 M photos in an ImageNet collection, with approximately 1000 different categories, are available. Additionally, it received higher rank among the submitted models to ILSVRC-2014. T. Saranya et al. [17] provided a method for extracting bootstrap features that involves freezing the VGG16 hidden layers, extracting the features, and merging them with a newly improved fully connected layer. The creation of the suggested framework involves three steps. Preprocessing of the pest image comes first, followed by freezing and unfreezing of the VGG 16 model and then an ideal fully connected layer with the hyper-parameter Adam optimizer is the third step.

4 Performance Evaluation

4.1 Dataset

The previous section discussed various research papers, each of these papers uses different datasets for their studies, and Table 1 provides a detailed summary of these works, offering detailed information about the datasets (Table 2) they used. Researchers consistently use certain datasets across multiple papers, highlighting their crucial role in exploring various research aspects. This emphasizes the significant impact of these datasets on advancing research in different directions.

Table 2. Dataset description

Author Name	Year	Dataset Used	Description	Type and Annotation
Lames Ki et al.	2017	Carrot-weed	Weed detection	Pixel, RGB
Sudars et al.	2020	Weeds, food crop	Six crops-Weed detection	Bounding Box, RGB
Haug and Osterm	2014	CWFI	Weed detection-carrot	Pixel, Multispectral
Sa et al.	2018	Weed Map	Weed detection–sugar beet	Pixel, Multispectral
Häni et al.	2020	Minne Apple	Segmentation and fruit detection for Apple	Pixel, RGB
Kamal et al.	2019	Plant dataset	Total diseases-38	Pixel, RGB
Fenu and Malloci	2021	DiaMOS	Pear fruit and leaf	Csv, Bounding Box, RGB
Singh et al.	2020	Plant Doc	13 plant and 30 diseases	RGB, Bounding box
Wang et al.	2020	Pest24	24 types of plant pest	RGB, Bounding box
Altaheri et al.	2019	Date Fruit	350 and 13palms	RGB

4.2 Performance Measures

The studies evaluated the classifiers, as outlined in Sect. 3, to assess their performance using the dataset. The following performance metrics have been commonly used to evaluate the models:

$$1. Accuracy\ Score = \frac{TP + TN}{TP + FP + FN + TN}$$

$$2. Specificity = \frac{TN}{FP + TN}$$

$$3. Sensitivity = \frac{TP}{TP + FN}$$

$$4. Precision = \frac{TP}{TP + FP}$$

$$5. F1 - Measure = \frac{2 * Precision * Recall}{Precision + Recall}$$

4.3 Proposed Architecture: Performance Analysis

The confidence curve presents a best F1 score of 0.76 with a confidence threshold of 0.255 on the dataset on which YOLOv8 is trained. Figure 2 showcases the performance in terms of accuracy of YOLOv8 architecture.

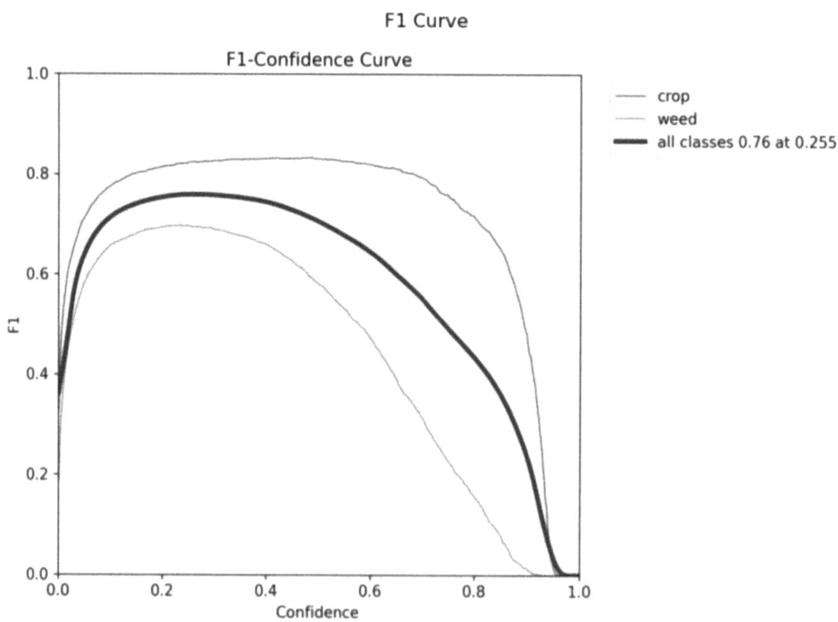

Fig. 2. F1 confidence curve for YOLOv8

5 Goals and Objectives

The "Advancements in Precision Farming" project's goals and objectives are essential for outlining its objectives, scope, and anticipated results. The project team has a clear direction thanks to these goals and objectives, which also provide the basis for project planning and implementation. The project's three goals and objectives are as follows:

- **Weed detection:** With Internet of Things (IoT) technology, weed infestations in agricultural areas are identified and managed. This technique is known as "weed detection using IoT." With this method, several characteristics of the agricultural environment related to the presence and growth of weeds are monitored and analysed using sensors, data processing algorithms, and communication networks.
- **Crop Recommendation:** Personalized crop recommendations are given to farmers based on a range of criteria, including soil characteristics, climate data, past yield data, and market demand, by utilizing Internet of Things (IoT) technologies. This project uses data on nitrogen (N), phosphorus (P), and potassium (K). It entails combining crop specific nutrient requirements with soil nutrient data gathered by IoT sensors to give farmers individualized fertilizer recommendations.
- **Yield Prediction**: The process of forecasting crop yields in agricultural fields with the use of Internet of Things (IoT) technologies includes gathering, analysing, and interpreting data from multiple sources. With IoT-powered yield prediction, farmers can optimise their farming methods, increase productivity, and boost profitability by gaining useful information and decision-support tools. Farmers can use IoT technologies to make data-driven decisions that result in sustainable crop production, less environmental impact, and more effective use of resources.

Together with an emphasis on model training and improvement, these goals and objectives outline the crucial areas and applications that are extremely important.

6 Methodology

This paper aims to use the YOLOv8 (You Only Look Once) for Weed Detection algorithm which is a groundbreaking deep learning technique for object detection within images. It is known for its high speed and accuracy, making it highly suitable for real-time applications, including surveillance. Some of the features of YOLO Algorithm includes:

- YOLO's most well-known feature is its single-shot detection method. In contrast to conventional object detection techniques, which need several image passes, YOLO analyses the entire image only once and concurrently forecasts class probabilities and item bounding boxes. Because of the quicker object recognition that follows, this makes it especially suitable for real-time monitoring.
- Bounding Box Predictions - YOLO predicts bounding boxes that tightly enclose detected objects. These bounding boxes indicate the precise location and extent of objects within the image or video frame. This accuracy is crucial for object tracking and event analysis in surveillance scenarios.
- Class Probability - In addition to bounding boxes, YOLO predicts class probabilities for each detected object.

- Real-Time Processing - Yolo is perfect for real-time applications like video surveillance because of its efficiency and speed. Its ability to process video frames at high frame rates guarantees real-time object tracking and detection as events take place.
- Adaptability - Because of its versatility, YOLO may be adjusted and improved for object detection applications. This flexibility is useful in surveillance situations when the surroundings and object types can change.

7 Results and Discussion

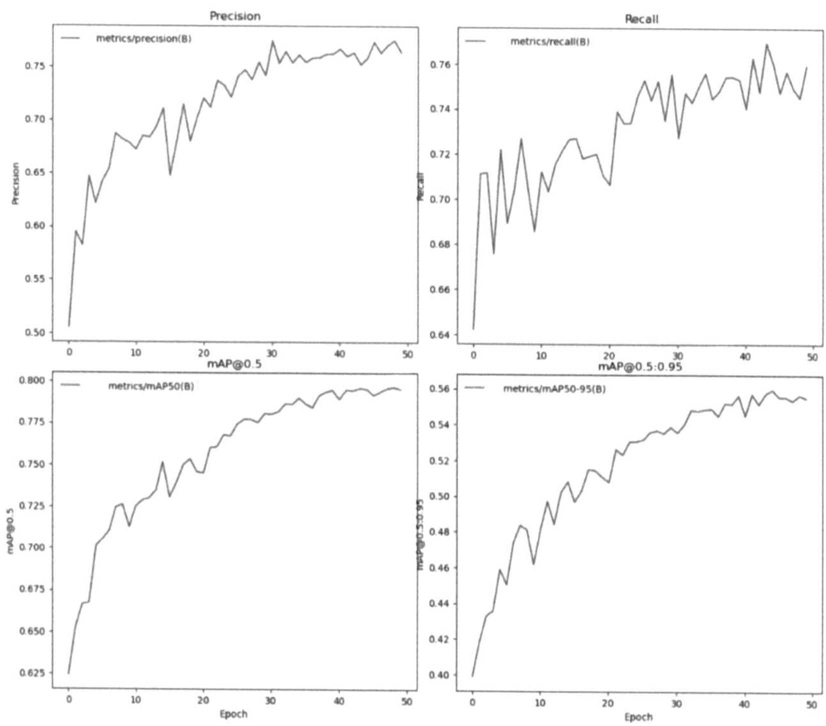

Fig. 3. Performance Metrices Curve

The graphs shown in Fig. 3 are based on performance metrices such as precision, recall, etc. They are crucial tools for evaluating the effectiveness of machine learning model, provides valuable insights, model's ability to make accurate predictions.

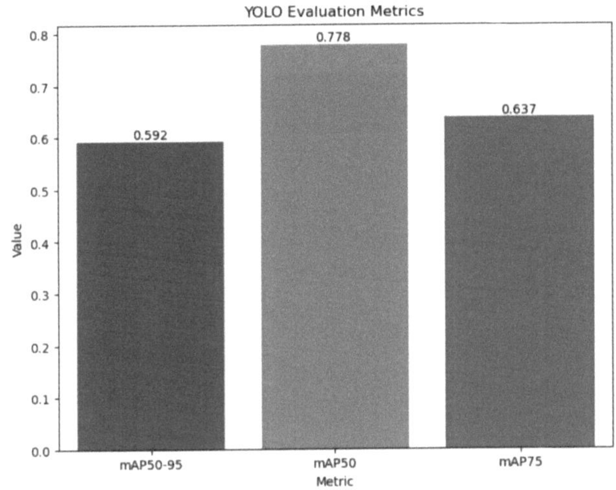

Fig. 4. YOLOv8 Evaluation Metrices

The histogram shown in Fig. 4 outlines YOLOv8's evaluation metrics, including mean Average Precision (mAP) at IoU thresholds of 0.50–0.95 (0.592), 0.50 (0.778), and 0.75 (0.637). These values signify the model's overall object detection performance, high precision at a lenient IoU threshold, and sustained effectiveness at a stricter threshold.

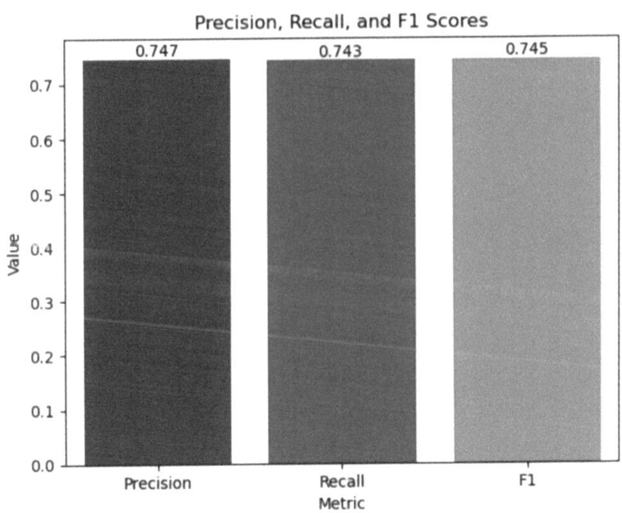

Fig. 5. Performance Metrices

The histogram in Fig. 5 presents key metrics (F1 score: 0.745, Precision: 0.747, Recall: 0.743) for YOLOv8. The balanced F1 score underscores the model's adoptive nature in object detection, with high precision and recall values showcasing its robust performance in accurately identifying and capturing objects.

Fig. 6. Sample of High-resolution image from Field

Fig. 7. Image sample from field detecting.

Figure 6 shows a sample in a high-resolution image for plant or weed with Bounding box for the detection purpose. Figure 7 shows a sample of a high-resolution image where detection of specific weed categories is done using bounding boxes for weed detection. This shows precision and clarity of identified weed types.

Figure 8 shows sample of image from the field.

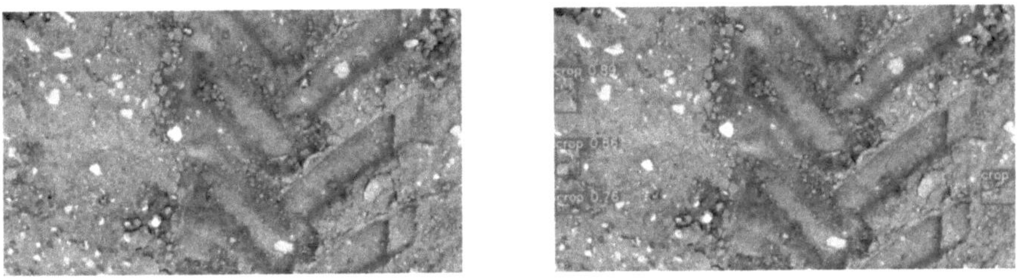

Fig. 8. Sample of the image from the field

YOLOv8, a real-time object identification system, can be used successfully in agriculture to find weeds. It is possible to develop a reliable weed detection system by gathering a variety of datasets, annotating them with bounding boxes to indicate the positions of weeds, training and optimising the YOLOv8 model, and applying post-processing methods. Identifying weed infested areas, directing targeted herbicide application, or supporting autonomous weed removal solutions are all possible with the successful integration of this technology into agriculture, all of which can lead to more effective and sustainable farming practises. However, to preserve the model's efficacy over time, it must be regularly improved and tailored to problems in the actual world.

8 Conclusion

In conclusion, this analysis highlights the significant potential of deep learning approaches to transform precision farming. By analysing how these technologies are applied across all facets of agriculture, it provides insightful information on the strengths and weaknesses of these technologies. For farmers, researchers, and industry stakeholders interested in maximising the advantages of data-driven decision-making in agriculture, these findings provide essential direction. Additionally, this study serves as an example of how agriculture and technology are convergent and promotes continued multidisciplinary cooperation to integrate these developments into useful, sustainable farming practices. Deep learning in precision agriculture presents the promise of a number of new technological developments. Crop monitoring, pest identification, and yield prediction can all be improved by combining IoT, deep learning, and machine learning techniques. A thorough understanding of agricultural landscapes can be obtained by broadening the scope to incorporate cutting-edge technology like thermal imaging and drone-based data collection. Large-scale datasets and transfer learning can be used to alleviate data scarcity challenges and boost model robustness. Transparency and accuracy can be improved by using visualisation techniques to make models more interpretable and by combining various deep learning architectures with classical machine learning. Prior to using models in actual farming systems, careful field testing and consultation with farmers and agronomists are essential. Furthermore, the era of precision agriculture has the potential to bring forth more environmentally friendly methods, decreased environmental impact, and improved food security. In summary, adopting these cutting-edge technologies has the potential to revolutionise precision farming and open the door to more effective, sustainable, and data-driven agricultural practices that can effectively deal with the problems posed by a growing population and changing environmental conditions.

Now, mentioning the authors' contribution, Mohit and Swastik Sindhani contributed equally to the conception, design, analysis, and interpretation of data. They were involved in drafting the manuscript and revising it regularly. Vibha Nehra provided constant feedback and suggested amendments for the project. All authors have given final approval of the version to be published and agree to be accountable for all aspects of the work.

Declarations.

Funding. The authors declare that no funds, grants, or other support were received during the preparation of this manuscript.

Competing Interests. The authors have no relevant financial or non-financial interests to disclose.

Data Availability. All data supporting the findings of this study are available within the paper and otherwise no datasets have been generated.

References

1. Chamara, N., Islam, M.D., Bai, G.F., Shi, Y., Ge, Y.: Ag-IoT for crop and environment monitoring: past, present, and future. Agric. Syst. **203**, 103497 (2022)
2. Farooq, M.S., Riaz, S., Abid, A., Abid, K., Naeem, M.A.: A survey on the role of IoT in agriculture for the implementation of smart farming. IEEE Access. **7**, 156237–156271 (2019)
3. Lova Raju, K., Vijayaraghavan, V.: IoT technologies in agricultural environment: a survey. Wirel. Pers. Commun. **113**, 2415–2446 (2020)
4. Boursianis, A.D., et al.: Internet of Things (IoT) and agricultural unmanned aerial vehicles (UAVs) in smart farming: a comprehensive review. Internet Things. **18**, 100187 (2022)
5. Talavera, J.M., et al.: Review of IoT applications in agro-industrial and environmental fields. Comput. Electron. Agric. **142**, 283–297 (2017)
6. Zhu, N., et al.: Deep learning for smart agriculture: concepts, tools, applications, and opportunities. Int. J. Agric. Biol. Eng. **11**(4), 32–44 (2018)
7. Lu, G., et al.: AGI for agriculture. arXiv preprint arXiv:2304.06136. (2023)
8. Eli-Chukwu, N.C.: Applications of artificial intelligence in agriculture: a review. Eng. Technol. Appl. Sci. Res. **9**(4), 4377–4383 (2019)
9. Sharma, R.: Artificial intelligence in agriculture: a review. In: 2021 5th International Conference on Intelligent Computing and Control Systems (ICICCS), pp. 937–942. IEEE (2021)
10. Jha, K., Doshi, A., Patel, P., Shah, M.: A comprehensive review on automation in agriculture using artificial intelligence. Artif. Intell. Agric. **2**, 1–12 (2019)
11. Dhanya, V.G., Subeesh, A., Kushwaha, N.L., et al.: Deep learning-based computer vision approaches for smart agricultural applications. Artif. Intell. Agric. **6**, 211–229 (2022)

12. Tripathi, P., Kumar, N., Rai, M., Khan, A.: Applications of deep learning in agriculture. In: Artificial Intelligence Applications in Agriculture and Food Quality Improvement, pp. 17–28. IGI Global (2022)
13. Kamilaris, A., Prenafeta-Boldú, F.X.: Deep learning in agriculture: a survey. Comput. Electron. Agric. **147**, 70–90 (2018)
14. Lu, Y., Chen, D., Olaniyi, E., Huang, Y.: Generative adversarial networks (GANs) for image augmentation in agriculture: a systematic review. Comput. Electron. Agric. **200**, 107208 (2022)
15. Rezk, N.G., Hemdan, E.E.-D., Attia, A.-F., El-Sayed, A., El-Rashidy, M.A.: An efficient IoT based smart farming system using machine learning algorithms. Multimed. Tools Appl. **80**, 773–797 (2021)
16. Ren, C., Kim, D.-K., Jeong, D.: A survey of deep learning in agriculture: techniques and their applications. J. Inf. Process. Syst. **16**(5), 1015–1033 (2020)
17. Saranya, T., Deisy, C., Sridevi, S., Anbananthen, K.S.M.: A comparative study of deep learning and Internet of Things for precision agriculture. Eng. Appl. Artif. Intell. **122**, 106034 (2023)
18. Muangprathub, J., Boonnam, N., Kajornkasirat, S., Lekbangpong, N., Wanichsombat, A., Nillaor, P.: IoT and agriculture data analysis for smart farm. Comput. Electron. Agric. **156**, 467–474 (2019)
19. Gowd, R.B., Rama, A.N., Shilpa, N., Sridhar, L., Niranjan, K.E., Sajithra Varun, S.: A novel based crop prediction using machine learning and Internet of Things. In: 2023 International Conference on Smart Systems for Applications in Electrical Sciences (ICSSES), pp. 1–5. IEEE (2023)
20. Oikonomidis, A., Catal, C., Kassahun, A.: Deep learning for crop yield prediction: a systematic literature review. N. Z. J. Crop. Hortic. Sci. **51**(1), 1–26 (2023)
21. Dhall, R., Agrawal, H.: An improved energy efficient duty cycling algorithm for IoT based precision agriculture. Procedia Comput. Sci. **141**, 135–142 (2018)
22. Arumugam, A.: A literature review on smart agriculture using neural network and Internet of Things. Int. J. Multidiscip. Res. Arts Sci. Commer. **3**, 47–56 (2023)
23. Nevavuori, P., Narra, N., Lipping, T.: Crop yield prediction with deep convolutional neural networks. Comput. Electron. Agric. **163**, 104859 (2019)
24. Bah, M., Dian, E.D., Hafiane, A., Canals, R.: Deep learning-based classification system for identifying weeds using high-resolution UAV imagery. In: Intelligent Computing: Proceedings of the 2018 Computing Conference, vol. 2, pp. 176–187. Springer International Publishing (2019)
25. Ferentinos, K.P.: Deep learning models for plant disease detection and diagnosis. Comput. Electron. Agric. **145**, 311–318 (2018)
26. Suchithra, M.S., Pai, M.L.: Improving the prediction accuracy of soil nutrient classification by optimizing extreme learning machine parameters. Inf. Process. Agric. **7**(1), 72–82 (2020)
27. Qiao, M., et al.: Crop yield prediction from multi-spectral, multi-temporal remotely sensed imagery using recurrent 3D convolutional neural networks. Int. J. Appl. Earth Obs. Geoinf. **102**, 102436 (2021)
28. Jeong, S., Ko, J., Yeom, J.-M.: Predicting rice yield at pixel scale through synthetic use of crop and deep learning models with satellite data in south and North Korea. Sci. Total Environ. **802**, 149726 (2022)
29. Sagan, V., et al.: Field-scale crop yield prediction using multi-temporal WorldView-3 and PlanetScope satellite data and deep learning. ISPRS J. Photogramm. Remote Sens. **174**, 265–281 (2021)
30. Yang, L., Cai, Y., Zhang, L., Guo, M., Li, A., Zhou, C.: A deep learning method to predict soil organic carbon content at a regional scale using satellite-based phenology variables. Int. J. Appl. Earth Obs. Geoinf. **102**, 102428 (2021)

31. Nehra, V., Anand, A., Kumari, N.: Fertilizer and crop recommendation using IoUT and machine learning. In: 2023 13th International Conference on Cloud Computing, Data Science and Engineering (Confluence), pp. 629–634. IEEE (2023)
32. Nehra, V., Sharma, M., Sharma, V.: IoT based smart plant monitoring system. In: 2023 13th International Conference on Cloud Computing, Data Science and Engineering (Confluence), pp. 60–65. IEEE (2023)
33. Chen, C.-J., Huang, Y.-Y., Li, Y.-S., Chen, Y.-C., Chang, C.-Y., Huang, Y.-M.: Identification of fruit tree pests with deep learning on embedded drone to achieve accurate pesticide spraying. IEEE Access. **9**, 21986–21997 (2021)
34. Tetila, E.C., et al.: Detection and classification of soybean pests using deep learning with UAV images. Comput. Electron. Agric. **179**, 105836 (2020)
35. Afonso, M., et al.: Tomato fruit detection and counting in greenhouses using deep learning. Front. Plant Sci. **11**, 571299 (2020)

"Integrating AI with Random Forest Regression and SGD Classifier Algorithm in Medical Diagnosis and Medicament"

Krish Sen[1(✉)], Ipseeta Nanda[1], Taruna Gautam[2], and Harsh Kasana[1]

[1] School of Computer Science and Engineering, IILM University, 16, Knowledge Park-II, Greater Noida, UP 201306, India
k.krishsen@gmail.com

[2] Faculty School of Management, IILM University, 16, Knowledge Park-II, Greater Noida, UP 201306, India

Abstract. The integration of Artificial Intelligence (AI) into medical diagnosis and medication represents a significant advancement towards personalized healthcare. This chapter presents a comprehensive review of recent developments and challenges in leveraging AI technologies to enhance medical diagnosis and treatment recommendations. By analyzing large volumes of medical data, AI systems can identify patterns and correlations that may not be apparent to human practitioners, leading to more accurate and timely diagnoses. Additionally, AI-driven predictive models can assist healthcare providers in recommending personalized treatment plans tailored to individual patient needs, thereby improving patient outcomes, and reducing healthcare costs. However, the widespread adoption of AI in healthcare also raises important ethical, regulatory, and privacy concerns that must be addressed to ensure patient safety and data security. This chapter discusses key considerations for the responsible deployment of AI technologies and Random Forest Regression in healthcare settings, including transparency, accountability, and patient consent. Furthermore, it explores emerging trends such as explainable AI and federated learning, which aim to enhance the interpretability and privacy of AI models Random Forest Regression (RFR), and Stochastic Gradient Descent (SGD) Classifier Algorithm while preserving their predictive power. Overall, this chapter highlights the transformative potential of AI in revolutionizing medical diagnosis and treatment recommendation, while emphasizing the importance of ethical and regulatory frameworks to guide its responsible implementation.

Keywords: Personalized Healthcare · Medical Diagnosis · Treatment Recommendation · Ethical Considerations · Random Forest Regression and Stochastic Gradient Descent Classifier Algorithm

1 Introduction

The introduction sets the context for the research chapter by discussing the significance of personalized healthcare and the role of AI in medical diagnosis and treatment. It provides background information on the challenges faced in traditional healthcare systems

M. Paprzycki et al. (Eds.): ICACIS 2024, CCIS 2405, pp. 65–79, 2027.
https://doi.org/10.1007/978-3-032-30990-7_5

and the potential benefits of integrating AI technologies. With the rapid advancement of technology, especially in the field of artificial intelligence (AI), the healthcare industry is at the forefront of a revolution. Combining AI with personalized medicine promises to overcome long-standing deficiencies in traditional healthcare systems. Historically, healthcare systems have struggled with systemic inefficiencies, resulting in delayed diagnoses and suboptimal treatment outcomes. The emergence of AI technology represents a revolutionary change in this landscape, offering many computational tools that can determine the contours of medical diagnosis and treatment. Machine learning algorithms, neural networks, and deep learning techniques form the backbone of AI systems and have unparalleled capabilities in analyzing large amounts of medical data. These analytical capabilities allow AI systems to identify complex patterns and correlations in medical data, thereby enabling healthcare professionals to make clinical decisions with a level of accuracy that is otherwise unattainable. However, introducing AI into healthcare will not be without its challenges. Privacy issues, ethical challenges, and regulatory considerations are barriers to adopting AI-driven technology. The medical data repositories required to train AI models raise significant privacy concerns regarding patient privacy and data security. In addition, the transparent nature of AI algorithms raises ethical challenges regarding algorithmic bias and accountability in clinical decision making. In addition, the regulatory framework governing the implementation of AI in healthcare is still in its infancy, requiring strong governance mechanisms to ensure compliance with established standards and guidelines. Thus, navigating the ethical and regulatory landscape of AI integration in healthcare requires a delicate balance between technological innovation and ethical responsibility. Given these challenges, there is a need to chart a course for responsible AI integration in healthcare based on the principles of transparency, equity and patient centricity. Transparency in AI algorithms and decision-making processes is essential to building trust between healthcare providers and patients. In addition, efforts to reduce algorithmic bias and ensure fairness in AI-driven healthcare interventions are priorities to maintain ethical standards and ensure fair access to healthcare. In addition, a secure data management framework must be established to protect patient privacy and reduce the risk of data breaches and misuse. In addition, cross-collaboration between healthcare professionals, data scientists, ethicists, and policy makers is needed to develop integrated strategies to address the multifaceted challenges posed by the integration of AI in healthcare. Through rigorous research and empirical analysis, we aim to explain the opportunities and challenges associated with the integration of artificial intelligence, and aim to lead the way to a future characterized by accuracy, efficiency, and compassion in healthcare.

Table 1. Comparison of AI Integration in Medical Diagnosis and Medication"

Aspect	AI Integration in Medical Diagnosis	AI Integration in Medication
Technology	Machine Learning, Neural Networks,	Natural Language Processing,

(*continued*)

Table 1. *(continued)*

Aspect	AI Integration in Medical Diagnosis	AI Integration in Medication
	Deep Learning	Predictive Analytics, Recommender Systems
Process Improvement	Faster and more accurate diagnosis	Personalized treatment plans based on
		patient data
Diagnosis Accuracy	Can detect patterns in medical images and	Can analyze vast amounts of patient
	data that humans might miss	data to predict potential medication
		responses and adverse effects
Patient Outcomes	This may lead to earlier detection of diseases	It can help avoid adverse drug reactions
	and improved treatment decisions	and optimize drug regimens
Challenges	Requires large amounts of quality data for	Integration with existing healthcare
	training models; potential for bias	systems; privacy and security concerns
Future Potential	Continuously improving with advancements	Could revolutionize treatment through
	in AI technologies; potential for	personalized medicine approaches

2 Literature Review

The literature review section examines existing research and studies related to AI-based medical diagnosis and treatment recommendations in Table 1. It provides a comprehensive overview of the current state-of-the-art techniques, methodologies, and applications in the field. One of the most promising applications of AI in healthcare is in medical diagnosis. AI-driven algorithms have shown remarkable skill in improving diagnostic accuracy and facilitating early disease detection. Using advanced computing methodologies, AI systems can overcome the inherent limitations of human perception and detect subtle anomalies in medical images and patient data that otherwise would escape human knowledge. This ability has profound implications for proactive intervention strategies that allow healthcare providers to initiate appropriate treatment and slow disease progression. Furthermore, integrating AI into drug management represents a watershed moment for therapeutic approaches. By using natural language processing and predictive analytics, AI-powered systems can predict drug reactions and prevent adverse drug reactions, thereby optimizing treatment regimens and improving patient safety. The paradigm of precision medicine tailored to the unique physiological profile of the individual patient holds the promise to transform healthcare and improve patient outcomes. The literature review should identify gaps in existing research and highlight areas where further investigation is needed Table 2.

Table 2. Comparative Analysis of AI Applications in Healthcare

Aspect	Esteva et al. (2017)	Rajkomar et al. (2019)	Obermeyer & Emanuel (2016)	Beam & Kohane (2018)	Aliper et al. (2016)
Technology	Deep Learning	Machine Learning	Machine Learning	Machine Learning	Deep Learning
Application	Skin Cancer Diagnosis	General Medical Diagnosis	Predictive Analytics	Healthcare Management	Pharmacological
					Properties Prediction
Data Used	Dermatologist-level	Electronic Health Records	Electronic Health Records	Electronic Health	Transcriptomic Data
	skin cancer images	(EHRs)	(EHRs)	Records (EHRs)	
Performance	Dermatologist-level	Comparable to human	Predictive value of	Application-specific	Predictive accuracy
	classification	radiologists	machine learning models	improvements	of drug properties
Challenges	Quality and quantity	Data quality,	Data quality and	Data integration,	Predicting
	of training data	interpretability,	interpretability,	interoperability,	pharmacological
		model generalizability	privacy concerns	scalability	properties based on
					transcriptomic data
Future Potential	Early disease	Enhanced diagnostic	Enhanced clinical	Improving patient	Drug repurposing,
	detection,	accuracy,	decision-making,	outcomes, reducing	precision medicine
	improved treatment	personalized treatment	population health	healthcare costs	
	decisions	plans	management		

This comparison table highlights various aspects of AI integration into medical diagnosis and medication based on the provided references. It covers the technology used, applications, data sources, performance, challenges, and future potential of AI in healthcare.

3 Methodology

The dataset serves the critical purpose of applying existing knowledge in machine learning and deep learning to benefit humanity, particularly in the field of medical science [1–4]. It comprises analytical results that focus on parameters mentioning diseases, one for training and the other for testing the model [13–15]. Each file contains 133 columns, with 132 representing various symptoms experienced by individuals and the final column denoting the prognosis. Through the mapping of these symptoms to 42 different diseases, the dataset facilitates the prediction of medical conditions [3]. The primary objective of this dataset is to streamline the diagnostic process for physicians by leveraging machine learning and deep learning techniques [2]. With 132 parameters, it provides a comprehensive range of symptoms, enabling the accurate prediction of a diverse set of diseases [4]. By utilizing this dataset, healthcare professionals can enhance their decision-making processes, potentially leading to earlier disease detection and improved treatment outcomes [1] (Table 3).

Table 3. Symptom-Disease Mapping in Medical Diagnosis"

Parameters	Diseases
Continuous_Sneezing	Fungal Infection
Shivering	Allergy
Chills	Gerd
Joint_Pain	Chronic Cholestasis
Stomach_Pain	Drug Reaction
Acidity	Peptic Ulcer Disease
Ulcers_On_Tongue	Aids
Muscle_Wasting	Diabetes
Vomiting	Gastroenteritis
Burning_Micturition	Bronchial Asthma
Spotting_Urination	Hypertension
Fatigue	Migraine
Weight_Gain	Cervical Spondylosis
Anxiety	Paralysis (Brain Hemorrhage)
Cold_Hands_And_Feets	Jaundice
Mood_Swings	Malaria
Weight_Loss	Chicken Pox
Restlessness	Dengue
Lethargy	Typhoid
Patches_In_Throat	Hepatitis A
Irregular_Sugar_Level	Hepatitis B
Cough	Hepatitis C
High Fever	Hepatitis D
Sunken Eyes	Hepatitis E
Breathlessness	Alcoholic Hepatitis

(continued)

Table 3. (*continued*)

Parameters	Diseases
Sweating	Tuberculosis
Dehydration	Common Cold
Indigestion	Pneumonia
Headache	Dimorphic Haemorrhoids(Piles)
Yellowish_Skin	Heart Attack
Dark_Urine	Varicose Veins
Nausea	Hypothyroidism
Loss_Of_Appetite	Hyperthyroidism
Pain_Behind_The_Eyes	Hypoglycemia
Back_Pain	Osteoarthritis
Constipation	Arthritis
Abdominal_Pain	(Vertigo) Paroxysmal Positional Vertigo
Diarrhea	Acne
Mild_Fever	Urinary Tract Infection
Yellow_Urine	Psoriasis
Yellowing_Of_Eyes	Impetigo

The pie chart describes the table described above:

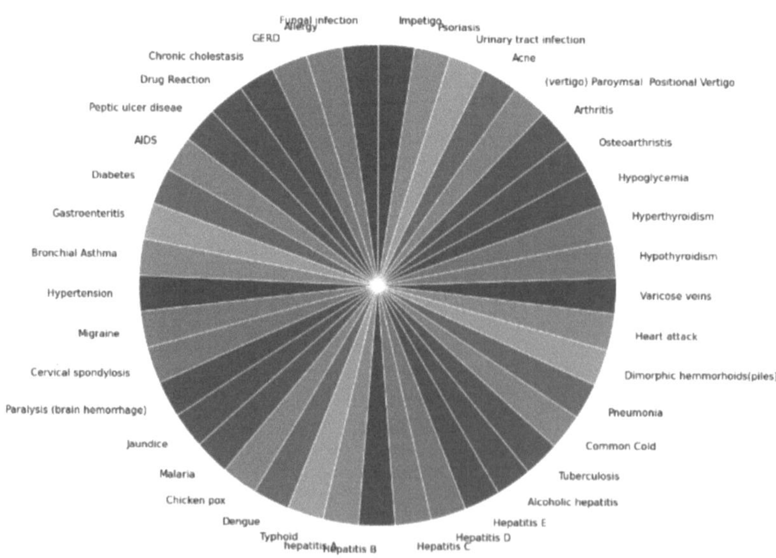

Fig. 1. Spectrum of Common Diseases

The model on training data and test it on testing data

4 Algorithm Used

This chapter focuses on these algorithms in the analysis of the results. Those are SGD Classifier: Stochastic Gradient Descent (SGD) Classifier is an efficient linear classification algorithm. It updates the model parameters iteratively using a gradient descent optimization method, making it suitable for large-scale and sparse datasets. Passive Aggressive Classifier: This online learning algorithm is adept at handling large-scale classification tasks, particularly in scenarios where data streams continuously. It updates model parameters aggressively when the model makes mistakes and passively otherwise, making it useful for dynamic environments. Ridge Classifier: A Ridge Classifier is a linear classification algorithm that applies L2 regularization to prevent overfitting. It's particularly effective when dealing with multicollinearity in feature variables, providing stable [4–7] solutions for classification problems. Linear SVC: Linear Support Vector Classification (Linear SVC) is a linear classification model that finds the optimal hyperplane to separate classes in the feature space. It's widely used for binary classification tasks and scales well to large datasets. NuSVC: Nu-Support Vector Classification (NuSVC) is a non-linear classification algorithm based on Support Vector Machines (SVM). It allows for flexibility in controlling the number of support vectors and the margin width, providing a robust solution for classification problems. Nearest Centroid: The nearest Centroid classifier calculates the centroid for each class and assigns new instances to the class whose centroid is closest to the instance's feature vector [5–8]. It's a simple and efficient classification algorithm suitable for high-dimensional data. Linear Discriminant Analysis: Linear Discriminant Analysis (LDA) is a dimensionality reduction technique often used for classification tasks. It finds the linear combination of features that best separates multiple classes, providing a robust decision boundary for classification. Quadratic Discriminant Analysis: Quadratic Discriminant Analysis (QDA) is a classification algorithm that assumes each class has its covariance matrix. It models the distribution of each class using a quadratic decision boundary, making it suitable for non-linear separations [9–12]. Bagging Classifier: Utilizes bootstrap sampling to train multiple base estimators, reducing variance and improving stability by aggregating predictions.

5 Comparative Analysis

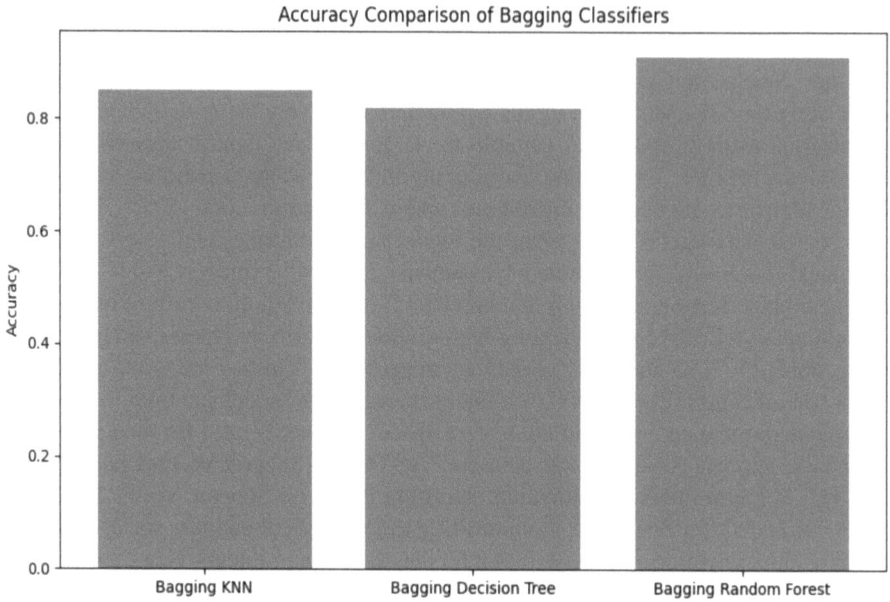

Fig. 2. Accuracy Comparison of Bagging Classifiers

In this graph in Fig. 2, justifies the Gradient Boosting Classifier: Ensemble technique building additive models sequentially, correcting errors of preceding models by fitting new models to residuals, producing a strong learner. Federation learning: Federated learning (also known as collaborative learning) is a sub-field of machine learning focusing on settings in which multiple entities (often referred to as clients) collaboratively train a model while ensuring that their data remains decentralized. A deep learning model using Keras and TensorFlow to classify diseases into various medical conditions. The methodology can be broken down into the following steps:

1. **Import necessary libraries**: The script imports essential libraries, including Keras, TensorFlow, Matplotlib, Pandas, NumPy, and scikit-learn, to support data manipulation, visualization, and deep learning model development.
2. **Mount Google Drive**: The script uses Google Drive to store and access the dataset. By mounting Google Drive, the script can read CSV files containing metadata about the images and load the images using Keras' Image Data Generator.
3. **Data Preparation**: The script reads CSV files containing training, validation, and test data using Pandas in Fig. 1. This step ensures that the data is properly loaded and structured for further processing.
4. **Data Visualization**: In Figs. 3 and 4, the script displays random images from the dataset using Matplotlib. This step helps to visually inspect the data and understand its appearance and quality.

5. **Data Augmentation**: The script uses Keras' ImageDataGenerator to perform real-time data augmentation during training. Data augmentation can increase the model's robustness and prevent overfitting by generating modified versions of the original images, such as rotations, width and height shifts, shearing, zooming horizontal flipping, and brightness adjustments.
6. **Model Architecture**: The script defines a custom deep learning model based on the DenseNet121 architecture, pre-trained on ImageNet for transfer learning. This approach leverages the power of pre-trained models, reducing the need for a large dataset and training time.
7. **Loss Function**: The script defines a custom weighted loss function to handle a class imbalance in the dataset. This is common in medical image analysis tasks, where certain classes may have significantly more or fewer samples than others. A weighted loss function adjusts the importance of each class during training, ensuring that the model pays equal attention to all classes.
8. **Model Training**: The script trains the model using data generators to efficiently load and process data in batches [7–9], applying data augmentation and normalization on the fly. The fit generator method in Kera's is used for training, allowing the script to specify essential training parameters, such as the number of epochs, batch size, and validation data.
9. **Performance Visualization**: The script plots the training loss curve to monitor the model's performance and ensure successful convergence during training. This visualization helps to identify potential issues, such as overfitting, underfitting, or poor convergence, the performance is shown in Table 4.

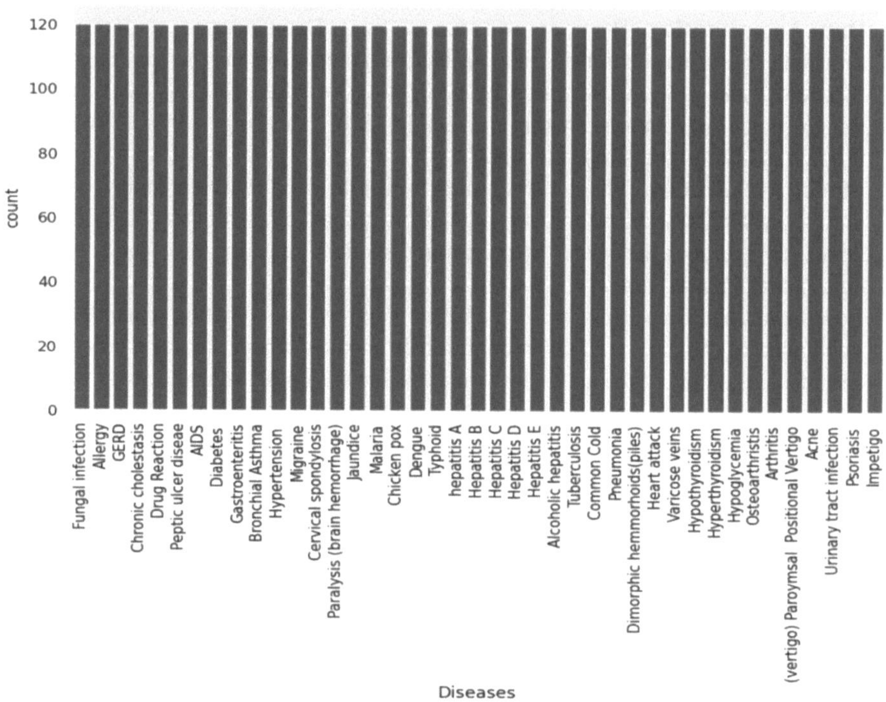

Fig. 3. Disease Count by Category

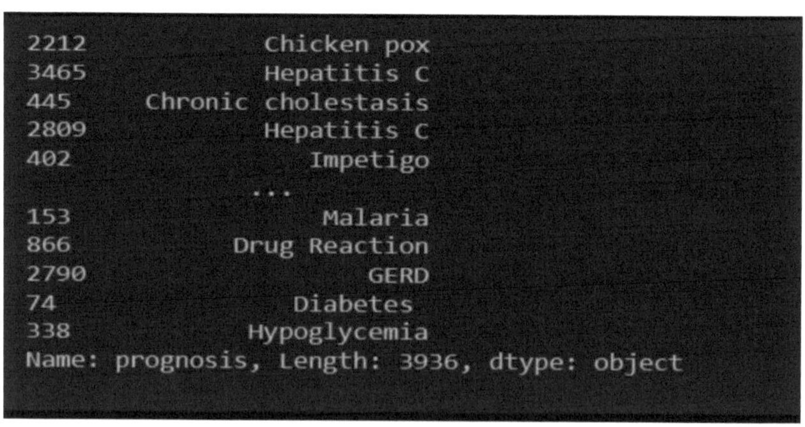

Fig. 4. Prognosis Report

Table 4. Model Accuracy Comparison for Medical Diagnosis

Model	Accuracy
Random Forest Classifier	0.85
SGD Classifier	0.78
Logistic Regression	0.82
Decision Tree	0.75
KNN	0.7

The methodology provides Python script and is designed efficiently to train a deep-learning model for medical image analysis. The script leverages pre-trained models, data augmentation, and custom loss functions to tackle class imbalance, ensuring the model's robustness and ability to generalize well to new data.

6 Result and Discussion

The output Figs. 6 and 5 present a comprehensive evaluation of various machine learning models on a dataset, facilitating informed model selection. A tabulated 4 summary in Fig. 2 displays model accuracies, with the Random Forest Classifier emerging as the top performer, closely followed by the SGD Classifier, Logistic Regression, Decision Tree, and KNN. This chapter signifies reinforcement by a succinct NumPy array encapsulating the data. Additionally, the authors of the chapter say that a visually compelling 3D plot showcases prediction lines, affirming the Random Forest Classifier's superior performance, trailed by the SGD Classifier and Logistic Regression [11–15]. This holistic analysis equips practitioners with crucial insights for optimal model choice, underscoring the Random Forest Classifier's prowess in this context. Such outputs serve as invaluable tools for navigating machine learning tasks effectively and enhancing decision-making processes.

Model	Accuracy
Random Forest Classifier	0.85
SGD Classifier	0.78
Logistic Regression	0.82
Decision Tree	0.75
KNN	0.70

Fig. 5. Machine Learning Model Classification Accuracy

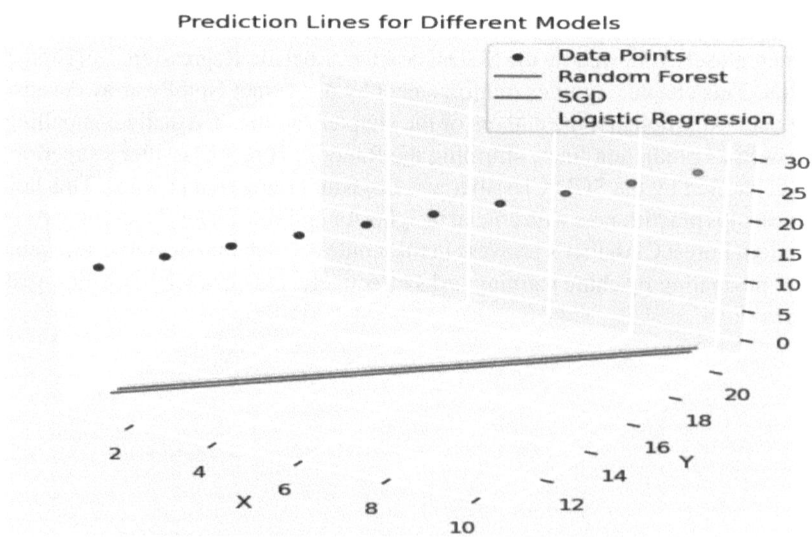

Fig. 6. SGD Prediction Lines for Different Models

.NSCV (Nested Split cross-validation) is best in this scenario because it provides a more reliable and accurate estimate of model performance compared to other cross-validation techniques. This chapter deals with the Reduced Bias: NSCV reduces bias by performing multiple iterations of inner and outer cross-validation folds. This helps to average out the impact of any specific data split on the performance metrics. Improved

Generalizability: By using multiple folds for both training and validation, NSCV provides a more comprehensive evaluation of the model's ability to generalize to unseen data. Better Handling of Small Datasets: NSCV is particularly advantageous when working with smaller datasets. By iterating over multiple folds, it ensures that the model is trained and evaluated on a larger portion of the available data, leading to more stable and reliable performance estimates. Identification of Optimal Hyperparameters: NSCV can be used to select the optimal hyperparameters for user model. By evaluating the model's performance across multiple folds with different hyperparameter combinations, us can identify the settings that yield the best results. Reduced Overfitting and Underfitting: NSCV helps to prevent both overfitting and underfitting by providing a more robust assessment of the model's ability to learn from and generalize to the data. Overall, NSCV is the best choice in this scenario because it provides a more reliable and accurate estimate of model performance mentioned in Fig. 7, particularly when working with smaller datasets or when selecting optimal hyperparameters. The results and discussion section presents the findings of the research and interprets them implications. It discusses the performance of AI models in medical diagnosis and treatment recommendation, including accuracy, sensitivity, specificity, and other relevant metrics. The section also explores the factors influencing the effectiveness of AI-based healthcare systems and identifies opportunities for improvement.

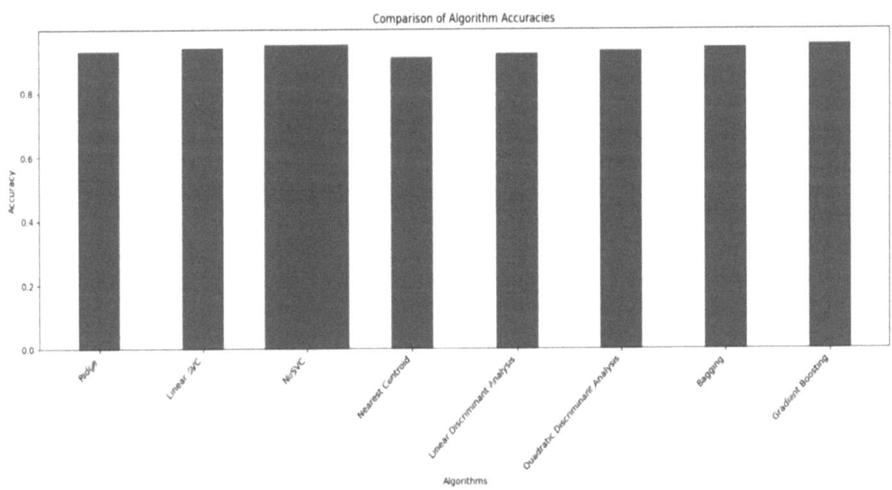

Fig. 7. Bar Graph of Model Performance

7 Conclusion

Integrating AI into medical opinion and drugs represents a significant advancement toward substantiated healthcare, leading to more accurate judgments and substantiated treatment plans. still, ethical, nonsupervisory, and sequestration enterprises must be addressed. The literature review highlights the current state-of-the-art ways, methodologies, and operations in AI-grounded medical opinion and treatment recommendations. AI has the implicit to revise medical opinion and treatment while emphasizing the significance of ethical and nonsupervisory fabrics. Here they strive to harness the full potential of AI technology to improve patient care, improve clinical outcomes, and usher in a new era of personalized medicine by fostering interdisciplinary dialogue and promoting ethical AI governance.

References

1. Aliper, A., Plis, S., Artemov, A., Ulloa, A., Mamoshina, P., Zhavoronkov, A.: Deep learning applications for predicting pharmacological properties of drugs and drug repurposing using transcriptomic data. Mol. Pharm. **13**(7), 2524–2530 (2016)
2. Beam, A.L., Kohane, I.S.: Big data and machine learning in health care. JAMA. **319**(13), 1317–1318 (2018)
3. Chen, M., Hao, Y.: Internet of Things: applications, challenges, and opportunities. J. Wirel. Mob. Networks Ubiquitous Comput. Dependable Appl. **6**(3), 11–35 (2015)
4. Nanda, I., Adhikari, N.: System on chips design for Internet of Things using partial reconfiguration. J. Adv. Res. Dyn. Control Syst. **11**(1), 10231029 (2019)
5. Nanda, I., Adhikari, N.: Application and performance of FPGA using partial reconfiguration with Xilinx PlanAhead. In: 2017 IEEE Transportation Electrification Conference, ITEC-India 2017, vol. 2018, p. 14. Institute of Electrical and Electronics Engineers Inc. (2018). https://doi.org/10.1109/ITECIndia.2017.8333891
6. Cho, K., et al.: Learning phrase representations using RNN encoder-decoder for statistical machine translation. arXiv preprint arXiv:1406.1078. (2014)
7. Davenport, T.H., Kalakota, R.: The potential for artificial intelligence in healthcare. Future Healthc. J. **6**(2), 94–98 (2019)
8. Doshi-Velez, F., Perlis, R.H.: Evaluating machine learning articles. JAMA. **322**(18), 1777–1779 (2019)
9. Chaganti, S.Y., Nanda, I., Pandi, K.R.: Cloud-based weather monitoring system. In: Lecture Notes on Data Engineering and Communications Technologies, vol. 37, p. 235245. Springer (2020). https://doi.org/10.1007/978-981-15-0978-0_23
10. Esteva, A., et al.: Dermatologist-level classification of skin cancer with deep neural networks. Nature. **542**(7639), 115–118 (2017)
11. Nanda, I., Singh, M., Khatua, L.: Automated irrigation system using IoT cloud computing. Int. J. Intell. Syst. Appl. Eng. **11**(2s), 360–365 (2023)
12. Esteva, A., et al.: A guide to deep learning in healthcare. Nat. Med. **25**(1), 24–29 (2019)
13. Litjens, G., et al.: A survey on deep learning in medical image analysis. Med. Image Anal. **42**, 60–88 (2017)
14. Nanda, I., Adhikari, N.: Analysis and design of ethernet to HDMI gateway using Xilinx Vivado. In: Lecture Notes on Data Engineering and Communications Technologies, vol. 37, p. 463477. Springer (2020). https://doi.org/10.1007/978-981-15-0978-0_46
15. Lundberg, S.M., Lee, S.I.: A unified approach to interpreting model predictions. Adv. Neural Inf. Proces. Syst. **30**, 4765–4774 (2017)
16. Nanda, I., M. Sharma, And G. Singh Gill, Trilateral plane estimation between nodes for the improved home automation system performance with the integrated Internet of Things, Int. J. Intell. Syst. Appl. Eng., 10, 2s, pp. 217, 2022.
17. Obermeyer, Z., Emanuel, E.J.: Predicting the future—big data, machine learning, and clinical medicine. N. Engl. J. Med. **375**(13), 1216–1219 (2016)

18. Rajkomar, A., Dean, J., Kohane, I., Butte, A.: Machine learning in medicine. N. Engl. J. Med. **380**(14), 1347–1358 (2019)
19. Silver, D., et al.: Mastering the game of go with deep neural networks and tree search. Nature. **529**(7587), 484–489 (2016)
20. Ting, D.S.W., et al.: Artificial intelligence and deep learning in ophthalmology. Br. J. Ophthalmol. **103**(2), 167–175 (2019)
21. Topol, E.J.: High-performance medicine: the convergence of human and artificial intelligence. Nat. Med. **25**(1), 44–56 (2019)

A Deep Learning Model with Hybrid Feature Synthesis for Improved Crop Yield Forecasting

P. Mano Paul[1], R. Shekhar[2], A. Ezil Sam Leni[2], and I. Diana Jeba Jingle[3](✉)

[1] Department of CSE-AI, Dayananda Sagar Academy of Technology and Management, Bengaluru, India
mano.paul@gmail.com

[2] Alliance School of Advanced Computing, Alliance University, Bengaluru, India
{shekhar.r,ezil.leni}@alliance.edu.in

[3] School of Engineering and Technology, Christ University, Bengaluru, India
diana.jebajingle@christuniversity.in

Abstract. In the current era of the internet and swift advancements in technology, the agricultural sector demands focus to optimise farmers' productivity and earnings. Half of India's population depends on agricultural output for their daily needs, making agriculture one of the country's strengths in both economic growth and rural development. The crop's yield has a significant impact on both the farmer's income and the government's plans for rural development to ensure food security. Farmers will benefit from improved crop cycle planning, including crop selection, pesticide detection, fertiliser prediction, and so forth, thanks to crop yield-based prediction. One such method used in agriculture to increase crop yield is machine learning. Researchers all over the world are employing a variety of ML and DL methods, including Classification, Artificial Neural Networks, regression, clustering, and prediction of crop yield are used to increase crop yield, and various techniques have been proposed to increase crop yield and help farmers increase their profits by improving their data from the assigned datasets. A method for machine learning and deep learning with DL and CatBoost and KNN approaches for agricultural prediction has been proposed. In this chapter, we aim to help farmers select the best crop, identify pesticides, and suggest fertilisers and pests. We are doing this by utilising a variety of deep learning and machine learning techniques, like CNN, CatBoost Algorithm, and KNN, which help farmers predict their losses and increase crop yield.

Keywords: deep learning · crop yield prediction · agriculture · catboost

1 Introduction

In India, 42% of workers are employed in the agriculture industry. The agricultural sector is the main driver of rural development. Thus, a productive crop cycle is critical to the nation. Since most Indian farmers are illiterate, they struggle to select the appropriate crops for the given season and have little idea of soil hygiene. The purpose of this system is to improve yield and profit while assisting Indian farmers in reducing issues related to their agricultural land. Because the system provides a list of crops that are suitable

M. Paprzycki et al. (Eds.): ICACIS 2024, CCIS 2405, pp. 80–93, 2027.
https://doi.org/10.1007/978-3-032-30990-7_6

for growing on farms, it will aid farmers in planning agricultural activities for effective implementation that will maximise yield rates and increase their return on investment. Farmers can also use this system to grow new crops, which keeps the soil from becoming unfruchtable. Farmers will benefit from this system by having more crop accuracy, higher farm profits, and an easier life. India's rural and urban development heavily depends on the agricultural sector, which is the nation's most important industrial sector. Better agricultural outcomes necessitate seasonal guidance in order to increase farmers' success and crop yield. This can be accomplished through selecting the appropriate crop for the appropriate session and location, identifying the pest, suggesting a pesticide to get rid of the pests, and suggesting fertilisers to increase crop productivity. Crop yield prediction is a significant issue in agriculture. India's agriculture produces a lot of data.

The field of agriculture frequently uses machine learning. Farmers used to forecast by drawing on their past experience in a given field, but this approach has been shown to be ineffective due to shifting weather patterns and soil fertility. This conventional approach can be replaced by machine learning, which can also help farmers select the best crops. The process of extracting knowledge from data sets containing patterns that the algorithm uses and converting them into useful structures for later use is known as machine learning. Two primary applications of machine learning are classification and prediction. Models learn from given data and apply that knowledge to the unknown value.

Climate change, erratic rainfall patterns, an increase in pest attacks in the county, and other factors have all contributed to a decline in crop yield and record losses for farmers in recent years. The goal of the chapter is to raise public awareness and educate farmers about the significance of selecting the proper crops, fertilisers, and pesticides. To this end, we are utilising machine learning and deep learning, which is a subset of artificial intelligence. To get the desired outcome and help farmers increase plant yield, we suggested models like CNN, catboost classifier, and KNN.

2 Related Works

In order to perform the prediction, the author Kavita et al. [1] talks about decision trees and stacked regression. It claims that India's agriculture is crucial to the nation's stability and economy. A poor crop cycle will have an impact on the food bank. Here, an article by Daniel et al. [6] describes how IoT analysis can be used for smart irrigation, which will help with production growth. Farmers must produce more from the same amount of agricultural land in order to increase availability as a result of the growth in agriculture and its success rate, as reported by Kale et al. [2]. Farmers will benefit from machine learning technology by being able to predict harvest yields more accurately.

The objective is to use remote sensing data to precisely identify the profit in crop yield. Technologies used include Decision Trees, rectilinear regression, various concepts of regression like Lasso regression, and another type of regression called Ridge Regression, which will aid in estimating the crop yield. These concepts are from Machine Language Concepts, written by Rashid et al. [3]. The decision tree outperformed all other prediction algorithms in terms of accuracy, according to cross-validation. This article's strengths include its accurate crop yield prediction and its simple, easy-to-understand model. The decision tree method is one of its drawbacks; it is also prone to overfitting, and even minor adjustments have an impact on both the tree and the trained model as a whole will change its predictions.

ANNs, Random Forest algorithms, and neural network algorithms are used in an article by S. Bhanumathi et al. [7] to carry out the improvement strategy. It claims that because agriculture occupies the majority of India's land, a successful harvest cycle and high-quality agricultural products are essential to the country's economy. Shafi et al.'s [4] use of deep learning and data processing allows for multi-modal prediction. Every farmer wants to know what their yield percentage will be and how successful their crop cycle will be. This analysis identifies the location and pH value of the soil, among other related attributes. Here, the percentage of nutrients from phosphorus P, potassium K, and nitrogen N was calculated using the soil, weather, and rainfall with different seasons.

The model will be trained after these informational attributes are examined. With the input data provided, the system predicts the crop yield with accuracy. This paper exhibits strong performance, excellent prediction accuracy, and high fault tolerance. The fact that extensive preprocessing is necessary to produce accurate results is a drawback. The model's reliance on Artificial Neural Networks makes it excessively hardware-dependent and costly to develop and train. Potnuru Sai Nishant et al.'s article "An Ensemble Algorithm for Crop Yield Prediction" [8] employs Lasso, Kernel Ridge, ENet, and stacked regression to make the prediction. It claims that India's economy and stability greatly depend on the country's agriculture.

A poor crop cycle will have an impact on the food bank. As agriculture expands, demand rises and farmers must produce more on the same amount of land in order to keep it relevant and increase availability. This model makes highly accurate crop yield predictions using remote sensing and geographic data. This paper's strengths include its high prediction accuracy, fault tolerance, and ability to avoid overfitting of the data because of Kernel Ridge. Its shortcomings include not working for smallCrop Yield Prediction using Machine Learning Algorithms is the title of a paper written by Aruvansh et al. [4, 9]. The prediction is made using xgboost, random forest, simpleRNN, and long short-term memory (LSTM).

According to this, the most common and lowest paid occupation in the last ten years has been agriculture. Machine learning has the potential to be the catalyst that advances the agricultural industry and generates enormous financial gains for farmers. The crop yield is predicted using random forest, RNN, and long short-term memory, and the mean square error of the results is used to compare the results. Using information on temperature, area, rainfall, and other variables, this paper will assist farmers in selecting the appropriate crop. This algorithm, which is highly fault-tolerant and accurately predicts crop yield, works well and provides high performance in this regard, according to Daniel et al.'s [6] features regarding water resources. The drawbacks are that computing it demands a significant amount of memory bandwidth and training time is more.

In Daniel et al. [6, 18], a model was created with IoT meant to identify the crop with a distance metrics and share the process to identify the chemical content using sensor turns an optimal growth in outcome with its yield. To speed up the process, we use a model given by Diana et al. [12, 19, 25] called "Qubit process" which was given to speed up the execution of the system. In the advancement phases there are so many references advances for the improval version of yield prediction. According to Rani et al. [10] given a cluster head approach in WSN, also Ram et al. [11] provides a classification technique with fog computing approach given in Diana et al. [24], which is required for the advancement in learning process for the yielding of crops in vegetation process. According to Shylu, Ajay and Paul et al. [13, 14, 17] a collaborative work given with sensor and digital model makes our learning process automated and efficient to utilize with cyberspace environment via web [15, 16]. Filtering also is an efficient way to identify the nutritious calculations and based on the fertilizer yield will be produces more and this type of learning models categorizes feature extraction and feature prediction in largescale networks which was given in Paul et al. [20–23]. Also the application for creating a new crop yield prediction web app will be delivered as smart social media application for crop prediction and given with a sample given by Sahil et al. [26] provides the application easier to deploy it in social media. So that all users get benefitted with this application. The problem and its approaches were dealed with CNN in the other chapters.

3 Proposed System

The overfitting issue that the current model causes is reduced by the suggested algorithm, which makes use of the CatBoost model. CNN usage reduces system performance while improving the crop yield model's accuracy. Three models comprise the manuscript:

3.1 Pest Identification and Pesticide Recommendation Using CNN

Convolution Neural Networks, or CNNs, are a popular deep learning algorithm-based technique for classifying, identifying objects in images, and recognising different types of images. In training modules, CNN classifies the data according to a designated feature and distinguishes between them. CNN uses a lot less preprocessing than other deep learning methodologies, which results in a much faster training process. Convolution, pooling, and fully connected layers make up CNN's three layers, which are used to identify and extract data. The ability to extract features like edges, colours, corners, and so forth is the convolutional layer's benefit. The primary goal of the pooling layer is to lower the processing power needed for data processing. This can be achieved by lowering the input matrix's dimension is given with the block as shown in Fig. 1.

The final layer, known as the connected layer, flattens the convectional layer's image before feeding it to a neural network that is used at each step over a sequence of epochs. In order to categorise photos, the model will discern between high and low features that predominate.

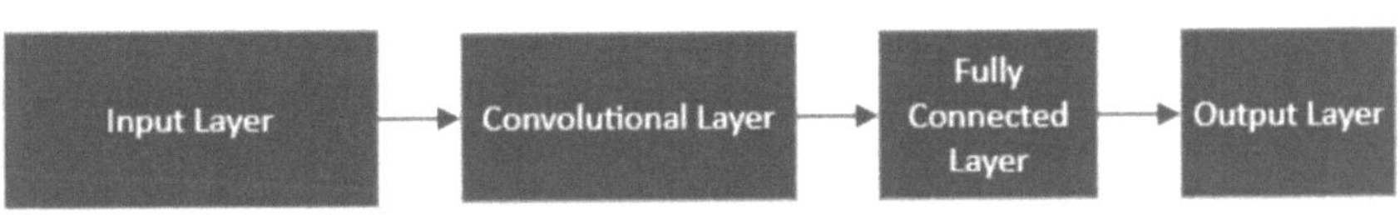

Fig. 1. Basic CNN Architecture

CNN needs a tonne of data in order to produce predictions with a high degree of accuracy. Selecting a database is crucial since Crop Yield must operate in real-time, making accuracy a crucial component. Training data and test data are the two sections of the database. Training Database with 3000 photos organised into ten groups. A test database with five hundred images divided into ten groups. Aphids, armyworms, bollworms, beetles, mites, mosquitoes, earthworms, grasshoppers, and so on are among the ten classification categories of pests as shown in Fig. 2.

Fig. 2. Images from pest dataset

CNN features various layered types, each with its own featured shapes. Here is a summary of the CNN model that predicts pests and classes pesticides using three conventional layers, three max-pooling layers, and a fully connected CNN layer. It also shows various activation methods, such as conv2d, max-pooling, dense-43, etc.

3.2 Soil Defect Identification and Crop Recommendation

3.2.1 Crop Recommendation Using CatBoost Classifier

Yandex created Cat Boost, a novel gradient boosting algorithm, in 2017. It has been demonstrated that this algorithm produces very accurate results quickly during training. The primary applications of this algorithm include self-driving cars, recommendation systems, and artificial assistants. It has been demonstrated that this model outperforms other models, including XGBoost and LightGBM. The testing parameters included training speed, accuracy, computing power, hyperparameter tuning, and more. Although CatBoost is most effective in handling techniques for categorical data, it is not limited to categorical features alone. In Cat Boost, the terms "Cat" and "Boost" denote categories and boosting, respectively.

CatBoost Classifier uses symmetric trees, which is the primary distinction between it and other boosting or classifier algorithms. And raises them one step at a time. To produce results with a high degree of accuracy, Cat Boost needs well-defined categorical data. Accuracy is crucial because crop yield needs to function in real-time, so selecting a database is crucial. The training and test data sections of the database are separated into two sections. Both the train data for 660×8 and the train data for 2200×8 are used for classification in this analysis as given in block diagram Fig. 3.

The input data is sent through a data cleaning process where it checks if the data is in the correct order and not corrupted. The process for the data set is shown in Table 1, this cleaned data is sent through for feature selection this decides which features mostly impact our processes and our training data this data is divided into test and train datasets. The training dataset is shown to the model during training but the test dataset is used for

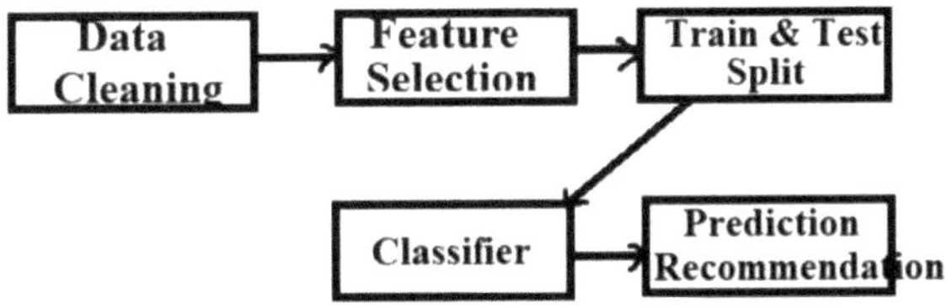

Fig. 3. Crop Recommendation Architecture

validation. The training data is sent through to the cat boost classifier which outputs a prediction on which crop to grow according to input data.

Table 1. Calculated dataset for prediction in CNN

Sl No	NitrogenN	PhosphorusP	PottasiumK	Temperature	Humidity	Ph value	Rainfall	Label
0	86	51	53	19.445677	80.913744	6.545670	203.966536	Rice
1	81	63	48	19.886543	79.919644	6.945696	227.005537	Rice
2	63	61	51	22.657079	81.987637	8.005677	264.099642	Rice
3	77	43	39	27.000345	79.998363	7.120301	243.956403	Rice
4	81	39	39	19.987543	82.004873	7.925673	263.112340	Rice

3.2.2 Soil Defect Identification and Crop Recommendation Using K-Nearest Neighbors

This is a non-parametric, supervised learning classifier, which utilizes closeness to make characterizations or expectations about the gathering of a confidential data. While it could be utilized for one or the other relapse or grouping issues, it's normally utilized as a characterization calculation, working off the possibility that comparative focuses might be viewed as close to one another which was given in Fig. 4.

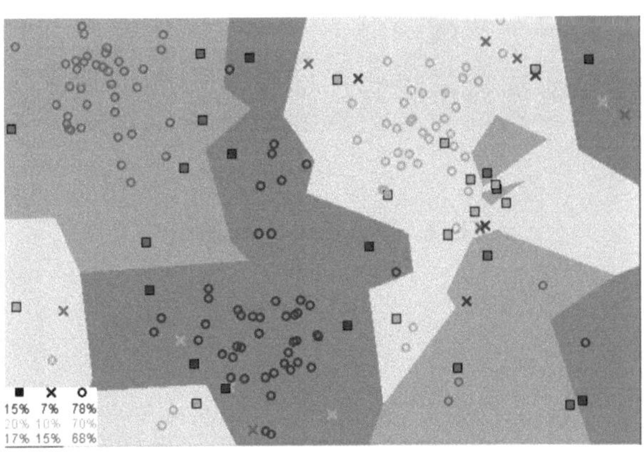

Fig. 4. Basic KNN classification

The image above shows the working of KNN algorithm it makes assumption that similar data points are near one another which was given in Fig. 5. The training data is sent through to the KNN classifier this outputs a prediction on which crop to grow according to input data. KNN requires well defined categorical data to result in high accuracy result. The database is divided into two parts training data and test data. Train Data with 2800 × 8 and Train Data with 660 × 8 classification of the datasets were used

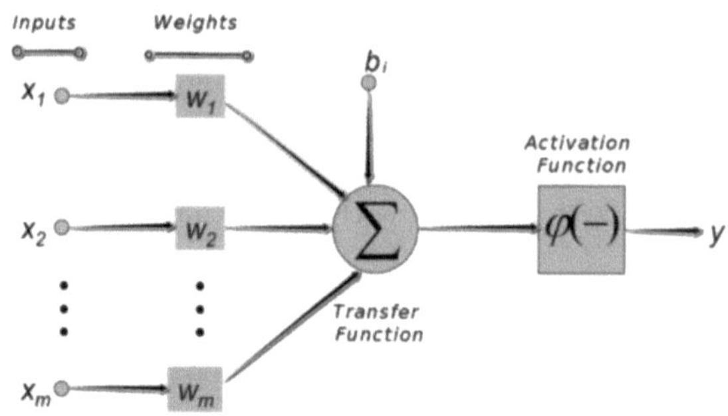

Fig. 5. KNN Classifier Architecture

3.3 Crop Recommendation

To represent the recommendation for the crops, we need to identify the input data set which will be given with different varieties which was given in Fig. 6.

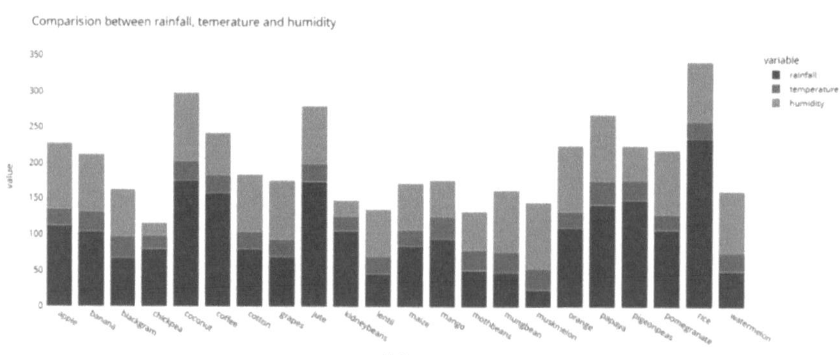

Fig. 6. Crop Dataset Analysis

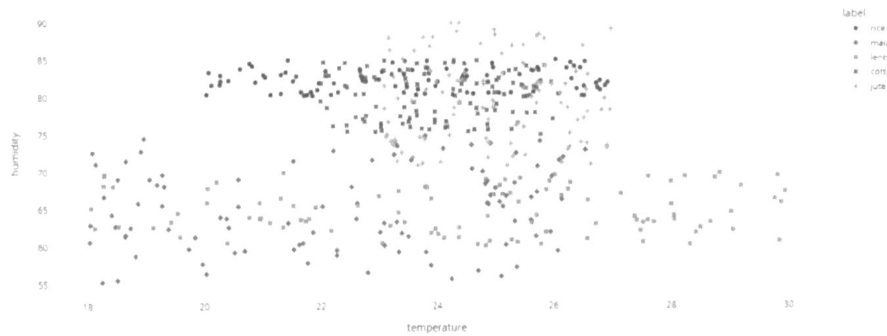

Fig. 7. Crop Dataset Analysis scatterplot

Also the given Fig. 7 depicts the scatter plot analysis for the given dataset with various crop labels. The above graph shows the relation between humidity and temperature which are the main features that effect the output of the system. The given Fig. 8 depicts the dataset analysis with various fertilizer to show the comparison of different values with Nitrogen, phosporus and potash to yield more outputs. Here is the NPK ratio for the fruit for designing the front end of the application, we have decided to choose HTML, CSS, and JavaScript (Fig. 9).

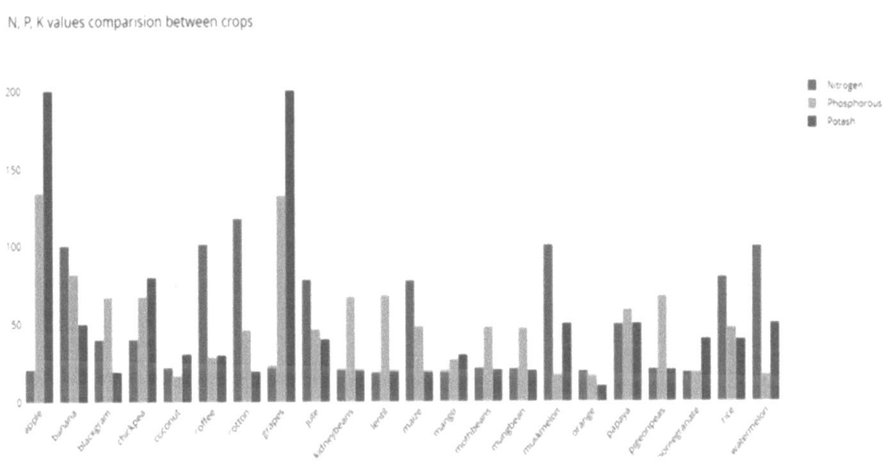

Fig. 8. Fertilizer dataset analysis

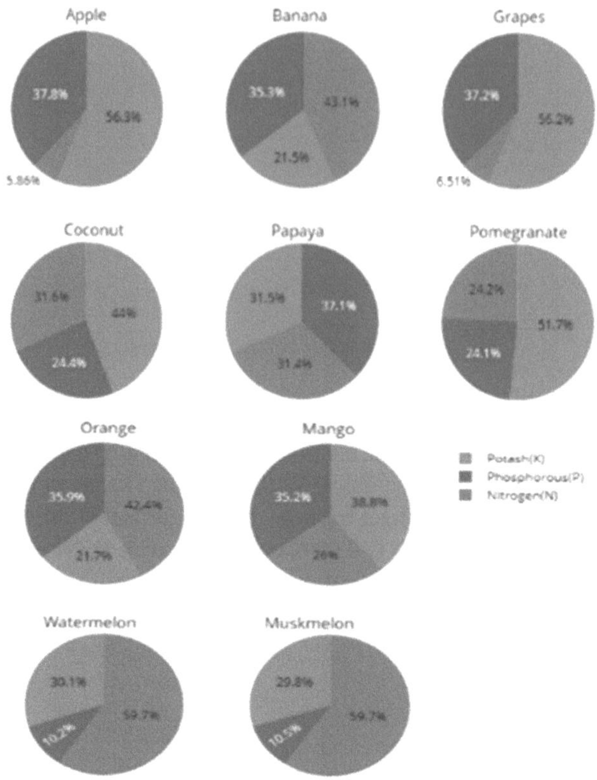

Fig. 9. Fertilizer dataset with piechart

These languages are beginner-friendly and have good online documentation. HTML or Hyper Text Markup Language is the building block of 90% of the internet as of today. To write code in HTML we have to use mark-up code also known as HTML tags. HTML also supports embedding programs written in JavaScript. JavaScript provides the functionality required for the web application.

CSS or Cascading Style Sheets demonstrates the dynamic styles used for HTML and written with property name and property value with the selector string tags and make it application friendly.

JavaScript is a cross-platform, Object-oriented (oops) language used mainly to design web applications. JavaScript has many open-source frameworks and a huge community backing it up, it is one the most popular language in the world.

Here the fertilizer dataset was given in piechart with various yield category identifies the yield prediction through our learning methods. While frontend makes the application user friendly the backend provides the structure to the application. We have decided to use Django as the backend framework. Django is an open source python backend web framework. It makes the process of web development easier by providing inbuild libraries that makes the process easier. This provides functionality to our application and acts as API or interface between Frontend i.e. users and machine learning models.

4 Experimental Analysis

We use python to design the three-machine learning/deep learning models. Python as lot of in-build library classes and algorithm this makes developing this model easier which otherwise should have been done from scratch.

Model 1: Pest Identification and Pesticide Recommendation.

This model should take an image as input and identify the pest present in that image and output he pesticide that can eradicate the pests. To design this model, we used TensorFlow and Keres API. TensorFlow is a open source API developed by google that enables us to build complex machine learning and deep learning models.

4.1 Pest Identification and Pesticide Prediction (Fig. 10 and Table 2)

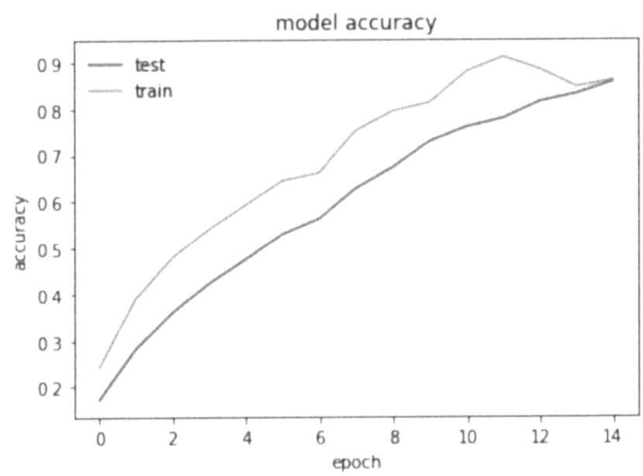

Fig. 10. Accuracy vs epoch Catboost classifier

Table 2. Result Table Catboost classifier

Task	Accuracy	Loss	Precision	Recall	F1 score
Train	0.8804	0.414	0.894	0.8438	0.86
Validation	0.8565	0.6	0.893	0.8134	0.84

The above table shows the performance of CNN architecture in classification of pests on training and validation datasets. We have received an accuracy of 88.04% for training and 0.85% for validation respectively.

4.2 Crop Recommendation

This model should take remote sensed data as input and outputs he crops that will result in best crop yield with respect to inputted data. To design this model, we used scikit-learn.

Scikit-learn is an open source API that enables us to build complex machine learning and deep learning models (Table 3).

Table 3. Result Table comparing different classifers

SL NO	Model	Training Accuracy	Test Accuracy
1	CatBoost Classifier	0.993939	1.0000000
2	XGBoost	0.989394	1.00000000
3	Random forest	0.986364	1.00000000
4	Decision tree	0.983333	1.0000000
5	KNN	0.978788	0.985714

The above table shows the training and test accuracies of various classifier. We have received training accuracy of 0.99 for training dataset and 1.000 for test dataset for catboost algorithm which is proved to be the best and the fastest classifier for the given dataset.

4.3 Fertilizer Recommendation

This model should take remote sensed data as input and outputs he crops that will result in best crop yield with respect to inputted data. To design this model, we used scikit-learn. Scikit-learn is an open source API that enables us to build complex machine learning and deep learning models (Fig. 11).

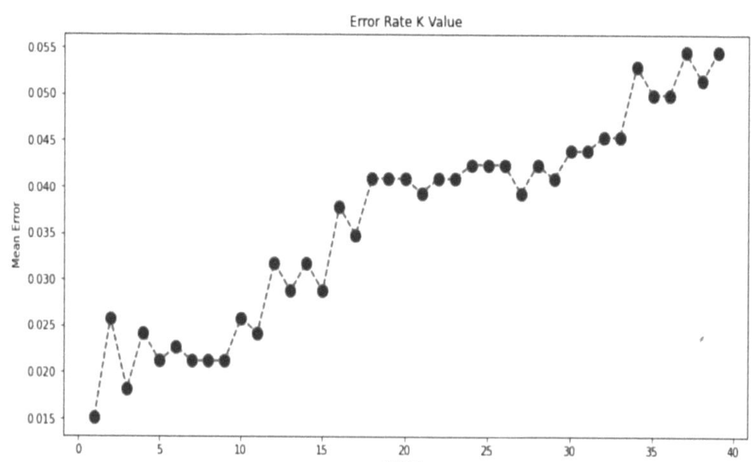

Fig. 11. K value vs Mean Error graph model

In the above graph between Mean Error and K Value, we can observe the mean error value for various K values. We can observe K value 18 to 28 gives a constant line with k value 21 giving the lowest mean error value. So, we have taken the K value has 21 which resulted in an accuracy of 97.83 for the test set.

5 Conclusion

In this work, we have developed an application that supports farmers throughout the crop development life cycle. This will help farmers choose the best crops and suggest the best fertilizers and pesticides by accounting for the soil, weather, location, and data. We have developed a CNN model that can identify a pest from an image and recommend a pesticide because pests are the primary cause of crop failure in India. This should aid farmers in safeguarding their harvests. The fertilizer recommendation will help farmers, and they will learn more about the state of the soil. We further recommend using fertilizers to help the soil overcome this deficiency. The web application's features will help close the gap between farmers and machinery has an intuitive interface that makes it easy for anyone to use and interact with the machine-learning models. Consequently, the system will assist farmers in more efficiently planning their crops and reduce the daily challenges they face. The technology helps farmers grow new crops, which prevents the soil from becoming infertile, by giving them a list of crops that should be planted on the property. The system also makes recommendations for the crop that best suits the farmer's land, assisting in maximizing crop yield and reducing losses. The system's support and assistance for farmers will result in an increase in both crop yield and return on investment.

References

1. Kavita, P.M.: Crop yield estimation in India using machine learning. In: 2020 IEEE 5th International Conference on Computing Communication and Automation (ICCCA). IEEE (2020)
2. Kale, S.S., Patil, P.S.: A machine learning approach to predict crop yield and success rate. In: 2019 IEEE Pune Section International Conference (PuneCon). IEEE (2019)
3. Rashid, M., Bari, B.S., Yusup, Y.B., Kamaruddin, M.A., Khan, N.: A comprehensive review of crop yield prediction using machine learning approaches with special emphasis on palm oil yield prediction. IEEE Access. **9**, 63406–63439 (2021)
4. Shafi, U., et al.: A multi-modal approach for crop health mapping using low altitude remote sensing, Internet of Things (IoT) and machine learning. IEEE Access. **8**, 112708–112724 (2020)
5. Feng, S., Zhao, J., Liu, T., Zhang, H., Zhang, Z., Guo, X.: Crop type identification and mapping using machine learning algorithms and sentinel-2 time series data. IEEE J. Sel. Top. Appl. Earth Obs. Remote Sens. **12**(9), 3295–3306 (2019)
6. Selvaraj, J.D.F., Paul, P.M., Jingle, I.D.J.: Automatic wireless water management system for smart vineyard irrigation using IoT technology. Int. J. Oceans Oceanogr. **13**(1), 211–218 (2019) ISSN 0973-2667. (Web of Science indexed), Research India Publication
7. Bhanumathi, S., Vineeth, M., Rohit, N.: Crop yield prediction and efficient use of fertilizers. In: IEEE International Conference on Communication and Signal Processing, pp. 4–6 (2019)
8. Nishant, P.S., Venkat, P.S., Lakshmi, B., Jabber, A.B.: Crop yield prediction based on Indian agriculture using machine learning. In: Conference: 2020 International Conference for Emerging Technology (INCET) (2020)

9. Nigam, A., Garg, S., Agrawal, A., Agarwal, P.: Crop yield prediction using machine learning algorithms. In: 2019 Fifth International Conference on Image Information Processing (ICIIP) (2019)
10. Rani, T.P., Vemireddi Srinadh, Mano Paul, P., Ananth, J.P.: CH selection and compressive sensing-based data aggregation in WSN using hybrid golden circle-inspired optimization. Int. J. Commun. Syst. **36**(15), 1099–1131., Wiley Publications (2023). https://doi.org/10.1002/dac.5574
11. Ram Kumar, M.P., Daniya, T., Mano Paul, P., Raja kumar, S.: Intrusion detection using optimized ensemble classification in fog computing paradigm. Knowl.-Based Syst. (2022). https://doi.org/10.1016/j.knosys.2022.109364., Elsevier, ISSN: 0950-7051, IF – 8.138, SCIE
12. Jingle, I.D.J., Sam, S., Paul, P.M., Jude, A., Selvaraj, D.F.: Design of Grover's algorithm over 2, 3 and 4-qubit systems in quantum programming studio. Int. J. Electron. Telecommun. **68**(1), 77–82 (2022). https://doi.org/10.24425/ijet.2022.139851. http://ijet.pl/index.php/ijet/article/view/10.24425-ijet.2022.139851/930, ISSN: 2300-1933
13. Shylu Sam, D.S., et al.: Design of low–power 4-bit flash ADC using multiplexer based encoder in 90nm CMOS process. Int. J. Electron. Telecommun. **68**(3), 565–570 (2022). https://doi.org/10.24425/ijet.2022.141275., ISSN: 0867-6747
14. Ajay Vasanth, P., Paul, S., Shylu, D.S., Paul, P.M.: IoT based prognostics using MEMS sensor with single board computers for rotary machines. Przeglad Elektrotechniczny. **97**(11), 170–174 (2021). https://doi.org/10.15199/48.2021.11.31., ISSN 0033-2097, (Scopus Indexed)
15. Paul, P.M., Jingle, I.D.J.: A privatized approach in enhanced spam filtering techniques using TSAS over cloud networks. Int. J. Intell. Enterprise. **9**(3), 332–343 (2022). https://doi.org/10.1504/IJIE.2020.10030567. Inderscience Publishers (Scopus indexed), ISSN: 1745–3232
16. Jingle, I.D.J., Paul, P.M.: A collaborative defense protocol against collaborative attacks in wireless mesh networks. Int. J. Enterprise Netw. Manag. **12**(3), 199–220. Inderscience Publishers (Scopus indexed), ISSN: 1748-1260 (2021). https://doi.org/10.1504/IJENM.2021.10030549
17. Sam, S., Paul, S., Jingle, D.J., Paul, M., Anuradha, Rani, J.S.: Design techniques in carry select adder using parallel prefix adder for improved switching energy. Przeglad Elektrotechniczny J. **97**, 152–155. Wydawnictwo Sigma publishers, (Scopus Indexed), ISSN: 0033-2097 (2021)
18. Selvaraj, J.D.F., Jingle, I.D.J., Mano Paul, P.: EShield: an effective detection and mitigation of flooding in DDoS attacks over large scale networks. Int. J. Eng. Adv. Technol. (IJEAT). **8**(5) (Scopus Indexed), ISSN: 2249-8958 (2019)
19. Paul, P.M., Ravi, R.: Cooperative vector based reactive system for protecting email against spammers in wireless networks. J. Electr. Eng. **18**., Annexure I, Edition 4, ISSN: 1582-4594, University Politechnica, Timisoara, Romania, faculty of Electrical and Power Engineering (2018)
20. Mano Paul, P., Ravi, R.: A collaborative reputation-based vector space model for email spam filtering. J. Comput. Theor. Nanosci. **15**(2), 474–479 (2018). https://doi.org/10.1166/jctn.2018.7128., American Scientific Publishers (Scopus Indexed)
21. Mano Paul, P., Diana Jeba Jingle, I.: A novel Optimal Email Feature Selection Protocol (OEFS) for detecting spam emails. Int. J. Comput. Sci. Eng. **07**(16), 34–39 (2019). https://doi.org/10.26438/ijcse/v7si16.3439. UGC Approved Journal
22. Paul, P.M., Ravi, D.R.: A novel email spam detection protocol for next generation networks. TAGA J. Graph. Technol. Tech. Assoc. Graph. Arts. **14**, 124–133., Annexure I, Swansea Printing Technology Ltd (2018)
23. Jingle, I.D.J., Blessing, E., Paul, P.M.: Distributed detection of DoS using clock values in wireless broadband networks. Int. J. Eng. Adv. Technol. (IJEAT). **1**(5) ISSN: 2249 – 8958 (2012)

24. Shekhar, R., Mano Paul, P., Jeba Jingle, D.: AI applications at the scheduling and resource allocation schemes in web medium. In: Towards Wireless Heterogeneity in 6G Networks, pp. 107–126. CRC Press, Taylor and Francis Group (2024) eBook ISBN9781003369028
25. Shelke, C.S., Jingle, D.J., Paul, P.M.: Achieving reliability of quantum state in cloud and infrastructure. In: Cloud Reliability Engineering Technologies and Tools, vol. 5., ISBN 9780367713737, Scopus Indexed. CRC Press, Taylor and Francis Group (2021)
26. Sahil Raj, P., Paul, M., Hegde, C.: A sustainable social media smart model for the deployment of learning skills in universities. In: Alliance Technology Conference (ATCON) - International Conference on Artificial Intelligence and Applications (ICAIA-2023). Alliance University, Bengaluru (2023)

Classification of Diseases in Common Food Crops Using Custom Designed Convolutional Neural Network

Vidyadevi G. Biradar(✉), H. Hanumanthappa, and Roshnica Selva

Nitte Meenakshi Institute of Technology (NMIT), Nitte (Deemed to be University), Bengaluru 560064, India
{vidyadevi.g.biradar,hanumanthappa.h}@nmit.ac.in

Abstract. The quality and productivity of agricultural products are greatly reduced by plant diseases, highlighting the critical need for early identification for global health. Benefits like higher crop yields can be obtained by utilizing computer vision and deep learning together as a dependable method of automatic plant disease diagnosis. In this study, a novel deep-learning model for crop disease diagnosis via image analysis of plant leaves is presented. The model uses an 80: 20 dataset split for training and testing. It was trained using the Plant Village dataset, which includes 61,486 leaf pictures and 39 plant illnesses. Six layers make up the convolutional neural network, which uses batch normalization, max pooling, ReLu activation, and SoftMax activation for classification. With training parameters set at 150 epochs, batch size 32, Adam optimizer, and binary cross-entropy loss function, the model demonstrates satisfactory performance, boasting an accuracy of 95.47%, F1 score of 0.95, precision of 1.00, and recall of 1.00. Confusion matrix analysis reveals exceptional accuracy across crops, except for tomatoes and potatoes, where false positives and false negatives are minimal.

Keywords: Deep learning · CNN · Convolution layer · Activation

1 Introduction

Plant diseases negatively affect world agriculture and pose a danger to both food supply and food security. [1], Effective disease management and the reduction of financial losses depend on the timely and precise diagnosis of plant diseases. Convolutional neural networks (CNNs) have demonstrated considerable promise for automating plant disease diagnosis. The goal of this re-search is to construct a reliable and scalable system that can correctly diagnose plant illnesses based on visual symptoms captured in photos. This research proposes a comprehensive approach to plant disease identification using deep learning. The methodology includes important processes including dataset gathering, pre-processing, model choice (such as ResNet, Inception, or Dense Net), transfer learning, model optimization, and evaluation using measures like accuracy, precision, and recall. Additionally, a user-friendly interface is developed to facilitate easy deployment and utilization of the trained model, enabling farmers, agricultural experts, and

M. Paprzycki et al. (Eds.): ICACIS 2024, CCIS 2405, pp. 94–109, 2027.
https://doi.org/10.1007/978-3-032-30990-7_7

researchers to assess the health of plants and make informed decisions for disease control measures. The proposed approach offers a promising solution to address the challenges of plant disease detection, contributing to improved disease management and sustainable agriculture practices. Table 1 shows the various crop types and the diseases in the plant village dataset.

In this study improvement in model performance on the classification of common food crops based on plant leaf's images is proposed.

Contributions of this study

- A custom design CNN is developed for the identification of diseases for crops available in the plant village dataset. Various diseases as shown in the table.
- The performance evaluation of the model is done using metrics accuracy, F1 score, Recall and Precision.
- Comparative analysis of the proposed model is carried out by comparing it with state–of–the–art existing methods.

This study is organized into various sections, chapter II gives a literature survey, chapter III describes methodology, chapter IV gives results and discussion and chapter V gives conclusion and future scope.

2 Literature Review

A novel deep-learning approach to plant disease detection is presented with an emphasis on the accurate diagnosis and categorization of plant diseases from photographs that show their visible symptoms. The suggested approach uses convolutional neural networks (CNNs) to train models to recognize and extract relevant features from a large collection of plant photos for illness detection. The VGG16 model achieves noteworthy metrics with an accuracy of 96.50%, an F1 score of 96.40%, a precision of 96.45%, and a recall of 96.35% when applied to the Plant Village dataset including 54,305 pictures. [1]. A hybrid model based on the Faster R-CNN (Region-based Convolutional Neural Network) model in conjunction with the Support Vector Machine (SVM) classifier is presented to identify and categorize wheat leaf spot disease into healthy and unhealthy leaves [2].

This research used the InceptionV3 model for the classification of plant village dataset to identify the diseases in common crops. Novel integration of convolutional neural networks (CNNs) with machine learning for crop recommendation and disease detection to improve agricultural practices and the control of plant diseases. Two key components of the system are included: machine learning algorithms for customized crop recommendations based on disease information and environmental conditions, and a CNN model trained on plant photos for accurate disease identification. The InceptionV3 model performs best with 98.42% accuracy. The InceptionV3 model performance was compared with ResNet50 and EfficientNetB0 and found that Res-Net50 gave better performance [3]. The Xception model is used to classify the CPH-Dataset which has 38,343 pictures and the results obtained were 96.20% accuracy, 96.05% F1 score, 96.10% precision, and 96.00% recall. The suggested system holds promise for rice agriculture by providing farmers and agricultural specialists with a valuable tool for early disease detection, accurate diagnosis, and prompt intervention, ultimately improving crop health and increasing rice production [4].

Table 1. Plant village dataset: crops and diseases

Sl.No	Crop Name	Disease
1	Apple	Apple Scab
2	Apple	Black rot
3	Apple	Cedar rust
4	Blueberry	Anthracnose
5	Blueberry	Leaf blight
6	Cherry	Healthy
7	Cherry	Leaf spot
8	Corn	Common rust
9	Corn	Gray leaf spot
10	Corn	Northern leaf blight
11	Grape	Black rot
12	Grape	Esca (Leaf curl)
13	Grape	Leaf blight
14	Orange	Citrus Black Spot
15	Orange	Citrus Canker
16	Peach	Bacterial spot
17	Peach	Scab
18	Bell Pepper	Bacterial spot
19	Bell Pepper	Healthy
20	Potato	Early blight
21	Potato	Late blight
22	Raspberry	Anthracnose
23	Raspberry	Healthy
24	Soybean	Frogeye leaf spot
25	soyabean	healthy
26	Strawberry	Leaf scorch
27	Strawberry	Powdery mildew
28	Tomato	Bacterial spot
29	Tomato	Early blight
30	Tomato	Late blight
31	Tomato	Leaf mold
32	Tomato	Tomato Spotted-Wilt Virus

An automated disease identification of cotton plants is worked out using DenseNet121. Accurate disease diagnosis and classification are made possible by training the CNN model on a dataset of cotton leaf photos labelled with diseases. This is measured by metrics like accuracy, precision, and recall. Applying the DenseNet-121 model to the 54,305 picture Plant Village dataset yields some impressive results: 98.80% accuracy, 98.75% F1 score, 98.78% precision, and 98.73% recall. The Dense-Net-121 model demonstrates good accuracy and efficient feature extraction, making it appropriate for resource-constrained contexts. The results were compared with Inception ResNetV2 and DenseNet-121 outperformed [5].

The model Inception-ResNetV2 model is used for the classification of diseases in common food crops. The model was trained using the transfer learning technique. It was found that the Inception-ResNetV2 model requires more computational resources, even though it achieves an accuracy of 99.11%, an F1 score of 99.05%, a precision of 99.08%, and a recall of 99.03%. These results were compared with MobileNetV2 and Inception V3 and concluded that Inception-ResNetV2 out performs the other two deep learning models [6].

The ShuffleNet model was used to train robust models that can precisely recognize and classify illnesses in pomegranate leaves. A sizable dataset of pomegranate leaf photos annotated with disease diagnoses is used to train CNN models, which allows for accurate disease identification by extracting discriminative features. Applying the ShuffleNet model to the Plant Leaf Disease Dataset (3,657 pictures), notable metrics are shown: 94.50% accuracy, 94.35% F1 score, 94.40% precision, and 94.30% recall. The Shuffle Net model emphasizes its fit for resource-constrained contexts by sacrificing some accuracy for efficiency [7].

The Efficient Net B0 model is used for Plant Village dataset classification, the research was carried out on large datasets that included a variety of plant species and disease types. The model performed 99.56% accuracy, 99.50% F1 score, 99.53% precision, and 99.47% recall. Researchers claimed that this method is suitable for mobile apps. When weighing the pros and negatives of ResNet50, it's crucial to take into account the less-developed architecture. Overall, this research contributes to the development of automated and effective plant disease management systems, empowering farmers and agricultural specialists to identify diseases early and implement prompt actions, thereby enhancing crop health and increasing agricultural productivity-ty [8].

A Super Resolution Convolutional Neural Network (CNN) MobileNetV2 model is employed to tackle issues related to accurate and high-resolution crop disease detection. The work uses deep learning approaches to improve low-quality photographs' resolution to improve illness diagnosis in crop shots. Results from experiments show that it is more effective than traditional techniques at identifying agricultural illnesses. Furthermore, the Plant Village dataset containing 54,305 photos yields 97.02% accuracy, 96.95% F1 score, 97.00% precision, and 96.90% recall for the MobileNetV2 model [9].

A ResNet50 model is used for timely disease identification and customized crop suggestions on the Plant Village dataset and the study also presents a thorough crop recommendation system that makes use of disease data and takes into account a variety of parameters, including soil properties, environmental variables in the model achieves accuracy of 99.75%, F1 score 99.68%, precision 99.72%, and recall 99.64%. However, the computational demands of ResNet50 raise concerns for resource-constrained environments, underscoring the crucial trade-off between accuracy and efficiency in practical applications [10].

Convolutional Neural Networks (CNNs) model YOLOv5 model was used for tomato disease classification. By pre-processing a collection of photographs of tomato leaves with overlapping ailments, researchers improve the quality of the images by training a CNN network to accurately recognize and classify these disorders. The efficacy of the method is demonstrated by performance indicators such as accuracy 98.12%, precision 98.10%, recall 98.05%, and F1-score 98.07%. The Tomato Diseases Dataset is used to test the YOLOv5 model, which shows good accuracy for real-time object recognition but greater computing resource requirements, highlighting the trade-off between efficiency and precision and making it less appropriate for devices with limited resources [11].

The literature survey shows that there limitations of pretrained model in the classification performance of common food crop diseases. It is observed that always there is a trade-off between the model performance and computational overhead. Therefore, to overcome these limitations, this research work aims at designing a shallow architecture custom convolutional neural network model.

3 Methodology

This chapter describes the methodology of the proposed research work. It gives details of the dataset used, deep learning model design, pre-processing of images and model—training parameters. The approach in this paper is based on the CNN model. CNN model is explored in various research works and found encouraging results [12–14]. Tomato plant disease prediction is done using the CNN model in [15–17]. There exist some Machine learning-based plat disease prediction methods [18]. This work aims to design a CNN model with shallow architecture.

A. Dataset

This work uses the Plant Village dataset which has 39 plant diseases that covers common food crops [5].

B. Pre-processing

Various pre-processing steps applied are;

- image resize
- image normalisation
- Image augmentation – image flipping, rotation, scaling, PCA (principal component analysis) color augmentation.

The convolutional neural network used in this work with design details are discussed here in this section. Figure 1 shows the architecture of the proposed CNN.

The model consists of two main components:

- Feature extraction model: This model takes an input image of a plant leaf and extracts features from it. These features are likely to be numerical values that represent the colour, texture, and shape of the leaf.

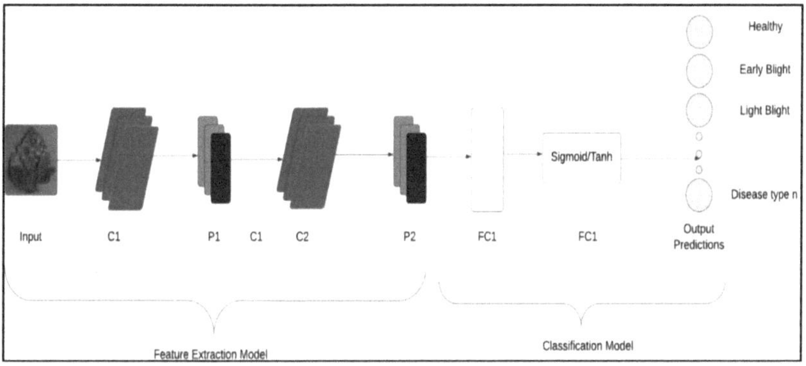

Fig. 1 Proposed model CNN architecture.

- Classification model: This model takes the features extracted by the first model as input and predicts the type of dis-ease that the plant has. The diagram shows two possible outputs: "Healthy" and "Disease type n".
- Convolutional Layer : The Convolutional Layer is the essential part of a Convolutional Neural Network (CNN) that initiates the process of extracting features from input images.
- Pooling layer: The CNN architecture's Pooling Layer, which comes after the Convolutional Layer, is essential in reducing the convolved feature map's size to save computational expenses.
- Fully connected layer: A key part of the CNN design, the Fully Connected (FC) layer is made up of neurons, weights, and biases that work together to create vital connections between layers.
- A Dropout layer: It is purposefully included in the CNN design to combat the problem of overfitting, which occurs when a model overly aligns with the training data, thereby impairing its performance on fresh data.
- Activation function: A Dropout layer is purposefully included in the CNN design to combat the problem of overfitting, which occurs when a model overly aligns with the training data, thereby impairing its performance on fresh data. In particular, overfitting hazards increase when all characteristics are linked to the Fully Connected (FC) layer.

C. Steps to build CNN model with values for hyper parameters
   1. Sequential Model Creation: Using the 'Sequential} API, layers are added one after the other to generate a sequential model in Keras. This guarantees the data moves through each layer in a sequential manner.
   2. Input form: The size of the input images and the channel order (for example, RGB images have three channels) determine the input form of the CNN.
   3. Initial Convolutional Layer: The input images' features are extracted by the first convolutional layer. To convolve over the input data, it makes use of 32 filters, each measuring three by three. This procedure aids in identifying fundamental traits and trends.

4. Activation and Batch Normalization: An activation function, also known as a Rectified Linear Unit, or ReLU, is applied follow-ing each convolutional layer. ReLU adds non-linearity, which enables the network to pick up intricate patterns.
   - Next, the input to a layer for every mini-batch is normalized by batch normalization. This method aids in both quickening and stabilizing the training process.
5. Max Pooling and Dropout Layers: Max pooling is a technique for spatial down sampling that minimizes the feature maps' spatial dimensions without sacrificing any significant information. It contributes to the network's increased resilience to changes in input data.
   - For regularization, dropout layers are incorporated. In order to prevent overfitting by adding noise and lowering inter-dependencies between neurons, they "drop out" a fraction of neurons at random during training.
6. More Convolutional Blocks: Two additional convolutional blocks, each with 64 filters, are added. As the network gets deeper, these blocks extract more hierarchical features from the data and capture increasingly complicated patterns.
7. Final Convolutional Block: With 128 filters in this final convolutional block, the network may extract even more complex and abstract characteristics, which are essential for precise categorization.
8. Flattening and Dense Layers: The network is flattened to create a one-dimensional vector from the multi-dimensional feature mappings after the convolutional layers. To represent the feature space, a dense layer comprising 1024 neurons is constructed. To create meaningful representations of the retrieved characteristics, this layer uses an activation function and performs a weighted sum of its inputs.
9. Output Layer: The number of neurons in the final dense layer, given as n_classes, is equal to the number of illness classes. For every input image, the class probabilities are predicted by this layer.

This layer is fitted with a softmax activation function, which normalizes the output values into probabilities. This facilitates the interpretation of the model's predictions as class probabilities.

4 Results and Discussion

The custom CNN is trained on the Plant Village dataset with the training parameters shown in Table 2. The CNN model is trained with 80:20 cross-validation with a total number of images of 61,486. The model hyper parameters are optimizer Adam and learning rate 0.001.

The model performance is evaluated with performance metrics accuracy, Recall, Precision and F1 score, the model gave satisfactory results and values of model performance metrics are tabulated in Table. 3

Convolutional Layers Equations

The convolution operation for a 2D input feature map X with a filter (kernel) W is

Table. 2 Proposed model training parameters

Name of the model	CNN
Batch size	32
No of epochs	150
Learning rate	0.001
Name of the dataset	Plant Village Dataset
Total number of images	61,486
No of images used for training	80:20
No of images used for testing	80:20
Activation function	ReLu
Loss function	Binary cross entropy
optimizer	Adam

represented as follows:

$$Y[i, i] = \sum m \sum n \; X\left[i + m, j + n\right].W[m, n] + b \tag{1}$$

Here, Y is the output feature map, i and j are the spatial indices, m and n are the filter indices, and b is the bias term.

Max Pooling Equation

Max pooling is a down sampling operation that extracts the maximum value from a local region in the input feature map. The operation for a 2x2 pooling window is represented as:

$$Y\left[i, j\right] = \max\left(X\left[2i, 2j\right], X\left[2i.2j + 1\right\}, X\left[2i + 1, 2j\ \right], X\left[2i + 1.2j + 1\right] \tag{2}$$

Relu Equation ReLU is an activation function that introduces non-linearity to the model. The ReLU function is defined as:

$$f(x) = \max(0, x) \tag{3}$$

Equation (1), (2), and (3) are used to calculate the convolution layers, max pooling and the activation function ReLu.

Figure 2 shows the model accuracy graph for 150 epochs, Adam optimizer and loss function binary cross entropy with batch size 32. Figure 3 shows the model loss graph and Fig. 3 shows the model confusion matrix respectively.

From the confusion matrix in Fig. 4 we found that the model gave the best performance with negligible false positives and false negatives for all the food crop leaves, however showed slightly poor performance for tomato and potato crops.

Table 3. Model performance metrics

F1	1.00
accuracy	95.46%
precision	0.95
recall	1.00

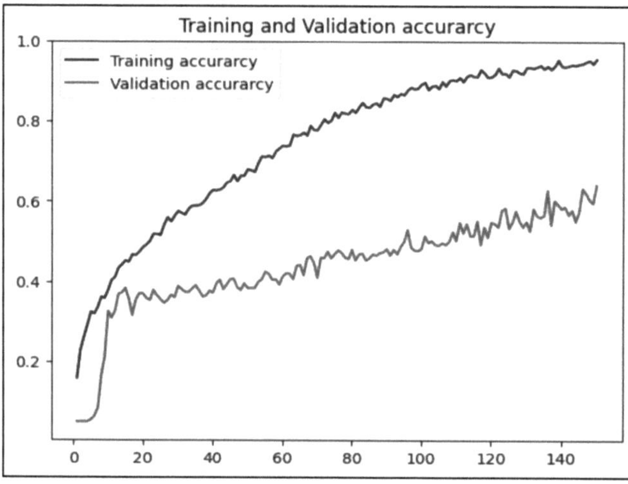

Fig. 2 Model accuracy Vs. Epochs

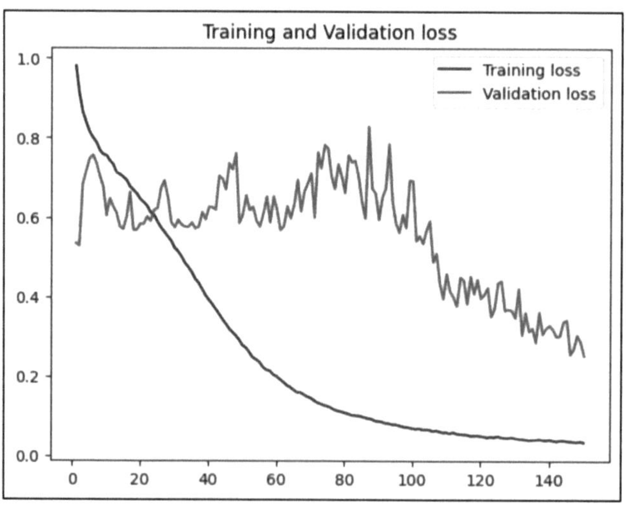

Fig. 3 Model Loss vs. Epochs

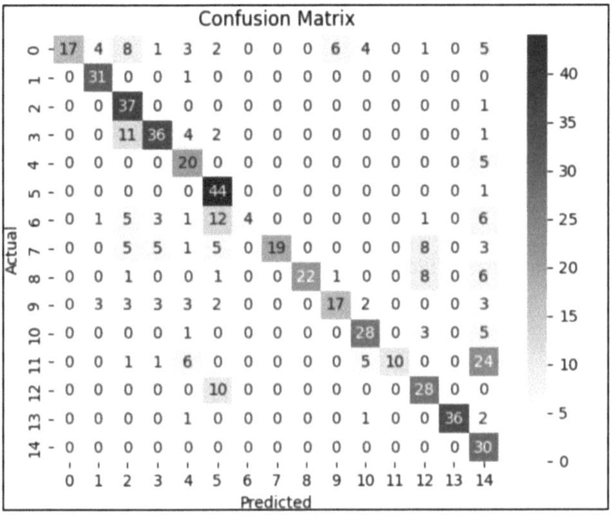

Fig. 4 Model confusion Matrix.

5 Performance Analysis

This section gives a comparison of existing methods with the performance of custom custom-designed CNN model in this work. Figures 5, 6, 7, and 8 shows a comparison of the performance of models which are studied during the literature survey. It is found that among the existing ones, ResNet50 gave the best performance, however, it gave poor indicators for Recall and F1 score. The performance of the proposed custom-designed shallow architecture CNN model in this research work is compared with ResNet50, it is found that the proposed model has given the best values with F1 100% and Recall 100%. There is a slight de-crease in accuracy and precision. This comparison is shown in Figs 9, 10, 11 and 12 and Table 4.

Table 4. Model performance comparison analysis

Model Name	Dataset	Accuracy	F1 Score	Precision	Recall
ResNet50 [1] [2021]	Plant Village (54,305 images)	99.75%	99.68%	99.72%	99.64%
EfficientNetB0 [2] [2023]	Plant Village (54,305 images)	99.56%	99.50%	99.53%	99.47%
InceptionV3 [8] [2022]	Plant Village (54,305 images)	98.42%	98.35%	98.40%	98.30%
MobileNetV2 [5] [2022]	PlantVillage (54,305 images)	97.02%	96.95%	97.00%	96.90%
VGG16 [3] [2022]	PlantVillage (54,305 images)	96.50%	96.40%	96.45%	96.35%
Inception-ResNetV2 [4] [2022]	PlantVillage (54,305 images)	99.11%	99.05%	99.08%	99.03%
DenseNet-121 [10] [2022]	PlantVillage (54,305 images)	98.80%	98.75%	98.78%	98.73%
Xception [2] [2023]	CPH-Dataset (38,343 images)	96.20%	96.05%	96.10%	96.00%
ShuffleNet[1] [2021]	Plant Leaf Disease Dataset (3,657 images)	94.50%	94.35%	94.40%	94.30%
YOLOv5 [6] [2021]	Tomato Diseases Dataset (3,673 images)	98.12%	98.07%	98.10%	98.05%
NASNetMobile [9] [2022]	Plant Village (54,305 images)	97.70%	97.65%	97.68%	97.63%
DenseNet169 [10] [2022]	Plant Village (54,305 images)	98.30%	98.25%	98.28%	98.23%
DeiT-Tiny [3] [2022]	Plant Village (54,305 images)	98.60%	98.55%	98.58%	98.53%
ConvNext Tiny [7] [2022]	Plant Village (54,305 images)	98.70%	98.65%	98.68%	98.63%

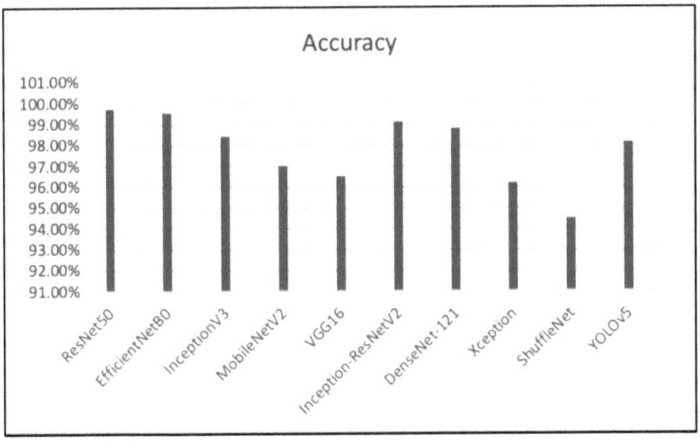

Fig. 5 Accuracy comparison of existing models

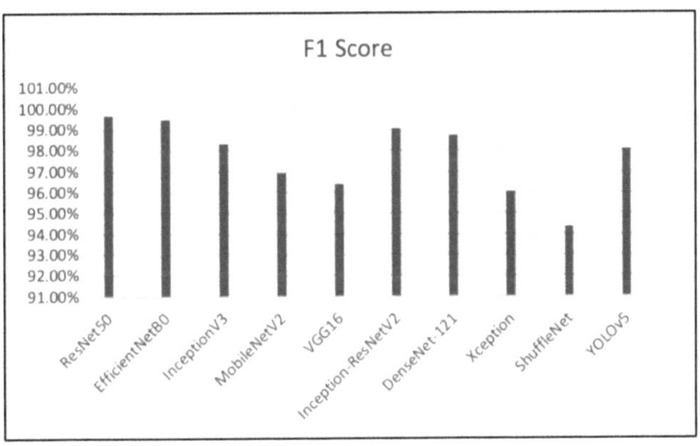

Fig. 6 F1 Score comparison of existing models

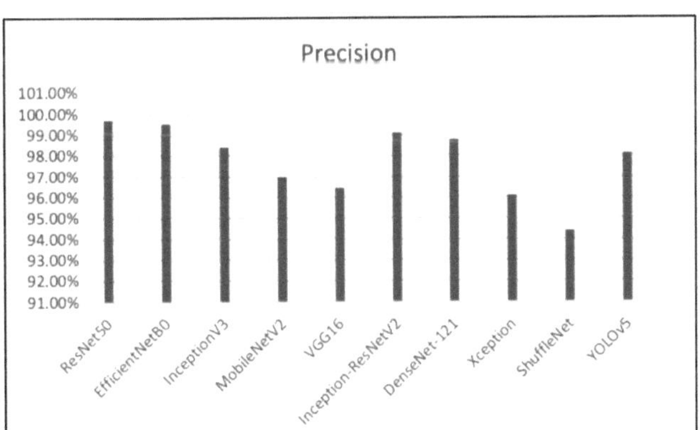

Fig. 7 Precision comparison of existing models

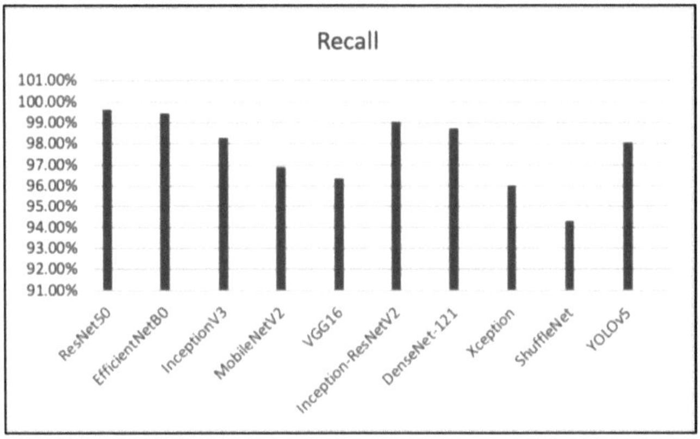

Fig. 8 Recall comparison of existing models

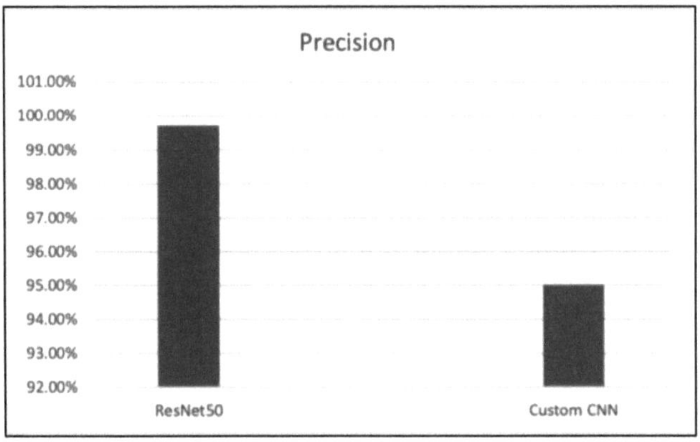

Fig. 9. Models accuracy comparison of ResNet50 and proposed CNN model.

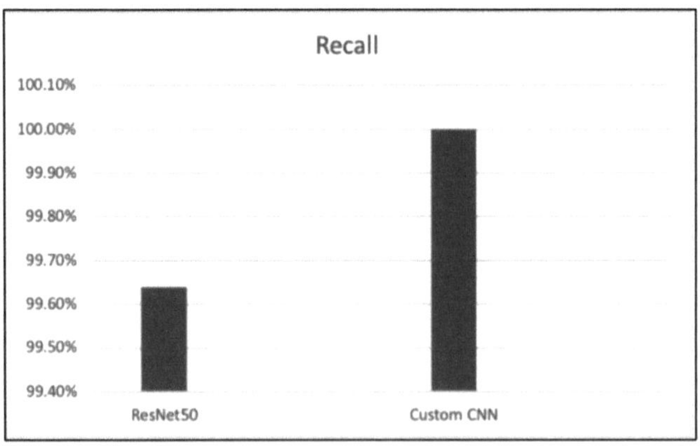

Fig. 10. Models accuracy comparison of ResNet50 and proposed CNN model.

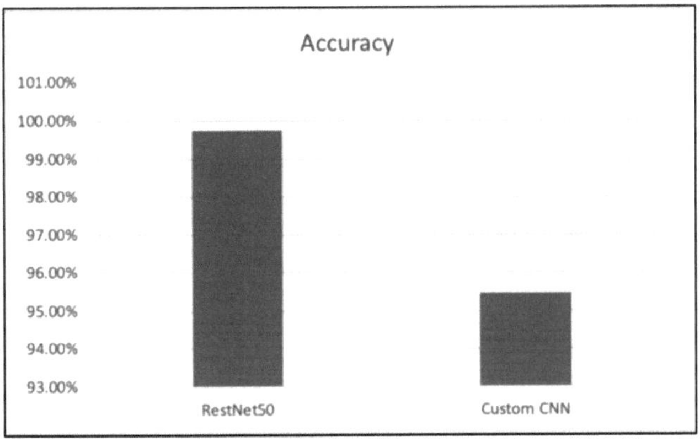

Fig. 11. Models accuracy comparison of ResNet50 and proposed CNN model.

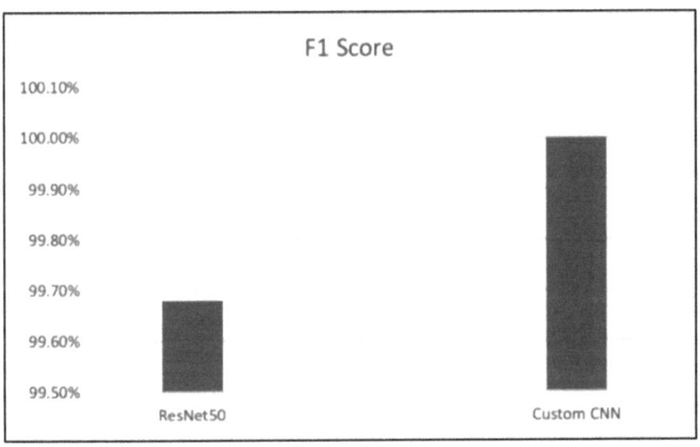

Fig. 12. Models accuracy comparison of ResNet50 and proposed CNN model.

6 Conclusion

In this research wsork plant disease in common food crops are classified using a custom designed CNN model. The contributions of the paper include a brief survey on state of the art deep learning models used for plant disease classification and their performance compassion is presented. The model gave a satisfactory performance with performance metrics with accuracy of 95.47%, F1 score 0.95, precision 1.00 and recall 1.00. The future scope of this work to improve model performance.

References

1. Akhtar, F., Partheeban, N., Daniel, A., Sriramulu, S., Mehra, S., Gupta, N.: Plant disease detection based on deep learning approach. In: 2021 International Conference on Advance Computing and Innovative Technologies in Engineering (ICACITE), pp. 74–77. IEEE (2021)

2. Bansal, A., Sharma, R., Sharma, V., Jain, A.K., Kukreja, V.: A deep learning approach to detect and classify wheat leaf spot using faster r-cnn and support vector machine. In: 2023 IEEE 8th International Conference for Convergence in Technology (I2CT), pp. 1–6 (2023)
3. Kumar, R., Shukla, N., et al.: Plant disease detection and crop recommendation using cnn and machine learning. In: 2022 International Mobile and Embedded Technology Conference (MECON), pp. 168–172. IEEE (2022)
4. Moiz, M., Akmal, M., Ishtiaq, M.S., Javed, U.: Classification of rice leaves diseases by deep cnn-transfer learning approach for improved rice agriculture. In: 2022 International Conference on Emerging Trends in Electrical, Control, and Telecommunication Engineering (ETECTE), pp. 1–6 (2022)
5. Negi, A., et al.: A detection and classification of cotton leaf disease using a lightweight cnn architecture. In: 2022 Fourth International Conference on Emerging Research in Electronics, Computer Science and Technology (ICERECT), pp. 1–5. IEEE (2022)
6. Ng, H.F., Lin, C.-Y., Chuah, J.H., Tan, H.K., Leung, K.H.: Plant disease detection mobile application development using deep learning. In: 2021 International Conference on Computer & Information Sciences (ICCOINS), pp. 34–38. IEEE (2021)
7. Nirmal, M.D., Jadhav, P., Pawar, S., Kharde, M., et al.: Deep learning-based disease detection using pomegranate leaf image. In: 2022 Smart Technologies, Communication and Robotics (STCR), pp. 1–5. IEEE (2022)
8. Vishnu Raja, P., Sangeetha, K., Ninisa, B.A., Samiksha, M., Sanjutha, S.S.: Convolutional neural networks based classification and detection of plant disease. In: 2022 6th International Conference on Computing Methodologies and Communication (ICCMC), pp. 1484–1488. IEEE (2022)
9. Sitha Ram, M., Krishna Priya, N., Sujith, M., Basha, S.S., Prashanth, J.: A super resolution cnn based model for crop disease detection. In: 2022 7th International Conference on Communication and Electronics Systems (ICCES), pp. 1532–1537. IEEE (2022)
10. Sajitha, N., Sourabh Nema, K.R., Bhavya, P.S., Pant, K.: The plant disease detection using cnn and deep learning techniques merged with the concepts of machine learning. In: 2022 2nd International Conference on Advance Computing and Innovative Technologies in Engineering (ICACITE), pp. 1547–1551. IEEE (2022)
11. Syed, R., Gadade, H.D., Kirange, D.K.: An approach to detect overlapping diseases in tomato leaf using cnn. In: 2022 4th International Conference on Advances in Computing, Communication Control and Networking (ICAC3N), pp. 1180–1184. IEEE (2022)
12. Deepalakshmi, P., Lavanya, K., Srinivasu, P.N.: Plant leaf disease detection using CNN algorithm. Int. J. Inf. Syst. Model. Des. **12**(1), 1–21 (2021)
13. Yadhav, S.Y., et al.: Plant disease detection and classification using cnn model with optimized activation function. In: 2020 International Conference on Electronics and Sustainable Communication systems (ICESC). IEEE (2020)
14. Saleem, M.H., Potgieter, J., Arif, K.M.: Plant disease detection and classification by deep learning. Plants. **8**(11), 468 (2019)
15. Tm, P., et al.: Tomato leaf disease detection using convolutional neural networks. In: 2018 Eleventh International Conference on Contemporary Computing (IC3). IEEE (2018)
16. Mokhtar, U., et al.: Tomato leaves diseases detection approach based on support vector machines. In: 2015 11th International Computer Engineering Conference (ICENCO). IEEE (2015)
17. Kibriya, H., et al.: Tomato leaf disease detection using convolution neural network. In: 2021 International Bhurban Conference on Applied Sciences and Technologies (IBCAST). IEEE (2021)

18. Ramesh, S., et al.: Plant disease detection using machine learning. In: 2018 International conference on design innovations for 3Cs compute communicate control (ICDI3C). IEEE (2018)
19. Mridha, K., et al.: Plant disease detection using web application by neural network. In: 2021 IEEE 6th International Conference on Computing Communication and Automation (ICCCA) (2021)

Underwater Single Image Restoration Using Modified Cycle GAN

Balaji Banothu[1(✉)] and B. Krishna Priya[2]

[1] Department of Computer Applications, NIT, Trichy, India
balaji@nitt.edu
[2] Department of Computer Science and Engineering, IITDM, Kancheepuram, India
krishnapriya@iiitdm.ac.in

Abstract. Underwater single-image restoration poses a significant obstacle because of the inherent degradation of images in aquatic environments, characterized by color distortion, blurring, and poor visibility. In this work, we have suggested a modified underwater single-image restoration strategy using a Cycle-GAN-based architecture. In the presented model we are using a generator structure similar to a DCGAN, our modified Cycle-GAN architecture effectively uses transposed convolutional layers for up sampling. Meanwhile, the discriminators are designed as Patch-GANs to evaluate the realism of translated pictures locally. The GAN guarantees the maintenance of essential picture features during translation by combining adversarial and cycle-consistency loss. The experiment's outcomes highlight our approach's efficacy in addressing problems like color distortion in various underwater scenarios as compared to the existing methods. The proposed technique makes an essential addition to underwater picture restoration, with implications for enhanced image quality in marine type applications.

1 Introduction

Research on the underwater environment has garnered more focus in the past year, leading to visual tasks centered around underwater scenes. For instance, an underwater concurrent mapping and localization system was introduced by Rahman et al. [1] for closed-loop underwater scene detection and relocation. A technique for identifying a diver's gestures with their hands in underwater situations was presented by Jiang et al. [2]. However, the intricacy of undersea scenery limits how accurate these jobs can be, where water selectively absorbs light, resulting in a prevalent blue-green appearance in underwater images. This phenomenon significantly hampers the visual experience and the precision of different visual activities. As a result, processing underwater photos is required to enhance the clarity of their images.

Regarding the state of the atmosphere, dark channel prior (DCP) was suggested by Kaiming He et al. [3] after analyzing several photographs of outdoor haziness. However, underwater situations are unsuitable for this approach. Then next Drew et al. [4] developed an underwater dark channel prior (UDCP) technique that combined DCP with the underwater physical model (UPM) designed explicitly for underwater scenes. Although this method works better in certain situations, it also has drawbacks. The contrast-limited

M. Paprzycki et al. (Eds.): ICACIS 2024, CCIS 2405, pp. 110–122, 2027.
https://doi.org/10.1007/978-3-032-30990-7_8

adaptive histogram equalization technique was presented by Kim et al. [5] as a way to improve picture contrast. However, this strategy may not produce the best results in more complicated underwater scenarios.

In recent years, methods grounded in deep learning have gained popularity. Compared to traditional approaches, these methods produce higher-quality restored images, better meeting user needs. The application of Generative Adversarial Networks (GANs) [6], initially employed for tasks such as image translation [7] and super-resolution [8], has extended to underwater image restoration, aligning with the broader category of image migration. Consequently, training networks with image pairs offers a potential solution. However, acquiring image pairs is challenging, given such samples' difficulty and limited availability.

We suggest using the modified Cycle GAN to overcome this obstacle for real-time improvement of underwater photographs. The model aims to familiarize itself with the various effects inherent in an underwater photograph and subsequently generate an enhanced image devoid of these effects. Our contribution for image restoration and applies adaptable modified Cycle GAN architecture for underwater low visibility images as follows.

- The Generator in our modified Cycle GAN architecture adopts a DCGAN-like structure, employing transposed convolutional layers for efficient up-sampling.
- The Discriminators are designed as Patch GANs to evaluate the realism of translated images locally.
- The GAN is trained using a combination of adversarial and cycle-consistency loss, enforcing the preservation of essential image characteristics during translation.

2 Previous Works

2.1 Conventional Techniques

The introduction of the Underwater Physical Model (UPM) [9] attempts to restore underwater images, primarily relying on straightforward image processing techniques involving alterations to the pixel values of the images. Iqbal et al. [10] presented a method for image enhancement through an Integrated Color Model (ICM) and Huang et al. [11] presented a method known as Relative Global Histogram Stretching (RGHS). Additionally, Bai et al. [12] employed a technique that involved regionalism of the pixel intensity center, employing multi-scale fusion and global and local equalization of the histogram for underwater image restoration. These methods operated in diverse color spaces, offering swift processing speeds and low computational complexity. However, they were not without drawbacks, requiring manual selection of parameters to achieve optimal image outcomes.

Some UPM-based picture restoration techniques then surfaced. The primary concept is to estimate the image's transmission value and background light intensity to invert the model. To estimate the parameters, Akkaynak et al. [13] analyzed changes in the picture's light source and dark pixels. Better repair results are achieved, although specific tools are needed. Peng et al. [14] proposed a technique for leveraging pictures. In order to finish picture restoration, blurriness and light absorption are used to measure scene depth. Its estimating accuracy is better than that of DCP. The precision of underwater model parameter estimation limits the picture quality retrieved by these approaches.

2.2 Deep Learning Methodologies

Deep learning-based methodologies uses data-driven strategies to recover underwater photos. Hashisho et al. [15]. suggested reconstructing the picture using an autoencoder called U-Net denoising. A small collection of underwater images was created by Li et al. [16]. He also developed the Underwater Convolutional Neural Network [17] model. Water-GAN was suggested by Li et al. [18] and is utilized to produce real underwater photos. However, obtaining the image's depth information is necessary, and it is challenging. A dual-branch discriminator was employed in Chen et al.'s [19] suggested GAN restoration approach to maintain the picture content. High-quality photos can be obtained with the help of deep learning algorithms, but training them is challenging due to their complicated network structure.

3 Proposed Method

A deep learning-based model called Cycle GAN is employed for image-to-image translation problems. When it comes to underwater single-picture restoration, Cycle GAN may be utilized to improve the underwater photo quality. The core idea behind Cycle GAN is to have two Generators and two Discriminators working in a cycle. The Generators target to transform images from one domain to another and vice versa when the Discriminator works to discern between artificially created and actual pictures. Our proposed model architecture as shown in Fig. 1. Let us thoroughly explain how and why this method is effective for underwater single-image restoration.

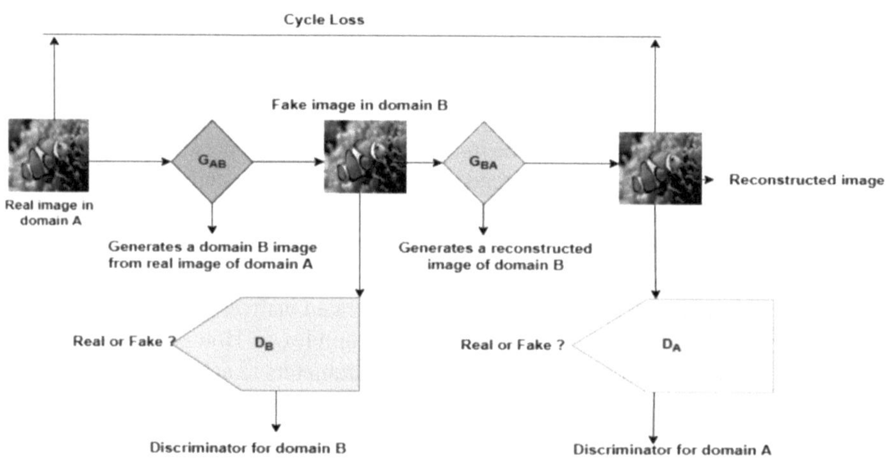

Fig. 1. Architecture of Modified Cycle GAN Model

3.1 Adversarial Training

The primary objective of adversarial training in Cycle GAN is to train competitively two Generators (G_A and G_B) and Discriminators (D_A and D_B). The Generator aims to transform underwater images into clear images to trick the Discriminator. The Discriminators aim to differentiate between pictures produced by G_A and actual, clear images.

- **Minimax Game:** Through adversarial training, a minimax game is created in which the Discriminators want to improve their ability to discriminate between genuine and produced pictures. At the same time, the Generators try to produce realistic images that mislead them.
- **Image Realism Improvement:** As the Generators and Discriminators play this game interactively, the Generators get better at creating realistic images, improving image quality.

3.2 Cycle Consistency

The cycle consistency loss guarantees that the translation is consistent between domains when a picture is transformed from domain A to domain B and back again. So the output should resemble the original.

Forward Cycle (E.g., $G_A \rightarrow G_B$): G_A is used to transform a picture from domain A (underwater) to domain B (clear).

Backward Cycle (E.g.$G_B \rightarrow G_A$): G_B is then used to translate the translated picture from domain B back to domain A.

- Preservation of Structure: Cycle consistency ensures that important structural information in the image is preserved during translation.
- Avoiding Information Loss: It prevents information loss during the translation process, making sure that the restored image is consistent with the original.

Complementary Objectives: Adversarial training and cycle consistency are complementary objectives. Adversarial training focuses on image realism, while cycle consistency focuses on maintaining structural information.

Balancing Realism and Consistency: Together, these objectives balance generating realistic images and ensuring that the produced visuals exhibit coherence with the first ones.

3.3 Generator

We include our Generative networks' architectural design from DCGAN as shown in Fig. 2. There are many residual blocks and three convolutional layers in the generator model. It also has a final convolutional layer that maps feature to the RGB space and two fractionally-strided convolutions with a stride of half. We utilized six blocks for 128 × 128 photographs, nine blocks for 256 × 256, and better-quality training images.

Our design uses a Leaky ReLU activation layer and integrates instance normalization. Hyperbolic tangent serves as the last layer's activation function. These decisions are made to provide a consistent and functional model design that remains true to the cited literature.

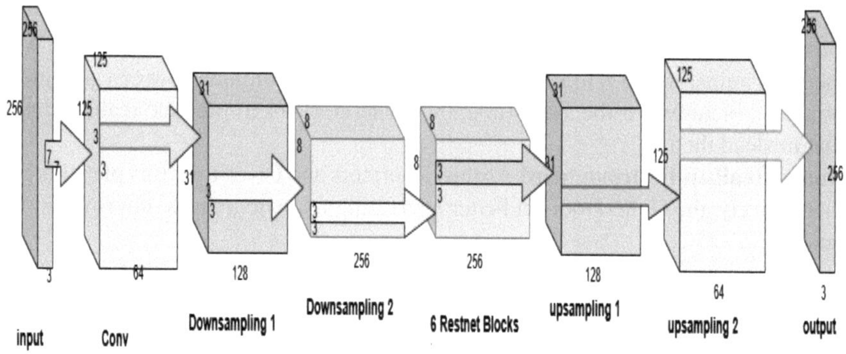

Fig. 2. Framework of Generator

3.4 Discriminator

Convolutional neural networks (CNN) serve as the foundation for Discriminator networks. In order to identify between two sets of photos and extract deep characteristics from the image, it employs five convolutional layers. The architecture of Discriminator is described in Fig. 3.

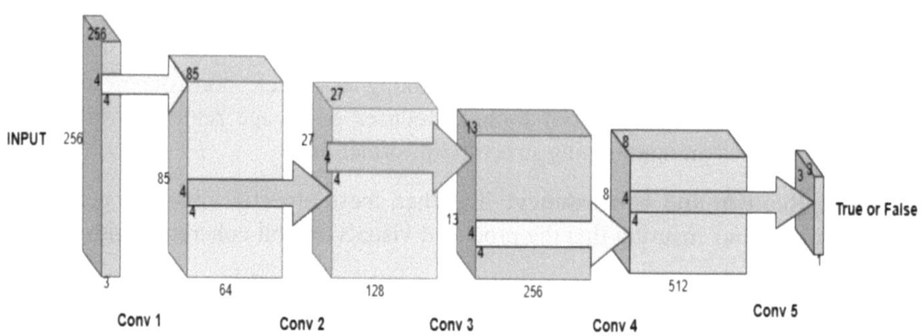

Fig. 3. Framework of Discriminator

3.5 Objective Function Formulation

Using training samples x_i, where $x_i \in X$, and y_i, where $y_j \in Y$, we want to get mappings X and Y two domains together. The data distribution is represented as y ~ pdata(y) and x ~ pdata(x). Our model includes two mappings: F: Y → X and G: X → Y. Furthermore, we present adversarial discriminators. In underwater image restoration using Cycle GAN, pdata represents the distribution of underwater images (x) and their corresponding clear images (y). It characterizes the likelihood of encountering various types of underwater scenes and their corresponding clear counterparts within the dataset. The term "pdata" refers to the probability distribution of data within a specific domain.

Cycle consistency losses, which try to avoid conflicts between the learn mappings G and F, and adversarial losses, which attempts to balance the target domain's data distribution with the produced picture distribution, are the two critical parts of the objective function.

3.5.1 Adversarial Loss

The goal of a traditional conditional A, Z → B is a mapping that the Generative Adversarial Network (GAN)-based model is supposed to learn., where Z stands for random noise, and P is the source (desired) domain. The following is the formulation of the conditional adversarial loss function is given in Eq. (1).

$$L(GAN)N(A, B[c], P, Q) = E_{(P,Q)}\left[\log B[c](Q) + E_{(P,Q)}\left[\log 1 - B(P, A(P, Z))\right)\right. \quad (1)$$

In this case, the Discriminator B[c] seeks to maximize L, while the Generator A seeks to minimize it.

3.5.2 Cycle Consistency Loss

Theoretically, using adversarial training, one may map A and B so that the outputs have distributions that precisely match those of the related resultant domains, P and Q. If the network has sufficient capacity. However, transport the same collection of input images to any arbitrary picture permutation inside the designated domain. In this case, an output distribution may resemble the target distribution by any of the learned mappings. Due to this, it is impossible to guarantee that the trained function transfers correctly when depending solely on adversarial losses to change one input (x_i) into the desired output (y_i). The learned mapping functions should exhibit cycle consistency to reduce the number of feasible mapping functions. The image translation cycle should be able to restore any picture x from domain P to its initial state. This criterion improves the mapping functions ability to reliably and precisely convert different inputs into the intended outputs as given in Eqs. (2) and (3) respectively.

$$\text{i.e., } x \rightarrow A(x) \rightarrow B(A(x)) \approx x \quad (2)$$

$$L_{cyc}(A, B) = E(x \sim p(data))(P)[\|B(A(x)) - x\|] + E(y \sim p(data(Q))\left[\|B(A(y)) - y\|\right. \quad (3)$$

3.5.3 Combined Objective Functions

The Eqs. (4) and (5) showing our full objective loss and min-max game for this loss respectively. Our Full objective function is given below:

$$L(A, B, D(P), D(Q)) = L(GAN)(A, D(Y), P, Q) + L(GAN)(B, D(X), Q, P) + \lambda L(Cyc)(A, B) \quad (4)$$

where the relative relevance of the two objectives is controlled by λ. Our goal is to resolve:

$$A^{*}, B^{*} = \arg\min_{A,B} \max_{D(P),D(Q)} L(A, B, D(P), D(Q)) \quad (5)$$

3.6 Training

The objective function is denoted by the number five, was minimized using the Adam optimizer. All networks were trained with a 0.0002 learning rate from the start. The learning rate drops linearly diminishing nearly to zero over the course of the following 100 epochs after being constant for the first 100. Efficiently optimizing the model variables during the training phase is the aim of this arrangement.

4 Experimental Analysis and Discussions

4.1 Dataset

4.1.1 EUVP Dataset

The EUVP collection consists of discrete sets of pair and unpaired picture samples demonstrating different levels of perceptual quality, encompassing high and low-quality examples. The purpose of the dataset is to make supervised training easier. Algorithms help enhance the quality of photos taken from underwater. The Tables 1 and 2 represents details of the datasets.

Table 1. Paired Dataset

Name	Train Pairs	Valid	Sum
Underwater Dark	5500	500	11500
Underwater Imagenet	3700	1200	8600
Underwater Scenes	285	130	4500

Table 2. Unpaired Dataset

Poor Quality	Good Quality	Validation	Total
3195	3140	330	6665

4.1.2 UIEB Dataset

The UIEB [20] consists of two subsets. There are 890 raw underwater photos in the first collection, along with accompanying high-quality reference photographs. The second subset comprises 60 challenging underwater images that present more complex scenarios for bench-marking image enhancement algorithms.

4.2 Evaluation Metrics

In this work, we utilize four conventional metrics, namely Peak Signal to Noise Ratio (PSNR) [20], Structural Similarity (SSIM) [20], and Underwater Image Quality Metric (UIQM) [21]. These metrics provide a quantitative comparison between the restored photos and the related ground truths, providing a thorough evaluation of the image enhancement execution.

4.2.1 Peak Signal-to-Noise Ratio (PSNR)

When we contrasted to its ground truth, the PSNR roughly represents the quality of the reconstruction of a produced picture. It is computed using the formula below in Eq. (6), this is determined by looking at their Mean Squared Error (MSE).

$$\mathrm{PSNR}(u, v) = 10\log_{10}\left[255^2/\mathrm{MSE}(u, v)\right] \tag{6}$$

4.2.2 Structural Similarity Index Measurement (SSIM)

The SSIM [20] (referring to Structural Similarity) compares three attributes across picture patches: brightness, contrast, and structure. It is defined by Eq. (7).

$$\mathrm{SSIM}(u, v) = \left(\frac{2\mu(u)\mu(v) + c1}{\mu(u)^2 + \mu(v)^2 + c1}\right)\left(\frac{2\sigma(uv) + c2}{\sigma(u)^2 + \sigma(v)^2 + c2}\right) \tag{7}$$

4.2.3 Underwater Image Quality Metric

The Underwater image colorfulness measure (UICM) [21], underwater image sharpness measure (UISM) [22], and underwater image contrast measure (UIConM) [23] are the three attribute metrics that make up the UIQM. UICM attempts to solve the color casting issue frequently present in underwater images. The water becomes more profound as it goes, and colors progressively losing intensity based on their distinct wavelengths.

Specifically, red fades first because of its shorter wavelength. Because of this, images captured underwater usually have a blue or greenish hue. Limited light is another element that contributes significantly to color desaturation in underwater images.

We employ the two rival color components associated with brightness, RG and YB, to measure the UICM by using Eqs. (8) and (9) respectively.

$$R_0G_0 = R_0 - G_0 \tag{8}$$

$$Y_0B_0 = \frac{R_0 + G_0}{2} - B_0 \tag{9}$$

Underwater images commonly experience substantial noise. Instead of employing conventional statistical values, measuring underwater image colorfulness relies on asymmetric alpha-trimmed statistical values. The mean in this context is defined in Eq. (10).

$$\mu(\alpha, \mathrm{R_0G_0}) = \frac{1}{\mathrm{K} - \mathrm{T}(\alpha\mathrm{L}) - \mathrm{T}(\alpha\mathrm{R})} \sum\nolimits_{\mathrm{i=T(\alpha L)+1}}^{\mathrm{K-T(\alpha R)}} \mathrm{Intensity}(\mathrm{R_0G_0, i}) \tag{10}$$

The second-order statistic variance σ2 in Eq. (11).

$$\sigma(\alpha, R_0G_0)^2 = \frac{1}{N} \sum\nolimits_{p=1}^{N} Intensity(R_0G_0, p) - \mu(\alpha, R_0G_0)\Big)^2 \tag{11}$$

The comprehensive metric employed for gauging underwater image colorfulness is presented in Eq. (12).

$$\mathrm{UICM} = {}^{-0.0268}\sqrt{\mu(\alpha, R_0G_0)\mu(\alpha, R_0G_0)^2 + \mu(\alpha, Y_0B_0)^2} + {}^{0.1586}\sqrt{\sigma(\alpha, R_0G_0)^2 + \sigma(\alpha, Y_0B_0)^2} \tag{12}$$

Sharpness on edges is measured via several stages in the UISM. Initially, every RGB color component is subjected to an edge detector. A grayscale edge map is produced by multiplying the resultant edge map by the source picture. This method preserves just the pixels that were originally part of the edge of the underwater image. Photos with a consistent backdrop and non-periodic patterns are suitable candidates for the Enhancement metric Estimation (EME).

The Formulation of UISM and EME is defined in Eqs. (13) and (14) respectively.

$$\mathrm{UISM} = \sum_{c=1}^{3} \lambda(c)\mathrm{EME}(\mathrm{Greyscale, Edge(c)}) \tag{13}$$

$$\mathrm{EME} = \frac{2}{\mathrm{k_0k_1}} \sum\nolimits_{\mathrm{l=1}}^{\mathrm{k_0}} \sum\nolimits_{\mathrm{k=1}}^{\mathrm{k_1}} \log\left(\frac{\mathrm{I(max, k, l)}}{\mathrm{I(min, k, l)}}\right) \tag{14}$$

UIConM is designed to assess contrast, a factor known to correlate with underwater visual performance, including stereoscopic acuity. In the context of underwater images, the degradation of contrast is typically attributed to backward scattering. UIConM is defined by Eq. (15).

$$\mathrm{UIConM} = \mathrm{logAMEE(Intensiy)} \tag{15}$$

$$\text{UIQM} = \text{k1} * \text{UICM} + \text{k2} * \text{UISM} + \text{k3} * \text{UIConM} \tag{16}$$

where k1, k2, k3 are constants. To sum up, a high PSNR value means that the output is more in line with the content of the actual image, and a high SSIM score means that the production is more similar to the structure and texture of the actual image, and an output that is more in accordance Higher UIQM scores are associated with human visual perception.

4.3 Metrics Results Comparison

In our work, we compared the performance of UDCP, UWGAN, and Modified Cycle GAN using three metrics: SSIM, PSNR, and UIQM. which achieved superior results. The complete quantitative comparison is presented in Table 3 and Fig. 4.

Table 3. Quantitative Comparison of Various Methods

Metrics	UDCP	UWGAN	Modified Cycle GAN
SSIM	0.24	0.74	**0.87**
PSNR	14.32	23.74	**28.77**
UIQM	2.27	**3.10**	3.07

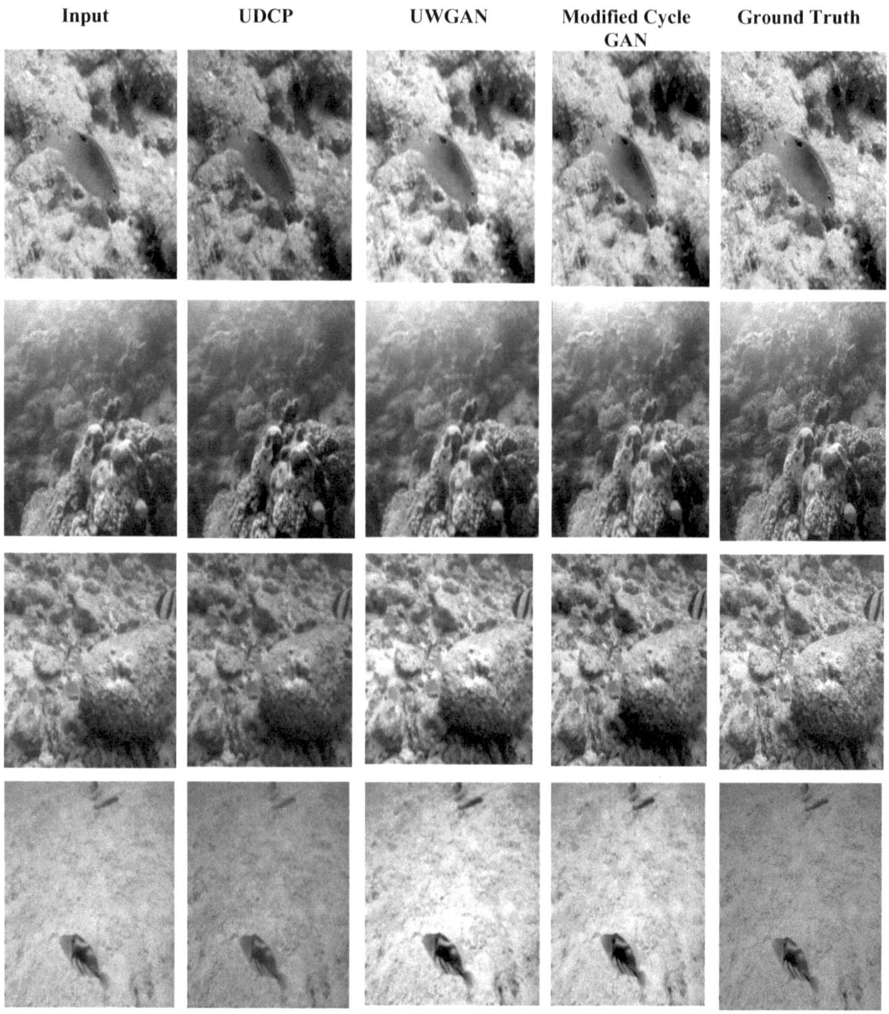

Fig. 4. Results of Various Methods

5 Conclusion

In conclusion, this research offers valuable insights into the effectiveness of diverse underwater image restoration techniques. While DCP fell short of expectations for underwater applications, UWGAN and Cycle GAN demonstrated notable potential. UWGAN excelled in generating synthetic underwater images. At the same time, Cycle GAN emerged as the preferred choice for restoring both paired and unpaired underwater datasets, showcasing superior performance across a range of evaluation metrics. Implementing modified Cycle GAN proved to be the most promising technique, yielding outstanding results across all three metrics, with notable excellence in PSNR evaluations.

Using two generators and discriminators, initially trained on paired datasets and later tested on unpaired data, underscored the effectiveness of modified Cycle Gan in tackling the complexities inherent in underwater image restoration. This approach highlighted the model's adaptability to unmatched data, enhancing its practical utility.

References

1. Rahman, S., Li, A.Q., Rekleitis, I.: Svin2: an underwater slam system using sonar, visual, inertial, and depth sensor. In: 2019 IEEE/RSJ International Conference on Intelligent Robots and Systems (IROS), pp. 1861–1868. IEEE (2019)
2. Jiang, Y., Zhao, M., Wang, C., Wei, F., Wang, K., Qi, H.: Diver's hand gesture recognition and segmentation for human–robot interaction on AUV. SIViP. **15**(8), 1899–1906 (2021)
3. He, K., Sun, J., Tang, X.: Single image haze removal using dark channel prior. IEEE Trans. Pattern Anal. Mach. Intell. **33**(12), 2341–2353 (2010)
4. Drews, P., Nascimento, E., Moraes, F., Botelho, S., Campos, M.: Transmission estimation in underwater single images. IEEE Int. Conf., 825–830 (2013)
5. Kim, J.Y., Kim, L.S., Hwang, S.H.: An advanced contrast enhancement using partially overlapped sub-block histogram equalization. IEEE Trans. Circuits Syst. Video Technol. **11**(4), 475–484 (2001)
6. Goodfellow, I., et al.: Generative adversarial nets. Adv. Neural Inf. Proces. Syst. **27** (2014)
7. Yan, L., Zheng, W., Wang, F.Y., Gou, C.: Joint image-to-image translation with denoising using enhanced generative adversarial networks. Signal Process. Image Commun. **91**, 116072 (2021)
8. Johnson, J., Alahi, A., Fei-Fei, L.: Perceptual losses for real-time style transfer and super-resolution. In: Computer Vision–ECCV 2016: 14th European Conference, Proceedings, vol. Part II 14, pp. 694–711. Springer International Publishing, Amsterdam, The Netherlands (2016)
9. Schettini, R., Corchs, S.: Underwater image processing: state of the art of restoration and image enhancement methods. EURASIP J. Adv. Signal Process. **2010**, 1–14 (2010)
10. Iqbal, K., Salam, R.A., Osman, A., Talib, A.Z.: Underwater image enhancement using an integrated colour model. IAENG Int. J. Comput. Sci. **34**(2) (2007)
11. Huang, D., Wang, Y., Song, W., Sequeira, J., Mavromatis, S.: Shallow-water image enhancement using relative global histogram stretching based on adaptive parameter acquisition. In: MultiMedia Modeling: 24th International Conference, MMM 2018, Proceedings, vol. Part I 24, pp. 453–465. Springer International Publishing, Bangkok, Thailand (2018)
12. Bai, L., Zhang, W., Pan, X., Zhao, C.: Underwater image enhancement based on global and local equalization of histogram and dual-image multi-scale fusion. IEEE Access. **8**, 128973–128990 (2020)
13. Akkaynak, D., Treibitz, T.: Sea-thru: a method for removing water from underwater images. In: Proceedings of the IEEE/CVF Conference on Computer Vision and Pattern Recognition, pp. 1682–1691 (2019)
14. Peng, Y.T., Cosman, P.C.: Underwater image restoration based on image blurriness and light absorption. IEEE Trans. Image Process. **26**(4), 1579–1594 (2017)
15. Hashisho, Y., Albadawi, M., Krause, T., von Lukas, U.F.: Underwater color restoration using u-net denoising autoencoder. In: 2019 11th International Symposium on Image and Signal Processing and Analysis (ISPA), pp. 117–122. IEEE (2019)
16. Li, C., et al.: An underwater image enhancement benchmark dataset and beyond. IEEE Trans. Image Process. **29**, 4376–4389 (2019)

17. Li, C., Anwar, S., Porikli, F.: Underwater scene prior inspired deep underwater image and video enhancement. Pattern Recogn. **98**, 107038 (2020)
18. Li, J., Skinner, K.A., Eustice, R.M., Johnson-Roberson, M.: WaterGAN: unsupervised generative network to enable real-time color correction of monocular underwater images. IEEE Rob. Autom. Lett. **3**(1), 387–394 (2017)
19. Chen, X., Yu, J., Kong, S., Wu, Z., Fang, X., Wen, L.: Towards real-time advancement of underwater visual quality with GAN. IEEE Trans. Ind. Electron. **66**(12), 9350–9359 (2019)
20. Hore, A., Ziou, D.: Image quality metrics: PSNR vs. SSIM. In: 2010 20th International Conference on Pattern Recognition, pp. 2366–2369. IEEE (2010)
21. Panetta, K., Gao, C., Agaian, S.: Human-visual-system-inspired underwater image quality measures. IEEE J. Ocean. Eng. **41**(3), 541–551 (2015)
22. Alenezi, F., Armghan, A., Mohanty, S.N., Jhaveri, R.H., Tiwari, P.: Block-greedy and CNN based underwater image dehazing for novel depth estimation and optimal ambient light. Water. **13**(23), 3470 (2021)
23. Guo, P., Liu, H., Zeng, D., Xiang, T., Li, L., Gu, K.: An underwater image quality assessment metric. IEEE Trans. Multimed. (2022)
24. Wang, N., Zhou, Y., Han, F., Zhu, H., Yao, J.: UWGAN: underwater GAN for real-world underwater color restoration and dehazing. arXiv preprint arXiv:1912.10269. (2019)

Cross-Domain Cardiac Arrhythmia Detection Using Deep Transfer Learning on ECG Signals

K. M. Namrata Bose[1], Soumyadeep Manna[1], Kshitij Goyal[1](✉), Sneha Sharma[2], and Bhupendra Singh[1]

[1] Department of Computer Science, Amity School of Engineering and Technology, Noida, Uttar Pradesh, India
7073731@gmail.com, bsingh5@amity.edu

[2] Amity Centre for Artificial Intelligence, Amity University, Noida, Uttar Pradesh, India
ssharma54@amity.edu

Abstract. Cardiac arrhythmia are serious medical conditions for which early identification is essential to successful treatment. When diagnosing arrhythmia, electrocardiograms (ECGs) are considered the gold standard. On the other hand, manual ECG analysis is laborious and prone to mistakes. This research suggests a novel deep transfer learning framework that uses ECG data to automatically detect cross-domain cardiac arrhythmia. The framework addresses the challenge of class imbalance in arrhythmia dataset by employing data up-sampling techniques.We evaluate the effectiveness of the proposed architecture with varying numbers of transferred layers from the pre-trained model to discover the best configuration for retraining the model. This investigation aims to identify the most effective balance between utilizing pre-trained knowledge and adapting the model to the unique properties of ECG data for improved arrhythmia classification.

Keywords: Cardiovascular diseases · Cardiac Arrhythmia · Electrocardiogram (ECG) · Deep learning · Transfer learning

1 Introduction

The Cardiovascular system (CVD) is one of the most important physiological systems in the human body. It is defined by the complex interplay of several human body organs, including the heart and blood arteries. A WHO report states that CVD is the world's top cause of death for people [1]. It is estimated that CVDs claim the lives of around 17 million people annually. Furthermore, middle- class and low-income nations account for 75% of all CVD related deaths [2].By 2030, it is anticipated that there would be 23 million fatalities from CVD. In addition, the cost of treating CVD is high, taking into account both the drug and diagnostic expenses. The expected cost of therapy in low- and middle- income countries

M. Paprzycki et al. (Eds.): ICACIS 2024, CCIS 2405, pp. 123–134, 2027.
https://doi.org/10.1007/978-3-032-30990-7_9

between 2011 and 2025 is $3.8 trillion [3]. Cardiac Arrhythmia-related deaths accounted for the majority of deaths caused by cardiovascular diseases. However, cardiac arrhythmia is defined as the abnormalities observed in the changes of heart rhythm caused by the defects in the electrical conduction of the heart muscle. Clinically, Electrocardiograms (ECG) are used to diagnose such irregularities. Traditionally, ECG signals are used by doctors to identify and evaluate cardiovascular disorders. This method involves professionals visually evaluating the ECG signal. Because ECG signals are non-stationary, abnormalities might not always appear during recording. As a result, prolonged analysis and observation of the recording are required for the proper diagnosis of a heart condition from the ECG signal. Thus, there is a significant chance of missing the data because of the volume of data. This makes the ECG signal's visual evaluation and analysis a challenging and time-consuming approach. Thus, there is a need for an automated system that can help doctors quickly identify arrhythmia.

In detecting cardiac arrhythmia using deep learning models, ECG signals have a significant as the major source of information. ECG is a non-invasive test that monitors the electrical impulses that cause the heart muscles to contract. A typical ECG signal displays characteristic waves as (P, QRS, T) that coincide with distinct parts of the cardiac cycle as shown in "Fig. 1". Any irregularity in heart rhythm or modifications to P-QRS-T wave patterns indicate the presence of cardiac arrhythmia.

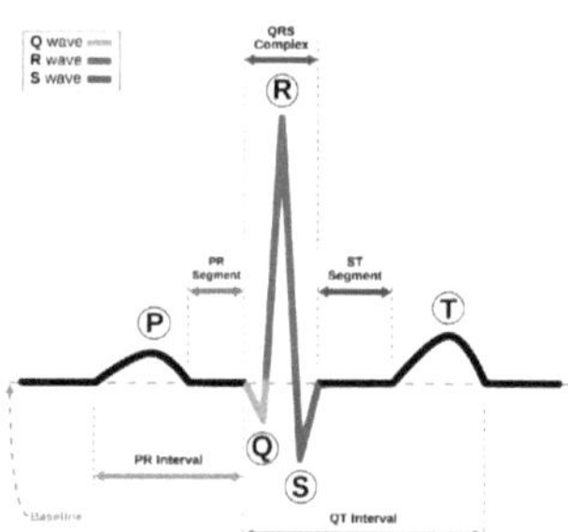

Fig. 1. Detailed ECG Waveform

Deep learning models trained on a large dataset of ECG signals can learn to recognize the subtle variations in these signals that differentiate between normal heart rhythms and various arrhythmia. Studies have shown that Deep learning models can achieve high accuracy in arrhythmia classification, potentially surpassing traditional methods [4]. CNNs (Convolutional Neural Networks) are specially useful for the analyses of the time-series data like ECG signals. They can effectively extract spatial features from the signal by learning filters that recognize specific patterns. In [5] the authors proposed a three blocked 1D-CNN model to effectively predict four arrhythmia classes. As recent advancement in this research, training the deep learning model with little or no data has become possible because of transfer learning. Reference [6] provides a comprehensive overview of deep learning approaches for ECG arrhythmia detection, including transfer learning techniques.

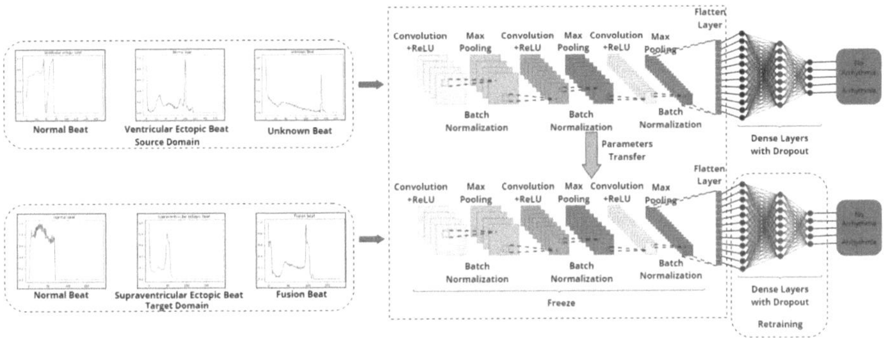

Fig. 2. Proposed crossed domain transfer learning framework for detection of cardiac arrhythmia using ECG signals

The authors emphasize the efficacy of transfer learning in cardiac arrhythmia classification tasks. Another implementation by [7] explored transfer learning with pre-trained models like AlexNet on time-frequency representations of ECG signals. There study suggests the effectiveness of transfer learning with different data representations for arrhythmia classification. The deep transfer learning approach helps to reduce the training time and provides improved performance even with the reduced labelled data requirement [8,9]. With this motivation in this chapter a novel cross domain transferring scheme is implemented where the proposed architecture is initially trained on Normal Beat, Ventricular ectopic beats and unknown beats. After this, the pre-trained model can be used to retrain only few top layers on the different domain of heart beats: fusion beat, supra-ventricular ectopic beat, and new observations of normal beats. "Fig. 2" represent the basic architectural view of proposed framework. The major contribution of this chapter are as follow:

- A Novel frame work for automatic Cross domain. Cardiac Arrhythmia detection is proposed by embedding deep transfer learning, with ECG signals.
- To address the class imbalance issue, the data was up-sampled using up sampling.
- The performance of proposed architecture has been analysed on different transferring layers to determine the number of layers required to be retrained.

2 Related Work

2.1 Challenges in Arrhythmia Classification

Cardiac arrhythmia detection, though crucial for timely diagnosis and intervention, presents significant challenges. ECG signals, the primary tool for arrhythmia detection, are susceptible to various noises like power-line interference, muscle movement artifacts, and baseline wander. These artifacts can obscure the underlying cardiac rhythm, making accurate interpretation difficult for both healthcare professionals and automated systems [4]. The challenge is further amplified by the presence of subtle arrhythmia that exhibit minor ECG variations, easily missed during visual inspection. Even deep learning models struggle with these nuances if not specifically designed to capture such intricacies. While deep learning offers promising avenues for automated arrhythmia detection, its implementation faces hurdles. A significant hindrance is the restricted accessibility of annotated ECG data for model training. Real-world datasets might be restricted in size and diversity, leading to a phenomenon called overfitting. Overfitted models perform well on the training data but fail to generalize effectively to unseen arrhythmia [10]. Additionally, the inherent imbalance in arrhythmia data poses another challenge. Arrhythmia are often rare events compared to normal sinus rhythm. Training a model on such imbalanced data can bias it towards the majority class (normal rhythm), hindering the detection of less frequent but critical arrhythmia [11]. Addressing these data-related challenges through data augmentation techniques and handling class imbalance during training is crucial for robust deep learning models in arrhythmia detection.

2.2 Application of Deep Transfer Learning on ECG Signal

Deep learning has emerged as an effective technique for analyzing ECG signals, which hold valuable information about heart health. However, a major hurdle in its implementation is the scarcity and expensiveness of large, labeled ECG datasets required to train deep learning models from scratch. This is where deep transfer learning comes to the rescue. Transfer learning capitalizes on pre-trained models developed on vast, generic datasets and fine-tunes them for specific tasks on smaller, specialized datasets like ECG signals. This approach offers significant advantages. Firstly, training time is significantly reduced as compared to building a fresh model from start because the already pre-trained model has all the essential knowledge. Secondly, transfer learning is especially helpful when working with limited ECG data, especially for less frequent arrhythmia. Compared to training a new model from start, using the already existing pre-trained model's knowledge we may enable it to perform better on smaller datasets. Finally, pre-trained networks excel at extracting features from the data. Even though ECGs are 1D time-series signals, transfer learning allows utilizing these pre-trained CNNs on large image datasets. Techniques like transforming ECGs into 2D representations or using 1D CNN architectures specifically designed for time-series data can be employed to bridge the gap between ECG data and the pre-trained models [12].

Deep transfer learning has demonstrated success in various ECG analysis tasks. A prominent application lies in automating arrhythmia classification, which is crucial for early diagnosis and intervention. Studies have shown promising results using transfer learning with pre-trained CNNs like VGG16 and

ResNet to classify various arrhythmia with high accuracy [13]. Beyond arrhythmia classification, transfer learning holds promise for ischemic heart disease detection by analyzing ECG signals to identify patients at higher risk. Additionally, ECG signals can be used for bio-metric identification purposes, and transfer learning can increase the accuracy and efficiency of such systems. This article implements cross-domain deep transfer learning in which the target and source domains have different data distributions and properties.

3 Method(s) and Material(s)

3.1 Dataset Description

MIT-BIH for the past five years, the MIT has served as a resource for creating and recommending algorithms to identify the greatest performance in the categorization of cardiac arrhythmia. When these models are learning and testing, they can handle a lot of data thanks to the knowledge in the MIT-BIH. This data was gathered from 47 patients who were examined at Boston's Beth Israel Hospital. Two or more cardiologists digitized and labeled these recordings, yielding 109,446 annotations, or cardiac arrhythmia. [14] The complete data set related to the MIT-BIH can be obtained for free through Physionet ATM Bank [15]. The data that was accessible in the Physionet ATM Bank was formatted and processed.

According to the Association for the Advancement of Medical Instrumentation (AAMI) EC57 standard, annotations in this dataset can be utilized to create five distinct beat categories [16].Table 1 summarizes the mappings between beat annotations within each category. Furthermore, Table 2 shows a significant variation in the number of incidences of various heartbeat types. With 90,083 samples, Normal (N) is the most prevalent class in this instance, while with the fewest samples, the minority class is Fusion Beat (F). To address class imbalance, we pre-processed the data using the resampling method [17].

Table 1. Data Description and Annotation

Class	Description	Annotation
N	NON ECTOPIC BEAT	Normal Block on the left bundle branch Beat on the right bundle branch block Atrial egress Nodal junction egress
S	SUPRA-VENTRICULAR ECTOPIC BEAT	Atrial premature contractions, premature nodal beats, atrial premature complexes, premature supra-ventricular contractions
V	VENTRICULAR ECTOPIC BEAT	Ventricular escape due to premature ventricular contraction
F	FUSION BEAT	Normal and ventricular fusion
Q	UNKNOWN BEAT	Paced combination of regular & paced classifiable

Table 2. Heartbeat frequency for each class in the dataset.

Class Abbreviation	Heartbeat Super Class	Number of Samples
N	Normal Beat	90,083
S	Supra-ventricular Ectopic Beat	2,779
V	Ventricular Ectopic Beat	7,009
F	Fusion Beat	15
Q	Unknown Beat	803

3.2 Data Pre-processing

Through processing, it was able to store 109,446 rows and obtain five distinct classes of cardiac arrhythmia (N, S, V, F, and Q): Of them, 87,554 (or 80%) match training data, while 21,892 (or 20%) match testing data. The class value for each annotation is located in the last column of every row, with each annotation comprising 187 columns. The normalized numerical values in the remaining 186 columns, which range from zero to one, are a part of the ECG trace. Annotations with values equal to zero are those that do not fill all 186 columns [18].

In this study, we have removed 2 classes of cardiac arrhythmia (S & F) in training data and testing data for making train and test data for proposed model. Also removed 2 classes of cardiac arrhythmia (V & Q) in testing data for making test data for transfer learning model. In this study, we have used oversampling to handle class imbalance. The resampling technique corrects class imbalance by increasing the amount of minority classes in training data. This helps the model learn more effectively from the minority classes and potentially improve its performance on those classes during prediction.

3.3 Proposed Network Architecture

This chapter proposes a 1D CNN architecture for detecting cardiac arrhythmia. The model is supplied with the pre-processed ECG signal as input. Figure 2 shows the suggested model architecture, which consists of three convolution layers, a batch normalization layer, and a max pooling layer. The kernel size of the first 1D CNN layer is 6, while the kernel sizes of the next two 1D CNN layers are 3. The 1D CNN layer's output is shown in Eq. 1.

$$y[i] = \sum_{K=0}^{K-1} (w[K] * x[i + K - 1]) \tag{1}$$

- `y[i]`: Output value at position `i` in the feature map.
- `w[k]`: Weight value at position `k` in the filter.
- `x[i + k - 1]`: Input value at position `i + k - 1` (considering zero-based indexing) in the input data.
- `K`: Size of the filter (kernel).

In addition to it each layer has an activation function as ReLU (Rectified Linear Unit) as given in Eq. 2.

$$f(x) = \max(0, x) \tag{2}$$

This activation function is required to introduce non-linearity into the network, allowing it to learn complex patterns. Next to the 1D CNN layer a batch normalization is applied which helps in normalizing transformations to the activation from the preceding layer. This improves training stability and gradient flow in the network. Following this, a max pooling layer with a pooling size of two is used to emphasize the most common feature. To reduce overfitting, a dropout layer of 0.30 was applied. To do this, certain nodes in the same layer are discarded probabilistically. Followed with this a flatten layer has been added to transformed the output into a single vector. The output of the flatten layer is fed as input to the first dense layer among the three consecutive dense layers. The equation for single dense layer is given as follows:

$$y = \sum_{i=1}^{N} (w[j] * x[i]) + b \tag{3}$$

- `y`: Output value of the neuron.
- `w[j]`: Weight value connecting the `ith` input neuron to this neuron (`jth` neuron).
- `x[i]`: Input value from `ith` input neuron in the previous layer.
- `b`: Bias term for this neuron.

Each dense layer had different number of neurons that is 64, 32, 3 respectively. The output vector from the dense layer is transformed into a probability distribution over all classes in the final layer using the softmax function. The softmax equation is:

$$softmax(z)_i = \frac{e^{z_i}}{\sum_{j=1}^{N} e^{z_j}} \tag{4}$$

- `softmax`$(z)_i$: The probability of the i-th class.
- `z[i]`: The dense layer's i-th neuron's output value prior to applying softmax.
- `e`: Euler's number (approximately 2.718).

After that, the model is built with Adam as the optimizer and categorical cross-entropy as the loss function. With a batch size of 32, the model performs 100 epochs on both the training and validation datasets.

4 Result

There must be a quantitative assessment of the proposed approach's performance. Initially, the accuracy with which a model can be trained to classify the considered classes of heart beats as N, S and V was determined. From each class, 186 features are extracted for each observation. Since there was the case of class imbalance data, the classes with lower number of observations are resampled.

For the pre-trained model, the test data comes from the same distribution as the training data, with a train-test split ratio of 70:30, respectively.

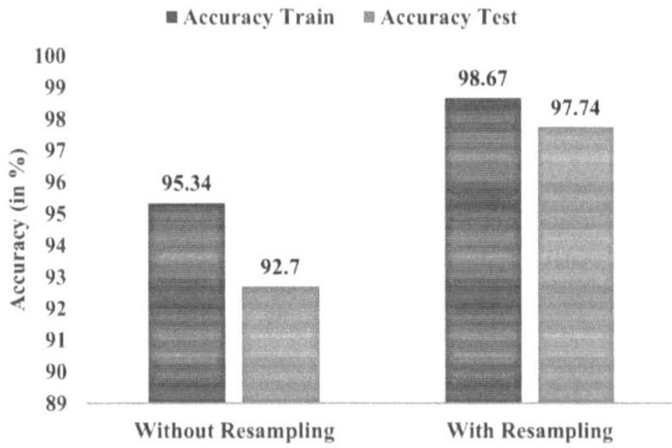

Fig. 3. Comparison of accuracy with & without Resampling

Figure 3 suggests that for the case of without resampling the accuracy on the training dataset is 95.34%. This suggests that the model performs well on the data it was trained on. Whereas, the accuracy on the testing dataset is significantly lower at 92.7%. This drop in performance when moving from training to testing could indicate that the model is overfitting the training data, meaning it is not generalizing well to new, unseen data. While in case of with resampling, the training accuracy is slightly higher at 98.67% compared to without resampling. This indicates that the model has learned the training data even more thoroughly. The testing accuracy also shows a notable improvement to 97.74%. This significant increase suggests that resampling has helped the model generalize better to new data. The gap between training and testing accuracy is much smaller, indicating reduced overfitting compared to the model trained without resampling.

To track the progression of model training over a period of time, accuracy curves are generated to visualize the performance of the models using the training as well as validation datasets. The accuracy curves had a positive correlation with the number of training cycles, indicating an upward tendency. Conversely, the loss curves demonstrated a negative correlation, suggesting a downward trend. These observations imply that the models' performance gradually reached a stable state over time. Figure 4 displays the loss curve of the pre-trained model, while Fig. 5 illustrates the accuracy curve.

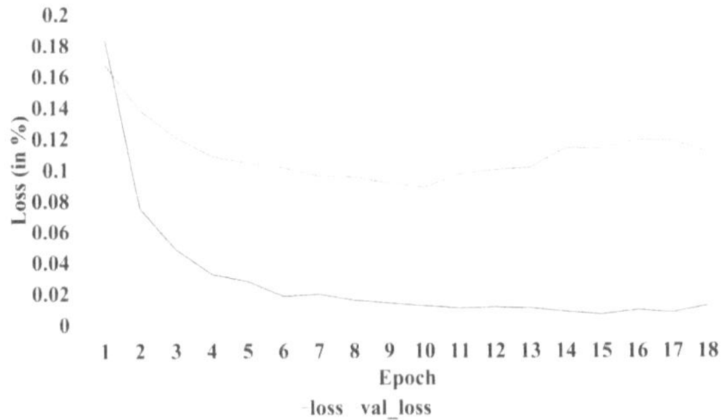

Fig. 4. Loss Curve for Pre-trained Model

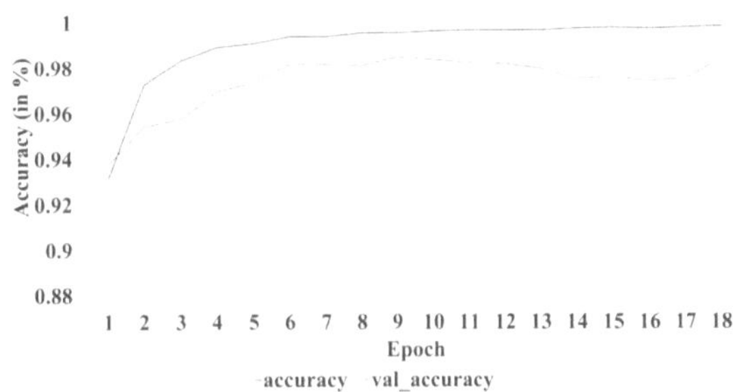

Fig. 5. Accuracy Curve for Pre-trained Model

Additionally, the effect of with and without transfer learning has also been observed. The model's performance is evaluated using either the base networks or our pre-trained network. At first the pre-trained model trained is used to evaluate its performance on different domain classes i.e., F and Q along with very few completely newer observations from class N. As a result of this analysis it has been observed that on different domain classes the model has degraded it performance from 97.74% to 85.73%. Whereas in case of with transfer learning when the pre-trained network parameters are transferred for initial layers and only last few layers or the last 3 dense layers in our case has be retrained on the new test data then there was an improvement in the accuracies. In Fig. 6 the bar chart compares the training and testing accuracies of a model with and without the application of transfer learning. Without transfer learning, both training and testing accuracies are exceptionally high and identical at 98.67%, suggesting possible overfitting or dataset limitations. However, when transfer learning is applied, while training accuracy decreases to 85.23%, testing accuracy remains high at 97.3%, indicating improved generalization. This scenario demonstrates that transfer learning can enhance a model's ability to perform well on unseen data by leveraging generalizable features learned from different datasets, making it a valuable technique for reducing overfitting and ensuring robust performance across various real-world applications.

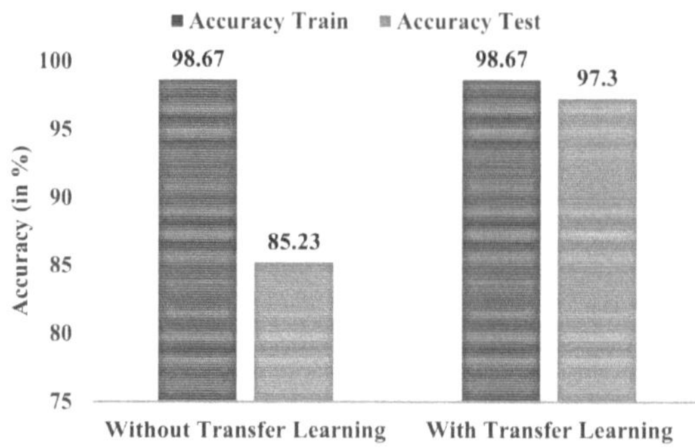

Fig. 6. Comparison of accuracy with & without Transfer Learning

Additionally, various optimizers, including Adam, SGD, and RMS Prop, have been implemented along with dropout rates of 10% 20%, 30%, and 40% in order to determine the most appropriate hyper-parameter. Consequently, it has been determined that the Adam optimizer with 30% dropout performs best with the given Arrhythmia dataset, as shown in Table 3. Moreover, It has been observed that using the transfer learning approach the proposed model have significantly reduced the training time as compared to the case of without transfer learning. For instance, the training time for proposed network has been reduced from 760.82 sec to 59.91 sec.

Table 3. Performance Comparison of Different Optimizers and Dropout Rates

Dropout	Optimizer		
	Adam(%)	*SGD(%)*	*RMSProp(%)*
10%	95.97	94.87	93.23
20%	96.38	93.79	94.63
30%	**97.74**	93.38	93.87
40%	95.16	92.12	92.54

5 Conclusion

This study effectively demonstrates the potential of pre-trained networks for accurate heart arrhythmia identification using the MIT-BIH Arrhythmia Database. The proposed method leverages transfer learning and data resampling to achieve significant improvements in classification accuracy. Transfer learning capitalizes on pre-existing knowledge from the pre-trained network, accelerating training and enhancing performance. Data resampling effectively tackles the challenge of imbalanced class distributions within the dataset, ensuring the model doesn't become biased towards the majority class. Through experimentation, we determined the optimal hyperparameter configuration for this specific dataset to be the Adam optimizer with a 30% dropout rate.

This chapter presents several key contributions that advance cardiac arrhythmia detection using pre-trained networks. We propose a novel framework that integrates deep transfer learning with ECG signals, enabling automatic cross-domain arrhythmia detection. To mitigate the common issue of class imbalance in medical datasets, we employed an up-sampling technique. This technique ensured the model was adequately trained on all classes, preventing bias towards the majority class. Additionally, to determine the optimal number of layers for retraining in the pre-trained network, we conducted a comprehensive analysis of the model's performance across different transferring layers.

Building upon these findings, several promising avenues for future research exist. Validation on larger and more diverse datasets can enhance the generalizability and robustness of our findings. Investigating the feasibility of implementing the model in real-time for continuous arrhythmia detection using wearable devices is another exciting direction for future exploration. This could revolutionize cardiac patient care by enabling early identification and intervention. By delving deeper into these potential avenues, pre-trained networks can be further refined as powerful tools for enhanced cardiac arrhythmia detection and improved patient treatment.

References

1. Daydulo, Y.D., Thamineni, B.L., Dawud, A.A.: Cardiac arrhythmia detection using deep learning approach and time frequency representation of ecg signals. BMC Med. Inf. Decis. Mak. **23**(1), 232 (2023)
2. Mc Namara, K., Alzubaidi, H., Jackson, J.K.: Cardiovascular disease as a leading cause of death: how are pharmacists getting involved? In: Integrated Pharmacy Research and Practice, pp. 1–11 (2019)
3. Luo, K., Li, J., Wang, Z., Cuschieri, A.: Patient-specific deep architectural model for ECG classification. J. Healthcare Eng. **2017** (2017)
4. Parvaneh, S., Rubin, J., Babaeizadeh, S., Xu-Wilson, M.: Cardiac arrhythmia detection using deep learning: a review. J. Electrocardiol. **57**, S70–S74 (2019)
5. Ahmed, A.A., Ali, W., Abdullah, T.A., Malebary, S.J.: Classifying cardiac arrhythmia from ECG signal using 1d CNN deep learning model. Mathematics **11**(3), 562 (2023)
6. Ansari, Y., Mourad, O., Qaraqe, K., Serpedin, E.: Deep learning for ECG arrhythmia detection and classification: an overview of progress for period 2017–2023. Front. Physiol. **14**, 1246746 (2023)
7. Sultan Qurraie, S., Ghorbani Afkhami, R.: ECG arrhythmia classification using time frequency distribution techniques. Biomed. Eng. Lett. **7**, 325–332 (2017)
8. Attia, Z.I., et al.: An artificial intelligence-enabled ECG algorithm for the identification of patients with atrial fibrillation during sinus rhythm: a retrospective analysis of outcome prediction. Lancet **394**(10201), 861–867 (2019)

9. Mohebbanaaz, Kumar, L.R., Sai, Y.P.: A new transfer learning approach to detect cardiac arrhythmia from ECG signals. Signal Image Video Process. **16**(7), 1945–1953 (2022)
10. Katal, N., Gupta, S., Verma, P., Sharma, B.: Deep-learning-based arrhythmia detection using ECG signals: a comparative study and performance evaluation. Diagnostics **13**(24), 3605 (2023)
11. Hong, S., Zhou, Y., Shang, J., Xiao, C., Sun, J.: Opportunities and challenges of deep learning methods for electrocardiogram data: a systematic review. Comput. Biol. Med. **122**, 103801 (2020)
12. Li, H., Wang, X., Liu, C., Li, P., Jiao, Y.: Integrating multi-domain deep features of electrocardiogram and phonocardiogram for coronary artery disease detection. Comput. Biol. Med. **138**, 104914 (2021)
13. Weimann, K., Conrad, T.O.: Transfer learning for ECG classification. Sci. Rep. **11**(1), 5251 (2021). https://doi.org/10.1038/s41598-021-84374-8
14. Baños, F.S., Romero, N.H., Mora, J.C.S.T., Marín, J.M., Vite, I.B., Fuentes, G.E.A.: A novel hybrid model based on convolutional neural network with particle swarm optimization algorithm for classification of cardiac arrhytmias. IEEE Access (2023)
15. George Moody, R.M.: PhysioBank, PhysioToolkit, and PhysioNet: components of a new research resource for complex physiologic signals (2008). https://physionet.org/content/mitdb/1.0.0/. Accessed 19 Dec 2023
16. Khalil, K., et al.: Efficient extreme learning machine (ELM) based algorithm for electrocardiogram (ECG) heartbeat classification. In: Ayaz, H., Asgher, U. (eds.) AHFE 2020. AISC, vol. 1201, pp. 312–318. Springer, Cham (2021). https://doi.org/10.1007/978-3-030-51041-1_41
17. Sakib, S., Fouda, M.M., Fadlullah, Z.M.: Harnessing artificial intelligence for secure ECG analytics at the edge for cardiac arrhythmia classification. In: Secure Edge Computing, pp. 137–153. CRC Press (2021)
18. Kachuee, M., Fazeli, S., Sarrafzadeh, M.: ECG heartbeat classification: a deep transferable representation. In: 2018 IEEE International Conference on Healthcare Informatics (ICHI), pp. 443–444. IEEE (2018)

Automated Conversion of Hand Signs to Text and Speech Using Deep Learning for Deaf Mute

S. Patrick Raja, V. R. Balasaraswathi(✉), and L. Mary Shamala

Vellore Institute of Technology, Chennai Campus, Chennai, Tamil Nadu, India
{balasaraswathi.vr,maryshamala.l}@vit.ac.in

Abstract. Communication is a fundamental aspect of human interaction, serving as the bridge that connects individuals and fosters understanding. Hearing-impaired and dumb people communicate with sign language which is hard for people to understand who are not familiar with it. Thus this creates a communication barrier between them. In this chapter we aims to address this problem with a solution using deep learning and natural language processing. The basic idea of this chapter is to train a Deep Learning model by extracting landmarks from the sign language as the attributes for prediction and using transformer for making it into a correct meaningful sentence with no grammatical error.

Keywords: Hand Sign Recognition · Natural Language Processing · Long Short Term Memory · Text-To-Text Transfer Transformer · Real Time Prediction · Convolution Neural Network

1 Introduction

The use of sign language by the deaf and the mute makes it difficult for people who are not familiar with it. Therefore There is a need for a system that can recognize and interpret sign language in real-time, facilitating seamless communication between the two communities. The primary aim of this chapter is to develop a real-time sign language recognition model. Also integrating Natural Language Processing can be helpful in predicting the meaningful sentence from the recognized signs.

In recent years advancements have opened up new possibilities for automating sign language recognition in domains such as computer visions and machine learning.

The proposed architecture has three main components: Using Media Pipe for extraction of hand landmark which is used as input for training and predicting. The LSTM model is used because the hand sign in motion has sequential relationship and other model find it hard to recognize. The predicted words is used as an input to the T5 model which is fine tuned for grammatical error correction task and sentence with correct grammar is obtained as output.

This chapter discusses the results of training and testing two model, challenges faced and future work.

M. Paprzycki et al. (Eds.): ICACIS 2024, CCIS 2405, pp. 135–146, 2027.
https://doi.org/10.1007/978-3-032-30990-7_10

2 Literature Review

Early systems proposed image processing and handcrafted rules for feature extraction and classification. Which struggles with low accuracy and limited vocabulary recognition. Some already proposed model use images for classification. Other methods uses hardware embedded gloves or wristband for collection of hand posture and classification. Development of mediapipe, proposed a different method of considered hand landmarks as an attributes for classification of hand gestures.

CNN algorithm was proposed [1] for hand sign recognition using depth images which contains information about the distance between the surface of the objects in a scene and position of Microsoft Kinect sensor. This model is trained using static hand sign images and the model attained an accuracy of 99.3% when tested with new data. The algorithm demonstrated effectiveness even in cluttered environments, such as skin color backgrounds, and when the hand overlaps the face. The use of CNN for feature extraction contributed to the robustness of the system, providing accurate recognition of Indian sign language gestures.

A CNN model was developed [2] for fingerspelling recognition of the Indian Sign language alphabet. Advanced techniques such as batch normalization, stochastic pooling, dropout, the diffusion based optimizer algorithm and data normalization are implemented. A substantial dataset comprising 62400 images representing 26 static signs from various users forms the basis of the research. The proposed system acquired a notable accuracy of 99.76% and 99.64% for training and validation.

A novel approach [3] was presented for static hand gesture recognition in sign language using hybrid model combining convolution neural networks with classical feature extraction methods such as ORB descriptors and gabor filters which aims to enhance accuracy and robustness to rotation and ambiguity in hand gesture recognition. Gabor filters are used for representation of texture and shape features in the hand gesture images and ORB descriptor is used for feature detection and matching images by which this model was able to attain an accuracy of 99.92% and 99.8%.

The challenges of real-time recognition in sign language [4] were addressed through a streamlined and efficient model. The proposed model integrates a single shot detector, 2D convolution neural network, Singular value recognition, and long short-term memory for real-time recognition of hand sign from RGB video. Proposed a novel method of extracting 3D hand keypoints co-ordinates for feature extraction. This model competes effectively with the state-of-the-art alternative in IHSLR, marking a significant contribution to real-time sign language recognition research.

The need for high recognition performance and user independence was discussed [5] particularly in dataset with limited labelled samples. The study proposes an end-to-end approach by fine-tuning pre-trained CNN model with score-level fusion technique for real-time hand gesture recognition. Also discussed the effectiveness of proposed approach in overcoming data limitation and achieving practical gesture recognition application.

A framework was presented [6] utilizing the bag of visual words (BOVW) model for recognizing ISL alphabets and digit in real-time video streams. The system incorporates segmentation through skin color and background subtraction, followed by feature extraction using speeded up robust features (SURF). Support vector Machine and Convolution Neural Network are used for classification. An interactive graphical user interface is implemented for accessibility and interactivity.

A novel approach [7] was proposed for robots to understand hand gestures from just images, without needing fancy gloves or joysticks. Their method works in two steps: first, it finds key points on the hands in the image, and then it uses those points to figure out what gesture the hand is making. They tested their method on a bunch of hand images, and it worked better than other methods that use more complicated steps. This new method is both accurate and fast, which makes it promising for helping robots interact with people in the real world. They achieved an accuracy of 87.5% and operating at 10 frames per second.

The researchers [8] presented an innovative, cost-effective, and highly accurate gesture recognition wristband designed to enhance human-computer interaction in virtual reality technology. The wristband demonstrated exceptional performance in recognizing gestures that correspond to a full keyboard and multi-command inputs. Through their proposed method, they achieved a maximum accuracy of 92.6% in recognizing 26 alphabetic letters. This wearable device holds significant promise for applications such as gesture command recognition, assistive technologies for individuals with disabilities, and wearable electronics. Overall, it offers a practical and accessible solution for improving human-computer interaction within immersive VR environments.

The authors [9] discussed about the challenges faced in recognizing gesture when the images are translated, rotated or scaled, limiting existing models. They proposed a robust sign word recognition system using CNN trained in rotated, translated and scaled version of sign language images. Their system achieves high accuracy of 99.3% on standard data and remains accurate 99.10% even with image transformations. This approach outperforms existing methods and shows potential for real-world use.

A new method for recognizing hand gestures from 3D skeleton data (joint positions). Researchers [10] used three channels: two using attention mechanisms to capture dynamic features and one for general features. The model is trained and tested using three different dataset and acquires accuracies of 94.12%, 92% and 97.01%. Benchmark dataset such as MSRA, DHG and SHREC'17 were used for training and validation. The combination of precise recognition and low computational cost positions the approach as an improvement over the other current approaches in the field of hand gesture recognition.

Extensive research on various algorithms was conducted by [11], the Long Short-Term Memory (LSTM) model is used for differentiating hand gestures. The MediaPipe Hand landmark detection algorithm is employed to identify hand landmarks and plot their coordinates, which are then converted into NumPy array format. These coordinates serve as input to the LSTM model, enabling real-time prediction and the conversion of the predicted text into speech. This model is trained using American hand signs.

The researchers [12] discussed on the advancement, challenges and methodologies from 2012 to 2022 for vision-based hand sign recognition systems. Key areas of exploration include image acquisition, camera orientations, tracking, image segmentation, gesture classification and feature extraction. They discovered a substantial variation in the accuracy of the proposed models from 68% to 97% with an average of 86.6%.

In the study [13], researchers proposed a method for recognition of movements for hand prosthesis control. They used RNN and LSTM model on the electromyography signal for recognizing the arm prosthesis movement as the user desire. The primary objective us to reduce the electrodes making its less expensive and less complex. The system achieved 99% accuracy in training and 87% accuracy in real-time.

A novel approach for human-robot communication using hand gestures and deep learning is implemented by [14]. Unlike existing methods requiring gloves or joysticks, it leverages only visual information, making it more natural and cost-effective. They used 2D landmarks on the hand and used it as an attribute for prediction. When model was evaluated on the latest benchmark dataset, the proposed model demonstrated commendable performance, attaining an accuracy rate of 87.5%.This operates at the 10 frames per second which is suitable for real-time application.

Computer vision based approach focusing on the ISL alphabet in python was proposed by [15]. Addresses the dynamic image problem by converting color image to grayscale streamlining image processing. Proposed a cost-effective and effective ISL recognition program where existing methods might have limitation in effectiveness and affordability.

3 Methodology

3.1 Novelty

This chapter not only aim to recognize static hand gestures but also dynamic movements of hand gestures. Which is more suitable for real-world applications. Fine tuning a T5 model for grammar correction adds unique dimension to the project. While many hand sign language recognition research focuses solely on predicting hand signs into texts. By integrating both models, this chapter aims to implement a real-world application for educational institute, healthcare and other users. None of the other proposed methods tried to integrate transformers for predicting meaningful sentence from incomplete sentence generate by the Hand sign recognition model.

3.2 Data Description

This chapter details two datasets for training and evaluating hand gesture and grammar error correction. The dataset for training the LSTM model was created by the authors itself by learning each and every hand sign and reciprocating the same. The Media Pipe package is used for extracting the landmarks of each and every frame. Totally 30 videos were collected for each hand sign and it is split into 30 frames and landmarks of each frames were used for prediction. For each hand sign, the model was provided with a dataset comprising 24 videos for training, while its performance was evaluated on a separate test set consisting of 6 videos.

JFLEG (JHU Fluency-Extended GUG) dataset is a grammatical error correction corpus dataset. The dataset consists of a source sentence and four correction which was converted into source text and target text format for fine tuning T5 Model. This dataset contains totally 1511 examples in total.

3.3 Algorithm and Models Used

There are three different models used for three different functions. Firstly, Media Pipe is an open-source framework developed by google which provides pre-trained models for various tasks which includes hand landmark detection (Fig. 1).

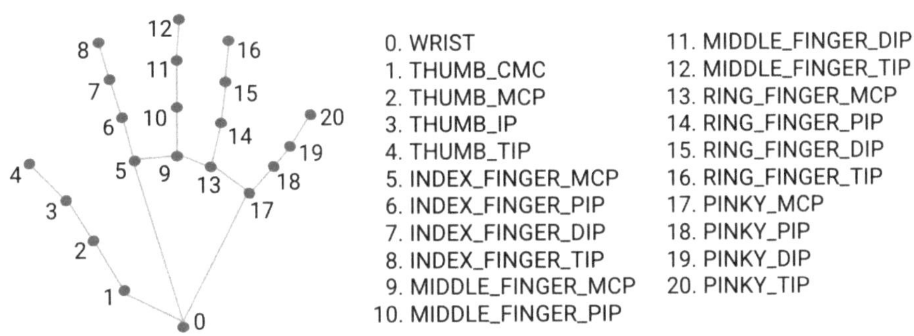

Fig. 1. Hand Landmarks that are used for identification of Hand Signs.

Media Pipe is a high precision model for hand and finger tracking. Which is based on a Convolution Neural Network (CNN) architecture trained on annotated hand images to accurately localize hand landmarks in real-time video streams. The Hand Landmarker employs a model bundle consisting of two distinct packaged models: One for palm and another for landmarks detection. The hand landmark model underwent training on a diverse dataset comprising approximately 30,000 real-world images, supplemented synthetic hand models imposed over different background.

LSTM is a type of variation of an RNN model which is designed to capture sequential and long-term dependencies in data. The motion of the hand gesture has sequential relationship which can be mapped for both training and prediction of hand gesture. By learning the patterns and dependencies of each hand gesture the LSTM model can accurately predict the corresponding sign language in real-time. By predicting each words labelled to hand gesture a sentence is formed which does not has articles, preposition and no correct tense.

The T5 model serves for the purpose of rectifying grammatical error correction within the sentence. The model is pre-trained on a task that involves abundant data before being fine-tuned on rectifying grammatical error task. Each data is formatted as text-to-text. During Training the model operates on the principle of teacher forcing, This means that for fine-tuning, we always need an input sequence along with its corresponding target sequence.

The T5 model comes in different size according to the amount of data by which it is pre-trained. For illustration, t5-base model is used. Similarly other T5 models which has been pretrained with larger dataset can also be used. Larger models like T5-large or T5-3b may require more computational resources (such as GPU memory and processing power) and longer inference times compared to smaller models. These larger models typically have more parameters and may offer improved performance compared to smaller variants like T5-small and T5-base model.

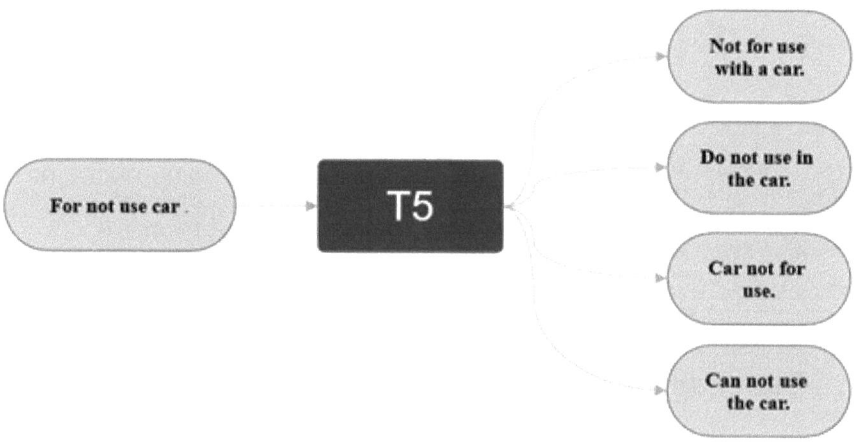

Fig. 2. Example of the data used for fine tuning T5 Model.

As mentioned in Fig. 2, The dataset has one incorrect sentence and four different corrected sentence which is converted into source text and target text format for fine tuning the T5 model.

3.4 Architecture Design

The Fig. 3 describes the architecture diagram of the proposed method. The modules of the proposed method includes

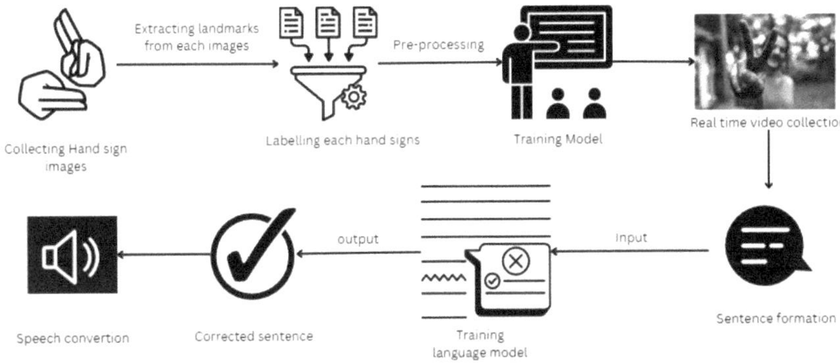

Fig. 3. Architecture Diagram of the proposed method.

1. Extracting landmarks from each images: The system development begins by collecting videos of hand signs, dividing it into frames and extracting landmarks from each frame. This sequence of landmarks is stored as numpy array of size (No. of landmarks x No. of frames). The model is then collects the same number of sequence of landmarks for prediction.
2. Labelling each hand sign: The hand signs are labelled by words they indicates.
3. Training the LSTM model: Training a model that can learn patterns from the sequential hand sign motion and storing the model.
4. Fine Tuning the Transformer: The T5 model is fine tuned for the grammar correction task and stored.
5. Real-time Prediction: An application is developed by integrating both the trained hand sign model and fine tuned T5 model to predict real-time hand sign, framing a sentence by combining the predicted word and predicting the grammatically correct and meaningful sentence.

3.5 Real Time Prediction

The Fig. 4 describes how the real time recognition of hand signs occur. The system is designed in such a way it add the predicted words and frame a incomplete sentence, when the predicted word is full stop then the sentence is used as an input for the T5 model so that the complete meaningful sentence is predicted and output is spelled to the users as speech.

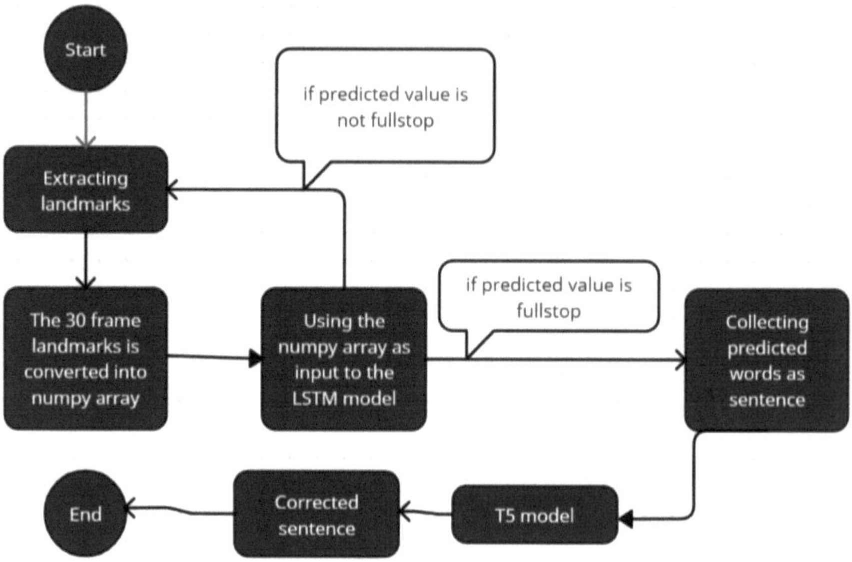

Fig. 4. State diagram describing real time prediction.

4 Experimental Results and Discussion

The LSTM based neural network model is used for training. The input layer which is LSTM layer takes in inputs with a notation of [None,30,126] where the first notation represents the batch size, the second denotes the sequence data and the third one is the number of features in each data. The dense layers are used in later stages to transform the outputs from LSTM layers into final prediction.

The Fig. 5 images depicts the visualization of layers of the model. The final output is the probability of all the labels that wants to be predicted. The predicted label with most percentage of accuracy is declared as predicted value.

Figure 6 and Fig. 7 depicts the categorical accuracy and loss while training in each epoch. An epoch is a complete pass through the entire training dataset by deep learning model which represents that all the data using to train your model has been seen and used to update the model's weight once. The model took about 230 epochs to reach 100% categorical accuracy.

The LSTM model is trained using landmarks from 30 frames extracted from 24 videos and tested with the data from other 6 videos (80% for training and 20% for testing the model). The model was able to achieve an accuracy of 97.61% for 7 handsigns. For error correction of the predicted words, The T5 base model is used. It is fine tuned using JFLEG dataset and the model is saved locally for accessing.

The Fig. 8 visualizes the training and validation loss of the T5 model while fine tuning it. By the image we can say that the validation loss is decreases with an increase in training data.

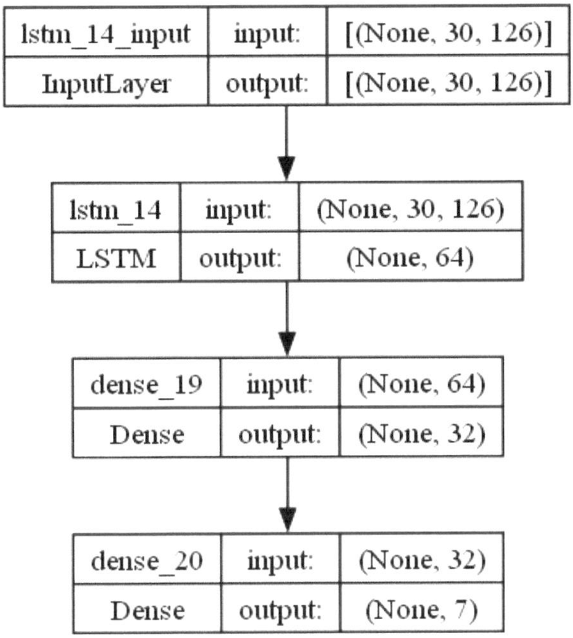

Fig. 5. Visualisation of Layers in the proposed model.

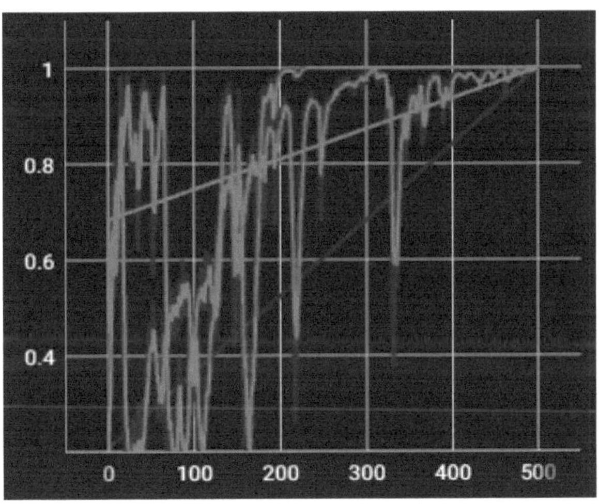

Fig. 6. Categorical Accuracy in each epoch

Table 1 illustrates the performance of the fine-tuned T5 base model in predicting grammatical error free sentence from the word gathered by prediction using LSTM model. There are instances where the corrections may not fully capture the intended meaning or structure of the original sentence. Overall, the

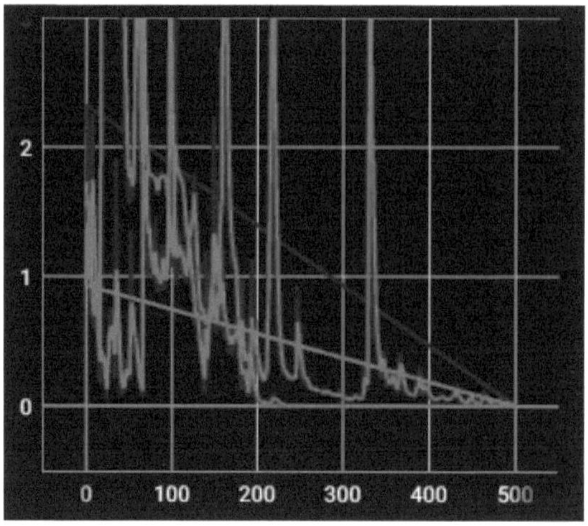

Fig. 7. Loss in each epoch

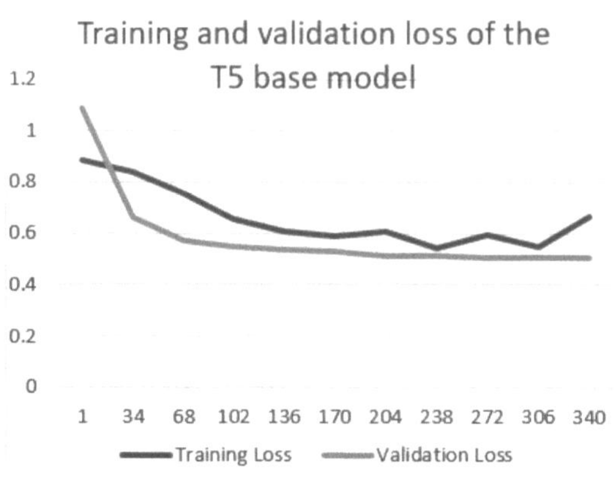

Fig. 8. Loss in each epoch

corrections made by the T5 base model align closely with the actual sentences, demonstrating its effectiveness in grammatical correction tasks. The average cosine similarity between the predicted sentences and actual sentences mentioned in table [1] is 0.87713.

Table 1. Results obtained

Predicted sentence by LSTM model	Corrected sentence by T5 base model	Actual sentence
I done fine	I did fine	I did fine
I want more how you	I want more, How you can help	I want more, How about you?
Hello I want learn sign communicate me father mother	Hello I want to learn sign communicate with my father mother	Hello! I want to learn sign language to communicate with my father and mother
thank you you help I learn more	Thank you for helping me learn more	Thank you for your help, I am learning a lot

5 Conclusion and Future Work

This chapter presents a comprehensive way for sign language recognition and translation, leveraging advanced technologies in computer vision and natural language processing. By combining Mediapipe for hand landmarks extraction and LSTM for dynamic hand gesture recognition. We were able to get continuous predicted words with less latency. The fine tuned T5 model plays a major role in predicting meaningful sentence for the user. The system demonstrates a novel approach of using transformers for making sentence grammar correction on the predicted sentence from the sequential model. The integration of Mediapipe, LSTM and T5 model is an novel approach proposed which achieves robust hand gesture recognition, capturing both static and dynamic movements with high accuracy and grammar correction for better understanding.

Future work of this chapter include taking videos of hand sign with camera with more frame rate so that it will be easy to extract exact sequence of hand sign and training the model will result in more accuracy. Because it is easy to find patterns with video of more frame rate. This increases total frames for training but since we will be using the same camera for prediction it will have higher accuracy with low latency. Adding landmarks of palm and face can also be done with which hand sign which uses facial expression can also be used as an attribute. Addition of attention mechanism can be done to focus on relavant part of the input and ignoring the others since in hand signs all the Fine tuning the T5 model with large number of English error correction dataset needs to be done so that the model the correct all kinds of grammatical error. Fine tuning complex T5 model like t5-large, t5-3b, t5-11b can be done for reducing loss. Fine tuning those model may take more time and more computing power which takes days by using laptops with lower specifications. This models which are fine tuned maybe in large size storing them in cloud and accessing it via API can be done. Training the Transformer with dataset with source text as the sentence formed by the words for which hand signs are available and target text as the actual sentence can also be done.

Acknowledgments. No funding (not applicable)

Disclosure of Interests. The authors declare no competing interests

References

1. Gangrade, J., Bharti, J.: Vision-based hand gesture recognition for Indian sign language using convolution neural network. IETE J. Res. **69**(2), 723–732 (2023)
2. Nandi, U., Ghorai, A., Singh, M.M., Changdar, C., Bhakta, S., Kumar Pal, R.: Indian sign language alphabet recognition system using CNN with diffGrad optimizer and stochastic pooling. Multimedia Tools Appl. **82**(7), 9627–9648 (2023)
3. Damaneh, M.M., Mohanna, F., Jafari, P.: Static hand gesture recognition in sign language based on convolutional neural network with feature extraction method using ORB descriptor and Gabor filter. Expert Syst. Appl. **211**, 118559 (2023)
4. Rastgoo, R., Kiani, K., Escalera, S.: Real-time isolated hand sign language recognition using deep networks and SVD. J. Ambient. Intell. Humaniz. Comput. **13**(1), 591–611 (2022)
5. Sahoo, J.P., Prakash, A.J., Pławiak, P., Samantray, S.: Real-time hand gesture recognition using fine-tuned convolutional neural network. Sensors **22**(3), 706 (2022)
6. Katoch, S., Singh, V., Tiwary, U.S.: Indian Sign Language recognition system using SURF with SVM and CNN. Array **14**, 100141 (2022)
7. Sagayam, K.M., Andrushia, A.D., Ghosh, A., Deperlioglu, O., Elngar, A.A.: Recognition of hand gesture image using deep convolutional neural network. Int. J. Image Graph. **22**(03), 2140008 (2022)
8. Tan, P., Han, X., Zou, Y., Qu, X., Xue, J., Li, T., et al.: Self-powered gesture recognition wristband enabled by machine learning for full keyboard and multicommand input. Adv. Mater. **34**(21), 2200793 (2022)
9. Miah, A.S.M., Shin, J., Al Mehedi Hasan, M., Rahim, M.A., Okuyama, Y.: Rotation, translation and scale invariant sign word recognition using deep learning. Comput. Syst. Sci. Eng. **44**(3), 1–16 (2023)
10. Miah, A.S.M., Hasan, M.A.M., Shin, J.: Dynamic hand gesture recognition using multi-branch attention based graph and general deep learning model. IEEE Access **11**, 4703–4716 (2023)
11. Beriya, R., Chhajed, K.K.: American hand sign recognition detection and recognition system. IEEE Access **11**, 1–1 (2023)
12. Al Farid, F., et al.: A structured and methodological review on vision-based hand gesture recognition system. J. Imaging **8**(6), 153 (2022)
13. Toro-Ossaba, A., Jaramillo-Tigreros, J., Tejada, J.C., Peña, A., López-González, A., Castanho, R.A.: LSTM recurrent neural network for hand gesture recognition using EMG signals. Appl. Sci. **12**(19), 9700–9714 (2022)
14. Sagayam, K.M., Andrushia, A.D., Ghosh, A., Deperlioglu, O., Elngar, A.A.: Recognition of hand gesture image using deep convolutional neural network. Int. J. Image Graph. **22**(03), 1–1 (2022)
15. Alaria, S.K., Raj, A., Sharma, V., Kumar, V.: Simulation and analysis of hand gesture recognition for Indian sign language using CNN. Int. J. Recent Innov. Trends Comput. Commun. **10**(4), 10–14 (2022)

Chroma Closet: Empowering Colorblind Persons with a Deep Learning-Based Color Recognition App

Areeg Fahad Rasheed[1(✉)], Huda Najm Alabbas[2], Safa F. Abbas[3], and Mahdi Zarkoosh[4]

[1] College of Information Engineering, Al-Nahrain University, Baghdad, Iraq
areeg.fahad@coie-nahrain.edu.iq

[2] Computing Department, Goldsmiths University, London, UK
halab001@gold.ac.uk

[3] Department of Cybersecurity Engineering, College of Information Engineering, Al-Nahrain University, Jadriya, Baghdad, Iraq
safa@alrasheedcol.edu.iq

[4] Software Engineering, Wellington, New Zealand

Abstract. Colour Blindness affects over 400 million people worldwide, hindering their ability to perceive and differentiate colours. This condition challenges colourblind individuals when coordinating and styling clothes, often resulting in embarrassment or discomfort. This chapter addresses these challenges by proposing a mobile-based colour adjustment solution utilizing a convolutional neural network (CNN). A comprehensive dataset has been constructed to train the CNN model, encompassing diverse clothing images from various sources, including online shops and personal collections. We evaluated the recognition system using multiple performance metrics, such as Recall, Precision, F1-score, Accuracy, and the Confusion Matrix. The results demonstrated the model's high performance across all metrics. Our proposed solution aims to enhance the comfort and convenience of colourblind individuals, enabling them to effortlessly and confidently select and wear clothes.

Keywords: Colorblind · Convolutional Neural Network · Machine learning

1 Introduction

Colour blindness, also known as colour vision deficiency, is a fairly common condition characterised by difficulty perceiving colours in the usual way [3]. This occurs when a cone (a type of nerve cell in the eye's retina) does not function properly. The cones process the light reflected from images and send it as a signal to the brain to perceive colour. Most individuals with colour blindness can perceive various colours, although their perception of specific colours may differ. Additionally, they might encounter difficulties distinguishing particular

M. Paprzycki et al. (Eds.): ICACIS 2024, CCIS 2405, pp. 147–160, 2027.
https://doi.org/10.1007/978-3-032-30990-7_11

colours or shades. In sporadic cases, certain forms of colour blindness can lead to a complete inability to perceive colours.

The human eye's retina has two types of photoreceptor cells: rods and cones. Rods are primarily responsible for vision in low-light conditions (scotopic vision) and do not mediate colour perception [9]. The human eyes possess a limited ability to distinguish slight details. Conversely, cones, active in higher light levels (photopic vision), are responsible for our perception of colours and provide us with a sharp visual sense. The central fovea, a specific area in the retina, exclusively contains cones [11].

Based on their sensitivity to various light wavelengths, cones can be classified into one of three groups (see Fig. 1). These groups are commonly referred to as red-sensing cones (L cones), green-sensing cones (M cones), and blue-sensing cones (S cones). L cones are sensitive to long wavelengths, typically around 560 nm, allowing humans to perceive red. M cones detect medium wavelengths, approximately 530 nm, enabling the perception of green. S cones, conversely, are attuned to short wavelengths, around 420 nm, facilitating the ability to see blue [8].

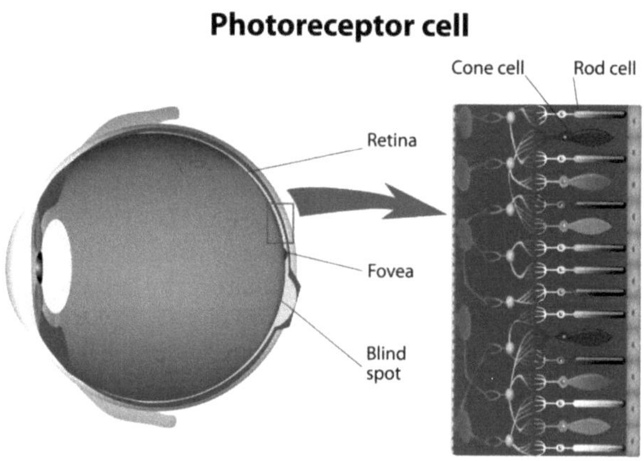

Fig. 1. Eye's Photo receptor cell types [4]

Based on this classification, colour Blindness is classified into four types. The following brief has a description of each type.

1. Trichromacy, or full-colour vision, is a remarkable characteristic of human visual perception. Individuals with Trichromacy have all three types of colour-sensitive cones present and functioning properly. This means they can traditionally perceive and distinguish all colours within the visible light spectrum. [13].
2. Anomalous Trichromacy is a form of colour vision in which all three types of colour-sensitive cones are present. Still, one or more of them respond atypically to certain light wavelengths. People with Anomalous Trichromacy may

still be able to distinguish between various colours; however, they might perceive some tints or hues as similar, in contrast to those with typical trichromatic vision. Anomalous Trichromacy is a relatively common colour vision deficiency, often manifesting as red-green colour blindness. In this condition, the functionality of either the middle-wavelength (M) or long-wavelength (L) cones is compromised, leading to difficulties in accurately perceiving and differentiating between shades of red and green. Nonetheless, individuals with Anomalous Trichromacy can still experience various colours. They may rely on other visual cues like brightness or saturation to compensate for their limited colour discrimination. [6].

3. Dichromacy is characterised by the absence or dysfunction of one type of colour-sensitive cone in the retina. Unlike Trichromacy, where three types of cones are present, individuals with Dichromacy have only two functioning cones, resulting in a reduced ability to perceive and distinguish specific colours. The most common form of Dichromacy is red-green colour blindness, where either the long-wavelength (L) or middle-wavelength (M) cones are absent or impaired. This condition makes it challenging for individuals to differentiate between shades of red and green accurately. Another less common form of Dichromacy is blue-yellow colour blindness, where the short-wavelength (S) cones are affected, leading to difficulties distinguishing between shades of blue and yellow [5].
4. Monochromacy, also known as total colour blindness, is a rare and severe colour vision deficiency in which an individual lacks functional colour-sensitive cones in their retina [16]. Unlike Trichromats or Dichromats, who possess two or three types of functioning cones, individuals with Monochromacy have only one cone or none at all, resulting in significantly impaired or absent colour perception. There are two primary types of Monochromacy: Rod Monochromacy and Cone Monochromacy. Rod Monochromacy, or Achromatopsia, involves having no functioning cones, with individuals relying solely on rods for vision. This leads to a complete inability to perceive colours, extreme light sensitivity, and poor visual acuity. Cone Monochromacy, conversely, involves having only one type of functioning cone, leading to a limited ability to perceive colour [7].

Deep learning and computer vision are two areas that work well together to solve complicated visual challenges [18]. Computer vision aims to allow computers to recognize and interpret visual data from photos or videos. On the other hand, deep learning is a subset of machine learning that uses multiple-layer artificial neural networks to learn hierarchical data representations automatically [17]. Convolutional Neural Networks (CNNs) [14,15] are highly successful in extracting significant characteristics from visual data. These networks train themselves to recognize patterns, objects, and structures in pictures, allowing them to perform tasks such as image classification, object recognition, and image segmentation [2].

This chapter presents a deep learning-based classification model to assist individuals with colour vision deficiencies in classifying coloured clothing items.

To accomplish this, we curated a specialised dataset of colour clothing images, which was used to train the model. Additionally, we developed a mobile application to implement and showcase the model's functionality.

The chapter is organised into different sections. Section 2 details the dataset's creation, including the selection and acquisition of clothing images. Section 3 is divided into two subsections: the first explains the architecture and training process of the proposed deep learning model. In contrast, the second demonstrates the functionality and features of the mobile application. Section 4 presents an evaluation of the performance of our proposed model, including metrics such as accuracy, precision, and recall. In Sect. 5, we engage in a comprehensive discussion of our findings and conclusions.

Contributions

1. Created a new dataset for image colour classification, specifically focused on clothes.
2. Defined and implemented a new Convolutional Neural Network (CNN) model for clothes colour classification, utilising convolutional layers, max pooling, and dense layers.
3. Developed a mobile application for iOS and Android platforms to empower colourblind individuals to classify clothes images based on their colours.

2 ChromaClosedDataset Dataset

In the realm of clothing image datasets, there is a notable absence of datasets that specifically cater to organizing images based on their colours. However, existing datasets classify clothes based on their types, such as t-shirts, pants, bags, and more, which can be found in [10]. To address this gap, we have taken the initiative to create a new dataset called ChromaClosedDataset[1] by curating a diverse collection of clothing images sorted by their colour. We have downloaded pictures from popular online shops like Amazon, LYST, eBay, and our collections to gather diverse clothing images. Additionally, we have utilized images from the reference [10] to augment the dataset. The dataset creation process involved organizing the collected images into eleven folders, each representing a different colour category. The folder names include black, blue, brown, green, orange, red, yellow, white, purple, grey, and pink. Each folder contains approximately 250 images showcasing a variety of clothing items, such as pants, skirts, and even shoes. By combining clothing items from different resources, we aimed to mitigate the issue of overfitting. Figure 2 shows a slice of our dataset.

3 Proposed System Overview

The proposed system architecture encompasses various stages: data collection, preprocessing, augmentation, splitting, and model training. The process begins

[1] https://github.com/AREEG94FAHAD/ChromaClosedDataset.

Fig. 2. Color-Categorised Clothing dataset slice

by gathering a diverse and representative dataset, ensuring data quality and integrity while incorporating adequate samples for each class. Next, the collected data undergoes preprocessing, involving techniques like resizing, normalisation, and noise reduction to standardise the input and enhance model performance. Augmentation techniques such as rotation, flipping, zooming, and cropping are then applied to expand the dataset's diversity, enabling the model to generalise better and handle variations in input images. The preprocessed and augmented dataset is split into training, validation, and testing subsets. The training set is used to train the model. The hyperparameters, including learning rate, batch size, and regularisation techniques, are fine-tuned during the model training phase. Once training is complete, the trained model is saved for later use. Users who want to classify an image using a mobile app capture it through its interface. The image is then sent to the server via an API call. The saved model is loaded into memory on the server side, and the image is classified based on learned patterns and features. The server generates a response indicating the predicted class or classes, which the API sends back to the mobile app. Finally, the mobile app displays the classification result to the user. Figure 3 depicts the proposed system procedure for classifying an image.

The following subsections explain the CNN network architectures used for training the dataset and the developed mobile app for classification purposes.

3.1 CNN Network Architecture

The dataset used in this project, as mentioned in the previous section, was collected from various sources. Consequently, the size of each image in the dataset differs. To address this issue, all images in the dataset were resized to a standard size of 224×224 pixels. We used the Nearest-Neighbour Interpolation method for resizing [1]. After resizing, the dataset was split into training and testing sets, with a ratio of 80% for training and 20% for testing. A Convolutional Neural Network (CNN) was employed to train the dataset. The CNN architecture consists of multiple layers. The initial layer is a 2D convolutional layer, utilising a filter size of 3×3, valid padding, and a stride of 1. Following that, there is a max pooling layer with a pooling size of 2×2. The third layer is an additional convolutional layer with a kernel size of 3×3, valid padding, and a stride of 1. This is followed by a max pooling layer with the same pooling parameters as the previous layer. The fifth layer is another convolutional layer with a kernel size of 3×3, valid padding, and a stride of 1. Subsequently, there is a max pooling layer with a pooling size of 2×2. After the convolutional layers, a dense layer with 128 units was used. Finally, the last layer is a softmax layer with ten units representing the number of colour classes in the dataset. All convolutional layers utilise the Rectified Linear Unit (ReLU) activation function. Figure 4 illustrates the CNN architecture.

3.2 Mobile App

The main objective of this work is to empower colourblind individuals to classify clothes quickly. To achieve this, we have developed a mobile app for effortless and efficient clothing classification. The mobile app was built using React Native, a cross-platform framework that allows for creating a single app compatible with Android and iOS devices [12]. When a user captures an image using the mobile app, it is sent to the server for classification. The server, implemented using the Django framework, processes the image and returns the corresponding colour as a response. The workflow of the mobile app and the main screens is illustrated in Fig. 5. In the following, we will provide a brief description of each screen.

a. Home Screen: The home screen serves as the initial screen of the application and provides a brief overview of the app's purpose. It includes two buttons to open the camera and access the device's image gallery.
b. Camera Screen: A simple camera interface is displayed when the user clicks on the camera icon from the home screen. The user can take a photo, switch between the front and back camera, and toggle the flash on or off.
c. Image Selection Screen: This screen appears when the user clicks the image icon. It displays the device's image gallery and prompts the user to select an image.
d. Image Review Screen: This screen is displayed after the user captures an image using the camera or selects an image from the gallery. It presents two icons - one for retaking or selecting a different image and the other for sending it to the server.
e. Loading Screen: This screen indicates that the image has been sent to the server and is awaiting a response. It serves as a loading indicator.
f. Result Screen: Once the image is received and processed by the server, this screen displays the processed image and a title specifying the detected colour. At the bottom of the screen are two icons - one to open the camera again if the user wants to capture another image and the other to select a different image from the gallery.

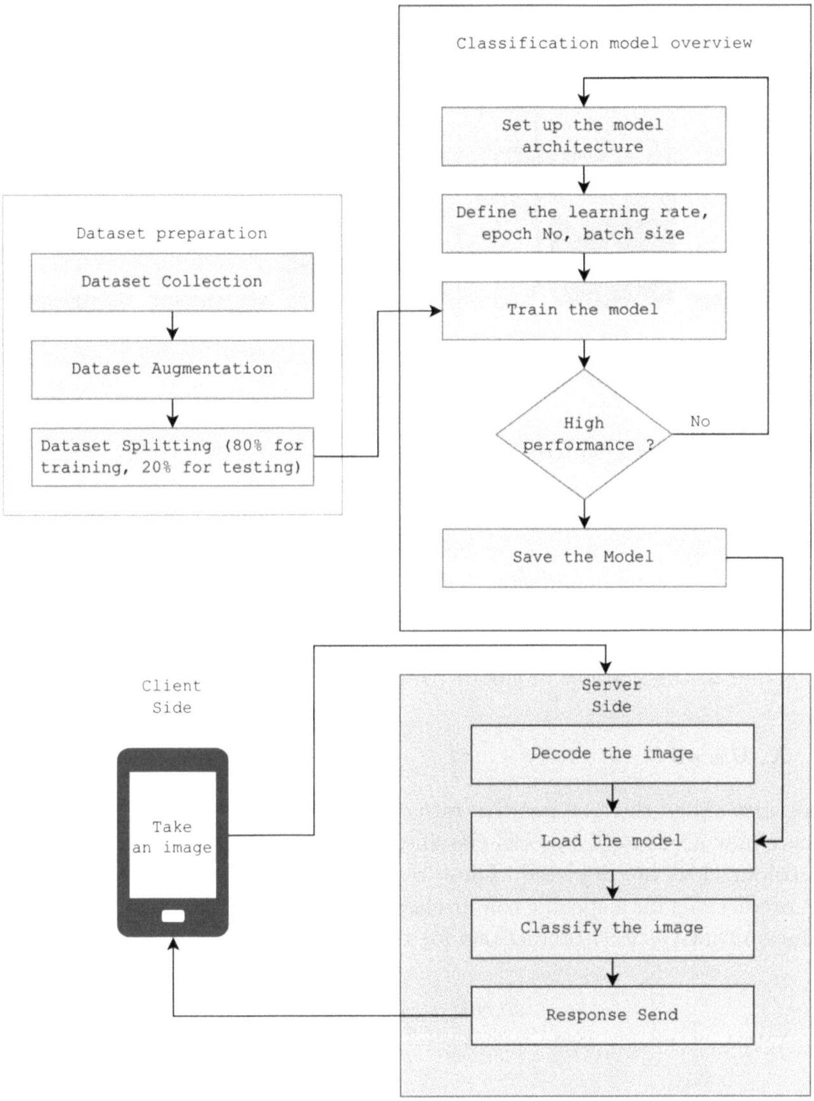

Fig. 3. The proposed system procedure for classifying an image

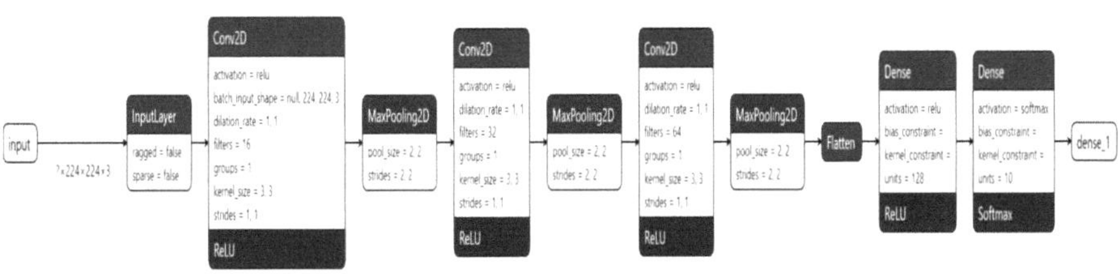

Fig. 4. The CNN Architecture for Image Classification

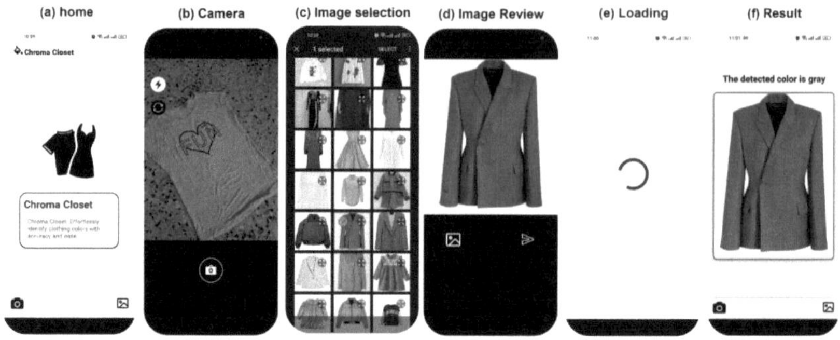

Fig. 5. Mobile apps' screens

4 The Model Performance

The proposed model for colour clothes classification has been evaluated using famous deep learning metrics, including Recall, Precision, F1-score, Accuracy, and confusion matrix, in addition to the feedback survey. In the following section, a description of each metric, along with its corresponding equation, is provided. It is worth noting that the proposed model has not been compared with other models due to the scarcity of colour clothes classification research.

4.1 A. Recall

Recall, also called the true positive rate or sensitivity, is a performance metric to evaluate how accurately a model classifies colours. In Fig. 6, the recall results for each colour class are depicted. These results indicate the ratio of true positive (TP) predictions for a specific colour class to the sum of true positive predictions and false negative (FN) predictions for that colour class as shown in Eq. (1)

$$Recall = \frac{TP}{TP + FN} \tag{1}$$

4.2 Precision

Precision serves as a performance metric to assess the model's accuracy in positive predictions. It is computed by dividing the number of true positive predictions for a particular colour class by the sum of true positive predictions and false positive (FP) predictions for that exact colour class. Figure 7 displays the precision results for each colour class, while Eq. (2) presents the mathematical expression for precision calculation.

$$Precision = \frac{TP}{TP + FP} \tag{2}$$

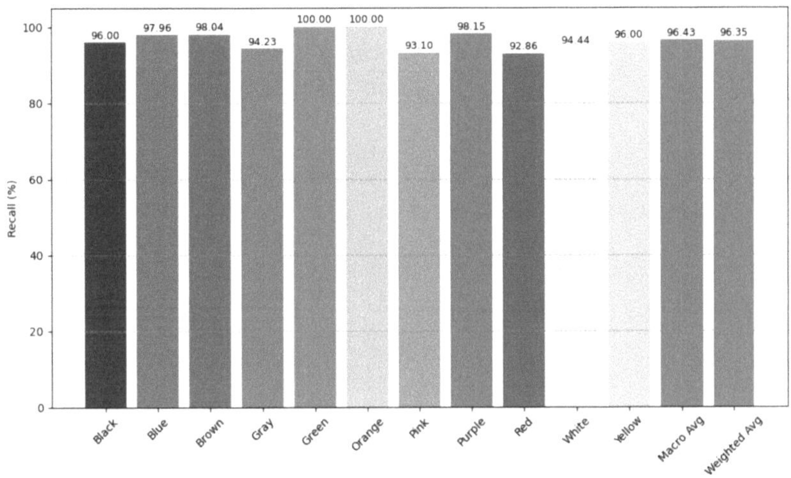

Fig. 6. Recall results for each colour class

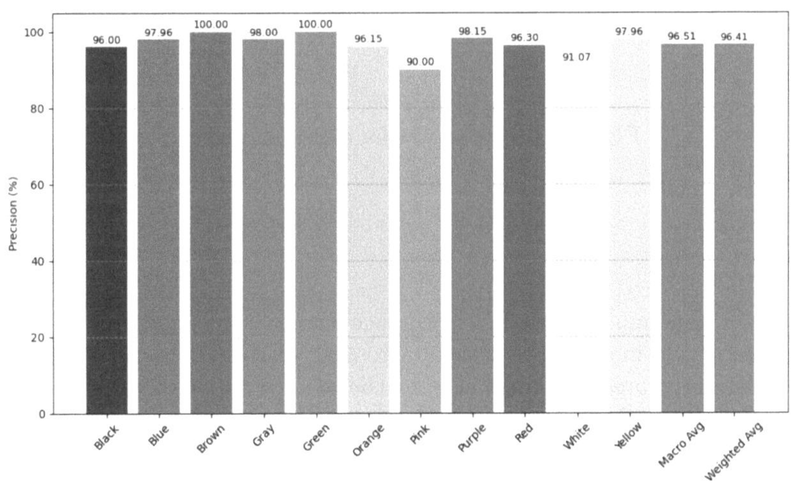

Fig. 7. Precision results for each colour class

4.3 F1-Score

The F1-score is a comprehensive measure that combines precision and recall to offer a balanced evaluation of a model's performance. It is determined by calculating the harmonic mean of precision and recall, taking into account true positive (TP), false positive (FP), and false negative (FN) predictions. Figure 8 presents the F1-score results for each colour class, while Equation (3) provides the mathematical formula for computing the F1-score.

$$F1 - score = \frac{2 \times (Recall \times Precision)}{Recall + Precision} \tag{3}$$

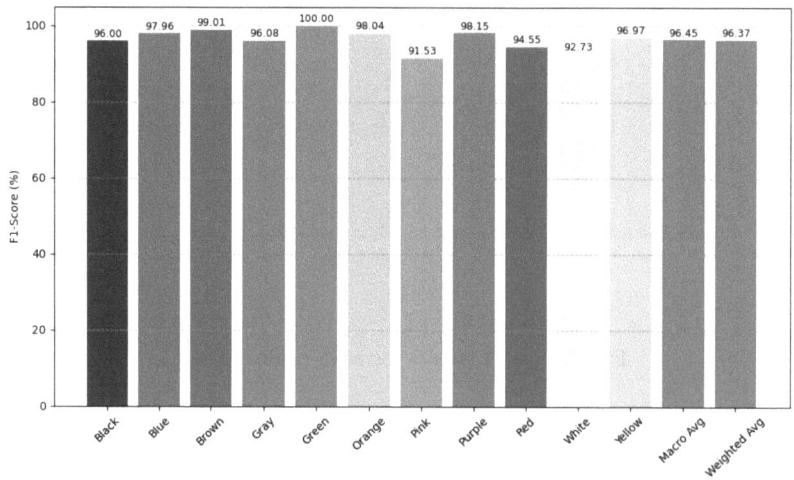

Fig. 8. F1-score results for each colour class

4.4 Accuracy

Accuracy is a commonly used performance metric that measures the overall correctness of the model's predictions across all classes. It is calculated as the ratio of correctly predicted instances to the total number of cases in the test dataset. In Fig. 9, the accuracy result is depicted. Equation (4) presents the mathematical formula for calculating accuracy:

$$Accuracy = \frac{TP + TN}{TP + FP + TN + FN} \tag{4}$$

4.5 Confusion Matrix

A confusion matrix is a tabular representation that comprehensively evaluates the model's predictions by comparing the predicted labels with the actual labels. It summarizes the performance of the model across different classes. Figure 10 depicts the confusion matrix, showing the distribution of expected and actual labels for each colour class.

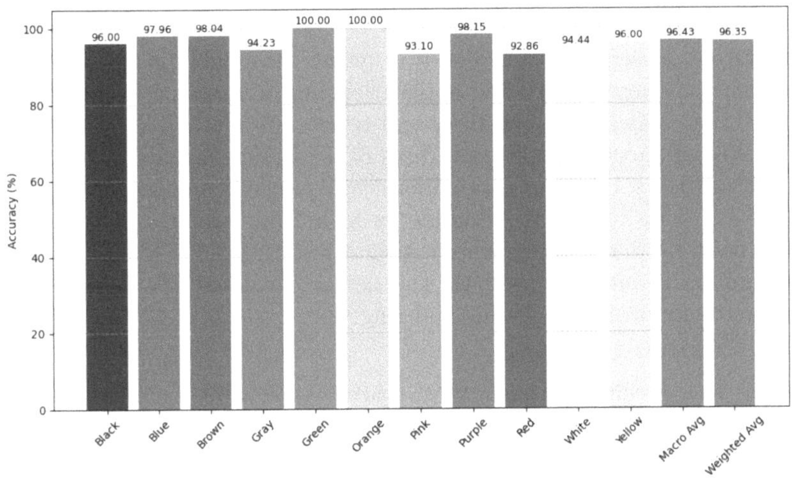

Fig. 9. Accuracy results for each colour class

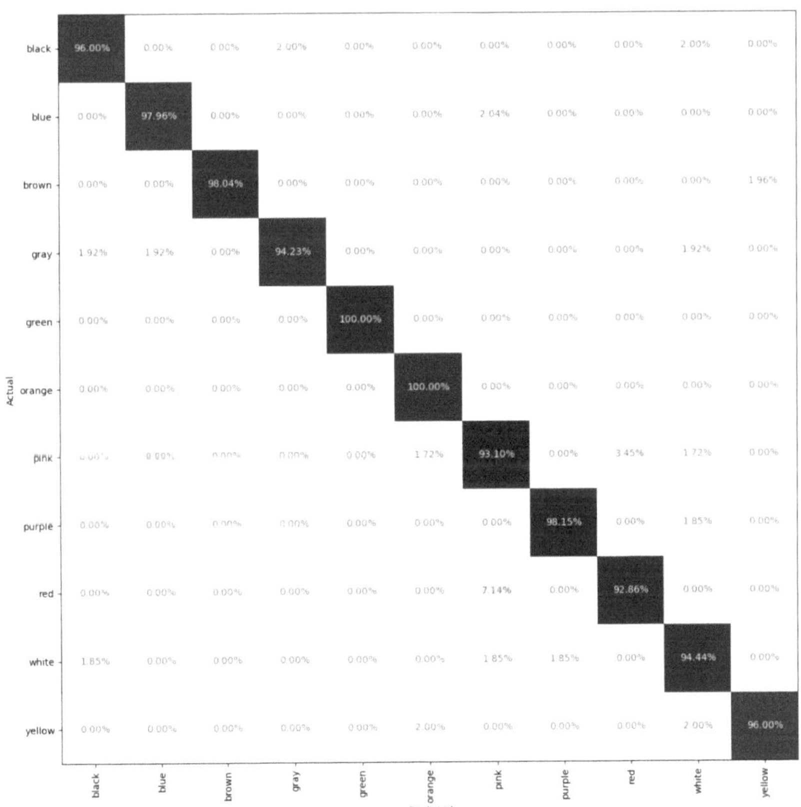

Fig. 10. Confusion Matrix: Evaluation of Model Predictions for Colour Classes

4.6 User Feedback Survey

We conducted a user feedback survey to gather invaluable insights from users about their experiences with the application, its performance, and their overall satisfaction. The survey questions and results are illustrated in Table 1. The survey included participants from various backgrounds, including doctors, engineers, and students, totalling approximately 25 participants, encompassing individuals with issues related to blindness or visual impairments. After gathering user feedback, we have implemented several improvements. These include the addition of audio pronunciation for the detected colours and releasing a new version that supports both Arabic and English.

Table 1. User Feedback on Color Classification App Features and Enhancements

Question	Results (%)
How accurate are you in finding the app's colour classification results?	93
How would you rate the user-friendliness and ease of use of the app?	97
How satisfied are you with the app's speed in providing colour classification results?	78
Have you experienced any technical issues or bugs related to the colour classification feature?	1
In your opinion, does the app's colour classification feature offer a practical advantage for individuals with colour blindness or other visual impairments?	95
Do you have any suggestions or feedback you would like to share to help improve our app and enhance your user experience?	– Hosting the Model on a Fast Server – Add Multiple Languages, Such as Arabic – Add a Voice to Pronounce the Color Name

5 Discussion and Conclusion

In conclusion, individuals worldwide, both women and men, encounter challenges associated with color blindness, impacting their ability to dress and achieve an ideal appearance. In response to this issue, we have proposed a comprehensive solution consisting of three integrated components. Firstly, we created a new dataset specifically designed to classify coloured clothes. This dataset is a valuable resource for training and evaluating models in the context of colour classification for fashion items. Secondly, we have developed a convolutional neural network (CNN) architecture tailored to handle the intricacies of colour classification by leveraging the created dataset. Thirdly, we have designed and implemented a mobile application that utilizes the trained CNN model to provide users with multiple, fast, and effortless colour classification experiences. This mobile app serves as a user-friendly interface, allowing individuals to determine the colours of their clothes quickly. The suggested model and system have been rigorously evaluated and tested, with several performance metrics such as recall, precision, F1-score, accuracy, and a confusion matrix, in addition to user feedback surveys. The findings show that our system performs well in categorizing colours like black, blue, brown, green, orange, purple, and yellow with an accuracy above 96%. Furthermore, with an accuracy of approximately 94%, the system also performs well for grey and white colours. However, it is vital to highlight that the model is less effective in categorizing the colours of pink and red clothes. This is due to the inherent difficulty distinguishing between pink and red, as indicated by the confusion matrix in Fig. 8. To address this issue, further improvements could be made by expanding the dataset with additional pink and red clothing images, allowing the model to learn subtle distinctions and increase its classification accuracy.

Author contributions. Areeg created and fine-tuned the dataset and model, Huda addressed colorblind challenges and contributed to writing, while Safa and M. assisted in creating the mobile app and developing the model.

References

1. Abbas, H.K., Al-Saleh, A.H., Al-Zuky, A.A.: Optical images fusion based on linear interpolation methods. Iraqi J. Sci. **60**(4), 924–936 (2019)
2. Albawi, S., Mohammed, T.A., Al-Zawi, S.: Understanding of a convolutional neural network. In: 2017 International Conference on Engineering and Technology (ICET), pp. 1–6. IEEE (2017)
3. Albrecht, M.: Color blindness. Nat. Methods **7**(775), 10–1038 (2010)
4. American Academy of Ophthalmology. Cones (2023). https://www.aao.org/eye-health/anatomy/cones. Accessed 7 June 2023
5. Barboni, M.T.S., et al.: Electrodiagnosis of dichromacy. Vis. Res. **158**, 135–145 (2019)
6. Bosten, J.: The known unknowns of anomalous trichromacy. Curr. Opin. Behav. Sci. **30**, 228–237 (2019)
7. Chao, J.R., et al.: S-cone function in blue cone monochromacy. Invest. Ophthalmol. Vis. Sci. **60**(9), 585–585 (2019)
8. Gasparini, S.J., et al.: Transplanted human cones incorporate into the retina and function in a murine cone degeneration model. J. Clin. Invest. **132**(12) (2022)
9. Gullett, L., West, T.V.: Understanding racial color blindness and multiculturalism in interracial relationships: cognitive and emotional tensions and their implications (2016)
10. Kaggle. Clothing dataset (2023). https://www.kaggle.com/datasets/agrigorev/clothing-dataset-full. Accessed 7 June 2023
11. Kevany, B.M., Palczewski, K.: Phagocytosis of retinal rod and cone photoreceptors. Physiology **25**(1), 8–15 (2010)
12. Masiello, E., Friedmann, J.: Mastering React Native. Packt Publishing Ltd (2017)

13. Nascimento, S.M.C., Foster, D.H.: Information gains from commercial spectral filters in anomalous trichromacy. Opt. Express **30**(10), 16883–16895 (2022)
14. Rasheed, A.F., Zarkoosh, M.: Unveiling derivatives in deep and convolutional neural networks: a guide to understanding and optimization (2024). working paper or preprint
15. Rasheed, A.F., Zarkoosh, M., Al-Azzawi, S.S.: Multi-CNN voting method for improved Arabic handwritten digits classification. In: 2023 9th International Conference on Computer and Communication Engineering (ICCCE), pp. 205–210. IEEE (2023)
16. Sechrest, E.R., Chmelik, K., Tan, W.D., Deng, W.-T.: Blue cone monochromacy and gene therapy. Vis. Res. **208**, 108221 (2023)
17. Szeliski, R.: Computer Vision: Algorithms and Applications. Springer, Cham (2022)
18. Tuffery, S.: Deep learning for computer vision (2023)

Integrating Data Augmentation in Deep Convolutional Neural Network for Enhanced Emotion Detection from Facial Expressions

Rohit Beniwal, V. V. S. D. Nagendra Anala(✉), Srijan Saurabh Jha, and Ujjwal Kakran

Department of Computer Science & Engineering, Delhi Technological University, Delhi 110042, India
rohitbeniwal@dtu.ac.in, nagendraanala@gmail.com

Abstract. Humans can express their emotions through various means, such as body language, verbal expressions, facial expressions, etc. Facial Expression Analysis is the most well-known component for Machine Learning models and robots to understand and interact with humans. In recent times, studies in human-robot interactions, psychology, mental health, and market research domains have also displayed an interest in identifying emotions using facial expressions. Therefore, we propose a facial emotion recognition method based on Deep Convolutional Neural Network (DCNN) to address the above domains. The proposed DCNN model is trained using FER2013 and to overcome the biased structure of the dataset, we performed several Data Augmentation Loops, consisting of augmenting image pixels, resizing and padding of the image, cropping the required image size out of the padded image, adjusting of brightness and contrast of the image, on the dataset to normalize it. Results show that we achieved an accuracy of 80.06% that outperforms the best performance of other models such as traditional CNN, VGGNet16-D, AlexNet, Xception, Inception v3, ResNet, RRCNN, and DenseNet by a margin of 3.14%.

Keywords: Data Augmentation · Deep Convolutional Neural Network · Emotion Detection · Facial Expression · Facial Recognition

1 Introduction

Facial expression is the most natural way to express the emotional state and intent to others [1]. When people engage with one another, the blend of verbal communication and facial expressions makes the interaction more captivating and allows others to better comprehend the objectives of the speaker. In the modern age, people spend a lot of time using smart gadgets and AI-powered assistance tools such as chatbots [2] to have virtual interactions as compared to the physical ones. The ability of AI to accurately predict human emotions and respond appropriately would significantly improve the user experience. This development will enable a better understanding of emotions in human and machine interactions [3] which might result in more natural and responsive communication between users and machines. We can use the most relevant method for emotion recognition using Facial Expressions.

M. Paprzycki et al. (Eds.): ICACIS 2024, CCIS 2405, pp. 161–172, 2027.
https://doi.org/10.1007/978-3-032-30990-7_12

Facial Emotion Recognition (FER) technology has emerged as a critical tool in a variety of industries, particularly in the field of health care where it aids in the diagnosis of mental stress [4] and improves psychological examinations. Some of its uses include market research where understanding consumer emotions can lead to better product development and advertising techniques. FER also has creative applications in personalized entertainment, such customizing music suggestion algorithms [5] to suit the emotional state of the listener, which results in improved user experience. Pertinent literature has shown that techniques for detecting emotions through facial expressions have evolved significantly over the time. Progress in this field resulted in the invention and improvement of several approaches that improve the accuracy along with the efficacy in detecting emotional states based on facial indicators.

In the initial years, traditional Machine Learning techniques such as Support Vector Machine, Principal Component Analysis, Linear Discriminant Analysis and Ensemble methods were used to construct FER systems. These traditional methods relied heavily on manually built features relevant to the FER task, such as Local Binary Patterns, Scale-Invariant Feature Transform, and Histogram of Oriented Gradients. As a result, these strategies faced major problems during the feature selection and extraction process, and were less efficient in classifying facial emotions. Because of this inefficacy, Deep Learning techniques have emerged, making it easier to automatically extract features. Convolutional Neural Networks (CNN) [6, 7] are one of the prominent Deep Learning approaches for improving the performance of FER models. However, widely utilized datasets such as FER2013 [8] show imbalances that compromise the accuracy of the model in practical settings. In order to tackle this problem, we suggest utilizing Deep Convolutional Neural Networks (DCNN) in conjunction with data augmentation techniques to significantly increase accuracy of FER systems.

The rest of the paper is organized as follows: the next section, Sect. 2 briefs about the related work within the domain of facial expression recognition; Sect. 3 provides an overview of the methodology; Sect. 4 discusses the result and analysis of the proposed methodology, followed by conclusion and future scope in Sect. 5.

2 Related Work

In the past few years, Convolutional Neural Networks (CNNs) have emerged as the primary technology for facial emotion recognition, beating older Machine Learning approaches that rely primarily on manually produced features. CNNs' power lies within its capacity to automatically train hierarchical representations straight from raw facial images, resulting in extracting relevant emotional indicators without extensive pre-processing.

Our research mainly focuses on integrating data augmentation techniques with DCNN frameworks to improve emotion detection skills that rely on previous studies and latest developments in this sector.

Singh and Nand [9] introduced a hybrid model that used a combination of image pre-processing and Deep Learning techniques. With this hybrid model, they managed to achieve an accuracy of 76.75%. The preprocessing is done by scaling up and normalizing the pictures and using Convolution Neural Networks on the FER2013 dataset. Their study demonstrates the effectiveness of this hybrid model and the improvement they managed to achieve by using precise pre-processing techniques on the dataset.

Wang et al. [10] enhanced the VGGNet architecture, which modified VGGNet16-D by including batch normalization, dropout methods, and data augmentation to improve model performance. These changes have managed their model to achieve an accuracy of 72.38%. Their report also notes the model's shortcomings, such as computational complexity and difficulty recognizing subtle expressions. This study is a milestone towards more accurate facial emotion identification techniques addressing both strengths and problems for further improvements that can be helpful and provide room for development for fellow researchers.

Le Nhu et al. [11] created a novel facial emotion identification approach that combines Deep Learning techniques with an average facial region weight. Their method proceeds by recognizing facial landmarks and then dividing the face into seven areas. Each region is then processed with a Convolutional Neural Network (CNN). This method substantially enhances the accuracy of the model by taking each facial region's unique contribution into account for emotion recognition. Their model outperformed cutting-edge approaches with an accuracy of 74.14% on the FER2013 dataset. This study indicates the effectiveness of region-specific analysis in improving face emotion recognition.

Rawat et al. [12] improved facial emotion recognition using hybrid model that combines Transfer Learning with DCNN models. Moreover, they fine-tuned a variety of pre-trained models that extensively increased the accuracy across various datasets. Particularly, DenseNet-161 has improved its accuracy by 7.23% on the JAFFE dataset, while the model achieved accuracy of 70.87% on the FER dataset. Their work highlighted the capability of Transfer Learning to significantly improve face emotion recognition accuracy and also marking the impact of fine tuning technique on the pre-trained model; thus, making an important advancement in the emotion analysis detection.

Reddy et al. [13] developed a method for recognizing facial expressions using a Recurrent Residual Convolutional Neural Network. Their approach, combined Recurrent Neural Networks and Residual Learning to capture both the spatial and temporal aspects of facial expressions. Furthermore, their model has achieved an accuracy of 61.86% on the FER2013 dataset. Additionally, they have also mentioned areas for further improvement, such as increasing dataset diversity and correcting overfitting challenges in the field of facial expression recognition.

Kwon et al. [14] developed an advanced technique for facial emotion recognition using landmark coordinate characteristics taken from photographs. Their technique was intended for uncontrolled situations and used 3D facial landmarks to overcome such typical issues that pose occlusion and lighting fluctuations. Using a transformer-based network that concentrates on these landmarks, they managed to achieve an accuracy of 73.7% on the FER+ dataset. Their approach represented a substantial development in facial expression recognition that provided a reliable solution for many real-world applications.

All these studies have emphasized the need for various datasets in facial emotion recognition research, with FER2013 being frequently used for validation due to its large data volume. If we possess a much bigger and unbiased dataset for training these models, we can achieve much better accuracy in the future. As a result, using FER2013 as the major dataset in the proposed study is consistent with this trend, allowing for more extensive research on incorporating data augmentation in DCNNs to improve emotion identification from facial expressions.

Addressing these crucial challenges of data imbalance and the need for better generalization in facial emotion recognition, as emphasized by H. V. et al. [15] and Avcı & Akay [16], our research integrates the advanced data augmentation techniques into DCNNs. This strategy intends to effectively improve the training of our model on a biased dataset while preserving the emotional content and improving the model's flexibility to new expressions. Our work uses a novel strategy to overcome all these constraints identified by the previous studies mentioned above and making a valuable contribution to the improvement of FER technology.

3 Methodology

The proposed architecture shown in Fig. 1 overcomes the imbalance in the dataset by using data augmentation techniques along with the DCNN model at its foundation. The procedure begins with the data pre-processing phase, which includes exploratory data analysis, which enables us to gain more insight into the features of the FER2013 dataset. It is followed by data augmentation that improves the diversity of the dataset and makes the model more resilient. The dataset is split into training and validation subsets in the next step. After that, the pixel values in training and validation subsets will be normalized into a uniform range between 0 and 1, as Neural Networks are very sensitive to unnormalized data. The course of action then moves on to the training phase, which involves feeding the dataset into the proposed DCNN model. Then, we move on to the result and analysis phase, where model efficacy is observed via several performance metrics. The proposed model not only addresses major issues such as bias in existing models but also gives better accuracy and efficiency than existing architectures.

3.1 Dataset

We used the FER2013 dataset [8] for this study. It contains 35,887 facial images, each in grayscale and at a resolution of 48×48 pixels. These images are processed in such a way that every face is centered within the frame, which leads to a uniform visual format for computation. Uniformity is essential for ensuring the efficacy of automated facial expression recognition systems.

The dataset includes seven discrete emotional classes that represent the globally recognized emotions of happiness, neutral, sadness, fear, surprise, anger, and disgust. As shown in Figs. 2 and 3, there is a clear imbalance in distribution among these categories. Happiness is the most abundant emotion in the dataset with 8,989 images. This is followed by neutral expressions, which account for 6,198 data points. The sadness emotion has 6,077 images, followed by the fear and anger class, with 5,121 and 4,953 instances respectively. The Surprise class consists of 4,002 samples. Disgust has the smallest representation, with only 547 samples, indicating a substantial disparity in the collection. This imbalanced distribution may cause substantial bias in Deep Learning

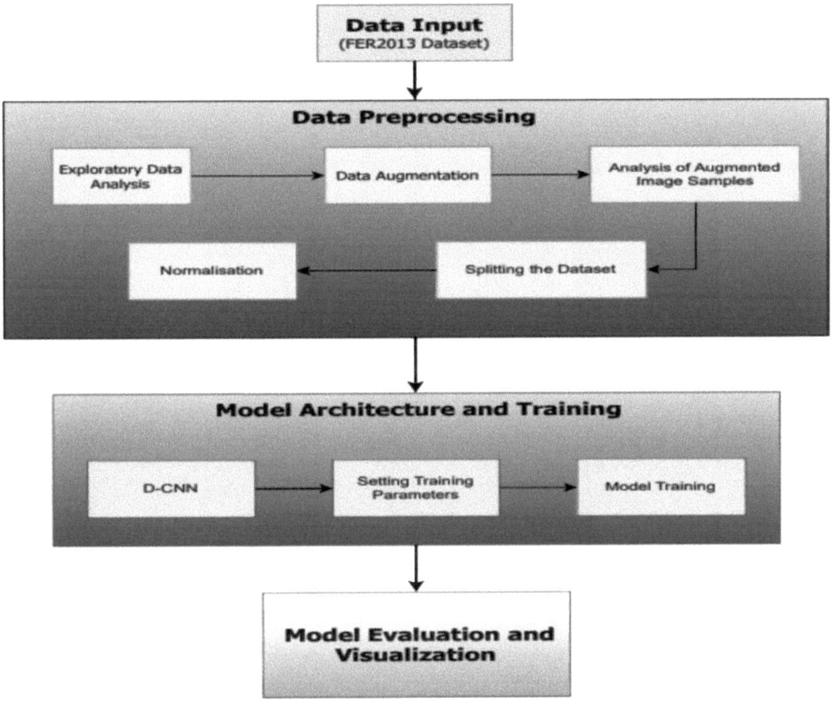

Fig. 1. Proposed D-CNN Architecture

models, leading to reduced accuracy for fewer represented classes due to a lack of training data. This may reduce the model's capacity to generalize across all classes, especially for emotions that have a low representation in the dataset. To overcome this issue, we used data augmentation techniques such as image rotation, zooming, flipping, and shifting in our proposed architecture. The objective is to deliberately enlarge the minority groups to attain a more consistent distribution throughout every class and strengthen the model's potential to learn from a more homogeneous dataset, which is likely to increase the accuracy for each emotion, particularly rarer. The augmentation approach improves the dataset diversity while maintaining the integrity of the underlying facial expressions

3.2 Data Preprocessing

In the circumstances of emotion detection from facial expressions using the FER-2013 dataset, preparing the dataset is very important to improve the quality and effectiveness of research methods. The data preparation workflow includes multiple crucial phases that are customized to handle different elements of the data preparation phase and support building strong and accurate emotion detection models. This phase includes exploratory data analysis, data augmentation, analysis of augmented image samples, and normalization occurs at the end. Each of these steps is described as follows:

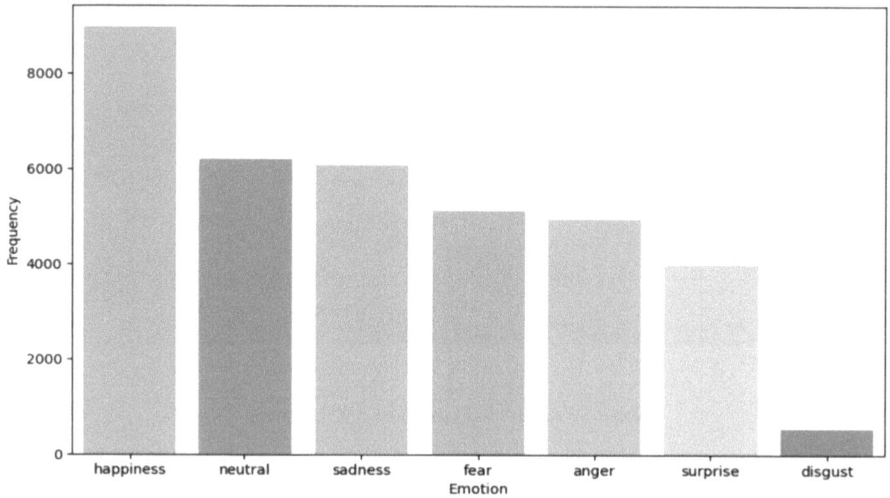

Fig. 2. Emotion Distribution in the FER2013 dataset

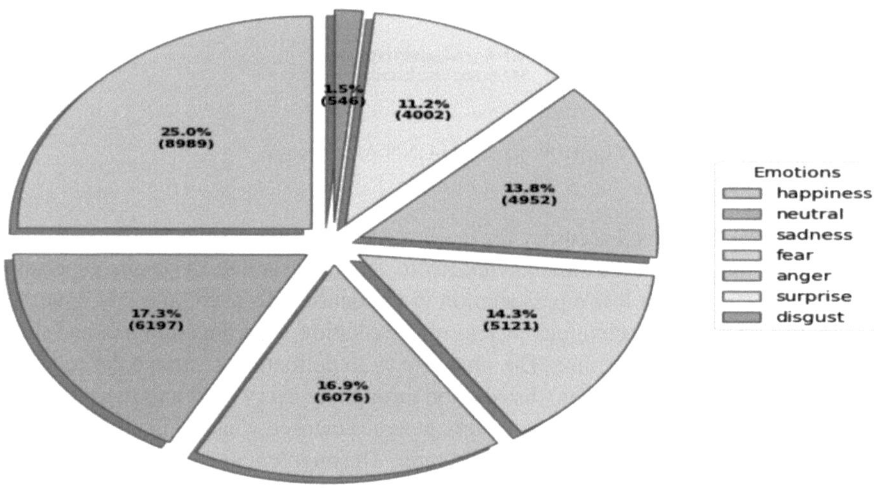

Fig. 3. Pie Chart Representation of Emotion Distribution in FER2013 Dataset

3.2.1 Exploratory Data Analysis (EDA)

The primary objective is to comprehend the dataset's important characteristics, like the classification of different emotions in different classes and the presence of abnormalities and possible partialities. This step includes checking the distribution of emotions, verifying image quality and recognizing any abnormalities that can influence the model's performance. Depiction tools like histograms and bar graphs are applied to observe the parity of different classes of emotions. Hence, approaches like principal component analysis can be applied to reduce the magnitude and depict high magnitude data in two or three dimensions, allowing the verification of patterns or collections.

3.2.2 Data Augmentation

To enhance the dataset's diversity and scale to resolve concerns like class imbalance and overfitting. Augmentation introduces variations in the training data, enabling the model to learn more generalized features. Geometric changes like rotation, translation, scaling, and flipping, as well as color space augmentation methods like brightness and contrast changes, cropping, and noise addition, are used in the proposed model. These approaches copy a variety of circumstances in which facial emotion is recorded, including different positioning, lighting, and obstructions.

3.2.3 Analysis of Augmented Image Samples

To evaluate the influence of different augmentation approaches on dataset, the architecture observes the enhanced images to verify the emotional data of the faces if recognized after augmentation. This phase involves qualitative assessments where augmented images are visually inspected.

3.2.4 Splitting the Dataset

To separate the dataset into training, validation, and testing sets so that every class of emotion has a representative allocation in all subsets. This is important for correctly quantifying the model's aptitude for abstraction from previously unseen data. The dataset is classified into 90% training and 10% validation sets.

3.2.5 Normalization

To make the pixel values up to the standard across all images in the dataset, the model's input data must be consistent. Normalization decreases the influence of light variations and increases convergence speed during training. Pixel values may be standardized by scaling them to a range of [0, 1] and dividing by 255, which is the maximum pixel value or by a more refined approach like Z-score normalization, which subtracts the average pixel value from each single pixel and divide it by the standard deviation pixel values in the dataset. Researchers can substantially enhance the dataset quality by systematically implementing these preparation processes, which enhances the performance and reliability of emotion detection models built by using the FER-2013 dataset.

3.3 Proposed Deep Convolutional Neural Network Model

The proposed model is a Deep Convolutional Neural Network, which processes the input data with a size of 48x48 pixels and a depth of one that is generic of grayscale images. The network structure begins with a Convolutional Layer having 64 filters that are important for characteristic retrieval. To enhance the training and to decrease internal independent variable shift, a batch normalization is performed. The second Convolutional Layer also has 64 filters that fine tunes the first layer's characteristic retrieval after which batch normalization is performed to preserve numerical stability. After this, a max pooling layer cuts the geometric parameters of the characteristic map by half, lowering the complexity and processing strain while preserving the most crucial features. Consequently, a dropout layer is added, setting a part of input units to zero, preventing overfitting and ensuring that the model adjusts effectively to new data. The model increases in depth with subsequent two convolutional layers, batch normalization, and a single set of max pooling after which a dropout layer is there with 128 and 256 filters, respectively. Every set of layers gradually records more theoretical and complicated features from the data. The final stages of convolutional neural networks involve flattening a layer that converts the three dimensional characteristic maps into one dimensional characteristic vector, allowing it to connect to a concentrated layer. This fully connected layer with 128 neurons assists a high-level reasoning engine that interprets the data collected by the convolutional layers. A batch normalization is performed again after which another dropout layer guarantees the model's reliability against overfitting. This convolutional neural network [13] design finishes with an output layer that uses the softmax activation function. Convolutional neural network's design jumps between convolution, batch normalization, pooling and dropout depicts cautious parity between characteristic retrieval and standardization intending to achieve high accuracy while safeguarding standardization among different datasets.

4 Result and Analysis

The proposed model has performed well on the FER2013 dataset with an 80.06% accuracy. This model also illustrated its strong predictive capabilities by correctly recognizing the outcomes of 5,013 out of 6,293 samples. The following Table 1 shows the performance of the proposed model.

Table 1. Performance of Emotion Recognition Model

Emotion Labels	Precision	Recall	F1-score
Anger	0.76	0.78	0.77
Disgust	0.99	1.00	0.99
Fear	0.71	0.61	0.66
Happiness	0.90	0.89	0.89
Sadness	0.67	0.61	0.64
Surprise	0.89	0.90	0.90
Neutral	0.66	0.79	0.72
Macro Avg.	0.80	0.80	0.80
Weighted Avg.	0.80	0.80	0.80

From Table 1, the comprehensive performance of our emotion recognition model is apparent. The average precision, recall, and F1-score are all approximately 0.80, showing that it is accurate when dealing with emotions. Thus, these scores demonstrate a good tradeoff between precision and recall to allow for more predictable emotional state recognition by boosting the confidence of emotional state recognition. Uniform

F1-scores over different emotions indicate that this model has been well-trained and can be applied to other emotional expressions. This kind of attainment points out how useful this model can be in real-life applications, where precise detection of emotions holds a lot of importance.

This DCNN model's performance was tested using a wide range of measures, including accuracy, loss, and a confusion matrix (Fig. 4). The confusion matrix also indicates the model's capabilities, from training to previously unseen validation data. The model accuracy distribution indicates that the model makes consistent predictions with minimal overfitting, since the validation accuracy closely tracks the training accuracy without an apparent decline.

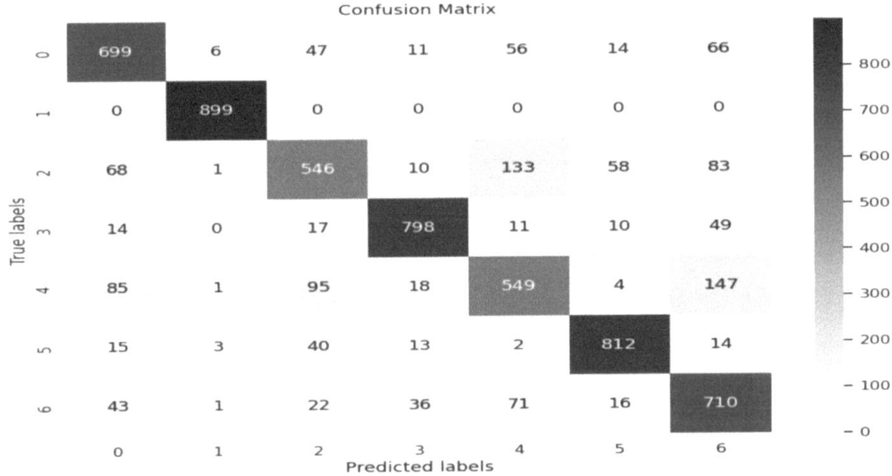

Fig. 4. Confusion matrix

Figure 5 displays epoch-wise training and validation accuracy trends across successive epochs. Both training and validation accuracy improved significantly in the early epochs, followed by a plateau, which indicates that the model has reached its peak learning capacity. The graph depicts strong generalization as training and validation accuracy curves eventually converge.

Similarly, the training and validation loss trend throughout epochs in Fig. 6 shows that the loss falls significantly at first and then gradually reaches a saturation point. These training and validation loss curves are near together at later epochs, indicating that the model is not overfitting and has acquired a standardized pattern from the training data. The confusion matrix (Fig. 4) depicts the model's classification performance across multiple classes. The diagonal elements represent the number of right predictions for each class, whereas the off-diagonal elements represent misclassifications. A significant concentration of values along the diagonal indicates a high true positive rate in all classes.

Table 2 shows the performance comparison of the proposed model compared to the existing state-of-the-art.

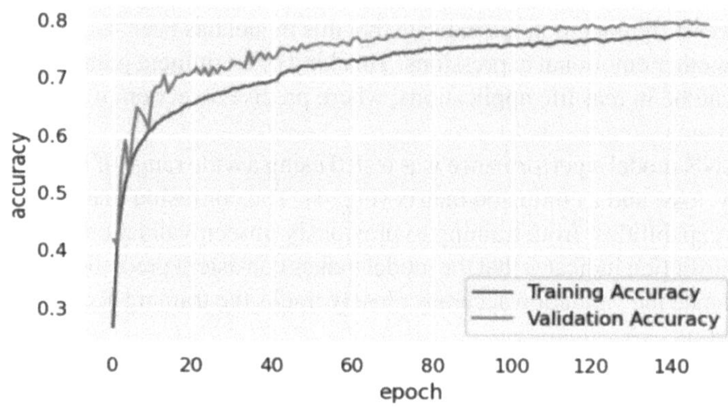

Fig. 5. Epoch-wise Training and Validation Accuracy Trend

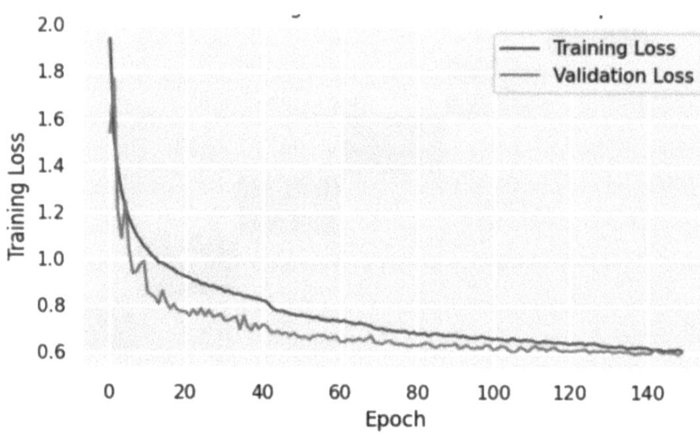

Fig. 6. Trend of Training and Validation Loss Across Epochs

Table 2 provides insight into the comparative analysis of the proposed model with existing state-of-the-art models. The state-of-the-art has used various models by employing different techniques for emotion recognition. Their accuracies range between 61.86% and 76.92%,. However, our proposed model achieves an accuracy of 80.06%; thus, it outperforms the results of state-of-the-art by a margin of 3.14%.

Table 2. Comparison of Results

Author [Ref.], Year	Accuracy	Model Description
Wang et al. [10], 2023	72.38%	Using improved VGGNet.
Le Nhu et al. [11], 2023	74.14%	Combining Deep Learning and Averaged Weight of Face-Regions.
Rawat et al. [12], 2023	70.87%	Using Transfer Learning with Deep Convolutional Neural Network (DCNN) Models.
Reddy et al. [13], 2023	61.86%	Using Recurrent Residual Convolutional Neural Network.
Kwon et al. [14],2023	73.7%	Using Landmark coordinate features.
H. V et al. [15], 2023	76.92%	CNN model using Canny Edge Detection.
Dowd et al. [17], 2022	74.6%	Simple CNN model using ML and On-Edge Computing Techniques.
Proposed Model	80.06%	Using Data Augmentation with Deep Convolutional Neural Network (DCNN) Models.

5 Conclusion and Future Work

In this paper, we proposed a facial emotion recognition method based on DCNN. The proposed DCNN model was trained using FER2013 and to overcome the biased structure of the dataset, we performed several Data Augmentation Loops, consisting of augmenting image pixels, resizing and padding of the image, cropping the required image size out of the padded image, adjusting of brightness and contrast of the image, on the dataset to normalize it. Results show that we achieved an accuracy of 80.06% that outperforms the best performance of state-of-the-art models by a margin of 3.14%. Future work in this area may include improving FER by using many diverse datasets and implementing applications that use FER in real-time scenario. Moreover, we can also incorporate speech and body language in addition to facial expressions for a more comprehensive model that can improve accuracy and applicability across a wide range of scenarios.

References

1. Mehrabian, A.: Communication without words. In: Communication Theory: Second Edition, pp. 193–200 (2017). https://doi.org/10.4324/9781315080918-15/COMMUNICATION-WITHOUT-WORDS-ALBERT-MEHRABIAN
2. Nirupa, V., Renuka, G.B., Naga Lakshmi, B., Sumanth Kumar, C.P., Rudra Sekhar Reddy, A., Paramesh, J.: Chatbot based on emotions using deep learning. In: 2023 1st International Conference on Optimization Techniques for Learning, ICOTL 2023-Proceedings (2023). https://doi.org/10.1109/ICOTL59758.2023.10435281
3. Ahmadi, N., Hammond, T.: Recognizing and responding to human emotions: a survey of artificial emotional intelligence for cooperative social human-machine interactions. In: Proceedings-Frontiers in Education Conference, FIE (2023). https://doi.org/10.1109/FIE58773.2023.10343328

4. Ming, F.J., Shabana Anhum, S., Islam, S., Hooi, K.K.: Facial emotion recognition system for mental stress detection among university students. In: International Conference on Electrical, Computer, Communications and Mechatronics Engineering, ICECCME 2023 (2023). https://doi.org/10.1109/ICECCME57830.2023.10252617
5. Chidambaram, G., Ram, A.D., Kiran, G., Shivesh Karthic, P., Kaiyum, A.: Music recommendation system using emotion recognition. Int. Res. J. Eng. Technol. (2021)
6. Dalal, R., Khari, M., Pandey, P., Jatana, S., Joshi, V.: Facial emotion recognition and detection using convolutional neural networks. In: 2023 3rd International Conference on Smart Generation Computing, Communication and Networking, SMART GENCON 2023 (2023). https://doi.org/10.1109/SMARTGENCON60755.2023.10442218
7. Lokeshnaik, S.K., et al.: Real time facial emotion recognition using deep learning and CNN. In: 2023 International Conference on Computer Communication and Informatics, ICCCI 2023 (2023). https://doi.org/10.1109/ICCCI56745.2023.10128259
8. Goodfellow, I.J., et al.: Challenges in representation learning: a report on three machine learning contests. In: Lecture Notes in Computer Science (Including Subseries Lecture Notes in Artificial Intelligence and Lecture Notes in Bioinformatics) 8228 LNCS, pp. 117–124 (2013). https://doi.org/10.1007/978-3-642-42051-1_16/COVER
9. Singh, E., Nand, P.: Enhancing facial emotion recognition through deep learning and image pre-processing. In: Proceedings-2023 3rd International Conference on Innovative Sustainable Computational Technologies, CISCT 2023 (2023). https://doi.org/10.1109/CISCT57197.2023.10351308
10. Wang, Y., Huang, L., Li, J., Sun, T.: Research on facial expression recognition based on improved VGGNet. In: ITOEC 2023-IEEE 7th Information Technology and Mechatronics Engineering Conference, pp. 1879–1882 (2023). https://doi.org/10.1109/ITOEC57671.2023.10291312
11. Le Nhu, H., Dang, H.V., Xuan, H.H.: Facial emotion recognition by combining deep learning and averaged weight of face-regions. In: Proceedings-International Conference on Knowledge and Systems Engineering, KSE (2023). https://doi.org/10.1109/KSE59128.2023.10299482
12. Rawat, U., Rai, C.S.: Improving Facial Emotion Recognition Through Transfer Learning with Deep Convolutional Neural Network (DCNN) Models, pp. 1335–1339 (2024). https://doi.org/10.1109/ICTACS59847.2023.10390186
13. Reddy, L.Y., Saranghi, P.K., Manaswini, C., Jabbar, M.A., Reddy, S.A.: Facial expression detection using recurrent residual convolutional neural network. In: 2023 IEEE 3rd Mysore Sub Section International Conference, MysuruCon 2023 (2023). https://doi.org/10.1109/MYSURUCON59703.2023.10396994
14. Mukhopadhyay, M., et al.: Facial emotion recognition based on textural pattern and histogram of oriented gradient, advanced communication and intelligent systems. In: ICACIS 2022. Communications in Computer and Information Science, vol. 1749. Springer, Cham. (2023). https://doi.org/10.1007/978-3-031-25088-0_9
15. Harshith, V., Shilpa, T., Siddappa, M.: Facial Emotion Recognition Method Based on Canny Edge Detection Using Convolutional Neural Network, pp. 425–430 (2024). https://doi.org/10.1109/ICCCIS60361.2023.10425079
16. Avcı, S.O., Akay, O.: Employment and Investigation of Various CNN Models and Datasets for Facial Expression Recognition and Classification, pp. 1–5 (2024). https://doi.org/10.1109/ELECO60389.2023.10415947
17. Dowd, A., Tonekaboni, N.H.: Real-time facial emotion detection through the use of machine learning and on-edge computing. In: Proceedings-21st IEEE International Conference on Machine Learning and Applications, ICMLA 2022, pp. 444–448 (2022). https://doi.org/10.1109/ICMLA55696.2022.00071

Counting Visual Elements: A Deep Learning Framework for Visual Question Answering Using Multimodal Data Approach

U. Nitish(✉), V. Sowmya, B. Premjith, and G. Jyothish Lal

Amrita School of Artificial Intelligence, Amrita Vishwa Vidyapeetham, Coimbatore, India
nitishu41@gmail.com, {v_sowmya,b_premjith, g_jyothishlal}@cb.amrita.edu

Abstract. Visual Question Answering (VQA) is a multidisciplinary task that includes both Computer Vision (CV) and Natural Language Processing (NLP). It aims to create an efficient model with the help of an object detection algorithm such as Yolov5 where the central objective is to achieve a detailed and simultaneous comprehension of both visual content from images and textual content from questions. This chapter deals only with counting tasks with the help of an encoder-decoder architecture to learn the contextual information in the given question and correlate it with the corresponding image to predict the answers with precision. The 'question features' are extracted using BERT and the 'image features' are then extracted using a pre-trained vision transformer model. A cross-attention mechanism is used to help the model learn where to focus more on the given question with respect to the image. The output from the attention mechanism and the 'question features' are then fused for further processing. We investigated the use of two different architectures, one with object detection (using Yolov5) and the other without it. The first model is without object detection and the second one is with object detection which was accomplished using Yolov5. The performance evaluation results on the popular Visual Question Answering version 2 (VQAv2) dataset in terms of Mean absolute error (MAE) shows that the model with object detection outperformed its counterpart. This signifies the impact of incorporating object detection in VQA tasks.

Keywords: Visual Question Answering (VQA) · BERT · vision transformer (ViT) · word embedding · Yolov5 · PCA

1 Introduction

Visual Question Answering (VQA) is a research area that combines computer vision and natural language processing to enable machines to understand and answer questions about visual content. It seeks to narrow the distance between textual questions and visual understanding by developing algorithms that can analyze images or videos and provide accurate answers to questions related to their content. VQA [1] is an intricate task involving multimodal learning that involves answering a question about the content

M. Paprzycki et al. (Eds.): ICACIS 2024, CCIS 2405, pp. 173–184, 2027.
https://doi.org/10.1007/978-3-032-30990-7_13

of a given image using natural language processing. Relative to other tasks in multimodal learning, VQA stands out as notably demanding. It necessitates a comprehensive grasp of the complex interplay between the presented question and the associated image to make accurate predictions for the answer. Over the past few years, there has been notable progress in enhancing the performance of VQA. This progress is attributed to advancements in feature extractors, attention mechanisms, and multimodal fusion approaches. These advancements have contributed to enhancing the accuracy and effectiveness of VQA systems.

The field of VQA gained prominence with the development of large-scale datasets, such as VQA v1 and v2, in 2015 and 2017 [2] respectively. These datasets contain pairs of images and associated questions along with corresponding answers, providing a valuable asset for the training and assessment of VQA models. The release of these datasets sparked significant research interest in the VQA domain. Initially, VQA systems relied on traditional computer vision techniques, such as object detection, image segmentation, and text analysis, to extract visual and textual features from images and questions. Machine learning algorithms were then employed to map these features and generate appropriate answers. However, these early approaches faced limitations in handling complex questions and achieving accurate results [3].

The VQA process typically involves three main components: image or video understanding, question processing, and answer generation. First, the visual component uses computer vision techniques to extract meaningful features and representations from the input visual data. This could involve object detection, image segmentation, scene recognition, or any other relevant visual analysis. Next, the textual component processes the question presented in natural language and converts it into a format suitable for machine comprehension. This step may involve parsing the question, understanding its semantics, and representing it in a structured format that the system can process. Finally, the answer generation component combines visual and textual information to produce the answer. It uses the extracted visual features and the processed question representation to reason and generate a relevant response. This can be achieved through various methods, such as machine learning models, neural networks, or knowledge-based approaches.

VQA has emerged as a versatile technology with applications spanning various domains, where the capacity to comprehend and respond to visual queries proves pivotal. In the realm of Assistive Technology, VQA serves as a valuable tool for individuals with visual impairments, offering answers to questions about their surroundings and facilitating effective navigation. Human-robot interaction benefits from VQA, enabling robots to understand and act upon verbal commands related to visual perception, fostering seamless communication and collaboration between humans and machines. Image Search Engines are transformed by VQA, allowing users to query images using natural language questions, revolutionizing the search process beyond traditional keyword reliance. In the domain of Content Understanding and Analysis, VQA plays a crucial role in deciphering the content of images and videos on platforms such as social media or surveillance systems, enabling automated analysis and information extraction. Furthermore, in Education and E-Learning, VQA finds utility by creating interactive learning environments where students can pose questions about visual content, receiving immediate answers and explanations, thereby enhancing the overall learning experience. The applications of VQA extend beyond these examples, with potential uses in fields such as healthcare, gaming, virtual reality, and more. The ability to comprehend and answer questions about visual content opens up new avenues for human-computer interaction and decision-making.

In conclusion, Visual Question Answering is a dynamic field that has witnessed significant advancements over the years. It has evolved from traditional computer vision techniques to powerful deep learning models capable of understanding and answering questions about visual content. The combination of image understanding and language comprehension has led to numerous applications across various domains, revolutionizing human-machine interactions and unlocking the potential of visual data analysis. As VQA continues to advance, we can expect further breakthroughs and practical implementations in the near future. VQA has gained significant attention due to its potential applications in numerous domains, including autonomous vehicles, robotics, image search engines, and human-computer interaction. By enabling machines to comprehend and respond to inquiries regarding visual content, VQA opens up possibilities for more intuitive and interactive interactions between humans and machines.

2 Literature Review

In the year 2022, J. Wu et al. [4] presented a Question-Driven Multiple Attention Model (QDMA). In this chapter, the visual features and textual features are obtained using Faster R-CNN and LSTM, respectively. Following that, a question-driven attention network was developed to identify specific areas in images relevant to the given question. This enables the model to accurately concentrate on relevant elements within complex scenes. To improve the interaction between the recognized image region and the question, a co-attentive network has been introduced. Comprising self-attentive and guided-attentive units, this network collaborates to establish a comprehensive understanding of the relationship between the image and the question. Finally, a module for prediction which is a two-layered Multi-Layer Perceptron (MLP), takes the extracted 'question features' and 'image features' as input to generate the correct answer, resulting in an overall accuracy score of 71.59% on the VQAv2 dataset.

In the year 2021, H. Zhong et al. [5] introduced the Self-Adaptive Neural Module Transformer (SANMT), which proposed a flexible framework that dynamically adjusts the encoding of 'question features' and the decoding of layout based on intermediate question and answer (Q&A) results. A transformer module was utilized to encode intermediate outcomes by leveraging the provided 'question features.' The encoding process generated a dynamic question feature embedding that dynamically evolves throughout the reasoning steps. By incorporating this adaptive mechanism, SANMT enabled the system to effectively adapt its processing based on the evolving Q&A context, leading to improved performance and flexibility in reasoning and layout decoding. They were able to get an accuracy of 64.5% in the VQAv2 dataset.

In the year 2018, D. -K. Nguyen and T. Okatani [6] proposed a simple architecture demonstrating complete symmetry between visual and language representations. Within this design, individual words in the question direct attention to specific regions of images, and reciprocally, each region attends to relevant words in the question. This bidirectional attention mechanism allows for comprehensive interactions between the image and question at every level. Also, they piled up this design to make a hierarchy, making it easier for the model to go back and forth between images and questions, allowing a better understanding of both pictures and text. As a result, they reached an accuracy score of 66.8%.

In the year 2018, M. Lao et al. [7] introduced a novel network named "Cross-modal Multistep Fusion (CMF)" which allowed the creation of multistep features that enabled multiple interactions between two modalities. This approach emphasized the generation of multistep features and their interactions. After conducting thorough experiments, they showcased that their suggested approach attains competitive performance with the best available techniques. They were able to achieve an overall accuracy score of 66.4%.

In the year 2020, C. Chen et al. [8] proposed an innovative approach, Multimodal Encoder-Decoder Attention Networks (MEDAN) which is tailored for multimodal tasks. MEDAN is composed of cascaded Multimodal Encoder-Decoder Attention (MEDA) layers, facilitating the extraction of rich and meaningful features from both questions and images. This involves effectively linking certain important words in the question with crucial regions in the image. In every MEDA layer, there's an Encoder module for focusing on questions and a Decoder module for managing both attentions, guided by questions and self-attention on images. The achieved overall accuracy for MEDAN stands at an impressive 71.01%.

In the year 2019, C. Yang [9] devised a mechanism to include co-attention within a deep neural network to concurrently learn features about both the questions and images. This approach includes textual attention using a self-attention model, helping filter out irrelevant details and improving distinctive features for question-level representations. The introduction of question type involves directly combining it with the multi-modal joint representation, efficiently reducing the potential answer options. The resulting network architecture, which merges the suggested co-attention mechanism and question type, establishes a unified model for Visual Question Answering (VQA). The achieved performance on the VQAv2 dataset attains a notable score of 64.25%.

The observed lower accuracy in the numbering task may be attributed to factors such as task complexity or inadequacies in the model architecture. Simultaneously, there is an unexplored avenue in NLP and computer vision by integrating the Vision Transformer (ViT) for image information and BERT for textual data. ViT, designed for computer vision, breaks down images into patches and processes them with transformer layers, while BERT excels in capturing contextualized word representations in language. The proposed multimodal approach involves utilizing ViT to extract features from images and BERT to process textual information, with the resulting embeddings being combined for a joint representation. This fusion of visual and textual information holds promise for enhancing performance in tasks such as visual question answering.

In tackling the challenges associated with numerical tasks, especially counting, a promising strategy involves merging image and text techniques while reframing counting as a regression problem. Notably, the integration of an object detection algorithm takes center stage, providing a crucial boost to the model's counting capabilities. This approach capitalizes on the collaboration between image and text understanding, aiming to significantly enhance overall performance, particularly in answering counting questions related to images. The utilization of object detection not only complements the regression-based approach but also contributes to addressing the complexity inherent in counting tasks.

3 Dataset Description

VQAv2 is a dataset containing open-ended questions about images developed and released by a collaboration between different organizations including Virginia Tech and Georgia Institute of Technology in the year 2017. The VQAv2 (Visual Question Answering) dataset (Fig. 1) is a widely used benchmark dataset for the task of visual question answering. It was created to enable research and development in the area of combining computer vision and natural language processing. The dataset consists of pairs of images and corresponding questions about the content of those images. Each question is associated with a human-generated answer. The dataset contains a diverse set of images from the MS COCO dataset, which includes a wide range of objects, scenes, and activities. The dataset is already divided into three: test, train, and validation. The training dataset contains 82,783 images and 443,757 questions about the images. The validation dataset contains 40,504 images and 214,354 questions. The training dataset contains 81,434 images and 447,793 questions. The training and validation datasets have annotations corresponding to the questions. Each question will have 10 answers answered by 10 different people. Therefore, training annotations will have 4,437,570 answers and validation annotations will have 2,143,540 answers. The dataset consists of three distinct answer types: yes/no responses which constitute around 37.6%, numerical answers (13%), and others which encompass one word or descriptive responses (49.4%) (Fig. 2).

Fig. 1. An example from the VQAv2 dataset

The questions and the answers are available in JSON format where each instance is clearly defined by its image id, question id and answer id. In this chapter, we only took the questions that started with the question "How many" during the training and testing. There were around 57000 annotations that came under the number category. Out of that, we used only those annotations whose questions started with "How many".

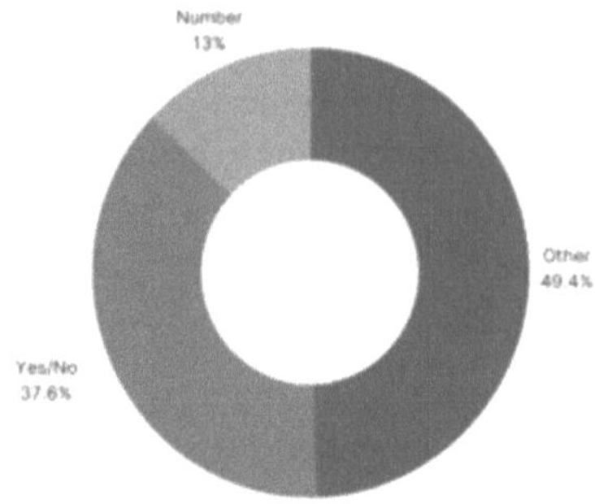

Fig. 2. Answer types and distribution

The distribution of answers that we got after filtering using the above criteria is 25.29% of answers are 1, then comes 2 with 24.67% and with 13.09% comes 3. The total distribution plot of the top 20 most occurred answers is given in Fig. 3.

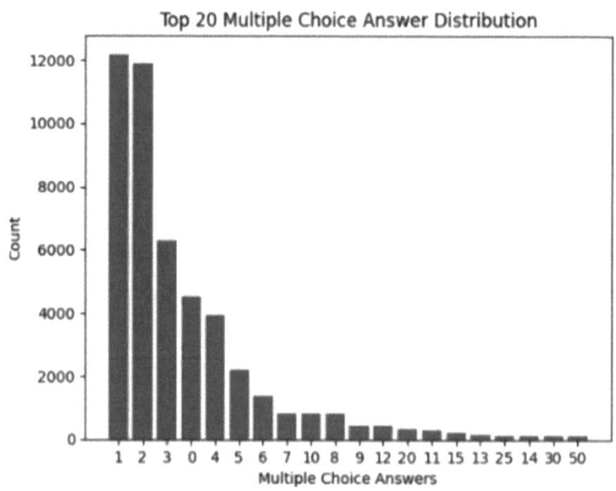

Fig. 3. Answer distribution from the filtered dataset

4 Proposed Methodology

The first step is the pre-processing stage which includes resizing the images to a standard dimension. Here the sizes have been fixed to (224 × 224 × 3). The resized images are normalized by dividing with the value 255.0 before extracting the 'image features'. The 'image features' are extracted using a pre-trained vision transformer [10] model "google/vit-base-patch16-224" released by Google. The "vit-base-patch16-224" variant of ViT has a base configuration and utilizes image patches of size 16 × 16 pixels for processing. The model consists of multiple transformer layers that enable it to capture both local and global contextual information from the image. These layers allow the model to attend to different image patches and learn representations that can be used for classification, object detection, image generation, and other vision-related tasks. It outputs a feature map of (1 × 196 × 768) for one image.

Next is the pre-processing stage for questions. All the text sequences are converted into lowercase and any non-alphanumeric characters are removed using regular expressions. The textual features are extracted using BERT [11]. The BERT base uncased model, provided by Hugging Face has been pre-trained on a large corpus of text data and is available for use in various NLP tasks through the Hugging Face Transformers library. The embeddings are generated for the input question completely. The max length of the output question sequence is set to be 25 since the max length of each question was found to be 21. and padding is done to those questions that have a length of less than 25 by setting the pad_to_max_length argument as true. Therefore, the resultant output for one question will be of size (25,768). In this work, we will be dealing with a regression problem since it is a counting task.

The encoder-decoder model is trained using the above pre-processed data. Two different models have been tried:

- Model-1: Without using any object detection algorithm.
- Model-2: Using YOLOv5 in the initial stage before feature extraction.

4.1 Architecture

Model-1

The pre-processed questions are tokenized using the 'BertTokenizer' API provided by Huggingface. The 'BertTokenizer' class offers a convenient way to convert text strings into sequences of tokenized vectors i.e. sequences of token IDs representing the input text. These tokenized vectors of questions are then passed through BERT to create vector representations or embeddings for each word. These embeddings capture semantic relationships, enabling models to understand textual data more effectively. The pre-processed images are sent through ViT to extract visual features. The dimension of the extracted features will be (196,768). PCA is used to reduce the dimensions to (196,128). PCA is mainly used because of the computational constraint. Using PCA will reduce the final size of features by a very huge proportion. The proposed architecture is given in Fig. 4.

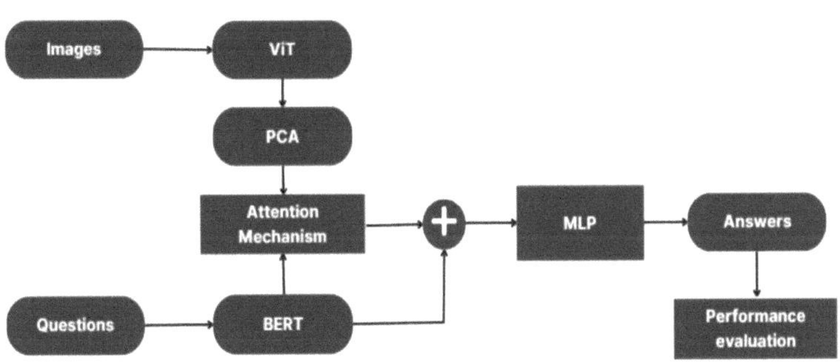

Fig. 4. Proposed Framework for model 1 for enhancing the performance in counting tasks

Both the 'question features' and 'image features' are then passed through an attention mechanism to perform cross-attention. Cross-attention aligns relevant image regions with corresponding text parts, enhancing semantic connections. It enables contextual understanding, improving representations for tasks like image captioning and VQA. It is implemented using TensorFlow (tf.keras.layers.MultiHeadAttention) where the query will be 'question features', value and key will be 'image features'. This will enable the model to focus on parts of the images relative to the questions. The number of heads is set to 2 and the output of the attention mechanism will be of the shape (25,768).

The output from the previous layer is then concatenated (added element-wise) with the 'question features' to get an output shape of (25,768). The output is reduced by adding the elements to get a final shape of (1,768). The final vectors are then passed through 3 dense layers with the activation function of the first two layers set as 'ReLu' and the final layers activation function is set as 'Linear' since it is a regression task. The number of units in the layers are 768, 256, and 1 respectively.

Model-2

The architecture is mostly similar to the first model. The only difference is that Yolov5 [12] is used as an object detection algorithm. The detected objects in each image are treated as a separate image and are passed through ViT. Figure 5 shows the architecture for the proposed model. The extracted features of each object are reduced to (1,768) and then concatenated together to form the final features of one image. For example, suppose an image has 10 objects detected. In that case, each object will have a feature size of (196,768) which is reduced to (1,768) and all the final features of these 10 objects are concatenated together to form a final feature of size (10,768) where 10 will be number of objects detected. The maximum number of objects detected is 64. Hence the final dimension is set to be (64,768). For those images without 64 objects zero padding is done. The rest of the process remains the same as in model-1. Here PCA is used to reduce the dimensions to (64,64). The trained weights and some sample data have been uploaded to the GitHub repository for both the models.

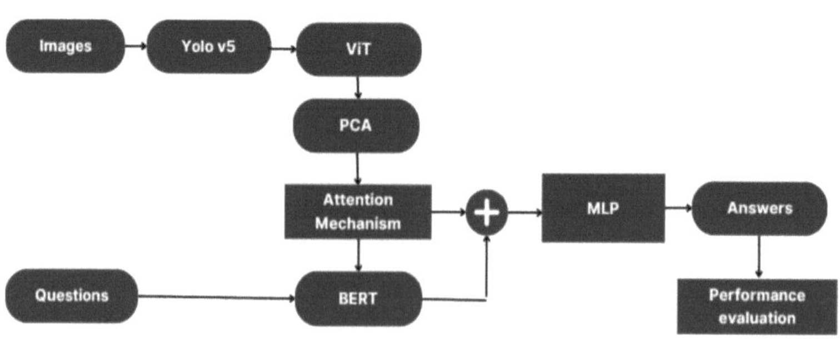

Fig. 5. Proposed Framework for model 2 for enhancing the performance in counting tasks

5 Experimental Results and Discussion

MAE score is used for performance evaluation. MAE (mean absolute error) is used in machine learning to measure the average magnitude of errors between predicted values and actual values. It is often used in regression analysis to assess the accuracy of a predictive model. The training data consists of 43271 pairs of questions and answers. Similarly, validation and testing were done on 4808 and 23017 pairs of questions and answers respectively.

5.1 Model-1

The model was trained for a total of 5 epochs. An MAE score of 6.8 was achieved when this particular model was tested on the testing dataset. The training was done on an RTX 4070 GPU with 12GB VRAM. It took around 8 min for one epoch during training. The epoch vs validation mean absolute error is shown in Fig. 6. We can observe that the MAE has decreased within the 5 epochs.

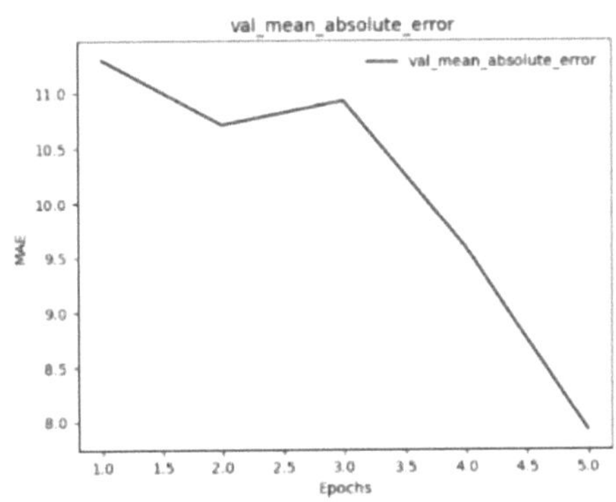

Fig. 6. MAE plot

Figure 7 denotes some results we got from model 1. In the first picture, the ground truth is 21 and we got the answer as 20, and in the second sample the ground truth is 2, but the answer we got is 2. This suggests that the model is not able to completely relate the question with the images.

5.2 Model-2

Similarly, the second model was trained for a total of 5 epochs. An MAE score of 5.62 was achieved when this particular model was tested on the testing dataset. The training was done on an RTX 4070 GPU with 12GB VRAM. It took around 6.5 min for one epoch during training. The epoch vs validation mean absolute error is shown in Fig. 8. Here also we can observe that the MAE has decreased within the 5 epochs but at a faster rate.

Fig. 7. Sample results from Model 1

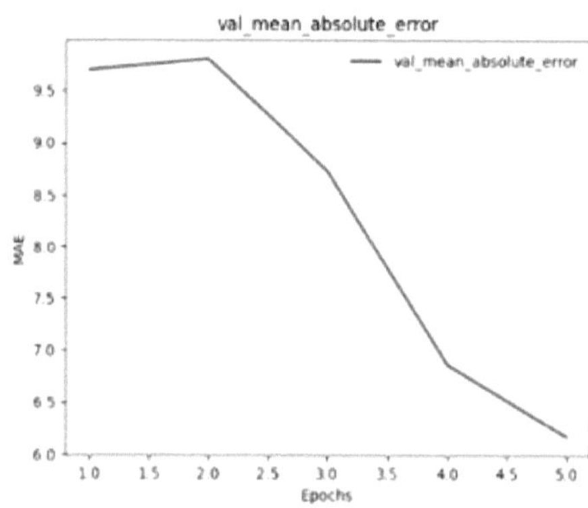

Fig. 8. MAE plot

Figure 9 denotes some results we got from model 2. In the first picture, the ground truth is 21 and the predicted answer is 18 and in the second sample the ground truth is 2 and the predicted answer is also 2. This suggests that the model can relate the question with the images better than model 1 since we are detecting the objects first.

Fig. 9. Sample results from Model 2

Table 1 contains the summary of the results for both the models as well as the information regarding the total trainable parameters.

Table 1. MAE scores based on the test data.

Sl No	Models	MAE	Total Trainable parameter
1	Model 1: (without Yolov5)	6.8	1.24 M
2	Model 2: (with Yolov5)	5.62	1.24 M

6 Conclusion and Future Works

In the absence of an object detection algorithm, Model 1 achieved an MAE score of 6.8. However, its performance was notably inferior when contrasted with a model that incorporated Yolov5 for object detection, obtaining a better MAE score of 5.62. This comparison implies that the inclusion of an object detection algorithm, such as Yolov5, significantly enhances the model's performance, leading to a lower mean absolute error. Consequently, the utilization of an object detection mechanism appears to be instrumental in improving the overall effectiveness of the model.

- As the present dataset has an imbalance in terms of the count of visual elements, efforts towards the creation of a balanced dataset is required for efficient modelling and analysis, The goal is to have a dataset that better represents the different value ranges, making it more dependable for future analyses or modelling efforts.
- A Text-to-Speech feature to expand the capabilities of the visual question-answering model for counting. This addition not only transforms the final results into audio but also makes our application an effective educational tool. This feature is especially beneficial for users with visual impairments, making our application more inclusive and versatile.

References

1. Goyal, Y., Khot, T., Summers-Stay, D., Batra, D., Parikh, D.: Making the V in VQA matter: elevating the role of image understanding in visual question answering. arXiv:1612.00837. https://doi.org/10.48550/arXiv.1612.00837
2. Ishmam, M.F., Shovon, M.S.H., Mridha, M.F., Dey, N.: From image to language: a critical analysis of visual question answering (VQA) approaches, challenges, and opportunities. Inf. Fusion. https://doi.org/10.48550/arXiv.2311.00308
3. Kafle, K., Kanan, C.: Visual question answering: datasets, algorithms, and future challenges. Comput. Vis. Image Underst. **163**, 3–20 (2017)
4. Wu, J., Ge, F., Shu, P., Ma, L., Hao, Y.: Question-driven multiple attention (DQMA) model for visual question answer. In: 2022 International Conference on Artificial Intelligence and Computer Information Technology (AICIT), Yichang, China, pp. 1–4 (2022). https://doi.org/10.1109/AICIT55386.2022.9930294

5. Zhong, H., Chen, J., Shen, C., Zhang, H., Huang, J., Hua, X.-S.: Self-adaptive neural module transformer for visual question answering. IEEE Trans. Multimed. **23**, 1264–1273 (2021). https://doi.org/10.1109/TMM.2020.2995278
6. Nguyen, D.-K., Okatani, T.: Improved fusion of visual and language representations by dense symmetric co-attention for visual question answering. In: 2018 IEEE/CVF Conference on Computer Vision and Pattern Recognition, Salt Lake City, UT, USA, pp. 6087–6096 (2018). https://doi.org/10.1109/CVPR.2018.00637
7. Lao, M., Guo, Y., Wang, H., Zhang, X.: Cross-modal multistep fusion network with co-attention for visual question answering. IEEE Access. **6**, 31516–31524 (2018). https://doi.org/10.1109/ACCESS.2018.2844789
8. Chen, C., Han, D., Wang, J.: Multimodal encoder-decoder attention networks for visual question answering. IEEE Access. **8**, 35662–35671 (2020). https://doi.org/10.1109/ACCESS.2020.2975093
9. Yang, C., Jiang, M., Jiang, B., Zhou, W., Li, K.: Co-attention network with question type for visual question answering. IEEE Access. **7**, 40771–40781 (2019). https://doi.org/10.1109/ACCESS.2019.2908035
10. Kumar, C.S.A., Maharana, A.D., Krishnan, S.M., Hanuma, S.S.S., Lal, G.J., Ravi, V.: Speech emotion recognition using CNN-LSTM and vision transformer. In: Abraham, A., Bajaj, A., Gandhi, N., Madureira, A.M., Kahraman, C. (eds.) Innovations in Bio-Inspired Computing and Applications. IBICA 2022 Lecture Notes in Networks and Systems, vol. 649. Springer, Cham (2023). https://doi.org/10.1007/978-3-031-27499-2_8
11. Sriharsha, C., Rithwik, S., Prahlad, K.P., Nair, L.S.: Intelligent learning assistant using BERT and LSTM. In: 2021 12th International Conference on Computing Communication and Networking Technologies (ICCCNT), Kharagpur, India, pp. 1–6 (2021). https://doi.org/10.1109/ICCCNT51525.2021.9579531
12. Dharneeshkar, J., Soban Dhakshana, V., Aniruthan, S.A., Karthika, R., Parameswaran, L.: Deep learning based detection of potholes in Indian roads using YOLO. In: 2020 International Conference on Inventive Computation Technologies (ICICT), Coimbatore, India, pp. 381–385 (2020). https://doi.org/10.1109/ICICT48043.2020.9112424

A Psychological Distress-Based Identification of the Factors Stress, Anxiety, and Depression Using Machine Learning Approach

Raminder Kaur Nagra(✉) and Vikram Kulkarni

Department of Information Technology, Mukesh Patel School of Technology Management and Engineering, SVKM's NMIMS (Deemed to be University), Mumbai, Maharashtra, India
{raminderkaur.nagra,vikram.kulkarni}@nmims.edu

Abstract. Over the past few decades, many people have encountered psychological health issues like stress, anxiety, and depression. It is critical to recognize mental health issues early on and begin treatment before they get worse. Some individuals, on the other hand, do acknowledge that they battle mental health conditions like stress, anxiety, and depression. Most people, however, associate it with mood swings. Numerous studies have examined whether user posts on social media can identify mental disorders. This essay forecasts psychological problems such as depression, anxiety, and stress. Additionally, cutting-edge pre-processing methods are used to examine various severity levels. This study implements the Logistic Regression (LR) algorithm and compares it to the Naïve Bayes, K-Star, and K-Nearest Neighbour models. To implement the algorithm, data is obtained from the publically accessible DASS42 tool. The outcome is shown along with evaluation metrics. The Logistic Regression's parameters are adjusted to achieve greater accuracy with the most appropriate settings. The results demonstrated that Logistic Regression outperformed other models in terms of accuracy. In this research, the proposed method helps people to self-evaluate their risk of psychological distress quickly and easily on a regular basis.

Keywords: Logistic Regression · DASS42 · Mental Health · Anxiety · Depression · Stress · Psychological Assessment · Machine Learning

1 Introduction

Mental health encompasses the overall state of emotional, psychological, and social well-being, which in turn affects one's cognitive abilities and interpersonal connections. Conducting prompt evaluations through self-report questionnaires [1] is essential for the diagnosis of mental health issues, enabling tailored therapies. Accurate assessment of psychological problems such as anxiety, sadness, and stress are crucial. These disorders are prevalent in contemporary society, underscoring the necessity for timely and precise diagnostic methodologies. Enhancing the availability and precision of psychological distress evaluations can have a substantial influence on both the personal well-being of individuals and the overall health of society. Medical predictive analytics [2] has the capacity to bring about substantial transformations in the healthcare sector.

M. Paprzycki et al. (Eds.): ICACIS 2024, CCIS 2405, pp. 185–197, 2027.
https://doi.org/10.1007/978-3-032-30990-7_14

The Depression Anxiety Stress Scales (DASS) questionnaire [3] is a crucial instrument for evaluating psychological discomfort. It is widely recognized for its effectiveness in assessing the complex aspects of mental well-being. The self-administered DASS42 questionnaire assesses the three interrelated negative emotional states: depression, anxiety, and stress. It skillfully differentiates between these emotional states, providing a thorough understanding of an individual's mental health. This differentiation is crucial, as depression, anxiety, and stress, despite sharing similar symptoms, necessitate distinct therapeutic strategies and interventions.

The purpose of including the DASS questionnaire into the study is to leverage its extensive and diverse technique for psychological assessment [4, 5]. The DASS42 questionnaire consists of 42 items, each calibrated to assess the intensity of symptoms. The well-organized questionnaire serves as a solid foundation for the implementation of contemporary analytical approaches [6, 7]. The integration of machine learning into psychological assessment signifies a notable progression in the field of mental health [8, 9]. Machine learning offers a significant possibility to enhance the precision and effectiveness of psychiatric diagnostics by efficiently handling large datasets and detecting complex patterns [10–12]. This unique approach is particularly relevant for analyzing responses from instruments like the DASS42 questionnaire, where the volume and intricacy of data can be overwhelming for traditional statistical methods.

This study employs machine learning to transform conventional approaches to psychological assessment. The goal is to use logistic regression on the DASS42 questionnaire to make a tool that combines the strong empirical basis of DASS42 with the accuracy and flexibility of modern computer methods. The combination of traditional psychological assessment methods with sophisticated machine learning algorithms demonstrates the future potential of mental health diagnoses [13]. This picture of the future envisions exams that are readily available, efficient, and customized to the complex details of individual mental health characteristics.

In the current investigation, Logistic Regression is utilized to classify sub-categories, including the intensity of depression, anxiety, and stress. This classification is accomplished by computer-based analysis, which helps in early intervention and get people the support they need. The dataset employed was acquired from https://openpsychometrics.org/_rawdata/ and was assembled via online questionnaires completed by a heterogeneous group of users from 2017 to 2019.

2 Data Acquisition

The Depression Anxiety Stress Scales (DASS) questionnaire is a crucial instrument for evaluating psychological discomfort. It is widely recognized for its effectiveness in assessing the complex aspects of mental well-being. The DASS42 questionnaire is a self-administered tool specifically created to assess the three interconnected negative emotional conditions of depression, anxiety, and stress. The complete scope and validated psychometric features of this research and practice make it highly relevant in contemporary mental health. The DASS questionnaire successfully differentiates between these three conditions, offering a detailed comprehension of an individual's psychological well-being. This differentiation is crucial, as depression, anxiety, and stress, despite their similarity in symptoms, necessitate distinct therapy methodologies and strategies.

2.1 The DASS Questionnaire: Development and Usage

The Depression Anxiety Stress Scales (DASS) questionnaire is a fundamental component of the psychological assessment tool landscape. In this research, dataset is derived from the open-source Internet survey. The original source of the dataset was the URL (//openpsychometrics.org/_rawdata), containing data collected from online questionnaires completed by various individuals between 2017 and 2019. Developed by Lovibond and Lovibond (1995), the DASS is a 42-item self-report instrument designed to measure the three related negative emotional states of depression, anxiety, and stress as described in Table 1.

Table 1. DASS42 Questionnaire Description

Subscale	Description	Number of Items
Depression	Measures dysphoria, hopelessness, lack of interest or pleasure	14
Anxiety	Assesses physiological arousal, situational anxiety, panic symptoms	14
Stress	Evaluates difficulty in relaxing, nervous arousal, easily agitated	14

Each of these states is represented by 14 questions within the questionnaire. Each item was sequentially presented in a randomized order to each new participant, accompanied by a 4-point rating scale prompting users to indicate the frequency of their experiences over the past week. These responses are scaled between 1 and 4, with the following coding:

1. = Did not apply to me at all
2. = Applied to me to some degree, or some of the time
3. = Applied to me to a considerable degree, or a good part of the time
4 = Applied to me very much, or most of the time

The categorization of the questions is given below:

Question number 1, 6, 8, 11, 12, 14, 18, 22, 27, 29, 32, 33, 35 & 39 for Stress symptoms
Question number 2, 4, 7, 9, 15, 19, 20, 23, 25, 28, 30, 36, 40 & 41 for Anxiety symptoms
Question number 3, 5, 10, 13, 16, 17, 21, 24, 26, 31, 34, 37, 38 & 42 for Depression symptoms

The values connected to each class question's answer were added to determine the scores for stress, anxiety, and depression. After the final scores were determined, they were categorized as Extremely Severe, Severe, Moderate, Mild, or Normal depending on how severe they were as shown in Table 2.

Incorporating the DASS questionnaire into the study, the aim is to leverage its detailed and multifaceted approach to psychological assessment. The questionnaire's structure, comprising 42 items (DASS42), each scaled to measure the severity of symptoms, serves

Table 2. Severity Level

Severity Level	Depression (D)	Anxiety (A)	Stress (S)
Normal	0–9	0–7	0–14
Mild	10–13	8–9	15–18
Moderate	14–20	10–14	19–25
Severe	21–27	15–19	26–33
Extremely Severe	28+	20+	34+

as a robust foundation for applying advanced analytical methods. This research capitalizes on the depth and breadth of data provided by the DASS42, aiming to refine and enhance the process of identifying and quantifying psychological distress. By applying logistic regression analysis to this rich dataset, this study seeks not only to uphold the rigor and accuracy of the DASS but also to streamline its application, making it more efficient and accessible for a wider range of users. The ultimate goal is to provide a more expedient yet equally reliable tool for mental health professionals, one that aligns with the fast-paced and resource-sensitive environments of modern healthcare systems.

3 A Proposed Method for Identification of Psychological Distress

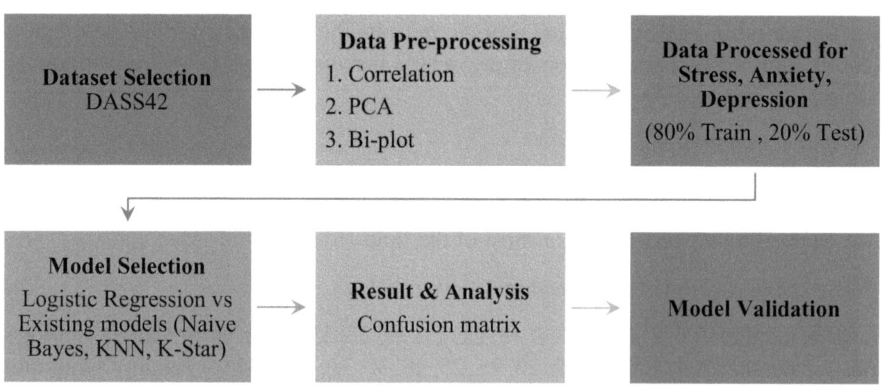

Fig. 1. Proposed method for identification of psychological distress

In this research, as per Fig. 1, a machine learning method for detecting psychological abnormalities [14]—specifically, Depression (D), Anxiety (A), and Stress (S)—based on the DASS42 survey—a 42-item assessment of these emotional states—is examined. In this context, the categorization of psychological states based on survey responses is the challenge that this research emphasizes the significance of clearly identifying. The objectives of this research are to:

- Identify and extract relevant set of features from data source (DASS42) using pre-processing techniques.
- Design and train machine learning model to predict stress, anxiety, and depression levels based on the extracted feature set
- Compare the performance of the proposed model against relevant existing methods to benchmark its efficacy and identify areas for improvement.

The use of machine learning (ML) in psychological testing indicates a significant advancement in the mental health domain. Machine learning offers a substantial opportunity to improve the precision and efficiency of mental health diagnosis by utilising its ability to analyze huge data sets and detect hidden trends [15]. This new approach is particularly useful for analyzing replies from questionnaires like the DASS, where the volume and complexity of the data might be too much for traditional statistical techniques to handle. By applying machine learning techniques [16, 17], such as logistic regression, and other techniques, it is possible to examine and understand the finer points of survey responses, leading to a more precise assessment of psychological distress levels. This work revolutionizes psychological evaluation through the use of machine learning. The future of mental health diagnosis lies in the combination of cutting-edge machine learning algorithms with traditional psychological assessment methods. Exams that are more easily accessible, efficient, and customized to the complex subtleties of each person's mental health profile are what this future holds.

4 Implementation

4.1 Dataset Selection

In recent years, there has been an increased interest in combining traditional psychological examinations with current technologies, particularly machine learning and artificial intelligence. Machine learning has the capacity to analyze complicated datasets, such as those obtained from the DASS questionnaire, more precisely and efficiently. This integration promises to improve the accuracy of psychological examinations while also making them more accessible and user-friendly, especially in areas where mental health providers' resources are limited. A brief summary of dataset DASS42 is shown in Fig. 2.

1. Stress Level is available from 0–4 all sub-classes
2. Anxiety Level is available 2(Mo), 3(S) and 4(Ex-S) sub-classes only
3. Depression Level is available in 2(Mo), 3(S) and 4(Ex S) sub-classes only

The DASS42 questionnaire stands out as a reliable, adaptable tool for assessing psychological distress. Its combination with machine learning technologies such as logistic regression marks a significant advancement in the field, with the potential to make mental health examinations more efficient, precise, and accessible.

4.2 Data Pre-processing and Model Selection

Data preparation for DASS42 involves a series of steps, such as normalisation, cleansing, and complexity reduction. To do this, various approaches, such as Principal Component

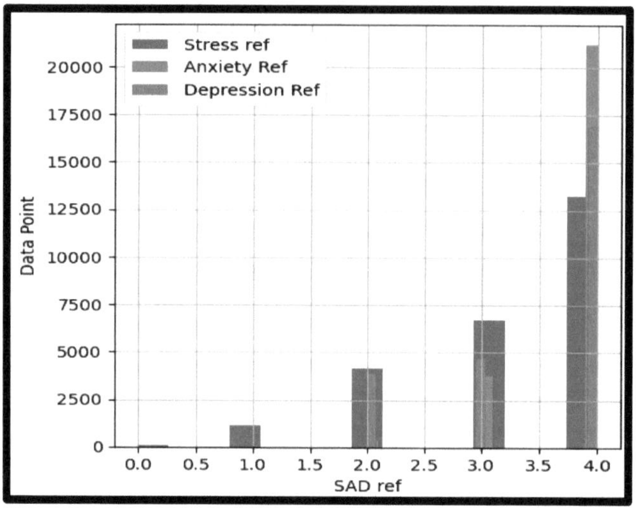

Fig. 2. DASS42 Dataset Distribution

Analysis (PCA), Bi-plots, and correlation heat maps, are employed. A correlation heat map visually represents the relationships between the different questions in the DASS42 questionnaire. It assists in identifying patterns among objects, such as when they move in opposite or complementary directions. High correlations highlight redundant elements and suggest removing them from the study to enhance its efficiency. Principal components, which are new, uncorrelated variables created using PCA, replace the original DASS42 variables. It is useful for reducing data dimensionality while maintaining the majority of the relevant information. This reduces computing effort and simplifies analysis. A bi-plot, which is especially helpful after PCA, is a graphical representation that displays both variables and observations in a reduced-dimensional space. It aids in understanding how factors contribute to component variation by visualising the links between original variables and main components. The applied steps consideration of a set's connections among its constituent points in a dataset:

Standard Deviation: Mean of the sample

$$\overline{X}1 = \frac{\sum_{i=1}^{n} X_i}{n} \tag{1}$$

Standard Deviation (SD) of a dataset is a measure of how spread out the data is

$$\text{sd} = \sqrt{\frac{\sum_{i=1}^{n} \left(X_i - \overline{X}\right)^2}{(n-1)}} \tag{2}$$

Variance: Variance is Similar as SD which is just the square of it. Both of them are measures of the spread of the data.

$$sd^2 = \frac{\sum_{i=1}^{n} \left(X_i - \overline{X}\right)^2}{(n-1)} \tag{3}$$

Covariance: Variance is a measure of the deviation from the mean for points in one dimension. Covariance is a measure of how much each dimension differs from the mean with respect to the other. It is used to measure the linear relationship between 2 dimensions.

$$\text{var}1(X) = \frac{\sum_{i=1}^{n}\left(X_i - \overline{X}\right)\left(X_i - \overline{X}\right)}{(n-1)} \tag{4}$$

$$\text{cov }1(\text{X}, \text{Y}) = \frac{\sum_{\text{i}=1}^{\text{n}} \left(\left(\text{X}_\text{i} - \overline{\text{X}}\right)\left(\text{Y}_\text{i} - \overline{\text{Y}}\right)\right.}{(\text{n} - 1)} \tag{5}$$

$$\text{cov}1(X, Y) = \text{cov}1(Y, X) \tag{6}$$

The Covariance Matrix: A matrix has the covariance of any two variables in a high dimension dataset.

$$C1^{n \times n} = \left(c_{i,j}, c_{i,j} = \text{cov}1\left(Dim_i, Dim_j\right)\right) \tag{7}$$

$$\text{C} = \begin{bmatrix} \text{cov }1(\text{X}, \text{X}) & \text{cov }1(\text{X}, \text{Y}) & \text{cov }1(\text{X}, \text{Z}) \\ \text{cov }1(\text{Y}, \text{X}) & \text{cov }1(\text{Y}, \text{Y}) & \text{cov }1(\text{Y}, \text{Z}) \\ \text{cov }1(\text{Z}, \text{X}) & \text{cov }1(\text{Z}, \text{Y}) & \text{cov }1(\text{Z}, \text{Z}) \end{bmatrix} \tag{8}$$

Correlation: It is obtained by dividing the covariance of the two variables by the product of their standard deviations.

$$\rho_{X,Y} = corr(X, Y) = \frac{\text{cov}(X, Y)}{\sigma_X \sigma_Y} = \frac{E\left[(X - \mu_X)(Y - \mu_Y)\right.}{\sigma_X \sigma_Y} \tag{9}$$

A crucial phase in getting data ready for machine learning models is preprocessing. Here, the above-mentioned techniques are applied on the data and get prepared for model training with properly formatted, and clean, which improves the generalization and performance of the model. In this work, 80% of the data is selected for training the models and 20% of the data is applied for testing. Based on the various models selected, below Sect. 5 shows the result and in-depth analysis.

5 Results and Analysis

Using a machine learning approach, the results and analysis of psychological distress-based factor identification, such as stress, anxiety, and depression, provided various insights. The model effectively found patterns and relationships in the data through feature selection and classification procedures, enabling precise psychological distress level prediction and classification. The study identified the major causes of each category of distress and offered insightful information for focused interventions and individualized care. Furthermore, by automating the distress assessment process, the machine learning approach showed promise in supporting mental health practitioners. This could lead to better patient outcomes and resource allocation in mental healthcare systems. Furthermore, the following sub-Sects. 5.1, 5.2 & 5.3 will show the result and analysis.

5.1 Pre-processing

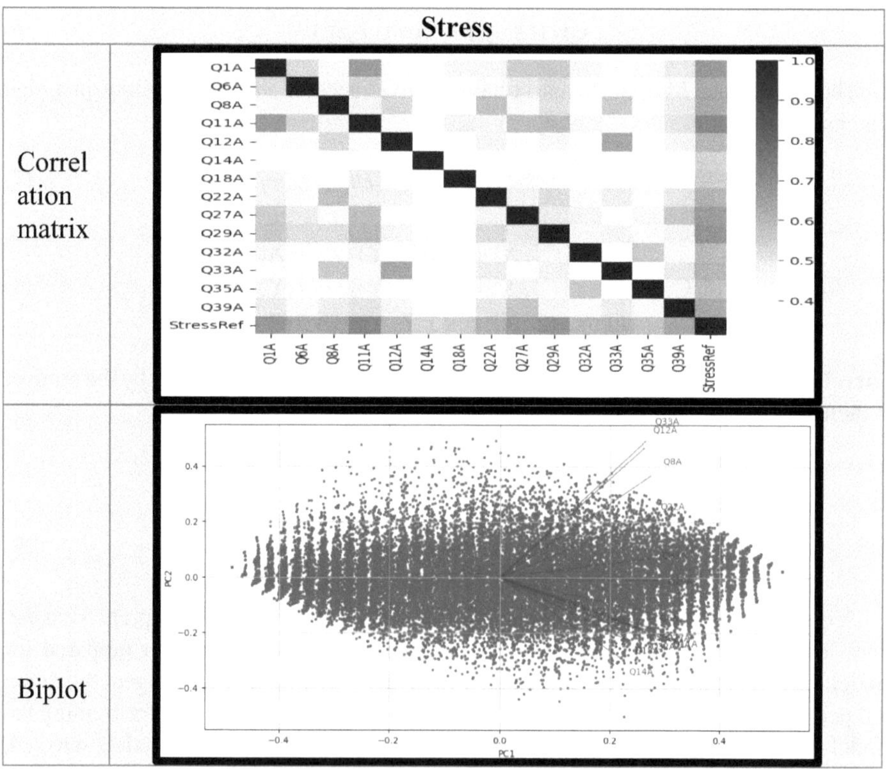

Fig. 3. Result of pre-processing for Stress

To optimize the DASS42 dataset for further analysis, an in-depth evaluation is carried out during preprocessing using correlation matrices and biplots for question selection.

The correlation matrix helps discover highly correlated variables (questions), which may imply redundancy, and it also shows the links between the variables. Through the visualization of these correlations and the reduction of dimensionality, biplots help to illustrate the important variables that contribute to the variance of the dataset. Making use of these insights, pertinent questions are chosen according to standards like non-redundancy, representation of distinct dimensions, and good correlation with target variables (such as stress, anxiety, and depression). The DASS42 dataset's psychological distress variables can be more accurately and effectively studied by using preprocessing and cleaning approaches to ensure that the data is suitable for future analysis and model training. The result of pre-processing is shown in Fig. 3 only for Stress, similarly the results of depression and anxiety is obtained.

5.2 Comparison of Models

In this section, based on the literature study, the following model classifier is selected and applied to the DASS42 dataset, i.e. Naïve Bayes, K-Star, K-nearest neighbour, and Logistic Regression after the pre-processing and result are obtained. The results of various models presented in Table 3 compare the accuracy, precision, recall, and F1-scores of different classifiers for identifying mental illness. The Logistic Regression implemented in this chapter, shows exceptional performance across all metrics for depression, anxiety, and stress with perfect accuracy and F1-scores of 1, 0.99, 0.78 respectively. Naïve Bayes [6], K-Star [6], and K-nearest neighbour [6] classifiers also exhibit decent performance across all mental illnesses, with relatively balanced precision, recall, and F-measure scores. Therefore, the best model with preprocessing is Logistic Regression and visualized in Fig. 4.

Table 3. Comparison of Models

CLASSIFIER	MENTAL ILLNESS	ACCURACY %	PRECISION (SCORE)	RECALL (SCORE)	F1-SCORE
Naïve Bayes [6]	Depression	74.89	0.747	0.749	0.747
	Anxiety	78.64	0.779	0.786	0.781
	Stress	75.73	0.752	0.757	0.753
K-Star [6]	Depression	75.9	0.759	0.759	0.746
	Anxiety	78.2	0.781	0.783	0.773
	Stress	75.87	0.755	0.759	0.743
K-nearest neighbour [6]	Depression	75.14	0.746	0.751	0.74
	Anxiety	78.26	0.775	0.783	0.773
	Stress	75.61	0.749	0.756	0.746
Logistic Regression (Our Approach)	Depression	100	1	1	1
	Anxiety	99.98	0.995	0.999	0.997
	Stress	99.35	0.775	0.798	0.786

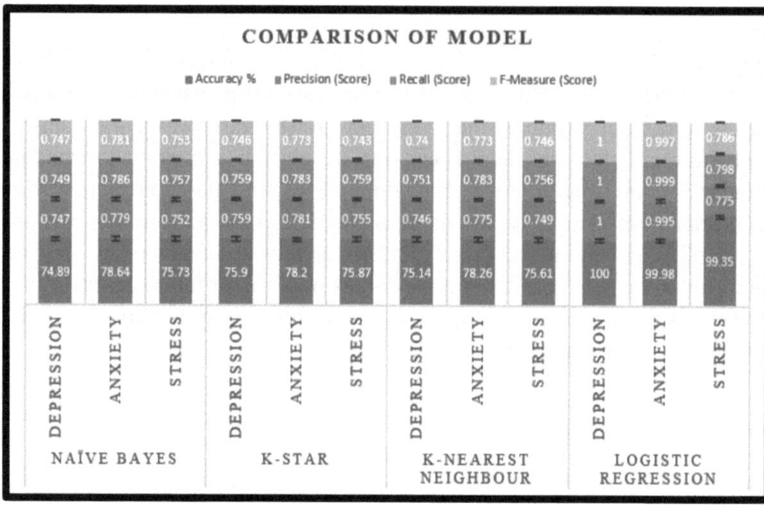

Fig. 4. Visualisation of Result

5.3 Model Validation

In several criteria, the model performs exceptionally well for a given state. The extremely low Mean Average Error (MAE), Mean Squared Error (MSE), and Root Mean Squared Error (RMSE) numbers indicate a high degree of precision in the predictions. The model shows a significant amount of variance in the data if the explained variance regression score and coefficient of determination (R^2) are both greater than 0.9. In terms of precise and accurate prediction of the target variable for the specified state, the logistic regression model performs exceptionally well overall. The result of the overall model performance for logistic regression is shown in Fig. 5.

Stress: Representation of Model Performance Evaluation using Confusion Matrix.	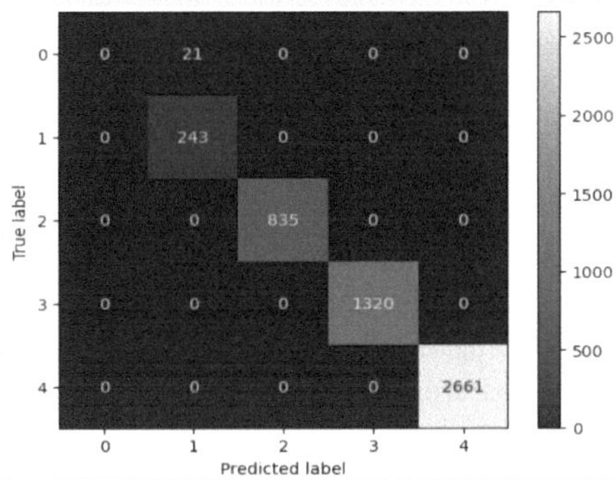
Anxiety: Representation of Model Performance Evaluation using Confusion Matrix.	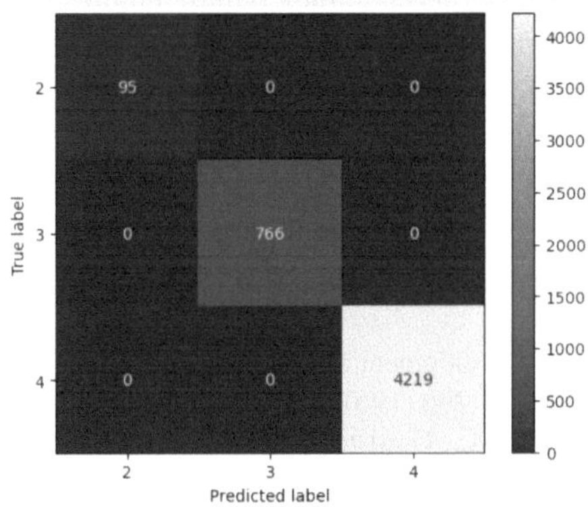
Depression: Representation of Model Performance Evaluation using Confusion Matrix.	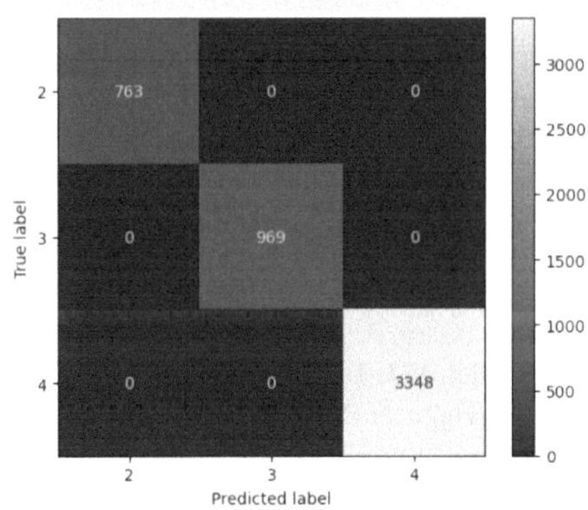

Fig. 5. Model Performance

6 Conclusion

The DASS42 dataset was analyzed using multiple classifiers, including Naïve Bayes, K-Star, K-nearest neighbour, and Logistic Regression. These classifiers were applied using an innovative preprocessing strategy, specifically tailored to the dataset. The preprocessing approach was used to enhance the quality of the data, control noise, outliers, and missing values, and ready the data for efficient model training and evaluation. Logistic Regression outperforms alternative models because of its robustness against overfitting, versatility in modelling nonlinear interactions, and ability to manage complex relationships between features and target variables. For modelling and analyzing datasets with several dimensions and complicated patterns, such as the DASS42 dataset, logistic regression is the preferred method. Future recommendations for the DASS42 dataset study include looking into complex feature engineering approaches, utilizing ensemble techniques like gradient Gradient Boosting and Random Forest, extensively optimizing hyper-parameters, and using cross-validation for reliable assessment. In addition, by leveraging machine learning techniques, potential correlations and dependencies can be uncovered that may exist among these psychological distress classes.

References

1. Hamilton, M.: Development of a rating scale for primary depressive illness. Br. J. Soc. Clin. Psychol. **6**(4), 278–296 (1967)
2. Miner, G., Miner, L., Goldstein, M., et al.: Practical Predictive Analytics and Decisioning Systems for Medicine: Informatics Accuracy and Cost-Effectiveness for Healthcare Administration and Delivery Including Medical Research. Academic Press, Inc., Cambridge, MA, USA (2016)
3. Lovibond, S.H., Lovibond, P.F.: Manual for the Depression Anxiety Stress Scales, 2nd edn. Psychology Foundation, Sydney (1995)
4. Crawford, J.R., Henry, J.D.: The depression anxiety stress scales (DASS): normative data and latent structure in a large non-clinical sample. Br. J. Clin. Psychol. **42**(2), 111–131 (2003)
5. Srinath, K.S., Kiran, K., Pranavi, S., Amrutha, M., Shenoy, P.D., Venugopal, K.R.: Prediction of depression, anxiety and stress levels using Dass-42. In: 2022 IEEE 7th International Conference for Convergence in Technology (I2CT), pp. 1–6. IEEE (2022)
6. Kumara, P., Garg, S., Garg, A.: Assessment of anxiety, depression and stress using ML models. Procedia Comput. Sci. **171**, 1989–1998 (2020)
7. Priya, A., Garg, S., Tigga, N.P.: Predicting anxiety, depression and stress in modern life using machine learning algorithms. Procedia Comput. Sci. **167**, 1258–1267 (2020)
8. Kene, A., Thakare, S.: Prediction of mental stress level based on machine learning. In: Machine Intelligence and Smart Systems: Proceedings of MISS 2021, pp. 525–536. Springer Nature Singapore, Singapore (2022)
9. Ratul, I.J., Nishat, M.M., Faisal, F., Sultana, S., Ahmed, A., Al Mamun, M.A.: Analyzing perceived psychological and social stress of university students: a machine learning approach. Heliyon. **9**(6), e17307 (2023). https://doi.org/10.1016/j.heliyon.2023.e17307
10. Nijhawan, T., Attigeri, G., Ananthakrishna, T.: Stress detection using natural language processing and machine learning over social interactions. J. Big Data. **9**(1), 1–24 (2022)
11. Zhu, L., et al.: Stress detection through wrist-based electrodermal activity monitoring and machine learning. IEEE J. Biomed. Health. Inf. **27**(5), 2155–2165 (2023). https://doi.org/10.1109/JBHI.2023.3239305

12. Sau, A., Bhakta, I.: Screening of anxiety and depression among seafarers using machine learning technology. Inform. Med. Unlock. **16**, 100149 (2019)
13. Richter, T., Fishbain, B., Fruchter, E., Richter-Levin, G., Okon-Singer, H.: Machine learning-based diagnosis support system for differentiating between clinical anxiety and depression disorders. J. Psychiatr. Res. **141**, 199–205 (2021)
14. American Psychiatric Association: Diagnostic and Statistical Manual of Mental Disorders. American Psychiatric Association, Reston, VA, USA (2013)
15. Ma, W., et al.: Detecting depression tendency based on deep learning and multi-sources data. Biomed Signal Process Control. **86**, 105226 (2023)
16. Mohamed, E.S., Naqishbandi, T.A., Bukhari, S.A., Rauf, I., Sawrikar, V., Hussain, A.: A hybrid mental health prediction model using support vector machine, multilayer perceptron, and random forest algorithms. Healthc Anal. **3**, 100185 (2023)
17. Nemesure, M.D., Heinz, M.V., Huang, R., Jacobson, N.C.: Predictive modeling of depression and anxiety using electronic health records and a novel machine learning approach with artificial intelligence. Sci. Rep. **11**(1), 1980 (2021)

Genetic Disorder Prediction Using Deep Learning

Thogati Naveen, Syed Yousuf, and S. Karthick(✉)

Department of Computational Intelligence, School of Computing, SRM Institute of Science and Technology, Kattankulathur, Tamil Nadu ,603203, India
{tn8790,sy6679,karthiks2}@srmist.edu.in

Abstract. Mutations in DNA can lead to genetic illnesses with potentially devastating consequences. Early prediction holds the key to improved patient care and intervention. This chapter investigates the potential of deep learning, particularly Long Short-Term Memory (LSTM) networks, for predicting genetic disorders. LSTMs excel in processing sequential data, making them ideal for analyzing the sequential nature of genetic data. The LSTM model will be trained on a meticulously curated dataset to evaluate its predictive performance across various disorders. Of particular interest is the LSTM's ability to capture long-term dependencies inherent in genetic data. Successful results from this experiment could empower doctors with a valuable tool for identifying at-risk patients and implementing preventive measures effectively.

Keywords: Genetic Disorders · Long Short-Term Memory · Single Gene Inheritance Disorder · Multifactorial Inheritance Disorder · Mitochondrial Inheritance Disorder

1 Introduction

Many human illnesses are caused by a single causative gene (monogenic syndromes). The unique phenotypic characteristics of each condition are derived from the genes that underlie it; minor differences set them apart. Clinicians and biologists must establish phenotype-gene correlations to understand the pathogenetic processes involved in these disorders fully. Finding the genes causing illnesses makes diagnosing patients easier and provides information on mutations and functional network linkages [1].

Genetic disorders can present as a variety of genetic abnormalities, including mutations, single nucleotide additions or deletions, whole gene loss, and variations. The identification of disease genes has been done using conventional techniques such as positional cloning and linkage analysis, which are then followed by mutation analysis. Positional cloning entails sequencing potential genes in the region and combines transcription and physical mapping, whereas linkage analysis determines the sensitive chromosomal interval.

Genetic disorders are classified as either single-gene disorders or complex, multifactorial diseases influenced by environmental, lifestyle, and genetic variables. Gene

M. Paprzycki et al. (Eds.): ICACIS 2024, CCIS 2405, pp. 198–210, 2027.
https://doi.org/10.1007/978-3-032-30990-7_15

mutations that result in a variety of clinical symptoms are the source of single-gene diseases. Despite differences in treatment approaches, they are biologically comparable and require similar genetic counseling, risk assessment, and access to management resources.

Mutations in nonnuclear mitochondrial DNA generate mitochondrial genetic disorders, which are only passed down from mothers. These illnesses include lactic acidosis, stroke-like episodes, mitochondrial encephalopathy, and ophthalmic problems [2]. Polygenic or complex disorders are another name for multifactorial genetic diseases, which result from mutations in several genes and are impacted by environmental and dietary variables. Examples of these conditions are diabetes, cancer, and Alzheimer's.

Deep learning has become a viable approach to genetic prediction by taking advantage of advances in statistical genetics, large data sets, and processing power. These methods are useful for studying complicated genetic illnesses because they can find interactions across loci and handle large dimensions without assuming additivity.

Genetic disorders affect people of all demographics and range from single gene defects to complicated combinations of genetic, environmental, and lifestyle variables. For management and intervention to be effective, early detection and precise diagnosis are essential. Previously, the identification of disease genes involved laborious techniques such as positional cloning and linkage analysis, which were subsequently followed by mutation analysis.

Genetic prediction has undergone a revolutionary change, nevertheless, thanks to advances in deep learning and machine learning. An effective method for evaluating sequential genetic data is to use deep learning models, such as Long Short-Term Memory (LSTM) networks. In contrast to other approaches, long-term dependencies in genetic sequences are well captured by LSTM networks, allowing precise prediction of a wide range of genetic illnesses. LSTM models can help physicians with early identification and intervention by extracting relevant patterns and producing dependable predictions through training on carefully selected datasets. Furthermore, the complexity of genetic illnesses and their intricate relationships across loci are particularly significant insights that deep learning may provide due to its capacity to manage complex genetic data. Thus, deep learning techniques have the potential to improve patient outcomes and advance genetic diagnostics in the field of genetic disorders.

2 Related Work

N. Brandes et.al in their work Genome-wide prediction of disease variant effects with a deep protein language model [3] looked into how well a deep protein language model might be used to predict the impact of disease variants on a broad scale. The project concentrated on ESM 1b; a potent model trained on enormous amounts of protein sequence data. To examine genetic changes throughout the human genome and forecast their effects on protein function, the researchers modified ESM 1b. This could fundamentally alter our knowledge of the role that mutations play in disease development. The study probably describes how well the model performs in comparison to current techniques and emphasizes how it can analyze every potential missense variant, surpassing the constraints of earlier methods.

In Accurate proteome-wide missense variant effect prediction with AlphaMissense J. Cheng et al., [4] proposed AlphaMissense, a deep learning model specifically designed to forecast the impact of missense variants—those involving single amino acid changes—across the entirety of human proteins [5]. Utilizing AlphaFold, an advanced protein structure prediction system, the model is finely tuned through integration with human and primate variant population frequency databases. This unique approach enables AlphaMissense to not only assess alterations in amino acid sequence but also consider potential structural modifications induced by the mutation. The researchers assessed AlphaMissense's performance against clinical benchmarks before utilizing it to gauge the pathogenicity, or disease-causing potential, of all conceivable missense variants within the human proteome. This extensive dataset of predictions provides invaluable insights into the potential repercussions of genetic variations on protein function and human health.

Atta-Ur-Rahman et al., in Advance Genome Disorder Prediction Model Empowered With Deep Learning [6] proposed a deep learning model, termed the Advanced Genome Disorder Prediction Model (AGDPM), designed to predict a range of genetic disorders. AGDPM addresses a critical challenge in genetic analysis by efficiently processing vast amounts of intricate genetic data to forecast diverse disorder categories. In contrast to prior approaches relying on specific gene sequences, AGDPM employs a deep learning architecture to analyze broader genetic information comprehensively. The researchers focus on convolutional neural networks (CNNs) as the underlying model type and customize its design for this purpose. AGDPM undergoes training on a meticulously curated dataset of genetic data stratified into various disorder types, followed by an evaluation of its efficacy in accurately predicting these categories. The findings indicate promising performance by AGDPM, underscoring its potential as an asset in genetic analysis and potentially enhancing our ability to identify individuals at risk for a spectrum of genetic disorders.

In Predicting Genetic Disorder and Types of Disorder Using Chain Classifier Approach A.Raza et al [7] have presented a novel method for predicting genetic disorders and their specific types, addressing the challenge of multi-label, multi-class issues where a single gene may be associated with multiple disorders. To overcome this challenge, the researchers propose a "chain classifier" approach, wherein multiple classifiers collaborate sequentially, with each leveraging predictions from preceding classifiers. Moreover, the study introduces a unique feature engineering strategy wherein probabilities from other machine learning models serve as additional features for the chain classifier. This enables the final classifier to make more informed predictions about the presence and types of genetic disorders by integrating knowledge from the entire chain. The findings demonstrate that this approach, particularly when employing Extreme Gradient Boosting (XGBoost) within the chain, yields promising results for accurate and specific prediction of genetic disorders.

K. Yang et al., in HerGePred: Heterogeneous Network Embedding Representation for Disease Gene Prediction [8] proposes a new method called HerGePred for predicting disease-associated genes. HerGePred utilizes a heterogeneous network embedding approach that incorporates biological knowledge from multiple sources, including protein-protein interactions, gene-disease associations, and gene ontology annotations.

This allows HerGePred to capture complex relationships between genes and diseases that may not be evident from any single source of data. The authors evaluated HerGePred on a benchmark dataset and showed that it achieved superior performance compared to existing methods.

Borja Calvo et al., in A partially supervised classification approach to dominant and recessive human disease gene prediction [9] presents a partially supervised classification approach for predicting dominant and recessive human disease genes. The authors propose a method that leverages both labeled and unlabeled data to improve the accuracy of gene prediction. Their approach utilizes a support vector machine (SVM) classifier to classify genes as disease-causing or not. The SVM is trained on a dataset of known disease genes, as well as a larger set of unlabeled genes. The unlabeled genes are used to learn the general properties of genes that are not associated with disease. The authors evaluated their method on a dataset of human disease genes and showed that it achieved promising results.

These works demonstrate the potential of deep learning techniques for genetic disorder prediction. However, there are still some challenges and limitations that need to be addressed, such as the quality and diversity of the data, the interpretability and explanation ability of the models, the privacy and security of the patient's data, and the integration and deployment of the models in clinical settings

3 Methodology

3.1 Proposed Flow

Data Acquisition. Gather a comprehensive genetic disorder dataset, ensuring it includes a diverse range of cases, including single gene inheritance disorder, mitochondrial inheritance disorder, and multifactorial inheritance disorder.

Preprocessing. The phase data is processed using multiple methods to remove anomalies and add missing values. Regression techniques are utilized on the preprocessed data to derive top-ranking features to predict genomic disorders once outliers have been eliminated. The data is separated into training and testing blocks for additional analysis after feature extraction.

Deep Learning Model. The LSTM model, specialized for sequential data analysis, holds promise for genetic disorder prediction. Its ability to capture long-term dependencies enables accurate predictions, offering valuable insights into genetic conditions and enhancing diagnostic capabilities in healthcare.

3.2 Dataset

The genome disorders dataset is from Kaggle which has open access for everyone. Genome disorder data contains 22083 patients' history of single-gene inheritance disorder, mitochondrial gene inheritance disorder, and multifactorial gene inheritance disorder. This data consists of three classes, 43 independent variables and 1 is the dependent variable. So, we applied several outliers, regression, and normalization techniques to get the best features. Table 1 describes the features of the genome disorder prediction dataset.

Table 1. Attributes in the genome dataset.

Si. No	Features
1	Patient Age
2	Genes in mother
3	Inherited from father
4	Maternal gene
5	Paternal gene
6	Status
7	Respiratory Rate
8	Heart Rate
9	Follow-up
10	Gender
11	Birth asphyxia
12	Autopsy birth defect
13	Folic acid
14	H/O serious maternal illness
15	H/O radiation exposure (x-ray)
16	H/O substance abuse
17	Assisted conception
18	History of anomalies in previous pregnancies
19	No. of abortion
20	Birth defects
21	Blood test result
22	Symptom 1
23	Symptom 2
24	Symptom 3

3.3 System Methodology

Methodology. The chapter's goal is to use the LSTM (Long Short-Term Memory) deep learning model to forecast genetic abnormalities. The LSTM architecture is well known for its specialized design, which includes memory cells that are essential for genetic data analysis since they can retain information over extended sequences. We downloaded our dataset, which included genetic information relevant to several illnesses, from the Kaggle website. To aid in model training, the LSTM method is then applied to the training dataset.

The unique design of the LSTM deep learning model is adapted to the intricacies of genetic illness prediction. It is the best option for efficiently analysing genetic data because of its capacity to identify long-term connections within sequential data.

The genetic data is pre-processed, including resizing, augmentation, and other essential operations to achieve optimal performance, before the model is trained.

To improve the LSTM model's resilience and efficiency, custom batch sizes are used in both the training and testing stages. The trained model is also scalable, meaning it can handle genetic datasets of various sizes.

System Architecture. The system architecture, as depicted in Fig. 1, is delineated within this section. It comprises a well-defined pipeline that encompasses dataset acquisition, data pre-processing, LSTM model defining and training, model evaluation, and the ultimate classification of genetic disorders into respective classes. In any deep learning project, the primary step involves procuring an appropriate dataset. In our case, this dataset encompasses patients' details encompassing a variety of fields. We source this data from the online repository Kaggle. Once the dataset is assembled, data pre-processing is executed.

The foundation of any deep learning model lies in the quality of the training data. Exploratory data analysis was conducted to gain insights into the distribution and characteristics of the training data, enabling informed decisions regarding data preprocessing and augmentation. The column titles were changed for better understating. Then the null values and outliers are removed. Finally, the columns were encoded using one hot encoder to facilitate uniform processing by the neural network. Finally, the training data was split into training and test subsets, ensuring a rigorous evaluation of the model's performance on unseen data.

Once the model is trained on a large dataset of genome data, it can be used to classify for new input. To predict a new input, it is first pre-processed to ensure that it is in the same format as the training data. The pre-processed input is then fed into the trained model, which outputs the genetic disorder class.

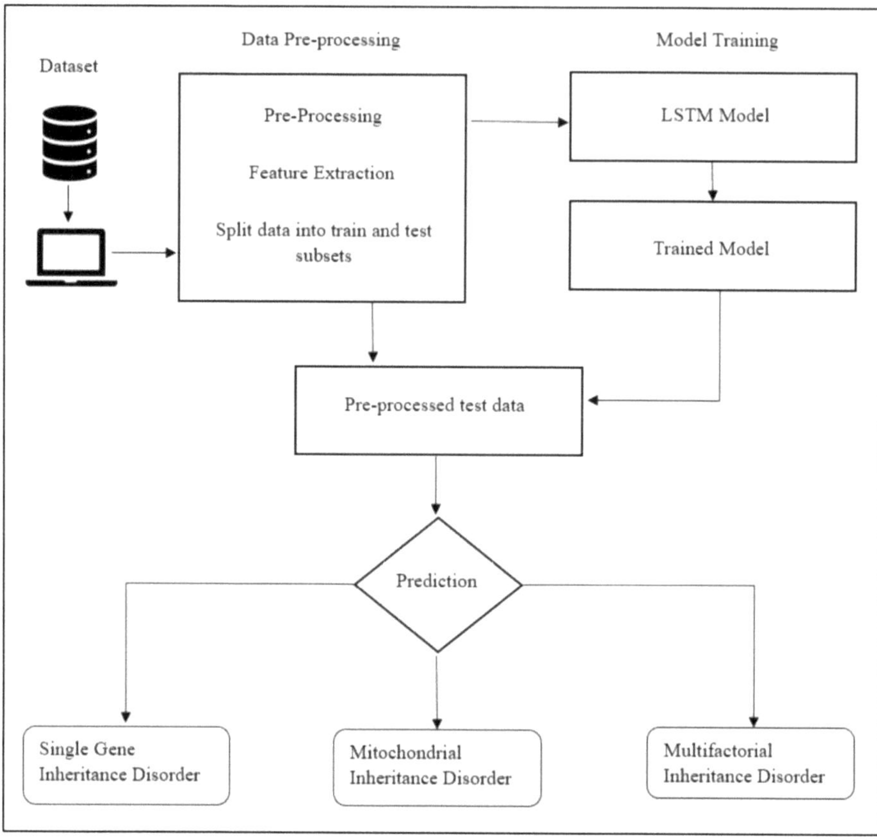

Fig. 1. System Architecture

LSTM Model. The LSTM (Long Short-Term Memory) model is a specialized class of recurrent neural networks (RNNs) that excels at capturing temporal dependencies in sequential data, making it particularly suitable for time series prediction tasks such as genetic disorder prediction [10].

In our context, we have chosen the LSTM model shown in Fig 2 as the foundation of our deep learning system for genetic disorder prediction. This choice stems from the LSTM's inherent ability to analyse sequential data, such as genetic sequences, and identify intricate patterns and dependencies within them. Genetic data often exhibits complex temporal relationships, and the LSTM's architecture, which includes memory cells capable of retaining information over long sequences, is well-suited to capture such dynamics.

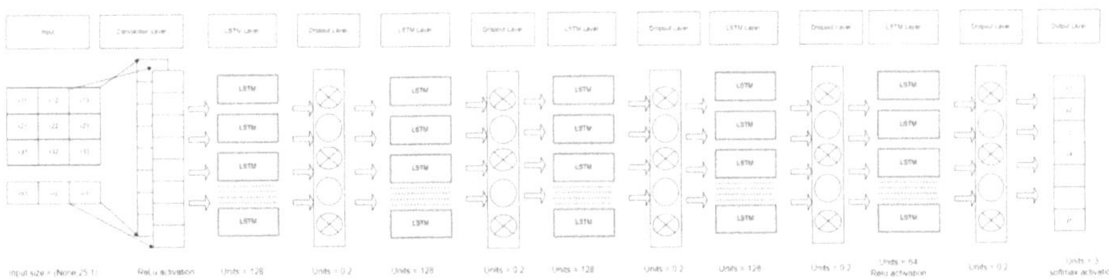

Fig. 2. Model Architecture

One significant advantage of using LSTM models for genetic disorder prediction is their adaptability to handle variable-length sequences. Genetic sequences can vary greatly in length, and traditional machine-learning models may struggle to effectively process them. However, LSTM networks, with their ability to maintain context information over time, can effectively handle sequences of varying lengths without the need for padding or truncation.

The workflow for training an LSTM model for genetic disorder prediction involves leveraging a dataset containing the patient details, along with any augmented data generated during preprocessing. During the training process, the LSTM model learns to discern patterns and dependencies within the genetic data, enabling it to make accurate predictions about the likelihood of genetic disorders based on input sequences.

Once trained, the LSTM model can be utilized to classify new genetic sequences. As a sequence is fed into the model, it undergoes a series of computations through the LSTM layers, culminating in a prediction regarding the presence or likelihood of a genetic disorder. This prediction is made based on the model's learned understanding of the relationships between genetic features and the manifestation of disorders.

Overall, the LSTM model serves as a powerful tool for genetic disorder prediction, enabling accurate classification of genetic sequences and facilitating early detection and intervention in clinical settings. Its ability to handle sequential data and capture temporal dependencies makes it an indispensable component of machine-learning systems aimed at genetic analysis and diagnosis.

4 Results

In this section, we explore the complexities of result generation and analysis, focusing on a class of genetic disorders from the medical report data.

Input and image analysis: Users provide medical test reports of genetics as input to start the process. This data goes through a thorough analysis process that includes preprocessing to make sure they are the right size and format for the model.

LSTM Model Inference: The LSTM model is used after the input data is ready. These previously trained model examines the input data and makes predictions based on their knowledge and training after learning to identify genetic patterns.

Genetic Disorder Prediction: This is the most important step in the analysis and result phase. The results of the input show users which type of genetic defect is present. The outcome of a trial test run with the trained LSTM model will be one of the 3 classes, they are 1. Single gene inheritance disorder, 2. Mitochondrial inheritance disorder or 3. Multifactorial inheritance disorder. The input is sent over the interface using the LSTM model, after which the necessary features are extracted. The model then makes a class prediction and assigns the class along with the final classification or forecast, giving users a thorough overview of the results.

The graphical representation in Figs. 3 and 4 sheds light on how training and validation loss and accuracy change over time in a dynamic manner. This visualization highlights the epoch where the loss is minimized and accuracy is maximized, demonstrating the ideal point in the training process, in addition to showing the convergence of the model over time.

Fig. 3. Training and Validation Accuracy

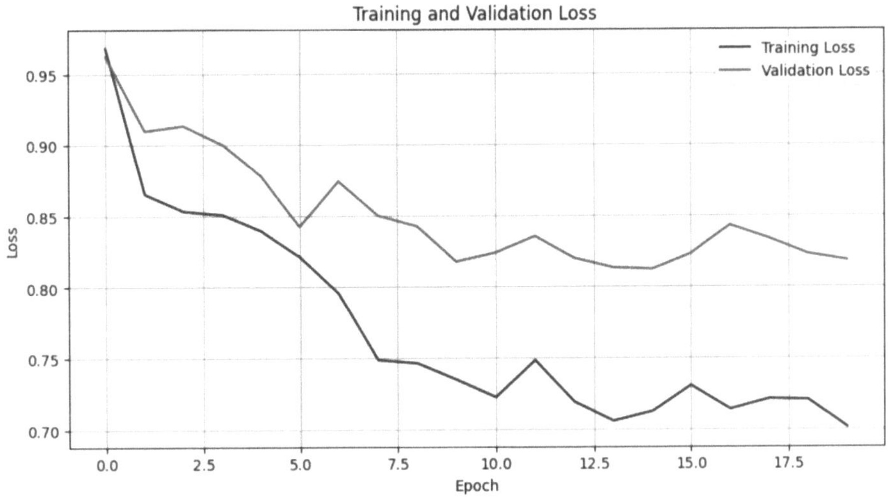

Fig. 4. Training and Validation Loss

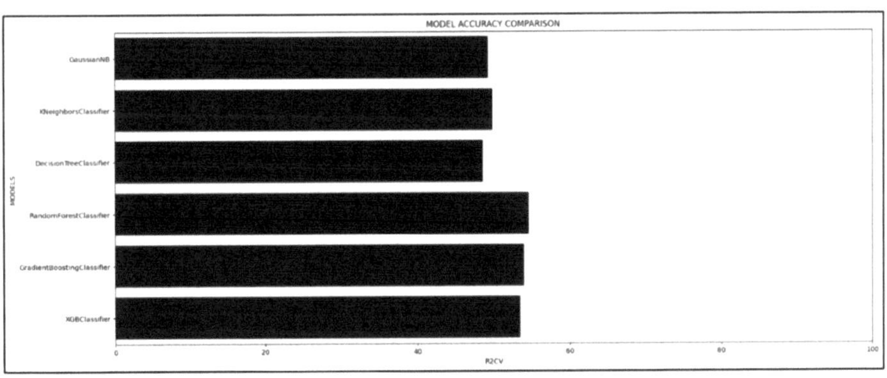

Fig. 5. Model accuracy comparison

Table 2. Average metric results for the LSTM model

Metric	Value
Training Accuracy	0.6315
Training Loss	0.7708
Validation Accuracy	0.5684
Validation Loss	0.8517

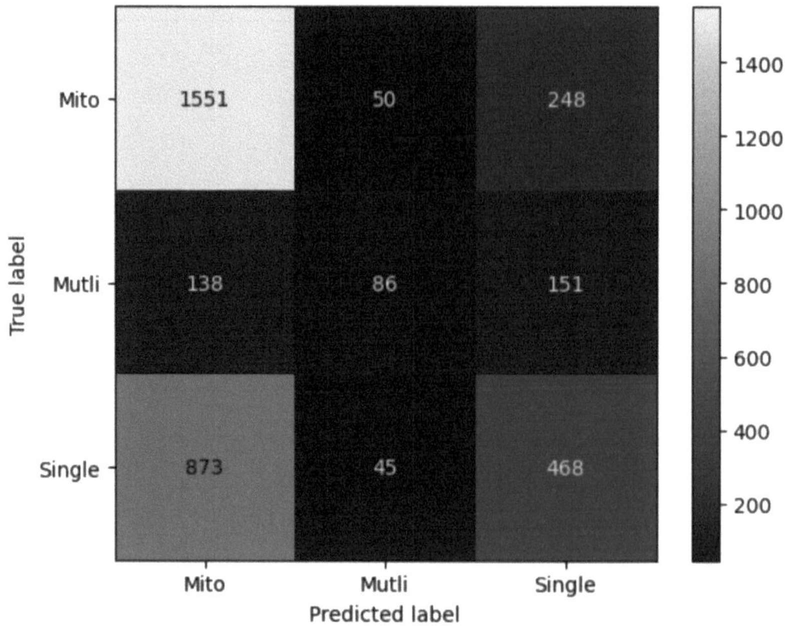

Fig. 6. Confusion Matrix

Table 3. Classification Report

Class	Precision	Recall	F1-score
Mitochondrial	0.61	0.84	0.70
Multifactorial	0.48	0.23	0.31
Single gene	0.54	0.34	0.42
Macro avg	0.54	0.47	0.48
Weighted avg	0.57	0.58	0.55
Accuracy	0.58	0.58	0.58

5 Discussions and Conclusion

From the previous section, we can conclude that while compared to the various machine learning approaches (Fig 5) LSTM model performed better as seen in Table 2. Figure 6 represents the confusion matrix for the training of the model for 20 epochs while Table 3 provides the classification report.

The classification report presents an evaluation of a model's performance in distinguishing between three types of genetic disorders: mitochondrial inheritance disorders (class 0), multifactorial inheritance disorders (class 1), and single-gene inheritance disorders (class 2). Across these classes, varying levels of precision, recall, and F1-score are observed. For single-gene inheritance disorders (class 0), the model achieves a moderate precision of 0.61 and a relatively high recall of 0.84, resulting in an F1 score of 0.70. Conversely, for mitochondrial inheritance disorders (class 1), precision and recall are notably lower at 0.48 and 0.23, respectively, leading to a lower F1 score of 0.31. Meanwhile, multifactorial inheritance disorders (class 2) demonstrate a precision of 0.54 and recall of 0.34, with an F1-score of 0.42. The macro and weighted averages provide an overall assessment, with macro average precision, recall, and F1-score at 0.54, 0.47, and 0.48, respectively, and weighted average precision, recall, and F1-score at 0.57, 0.58, and 0.55, respectively. The model achieves an accuracy of 0.58, indicating its ability to correctly predict the classification of genetic disorders for 58% of instances.

In conclusion, the proposed deep learning models for genetic disorder prediction show promising results in enhancing our understanding of genetic conditions and improving diagnostic accuracy. The integration of the LSTM network approach presents a multifaceted approach to addressing the complexity of genetic disorders, offering valuable insights into disease mechanisms and potential interventions.

However, challenges and limitations persist, such as data quality, interpretability of models, patient data privacy, and clinical deployment. Future research should focus on addressing these issues to ensure the reliability and usability of deep learning models in clinical settings.

Looking ahead, enhancements in deep learning techniques could further refine genetic disorder prediction models. Transfer learning approaches could be explored to leverage pre-existing knowledge from large-scale genetic datasets, thereby improving model generalizability and performance on smaller datasets. Additionally, attention mechanisms could be incorporated to enhance the focus on relevant genetic features, leading to more accurate predictions.

Overall, deep learning presents a promising avenue for advancing genetic diagnostics and improving patient outcomes in the field of genetic disorders. Continued research and development efforts are crucial to overcoming existing challenges and maximizing the potential of these innovative approaches in clinical practice.

Acknowledgments. We would like to express our gratitude to our guide and co-author, Dr. S. Karthick, for his valuable insights, as well as to the anonymous reviewers whose comments have greatly benefited this chapter.

References

1. Wang, X., Gulbahce, N., Yu, H.: Network-based methods for human disease gene prediction. Brief. Funct. Genom. **10**(5), 280–293 (2011). https://doi.org/10.1093/bfgp/elr024
2. Yang, P., Li, X.-L., Mei, J.-P., Kwoh, C.-K., Ng, S.-K.: Positive-unlabeled learning for disease gene identification. Bioinformatics. **28**(20), 2640–2647 (2012). https://doi.org/10.1093/bioinformatics/bts504
3. Brandes, N., Goldman, G., Wang, C.H., et al.: Genome-wide prediction of disease variant effects with a deep protein language model. Nat. Genet. **55**, 1512–1522 (2023). https://doi.org/10.1038/s41588-023-01465-0

4. Cheng, J., et al.: Accurate proteome-wide missense variant effect prediction with AlphaMissense. Science. **381**, eadg7492 (2023). https://doi.org/10.1126/science.adg7492
5. Luo, P., Li, Y., Tian, L.-P., Wu, F.-X.: Enhancing the prediction of disease-gene associations with multimodal deep learning. Bioinformatics. **35**(19), 3735–3742 (2019). https://doi.org/10.1093/bioinformatics/btz155
6. Atta-Ur-Rahman, et al.: Advance Genome Disorder Prediction Model Empowered With Deep Learning. IEEE Access. **10**, 70317–70328 (2022). https://doi.org/10.1109/ACCESS.2022.3186998
7. Raza, A., et al.: Predicting genetic disorder and types of disorder using chain classifier approach. Genes. **14**(1), 71 (2022). https://doi.org/10.3390/genes14010071
8. Yang, K., et al.: HerGePred: Heterogeneous network embedding representation for disease gene prediction. IEEE J. Biomed. Health Inform. **23**(4), 1805–1815 (2019). https://doi.org/10.1109/JBHI.2018.2870728
9. Calvo, B., López-Bigas, N., Furney, S.J., Larrañaga, P., Lozano, J.A.: A partially supervised classification approach to dominant and recessive human disease gene prediction. Comput. Methods Programs Biomed. **85**(3), 229–237. https://doi.org/10.1016/j.cmpb.2006.12.003
10. Men, L., Ilk, N., Tang, X., Liu, Y.: Multi-disease prediction using LSTM recurrent neural networks. Expert Syst. Appl. **177**, 114905. https://doi.org/10.1016/j.eswa.2021.114905

Enhancing Startup Success: Leveraging Machine Learning for Business Category Recommendation

Shashank Kumar, Pratik Jadon(✉), Lakshya Sharma, and Namita Sharma

Sharda University, Greater Noida, India
pratiking0@gmail.com, 2020544570.lakshya@ug.sharda.ac.in,
namita.sharma@sharda.ac.in

Abstract. Today recommendation systems in business are at the core of the personalization process for the mutual good of startups. This chapter introduces a cutting-edge system based on NLP and machine learning that uses NLP and machine-learning algorithms to provide the recommendations platform. Its foremost goal is to help businesses understand who can supply them with financially and the order in which this should take place. It examines one of the most important problems faced by startups that is finding the right investors. How to do it better and more efficiently, using the Word2Vec model for NLP by Google. The viable method to use the two given text input and grasp the meaning of their business is to convert user prompts into tokens and vectors, after which the mentions of individual business categories are notated and their similarities calculated. In addition, it also explains details the implementation of three machine learning models - Artificial Neural Networks (ANN), K-Nearest Neighbors (KNN), and Support Vector Machines (SVM) for precise recommendation models. Through rigorous evaluation and comparison, the ANN manifests as the optimal solution from the multiplicity of alert systems revealing the highest predictive accuracy magnets for investor engagement and business growth. Our business recommendation and investor engagement platform are deservingly called a solid tool for all those businesses who desire to improve investor engagement tactics and create economic growth in the market place.

Keywords: Recommendation systems · Natural Language Processing (NLP) · Machine Learning · Word2Vec embedding · Cosine similarity · Artificial Neural Networks (ANN) · K-Nearest Neighbors (KNN) · Support Vector Machines (SVM)

1 Introduction

Among modern business and firms, recommender systems become even more relevant and favored due to their powerful ability to adapt to new business trends, provide insightful information in various business domains and give tailored recommendations for these domains. These recommendation systems are, in fact, a useful tool for smart businesses

M. Paprzycki et al. (Eds.): ICACIS 2024, CCIS 2405, pp. 211–224, 2027.
https://doi.org/10.1007/978-3-032-30990-7_16

looking to profit from tailored recommendations made just for their current clientele. These suggestions aid in attracting customers and fostering the expansion of the business. In today's commercial market, big business firms utilize various machine learning and other advanced techniques like natural language processing (NLP) [1] and analytics to develop very potent tool that is utilized for decision-making, and consumer interactions based on their interest.

This chapter provides a thorough discussion of a recommendation system designed to solve the particular difficulties businesses encounter in finding and communicating with potential investors [2] in an easy and efficient manner. This project aims to create a robust recommendation system. Which utilizes the modern cutting-edge techniques such as natural language processing techniques (NLP) and machine learning to generate recommendation that are highly personalized as per the businesses, users so that they are in line with each user's unique needs and preferences.

The study starts with a review of the literature to examine the current state of research in recommendation systems. Through utilization of various information sources such as industry reports, academic papers and conference proceedings in the survey, a solid basis is created for comprehending the latest main trends and the areas of interest. innovation inside the field of recommendation.

Following the literature survey, a detailed explanation of the methodology which is utilized in creating this robust recommendation system is presented in the chapter. This methodology is divided into many different steps that begins with the extraction of the user prompts for their business requirements. These user prompts are very essential for further processes as they are a solid base for generating personalized recommendation. Various robust text processing techniques are performed on these extracted text prompts including tokenization and Word2Vec embeddings [3], These techniques help to transforms the prompt into a format which is machine understandable and suitable for analysis. Then a similarity score is calculated known as cosine similarity for identifying the optimal matching category for the given prompt and recommendation.

After the prompt is processed and a category is calculated, the next stages start which is known as data preparation. With the help of one-hot encoding technique, all the categorial information is converted to the numerical format. This conversion is an essential step as it clarifies the dataset for training as well as it ensures that the machine learning algorithms can comprehend user inputs with ease. This converted data is then utilized to train three different models, Artificial Neural Network (ANN), Support Vector Machine (SVM) [4], and K-Nearest Neighours (KNN) [5], to predict the possible investors to the user based on their prompts and encoded data.

This chapter concludes with the overall assessment of the recommendation system's effectiveness. To perform this evaluation many different metrics are utilized such as accuracy, precision and recall. After thorough training and testing, performance and efficacy of each model is evaluated based on these metrices. The results focus on providing the insights on the model's capabilities to produce appropriate recommendation as per the user requests and depicting the most optimal and efficient model for our recommendation system.

2 Literature Survey

Recommendation systems constitute a core factor in the contemporary business landscapes, they allow the companies to treat their clients or other stakeholders in a targeted and precise way. These bits of hardware use the power of machine learning algorithms, natural language processing and data analytics to understand users' habits, reactions and circumstances. Being founded on data-driven insight, recommendation systems permit companies to personalize suggestions, increasing user involvement and boosting corporate progress.

This literature review aims at overviewing and clarifying different approaches, methodologies and outcomes of other recent studies in this field. This review builds upon the integration of information from various sources such as academic papers, conference proceedings and industry reports, to lay a stable ground for such knowledge by addressing the current state of research development, important trends, and innovations and advancements in the domain of recommendation systems for business applications.

Pereira et al. [6], proposed a recommender system designed to optimize the accuracy of recommendations has been improved through the integrated use of the collaborative filtering and demographic filtering techniques. It will overcome drawbacks by a hybrid process which combines both interpersonal and digital exchange. Evaluation of the performance is done by precision level, recall level, and ROC curve analysis.

Lian et al. [7] suggested using two R-Transformer model to track users' state of equity and cash flow as they as change in the course of time. Generating the computed inner product between these states, we come up with the final score. It shows the most effective approach that beats collaborative filtering and RNN methods, which brings RMSE value lower and increments the F-measure to a much higher level.

Asemi et al. [8] proposed an investment recommender system with stroke neuro-fuzzy layer. It considers some of the most important decision-making processes, offers suggestions regarding the types of investments, deals with a fractional data, and implements other experts' standpoints. The system validated for reliability and correctness; it is reported to be more efficient than existing methods.

Takayanagi et al. [9] introduced a dynamic hybrid recommender system model PDRSI that incorporates the wishes of investors and the trend of the market from social networks and market data with simulations. The treatment to the consumed dataset would follow Twitter policy for the future research.

Hu et al. [10] proposed the optimization of a possible computational algorithm to investigate investment tourists' preferences in search of an appropriate financial item for representation. They took a different way in approaching the question of why some products are selected together and in order to verify their method they applied it to noisy data collected from an online financial platform revealing their improved steering mechanics in missing data compared to existing approaches (Table 1).

Table 1. Recent Advances in the area of Recommendation System

Author Name	Year	Methodology	Result
Kapoor et al. [11]	2020	Utilized SVM for sentiment analysis of user movie reviews, updating movie ratings based on sentiments.	Achieved 85% accuracy with SVM model for sentiment analysis, enhancing movie ratings based on user reviews.
Cai et al. [12]	2020	KD-KNN-LR algorithm combines KD-KNN and Logistic Regression for marriage recommendation. KD-KNN optimizes KNN with KD-Tree for efficient neighbor search.	KD-KNN-LR achieves 86% accuracy in recommending marriage candidates.
V. Malik et al. [13]	2022	EPR-ML utilized NLP and ML algorithms for e-commerce product recommendation. Features are extracted via LR, and LSVM.	LSVM achieves a maximum accuracy of 96% in predicting the trending duration of videos.
Kumar et al. [14]	2022	Recommendation model employs NLP for data processing and feature extraction, followed by transformer subsystem for prescription generation.	Model displayed an accuracy, ranging from 70% to 75%, outperforming other existing algorithms.
Brintha et at. [15]	2022	Food recognition using transfer learning with VGG16; diabetes prediction with a three-dense layer ANN; food tracking system with home and add food items functionality.	Food recognition achieved 96% accuracy; diabetes prediction achieved 83% accuracy; efficient food tracking system implemented.
Picado et al. [16]	2022	Proposed a recommendation system for MOOCs based on a hybrid architecture, integrating collaborative filtering and content-based approaches.	Validated the system across multiple MOOCs, utilizing student interaction logs and learning resource descriptions to provide personalized recommendations and enhance learner engagement.
Dixit et al. [17]	2023	The movie recommendation chatbot utilizes cosine similarity and NLP to provide personalized recommendations based on user inputs.	Achieved accuracy rates of 80-92.5% using various recommendation techniques, enhancing user experience and diversity.

3 Methodology's

This project focuses on to develop a modern recommendation system which provides businesses the power to easily identify and engage with suitable investors for the growth of their business. Through the fusion of advanced natural language processing (NLP) methodologies and machine learning algorithms, this system endeavors to deliver highly customized suggestions, ensuring alignment with the diverse requirements and preferences of each user.

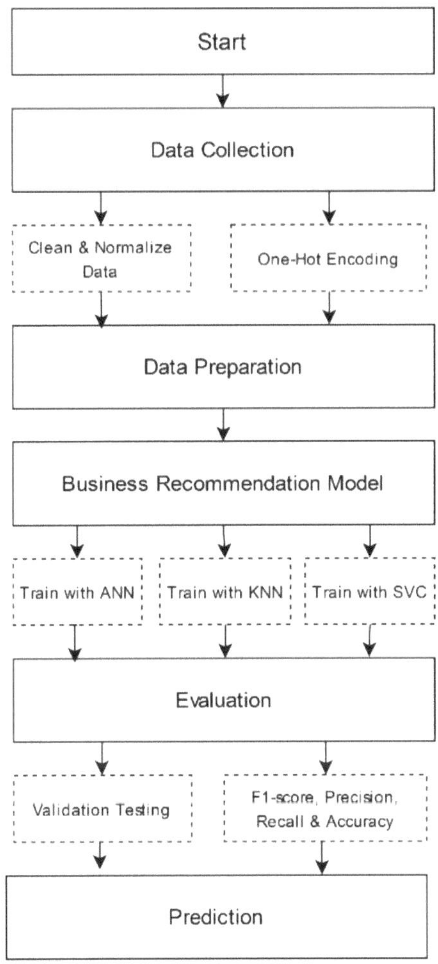

Fig. 1. Methodology Flowchart

Below is the detailed explanation of the steps shown in Fig. 1.

Data Collection. In this stage, relevant data pertaining to businesses and investors is gathered from various sources, serving as the foundation for subsequent analysis and model training.

Data Preparation. In this phase, we carefully filter out any noise from the data that has been gathered. We also carry out necessary operations, such as one-hot encoding, to translate category, location and various other features into numerical representations so that they are compatible with later model training procedures.

Business Recommendation Model. The core of the methodology lies in the application of machine learning models – Artificial Neural Networks (ANN), k-Nearest Neighbors (KNN), and Support Vector Machines (SVM) to learn patterns and make predictions based on the prepared data.

Evaluation. After the models are trained under different datasets, various evaluation metrics of the models are generated such as F1 score, recall, and precision. These metrics assists in evaluation and understanding of the performance of the recommendation model and ensure its effectiveness in providing accurate investor recommendations.

4 Proposed Model

In this proposed model, we will examine the detailed explanation of the techniques that we used to recommend investors based on our user input and business data. To achieve such recommendation, we utilized advanced algorithms such as, Artificial Neural Networks (ANN), K-Nearest neighbors (KNN), and Support Vector Machine (SVM), to generate useful and insightful recommendations. For fine-tuning our model, we have used various evaluation metrics such as F1-score, recall and precision to introspect the overall performance of the models. By utilizing such techniques, we can ensure our recommendation systems robustness and reliability. For the dataset we have utilized the Indian Startup dataset.

Data Used. In our study, data we utilized a dataset consisting of 3044 rows and 10 columns incorporating some cells with missing data in having NaN value in them. Additionally, it replete with the diverse features, including many investors who cater to startup company initiations and spanning the wide range of businesses classes. These variations of businesses make the dataset richer, which could result in expansive analysis points and recommendation generations.

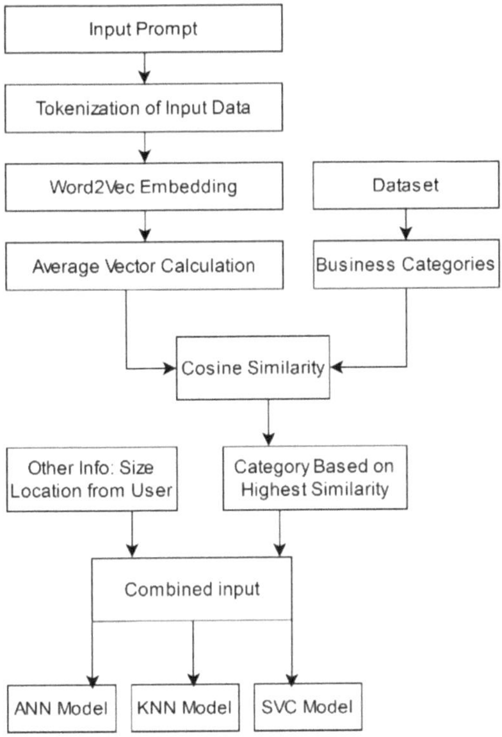

Fig. 2. Flowchart of proposed model

Below is the detail explanation of the proposed model shown in the Fig. 2.

Taking User Input. User input covered two main parameters: business prompts and other extra information such as business size and location. These inputs undergo distinct processing methods: textual prompts are subjected to text processing techniques, while other information is transformed into numerical feature representations. These processed inputs collectively form the foundation for generating personalized recommendations, finely tuned to meet the unique requirements of each user.

Prompt Text Processing and Similarity Calculation. Text processing function enables transformation of user prompts into numerical form for further processing. This technique includes word tokenization and Word2Vec embedding so that prompts semantics can be interpreted by ML algorithms. Then the Cosine Similarity utilizes processed text and correctly aligns the user prompts with the appropriate business categories. Based on these categories users are given personalized recommendations.

- *Tokenization.* The user prompts are segmented into individual words, permitting the process of further breakdowns.
- *Word2Vec Embeddings.* Each particular word is substituted into a numerical equivalent through the Word2Vec embedding in order to develop semantic conception.

- *Cosine Similarity Calculation.* The system calculates cosine similarity between a vector representing user prompts and a vector which represents pre-defined business categories.
- *Category Alignment.* The system makes use of cosine similarity to find out the business category that closely resembles the one that is stated by the user and offers customized suggestions to them.

Combined Input. In data preparation step, we combine business category generated from cosine similarity over user prompt, with additional information's provided by the user such as business location, size etc... We then use one-hot encoding to encode categorical variables, such as business categories and locations, into a numerical format. For each category, binary variables must be created; each variable must represent a distinct category. For example, three binary variables are created if there are three categories (e.g., Technology, Finance, Healthcare). The corresponding binary variable is set to 1 and the others to 0 if a business is classified as Technology. In order to allow machine learning algorithms to properly learn from the data during model training, this transformation guarantees compatibility with those algorithms.

Model and Accuracy. Multiple machine learning models were utilized for training on the ready dataset- KNN model, SVM model, and ANN model were specifically used. All the models were trained intensively to let them recognize these complicated connections and correlations contained in the information so that their investors recommendations could be as accurate as possible. As the models completed their training, each one went under detailed verification, and objective was assessing accuracy, precision, and recall. Through a rigorous evaluation process, we were able to determine which model produced the most accurate and trustworthy recommendations in response to the user's prompt. Through a comparative analysis of these models' performances, our goal was to identify the best option that would satisfy the particular demands of this recommendation system.

Brief descriptions of the prior mentioned algorithms are provided here, along with the training and validation accuracies that each model underwent. This description allows us to take a quick glimpse of the performance and properties of the algorithms, thus helping us to understanding the effectiveness and applicability of each algorithm to the task.

Artificial Neural Network. It welled forth from the architecture of the human brain. Artificial Neural network (ANN), which is a subgroup of machine learning algorithms, is based on neural networks of the human brain. These networks models consist of the interconnections between nodes or neurons which are arranged in a layer. The layered architecture represents the greatest advantage of ANN, due to the ability of the networks to accurately determine the complex patterns and correlations within the data. On this basis, ANN is best suitable for classification and regression tasks.

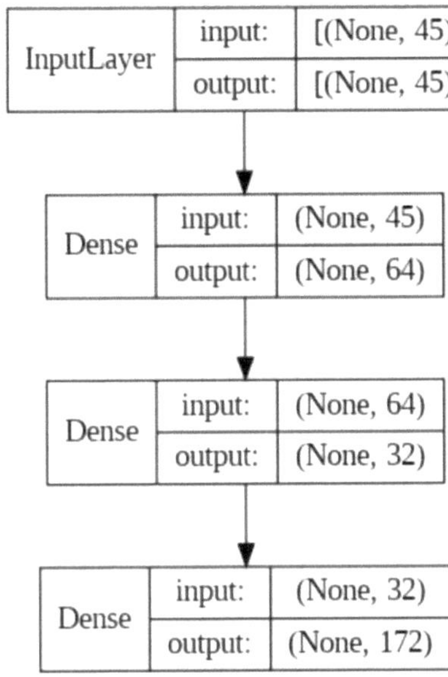

Fig. 3. Architecture diagram of ANN model used

The Fig. 3. illustrates the way the layers in the Artificial Neural Network model are organized sequentially. The network consists of layers with ReLU activation functions that are densely coupled, leading to an output layer having SoftMax activation. This designed structure allows the model to easily understand and learn the complex patterns and structures inside the data and produce accurate predictions.

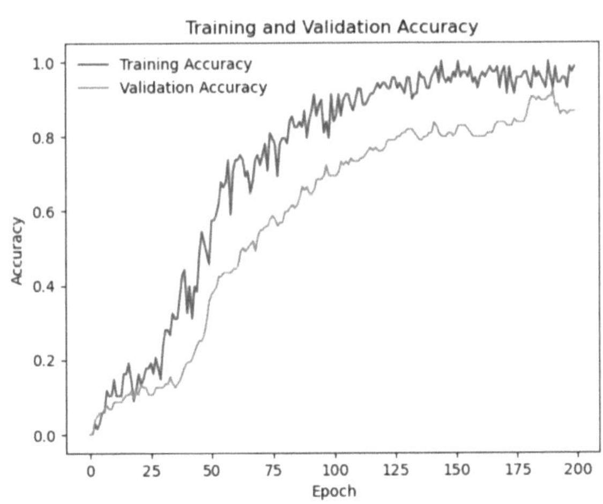

Fig. 4. Training and Validation Accuracy of ANN model

The Fig. 4. Illustrates that our ANN model has performed exceptionally good as its accuracy has remained continuously above 90%. Model's accuracy shows us that our model was flexible and was able to adapt to the training data. Though it's validation accuracy slightly lags behind with validation accuracy being around 85%. Overall, it suggests our model's good performance, generalization and potential to accurately predict upon the unseen data.

K-Nearest Neighbour. K-Nearest Neighbors (KNN) is relatively very simple and straight-forward technique and is used in both areas of classification and regression. KNN uses a terminology called closeness, where the prediction or classification is done and affected by the K-Nearby points to the new data point to be classified. KNN follows an intuitive approach but it serves and performs well and is very flexible to adapt to diverse datasets.

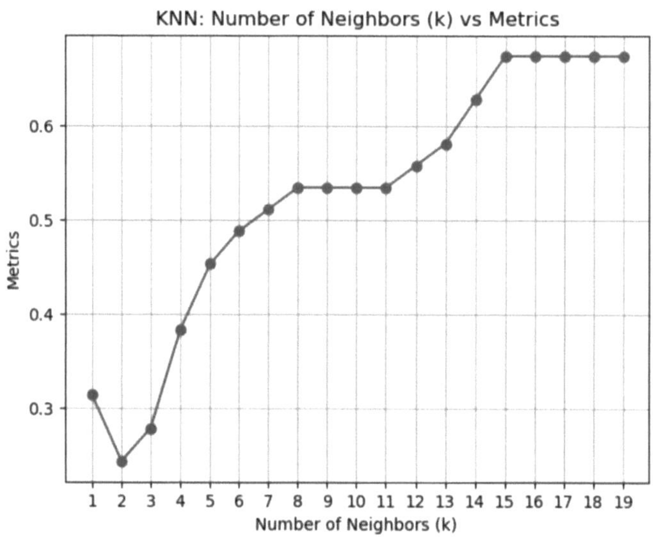

Fig. 5. KNN accuracy for various K-values

Figure 5 Shows the graph plot of the KNN model accuracy under various K-Values. The graph displays fluctuation in the accuracy of the same KNN model showing that how much its sensitive towards K-value or the local value pattern. This accuracy pattern or behavior shows the trade-off over choosing K-values between bias and variance.

Support Vector Machine. Support Vector Machine (SVM) is a supervised learning technique. SVM is a robust technique and is extensively applied in classification and regression endeavors. Inside our project we have utilized a special variant of SVM known as Support Vector Classifier (SVC). SVC is a specialized variant which is more focused and designed for classification tasks. SVC functions by knowing the optimal hyperplane to depict classes within the feature space, thus making it an optimal choice for our recommendation.

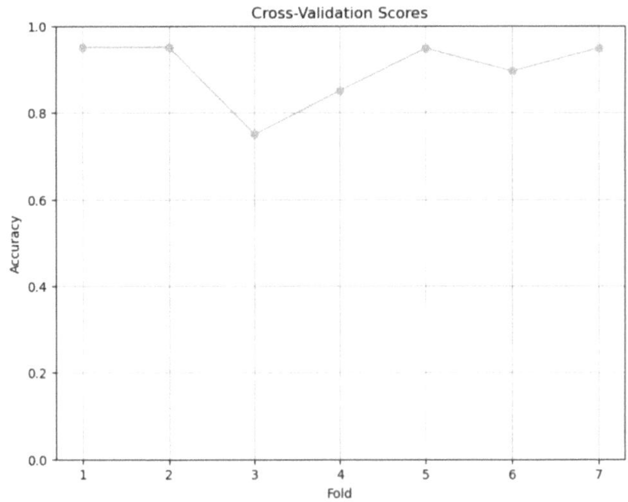

Fig. 6. SVC different fold's validation accuracy

Figure 6 Illustrates the accuracy graph plot of (Support Vector Model) SVC model over different fold values for cross-validation. These small variations in the accuracy over different fold values shows that our model is very flexible, robust and it's not depended on any dataset, thus illustrating that our SVC model is very good in generalization and optimal for our recommendation.

5 Result

In this section we will discuss the findings and insights of our recommendation system along with a detailed discussion over system's performance and comparison between different models. After rigorous training, testing as well as thorough analysis we have comprehended the overall efficiency of our approach as well as performance differences of each model utilized. Through this comprehension we can see how good and efficient our recommendation system is in terms of providing personalized recommendation.

Table 2. Performance metrics of ANN model

Metrics	Value
Recall	0.91
Precision	0.90
F1-Score	0.88
Accuracy	0.91

The given metrics Table 2 showcases overall performance and evaluation of our ANN model. With an accuracy of 91% our model depicts its strong capability to predict correct recommendations across different datasets. Apart from this, our model also achieved high recall, precision, f1-score which also showcases the robustness and effectiveness of our model in terms of identifying and classifying the datasets.

Table 3. Performance metrics of KNN model

Metrics	Value
Recall	0.72
Precision	0.70
F1-Score	0.70
Accuracy	0.67

The above performance metrics Table 3 gives an insight into the KNN classifier effectiveness in classifying. The model is overall correct 67.44%; it reveals that the model reached a fair balance between precision, recall, and an F1-score, indicating that the model can classify objects in multiple classes correctly. Each of those metrics gives clear understanding of how the classifier recognizes the patterns in the dataset.

Table 4. Performance metrics of SVC model

Metrics	Value
Recall	0.77
Precision	0.77
F1-Score	0.75
Accuracy	0.77

The above Table 4 represents the complete evaluation of Support Vector Classifier's performance. Having an overall accuracy of 77.14%, the precision and recall of 77%, and the F1-Score measuring at 75.87%, the classifier demonstrates both the ability to achieve high levels of accuracy and the precision to correctly label positive instances. These metrics show therefore its credibility in making confident predictions.

Among the recommendation system's evaluation methods, Artificial Neural Network (ANN) proved to be the most impressive, as it was able to achieve an accuracy of 91.86% and set good precision, recall, as well as F1-score parameters. While the success of the ANN can be attributed to its ability to pick up minute details and complex relationships embedded within the data, its shortcomings lie in the difficulty of understanding the decision-making process behind the AI. Unlike this, K-Nearest Neighbors (KNN) with the lower accuracy of 67.44% could be the reason its inherent problem is in the local similarity-based approach and maybe this could not be generalized when dealing with high-dimensional and/or noise data. And the Support Vector Classifier (SVC) had an accuracy of 77.14%, but its performance went slighter behind the ANN, most likely due to the problem of getting an optimal hyperplane on modified dataset. One important note from these results is a proper model which is fine-tuned to the task of making recommendations should be used when recommending.

6 Conclusion

In conclusion, the proposed recommendation system shows high efficiency as it integrates NLP techniques alongside with intelligent learning algorithms, it eventually enables a new level in business and investors interactions via the availability of personalized interactions. The result of performance measures shows that the ANN model leads other methods, scoring overall accuracy of 91.86%. This higher accuracy illustrates the powerful predictive capabilities of the ANN model, as it is shown by its high recall, precision, and F1-score metrics. However, the KNN and SVC models showcased a slightly weaker accuracy that indicates the difficulty in handling the more complex data, which can be messy like in high-dimensional data. Implicating the studies, it is to choose the best models which are specific to the recommendations in order to give businesses a good basis to make informed decisions and for the engagement of the stakeholders. In the following, exact study of model precision and aspect the difficulties of the different recommendation tasks that might aid to upgrade the field of personalized recommendation system.

References

1. Mondal, S., Kumar, S., Shireen, B., Singh, S., Barik, R.C.: Enhancing cross-domain recommendation system using a novel hybrid NLP based text vectorization and unsupervised machine learning model. In: 2024 IEEE International Students' Conference on Electrical, Electronics and Computer Science (SCEECS), pp. 1–6. IEEE (2024)
2. Bu, C., Zhang, J., Xingchen, Y., Le, W., Xindong, W.: Which companies are likely to invest: knowledge-graph-based recommendation for investment promotion. In: 2022 IEEE International Conference on Data Mining (ICDM), pp. 11–20. IEEE (2022)
3. Liu, W., Peng, Z., Zhao, S., Liu, J.: Similarity analysis in data element matching based on Word2vec. In: 2022 IEEE 22nd International Conference on Software Quality, Reliability, and Security Companion (QRS-C), pp. 319–323. IEEE (2022)
4. Sihombing, D.J., Cross, D.C., Othernima, A.K., Artpinkkan, T.H.: Application of artificial neural network (ANN) and support vector machine (SVM) for government policy recommendations to allow people to do activities without masks. In: 2021 IEEE 5th International Conference on Information Technology, Information Systems and Electrical Engineering (ICITISEE), pp. 197–201. IEEE (2021)
5. Li, B., Wan, S., Xia, H., Qian, F.: The research for recommendation system based on improved KNN algorithm. In: 2020 IEEE International Conference on Advances in Electrical Engineering and Computer Applications (AEECA), pp. 796–798. IEEE (2020)
6. Pereira, N., Varma, S.L.: Financial planning recommendation system using content-based collaborative and demographic filtering. In: Smart Innovations in Communication and Computational Sciences: Proceedings of ICSICCS 2017, Volume 1, pp. 141–151. Springer Singapore, Singapore (2018)
7. Lian, M., Li, J.: Financial product recommendation system based on transformer. In: 2020 IEEE 4th Information Technology, Networking, Electronic and Automation Control Conference (ITNEC), vol. 1, pp. 2547–2551. IEEE (2020)
8. Asemi, A., Asemi, A., Ko, A.: Investment recommender system model based on the potential investors' key decision factors. Big Data. **11**, 195–207 (2023)
9. Takayanagi, T., Chen, C.-C., Izumi, K.: Personalized dynamic recommender system for investors. In: Proceedings of the 46th International ACM SIGIR Conference on Research and Development in Information Retrieval, pp. 2246–2250 (2023)

10. Hu, X., Chen, Y., Ren, L., Zeshui, X.: Investor preference analysis: an online optimization approach with missing information. Inf. Sci. **633**, 27–40 (2023)
11. Kapoor, N., Vishal, S., Krishnaveni, K.S.: Movie recommendation system using nlp tools. In: 2020 5th International Conference on Communication and Electronics Systems (ICCES), pp. 883–888. IEEE (2020)
12. Cai, Z., Zhang, X.: Marriage recommendation algorithm based on KD-KNN-LR model. In: 2020 IEEE International Conference on Artificial Intelligence and Computer Applications (ICAICA), pp. 569–572. IEEE (2020)
13. Malik, V., Mittal, R., S. Vikram SIngh.: EPR-ML: E-Commerce product recommendation using NLP and machine learning algorithm. In: 2022 5th International Conference on Contemporary Computing and Informatics (IC3I), pp. 1778–1783. IEEE (2022)
14. Kumar, C.S., Sirisati, R.S., Gudditti, V., Rao, K.S., Challa, R.K.: A Smart recommendation system for medicine using intelligent NLP techniques. In: In 2022 International Conference on Automation, Computing and Renewable Systems (ICACRS), pp. 1081–1084. IEEE (2022)
15. Brintha, N.C., Nagaraj, P., Tejasri, A., Durga, B.V., Teja, M.T., Kumar, M.N.V.P.: A food recommendation system for predictive diabetic patients using ANN and CNN. In: 2022 7th International Conference on Communication and Electronics Systems (ICCES), pp. 1364–1371. IEEE (2022)
16. Picado, A., Finamore, C., Santos, A.M., Antunes, C.: Students temporal profiling and e-learning resources recommendation based on NLP's terms extraction. In: 2022 IEEE International Conference on Data Mining Workshops (ICDMW), pp. 264–273. IEEE (2022)
17. Dixit, A., Gupta, K., Dinesh, G.: Movie recommendation chatbot using cosine similarity and NLP tools. In: 2023 14th International Conference on Computing Communication and Networking Technologies (ICCCNT), pp. 1–7. IEEE (2023)

CMDDL: A Novel Coconut Maturity Detection Model Using Deep Learning

Suman Das[1], P. P. Afeefa[1], K. H. Aparna[1], Raju Hazari[1], and Pranesh Das[2](✉)

[1] Machine Learning Laboratory, Department of Computer Science and Engineering, National Institute of Technology Calicut, Kozhikode, Kerala, India

[2] Department of Computational and Data Science, National Institute of Technology Warangal, Hanamkonda 605004, India

pranesh@nitw.ac.in

Abstract. Coconut plays a significant role in the agrarian economy of India. It has a huge industrial value all over the world. Coconut harvesting is mainly done by judging their maturity stages based on shape, color, time frame, shaking sound, and other growth characteristics of change as they grow. One of the significant reasons to detect coconut maturity is because the maturity is directly related to the quality and could affect the commercialization of the product. It is also essential to timely harvest the coconut. But the detection of coconut maturity is a very difficult task as it depends on various attributes. To detect coconut maturity, a custom dataset of coconut is created. A deep learning-based algorithms, specifically the YOLOv5 and Yolov8 Neural Networks are used to train the models. To create the dataset, on-tree coconut images are collected from local coconut harvesters. The dataset was composed 948 images were collected in complex backgrounds on different days and times. As the dataset is not too big, the knowledge of transfer learning is used at the time of training to extract the features. The effectiveness of the proposed model is validated with some existing work, which performs better than the previous models (mAP_0.5 0.929). The developed model can detect the maturity state of a bunch of coconuts in real-time.

Keywords: Detection of Coconut Maturity · Object Detection · Image Processing · Deep Learning · Convolutional Neural Network (CNN) · YOLOv5 · YOLOv8

1 Introduction

Fruit maturity classification can be done through both destructive and non-destructive techniques. However, non-destructive approaches are preferable over destructive approaches as they allow for assessment without damaging the fruit. To detect the maturity state of coconut, we will use image-based methods which employ computer vision algorithms and image processing techniques to extract features related to fruit maturity. India is the third-largest producer of coconuts in the world, both in terms of the area used and the quantity produced; Tamil

M. Paprzycki et al. (Eds.): ICACIS 2024, CCIS 2405, pp. 225–243, 2027.
https://doi.org/10.1007/978-3-032-30990-7_17

Nadu accounts for 31% [1] of India's total production. Coconut has so many commercial benefits. Coconut oil can be extracted from the dried meat of coconut. After extracting the oil, we will get a side product called copra cake, which can be used as animal food. The meat of coconut can also be used in many dishes. For the above purposes, we need matured coconut. Coconut water is also health beneficial. But, tender coconut is better for this purpose. So, maturity detection is one of the main challenges experienced by the coconut harvesting system. Due to the direct correlation between a fruit or vegetable's mature stage and the quality of the final product, maturity detection and classification were seen as crucial considerations. Therefore, in order to fulfil its purpose and keep its quality, a coconut must be harvested at the precise stage of maturity. The difficulties of harvesting coconuts include a lack of labour and high labour expenses due to the crop's height and intricate trunk structure. Despite rising coconut demand, producers risk suffering significant financial losses.

To solve this issue and to ensure that coconuts are harvested on schedule, clever solutions must be used to determine the nut's level of maturity. Image processing software is the foundation of the technology used for real-time object detection. There are difficulties in developing a quick and accurate coconut detection method utilizing image analysis and machine vision because of the nut's colour, size, texture, form, illumination, and reflectance characteristics [2]. Occlusions and shadows in the tree crown are also crucial because they greatly impact target detection.

2 Related Works

Coconut maturity detection is crucial in the agricultural industry to ensure optimal harvesting and quality control. Traditional methods of assessing coconut maturity rely on manual inspection, which can be subjective and time-consuming. Deep learning techniques have shown great potential in automating fruit maturity detection tasks in recent years. This literature survey aims to provide an overview of the existing research and advancements in deep learning-based coconut maturity detection models.

In [3], to classify coconut maturity levels into three classes (young, mature, and old), various Convolutional Neural Network(CNN) models were chosen and compared the results among each other. The original RGB colour data from the input photographs were pre-transformed to reduce the complexity of the feature extraction layers. The outcomes of model creation were validated using K-fold cross-validation. The complete training of the speed-up CNN was used to develop DL to prevent the overfitting issue. Resnet50 and Googlenet, two pre-trained networks, were also used to refine it.

Automatic categorization of coconut maturity lowers production costs. It assists producers in meeting coconut selection quality standards, promoting the expansion of the coconut market and export for Thailand. In earlier studies, computer vision and sensor technology have been used to classify coconuts. For instance, a Polynomial Regression model is used to analyze the bottom of a coconut shell collected in the yamamoto2014plant to categorize coconuts according to their age. However, a light variation affects image processing [4].

Later, the Faster R-CNN method was used for Coconut maturity detection in complex background [1]. This model divides the object detection process into two stages: RPN and a categorization network. To create a feature map for the extraction of features, the convolutional layer employs a hierarchical feature extraction technique and semi-supervised learning. The deep convolutional neural network significantly improves over conventional object detection techniques. The accuracy of recognition significantly increased as convolutional network depth was increased.

There have been notable attempts to implement coconut harvesting robots with machine vision grounded in picture identification and analysis. Their method uses image processing with the Particle Swarm Optimisation (PSO) algorithm, which instantly determines where the coconuts should be placed in the tree. The coconut's base was sliced with a robotic arm that included a grinder on the end. Their model was 80.0 per-cent accurate in identifying and locating the coconuts. A different piece of work was examined, and their method involved creating a coconut detecting that would allow a cable robot to pick up and deposit coconuts into a dehusked without human assistance [5].

Another piece was created using an image or video with coconut and on-tree fruits as input. The following stage involves employing a UAV to take sufficient photos for training the YOLOv5 network. The images were submitted after consolidation to carry out the annotations and extract the features. These annotations will establish the fundamental parameters for the mature coconut's bounding boxes and labels. The network is prepared to be trained using the customized data once the annotations are finished. The model can identify and categorize mature coconut from the input image or video after training [2].

The segmentation of apple flowers was one example of a similar study carried out by [6] using the R- CNN model. After analysing their growth characteristics, the training set photos are enhanced in accordance with the growth features of apple blooms. For the dataset, they employed side flowers with buds, semi-open, fully-opened shapes, and central flowers. By including a mask prediction head, Mask R CNN expands the capabilities of Faster R CNN. Three primary components make up the Mask Scoring R-CNN model. The shared convolutional layer is the initial component. The standard convolutional layer is used to extract picture characteristics. The second component is the region proposal neural network (RPN), which is used to create bounding boxes and perform the initial correction on them. The third component of the model is in charge of classifying the targets discovered, correcting the bounding boxes, and producing masks.

Some automated coconut harvesting models are already there. One of them is a climbing robot [7]. Here, they build a cutting arm with a climbing robot as hardware and coconut detection is done using a genetic algorithm. They designed the model using CAD, which is hexagonal in shape with three wheels. The device connects with Bluetooth and can be operated wirelessly. But it takes too much time to cut the coconut.

In previous research, as discussed above, some tried to detect coconut maturity by applying machine learning and digital image processing. Most of the previous works on coconut maturity detection were done on grounded coconuts. Some research is carried out to cut down coconuts for harvesting, which are time-consuming and not that much efficient. In all these precious works, some common observations are the unavailability of a proper dataset, hard-to-detect images in complex backgrounds, and coconuts maturity may vary based on daylight (sunny, cloudy) or on their size, shape, brightness, shadow, etc., which makes the detection complex. So in this study, our primary focus is to address all these challenges and build a coconut maturity detection model which can be used in any intelligent device.

In this chapter, a model called CMDDL is proposed. The objectives are listed as follows:

- To create a dataset of coconut images with different maturity states.
- Develop the CMDDL model which can detect and classify the coconut maturity in complex background.
- To reduce the labor cost of coconut harvester by identifying coconut maturity so it can be harvested timely.

3 Proposed Work

3.1 Conceptual Framework of Coconut Maturity Detection

The conceptual framework is shown in Fig. 1. The YOLOV5 model is trained with a custom dataset of coconut images with various maturity states. The input images of coconut are to be given in a trained model for detection and classification of coconut maturity. The model detects the coconuts present in the input image and classifies it based on their maturity.

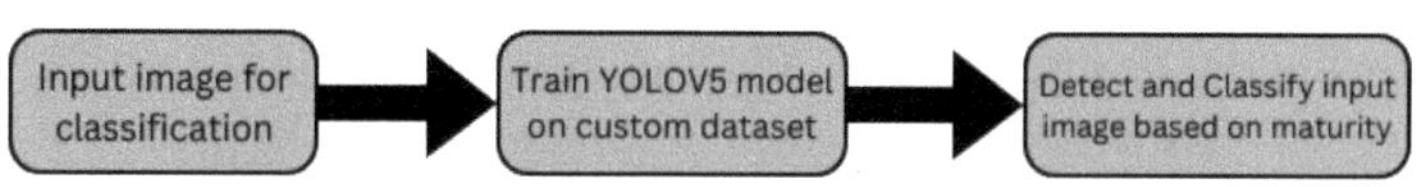

Fig. 1. Block diagram of conceptual framework

3.2 Block Diagram of Proposed Model

Detection of coconut maturity without cutting the coconuts is really hard to implement using available datasets as most of the datasets are made from the already grounded coconut images. So the proposed model's block diagram Fig. 2 starts with the collection of coconut images with various maturity states to make a custom dataset. The next step is to make the image dataset ready to train the YOLOV5 model. For that, the images are labeled based on their maturity to extract the features. We will also apply various augmentation techniques. In the next step, we will train the model using the custom dataset of annotated images. After completion of training the model can be used to detect and classify the maturity state of the coconut.

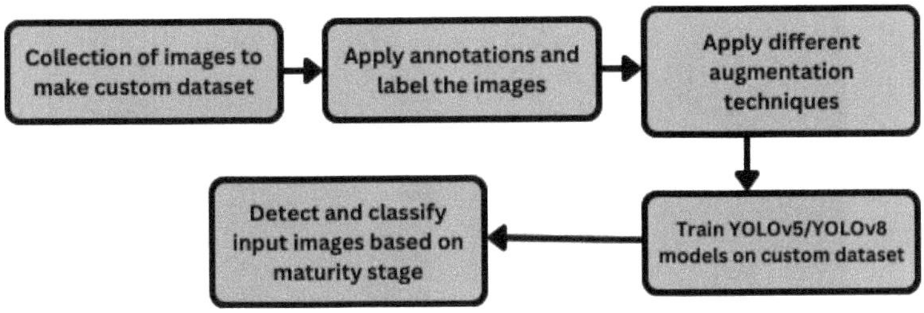

Fig. 2. Block diagram of Proposed Model

4 Dataset Creation

The growth of coconut is observed and analyzed so that images can be labeled properly to create the dataset for training the model.

To make a proper custom dataset of coconut, the images are collected in two different ways. One from the local coconut climber and another from the internet. Images that contain coconuts with different maturity stages were collected by local coconut climbers of Kerala. The images are collected by using a mobile phone and its resolution is 2252×4000. The pictures are taken from a certain distance so that the coconuts, as well as the background both, are clearly visible. The images are taken at different times of day in complex backgrounds in different lighting conditions. A total of 948 images are collected which are different in type(tender/mature/dry).

After collecting the images the next step is to label it. In the case of dried coconut, we could say that it is matured. But, in the case of green coconut, it is a challenging task to determine the maturity level of the coconut. For that reason, we have collected information related to coconut maturity from local coconut climbers to set the Ground Truth of dataset.

According to that information, the brown shades present in the coconut do not indicate it is matured. This is because most unripe coconuts contain these shades of brown (Fig. 3a). These shades are indicative of a coconut disease called Mandari. As shown in Fig. 3b, if there are any horizontal wrinkles in the coconut or brown spots on the lower part of the coconut, the coconut is ripe. Some other factors are also there, like the coconut bundles which are located at lower level of the tree probably matured. If the top of the coconut has a smooth finish, it is probably a tender coconut. A coconut with few vertical stripes is neither ripe nor tender. The maturity level of these coconuts is between these two categories. i.e., such coconuts can be classified as not matured coconuts.

Even if we use all the above methods for maturity level identification, sometimes we get confused. In such a situation, coconut climbers use two traditional methods for testing its maturity. Those are the shaking sound of the coconut and by cutting some portion of the coconut with a knife.

Based on the given information the collected images are labeled into three classes (tender coconut, green coconut, dry coconut) using a labeling tool. Roboflow software [8] is used as a tool for labeling the data to train YOLOV5

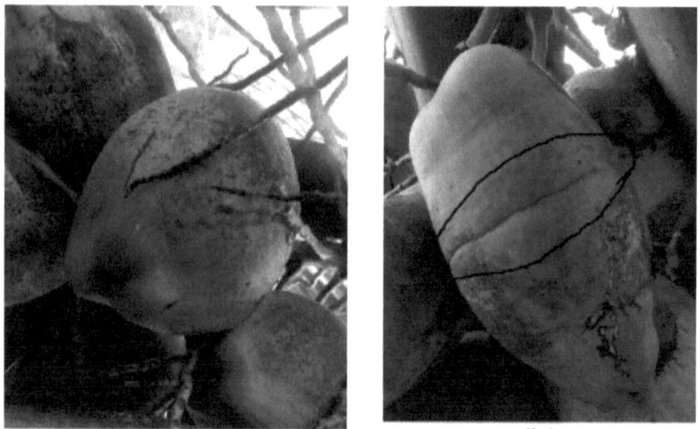

Fig. 3. Coconut with brown dots and wrinkles

model. Here bounding boxes are created around the objects of interest and assign class labels to each box.

As suggested in [9] the HSV (Hue, Saturation, and Value) of the images adjusted in a range. Here hue indicates the color, saturation denotes range of gray color space and value is the brightness of the color. For image augmentation, HSV is set to a range. Hue kept between $-15°$ and $+15°$, saturation between -25% to 25% and brightness adjusted between -30% to 30%.

After labeling all the collected images, it split into training, test and validation set. 70% (679 images) of the total images are used for training the model. From the remaining images, 10% (86 images) were used for testing and 20% (183 images) were used for validation. Then the dataset is exported in YOLOV5 format [10] which generates YOLO-compatible annotation files (.txt) along with the corresponding image files. The newly created dataset is published in Kaggle [10].

5 Methods and Procedures

The workflow of this study is shown in the Fig. 4. First step is to collect images and then label them using a labeling tool to set the ground truth. The whole dataset is divided into three classes (tender coconut, green coconut, and dry coconut). Then the labeled images are downloaded to train the YOLOv5 and YOLOv8 models. For that, we have divided the dataset into three parts training(70%), validation(20%) and testing(10%). It contains .txt files corresponding to each image and a .yaml file, which stores the information related to classes. We have trained both models for 150 epochs with batch size 16 and fixed image size 640. As the dataset is not too large, we have used the knowledge of transfer learning for better results. To extract the features, the model's weight is initialized with pre-trained model yolov5s.pt which is trained with COCO dataset, provided by Ultralytics [11]. YOLO models have basically two parts. Those are the backbone layers and the head layers. Backbone layers serve as feature extractors and head layers compute the output predictions. Here the same backbone is used as the pre-trained COCO model. YOLOv5s backbone consists of 12 layers, which will be fixed by the 'freeze' argument. The model is developed using Google Colab with GPU support. After training, the model is validated using a validation set that produces good results. It was further fine-tuned using the current model as the weight with a very small learning rate. The performance of the model increases a bit after finetuning. Finally, the model is tested with a webcam which is able to detect the maturity and plot bounding box (Table 1).

Table 1. Parameters used to train the models

Batch size	16
Image size	640
Number of epochs	150
Weights	yolov5s.pt

6 Architecture of YOLOv5 (You Only Look Once)

CNNs are classifier-based systems that can analyze incoming images as organized arrays of data and identify relationships between them. The benefit of YOLO is that it is faster than other networks while still maintaining accuracy. Because it enables the model to view the entire image during testing, its predictions are influenced by the image's overall context. It uses a grid approach to divide up the photos. In the grid, each cell is in charge of finding objects within of it. For each cell of the grid, some information is stored in the form of an array.

The architecture of YOLOv5 is shown in Fig. 5. It has three major sections, Backbone Network, Neck Network and Head Network. The input to the YOLOv5 architecture is an image of fixed size. The backbone network is a CNN responsible for extracting high-level features from the input image. YOLOv5 utilizes a modified version of the CSPDarknet53 architecture as its backbone. CSPDarknet53 is a deep convolutional neural network that consists of convolutional layers, residual blocks, and down-sampling operations. The backbone network gradually reduces the spatial dimensions of the feature maps while increasing the number of channels. The neck network is inserted between the backbone and head networks to further process and fuse feature maps. YOLOv5 employs a PANet (Path Aggregation Network) as its neck network. PANet combines feature maps at different scales to capture both low-level and high-level features effectively. The PANet architecture consists of bottom-up and top-down pathways along with lateral connections for feature fusion. The head network takes the fused feature maps from the neck network and generates bounding box predictions and class probabilities. YOLOv5 uses a modified version of the YOLO head, which consists of a series of convolutional layers and final prediction layers. The head network predicts bounding boxes by dividing the image into a grid of cells and predicting bounding box attributes (coordinates, confidence scores, class probabilities) for each cell. Each bounding box prediction consists of a set of attributes, including the coordinates of the bounding box, a confidence score representing the likelihood of the presence of an object, and class probabilities indicating the predicted object class.

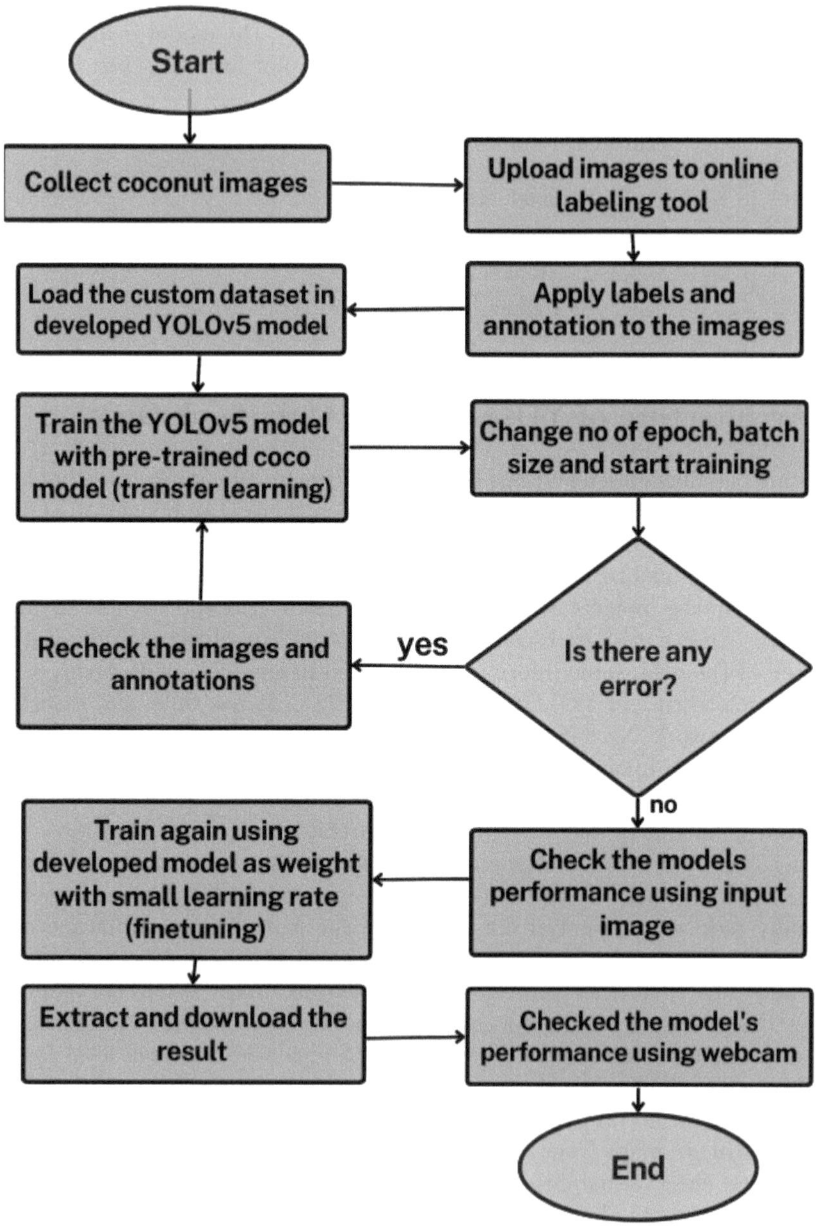

Fig. 4. Flowchart of developed model

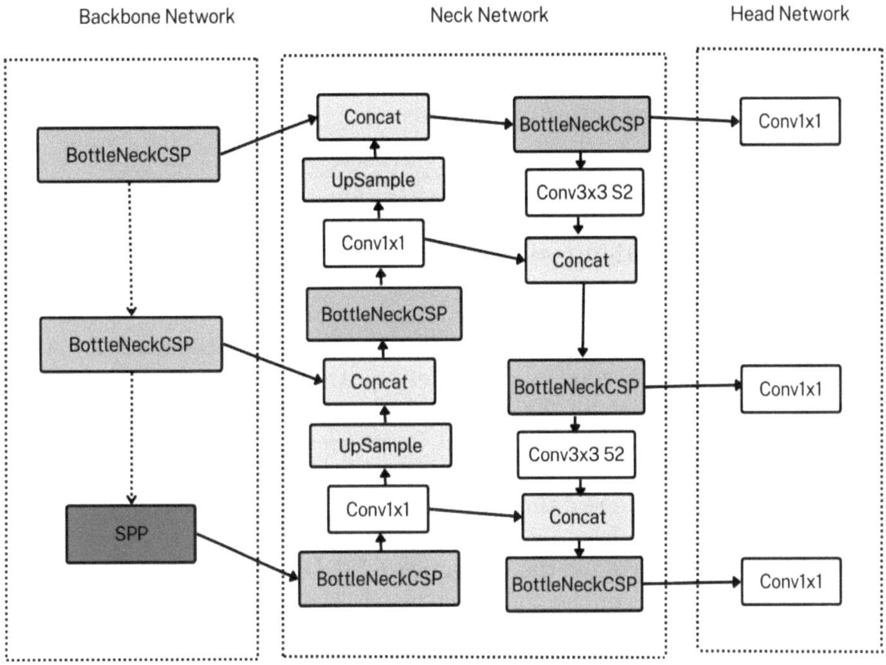

Fig. 5. Archuitecture of YOLOv5 [12]

7 Working Principle of YOLO

YOLO algorithm is based on the principle of single-shot object detection. It aims to detect objects in an input image by making predictions directly from the raw image pixels in a single pass through the network. YOLOv5 utilizes a deep convolutional neural network (CNN) architecture. YOLOv5 divides the input image into a grid of cells. Each cell is responsible for predicting bounding boxes for objects located within its boundaries. For each grid cell, YOLOv5 predicts multiple bounding boxes with different sizes and aspect ratios, allowing it to handle objects of various shapes. The information stored for each grid cell is shown in Eq. 1.

1. If the object is present in the grid then x = 1 otherwise x = 0
2. b_x and b_y denotes the center point of bounding box.
3. b_h and b_w denotes height and width of bounding box.
4. $c_1 ... c_n$ denotes number of classes. Its value is 1 for the class to which the object belongs. The rest are 0.

$$y = \left[x\ b_x\ b_y\ b_h\ b_w\ c_1\ nc_2\ ...\ c_n\right]^T \tag{1}$$

To predict the object we will use a method called Intersection Over Union (IOU). IOU computes the ratio of intersection and union of actual and predicted bounding boxes. If it is greater than 0.5 then we will consider the prediction. A higher IOU means more correct predictions.

$$IOU = \frac{sizeofintersection}{sizeofunion} \tag{2}$$

8 Results and Discussion

Both YOLOv5 and YOLOv8 models are open source provided by Ultralytics. The developed models are able to detect as well as classify the maturity states of coconut on-tree with good accuracy for the training and validation images using our custom dataset. In this section performance of the models are shown through precision, recall, F1 score, and mean average precision. Also showed graphical representations of the system's performance for better visualization of the results. Finally, some real-time testing images are also provided to show the output of developed models.

The confusion matrix for the developed CMDDL model using YOLOv5 is shown Fig. 6. Each cell in the confusion matrix represents a specific combination of predicted and actual class labels. The four important components of the confusion matrix are-

- True Positive (TP): All the positive instances that are predicted correctly by the model.
- False Positive (FP): Instances that are predicted as positive but actually they are negative.
- True Negative (TN): All the negative instances that are predicted correctly by the model.
- False Negative (FN): The positive instances that are predicted as negative by the model.

The parameters which are used to evaluate the model's performance are Precision, Recall, F1-score, and mean Average Precision (mAP).

Precision, Recall and F1 Score: Precision measures the amount of correctly predicted positive instances out of all predicted positive instances. Whereas recall measures the proportion of actual positive instances that are correctly identified by the model. The F1 score is the harmonic mean of precision and recall. It is a way of calculating the average value which provides a balanced measure that considers both precision and recall [13].

$$Precision = \frac{TP}{(TP + FP)} \tag{3}$$

$$Recall = \frac{TP}{(TP + FN)} \tag{4}$$

$$F1score = \frac{2 * (Precision * Recall)}{(Precision + Recall)} \tag{5}$$

8.1 Evaluation Matrices and Curves

In the Fig. 6a, the diagonal from the top-left corner to the bottom-right corner of the matrix shows the percentage of correctly predicted objects. 95% dry coconuts are detected correctly whereas 5% dry coconuts are predicted as green coconut. In the case of green coconut 90% predictions are correct but for tender coconut, the accuracy is lesser than dry or green coconuts.

The precision-Recall curve of the CMDDL model using YOLOv5 is shown in Fig. 7. The mAP at IoU threshold of 0.5 is 0.929, that is the mAP_0.5 value is 92.9%.

The confusion matrix for the developed CMDDL model using YOLOv8 is shown in Fig. 6b. Accuracy of this model is 83.5%.

The precision-Recall curve of the CMDDL model using YOLOv8 is shown in Fig. 8. The mAP at IoU threshold of 0.5 is 0.89, that is the mAP_0.5 value is 89%.

8.2 Results and Comparative Analysis

The precision value, recall value and F1 score for all three classes (tender coconut, green coconut, dry coconut) of CMDDL model by using both the YOLOv5 and YOLOv8 models are shown in Table 2 and Table 3 respectively.

We have used the parameter mean Average Precision (mAP) to compare the proposed model's performance with existing models. It summarizes the precision-recall curve into a single value. The value of Average Precision (AP) is given by Eq. (6).

$$AP = \sum_{k=0}^{k=n-1} [Recalls(k) - Recalls(k+1)] * [Precision(k)] \tag{6}$$

where n is the number of thresholds, Recalls(n) = 0, and Precisions(n) = 1.

As we have more than one class, we need to calculate the mean of AP. The equation for calculating mean AP (mAP) is shown in 7.

$$mAP = \frac{1}{n} \sum_{k=1}^{k=n} AP_k \tag{7}$$

where AP_k is the value of AP of class k and n is the number of classes.

To calculate the mAP value, the IOU threshold is considered as 0.5. Because if the IOU value is less than 0.5, then it is more likely the detected class of the object is incorrect.

The comparative analysis between the papers [1,2] and our developed model is shown in Table 4. The mAP_0.5 value of YOLOv5 is 92.9% whereas in [2] the mAP_0.5 value is 88.4%.

8.3 Training and Validation Results

The result graphs of CMDDL model are plotted for visualizes the performance metrics during training or evaluation. It provides a graphical representation of how the model's performance changes over time or with different configurations. CMDDL model's result graph for bounding box loss, object loss, classification loss, precision, and recall at the time of training and validation are shown in the below figures. After training the model with a pre-trained weight of the COCO model, we have further finetuned it. For that, we have used our model's output as weight and re-trained it with a small learning rate.

The training curve (Fig. 9) shows how the performance metric changes over iterations/epochs during the training process. It demonstrates the model's ability to learn and improve over time. Here the losses are gradually decreasing with more iterations, and the accuracy is increasing, as training progresses.

In Fig. 10, validation curve is shown, which shows the performance metric on a separate validation dataset. This curve helps assess how well the model generalizes to unseen data and can provide insights into overfitting or underfitting issues.

The performance of CMDDL model and how it's improving with more epochs is shown in Fig. 11. Precision, recall, and mAP indicate how well the model is performing.

Training and validation loss of the finetuned model are shown in Fig. 12 and Fig. 13 respectively. It is clearly visible that losses are still improving during finetune.

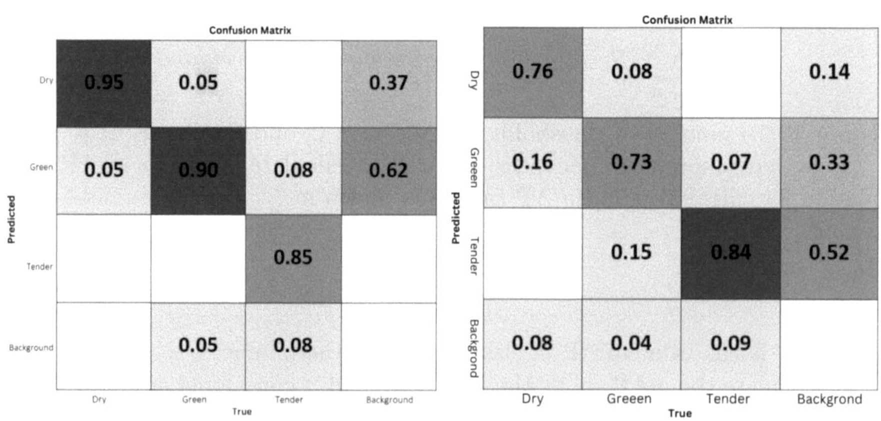

(a) Confusion Matrix of CMDDL Model Using YOLOv5 (b) Confusion matrix of CMDDL Model Using YOLOv8

Fig. 6. Confusion matrices of CMDDL Model

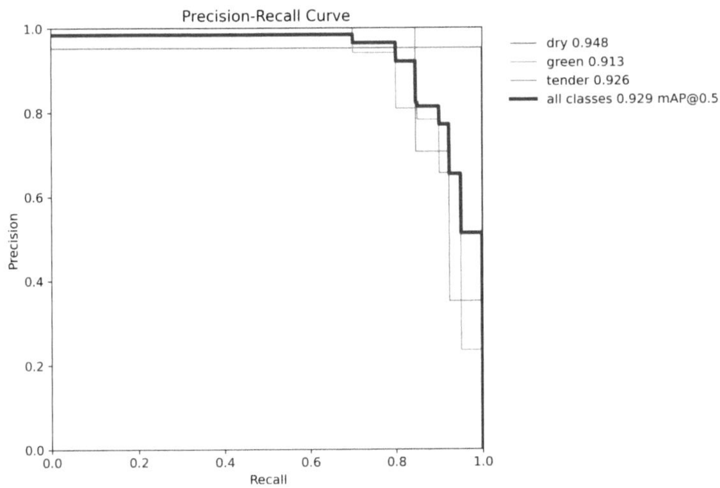

Fig. 7. Precision-Recall curve of CMDDL Model Using YOLOV5

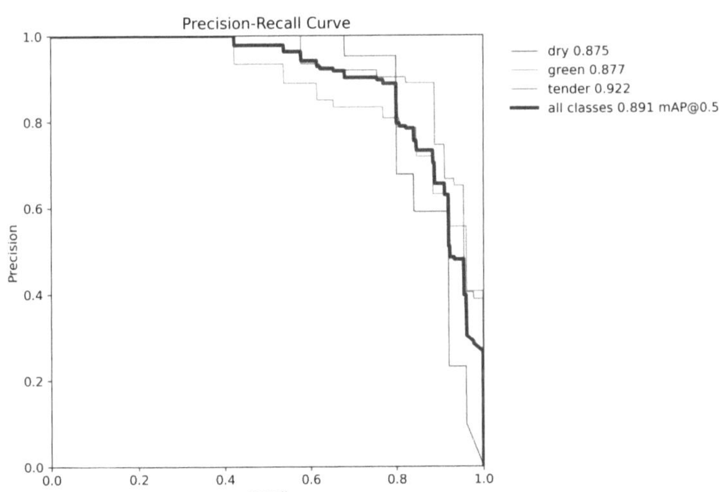

Fig. 8. Precision-Recall curve of CMDDL Model Using YOLOV8

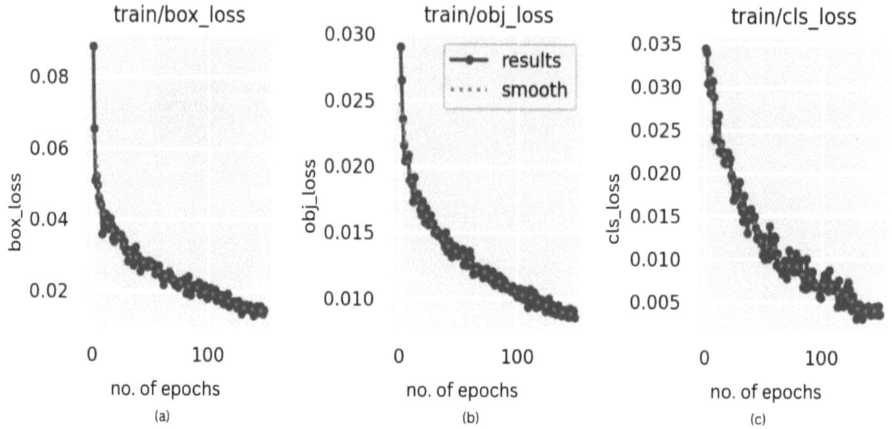

Fig. 9. Training Losses of CMDDL Model Using YOLOv5 (a). Bounding box loss, (b). Object loss, and (c) Classification loss

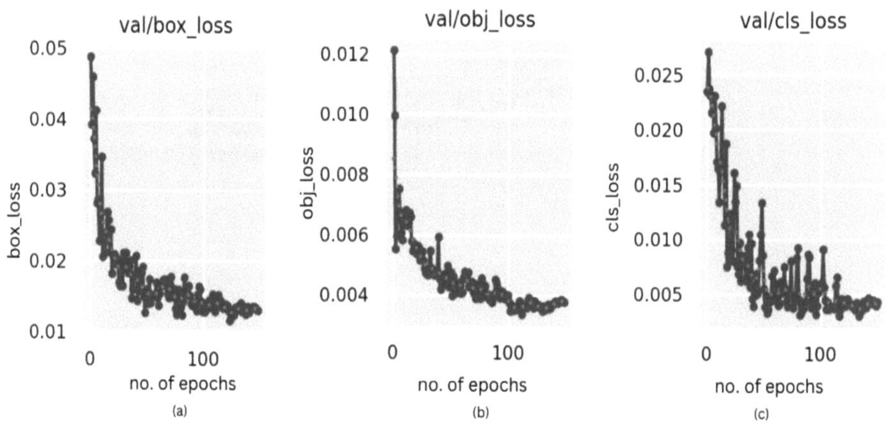

Fig. 10. Validation Losses of CMDDL Model Using YOLOv5 (a). Bounding box loss, (b). Object loss, and (c)Classification loss

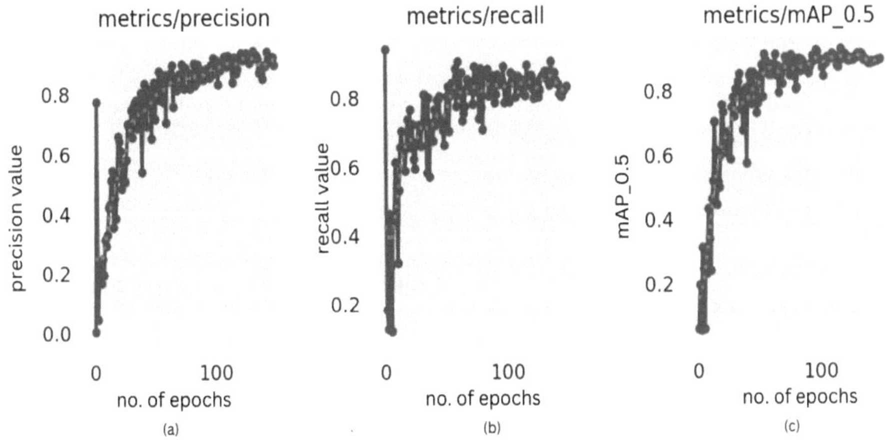

Fig. 11. (a). Precision, (b). Recall and (c). mAP values

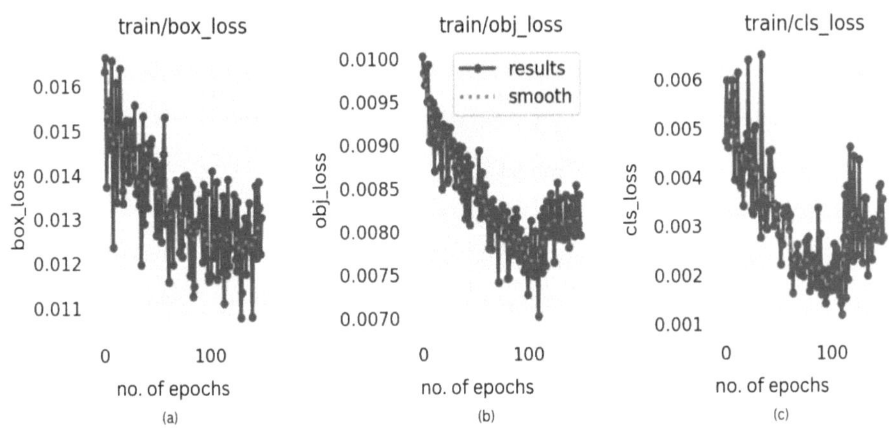

Fig. 12. Losses during training phase of finetuning of CMDDL Model (a). Bounding box loss, (b). Object loss, and (c) Classification loss

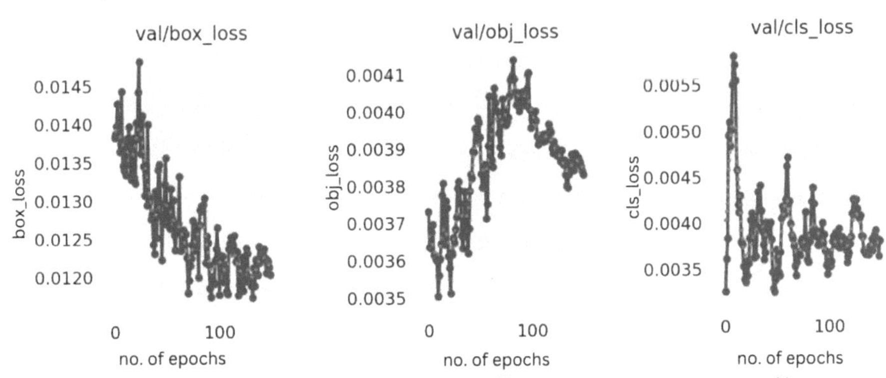

Fig. 13. Losses during validation phase of finetuning of CMDDL Model (a). Bounding box loss, (b). Object loss, and (c) Classification loss

Table 2. Precision, Recall and F1 Score of different maturity stage coconuts using CMDDL-YOLOv5 model.

Evaluation Parameters	Tender Coconut	Green Coconut	Dry Coconut
Precision	88.5%	72.2%	94.7%
Recall	77%	85%	90%
F1 Score	82.3%	78%	92.2%

Table 3. Precision, Recall and F1 Score of different maturity stage coconuts using CMDDL-YOLOv8 model.

Evaluation Parameters	Tender Coconut	Green Coconut	Dry Coconut
Precision	84.8%	76%	90.4%
Recall	92.3%	76%	82.6%
F1 Score	88.3%	76%	86.3%

Table 4. Comparative analysis of mAP_0.5

Detection Algorithm	mAP_0.5 IoU
YOLOv5 model [2]	0.884
Faster RCNN model [1]	0.894
YOLOv3 model [1]	0.654
Proposed CMDDL-YOLOv8 model	0.891
Proposed CMDDL-YOLOv5 model	0.929

8.4 Detection of Test Images

For visualization of the result, here are some images (Fig. 14, Fig. 15) in which the maturity state is detected by the model.

Fig. 14. Visualisation of the result after detecting coconut images with different maturity stages using CMDDL-YOLOV5

Fig. 15. Visualisation of the result after detecting coconut images with different maturity stages using CMDDL-YOLOV8

9 Conclusion and Future Scope

In this work, a custom dataset of coconut is created, which is used to train the models. Two deep learning-based algorithms (YOLOv5 and YOLOv8) are used to detect and classify coconut maturity in real-time. Although both models are able to detect and classify coconut maturity stages very well, CMDDL-YOLOv5 performs slightly better than CMDDL-YOLOv8. The developed CMDDL model can be used in any intelligent device for coconut harvesting, which will save both time and effort. It also can be used for yield estimation of coconut crops.

In the training process, transfer learning is used. The model provides very good results even though the dataset is not too large. Also, various data augmentation techniques were applied to enhance the model's robustness and generalization capabilities. The model's performance was evaluated using various metrics to assess its accuracy in differentiating between tender, green, and dry coconuts. The results demonstrated high accuracy levels, indicating the potential of the proposed model for real-world applications.

However, this model has some limitations, like it does not deal with different types of coconuts that are present in different geographical locations. For that, more images need to be collected with different maturity in other geographical regions. So, more images of coconuts with various maturity states and different types need to collect to improve the performance of the developed model.

Acknowledgement. This work was carried out as a part of SRG(SERB) funded project work (ID: SRG/2021/001593) by the M. Tech final year student Mr. Suman Das under the guidance of Dr. Pranesh Das as part of his thesis work.

References

1. Parvathi, S., Selvi, S.T.: Detection of maturity stages of coconuts in complex background using faster r-CNN model. Biosys. Eng. **202**, 119–132 (2021)
2. Novelero, J.M., Dela Cruz, J.C.: On-tree mature coconut fruit detection based on deep learning using UAV images. In: 2022 IEEE International Conference on Cybernetics and Computational Intelligence (CyberneticsCom), pp. 494–499. IEEE (2022)
3. Noppon, L., Nipon, P.: The application of convolution neural network for coconut maturity classification. In: 2021 18th International Conference on Electrical Engineering/Electronics, Computer, Telecommunications and Information Technology (ECTI-CON), pp. 112–115. IEEE (2021)
4. Titus, A.B., Narayanan, T., Das, G.P.: Vision system for coconut farm cable robot. In: 2017 IEEE International Conference on Smart Technologies and Management for Computing, Communication, Controls, Energy and Materials (ICSTM), pp. 443–450. IEEE (2017)
5. Devakumar, T., Avudai Nayagam, T.: Intelligent system for matured coconut identification. Int. J. Recent Technol. Eng. **9**, 57–61 (2020)
6. Tian, Y., Yang, G., Wang, Z., Li, E., Liang, Z.: Instance segmentation of apple flowers using the improved mask r-cnn model. Biosys. Eng. **193**, 264–278 (2020)

7. Wibowo, T.S., Sulistijono, I.A., Risnumawan, A.: End-to-end coconut harvesting robot. In: 2016 International Electronics Symposium (IES), pp. 444–449. IEEE (2016)
8. https://roboflow.com/
9. Tantrakansakul, P., Khaorapapong, T.: The classification flesh aromatic coconuts in daylight. In: 2014 11th International Conference on Electrical Engineering/Electronics, Computer, Telecommunications and Information Technology (ECTI-CON), pp. 1–5. IEEE (2014)
10. https://www.kaggle.com/datasets/madsd123/coconut-dataset-for-cmddl-model
11. Jocher, G., et al.: ultralytics/yolov5: v6. 0—yolov5n 'nano'models, roboflow integration, tensorflow export, opencv dnn support (2021). https://github.com/ultralytics/yolov5
12. Snegireva, D., Perkova, A.: Traffic sign recognition application using yolov5 architecture. In: 2021 International Russian Automation Conference (RusAutoCon), pp. 1002–1007. IEEE (2021)
13. Goutte, C., Gaussier, E.: A probabilistic interpretation of precision, recall and F-score, with implication for evaluation. In: Losada, D.E., Fernández-Luna, J.M. (eds.) ECIR 2005. LNCS, vol. 3408, pp. 345–359. Springer, Heidelberg (2005). https://doi.org/10.1007/978-3-540-31865-1_25
14. Fadchar, N.A., Dela Cruz, J.C.: A non-destructive approach of young coconut maturity detection using acoustic vibration and neural network. In: 2020 16th IEEE International Colloquium on Signal Processing & Its Applications (CSPA), pp. 136–137. IEEE (2020)
15. Zheng, J., Wu, W., Yu, L., Fu, H.: Coconut trees detection on the tenarunga using high-resolution satellite images and deep learning. In: 2021 IEEE International Geoscience and Remote Sensing Symposium IGARSS, pp. 6512–6515. IEEE (2021)
16. Yamamoto, K., Guo, W., Yoshioka, Y., Ninomiya, S.: On plant detection of intact tomato fruits using image analysis and machine learning methods. Sensors **14**(7), 12191–12206 (2014)
17. Sethy, P.K., Panda, S., Bhoi, N.: On-tree detection and counting of mature and immature fruit of carica papaya using image processing. Int. J. Comput. Appl. **975**, 8887 (2016)
18. Bharathi, S., Harini, P.: Early detection of diseases in coconut tree leaves. In: 2020 6th International Conference on Advanced Computing and Communication Systems (ICACCS), pp. 1265–1268. IEEE (2020)

Lightweight Deep Learning Accelerators for Real-Time Object Detection in Resource-Constrained IoT Devices

Shrayanshi[1], P. Geethanjali[2], Metun[3], Darshan Upadhyay[4], Khunaal Aryan[5], Jyoti Parashar[6], and Kamal Upreti[7](✉)

[1] Rapipay Fintech Private Limited, Noida, India
[2] Bangalore Institute of Technology, Bangalore, India
1BI19ET016@bit-bangalore.edu.in
[3] Masters in Computer Science, New York University, Brooklyn, NY, USA
[4] Department of Civil engineering, S. V. National Institute of Technology, Surat, India
[5] Department of Information Science and Engineering, R V College of Engineering, Bengaluru, Karnataka, India
[6] Department of Computer Science and Engineering, Panipat Institute of Engineering and Technology (PIET), Panipat, Haryana, India
[7] Department of Computer Science, CHRIST University Delhi NCR, Ghaziabad, India
kamalupreti1989@gmail.com

Abstract. As Internet of Things (IoT) & the mobile edge computing (MEC) continue to advance, the need for energy-efficient solutions becomes paramount. This research introduces a comprehensive approach by merging a Cross DL Model & a Lightweight Energy-Efficient Accelerator to address challenges in both MEC and IoT devices. The proposed Hybrid Deep Learning Model leverages a modified k-mean clustering (MKM) algorithm & Convolutional Neural Networks (CNNs) for energy-efficient head selection & cluster formation in MEC. The CNN is employed to optimize communication paths and task partitioning, while the MKM method reduces re-clustering cycles, overcoming energy consumption and delay issues. The integration of MKM with CNN ensures accurate identification and application of cluster heads, even in dynamic cluster environments. This accelerator employs model simplification and compression techniques, optimizing the network model for h/w implementation. The anticipated hardware architecture achieves significant reductions in logic and BRAM size, resulting in approximately 11.25× lower energy consumption compared to previous works. Experimental results demonstrate successful real-time object detection at 98.7 fps on a ZC702 FPGA, showcasing the practicality and efficiency of the proposed approach. This unified approach presents a promising solution for energy-efficient edge computing, combining the strengths of a Hybrid Deep Learning Model tailored for MEC & a Lightweight Accelerator optimized for IoT devices. The findings highlight improvements in power utilization, overhead, throughput, packet delivery ratio, energy consumption, and packet loss rate, making it a compelling alternative to existing methodologies in the evolving landscape of edge computing and IoT.

M. Paprzycki et al. (Eds.): ICACIS 2024, CCIS 2405, pp. 244–259, 2027.
https://doi.org/10.1007/978-3-032-30990-7_18

Keywords: CNN (Convolutional Neural Networks) · K-Mean Clustering · Energy Efficiency · Mobile Edge Computing (MEC) · Lightweight Accelerator · and Hardware Optimization

1 Introduction

The proliferation of mobile edge computing (MEC) & the Internet of Things (IoT) has escorted in a new era of connectivity & computation, enabling various applications ranging from smart cities to industrial automation. However, the rapid growth in these technologies has brought forth significant challenges, particularly regarding energy efficiency and real-time processing capabilities. This research addresses these challenges through a comprehensive approach combining a Hybrid Deep Learning Model and a Lightweight Energy-Efficient Accelerator. In MEC environments, the efficient utilization of energy resources is crucial due to the constrained nature of mobile devices and the need for seamless communication. Recognizing the intricacies of cluster formation and head selection, we propose a "Hybrid Deep Learning Model that combines Convolutional Neural Networks (CNNs) with a modified k-mean clustering (MKM) algorithm." This model aims to optimize communication paths and task partitioning, reducing energy consumption and mitigating delays associated with the dynamic nature of MEC clusters.

Simultaneously, the paradigm of IoT introduces unique challenges, especially concerning resource-constrained devices. Current deep learning algorithms often prove impractical for IoT devices due to their complexity and high energy consumption. To bridge this gap, we present a "Lightweight and Energy-Efficient Deep Learning Accelerator" designed for real-time object detection. This accelerator leverages model simplification and compression techniques to augment the network model for h/w implementation, ensuring compatibility with battery-operated IoT devices. The integration of these two components forms a unified approach to tackle energy efficiency concerns in both MEC and IoT. By combining the strengths of a Hybrid Deep Learning Model tailored for MEC and a Lightweight Accelerator optimized for IoT devices, we aim to provide a holistic solution that addresses the evolving landscape of edge computing. Through experimental validation, we showcase the practicality and efficiency of our proposed approach, demonstrating improvements in overhead, throughput, packet delivery ratio, energy consumption, and packet loss rate. This research contributes to the ongoing discourse on sustainable and efficient edge computing solutions, with potential implications for diverse applications in the realm of Edge IoT.

MEC embodies a strategic approach aimed at optimizing partial computational offloading to minimize energy consumption in client devices (CDs) and alleviate service quality delays. This involves breaking down a sole duty into multiple tasks within the MEC framework, enabling efficient data analysis of extensive information with real-time, latency-free processing. With the widespread integration of IoT technologies, this intelligent approach finds application across various domains where interconnected components, equipped with sensors, enable real-time environmental data detection. Smartwatches, laptops, monitoring gadgets, linked cars, and innovative manufacturing components are just a few examples of the networked intelligent items that have emerged as a result of the Internet of Things' widespread adoption. These devices, which include predictive analytics and are connected via a network of channels, are completely changing the way we work, live, and interact [1]. However, the expansion of the IoT presents new challenges, particularly concerning the use of battery-operated devices for data collection and analysis. To ensure data integrity, IoT systems connect objects and sensors into multiple clusters, resulting in increased energy demands [2]. The design and evaluation of edge computing-based architectures play a pivotal role in shaping the future evolution of IoT infrastructure. Efficient clustering algorithms can extend network lifespan and decrease energy consumption. To address these challenges, researchers extensively employ AI-based IoT techniques, including DL, ML, and FC, to develop more resilient, adaptable, efficient, and accurate solutions [3].

In the context of mobile computing—which includes smartphones, the Internet of Things, sensors, cloud computing, data processing, and storage infrastructure—edge computing emerges as a discrete, decentralized online ecosystem. Its main objective is to supply end nodes, mostly found at the network's edge, with high data processing, data transfer, and excellent connectivity services. The constraints associated with limited processing power and storage in client devices (CDs) are addressed by Mobile Edge Computing (MEC), which integrates mobile and edge computing features. However, because client devices have limited capacity, installing MEC systems may provide difficulties that result in increased energy usage and decreased reliability [4]. MEC offers a cutting-edge remedy for important problems related to cloud computing. MEC seeks to improve system performance, maximize bandwidth, provide greater dependability and high throughput, and lower client device energy consumption by placing computation servers and specific applications close to edge servers. This method increases the processing capacity of client devices, which is especially helpful in situations where complicated and power-hungry services and applications are involved. MEC provides client devices with highly distributed computing resources and storage from its position at the cutting edge of wireless communication [5].

The rise of deep learning has been surged by advancements in computing power and the emergence of big data [20]. Recent years have seen extensive reviews and discussions on deep learning [21–25], finding applications across various fields including image recognition [26], object detection [27], autonomous driving [28, 29], and robotics [30]. Its success in these domains has highlighted the importance of deep learning networks, which have become increasingly integral, particularly in the Internet of Things (IoT) landscape, due to the rapid proliferation of IoT devices and network infrastructure [31]. The need for real-time, energy-efficient deep learning operations on resource-constrained edge devices has become critical in the IoT era [32]. However, the inherent complexity of deep learning models poses challenges, requiring substantial data and computational resources [33]. This complexity spans model architecture, size, optimization processes, and data intricacy. Many deep learning models, such as convolutional neural networks (CNNs), feature intricate architectures, resulting in large model sizes due to numerous parameters, layers, and filters. Configuration parameters, like layer width and filter size, also contribute to the overall model size. Consequently, consecutively these models demand significant memory for parameter storage and involve substantial energy consumption for computational processes and data transfer to/from memory.

The central objective of this study is to address energy-related challenges in the selection of cluster heads and the formation of clusters by devising optimal decision-making policies for Mobile Edge Computing (MEC). To fulfill this objective, we introduce a novel approach termed the "Energy-efficient Cluster Formation and Head Selection Algorithm (E-CFSA)," which employs a hybrid deep learning model integrating [Convolutional Neural Networks (CNNs) and a modified k-mean clustering (MKC) method]. To partition data, the suggested model incorporates a partial loading strategy. It then calculates the costs of different partitioning and loading strategies and chooses the best one. To promote self-organization and guarantee high availability, our system design uses a rotation-based strategy for the cluster head generation and selection process. An efficient team that transmits data to the base station is supervised by a central cluster head block. Moreover, our method employs a modified k-mean clustering (MKM) technique to choose balanced cluster heads, allowing for the leadership of multiple cluster heads within a cluster. Cluster head selection depends on the duration and timeliness of cluster nodes, accommodating the presence of more than two clusters in the group. This method minimizes re-clustering cycles, thereby enhancing energy and time efficiency. Experimental analyses compare our proposed E-CFSA with existing methods, such as the Weighted Clustering Algorithm (WCA) and the Agent-Based Secure Enhanced Performance approach (AB-SEP). Additionally, this study facilitates collaborative forecasting among mobile devices & IOT, fostering a shared predictive environment.

Conducting model reduction and parameter simplification on the backbone model network entails simplifying the model and incorporating activation and parameter quantization for model compression. Moreover, a low-weight and energy-efficient hardware architecture is proposed, with a planned implementation that employs a 3D tensor-like Processing Element (PE) structure to enable parallel processing between layers and channels. This design leads to decreased latency and energy usage. The proposed on-chip memory management strategy reduces the requirement for on-chip memory, contributing to the lightweight and low-power nature of the design. Experimental results highlight the success of the optimized model in object detection. The proposed hardware design achieves significant reductions, with a logic size 1.35× smaller and a Block RAM (BRAM) size 5.16× smaller compared to previous related works. Additionally, the energy consumption of the design is approximately 11.25× lower, while maintaining real-time processing at 98.7 frames per second under an operating frequency of 221 MHz on a ZC702 FPGA.

2 Literature Review

This study involves evaluating energy usage performance, developing a model for energy conversion, and improving power quality in Mobile Edge Computing (MEC) systems. The proposed approaches tackle energy-related challenges through collaborative block descent and fuzzy linear programming concepts. Currently, significant research focuses on designing offloading schemes for MEC networks. Although deep learning (DL) techniques are powerful, they often demand considerable processing power and memory for storing extensive training data and large models. A novel DL model introduced in [6] is customized to operate efficiently on edge devices, incorporating shallow features suitable for IoT equipment with limited processing capacity. Another model, discussed in [7], targets scenarios where precise decisions are crucial. This deep learning model accelerates knowledge acquisition and convolution layers on edge devices while reducing component width for multiclass classification [8]. Addressing the challenge of early feature loss in MEC systems with limited learning outcomes, [9] proposes an enhanced Convolutional Neural Network (CNN) model, employing a modified layering technique specifically tailored for edge devices. In [10], three component-based models are introduced to predict optimal computational and storage transfer techniques. The suggested model successfully separates the MEC process into static and dynamic transfers by utilizing state variables, decision behavior, and scheme utility. It presents "I-Devices," or intelligent terminals, which are ideal for network infrastructure applications and services [11].

MEC systems exhibit improved processing power, efficiently managing large-scale data processing assignments [12] explores a deep reinforcement learning approach for adaptive MEC, aiming to optimize MES data sampling and improve transfer rates. The proposed model in [13] employs a comprehensive replica learning strategy to alleviate MD service delays. By integrating a cost function, this model addresses service processes, resulting in enhanced communication and reduced service delays. The application of practical deep learning-based computing in MEC systems, especially with limited training datasets, presents challenges [14] introduces a high-rate binary transfer process in dynamic MEC networks to tackle associated difficulties. This study addresses energy uncertainty issues using Convolutional Neural Networks (CNNs). The model makes use of a binary task allocation technique based on time-varying processes and other analysis features to reduce energy consumption and latency. In order to address global optimization difficulties, a gradient-based deterministic strategy in MEC systems is used in [15], an energy-efficient method based on deep learning techniques. A dense decentralized cellular network with numerous users, servers, and activities is assessed in this article. It takes into account both MES and CD mobility, resulting in the creation of a task-transfer model that is region-parallel and enables dependable communication for low-latency application regions.

[16] provides a comprehensive examination of the expanding multimedia Internet of Things (IoT), highlighting the potential for innovative applications to enhance overall quality of life through interconnected devices and emerging technological solutions [17]. The primary focus of the model proposed in [18] is to emphasize the architecture of Mobile Edge Computing (MEC) and its diverse applications. MEC facilitates the seamless integration of edge devices between node sources and the cloud, thereby extending the reach of cloud services. This study concentrates on addressing energy-related challenges within MEC, with a specific emphasis on improving capabilities and optimizing workload [19].

Several studies have investigated ways to accelerate Squeeze Net on FPGA, as documented in the literature [34–36]. In [34], efforts were made to enhance the performance of hardware processing convolution operations by employing strategies like flattening, loop unrolling, and pipelining. Though, these approaches didn't significantly improve performance due to bandwidth limitations. Despite combining convolution and maxpool operations at the layer level, the implementation's resource utilization was excessively high, making it impractical for deployment on edge devices due to high power consumption. In order to prioritize scalability when building Convolutional Neural Networks (CNNs), another Squeeze Net design was presented in [35]. This allowed for the flexible and scalable deployment of the CNN as a whole. Even with a (8–16)-bit fixed quantization method, the architecture was resource-intensive and high power, making it difficult to embed and operate on devices with limited resources. Eight multiply-accumulate (MAC) −16 units were included in an accelerator implementation in [36], completing 16 MACs in a clock cycle. To optimize the accelerators, a quantization technique with 8-bit weights, bias, and 16-bit feature maps was used. To cut down on unnecessary memory accesses and extra power usage, a variety of buffers, including the input feature map tile buffer (ITB) and input feature map tile buffer window (ITBW), were used. The design was impractical for real-time deployment on battery-operated edge devices because to its enormous memory capacity, lengthy execution time, and high energy consumption, even if its power consumption allowed it to function on embedded devices.

3 Research Methodology

In the context of Mobile Edge Computing (MEC), this study introduces an innovative "Energy-efficient model" termed E-CFSA. The proposed hybrid model integrates 'Convolutional Neural Networks (CNN) & modified k-mean clustering (MKC).'

(A) **Network Initialization Phase:** This phase involves the declaration and initialization of network variables, breaking down the grid into smaller subcategories.
(B) **Evolution of Nodes:** This phase, tasked with node selection, evaluates trust levels among nodes by utilizing a customized variant of the k-means clustering algorithm to create clusters that most accurately reflect the network's dynamics.
(C) **Cluster Head Selection:** Utilizing the CNN method, this phase identifies optimal cluster head, contributing to power savings.
(D) **Data Transmission:** The final segment of the proposed model is dedicated to *data transmission*, ensuring efficient communication within the network.

Achieving optimized hardware suitable for edge device deployment requires transforming deep learning models into compact versions and utilizing lightweight algorithms. Data quantization is an effective method for compressing models to operate on hardware with limited resources. Model simplification is also essential for hardware optimization, which guarantees that the hardware is light and energy-efficient. As a result, we suggest a model simplification approach that combines data quantization for model compression with a reduction in model size and an ease of parameter setting. The use of data quantization, as an effective compression technique, is essential for resource-constrained, low-latency, and low-energy devices. These devices, constrained by factors such as compactness and battery capacity, require data quantization for efficient model compression. Given the limitations of memory, computation, and power in these devices, quantizing data from floating-point numbers ensures smaller size, reduced computational load, and lower power consumption during data movement and processing.

Figure 1 depicts the process of data quantization for the convolution operation, providing details on the quantized bit arrangements for each element. The weight parameter

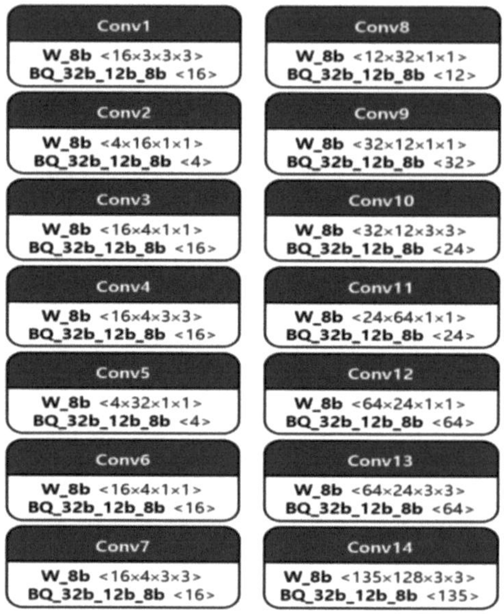

Fig. 1. Model compression through data quantization on convolutions.

undergoes quantization to 8 bits, while the bias, multi-scale, and shift-scale factors are quantized to 32, 12, and 8 bits, respectively, following the BQ order (bias and quantization). Additionally, the activation component is quantized to 8 bits. These quantized parameters can be acquired offline, enabling their utilization in the inference process and simplifying the deployment of the deep learning model on devices. As a result, the reduction in memory size and computational complexity facilitates the model's deployment on cost-effective edge devices. When implementing deep learning models on edge devices with limited resources, hardware design and implementation play a crucial role, especially when using a lightweight approach that incorporates model reduction and compression. In other words, it becomes difficult to build a lightweight model on these devices if the hardware is heavy, has redundant logic and memory needs, and is not well-optimized. This situation leads to substantial hardware resource utilization, increased latency, and higher energy & power consumption. In order to propose an optimized hardware architecture for the previously mentioned lightweight deep learning model, it is necessary to implement a "memory-efficient on-chip memory management strategy" and make use of parallel processing between layers and channels via a 3D tensor-like Processing Element (PE) structure.

Exemplified in Fig. 2 is an outline of the proposed hardware architecture. We have implemented an advanced extensible interface 4 (AXI4) protocol-enabled custom direct memory access (DMA) design that interfaces with external memory. The inform layer unit governs layer sequence, while the *ifmap* (input feature map) driver unit retrieves 'input feature map data from external memory' through DMA. It manages 'read/write operations to on-chip memories' for the *ifmap*, subsequently supplying this data to the 'arithmetic core unit'.

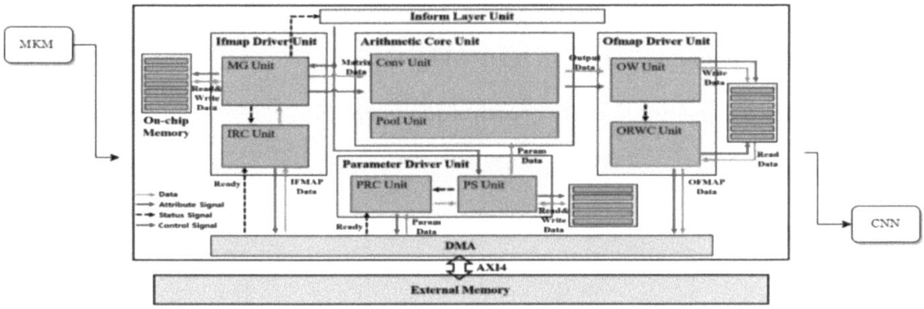

Fig. 2. Proposed hardware architecture overview.

Furthermore, the parameter driver component is responsible for fetching parameter data such as weights, bias, shift-scale factors, and multi-scale factors. The resulting parameter data is read and written to on-chip memory specifically designated for parameters. Using ifmap data from the ifmap driver unit and parameter data from the parameter driver unit, the arithmetic core unit performs convolution and maxpool operations. The ofmap driver unit is the next unit to receive the output from the arithmetic core unit. Last but not least, the ofmap driver unit handles "read/write" operations for data output from the arithmetic core unit and controls communication with the on-chip memories assigned to the ofmap. A comprehensive breakdown of the operations conducted by each unit is provided below.

4 Results and Discussion

Performance Measuring Parameters

This subsection outlines the performance evaluation specifications for both the conventional and the proposed *E-CFSA*. Experimental investigations were carried out to contrast *E-CFSA* with the traditional method, evaluating variables such throughput, packet delivery ratio, stability period, routing overhead, and packet delivery ratio of the cluster head. The ratio of data packets received by sources is known as the packet delivery ratio, or PDR. It can be mathematically defined as follows: S1 is the "number of packets" delivered, and S2 is the "number of packets" received for nodes. Eq. (1) defines it.

$$PDR = \left[\frac{S1}{S2} * 100\right] \tag{1}$$

According to Eq. (2), throughput (Th) is defined as the ratio of cumulative distributed packets coming from the source to the total simulation duration.

$$Th = \left[\frac{No.of\ \ received\ packets}{Simulation\ time}\right] \tag{2}$$

The number of routing and controlling packets required for network communication is known as routing or network overhead (RO), delineated by Eq.(3).

$$RO = \left[\frac{No.of\ \ routing\ packets}{packets\ received}\right] \tag{3}$$

Energy consumption (EC) is total energy expended by the system for data transformation, & communication, delineated by Eq.(4).

$$EC = \left[\frac{Energy\ used\ in\ comm.}{Total\ Energy} \right] \tag{4}$$

Table 1. Simulation outcomes (Influence of Network Size).

No. of nodes	Throughput (kbps)	Routing Overhead
200	198	0.528
400	188	0.493
600	196	0.689
800	236	0.869
1000	277	0.972
1200	282	0.991

Table 1 presents simulation outcomes examining 'the impact of network size' on network performance, considering the no. of nodes, throughput measured in kilobits per second (kbps), and routing overhead. The table categorizes results based on varying numbers of nodes, ranging from 200 to 1200. As the network size increases, the throughput demonstrates fluctuations, starting at 198 kbps for 200 nodes, dipping to 188 kbps for 400 nodes, followed by an increase to 277 kbps for 1000 nodes. Simultaneously, the routing overhead, representing the proportion of routing and controlling packets in the network, shows variations. For instance, with 200 nodes, the routing overhead is 0.528, and it reaches 0.991 for 1200 nodes. This analysis reveals the intricate relationship between network size, throughput, and routing overhead, emphasizing the need for careful consideration when scaling network infrastructures to achieve optimal performance.

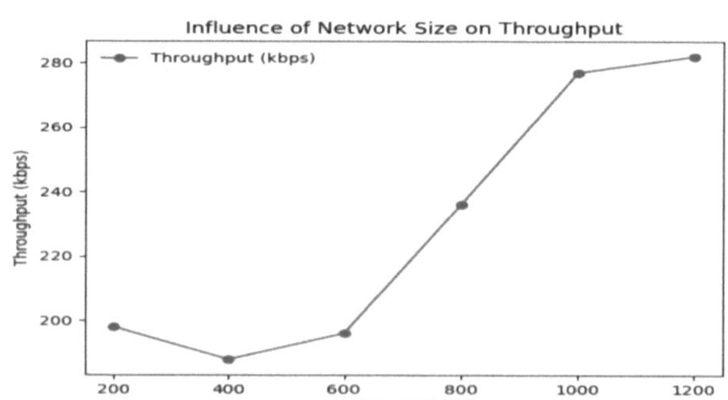

Fig. 3. Influence of Network Size on Throughput

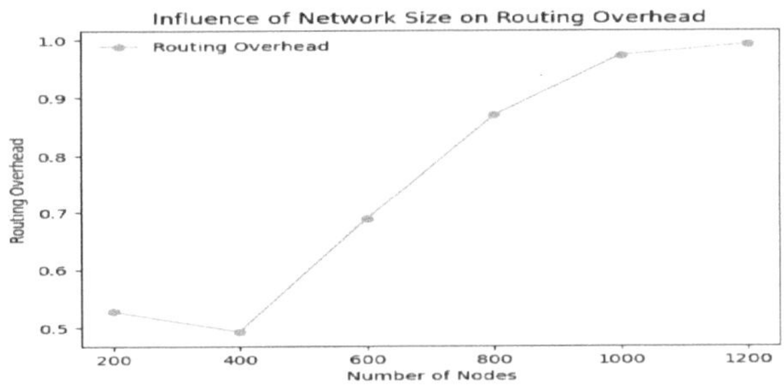

Fig. 4. Influence of Network Size on Routing Overhead

Above Figs. 3 and 4 as shown two distinctive line charts illustrating the influence of *network size* on network 'performance metrics.' The first chart depicts the relationship between the number of nodes and throughput in kilobits per second (kbps). As the quantity of nodes upsurges, the throughput experiences fluctuations, reaching a peak at around 1000 nodes before a slight decrease. This visual representation provides insights into the dynamic nature of data transfer efficiency concerning the network size. The second chart focuses on the routing overhead, represented by the proportion of routing & controlling packets in the network. It demonstrates an upward trend in routing overhead as the quantity of nodes upsurges. This inclination suggests that larger networks may incur a higher proportion of overhead due to increased complexity in routing control packets. These visualizations serve as valuable tools for understanding the intricate relationships between network size, throughput, and routing efficiency.

Table 2. Simulation outcomes (Influence of Node speed).

No. of nodes	Throughput (kbps)	Packet Loss Rate (%)
5	116.93	12.67
10	114.23	18.45
15	103.97	17.42
20	101.49	22.42
25	98.83	26.73
30	97.12	24.21

Table 2 provides simulation outcomes that explore the impact of 'node speed' on the performance metrics, specifically throughput in kilobits per second (kbps) and packet loss rate in percentage. The table categorizes the results based on varying numbers of nodes, ranging from 5 to 30. 'As the number of nodes increases, the throughput exhibits a declining trend, starting at 116.93 kbps for 5 nodes and decreasing to 97.12 kbps for 30 nodes.' Simultaneously, the *packet loss rate*, representing the % of lost *data packets*, tends to increase with a higher number of nodes. For instance, at 5 nodes, the packet loss rate is 12.67%, whereas it rises to 24.21% at 30 nodes. This suggests that an increase in node speed has an impact on both throughput and packet loss rate, emphasizing the need to carefully consider the trade-offs between these two-performance metrics when designing and configuring networks with varying node speeds.

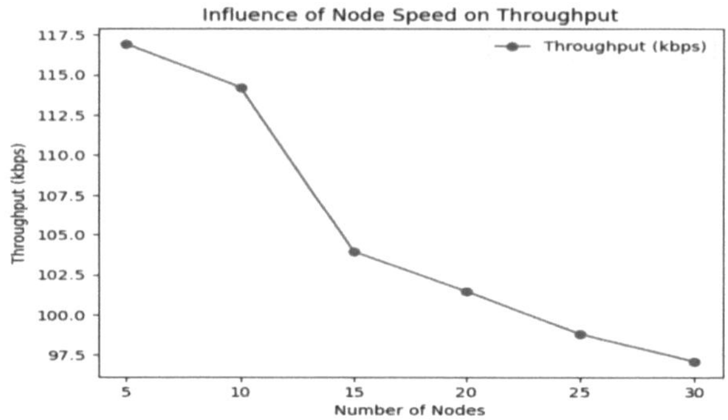

Fig. 5. Influence of Node Speed on Throughput

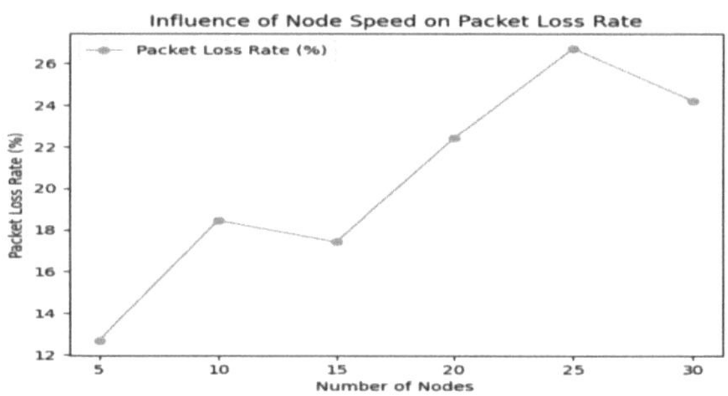

Fig. 6. Influence of Node Speed on Packet Loss Rate

As Figs. 5 and 6 as shown two distinct line charts depicting the influence of node speed on network performance metrics. The first figure illustrates the relationship between the number of nodes and throughput, measured in kilobits per second (kbps). As *the number of nodes increases from 5 to 30*, a gradual decline in throughput is observed, highlighting the impact of node speed on data transfer efficiency. The second figure focuses on the *packet loss rate*, expressed as a percentage, the varying quantity of nodes. A similar trend emerges, revealing an upward trajectory in packet loss rates as the number of nodes increases. This visual representation effectively captures the trade-offs between node speed and network performance, providing valuable insights for network optimization and configuration decisions.

Table 3 presents a comparison of latency and throughput performance between the conventional approach and the proposed method, which incorporates *parallel processing* across layers & introduces a 'maxpool layer in the convolution procedure'. In this approach, the latency is measured at 272.5, indicating the time taken for the system

Table 3. Improving latency and throughput performance

Parameter	Conventional	Proposed
Latency	272.5	125.69
Throughput	90.9	198.3

to process data. In contrast, the proposed method significantly enhances performance, reducing latency to 125.69. This substantial reduction in latency demonstrates the efficacy of parallel processing and the incorporation of a maxpool layer in expediting data processing. Moreover, the throughput, representing the amount of data processed within a given timeframe, exhibits a notable improvement in the proposed approach, with a throughput value of 198.3 compared to the conventional value of 90.9. The proposed method's superior throughput underscores its efficiency in handling data and achieving higher processing rates.

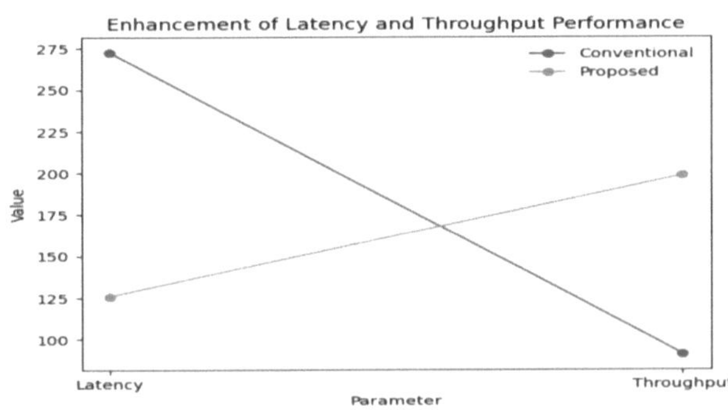

Fig. 7. Enhancement of Latency & Throughput Performance

Figure 7 illustrates a line chart visualizing the enhancement of throughput & latency performance by employing parallel processing among layers & integrating a 'maxpool layer in the convolution procedure'. The *x-axis* represents the parameters, specifically 'Latency' & 'Throughput,' while the *y-axis* corresponds to values measured for apiece parameter. Two lines on the chart distinguish between the conventional approach and the proposed method, marked with circular indicators. The blue line represents the conventional values, showcasing a latency of 272.5 and a throughput of 90.9. In contrast, the orange line represents the proposed values, demonstrating a substantial reduction in latency to 125.69 and a significant increase in throughput to 198.3. This visual representation effectively conveys the performance improvements achieved by the proposed approach, emphasizing the impact of parallel processing and the inclusion of a maxpool layer on latency and throughput metrics.

Table 4 provides a comprehensive overview of the performance outcomes, specifically latency and frames per second (FPS), corresponding to various clock frequencies. The table delineates three distinct clock frequency settings, namely 168 MHz, 201 MHz, and 221 MHz. At a clock frequency of 168 MHz, the system exhibits a latency of 14.72

Table 4. Outcomes of FPS and latency performance conferring to numerous clock frequencies

Frequency (MHz)	Latency (ms)	FPS (frame/s)
168	14.72	74.56
201	12.4	89.6
221	11.25	98.7

milliseconds and achieves a frame rate of 74.56 frames per second. As the clock frequency increases to 201 MHz, there is a notable improvement in performance, with reduced latency to 12.4 milliseconds and an increased frame rate of 89.6 frames per second. Further enhancement is observed at the highest clock frequency of 221 MHz, where latency decreases to 11.25 milliseconds, and the frame rate peaks at 98.7 frames per second. The table underscores the impact of clock frequency on system performance, illustrating a trade-off between latency and FPS as the clock frequency varies, providing valuable insights for optimizing the system based on specific performance requirements.

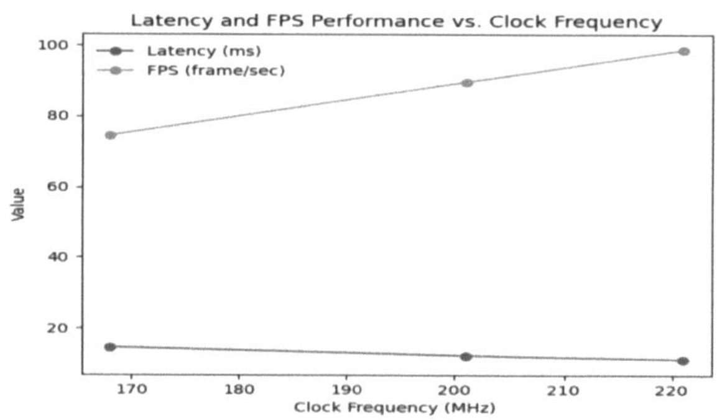

Fig. 8 Latency & FPS performance vs Clock frequency

Figure 8 represents clock frequencies (in MHz), ranging from 168 to 221, while the left y-axis corresponds to latency (in milliseconds) and the right y-axis represents frames per second (FPS). The blue line with circular markers illustrates the trend in latency values, demonstrating a decrease as the clock frequency increases. Simultaneously, the orange line with circular markers depicts the trend in FPS, showcasing an upward trajectory with higher clock frequencies. The legend distinguishes between latency and FPS, aiding in the interpretation of this visual representation of how latency and FPS vary in response to different clock frequencies.

5 Conclusion

Within the realm of 'Mobile Edge Computing (MEC)', this research presents an "energy-efficient algorithm termed E-CFSA for cluster formation and head selection, employing Convolutional Neural Networks (CNN) and modified k-means clustering". The proposed method utilizes machine learning to establish stable clusters with proficient cluster heads, where nodes form clusters using the k-means algorithm. The competent archetypal exhibits accurate predictions, with a test dataset error margin of +/−0.075. This approach addresses the issue of recurrent cluster head selection, thereby promoting prolonged enhanced lifespan & stability for member nodes within a cluster, evaluated through 'cluster head stability time'. The overall functioning is assessed based on the optimal model, considering factors such as throughput, packet delivery ratio, and overhead, while accommodating disparities in node speed & network size. Within the domain of deep learning technology and the expanding frontier of the Internet of Things (IoT), the deployment of deep learning models on IoT devices has emerged as a growing area of interest, especially with the rise of TinyML.

The optimized model's success in object detection is confirmed by experimental results, which are assessed both qualitatively and quantitatively. Furthermore, a proposed hardware architecture is introduced, characterized by its lightweight and energy-efficient design. This design uses an effective on-chip memory management technique, enables the creation of input feature map matrices, and includes a 3D tensor-like Processing Element (PE) structure. Reduced latency and energy usage result from the simultaneous processing of numerous input feature map matrices made possible by the 3D tensor-like PE structure. Additionally, the integration of this PE structure with input feature map matrix generation allows for parallel processing across layers and channels, thereby reducing logic size. Utilizing an strategy related to memory management of on-chip allows for gradual external memory access, reducing operations which are irregular and frequent related to read and write. This approach minimizes the dependency on smaller on-chip memories, resulting in decreased power consumption. The suggested hardware design demonstrates significant reductions of 1.35× and 5.16× in logic and BRAM sizes, respectively. Moreover, it consumes about 11.25× less energy compared to previous iterations. These outcomes were attained with a real-time processing speed of 98.7 fps at an operating frequency of 221 MHz on a ZC702 FPGA. Such results highlight the potential integration of this hardware into edge devices with limited resources, especially those powered by batteries in IoT applications.

References

1. Song, S., Ma, S., Zhao, J., Yang, F., Zhai, L.: Cost-efficient multi-service task offloading scheduling for mobile edge computing. Appl. Intell. **52**, 4028–4040 (2022)
2. Zhou, W. et al.: Offloading strategy with PSO for mobile edge computing based on cache mechanism. Clust. Comput. **25**, 2389–2401 (2022)
3. Irshad, A., Chaudhry, S.A., Ghani, A., Mallah, G.A., Bilal, M., Alzahrani, B.A.: A low-cost privacy-preserving user access in mobile edge computing framework. Comput. Electr. Eng. **98**, 107692 (2022)
4. Zhao, F., Chen, Y., Zhang, Y., Liu, Z., Chen, X.: Dynamic offloading and resource scheduling for mobile-edge computing with energy harvesting devices. IEEE Trans. Netw. Serv. Manag. **18**, 2154–2165 (2021)
5. Al-Shuwaili, A., Simeone, O.: Energy-efficient resource allocation for mobile edge computing-based augmented reality applications. IEEE Wirel. Commun. Lett. **6**, 398–401 (2017)
6. Wang, Q., Tan, L.T., Hu, R.Q., Qian, Y.: Hierarchical energy-efficient mobile-edge computing in IoT networks. IEEE Internet Things J. **7**, 11626–11639 (2020)

7. Tun, Y.K., Park, Y.M., Tran, N.H., Saad, W., Pandey, S.R., Hong, C.S.: Energy-efficient resource management in UAV-assisted mobile edge computing. IEEE Commun. Lett. **25**, 249–253 (2020)
8. Cao, X., Wang, F., Xu, J., Zhang, R., Cui, S.: Joint computation and communication cooperation for energy-efficient mobile edge computing. IEEE Internet Things J. **6**, 4188–4200 (2018)
9. Wu, G., Miao, Y., Zhang, Y., Barnawi, A.: Energy efficient for UAV-enabled mobile edge computing networks: intelligent task prediction and offloading. Comput. Commun. **150**, 556–562 (2020)
10. Zhang, K., et al.: Energy-efficient offloading for mobile edge computing in 5G heterogeneous networks. IEEE Access. **4**, 5896–5907 (2016)
11. Zhang, L., Lai, S., Xia, J., Gao, C., Fan, D., Ou, J.: Deep reinforcement learning based IRS-assisted mobile edge computing under physical-layer security. Physical Commun. **55**, 101896 (2022)
12. Ning, Z., Huang, J., Wang, X., Rodrigues, J.J.P.C., Guo, L.: Mobile edge computing-enabled internet of vehicles: toward energy-efficient scheduling. IEEE Netw. **33**, 198–205 (2019)
13. Ale, L., Zhang, N., Fang, X., Chen, X., Wu, S., Li, L.: Delay-aware and energy-efficient computation offloading in mobile-edge computing using deep reinforcement learning. IEEE Trans. Cogn. Commun. Netw. **7**, 881–892 (2021)
14. Lyu, X., Tian, H., Ni, W., Zhang, Y., Zhang, P., Liu, R.P.: Energy-efficient admission of delay-sensitive tasks for mobile edge computing. IEEE Trans. Commun. **66**, 2603–2616 (2018)
15. Guleria, K., Prasad, D., Lilhore, U.K., Simaiya, S.: Asynchronous media access control protocols and cross layer optimizations for wireless sensor networks: an energy efficient perspective. J. Comput. Theor. Nanosci. **17**, 2531–2538 (2020)
16. Zaman, S.K.U., et al.: LiMPO: lightweight mobility prediction and offloading framework using machine learning for mobile edge computing. Clust. Comput. **26**, 99–117 (2022)
17. Lilhore, U.K., Khalaf, O.I., Simaiya, S., Tavera Romero, C.A., Abdulsahib, G.M., Kumar, D.: A depth-controlled and energy-efficient routing protocol for underwater wireless sensor networks. Int. J. Distrib. Sens. Netw. **18**, 15501329221117118 (2022)
18. Trinh, H., et al.: Energy-aware mobile edge computing and routing for low-latency visual data processing. IEEE Trans. Multimed. **20**, 2562–2577 (2018)
19. Mukherjee, M., Kumar, V., Lat, A., Guo, M., Matam, R., Lv, Y.: Distributed deep learning-based task offloading for UAV-enabled mobile edge computing. In: Proceedings of the IEEE INFOCOM 2020—IEEE Conference on Computer Communications Workshops (INFOCOM WKSHPS), Toronto, ON, Canada, 6–9 July, pp. 1208–1212 (2020)
20. Mijwil, M.M., Abttan, R.A.: Artificial intelligence: a survey on evolution and future trends. Asian J. Appl. Sci. **9**, 87–93 (2021)
21. Schmidhuber, J.: Deep learning in neural networks: an overview. Neural Netw. **61**, 85–117 (2015)
22. Deng, L.: A tutorial survey of architectures, algorithms, and applications for deep learning. APSIPA Trans. Signal Inf. Process. **3**, e2 (2014)
23. Bengio, Y., Courville, A., Vincent, P.: Representation learning: a review and new perspectives. IEEE Trans. Pattern Anal. Mach. Intell. **35**, 1798–1828 (2013)
24. Bengio, Y.: Deep learning of representations: looking forward. In: Proceedings of the International Conference on Statistical Language and Speech Processing, Tarragona, Spain, 29–31 July, pp. 1–37 (2013)
25. Bengio, Y.: Learning deep architectures for AI. Found. Trends Mach. Learn. **2**, 1–127 (2009)
26. Qijie, Z., et al.: M2Det: a single-shot object detector based on multi-level feature pyramid network. In: Proceedings of the Thirty-Third AAAI Conference on Artificial Intelligence, Honolulu, HI, USA, 27 January–1 February (2019)

27. Zhao, Z., Zheng, P., Xu, S., Wu, X.: Object detection with deep learning: a review. IEEE Trans. Neural Netw. Learn. Syst. **30**, 3212–3232 (2019)
28. Jeong, Y., Son, S., Lee, B., Lee, S.: The braking-pressure and driving-direction determination system (BDDS) using road roughness and passenger conditions of surrounding vehicles. Sensors. **22**, 4414 (2022)
29. Andre, L., Matthew, C., Nathan, A., Edwin, W., Emil, D., Bennie, V.: Deep learning in the automotive industry: applications and tools. In: Proceedings of the IEEE International Conference on Big Data (Big Data), Washington, DC, USA, 5–8 December, pp. 3759–3768 (2016)
30. Chun-Hsian, H., Po-Jung, C., Yi-Jie, L., Bo-Wei, C., Jia-Xuan, Z.: A robot-based intelligent management design for agricultural cyber-physical systems. Comput. Electron. Agric. **181**, 105967 (2021)
31. Liangzhi, L., Kaoru, O., Mianxiong, D.: Deep learning for smart industry: efficient manufacture inspection system with fog computing. IEEE Trans. Ind. Inform. **14**, 4665–4673 (2018)
32. Mehdi, M., Ala, A., Sameh, S., Mohsen, G.: Deep learning for IoT big data and streaming analytics: a survey. IEEE Communications Surv. Tutor. **20**, 2923–2960 (2018)
33. Xia, H., Lingyang, C., Jian, P., Weiqing, L., Jiang, B.: Model complexity of deep learning: a survey. Knowl. Inf. Syst. **63**, 2585–2619 (2021)
34. Arora, M.; Lanka, S.: Accelerating SqueezeNet on FPGA. Available online: https://lankas.github.io/15-618Project. Accessed on 7 July 2022
35. Huang, C., Ni, S., Chen, G.: A layer-based structured design of CNN on FPGA. In: Proceedings of the 2017 IEEE 12th International Conference on ASIC (ASICON), Guiyang, China, 25–28 October, pp. 1037–1040 (2017)
36. Mousouliotis, P.G., Panayiotou, K.L., Tsardoulias, E.G., Petrou, L.P., Symeonidis, A.L.: Expanding a robot's life: low power object recognition via FPGA-based DCNN deployment. In: Proceedings of the 2018 7th International Conference on Modern Circuits and Systems Technologies (MOCAST), Thessaloniki, Greece, 7–9 May, pp. 1–4 (2018)

Data Science

Beyond the Lyrics: Comparative Analysis of Deep Learning Approaches for Sentiment Classification in Song Lyrics

Avni Tonger, Gauri Tyagi, Archana Singh, and Sofia Singh(✉)

Department of Artificial Intelligence, Amity School of Engineering and Technology, Amity University Noida, Noida, India

gauri.tyagi@s.amity.edu, {asingh27,ssingh5}@amity.edu

Abstract. This chapter presents a comparative analysis of deep learning models including BERT, LSTM, SVM, LNet, etc., for sentiment classification in song lyrics. We are utilizing a dataset extracted from the Billboard Top 100 songs spanning from 2012 to 2022. The study explores various deep learning architectures' efficacy in capturing sentiment nuances expressed in diverse music genres. Each model is trained, validated, and tested using appropriate metrics to evaluate performance. Comparative assessments based on accuracy, precision, recall, and F1-score metrics provide insights into model strengths and weaknesses. Findings contribute to advancing sentiment analysis techniques in song lyrics and offer practical guidance for leveraging deep learning in music-related applications such as personalized recommendations and marketing strategies.

Keywords: Sentiment analysis · Deep learning · Song lyrics · Comparative analysis · BERT · LSTM · SVM · XLNet · Billboard Top 100 songs

1 Introduction

Sentiment analysis involves analysing text to determine the emotional tone expressed, such as positive, negative, or neutral sentiments; in song lyrics it has emerged as a vital area of research due to its potential applications in understanding user choices and preferences, enhancing music recommendation systems, and informing sentiment-driven marketing strategies [10, 11].

With the exponential growth of digital music platforms and the availability of vast amounts of song data, there is a growing need to develop robust techniques for automatically analysing the sentiment expressed in song lyrics. Deep learning models have shown remarkable success in various natural language processing tasks, making them promising candidates for sentiment classification in song lyrics [17].

This chapter focuses on conducting a comparative analysis of deep learning approaches for sentiment classification in song lyrics, utilizing a dataset comprising Billboard Top 100 songs spanning from 2012 to 2022.

The selected models, including BERT, LSTM, SVM, XLNet, among others, offer diverse architectural paradigms and learning mechanisms, enabling a comprehensive

M. Paprzycki et al. (Eds.): ICACIS 2024, CCIS 2405, pp. 263–274, 2027.
https://doi.org/10.1007/978-3-032-30990-7_19

evaluation of their effectiveness in capturing sentiment nuances inherent in song lyrics across different genres and themes [15, 26].

Through this comparative study, we aim to not only assess the performance of these models but also identify their strengths and limitations in handling sentiment analysis tasks specific to song lyrics. Additionally, we explore the impact of various factors such as hyperparameters, training methodologies, and feature representations on model performance, providing valuable insights for optimizing sentiment analysis in the realm of music.

Ultimately, the findings of this research endeavour are expected to contribute significantly to advancing sentiment analysis techniques in song lyrics and fostering innovation in music-related applications, including the enhancement of recommendation systems.

2 Literature Review

The literature in the field of sentiment analysis in song lyrics encompasses diverse approaches and methodologies aimed at understanding and classifying emotional content in music.

Revathy et al. (2023) [2] introduce LyEmoBERT, a model designed for multi-class classification of lyrical emotions and subsequent recommendations based on these emotions. Their work demonstrates the potential of transfer learning approaches and the importance of integrating domain-specific datasets for emotion classification.

Jin et al. (022) [3] propose an attention-based Bi-DLSTM model for sentiment analysis of Beijing Opera lyrics, leveraging dilated recurrent skip connections to capture long-sequence information effectively. Their model, complemented by attention mechanisms, addresses the scarcity of lyric sentiment analysis data by constructing a dedicated dataset, demonstrating the efficacy of their approach through extensive experimentation.

Xu et al. (021) [5] investigate the relationship between music emotion and lyric features, employing machine learning analysis to extract and analyse linguistic features in Chinese songs. Their findings underscore the significance of lyric features in music emotion recognition models, enhancing the predictive capability of existing models, particularly in valence recognition tasks.

Additionally, Xia et al. (2008) [6] propose a sentiment vector space model (s-VSM) tailored for lyric-based song sentiment classification, addressing key challenges such as word ambiguity and short lyric lengths. Their model outperforms traditional vector space models, highlighting the importance of considering contextual nuances in sentiment analysis.

Lastly, Martín-Gómez and Navarro Cáceres (2018) [7] introduce a data mining-based sentiment analysis method to infer emotions evoked by music. Leveraging various data mining algorithms, their approach extracts and classifies musical features to elucidate the influence of music parameters on human emotions, offering insights into the complex interplay between music and emotions.

Collectively, these studies underscore the diversity of approaches and methodologies in sentiment analysis in song lyrics, reflecting ongoing efforts to deepen our understanding of emotional content in music and its implications for various applications.

3 Dataset (Table 1)

Table 1. Dataset Attribute Description

Column Name	Data Type	Description
Top100Year	Integer	The year of the Billboard Top 100 list to which the song belongs.
SongTitle	String	Title of the Song
Artist	String	Name of the Artists
LyricsStatus	Boolean	Indicates whether the lyrics of the song are available (True) or not (False).
Lyrics	String	Lyrics of the Song

3.1 Description of the Dataset

The dataset comprises Billboard Top 100 songs spanning from 2012 to 2022, containing information on various attributes of each song. It consists of 1100 entries across seven columns.

The dataset primarily comprises songs in English, with a minority in other languages such as Spanish, Korean, Portuguese, and Hungarian. Among these, Spanish is the most prevalent, followed by Korean. This dataset provides a comprehensive collection of Billboard Top 100 songs over a decade, facilitating various analyses and insights into trends in popular music across different genres and languages.

3.2 Data Preprocessing

Several steps were undertaken to prepare the initial dataset to subsequently train our models, comprising 1100 rows and 7 columns, for sentiment analysis.

Initially, the dataset was filtered to include only entries with available lyrics. The 'LyricsStatus' column, deemed unnecessary for analysis, was subsequently dropped. Initially, we employed a pretrained Facebook model (fastText) to identify the language of each song's lyrics. Only English lyrics were retained for analysis, ensuring a consistent language base. To avoid redundancy, duplicates based on song titles were removed.

The next phase focused on text cleansing; this involved removing special characters, punctuation, and converting all text to lowercase to standardize the data format. A significant visualization included in our analysis Fig. 1. showcases the distribution of songs by artists in the Top 100 chart, highlighting the most frequently featured artists over the years.

Further refinement was achieved by removing stop-words along with specific, frequently occurring words that do not contribute significantly to sentiment analysis. This step was crucial for focusing the model on meaningful text.

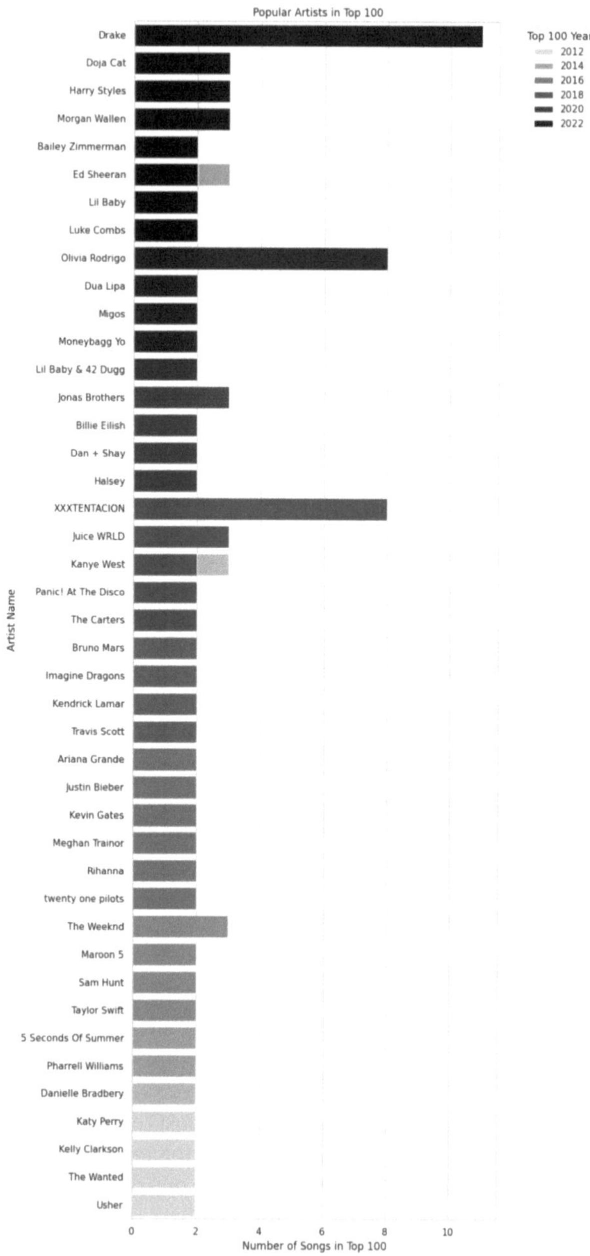

Fig. 1. Distribution of Songs by Artists in the Top 100 Chart

After cleansing, a sentiment analysis was performed on the cleaned lyrics using VADER, a lexicon and rule-based sentiment analysis tool that is specifically attuned to sentiments expressed in social media. This process involved generating compound sentiment scores for each song, which were then classified into positive, negative, or neutral categories based on predefined thresholds.

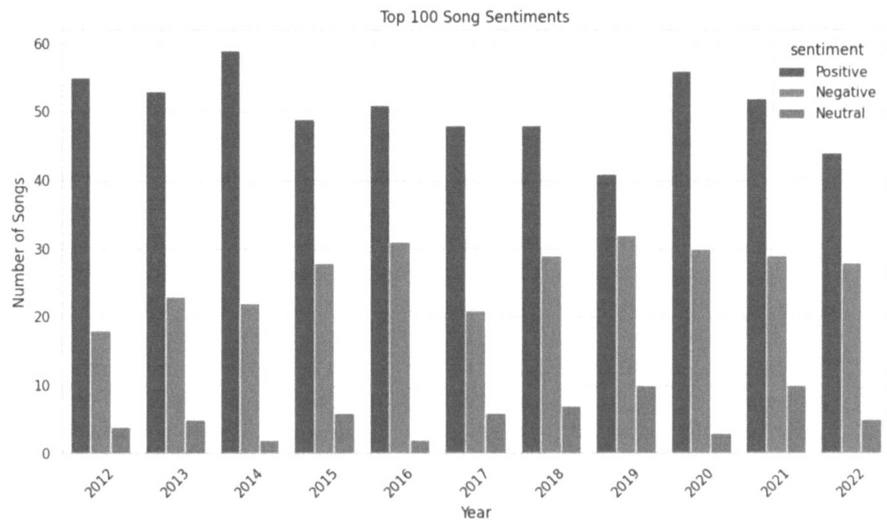

Fig. 2. Distribution of sentiments across the year 2012 to 2022

Additionally, we visualized the distribution of sentiments over the years with interactive bar charts, providing a clear visual representation of trends in song sentiments within the Top 100 charts as shown in Fig. 2. This comprehensive approach to preprocessing and analysis ensures our data is optimally prepared for accurate sentiment classification, yielding reliable insights into the emotional underpinnings of popular music lyrics.

The resulting clean lyrics were stored in a new column named ‘LyricsClean’. Finally, additional features such as the total number of words and unique words were computed to enrich the dataset.

The pre-processed dataset, consisting of 907 rows and 2 columns, was then ready for subsequent analysis and model training for sentiment classification.

4 Deep Learning Models for Sentiment Classification

4.1 BERT Model

Bidirectional Encoder Representations from Transformers is a powerful natural language processing model developed by Google. It utilises a transformer architecture, which enables it to capture contextual information from both left and right contexts in a text [14].

BERT is pre-trained on a large corpora of text data using unsupervised learning techniques, such as masked language modelling and next sentence prediction. After pre-training, BERT can be fine-tuned on downstream tasks like sentiment analysis, text classification, question answering, and more [28].

The model is being trained for a multi-class classification task with three classes (sentiments). The model is compiled for training using the Adam optimizer with a learning rate scheduler. The loss function used is 'Sparse Categorical Cross Entropy', which is suitable for multi-class classification tasks. It shuffles the dataset and batches it with a batch size of 8.

4.2 LSTM Model

Long Short-Term Memory (LSTM) is a type of recurrent neural network (RNN) architecture designed to handle the vanishing gradient problem, which occurs in traditional RNNs when trying to learn long-term dependencies in sequential data. LSTM models are well-suited for sequential data analysis, making them commonly used in tasks such as sentiment analysis [29].

The first LSTM layer has 128 units and returns sequences. Dropout is applied after the first LSTM layer to prevent overfitting. The subsequent LSTM layers have decreasing numbers of units (64 and then 32) and return sequences. A dense layer with 3 units and SoftMax activation is added for multi-class classification. The SoftMax activation ensures that the output values are normalized probabilities representing the likelihood of each class. It It is compiled with categorical cross-entropy loss, Adam optimizer, and accuracy metric.

4.3 Support Vector Machine

SVM is a supervised machine learning algorithm commonly used for classification tasks. It works by finding the optimal hyperplane that separates different classes in the feature space. SVM aims to maximize the margin between the classes, which helps improve generalization performance and robustness against noise [8].

It is used for its ability to handle high-dimensional data efficiently and effectively. By representing text data as numerical feature vectors (e.g., using techniques like TF-IDF or word embeddings), SVM can learn to classify text into different sentiment categories. Its ability to handle large feature spaces and find the optimal decision boundary makes it suitable for sentiment analysis tasks where the number of features (e.g., words or word embeddings) can be very high.

4.4 XlNet

XLNet, an extension of the Transformer architecture, is a state-of-the-art language model designed to capture bidirectional context by leveraging the permutation-based attention mechanism [20]. It offers several advantages, including its ability to model complex dependencies in text data and its superior performance in capturing long-range dependencies compared to traditional models. Moreover, XLNet's pre-trained representations of language enable effective transfer learning, allowing the model to adapt to sentiment analysis tasks with minimal fine-tuning [14].

For our research, we utilized the 'xlnet-base-cased' model, which is pre-trained on a large corpus of text data. The 'XLNetTokenizer' was employed to tokenize input text, and the 'XLNetForSequenceClassification' model was utilized for sentiment classification. The model was fine-tuned using 'AdamW' optimizer with a learning rate of 3e-5 over 10 epochs, with a linear scheduler for adjusting learning rates during training. These configurations enable effective utilization of XLNet's capabilities for sentiment analysis tasks on the given dataset, empowering the model to learn and capture sentiment nuances present in song lyrics.

5 Deep Learning Models for Sentiment Classification

Table 2. Comparative Analysis of the Deep Learning Models for Sentiment Analysis

Model	Test Accuracy	Precision	Recall	F1_Score
BERT	0.839	0.84	0.94	0.89
LSTM	0.800	0.78	0.82	0.80
SVM (*CNB*)	0.747	0.84	0.81	0.83
SVM (*MNB*)	0.747	0.84	0.81	0.83
SVM (*BNB*)	0.738	0.78	0.90	0.83

In the comparative analysis of four sentiment analysis models, namely BERT, SVM (ComplementNB, MultinomialNB, BernoulliNB), XLNet, and LSTM, significant differences in performance metrics were observed (Table 2).

BERT exhibited commendable results with a test loss of 0.474 and an accuracy of 83.88%. SVM models, including ComplementNB, MultinomialNB, and BernoulliNB, achieved accuracies ranging from 73.08% to 74.73%, with notable variations in precision, recall, and F1-score across sentiment classes. XLNet demonstrated competitive performance with a loss of 0.4427 and an accuracy of 82.96%, exhibiting high precision and recall values. LSTM, on the other hand, achieved an overall accuracy of 80% with balanced precision and recall scores for both sentiment classes.

The diverse performance of these models suggests that while BERT and XLNet excel in capturing nuanced sentiment nuances, traditional models like SVM and LSTM also offer robust performance, albeit with slight variations in precision and recall metrics. These findings underscore the importance of selecting an appropriate model architecture based on the specific requirements and characteristics of the sentiment analysis task at hand.

6 Practical Implications

The comparative analysis of deep learning models for sentiment analysis in song lyrics extends beyond academic curiosity, holding significant implications for various industries [9].

In the music industry, understanding the emotional content of songs can enhance personalized music recommendation systems, tailoring playlists to the listener's current mood or emotional state, thereby improving user engagement and satisfaction. For artists and record labels, sentiment analysis can guide the creative process, marketing strategies, and promotional activities by aligning song releases with current sentiment trends among target audiences [1].

In the broader context of media and entertainment, sentiment analysis of song lyrics can be integrated into content curation platforms, social media, and marketing analytics tools to gauge public sentiment, predict trends, and tailor content more effectively to diverse audience segments. Furthermore, this technology could play a role in mental health applications, where music is used as a therapeutic tool, by selecting songs that match or influence the emotional state of users positively [10].

As AI and machine learning continue to evolve, the integration of sentiment analysis in interactive and smart devices (e.g., smart speakers, virtual assistants) could offer more intuitive and context-aware functionalities, enhancing user experience through emotionally intelligent responses and interactions.

This research underscores the potential of deep learning in unlocking new avenues for engagement, personalization, and emotional connectivity, paving the way for innovative applications that transcend traditional boundaries between technology and human emotions.

7 Result

In this comparative analysis of deep learning models for sentiment analysis in song lyrics, we evaluated the performance of BERT, LSTM, and XLNet alongside SVM classifiers (Complement Naive Bayes - CNB, Multinomial Naive Bayes - MNB, Bernoulli Naive Bayes - BNB).

Among the deep learning models, XLNet exhibited the highest test accuracy (83.0%), precision (85%), recall (95%), and F1-score (87%). BERT followed closely with a test accuracy of 83.9% and robust performance across precision, recall, and F1-score metrics.

While LSTM demonstrated competitive performance, achieving a test accuracy of 80.0%, the SVM classifiers (CNB, MNB, BNB) showed slightly lower accuracy scores ranging from 73.8% to 74.7% (Fig. 3).

These findings suggest that XLNet and BERT are promising models for sentiment analysis in song lyrics for the chosen dataset, showcasing their effectiveness in capturing complex emotional nuances and outperforming traditional SVM classifiers in this task (Fig. 4).

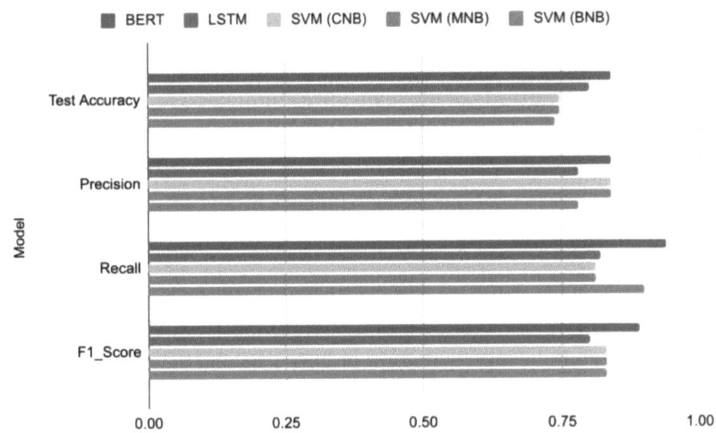

Fig. 3. Distribution of the comparative results of the BERT, LSTM and SVM models

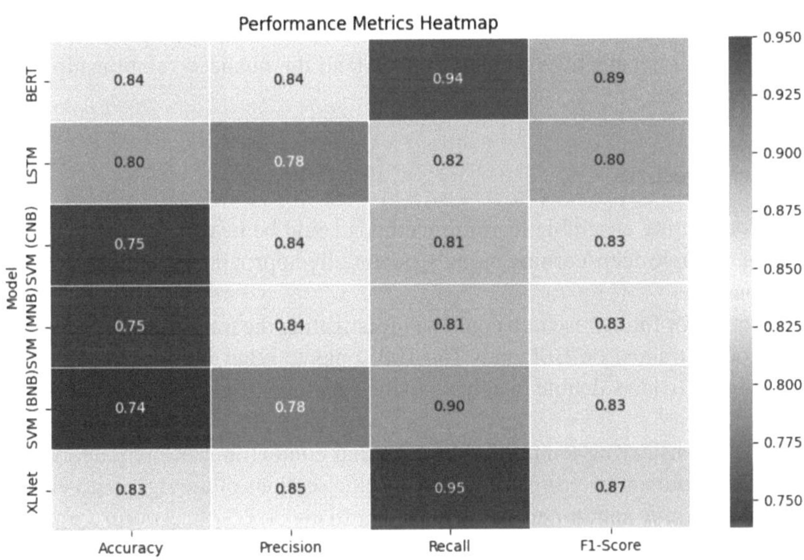

Fig. 4. Heatmap depicting the Accuracy, Precision, Recall and F1-score of the models

8 Conclusion

In the conclusion of our research, the contributions of each team member are distinctly highlighted. **Gauri Tyagi** led the data collection and preprocessing stages, ensuring the robustness of the dataset, and carried out the execution of SVM and the XLNet models. **Avni Tonger** was instrumental in implementing and fine-tuning the deep learning models, including BERT and LSTM, and carried out the computational experiments.

Sofia Singh provided expert guidance on the project's direction, particularly in refining the analytical methodologies and interpreting the data analysis results. **Archana**

Singh contributed significantly to the structuring and writing of the manuscript, ensuring that the study's findings were clearly articulated and aligned with academic standards. Together, the collaborative efforts of the team have culminated in a comprehensive study that advances our understanding of sentiment analysis in song lyrics and its practical applications.

8.1 Limitations of the Study

This study's exploration of sentiment analysis in song lyrics using deep learning models encompasses several limitations that warrant attention. Firstly, the inherent complexity of human emotions and their representation in music means that lyrics alone might not fully capture the intended sentiment, overlooking the influence of melody, rhythm, and instrumentation.

Additionally, the dataset used, while extensive, may not encompass the full diversity of genres, cultures, and languages, potentially limiting the generalizability of the findings across different musical traditions. These constraints highlight the need for a more holistic approach to sentiment analysis in music, incorporating multimodal data and cross-cultural perspectives to better understand the nuanced relationship between music and emotion.

8.2 Future Directions

Firstly, incorporating ensemble learning methods could be investigated to combine the strengths of multiple deep learning models, potentially improving classification accuracy and robustness.

One avenue for future research could be investigating the transferability of sentiment analysis models trained on Billboard Top 100 songs to other music genres or cultural contexts could provide valuable insights into the generalizability and robustness of these models.

Moreover, considering temporal dynamics and context in sentiment analysis, such as changes in sentiment over time or within specific sections of a song, could yield more nuanced and accurate sentiment predictions.

Finally, evaluating the practical implications of sentiment analysis in real-world music-related applications, such as personalized music recommendation systems or sentiment-driven marketing strategies, through user studies or field experiments, can provide valuable insights into the potential benefits and challenges of deploying sentiment analysis models in industry settings.

References

1. Wang, J., Yang, Y.. Deep learning based mood tagging for Chinese song lyrics. arXiv (2019). https://arxiv.org/pdf/1906.02135.pdf
2. Revathy, V.R., Pillai, A.S., Daneshfar, F.: LyEmoBERT: classification of lyrics' emotion and recommendation using a pre-trained model. Procedia Comput. Sci. **218**, 1196–1208 (2023) https://www.sciencedirect.com/science/article/pii/S1877050923000984

3. Jin, C., Song, Z., Xu, J., Gao, H.: Attention-based Bi-DLSTM for sentiment analysis of Beijing opera lyrics. 06 May 2022. Conference Issue: Intelligent Media Computing Technology and Applications for Mobile Internet. (2022). https://www.hindawi.com/journals/wcmc/2022/1167462/
4. Xu, L., Sun, Z., Wen, X., Huang, Z., Chao, C., Xu, L.: Using machine learning analysis to interpret the relationship between music emotion and lyric features. PeerJ Comput Sci. **7**, e785 (2021) https://www.ncbi.nlm.nih.gov/pmc/articles/PMC8627224/
5. Xia, Y., Wang, L., Wong, K., Xu, M.: Sentiment Vector Space Model for Lyric-based Song Sentiment Classification (2008). https://aclanthology.org/P08-2034.pdf
6. Martín-Gómez, L., Cáceres, M.N.: Applying data mining for sentiment analysis in music. Adv. Intell. Syst. Comput. (2018). https://doi.org/10.1007/978-3-319-61578-3_20. Conference: International Conference on Practical Applications of Agents and Multi-Agent Systems. https://www.researchgate.net/publication/318510880_Applying_Data_Mining_for_Sentiment_Analysis_in_Music
7. Chen, X., et al.: A Novel Approach for Explicit Song Lyrics Detection Using Machine and Deep Ensemble Learning Models (2023). https://doi.org/10.7717/peerj-cs.1469. https://peerj.com/articles/cs-1469.pdf
8. Zainuddin, N., Selamat, A.: Sentiment analysis using support vector machine. In: I4CT 2014 - 1st International Conference on Computer, Communications, and Control Technology, Proceedings, pp. 333–337 (2014). https://doi.org/10.1109/I4CT.2014.6914200. https://www.researchgate.net/publication/286583940_Sentiment_analysis_using_Support_Vector_Machine
9. Xituo(Vito) Chen and Tiffany, Y. Tang. Combining Content and Sentiment Analysis on Lyrics for a Lightweight Emotion-Aware Chinese Song Recommendation System. DOI:10.1145/3195106.3195148, Conference: ICMLC 2018:10th International Conference on Machine Learning and Computing (2018). https://www.researchgate.net/publication/347751569_Combining_Content_and_Sentiment_Analysis_on_Lyrics_for_a_Lightweight_Emotion-Aware_Chinese_Song_Recommendation_System
10. Jia, X.: Music emotion classification method based on deep learning and improved attention mechanism. Comput Intell Neurosci. (2022). https://doi.org/10.1155/2022/5181899. PMID: 35769273; PMCID: PMC9236837. https://www.ncbi.nlm.nih.gov/pmc/articles/PMC9236837/
11. Jiang, T., Deng, S., Wu, P., Jiang, H.. Real-time human-music emotional interaction based on deep learning and multimodal sentiment analysis. Conference Issue: Intelligent Media Computing Technology and Applications for Mobile Internet 2022, Vol. 2023, 4939048 (2023). https://www.hindawi.com/journals/wcmc/2023/4939048/
12. Sumith, N., Wagle, S., Ghosh, P., Kishore, K.: Sentiment classification of english and hindi music lyrics using supervised machine learning algorithms. In: 2022 2nd Asian Conference on Innovation in Technology (ASIANCON). IEEE (2022). https://doi.org/10.1109/ASIANCON55314.2022.9908688. https://ieeexplore.ieee.org/document/9908688
13. Vásquez-Leon, M., Ugarte, W.. Sentiment analysis of song lyrics using clustering. https://doi.org/10.1007/978-3-030-75680-2_38, Conference: Brazilian Technology Symposium (2021). https://www.researchgate.net/publication/352395484_Sentiment_Analysis_of_Song_Lyrics_Using_Clustering
14. Danyal, M.M., et al.: Proposing sentiment analysis model based on BERT and XLNet for movie reviews. Multimed. Tools Appl. **83**, 1–25 (2024). https://doi.org/10.1007/s11042-024-18156-5. https://www.researchgate.net/publication/377410754_Proposing_sentiment_analysis_model_based_on_BERT_and_XLNet_for_movie_reviews
15. Shukla, S., Khanna, P., Agrawal, K.K.: Review on sentiment analysis on music. In: Dec. 18–20, 2017 International Conference on Infocom Technologies and Unmanned Systems (ICTUS'2017), ADET, Amity University Dubai, UAE. IEEE (2017) https://ieeexplore.ieee.org/stamp/stamp.jsp?arnumber=8286111

16. Raschka, S.: MusicMood: predicting the mood of music from song lyrics using machine learning. ArXiv. abs/1611.00138 (2016). https://www.semanticscholar.org/paper/MusicMood%3A-Predicting-the-mood-of-music-from-song-Raschka/0e0e9361fff86f87d964984d8001c90c68a1c3a9
17. Ellen G.Y., Manueke, L.L., Mangkey, L., Manueke, G.W.: Sentiment Analysis of Lyrics on Recycled and Recent Songs using Natural Language Processing Technology (2024). https://novateurpublication.org/index.php/np/article/view/179/169
18. Yudhik Agrawal, R., Shanker, Alluri, V.: Transformer-based approach towards music emotion recognition from lyrics. In: European Conference on Information Retrieval (2021). https://doi.org/10.1007/978-3-030-72240-1_12. Corpus ID: 230770386. https://www.semanticscholar.org/paper/Transformer-based-approach-towards-music-emotion-Agrawal-Shanker/8d9877694e990ea8bb26ecaf430fa41849a8aae7
19. Padmane, P., Agrahari, K., Kesharwani, R., Mohitkar, K., Khan, S., Kamale, N.: Prediction of song mood through lyrics. Int. Res. J. Mod. Eng. Technol. Sci. (2022) e-ISSN: 2582–5208. https://www.irjmets.com/uploadedfiles/paper/issue_4_april_2022/21305/final/fin_irjmets1650865496.pdf
20. Dhivyaa, C.R. et al.: XLNet Transfer Learning Model for Sentimental Analysis, 76–84 (2023). https://doi.org/10.1109/ICSCSS57650.2023.10169445. https://www.researchgate.net/publication/372207199_XLNet_Transfer_Learning_Model_for_Sentimental_Analysis
21. Kora, R., Mohammed, A.: An enhanced approach for sentiment analysis based on meta-ensemble deep learning. Soc. Netw. Anal. Min. **13**, 38 (2023) Springer. https://link.springer.com/article/10.1007/s13278-023-01043-6
22. Park, H.-j., Song, M., Shin, K.-S.: Deep learning models and datasets for aspect term sentiment classification: implementing holistic recurrent attention on target-dependent memories. Knowl.-Based Syst. **187**, 104825 (2020) https://www.sciencedirect.com/science/article/abs/pii/S0950705119303004
23. Mia, M., Das, P., Habib, A.: Verse-based emotion analysis of bengali music from lyrics using machine learning and neural network classifiers. Univ. Bahrain Sci. J. (2024) ISSN: 2210-142X, https://journal.uob.edu.bh/handle/123456789/4947
24. Ali, N.M., El Hamid, M.M.A., Youssif, A.: Sentiment Analysis For Movies Reviews Dataset Using Deep Learning Models. Int. J. Data Min. Knowl. Manag.Process (IJDKP). **9** (2019) https://web.archive.org/web/20200211172716id_/https://pdfs.semanticscholar.org/4510/27cc32ee1b91eb3c8773436c1da1132a8f64.pdf
25. Zhang, L.: Deep learning for sentiment analysis: a survey. Arxiv (2018). https://arxiv.org/pdf/1801.07883.pdf
26. Shilpa, P. C., Shereen, R., Jacob, S., & Vinod, P.: Sentiment analysis using deep learning. 930–937 (2021). https://doi.org/10.1109/ICICV50876.2021.9388382. https://www.researchgate.net/publication/350543179_Sentiment_Analysis_Using_Deep_Learning
27. Dang, N.C., Moreno-García, M.N., De la Prieta, F.: Sentiment analysis based on deep learning: a comparative study. Electronics 2020. **9**(3), 483 (2020). https://doi.org/10.3390/electronics9030483
28. Ain, Q.T., et al.: Sentiment analysis using deep learning techniques: a review. Int. J. Adv. Comput. Sci. Appl. (IJACSA). **8**(6) (2017). https://doi.org/10.14569/IJACSA.2017.080657. https://thesai.org/Publications/ViewPaper?Volume=8&Issue=6&Code=IJACSA&SerialNo=57
29. Umarani, V., Julian, A., Deepa, J.: Sentiment Analysis using various Machine Learning and Deep Learning Techniques. J. Nigerian Soc. Phys. Sci. **3**, 385–394 (2021). https://doi.org/10.46481/jnsps.2021.308. https://www.researchgate.net/publication/356624355_Sentiment_Analysis_using_various_Machine_Learning_and_Deep_Learning_Techniques

LAResNet50: Lesion Aware Detection Network for Dual Ocular Diseases

Sarvat Ali(✉) and Shital Raut

Department of Computer Science and Engineering, Visvesvaraya National Institute of Technology, Nagpur 440022, Maharashtra, India
sarvataliii@students.vnit.ac.in

Abstract. As the manual screening of medical images by physicians is time-consuming and there is a paucity of medical personnel, patients avoid regular screening until the disease is severe. Nowadays, computer-aided diagnosis is highly anticipated in the field of ophthalmology. Modern computationally intelligent systems are able to diagnose and treat ocular disease with greater speed and accuracy. However, their explicability remains a major concern. We have attempted to develop a trustworthy AI-powered dual ocular disease detection network cognizant of relative lesion segmentation and multi-head self-attention. The ensemble model integrates a UnetPlusPlus segmentation model with Squeeze-Excitation (SE) inclusive ResNet50 as an encoder to examine lesion anatomy and a ResNet50 with multi-head self-attention(MHSA) to highlight spatial locations of lesions. This lesion-aware ensemble architecture is trained and tested upon heterogeneous Diabetic Retinopathy(DR) and PM(pathological Myopia) datasets with a mean accuracy of 0.967 across datasets. This robust, explicable, usable and fair AI system can be entrusted by ophthalmologists and retinal surgeons as its lesion awareness module can help analyse and treat the disease further. This chapter aims to promote awareness, facilitate early diagnosis, and encourage proactive treatments.

Keywords: Explainable AI · Ocular disease · lesion segmentation · MHSA · ResNet50

1 Introduction

Ocular diseases encompass a diverse spectrum of disorders that affect various parts of the eye, including the cornea, lens, retina, optic nerve, and surrounding tissues. It can range from relatively common conditions like refractive errors (e.g., myopia, hyperopia, astigmatism) to more severe and potentially blinding diseases such as DR, PM, glaucoma, age-related macular degeneration (AMD), and cataracts. In this chapter, we have considered PM and DR diseases to generate an explainable lesion-aware framework to detect both. PM is characterized by extreme nearsightedness and is distinguished by its potential to

M. Paprzycki et al. (Eds.): ICACIS 2024, CCIS 2405, pp. 275–289, 2027.
https://doi.org/10.1007/978-3-032-30990-7_20

cause serious complications and vision-threatening issues. Potential characteristics associated with this condition are thinning of the sclera, stretched and thinned retina (myopic maculopathy), increased risk of retinal detachment, and increased risk of macular degeneration affecting the central part of the retina. Different forms of atrophy lesions are associated with PM such as Peripapillary atrophy(PPA) refers to the deterioration and thinning of the optic nerve, Chorioretinal atrophy(CRA) causes the retina to shrink and the surrounding cells to die, impairing vision, Patchy atrophy which resembles a greyish-white lesion of 2 optic disk diameters in the inferotemporal part of the centre of the macula and optic disk. PM also results due to breaks in the membrane separating the choroid (blood vessel layer) and retina causing lacquer cracks in the macula resulting in central vision loss [26,32]. DR is a multifaceted condition with various stages and manifestations. It typically begins with non-proliferative diabetic retinopathy (NPDR), characterized by lesions such as red saccular structured microaneurysms(MA) ranging 1–3 pixels, retinal haemorrhages (HE) which are structural distortions in the walls of blood vessels with an increased risk of blood leakage from the vessels and producing irregular shapes ranging in 3–10 pixels, soft and hard Exudates (EX) that are discrete yellowish-white intraretinal deposits containing extracellular lipids and proteins due to leakage of blood from abnormal retinal capillaries ranging in 1–6 pixels [9]. If not managed effectively, NPDR can progress to a more advanced stage called proliferative diabetic retinopathy (PDR), marked by the growth of abnormal blood vessels on the retina's surface, which can lead to bleeding, scarring, and retinal detachment [42]. In the past two decades, there has been an alarming rise in the prevalence of diabetes. According to the Diabetes Atlas [2], nearly a half-billion individuals of all ages have been diagnosed with diabetes worldwide. This is anticipated to reach 700 million by 2045. In addition, the IDF Diabetes Atlas warns that by 2040, one in three diabetics will develop DR. PM epidemiology goes upto 3% of the world population [48]. The current ratio of ophthalmologists to patients, especially in India, is 1:10000 [31], highlighting the necessity for an automated intelligent detection method for early DR and PM detection. A Fundus image is a medical image that captures a detailed view of the retina, the optic nerve, and the blood vessels in the eye's interior shown in Fig. 1. It is a valuable input for diagnosing and monitoring various eye conditions, including DR, PM, glaucoma, and other ocular disorders. Many PM and DR detection frameworks have relied upon fundus image datasets as an input to their architectures. Different methods such as image preprocessing, machine learning, deep learning, transfer learning, and lesion segmentation are addressed earlier to detect DR characteristics. Preprocessing activities for DR can extract MA, HE, EX lesions associated with DR as image pre-processing improves fundus image features for model interpretation, improving lesion feature extraction and categorization. It improves image contrast, lowers lighting error and blurriness, removes noise, balances structure intensity, finds minute patterns (subtle lesions) impeded by high-intensity structures, etc. It lets an intelligent system detect mild and intermediate DR. ML methods for DR detection include SVM [5,44], and Decision Tree [10], but they fail to provide optimal results for real-time, large and complex data as they lack domain knowledge and data representation. Other approaches employed for PM and DR detection are convolution neural network [11,40] Transfer learning(TL) models [7,13] have the advantage of leveraging knowledge learned from one domain to improve performance in another domain, especially when there is limited data for the target task, which is the most common scenario in the medical domain [21]. Many studies for PM detection and segmentation have used these TL models to report remarkable results. Other approaches include texture analysis [29,41] for region of interest extraction and analysis further, relative lesion segmentation driven classification [18,43], multiscale learning and prior information feature fusion [12] are other approaches followed. We have attempted to design a unified framework to identify PM and DR by first generating relative lesion information by using a segmentation approach and later fusion of lesion information in the classification architecture that again has MHSA in place of the last 3 bottleneck convolutions to capture lesion location information to distinguish PM, DR and normal fundus. The major contribution of this chapter includes

- An novel and explainable framework for dual disease(PM/DR) detection.
- Lesion awareness is generated by integrating lesion segmentation information and MHSA-inclusive ResNet50 features.
- This lesion-aware framework generates remarkable results on heterogeneous datasets for both PM and DR showcasing robustness.
- Activation maps generated by this LAResNet50 network promise a trustworthy tool for initial diagnosis and precise treatment thereafter.

The remainder of this chapter is organized as follows: Related works for individual PM and DR diagnosis. Datasets and the proposed LAResNet50 architecture are discussed in the section Methodology. Experimental and comparative study results on the heterogeneous datasets for both PM and DR are shown in the Results section. The Ablation study section highlights the importance of LAResNet50. The conclusion section concludes this chapter's significance and suggests future directions.

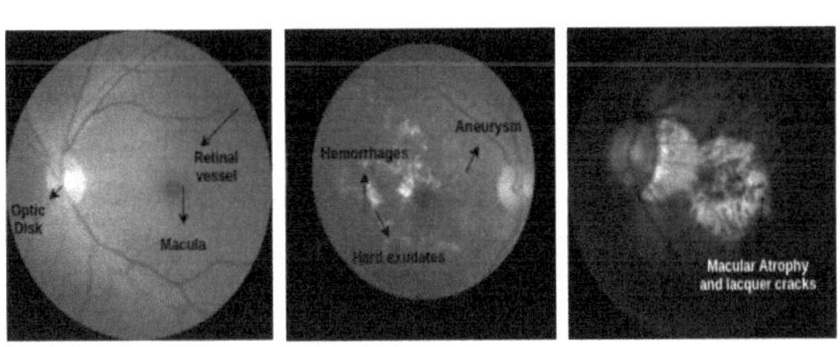

(a) Normal (b) DR (c) PM

Fig. 1. Fundus Images

2 Related Study

Many studies pertaining to DR and PM detection have been carried out earlier using Transfer Learning(TL) models such as Lam et al. [28] used GoogleNet and Xception models on Kaggle eyepacs dataset to achieve an accuracy of 0.745. Hagos et al. [20] used the InceptionV3 model on the same dataset to report an accuracy of 0.91. Yip et al. [49] used an ensembling of DCNN and TL to report an accuracy of 0.92 on the private dataset. Rishabh et al. [15] used custom CNN and Decision Tree classifiers to report an average sensitivity of 0.91 on three different datasets namely Eyepacs, Messidor2 and E-Optha. Rakhlin et al. [38] used enhanced VGGNet to report sensitivity of 0.92 and 0.99 on Eyepacs and Messidor datasets respectively. Quellec et al. [36] used Covnets with backpropagation and lesion detection for explainable DR detection and reported an area under ROC curve of 0.95. Jordi et al. [27] used a feature space score map to develop an interpretable classifier reporting an accuracy of 0.91 on the Messidor2 dataset. Gulshan et al. [17] used InceptionV3 to report 0.975 sensitivity on the Eyepacs dataset. Zhang et al. [50] used Ensemble of InceptionResnetV2, Xception [8] and InceptionV3 to report an accuracy of 0.9767 on private dataset. Ishtiaq et al. [22] used feature fusion of ResNet50 [25], GraphNet124 and Local binary patterns(LBP) to report a detection accuracy of 98.85 on Kaggle EyePacs dataset. Gour at al. [16] proposed the network XCapsNet, which combines Xception and Capsule networks for DR detection and reported an accuracy of 0.989 and 0.983 on Eyepacs and Messidor datasets respectively. PM detection frameworks also have used TL models extensively such as N Rauf et al. [40] developed 27 different CNN models employing different preprocessing and architectural variations and reported an AUC of 0.9845 on the test set of 400 images. Hemelings R et al. [37] developed a ResNet encoder [25] model to generate features from processed images and achieved an AUC of 0.993 on the validation dataset. Cefas Rodrigues Freire et al. [13] used additional dataset REFUGE [33], RIGA [4], and IDRiD [34] and used pre-trained model Xception with fine tuning to detect the probability of PM and achieved AUC score of 0.9987 on the test dataset. Lu L et al. [30] developed a deep learning system for PM detection using 17,330 colour fundus images and used Xception, VGG16, Resnet, and Densenet201 model to classify PM patients achieving the best AUC score of 0.993 with Xception model. Yun Sun et al. [47] used prior knowledge of tessellated fundus and brighter regions in a feature fusion framework to achieve an AUC score of 0.998 on the PALM dataset and an accuracy of 0.8921 on its private dataset of 714 images for the myopic maculopathy grading using Efficietnet and ResNet50 as the backbone. Yan Guo et al. [19] build an encoder-decoder network along with a feature fusion module to retain semantic information and a classification head attached to the encoder to report an AUC score of 0.999 on the test dataset. None of the mentioned studies have considered lesion information as a prior knowledge to capture lesion anatomy and attention mechanism to signify location of the respective disease lesions. To our knowledge this is the first chapter to address ternary classification of PM, DR and normal fundus images. In this capter, we have developed an explainable unified framework for dual disease detection by utilizing segmentation features for giving attention to respective lesions and later fusing these segmentation features in the Resnet50 model with MHSA. The model trained and validated on heterogeneous datasets reported clinically promising results.

3 Methodology

3.1 Datasets

For PM classification we have employed 3 different datasets namely PALM [14] consisting of 400 fundus images with 161 Normal and 213 PM images. Another dataset is ODIR [3] which is a multiclass dataset for ocular disease classification and we have shortlisted 300 images, 150 for both PM and Normal fundus for testing owing to notable field of view. Another dataset HPMI [45] is used to extract 1200 PM images. For DR detection, we have used the Kaggle Aptos dataset [1] having 1434 normal fundus and 1496 DR fundus images and Idrid dataset [46] with 129 normal fundus and 326 DR fundus images. For PM lesion segmentation, we have used 311 atrophy-annotated images from the PALM dataset and for DR lesion segmentation we have used 81 lesion-annotated images from the Idrid dataset. For Integrated model training, we have selected 1822 DR images from all the categories ranging from mild to PDR, 1563 normal fundus images and 1472 PM images varying from peripappilary atrophy to choroidal neovascularization. Out of total 4857 images we have kept 80% data for training and validation while the rest 20% is kept for testing.

3.2 Image Processing and Augmentation

The images were resized to the input dimension of $224 \times 224x3$ and contrast-limited adaptive histogram equalization (CLAHE) was applied to give uniform light conditions to all the images for input to the custom model. As PM lesion atrophy and DR lesion exudates are yellow lesions whereas MA and HE DR lesions are red, these image preprocessing steps make the visibility of the lesion uniform as shown in Fig. 2. To prevent overfitting, data augmentation techniques are applied, such as rotation of 30 degrees, random horizontal flip where all pixels of the random image are shifted horizontally, and gaussian blur that introduces random noise in the image while preserving edges and details for better feature learning by model. By applying random augmentation steps for each epoch, we varied the images so that the model learns generalized features and does not overfit. Images are normalized using the dataset's mean and standard deviation. For the related lesion segmentation, images are resized to $224 \times 224 \times 3$ and converted to grayscale, gaussian blur is added to remove noise and redundant details, and a laplacian filter is applied to emphasize the edges of lesion boundaries so that the model can learn better. Data augmentation steps like horizontal flip, horizontal shift, random scaling and random contrast adjustment are applied to feed the model with varied data on every epoch so that it generalizes well.

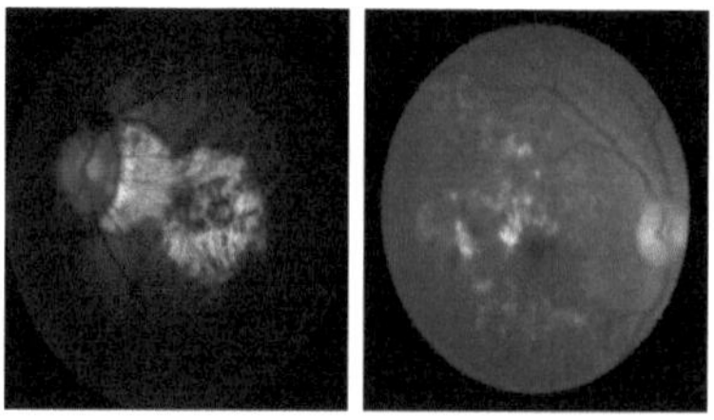

(a) PM (b) DR

Fig. 2. Pre-processed Images

3.3 Features Generation Using Lesion Segmentation(F1)

PM images have different forms of atrophy lesions present in them whereas in DR images lesions vary from small MA, and HE to soft and hard EX. UNet++ architecture [51] is an extension to the UNet architecture and improves upon it by adding skip pathways between different levels of the encoder and decoder that facilitate the flow of both low-level and high-level features across different scales, helping the network better capture context and details in the fundus image. Hence, we have used this architecture to segment PM and DR lesions, utilising a pre-trained squeeze-excitation inclusive ResNet50 encoder with preprocessed and augmented images to ensure that the model receives robust training data 3. Dice Loss is used as a criterion to train the segmentation model. Adam optimizer is used with an initial learning rate of 0.001. The model is trained for 50 epochs to report a mean Intersection over union(IOU) score of 0.85 for each of the Atrophy, Microaneurysm, Haemoharrages, Soft Exudates and Hard Exudates. The comprehensive segmentation architecture is used to extract features set F1 from the encoder for further classification as shown in Fig. 3.

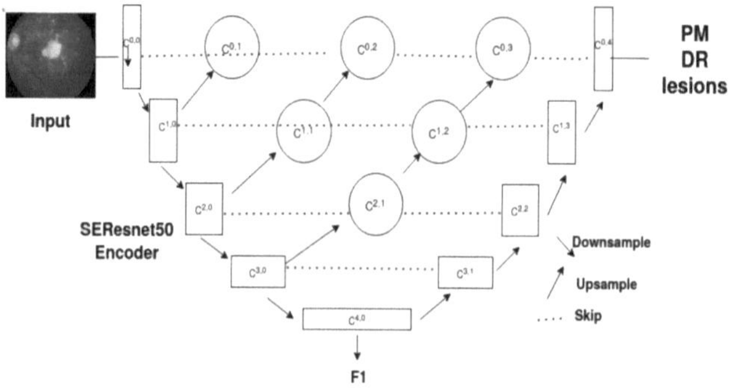

Fig. 3. Segmentation Architecture

3.4 Features Generation Using MHSA Inclusive ResNet50(F2)

Resnet50, also known as deep residual training networks, solves the vanishing gradient problem as they have a skip connection from the previous layer to keep training errors in check as we stack more layers into the model for better accuracy. ResNet50 consists of bottleneck blocks comprising of 1×1 convolutions for adjusting dimensions, 3×3 convolutions for capturing spatial features and 1×1 convolutions thereafter. We have used spatial convolutions in the initial bottleneck blocks to generate low-resolution feature maps from the fundus images and replaced spatial convolutions of the last 3 bottleneck blocks with MHSA to generate attention maps of the information contained in the feature maps captured by convolutions.

MultiHead Self Attention(MHSA). Due to attention's capacity to learn to concentrate on key areas within a context, it has become a crucial part of deep learning models for numerous modalities [39]. Self-attention is defined as attention applied to a single context instead of across multiple contexts. The ability of self-attention to directly model distanced interactions and its parallelizability has led to state of art results in many tasks [35]. Given a pixel $x_{\mathrm{i,j}} \in R^{\mathrm{din}}$, we first extract a local region of pixels in positions $ab \in N_{\mathrm{k(i,\ j)}}$ with spatial extent k centred around pixel x_{ij}. Single self-attention is then calculated as shown in the Eq. 1. Here the queries $q_{ij} = W_Q x_{ij}$, keys $k_{ab} = W_K x_{ab}$, and values $v_{ab} = W_V x_{ab}$ are the linear transformations of the pixel in position x_{ij} and the nearby pixels. Softmax $_{ab}$ denotes a softmax applied to all logits computed in the neighbourhood of pixel x_{ij}. $W_Q, W_K, W_V \in R^{dout \times din}$ are all learned transforms. In multiple head self-attention, distinct $W_Q, W_K, W_V \in R^{dout \times din}$ are used to learn multiple distinct representations of the input. It works by dividing the pixel features x $_{ij}$ depthwise into N groups $x_{ij}^n \in R^{din/N}$, computing single-headed attention on each group separately as above with different transforms $W_Q^n, W_K^n and W_V^n \in R^{dout/N \times din/N}$ per head, and then concatenating the output representations into the final output $y_{ij} \in R_{out}^d$. We have used relative positional embedding here, which marks the distance of pixel x_{ij} from each position ab in $N_k(i,j)$, where for each pixel x_{ij} its positional embedding is equivalent to its row offset as a-i, column offset as b-j and relative positional encoding is represented as $\mathrm{r}_{a-i,b-j}$ in Fig. 4.

$$y_{ij} = x_{i,j} * \Sigma_{ab \in Neighbour_{16}(i,j)} softmax_{ab}(p_{ij}^T n_{ab} + p_{ij}^T d_{a-i,b-j} r_{ab}) \quad (1)$$

As mentioned in [6], augmenting convolutional features with global self-attention features demonstrated significant improvements in object detection and image classification. Hence, we have decided to use MHSA in the last 3 bottleneck blocks, where spatial convolutions are replaced by MHSA to use the best primitives of both convolutions and self-attention as convolutions can generate low-resolution features of the fundus image and self-attention can focus on salient features from these convolutions. Feature Set F2 is generated by this MHSA-inclusive ResNet50.

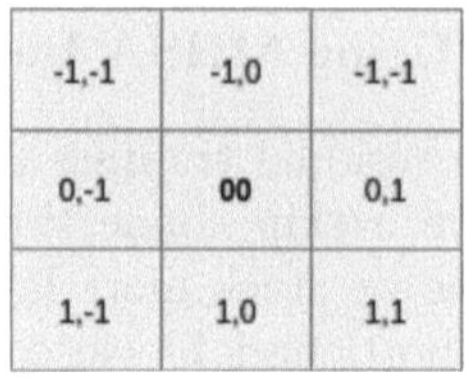

Fig. 4. Relative positional embedding

3.5 Feature Fusion Generated by ResNet50 Encoder(F1) and ResNet50 with MHSA(F2)

An integrated feature set of F1 and F2 features is created as shown in Fig. 5. $1 \times$ 1x2048 features each from the Global Average Pooling layer of MHSA-inclusive ResNet50 and SEResNet50 encoder of Unet++ architecture are concatenated to generate feature set F3 of 4096 features.

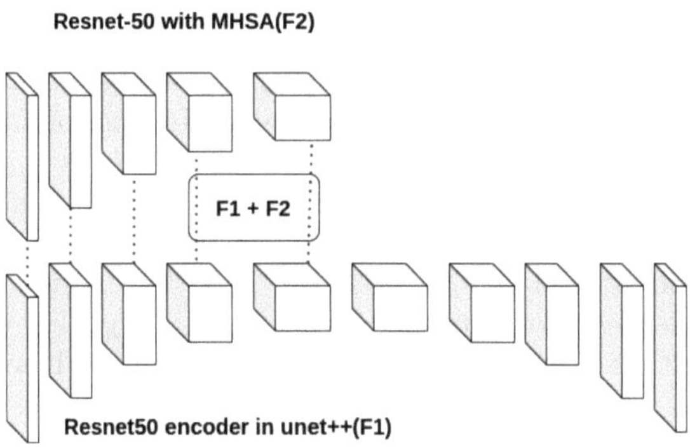

Fig. 5. F1+F2

3.6 Bayesian Optimization(BO)

Bayesian optimization technique uses a Gaussian process to explore the next step in the range of the hyperparameters, which starts with random initialization of hyperparameters and attempts to maximize negative validation loss as shown in the Eq. 2. Here hp is a set of selected hyperparameters from the parameters_space (A) given in Table 1.

$$f(hp) = max_{hp \in A}(-L_{CrossEntropy}(y', y)) \tag{2}$$

The Gaussian process 3 acting as a surrogate model attempts to find a prior distribution of hyperparameters to maximize our f(hp) 2.

$$P(hp) = [f(hp_1), f(hp_2)...f(hp_n)] \tag{3}$$

The prior is used by the Bayesian inference as given in the Eq. 4 to calculate posterior.

$$P(hp/f(hp)) = P(hp) * P(\frac{f(hp)}{hp}) \tag{4}$$

To select the best set of parameters in the next step, an Expectation Improvement(EI) technique is used based on the updated prior as shown in Eq. 7. Here Eq. 5 promotes exploitation in the current feature space region where f(hp)-f(hp') is the difference between the current maximum objective function and prediction and $\Phi\frac{f(hp)-f(hp')}{\sigma(hp)}$ is cumulative density function, representing area_under_curve. Equation 6 promotes exploration in another region of the distribution owing to uncertainty in the predictions. This way, BO achieves a global maximum for the objective function.

$$EI1(hp) = f(hp) - f(hp')\Phi\frac{f(hp) - f(hp')}{\sigma(hp)} \tag{5}$$

$$EI2(hp) = \sigma(hp)\phi\frac{f(hp) - f(hp')}{\sigma(hp)} \tag{6}$$

$$EI(hp) = EI1(hp) + EI2(hp) \tag{7}$$

We have assumed our parameter_space A as shown in the Table 1. In each iteration of the BO strategy, hyperparameter values that maximize the Expected Improvement (EI) using the Gaussian process are selected, and objective function f(hp) is calculated for those hyperparameters. Later, the surrogate Gaussian process is updated based on the feedback of the objective function. This integrated fusion model is trained for 50 epochs using hyperparameters given by BO shown in Table 1. The loss function used is CrossEntropy Eq. 8 and the fusion model is trained for 50 epochs. The comprehensive model architecture is shown in Fig. 6.

$$L_{Cross-Entropy}(y', y) = -\sum_{i=0}^{2} y_i.log(y_i') \tag{8}$$

4 Results

Our proposed model generated consistent and explainable results on the heterogeneous datasets showing robustness and clinical applicability as shown in Table 2. The kappa metric which shows the agreement between the actual and predicted diagnosis is maximum for our proposed LAResNet50. From these results, we can infer that merging of segmentation and MHSA inclusive ResNet50 features enhanced our classification results. The results are substantial to prove model superiority as compared to other related studies as represented in Table 3. Moreover, our model can detect two diseases demonstrating generalizability for

Table 1. Proposed and selected parameters

Parameter_Name	Parameter_Space(A)	Final
Number of dense layers for finetuning	[0,1,2]	1
Number of neurons in dense layers	[128–2050]	[2048]
Optimizers	[SGD, Adamax, Adam]	Adam
Learning Rate	[0.01 –0.000001]	0.001
Dropout	[0.1–0.5]	[0.4]
Activation	[relu, linear, tanh]	[relu]

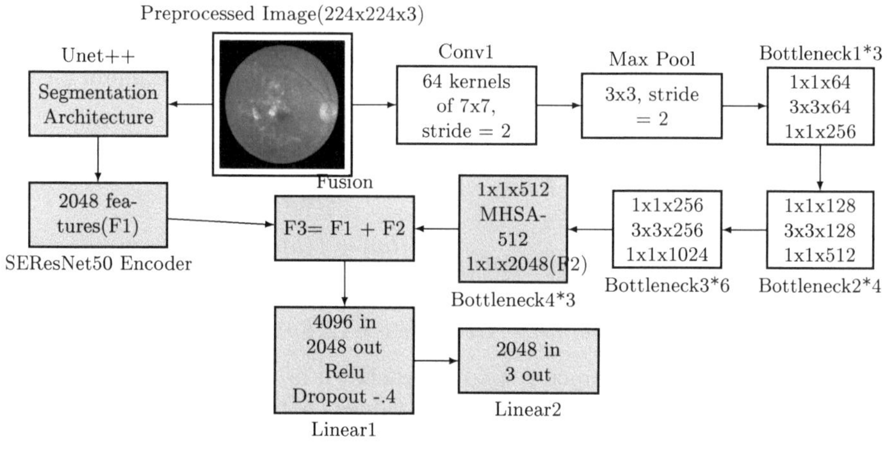

Fig. 6. LAResNet50 Architecture

ocular disease detection. The resultant confusion metrics of the test data are shown in Fig. 7. The final model gave better discrimination between the two diseases. The activations maps generated by our model for PM and DR fundus images are shown in Figs. 8 and 9 respectively. The activation map of LARes-Net50 effectively detected and represented atrophy, lacquer cracks, PPA in the case of PM, and haemorrhages, exudates in the case of DR more accurately than the baselines. It is also noteworthy that our LAResNet50 highlights prominent lesions areas of both PM and DR, which can further aid ophthalmologists for the targeted treatments.

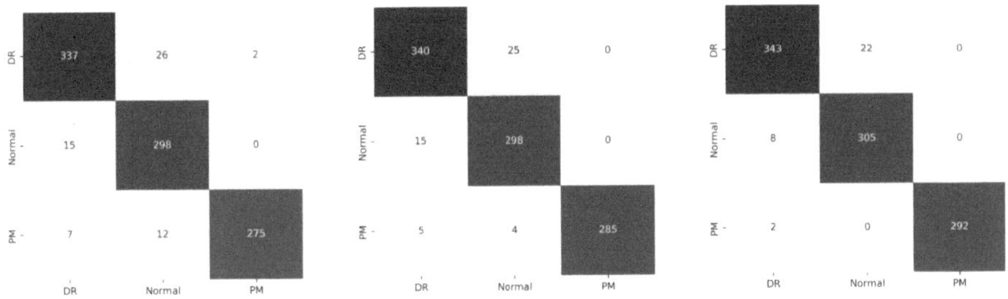

(a) ResNet50 (b) MHSAResNet50 (c) LAResNet50

Fig. 7. Confusion Metrics

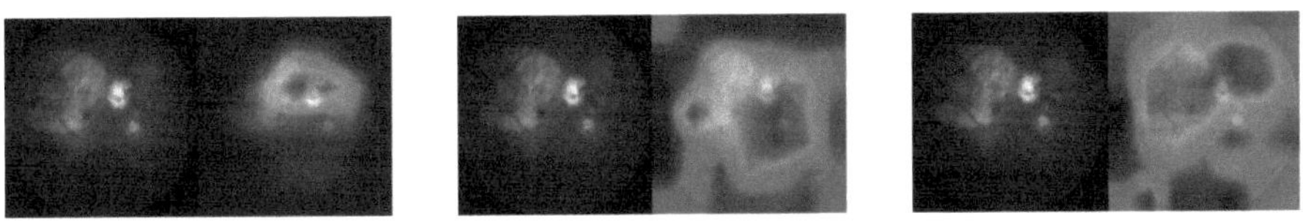

(a) ResNet50 (b) MHSAResNet50 (c) LAResNet50

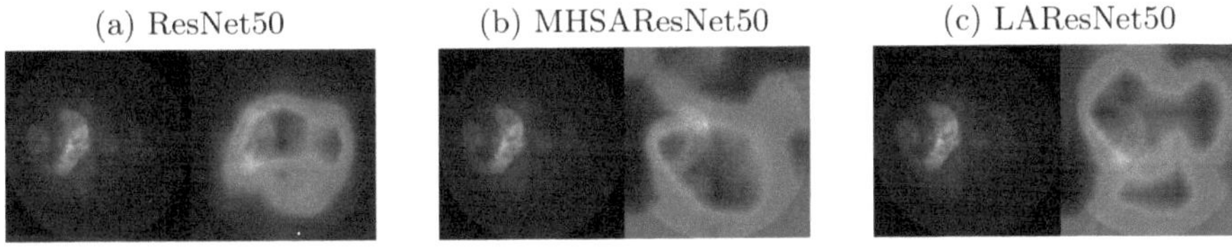

(d) ResNet50 (e) MHSAResNet50 (f) LAResNet50

Fig. 8. Class Activation Maps for PM

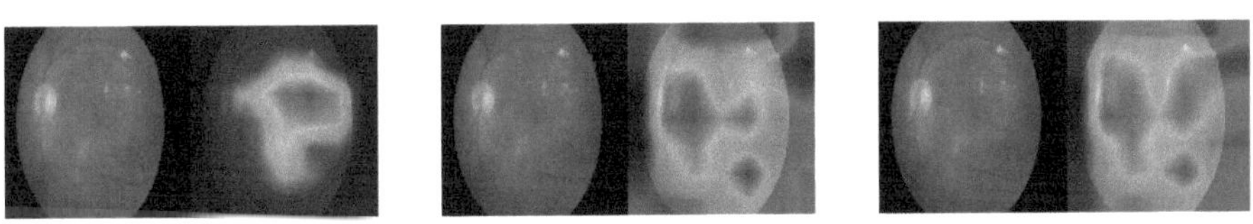

(a) ResNet50 (b) MHSAResNet50 (c) LAResNet50

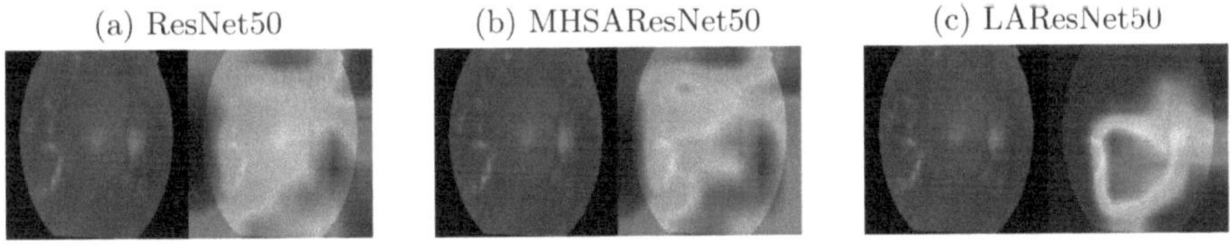

(d) ResNet50 (e) MHSAResNet50 (f) LAResNet50

Fig. 9. Class Activation Maps for DR

Table 2. Results

Model	Accuracy	kappa
ResNet50	0.9375	0.90
ResNet50+MHSA	0.9495	0.92
LAResnet50	0.9670	0.95

Table 3. Related work performance comparison

Author	Disease	Dataset	AUC score	Accuracy
N Rauf et al. [40]	PM	PALM	0.9847	-
R Hemelings et al. [37]	PM	PALM	0.9934	-
Li Lu et al. [30]	PM	Private	0.993	-
Cefas RL et al. [13]	PM	PALM	0.9987	-
Devda J et al. [23]	PM	PALM	-	0.978
Jaemin Son et al. [24]	PM	Private+PALM	.9974	-
Yun Sun et al. [47]	PM	PALM	0.9981	-
Yan Guo et al. [18]	PM	PALM	0.999	-
Lam et al. [28]	DR	Eyepacs	-	0.745
Hagos et al. [20]	DR	Eyepacs	-	0.91
Yip et al. [49]	DR	Private	-	0.92
Jordi et al. [27]	DR	Messidor2	-	0.91
Zhang et al. [50]	DR	Private	-	0.976
Ishtiaq et al. [22]	DR	Eyepacs	-	0.988
LAResNet50	PM+DR	Aptos+IDRID+PALM+ODIR+HPMI	.99	0.967

5 Conclusion

In this chapter, we have successfully deployed a dual ocular disease detection model LAResNet50 with lesion awareness to create a trustworthy screening AI system. Lesion awareness is created by the segmentation of lesions corresponding to each of the PM and DR diseases and then the fusion of segmentation encoder features with MHSA-inclusive ResNet50. The model has shown its superiority as compared to other related studies in terms of robustness, evaluation parameters and trustworthiness. This approach can be extended to identify and grade other ocular diseases such as Glaucoma, Age-related macular degeneration etc. The future directions of this study would be to grade the given PM and DR images into their respective categories, comprehensive analysis of fundus image for multilabel targets and further finetuning the segmentation and classification architectures with related feature importance on the real-time datasets to generate a reliable and holistic computer-aided diagnosis of major ocular diseases.

6 Contribution

Both the authors contributed equally to this chapter for the following: study conception and design, data collection, analysis and interpretation of results, and manuscript preparation.

References

1. https://www.kaggle.com/c/aptos2019-blindness-detection
2. Idf diabetes atlas 9th edition. https://diabetesatlas.org/atlas/ninth-edition/
3. Peking university international competition on ocular disease intelligent recognition, ODIR-2019 (2019)
4. Almazroa, A.: Retinal fundus images for glaucoma analysis: the riga dataset. Univ. Michigan - Deep Blue Data. (2018). https://doi.org/10.7302/Z23R0R29
5. Amin, J., Sharif, M., Yasmin, M., Ali, H., Fernandes, S.L.: A method for the detection and classification of diabetic retinopathy using structural predictors of bright lesions. J. Comput. Sci. **19**, 153–164 (2017)
6. Bello, I., Zoph, B., Vaswani, A., Shlens, J., Le, Q.V.: Attention augmented convolutional networks. CoRR abs/1904.09925 (2019). http://arxiv.org/abs/1904.09925
7. Chaurasia, B.K., Raj, H., Rathour, S.S., Singh, P.B.: Transfer learning–driven ensemble model for detection of diabetic retinopathy disease. Med. Biol. Eng. Comput. 1–17 (2023)
8. Chollet, F.: Xception: Deep learning with depthwise separable convolutions. In: Proceedings of the IEEE Conference on Computer Vision and Pattern Recognition (2017). https://doi.org/10.7302/Z23R0R29
9. Das, D., Biswas, S.K., Bandyopadhyay, S.: A critical review on diagnosis of diabetic retinopathy using machine learning and deep learning. Multimedia Tools Appl. **81**(18), 25613–25655 (2022)
10. Decenciere, E., et al.: Teleophta: Machine learning and image processing methods for teleophthalmology. Irbm **34**(2), 196–203 (2013)
11. Dutta, S., Manideep, B., Basha, S.M., Caytiles, R.D., Iyengar, N.: Classification of diabetic retinopathy images by using deep learning models. Int. J. Grid Distrib. Comput. **11**(1), 89–106 (2018)
12. Fan, R., Liu, Y., Zhang, R.: Multi-scale feature fusion with adaptive weighting for diabetic retinopathy severity classification. Electronics **10** (2021). https://doi.org/10.3390/electronics10121369
13. Freire, C.R., et al.: Automatic lesion segmentation and pathological myopia classification in fundus images. ArXiv **abs/2002.06382** (2020)
14. Fu, H., et al.: "Palm: Pathologic myopia challenge". IEEE Dataport (2019). https://doi.org/10.21227/55pk-8z03
15. Gargeya, R., Leng, T.: Automated identification of diabetic retinopathy using deep learning. Ophthalmology **124**(7), 962–969 (2017)
16. Gour, M., Jain, S., Kaushal, S.: Xcapsnet: A deep neural network for automated detection of diabetic retinopathy. Int. J. Imaging Syst. Technol. **33**(3), 1014–1027 (2023)
17. Gulshan, V., et al.: Development and validation of a deep learning algorithm for detection of diabetic retinopathy in retinal fundus photographs. jama **316**(22), 2402–2410 (2016)

18. Guo, Y., et al.: Lesion-aware segmentation network for atrophy and detachment of pathological myopia on fundus images. In: 2020 IEEE 17th International Symposium on Biomedical Imaging (ISBI), pp. 1242–1245. IEEE (2020)
19. Guo, Y., et al.: Lesion-aware segmentation network for atrophy and detachment of pathological myopia on fundus images. In: 2020 IEEE 17th International Symposium on Biomedical Imaging (ISBI), pp. 1242–1245. IEEE (2020)
20. Hagos, M.T., Kant, S.: Transfer learning based detection of diabetic retinopathy from small dataset. arXiv preprint arXiv:1905.07203 (2019)
21. Iman, M., Arabnia, H.R., Rasheed, K.: A review of deep transfer learning and recent advancements. Technologies **11**(2) (2023). https://doi.org/10.3390/technologies11020040, https://www.mdpi.com/2227-7080/11/2/40
22. Ishtiaq, U., Abdullah, E.R.M.F., Ishtiaque, Z.: A hybrid technique for diabetic retinopathy detection based on ensemble-optimized cnn and texture features. Diagnostics **13**(10) (2023). https://doi.org/10.3390/diagnostics13101816, https://www.mdpi.com/2075-4418/13/10/1816
23. J., D., R., E.: Pathological myopia image analysis using deep learning. Procedia Comput. Sci. **165** (2019). https://doi.org/10.1016/j.procs.2020.01.084
24. Son, J., Kim, J., Kong, S.T., Jung, K.H.: Leveraging the generalization ability of deep convolutional neural networks for improving classifiers for color fundus photographs. Appl. Sci. **591** (2021). https://doi.org/10.3390/app11020591
25. He, K., Zhang, X., Ren, S., Sun, J..: Deep residual learning for image recognition. ArXivorg Ithaca (2015)
26. Ohno-Matsui, K.: What is the fundamental nature of pathologic myopia? Retina **37** (2017). https://doi.org/10.1097/IAE.0000000000001348
27. de La Torre, J., Valls, A., Puig, D.: A deep learning interpretable classifier for diabetic retinopathy disease grading. Neurocomputing **396**, 465–476 (2020)
28. Lam, C., Yi, D., Guo, M., Lindsey, T.: Automated detection of diabetic retinopathy using deep learning. AMIA Summits Transl. Sci. Proc. **2018**, 147 (2018)
29. Lee, B., et al.: Fusion of pixel and texture features to detect pathological myopia. In: 2010 5th IEEE Conference on Industrial Electronics and Applications, pp. 2039–2042 (2010). https://doi.org/10.1109/ICIEA.2010.5515493
30. Lu L., et al.: Development of deep learning-based detecting systems for pathologic myopia using retinal fundus images. Commun. Biol. **4** (2021). https://doi.org/10.1038/s42003-021-02758-y
31. Medhi, J.P., Dandapat, S.: An effective fovea detection and automatic assessment of diabetic maculopathy in color fundus images. Comput. Biol. Med. **74**, 30–44 (2016)
32. Ohno-Matsui, K., Kawasaki, R., Jonas, J.B., et al.: International photographic classification and grading system for myopic maculopathy. Am. J. Ophthalmol. **159**(5), 877-883.e7 (2015)
33. Orlando, J.I., et al.: Refuge challenge: A unified framework for evaluating automated methods for glaucoma assessment from fundus photographs. Med. Image Anal. **59**, 101570 (2020)
34. Porwal, P.: Indian diabetic retinopathy image dataset (idrid): A database for diabetic retinopathy screening research. Data **3**(3) (2018)
35. Parmar, N., Vaswani, A., Uszkoreit, J., Kaiser, L., Shazeer, N., Ku, A.: Image transformer. CoRR abs/1802.05751 (2018). http://arxiv.org/abs/1802.05751
36. Quellec, G., Charriere, K., Boudi, Y., Cochener, B., Lamard, M.: Deep image mining for diabetic retinopathy screening. Med. Image Anal. **39**, 178–193 (2017)

37. Hemelings, R., Elen, B., Blaschko, M.B., Jacob, J., Stalmans, I., De Boever P.: Pathological myopia classification with simultaneous lesion segmentation using deep learning. Comput. Methods Programs Biomed. **199**, 105920 (2021). https://doi.org/10.1016/j.cmpb.2020.105920
38. Rakhlin, A.: Diabetic retinopathy detection through integration of deep learning classification framework. BioRxiv p. 225508 (2017)
39. Ramachandran, P., Parmar, N., Vaswani, A., Bello, I., Levskaya, A., Shlens, J.: Stand-alone self-attention in vision models. Adv. Neural. Inf. Process. Syst. **32** (2019)
40. Rauf, N., Gilani, S., Waris, A.: Automatic detection of pathological myopia using machine learning. Sci. Rep. **11**, 16570 (2021). https://doi.org/10.1038/s41598-021-95205-1
41. Sarwinda, D., Bustamam, A., Arymurthy, A.M.: Fundus image texture features analysis in diabetic retinopathy diagnosis. In: 2017 Eleventh International Conference on Sensing Technology (ICST). pp. 1–5 (2017). https://doi.org/10.1109/ICSensT.2017.8304447
42. Sebastian, A., Elharrouss, O., Al-Maadeed, S., Almaadeed, N.: A survey on deep-learning-based diabetic retinopathy classification. Diagnostics **13**(3), 345 (2023)
43. Sebastian, A., Elharrouss, O., Al-Maadeed, S., Almaadeed, N.: A survey on diabetic retinopathy lesion detection and segmentation. Appl. Sci. **13**(8) (2023). https://doi.org/10.3390/app13085111, https://www.mdpi.com/2076-3417/13/8/5111
44. Senapati, R.K., et al.: Bright lesion detection in color fundus images based on texture features. Bull. Electr. Eng. Inf. **5**(1), 92–100 (2016)
45. Shenghai, H., Zhongwen, L., Bing, L., Shaodan, Z., Quanyong, Y., Lei, W.: hpmi: A retinal fundus image dataset for identification of high and pathological myopia based on deep learning. (2023). https://doi.org/10.6084/m9.figshare.24800232.v1
46. Saw, S.M., et al.: Nearwork in early onset myopia. Invest Ophthalmol. Vis. Sci. **43** (2002)
47. Sun, Y., et al.: A deep network using coarse clinical prior for myopic maculopathy grading. Comput. Biol. Med. **154**, 106556 (2023)
48. Ueta, T., Makino, S., Yamamoto, Y., Fukushima, H., Yashiro, S., Nagahara, M.: Pathologic myopia: an overview of the current understanding and interventions. Global Health Med. **2**(3), 151–155 (2020)
49. Yip, M.Y.T., et al.: Enhanced Detection of Referable Diabetic Retinopathy via DCNNs and Transfer Learning. In: Carneiro, G., You, S. (eds.) ACCV 2018. LNCS, vol. 11367, pp. 282–288. Springer, Cham (2019). https://doi.org/10.1007/978-3-030-21074-8_23
50. Zhang, W., et al.: Automated identification and grading system of diabetic retinopathy using deep neural networks. Knowl.-Based Syst. **175**, 12–25 (2019)
51. Zhou, Z., Siddiquee, M.M.R., Tajbakhsh, N., Liang, J.: Unet++: Redesigning skip connections to exploit multiscale features in image segmentation. IEEE Trans. Med. Imaging **39**(6), 1856–1867 (2019)

Genetic Algorithm and EfficientNet-Based Diabetic Retinopathy Identification

Alka Singh[1,2](✉) and Rakesh Kumar[1]

[1] Department of Computer Science and Engineering, Madan Mohan Malaviya University of Technology, Gorakhpur, India
alkaa.singh523@gmail.com

[2] School of Computer Applications, Noida Institute of Engineering and Technology, Greater Noida, India

Abstract. Diabetic Retinopathy (DR) emerges as a chronic eye condition stemming from diabetes in individuals, leading to defects in retinal blood vessels. Early detection and accurate classification of DR are crucial for preventing vision impairment. Fundus images serve as primary diagnostic tools for retinal diseases, yet preprocessing of DR images is necessary to address issues like size contrast, data redundancy, and information irregularity. A promising approach involves leveraging the Residual Attention (RA) mechanism in conjunction with EfficientNet to highlight significant image features. RA-EfficientNet combines residual attention units with EfficientNet to capture more nuanced features, addressing variations among lesions. This method extracts features from grayscale retinal images, followed by feature selection using Genetic Algorithm, and classification using Support Vector Machine (SVM). On the APTOS 2019 dataset, this approach achieved a remarkable accuracy of 97.1% in a 5-class classification task: 0: No DR, 1: Mild DR, 2: Moderate DR, 3: Severe DR, and 4: Proliferative DR. The superiority of this model lies in its ability to effectively extract informative features from retinal images using EfficientNet, automatically select the most relevant features using a genetic algorithm, and classify diabetic retinopathy with high accuracy using an SVM classifier.

Keywords: Diabetic Retinopathy · EfficientNet · Genetic Algorithm · Residual Attention · Retinal Images · Support Vector Machine

1 Introduction

Diabetes mellitus is one of the world's many public and prevalent health problems which result due to insufficient production or inadequate use of insulin in humans. Prevalence of diabetes results in various health problems, such as cardiovascular disease, neural damage, renal failure, blindness, hearing impairment, and amputation [1]. According to IDF (International Diabetes Federation) [38] 2021, nearly 537 million adults suffer from diabetes as well as this figure may rise to 643 million by 2030 and 783 million by 2045. Worldwide 6.7 million deaths occur due to diabetes [38]. The paper [40] focuses

M. Paprzycki et al. (Eds.): ICACIS 2024, CCIS 2405, pp. 290–307, 2027.
https://doi.org/10.1007/978-3-032-30990-7_21

on a smart healthcare systems using data science and cloud-based platforms. It uses Data Science as a Service (DSaaS) to predict diabetes. Diabetic retinopathy (DR), one of the most prevalent nodus of diabetes, is a retinal disease and gradually progresses to blindness if medical help is not sought [2]. The retina, present at the back of the eye, is a light-sensitive zone that changes light into electric signals. These signals are then sent to the brain due to which we see the image. The layers of the retina request a constant supply of blood, which in turn is ended through tiny blood vessel networks which are prone to uncontrolled blood sugar levels. Duration of diabetes, hereditary factors, and metabolic control density are such variables that play a pivotal job in DR development [3]. Diabetes affects the capability of the body to absorb glucose or fructose, resulting in high blood sugar levels. The blood vessels start damaging due to inadequate distribution of oxygen to cells. The capillaries in the retina, become weak and start leakage. These form tiny dots like microaneurysms (MAs) or hemorrhages (HMs) [4]. The retinal blood vessel swells and starts to bleed the gel-like fluid called vitreous resulting in exudates (EXs). When the stage progresses, there occurs the growth of a weak and tiny network of blood vessels to fulfill the oxygen deprivation but instead leads to a more complicated condition called retinal neovascularization. These fragile blood vessels burst and leak into the eye, harming the macula and leading to blindness or vision loss [5]. Figure 1 shows the images of healthy eyes and eyes with DR.

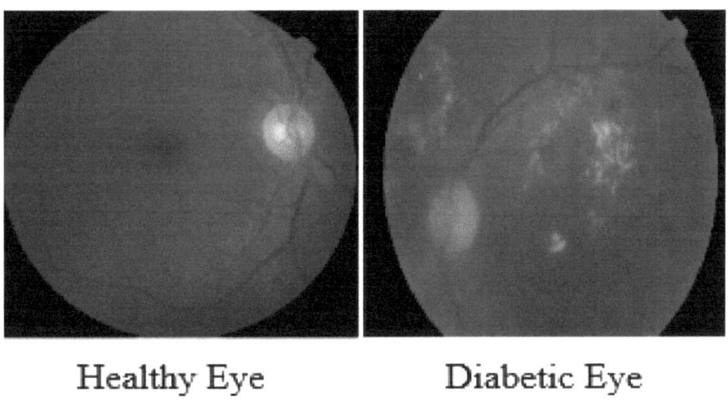

Fig. 1. Illustrates healthy vs diabetic eye [33]

DR is a progressive disease, health experts advise that it requires regular screening to diagnose the sign of illness. This detection process is very tiring and time-consuming which gears in more errors. As, diabetic patient figures are rising day by day across the globe and due to a lack of medical experts, DR patients are not diagnosed timely and treated, which ultimately leads to irreversible vision loss or blindness. So, monitoring diabetic patients regularly is helpful in the detection of DR at its earlier stage. The DR monitoring involves taking a retinal fundus picture which is then inspected by ophthalmologists for detection of microaneurysms or exudates. Based on severity DR mainly has two stages: Non-proliferative DR (NPDR) with a less severe form and Proliferative DR (PDR) with a highly severe form. In NPDR, the blood vessels present inside the retina get damaged as well as start leaking lipoprotein onto it, due to which the retina becomes damp and swollen. As the disease progresses, different signs of DR appear, like MAs, HMs, EXs, and inter retinal microvascular abnormalities (IRMA). PDR condition arises when there is a network of new abnormal growth of tiny and weak blood vessels in the retinal region. Table 1 summarizes the various stages of DR.

Table 1. Different severity levels of Diabetic Retinopathy

Levels	DR Severity Level	Findings from Retinal Fundus Photographs
0	No DR	No abnormalities, Healthy Eye.
1	Mild DR	Presence of Microaneurysms only.
2	Moderate DR	Presence of microaneurysms or blot hemorrhages or hard exudates and cotton wools but no sign of proliferative DR.
3	Severe DR	Each of the four quadrants possesses more than 20 intra-retinal hemorrhages, wherein two or more quadrants have venous beading and the presence of one or more intra-retinal microvascular abnormality (IRMA) but no sign of proliferative DR
4	Proliferative DR	Both or any of these - Neovascularization, pre-retinal haemorrhage

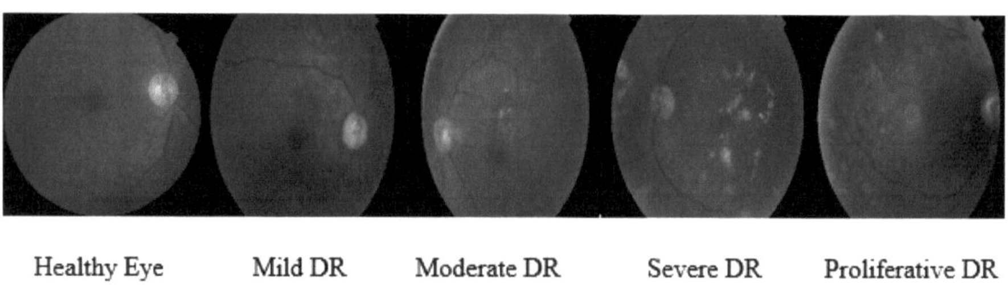

Fig. 2. Different classes of Diabetic Retinopathy [33]

Automating the tedious process gives the solution to improving the burden caused by DR on the economy and healthcare system. In the past ten years, outstanding attainments in computer vision and image processing have been achieved by deep Convolutional Neural Networks (CNN). Here, the mass screening of the disease is facilitated by Computer-aided diagnosis (CAD). In current years, multiple machine learning (ML), as well as deep learning (DL) approaches, have been explored and used by numerous researchers to report the issues in retinal fundus images related to the detection and classification of DR. EfficientNet was recently developed using the ImageNet dataset in light of motion learning innovation to overcome the DR's small sample size issue. Figure 2 shows different classes of Diabetic Retinopathy. The key contributions of this research for diabetic retinopathy identification are as follows:

- The key purpose of this research is to propose an automatic analysis and classification of DR using retinal images.

- The proposed model is highly efficient to automate the process of detecting the patient's condition by classifying the severity of DR.
- The accuracy measure of the proposed model has been deeply rooted via repeated experimental effort which was performed on publicly accessible datasets on Kaggle for competition.
- This proposed model utilizes a genetic algorithm that picks out the relevant as well as essential features in an attempt to reduce the dimensionality of the retinal image in real-time.
- The final element utilized is the SVM classifier which is highly effective for classifying the DR into 5-class as well as 2-class characterization (DR or No DR).

2 Literature Review

J. Wei et al. [6] proposed a novel computerized method known as Genetic U-net which helps in the generation of U-shaped CNN. The proposed genetic U-net method achieves enhanced retinal blood vessel breakdown with a smaller number of parameters which decreases the computational complication and also the problem of overfitting. The outcome indicates that this model developed utilizing the suggested process presents a greater performance having 1% of real U-Net parameters. N. Ullah et al. [7] developed an automated feature selection approach rooted in a very deep neural network along with a genetic algorithm. AlexNet, VGG-19, ShuffleNet, as well as NASNet-Large, and Inception V3 are used to pull out features from fundus pictures which are trailed by feature selection employing a genetic algorithm. Optimal features are rated as high rank whereas unsatisfactory features into low rank. Only optimal features are selected for further process. The classifier utilized here is based on the Support Vector Machine (SVM).

N. Tamim et al. [8] proposed an accurate system to detect any glaucoma or diabetic retinopathy from the retinal images. Firstly, the features are divided into three different groups: first-order statistics (FOS), histogram of oriented gradient (HOG), and higher-order statistics (HOS). Then, the most significant feature selection is made using a genetic algorithm. Finally, the classifier classifies one out of three classes i.e., glaucoma, diabetic retinopathy, and normal. The different classifiers the author has used for this purpose are Naïve Bayes (NB), as well as Decision Tree (DT), Linear Discriminant Analysis (LDA) as well as k-Nearest Neighbor (kNN). R. A. Welikala et al. [9] offered a dual vessel classification automated approach. Through this two-vessel separation approach, two different binary vessel maps which have important information are produced. Two separate 4-D feature vectors are produced from the local morphology features of the vessel. Via Support Vector Machine (SVM) as a classifier, classification on each vector is performed. Then, these separate results are combined to yield a final decision. Because of added features, it generates two 1-D feature vectors. Genetic algorithm-based feature selection selects the best feature subsets from these vectors, to enhance the performance of the classification.

R. Mansour in [10], proposed a novel hybrid model for the extraction of blood vessels using vertex chain code and genetic algorithm. This hybrid approach practices geo-metrical factors of the fundus vascular tree for detecting retinal exudates as well as hypertension from color fundus images. By thinning, it can create segmented tree skeletons. Three main kinds of points in the skeleton which are needed to be detected are, bifurcation, crossing points, and terminal points. These landmarks are then labeled and kept as chain codes. A. Kaur et al. in [11] formulated a technique that is useful in transferring the median filter to take away the outcome of extremely dense noise in fundus images. Then, from these retinal images, the genetic algorithm detects exudates. This technique outperforms sensitivity, accuracy, and error rate.

K. Gayathri Devi et al. [12] proposed an exudate and optic disk segmentation method from retinal fundus images using k-means clustering. The fitness function is computed using a genetic algorithm to implement crossover within the segmented pictures, acquired from the clustering. The greyscale image is changed to RGB, before mutation. The 3-segmented RGB channels are then united by the mutation to get the output from the genetic algorithm. The segment which is of high intensity is called the exudates and the low-intensity segment is called the optic disk. By using watershed segmentation, the optic disk elimination which is of similar intensity as of exudates is achieved. Parameter validation after the morphological operation is done as the final step.

P. Mohamed Jebran et al. [13], suggested an approach of microaneurysms detection in retinal images using an enhanced sub-class of features. Patches were used for more accurate identification. Identification of features like LBP and GLCM was done and subsets made were centered around SVM weights. The selection method used is a Genetic Algorithm-Neural Network (GA-NN), to enhance subsets of features. Classification using KNN, SVM, and DT is performed on these features. V. Popat et al. [14] proposed a method in which a genetic algorithm is used for selecting the model parameter and for image segmentation a U-net-based model is designed. Their results show that the genetic algorithm is capable of finding small architecture and a good accuracy compared to U-net created manually. A. B. Kadan et al. [15] proposed a novel method to automatically identify exudates. The segmentation of the optic disc is completed through edge detection and morphological method. Afterward, the selection of imperative features is inspired by the Grey wolf optimization algorithm. Finally, the application of the K-Nearest Neighbor (KNN) classifier is utilized to calculate hard exudates. S. K. Ghosh et al. [16] introduce an approach to an image enhancement algorithm in a fuzzy domain grounded on particle swarm optimization (PSO). The fuzzification utilizing PSO enhances the retinal image quality resulting in better performance and accomplishing the maximum points of all metrics related to traditional methods.

Z. Gao et al. [17] use deep neural networks and image processing for the automatic prediction of diabetic retinopathy grades and the model achieved 88.72% of accuracy in the experiments. They trained a deep neural network model to categorize the severities of diabetic retinopathy fundus images. They constructed a novel dataset of retinal fundus images. In the data set each image is labeled with one of four stages of the DR severity. They collected a total of 4476 images from three medical divisions (Endocrinology & Metabolism department, Health Management Center, and Ophthalmology Department).

Early identification of DR is the point of numerous analysts who have effectively contrived and proposed techniques and designs utilizing conventional AI (ML) strategies [18–20], Convolutional Neural Net [21, 22] is an amalgamation of convolutional brain organizations and conventional ML representations [23]. The efforts to utilize customary ML algorithms wherever choice trees are utilized on the optic pictures, being preceded by PCA smearing [24], did show hopeful outcomes having 73.4% precision, however, on a test set comprising 151 pictures.

Convolutional Neural Networks overwhelmed picture handling and later Alexnet [25] achieved extraordinary results on the ImageNet dataset [26]. The most recent group amongst the convolutional neural organizations, the EfficientNet [3] assists in taking advantage of three key perspectives in particular width, profundity, and goal of the design. They are less impacted by twists and mathematical changes after appropriate preparation. This double-dealing helps in assessing the parts of the human retina improved and helps in order of the seriousness of DR for right-on-time identification.

It has been seen that there is a lot of research on grouping blood vessels and hemorrhages utilizing profound brain organizations and weighty custom increases [27]. Every one of the performance models up to this point has not given great outcomes on various test datasets as contrasted with the gathering models of various CNN families which shows vigor.

As of now, some investigations on the determination of certain illnesses joined with electronic clinical record data for the most part utilize normal AI techniques such as Logistic relapse, irregular woods, choice tree, and so on. Evaluating certifiable information utilizing the condition of the workmanship AI calculations, getting accuracy esteem equivalent to 0.770 and a review equal to 0.775 applying the Hoeffding Tree calculation [28]. Herein review, a semi-directed learning-based calculation of the Laplacian support vector machine (LapSVM) was utilized in diabetes illness expectation [29].

Here, a supportive network is suggested that utilizes AdaBoost calculation along with Decision Stump as a base classifier for order. AI-associated models entail the physical extraction of elements, and then over the model grouping or relapse, which is tedious and difficult [30].

All things being equal, profound gaining calculations endeavor to advance additional theoretical elements from the information, wiping out the requirement for clients to do highlight extraction, and lessening the errand of growing new element filters for each issue. This learning decided to utilize the convolution brain network calculation inside and out learning technique joined with electronic clinical archives data to analyze diabetes convoluted with the retina, keep away from the course of fake highlight extraction, and work on symptomatic exactness.

A convolution brain network has a place with the counterfeit brain organization, which is near the genuine natural brain network framework, with an input, convolution layer, down-sampled layer, all-associated layer, and component yield. CNN's feedback layer can straightforwardly get two-layered visual means, for example, two-layered pictures without the need for inordinate human mediation to compute the legitimate qualities of the first picture and consequently separate highlights and grouping gained from the information [31].

The main issue with a deep neural network is its ability to transform into a black box with lots of weighted layers with slight or no facts about the features of the image level [32]. Additionally, the training involves a large number of images, which is not easily available. Another, major issue related to deep learning is that the computation is unusually prolonged not only during training but also in testing due to the presence of a lot of features. This chapter primarily rests on hand-crafted features and machine learning models in an attempt to overcome the entirety of the disadvantages listed.

3 Proposed Methodology

3.1 Dataset

In this chapter, the DR classification is tested on APTOS 2019 training dataset, downloaded from the Kaggle site [33]. Aravind Eye Hospital in India provided the dataset, which included 3662 high-resolution images with each example linked and examined by extremely trained professionals. According to the outcomes, these images have been classified into five classes ranging from 0 to 4, with class 0 containing 1805 ordinary images demonstrating the absence of diabetic retinopathy (DR), class 1 containing 370 images demonstrating gentle no-proliferative DR, class 2 containing 999 images demonstrating moderate no-proliferative diabetic retinopathy, and class 3 containing 193 images demonstrating extreme no-proliferative diabetic retinopathy. There are 295 pictures of proliferative DR. It is observed that a spread of five grades is critically imbalanced. Moreover, Fig. 3 portrays the distribution of the dataset into 5 grades.

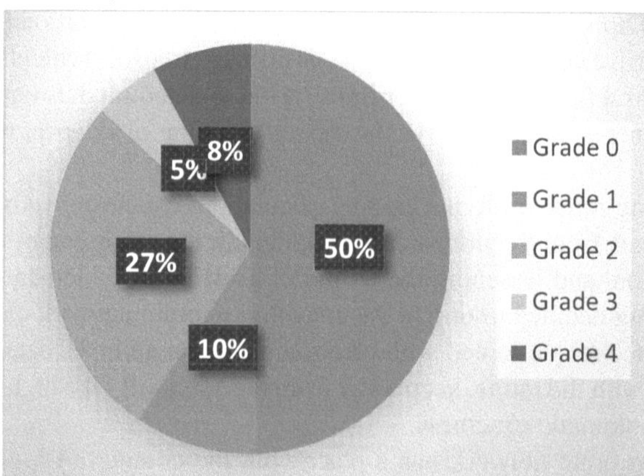

Fig. 3. Illustrates the dataset distribution into five grades.

3.2 Design

The suggested approach mainly has succeeding steps: feature extraction, normalization, feature selection using Genetic Algorithm (GA), and classification. In Fig. 4, the proposed DR model pipeline is portrayed.

As diabetic retinopathy treatment is very complicated, therefore it requires high attention and more accuracy during the screening procedure in the real-time diagnosis of the patients suffering from diabetic retinopathy disease. In this research, a new model for effective diabetic retinopathy diagnosis is presented which is based on the combined GA as well as EfficientNet approach and outperforms well while comparing to the previous diagnosis methods. The working procedure of the proposed model as depicted in Fig. 4 is described as follows. In this model, initially RGB images of size 224x224 pixels are provided as an input which is transformed into the grey image. After the image transformation procedure, feature extraction is done as means of the EfficientNet scheme. As for the kernel size, EfficientNet primarily utilizes 3x3 kernels in its convolutional layers. In the next phase, the normalization procedure is done for entire image datasets. Once normalization is completed properly, the feature selection is done as means of the GA algorithm. The image classification is done in the last phase using the support vector machine (SVM).

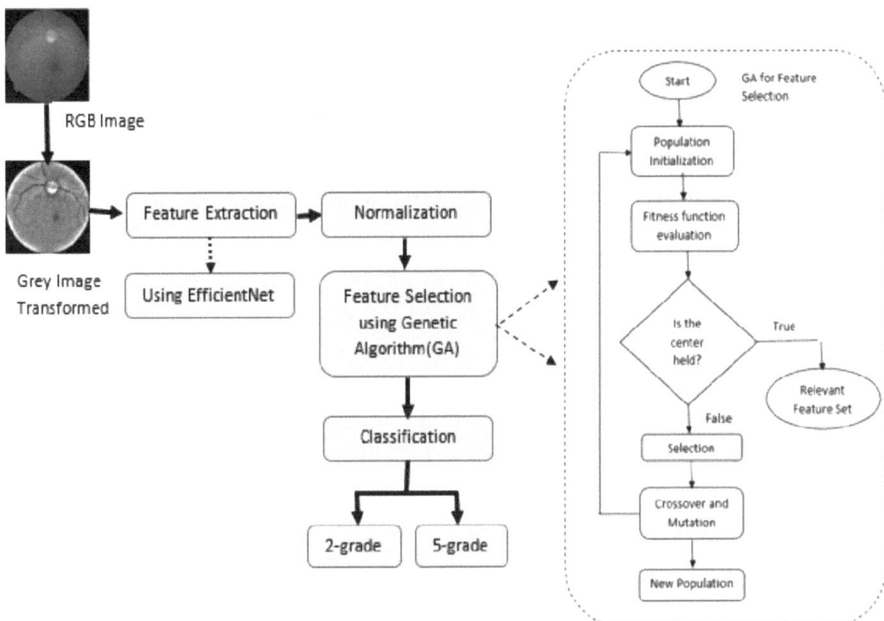

Fig. 4. Illustrates proposed DR diagnostic model.

3.3 Feature Extraction

In the feature extraction phase, the grey-scaled image is given to EfficientNet for an effective feature extraction process in real-time. The efficientNet approach is already pre-trained as means of ImageNet. Moreover, to form RA-EfficientNet, a Residual Attention (RA) unit is included with EfficientNet. The addition of the RA unit allows the extraction of more valid features from images efficiently.

3.3.1 EfficientNet

In machine learning, transfer learning is the means by which a pre-trained model is reutilized, becoming the initial point for any model on multiple jobs. Through transfer learning, a model can achieve higher performance than training with only a very small amount of data. EfficientNet is a good model for transfer learning. The effectiveness of the EfficientNet model relies on three important parameters i.e., resolution, depth, and width. It uniformly scales all dimensions using a compound coefficient. As a result, the EfficientNet models achieve better efficiency and higher accuracy. There are multiple versions of the network extending from B0 to B7. In the present article, we used EfficientNetB0 with RA as the feature extractor. The network uses a 224 × 224 image size as input. The architecture uses Mobile Inverted Bottleneck Convolution (MBConv) along with connection to squeeze and excitation added to it, similar to MobileNetV2 [22] and MnasNet, as an important building block.

Figure 5 gives an illustration of EfficientNetB0. The architecture has exactly 16 MBConv blocks having 3 × 3 or 5 × 5 kernels each. As an input, the retinal image is first treated over a 3 × 3 Conv2D layer, followed by 16 MBConv layers and 1 × 1 Conv2D layer in order as well as in the end the output is handed to the RA block.

The EfficientNet model measures all magnitudes of depth, width, and resolution uniformly and practices a compound coefficient ø so as to increase the model accuracy.

Depth is defined as $d = \alpha^{\phi}$
Width is defined as $w = \beta^{\phi}$
Resolution is defined as $r = \Upsilon^{\phi}$
s.t. $\alpha.\ \beta^2.\ \Upsilon^2 \approx 2$
$\alpha \geq 1$, *and* $\beta \geq 1$, *as well as* $\Upsilon \geq 1$

where ø is a user-specified coefficient that let us know several resources which are available whereas α, β and ϒ identify in what ways to allocate these resources to network depth, width and resolution respectively.

3.3.2 RA Block

The attention block in feature extraction lets the network choose the area which needs more attention and the sort of lesions that are considered after. Motivated by ResNet [34] and GCNet [35], a fresh segment generally named RA unit to extract fundus features with small variances is aimed. It is presented in Fig. 6.

The EfficientNet's input to the block is $F_{in} \in R^{H \times W \times C}$ wherein the defined variables W, H as well as C represent width, as well as height along with the channel number of the features plots. Furthermore, it has high semantic features of retinal images. Primarily, F_{in} is passed through two different convolutional paths and as a result, two different kinds of features arise, $F_{CONV1} \in R^{H \times W \times C}$ and $F_{CONV2} \in R^{H \times W \times C}$. F_{CONV1} outcomes from three convolution functioning which rises the cross-channel knowledge as well as decreases the elementary stages of computation. Therefore, it is forwarded toward the GC-based attention module. This GC-based attention module $F_{ATT} \in R^{H \times W \times C}$ is used to highpoint the important retinal lesion information and subdue less important information using channel-wise attention feature maps. At last, F_{ATT} with F_{CONV2} is added and the final feature map output $F_{out} \in R^{H \times W \times C}$ is attained.

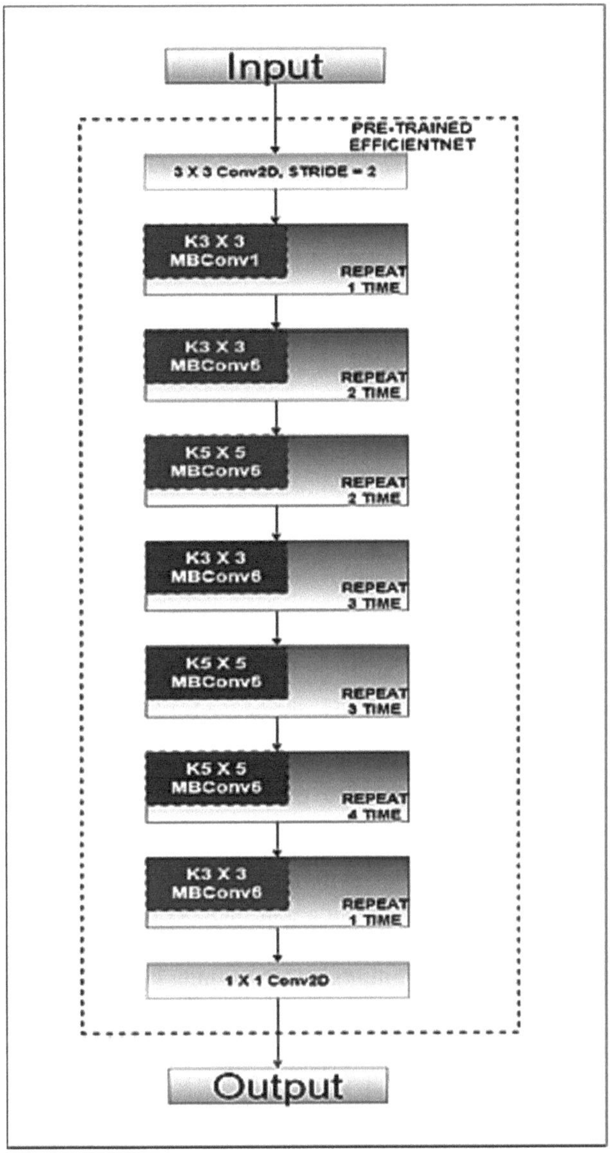

Fig. 5. Illustrates Efficient Net Model.

3.4 Normalization

To recomputed the features and restrict the amount to a mutual variety, the chapter uses the min-max normalization method. The use of limited range makes the values of the features turn out to be with smaller standard deviations which in turn suppress the outliers in different features. In this procedure, a linear transformation is accomplished on the original image.

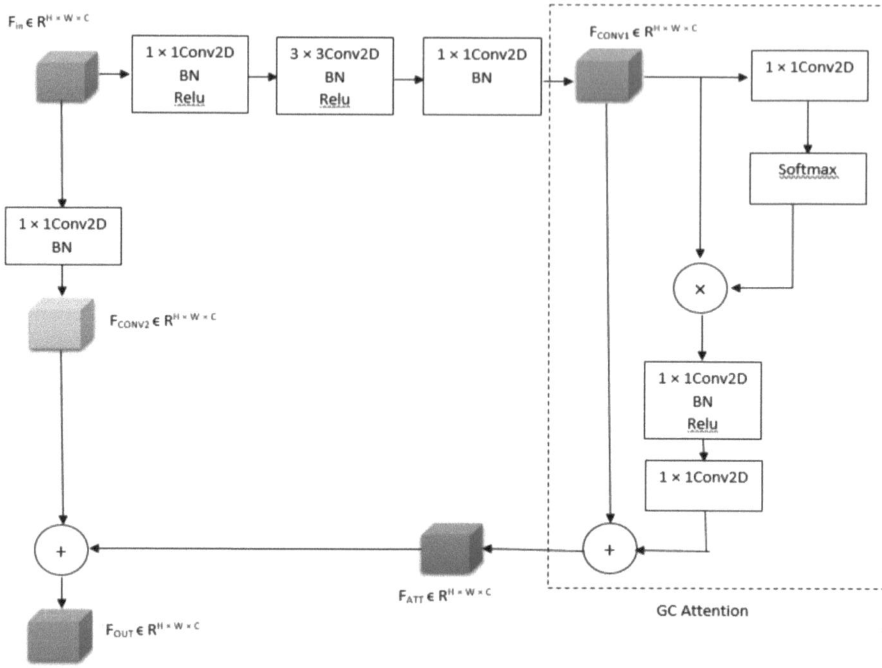

Fig. 6. Illustrates the structure of RA block.

3.5 Genetic Algorithm-Centered Feature Selection

This procedure of feature selection refers to the choice of the utmost consistent and distinguishable features which minimizes the multiple dimension of the feature cosmos to the least. In the previous step of feature extraction, there are drawbacks of dimensionality problems. In this work, 429 features are extracted in the previous step which not only affects the increase in computation in regards to training but also affects the accuracy. The irrelevant and redundant features may be due to overfitting issues. So, it is required to get rid of this. In the proposed chapter, the Genetic Algorithm (GA) helps in feature selection which improves the accuracy as well as decreases the computational time.

A genetic Algorithm is a highly random heuristic search algorithm used to solve optimization problems in deep learning. A genetic Algorithm is an evolutionary search technique that imitates natural selection, mutation, and crossover mechanisms. It is a metaheuristic search strategy that searches for many solutions and picks the optimized solution. In the first step, the system generates a random uniform population. The crossover, as well as mutation for each distinct, is 0.5. This proposed model initiates producing a random population. All of the chromosomes have been prepared through several genes that have real numbers. The chromosomes with the highest fittest value pass to the next generation. Table 2 illustrates the Pseudocode for GA.

Table 2. Illustrates the Pseudocode for Genetic Algorithm

Genetic Algorithm: Herein, GA variables (n, χ, μ)
// **Initialization of generation 0, First:**
1. A: = 0;
2. P_k: = n number of arbitrarily-generated individual's population;
//**Estimation of P_k:**
3. Computation of fitness(i) for all i ϵ P_k
4. do
5. {
// **Build generation** k + 1:
// **Next do the Copy:**
6. Choose $(1\text{-}\chi) \times n$ constituents of P_k as well as include into P_{k+1};
// **Next Perform Crossover:**
7. From P_k, choose $\chi \times n$ constituents; couple all these; production of offspring; include this offspring within the P_{k+1};
// **Next perform the Mutate**
8. From P_{k+1}, choose $\mu \times n$ constituents; in each the arbitrarily-selected bit is inverted;
// **Estimation of** P_{k+1};
9. Computation of fitness(i) for all i ϵ P_k;
// **Next Increment Again:**
10. K: = k + 1;
11. return this fittest individual from P_k

3.6 Classification

Genetic Algorithm once selects distinguishable features; this help to define the classification system. Utilizing the k-fold cross-validation technique proposed model can avoid ambiguity and inconsistency in the model performance. In the k-fold cross-validation, all of the important distinguishing features set is split into many k groups. These groups could be utilized as test and train sets. In this chapter, as the APTOS dataset has 3662 images, we have used 9-fold cross-validation. Different features are divided into 9 equal parts, out of which 8 are used for training and 1 for testing. This value of K plays a vital role in getting high accuracy with low bias and modest variance.

The Support Vector Machine (SVM) was employed for classification, as well as for regression. In this chapter, SVM is used for classification problems. In SVM, the support vector needs to be observed to discover the finest extrication hyperplane. SVMs can achieve high accuracy of classification by choosing the optimal parting hyperplane even with nominal training sets.

4 Implementation Details

In this chapter, we developed a Genetic Algorithm and EfficientNet based model for accurate DR detection. The proposed model comprises pre-processing, feature extraction, feature selection and classification.

- We compared our model to existing H.N. Huynh [36] MobileNetV2 model, and G. Zhang [37] Multi-Model Domain Adaptation model using the APTOS 2019 dataset to validate the results.
- Initially the retinal images are given as input.
- Then, the convolutional layers of EfficientNet are adept at extracting hierarchical representations from input images, enabling the model to capture features at various levels of abstraction. For down sampling layers stride of 2 is used.
- The most informative features extracted by EfficientNet are now selected by genetic algorithm.
- The selected features obtained from the genetic algorithm are used by Support Vector Machine for DR classifications.
- The sigmoid activation function is utilized to find different levels of DR.
- The value of learning rate used in our work is set to 0.001

5 Result and Discussion

5.1 Performance Metrics

In this work, we have used RA-EfficientNet, a Genetic Algorithm and to enhance the effectiveness of SVM as a classifier k-fold cross-validation. There are some important indicators that measure the performance of the suggested work. The values are some basic confusion matrix terms such as True Positive (TP), and False Positive (FP), as well as True Negative (TN), and False negative (FN). If the lesion pixel is accurately classified, then it's a TP; if not, then it's a FP. Although, if a non-lesion pixel is exactly categorized, then it's a TN, otherwise it's a FN.

5.1.1 Accuracy:

Accuracy is the simplest metric that processes the number of right predictions divided through the entire number of predictions.

$$Accuracy = \frac{TP + TN}{TP + FP + TN + FN} \tag{1}$$

5.1.2 Recall

Recall refers to the proportion between the number of positive samples predicted as true to the overall number of positive samples. It mainly aims at type-II errors.

$$Recall = \frac{TP}{TP + FN} \tag{2}$$

5.1.3 Precision

The precision metric is the quotient of the true positives and the total positive predicted. It focuses on type-I errors.

$$Precision = \frac{TP}{TP + FP} \tag{3}$$

5.1.4 Specificity

Specificity is the model's ability to predict true negatives in the sample. It is calculated as Eq. 4.

$$Specificity = \frac{TN}{TN + FP} \tag{4}$$

5.1.5 F1 Score

F1 score refers to the harmonic mean of recall and precision. It uses a combination of both. It works well on imbalanced classification problems as it presents a fine balance between precision and recall.

$$F1\ Score = 2 \times \left\{ \frac{Precision \times Recall}{Precision + Recall} \right\} \tag{5}$$

5.2 Performance Analysis

There are eight versions of EfficientNet, ranging from B0 to B7. Figure 7 summarizes the performance of all eight EfficientNet models. As we can observe EfficientNetB7 achieves the highest accuracy but the input size is 600 × 600 which is too large, whereas EfficientNetB0 gains 97.95% accuracy with the small input image dimension of 224 × 224 and also has lesser parameters. Due to issues in the hardware resource, we have chosen EfficientNetB0 as the feature extractor.

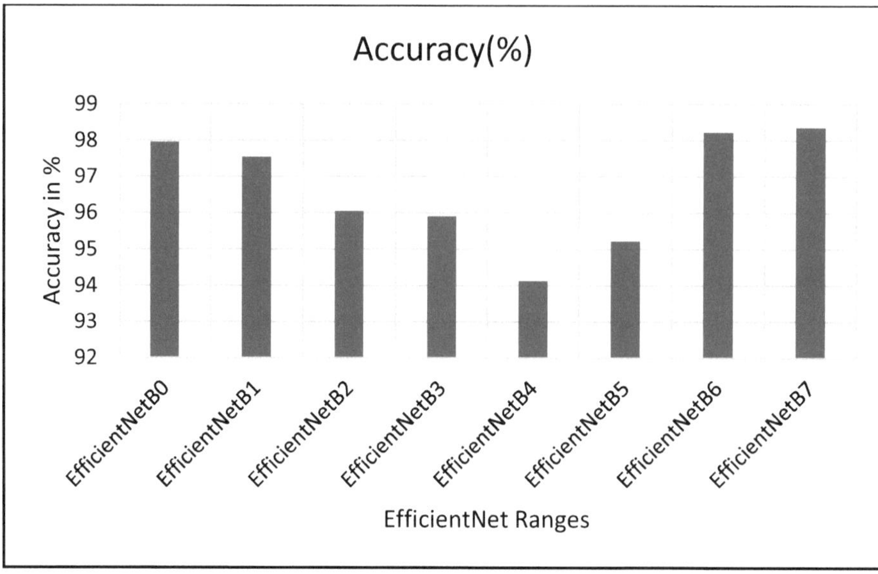

Fig. 7. Different EfficientNet model performance.

In this chapter, the suggested methodology was estimated using the Kaggle dataset. It was separated into two segments i.e., the training dataset as well as the testing dataset. This whole dataset was divided with a percentage of 70/30; 70% was utilized for training, whereas the rest of the 30% of the image data was utilized for testing. Extraction of features from the pictures was done via the EfficientNetB0 model. To minimize the dimensions of the feature vector, feature selection has been used. For feature selection, in the proposed methodology, GA was used with the tournament selection approach. This helps in the ranking of the features. Finally, to classify the images in classes, Support Vector Machine is used as a classification model. In this process, the multiclass dataset is being assessed for accuracy. The SVM algorithm categorize provided input images as well as yields a confusion matrix to portray the acuteness level of the illness. This proposed model achieves an accuracy of 97.1%, precision 91.18%, recall 96.58% and F1 measure 93.72%.

Table 3. Performance comparison of proposed model with existing methods.

S. No.	Model	Accuracy	Precision	Recall	F1 Score
1	H.N. Huynh et al. [36]	93.89%	94%	92%	90%
2	G. Zhang et al. [37]	90%	–	–	–
3	Proposed Model	97.1%	91.18%	96.58%	93.72%

Table 3 depicts the performance comparison of proposed model with existing methods. The existing model developed by H. N Huynh et al. [36], provides accuracy, precision, recall, and F1 score values 93.89%, 94%, 92%, and 90%, respectively. Another model developed by G. Zhang et al. [37], provides an accuracy level of 90%, however other parameters such as precision, recall, and F1 score have not been disclosed. Whereas the measured performance metrics of proposed models are improved in comparison to the existing models i.e., the proposed model offers accuracy of 97.1%, and precision, recall, and F1 scores were measured at 91.18%, 96.58%, and 93.72%, respectively.

6 Conclusion

The chapter presented an efficient retinal DR recognition system. In terms of the suggested system, the accuracy has been deeply rooted via repeated experimental effort which was performed on publicly accessible datasets on Kaggle for competition. The system takes the retinal image as input, converting it into a grey scale. The grey scale retinal image goes through various preprocessing steps and thereafter normalization is done. With the support of RA-EfficientNet, various features are extracted from the images for further action. RA-EfficientNet accomplishes better in correlation, with higher exactness, and requires fewer PC-based estimates than other organizations. The second section is designing a genetic algorithm that picks out the relevant and essential features in an attempt to minimize the dimensionality of the retinal image. The final element is the SVM classifier that classifies the DR into 5-class and 2-class characterization. Various performance matrices have been measured and it is found that the accuracy of the proposed model is 97.1%, precision is 91.18%, recall is 96.58% and F1 measure is 93.72%. When compared to existing DR order methodologies, the results show that our demonstration model yields the finest presentation as well as presents a superior assessment as an incentive for the APTOS 2019 dataset. Furthermore, we confirm the validity of the suggested RA-EfficientNet computation by producing and reviewing an EyePACS dataset containing retinal images, which is implemented perfectly. Although numerous methods have been investigated for accurately identifying diabetic retinopathy, there are still countless opportunities for additional studies to create novel methods of diabetic retinopathy evaluation.

Acknowledgments. Conflicts of Interest The authors declare no conflict of interest

Contributions Formal analysis, Writing, Visualization, Writing, original draft, Investigation, Resources, Conceptualization, Methodology - Alka Singh

Writing, review & editing, Investigation, Supervision - Rakesh Kumar

References

1. Ansari, P., et al.: Diabetic retinopathy: an overview on mechanisms, pathophysiology and pharmacotherapy. Diabetology. **3**(1), 159–175 (2022). https://doi.org/10.3390/diabetology3010011
2. Elgafi, M., et al.: Detection of diabetic retinopathy using extracted 3D features from OCT images. Sensors. **22**(20), 1–13 (2022). https://doi.org/10.3390/s22207833
3. Yi, S.L., Yang, X.L., Wang, T.W., She, F.R., Xiong, X., He, J.F.: Diabetic retinopathy diagnosis based on RA-efficientnet. Appl. Sci. (2021). https://doi.org/10.3390/app112211035

4. Cataldi, S., Tramontano, M., Costa, V., Aprile, M., Ciccodicola, A.: Diabetic retinopathy: are lncRNAs new molecular players and targets? Antioxidants. **11**(10) (2022). https://doi.org/10.3390/antiox11102021
5. Diabetes, D.W.: Dealing with diabetes. Modernod, 1–5 (2019) [Online]. Available: https://modernod.com/articles/2019-june/dealing-with-diabetes?
6. Wei, J., et al.: Genetic U-net: automatically designed deep networks for retinal vessel segmentation using a genetic algorithm. IEEE Trans. Med. Imaging. (2022). https://doi.org/10.1109/TMI.2021.3111679
7. Ullah, N., et al.: Diabetic retinopathy detection using genetic algorithm-based CNN features and error correction output code SVM framework classification model. Wirel. Commun. Mob. Comput. **2022**, 7095528 (2022). https://doi.org/10.1155/2022/7095528
8. Tamim, N., Elshrkawey, M., Nassar, H.: Accurate diagnosis of diabetic retinopathy and glaucoma using retinal fundus images based on hybrid features and genetic algorithm. Appl. Sci. (2021). https://doi.org/10.3390/app11136178
9. Welikala, R.A., et al.: Genetic algorithm based feature selection combined with dual classification for the automated detection of proliferative diabetic retinopathy. Comput. Med. Imaging Graph. (2015). https://doi.org/10.1016/j.compmedimag.2015.03.003
10. Mansour, R.: Using genetic algorithm for identification of diabetic retinal exudates in digital color images. J. Intell. Learn. Syst. Appl. **04**, 188–198 (2012). https://doi.org/10.4236/jilsa.2012.43019
11. Kaur, A., Kaur, P.: An Integrated Approach for Diabetic Retinopathy Exudate Segmentation by Using Genetic Algorithm and Switching Median Filter (2016). https://doi.org/10.1109/ICIVC.2016.7571284
12. Gayathri Devi, K., Dhivya, M., Preethi, S.: Detection of exudates and removal of optic disk in fundus images using genetic algorithm. In: Lecture Notes in Computational Vision and Biomechanics (2019). https://doi.org/10.1007/978-3-030-00665-5_129
13. Mohamed Jebran, P., Gupta, S.: Microaneurysm Detection by Multiple Feature Subset Extraction and Selection Based on SVM-Weights and Genetic Algorithm-Neural Network (2021). https://doi.org/10.1109/ICACCS51430.2021.9441746
14. Popat, V., Mahdinejad, M., Dalmau Cedeño, O.S., Naredo, E., Ryan, C.: GA-Based U-Net Architecture Optimization Applied to Retina Blood Vessel Segmentation (2020). https://doi.org/10.5220/0010112201920199
15. Kadan, A.B., Subbian, P.S.: Detection of hard exudates using evolutionary feature selection in retinal fundus images. J. Med. Syst. (2019). https://doi.org/10.1007/s10916-019-1349-7
16. Ghosh, S.K., Biswas, B., Ghosh, A.: A Novel Approach of Retinal Image Enhancement Using PSO System and Measure of Fuzziness (2020). https://doi.org/10.1016/j.procs.2020.03.446
17. Gao, Z., Li, J., Guo, J., Chen, Y., Yi, Z., Zhong, J.: Diagnosis of diabetic retinopathy using deep neural networks. IEEE Access. (2019). https://doi.org/10.1109/ACCESS.2018.2888639
18. Abràmoff, M.D., et al.: Automated early detection of diabetic retinopathy. Ophthalmology. (2010). https://doi.org/10.1016/j.ophtha.2010.03.046
19. Habashy, S.M.: Identification of diabetic retinopathy stages using fuzzy C-means classifier. Int. J. Comput. Appl. (2013). https://doi.org/10.5120/13420-1096
20. Hann, C.E., Revie, J.A., Hewett, D., Chase, J.G., Shaw, G.M.: Screening for diabetic retinopathy using computer vision and physiological markers. J. Diabetes Sci. Technol. (2009). https://doi.org/10.1177/193229680900300431
21. Johora, F.T., -Or-Rashid, M.M., Yousuf, M.A., Saha, T.R., Ahmed, B.: Diabetic Retinopathy Detection Using PCA-SIFT and Weighted Decision Tree (2020). https://doi.org/10.1007/978-981-13-7564-4_3
22. Philip, M.A.: Deep Neural Network for Diabetic Retinopathy Disease Severity Classification (2017)

23. Kanungo, Y.S., Srinivasan, B., Choudhary, S.: Detecting Diabetic Retinopathy Using Deep Learning (2017). https://doi.org/10.1109/RTEICT.2017.8256708
24. Tymchenko, B., Marchenko, P., Spodarets, D.: Deep Learning Approach to Diabetic Retinopathy Detection (2020). https://doi.org/10.5220/0008970805010509
25. Krizhevsky, A., Sutskever, I., Hinton, G.E.: ImageNet classification with deep convolutional neural networks. Commun. ACM. (2017). https://doi.org/10.1145/3065386
26. Deng, J., Dong, W., Socher, R., Li, L.-J., Li, K., Fei-Fei, L.: ImageNet: A large-scale hierarchical image database. In: 2009 IEEE Conference on Computer Vision and Pattern Recognition, pp. 248–255 (2009). https://doi.org/10.1109/CVPR.2009.5206848
27. Kaggle: Diabetic Retinopathy Detection. [Online]. Available: https://www.kaggle.com/c/diabetic-retinopathy-detection
28. Liskowski, P., Krawiec, K.: Segmenting retinal blood vessels with deep neural networks. IEEE Trans. Med. Imaging. **35**(11), 2369–2380 (2016). https://doi.org/10.1109/TMI.2016.2546227
29. R.Priya, R.P., Aruna, P.: SVM and neural network based diagnosis of diabetic retinopathy. Int. J. Comput. Appl. (2012). https://doi.org/10.5120/5503-7503
30. Mercaldo, F., Nardone, V., Santone, A.: Diabetes mellitus affected patients classification and diagnosis through machine learning techniques. Procedia Comput. Sci. (2017). https://doi.org/10.1016/j.procs.2017.08.193
31. Simanto, et.al. (2022). Diabetes Prediction Using Machine Learning Techniques. Advanced Computing and Intelligent Technologies. Lecture Notes in Electrical Engineering, 914. Springer, Singapore. https://doi.org/10.1007/978-981-19-2980-9_26.
32. Vijayan, V.V., Anjali, C.: Prediction and Diagnosis of Diabetes Mellitus - a Machine Learning Approach (2016). https://doi.org/10.1109/RAICS.2015.7488400
33. Kaggle: (2021). https://www.kaggle.com/c/aptos2019-blindness-detection/data Accessed on 21 May 2021
34. Hu, J., Shen, L., Albanie, S., Sun, G., Wu, E.: Squeeze-and-excitation networks. IEEE Trans. Pattern Anal. Mach. Intell. (2020). https://doi.org/10.1109/TPAMI.2019.2913372
35. Sandler, M., Howard, A., Zhu, M., Zhmoginov, A., Chen, L.C.: MobileNetV2: Inverted Residuals and Linear Bottlenecks (2018). https://doi.org/10.1109/CVPR.2018.00474
36. Huynh, H.N., Do, M.T., Huynh, G.T., Tran, A.T., Tran, T.N.: Classification of Stages Diabetic Retinopathy Using MobileNetV2 Model. **4**, 147–157 (2022)
37. Zhang, G., Sun, B., Zhang, Z., Pan, J., Yang, W., Liu, Y.: Multi-model domain adaptation for diabetic retinopathy classification. Front. Physiol. **13** (2022). https://doi.org/10.3389/fphys.2022.918929
38. https://idf.org/about-diabetes/what-is-diabetes/
39. Gangani, D., Thilini, J.N., Madhusha, B., Meddage, D.P.P., Upaka, R.: A novel machine learning approach for diagnosing diabetes with a self-explainable interface. Healthc. Anal. **5**, 100301 (2024). https://doi.org/10.1016/j.health.2024.100301
40. Guleria, P., Srinivasu, P.N., Hassaballah, M.: Diabetes prediction using Shapley additive explanations and DSaaS over machine learning classifiers: a novel healthcare paradigm. Multimed. Tools Appl. **83**, 40677–40712 (2024). https://doi.org/10.1007/s11042-023-17212-w
41. Singh, A., Kumar, R., Gandomi, A.H.: Adaptive isomap feature extractive gradient deep belief network classifier for diabetic retinopathy identification. Multimed. Tools Appl. (2024). https://doi.org/10.1007/s11042-024-19216-6

Sugarcane Crop Classification by Using Ensemble Learning and Remote Sensing Data

Rashmi Saini[1(✉)], Suraj Singh[1], and Prabhakar Semwal[2]

[1] G. B. Pant Institute of Engineering and technology, Pauri Garhwal 246196, India
rashmisaini@gmail.com

[2] THDC Institute of Hydropower Engineering and Technology, Tehri Garhwal, India

Abstract. Sugarcane holds paramount importance in Indian agriculture, with India ranking as the second-largest producer globally, following Brazil. This research paper delves into the intricate dynamics of sugarcane cultivation within the Indian con-text, focusing on the region of Roorkee, Uttarakhand. The study highlights the critical need for precise land use and land cover (LULC) classification, not only for sugarcane but also for six other prominent classes within the region. Situated in the foothills and plains of Haridwar district, Roorkee epitomizes the diverse agricultural landscape of India, necessitating accurate classification for informed land use planning and sustainable agricultural management. Leveraging Sentinel-2 satellite imagery has been used for sugarcane mapping, advanced machine learning classifiers including Extreme Gradient Boosting (XGBoosT) and Support Vector Machine (SVM) algorithms were deployed for classification. The study yielded high overall accuracies, with XGBoosT reaching 93.223% and SVM achieving 91.63%. Additionally, Kappa's values, with XGBoosT obtained 0.918 and SVM achieved 0.899 value. This research provides invaluable in-sights for enhancing agricultural productivity and sustainability in the region.

Keywords: Sugarcane · Ensemble learning · Crop Classification · Extreme Gradient Boosting (XGBoosT) · Support Vector Machine (SVM) · Remote Sensing

1 Introduction

Sugarcane (Saccharum officinarum) is a globally significant agricultural commodity. India, ranking as the world's second-largest producer after Brazil. India's recent ascendancy to the position of the world's largest sugar producer underscores the sector's rapid growth, attributed to expanded cultivation areas and improved yield rates [1]. This perennial crop, known for its efficient photosynthesis, thrives in tropical and subtropical climates characterized by high temperatures and humidity. Its extended growing season results in high yields, making it valuable for sugar production, as well as serving as a cash, feed, and industrial crop. Sugarcane exhibits remarkable versatility, finding application in various industries such as sucrose, yeast, paper, chemicals, bio-fertilizers, fodder, and renewable energy sources [2]. Within India, the northern states lead in sugarcane production, further solidifying the country's status as a key player in the industry.

M. Paprzycki et al. (Eds.): ICACIS 2024, CCIS 2405, pp. 308–319, 2027.
https://doi.org/10.1007/978-3-032-30990-7_22

Given its economic importance, accurate estimation of sugarcane yield at a fine scale is paramount for efficient production management [1, 2].

Uttarakhand, known for its hilly terrain, here, the key contributor's regions for sugarcane production are Dehradun, Haridwar, and Udham Singh Nagar. Ethanol, primarily derived from sugarcane, is increasingly integrated into fuel blends worldwide [3]. The Indian government aims to achieve more ethanol blending by 2025 to reduce dependence on fossil fuels. This dual-purpose approach aligns with sustainable practices and ensures the economic viability of sugarcane cultivation. In Brazil, ethanol makes up a significant portion of gasoline, reaching levels of up to 27.5%. Ethanol not only serves as a cleaner-burning fuel but also helps manage surplus sugarcane stocks [4]. To enhance sugarcane production, a comprehensive approach emphasizing improved productivity, expanded cultivation areas, and investment in research is necessary [5]. Efficient agricultural management requires a nuanced understanding of spatial and temporal factors, including climate and soil attributes. Agricultural systems evolve over time, influenced by dynamic interactions between crops and prevailing environmental conditions [3–5].

Remote sensing (RS) has become instrumental in agricultural research, particularly in mapping crops and estimating crop yields. Advanced satellite technology enables the mapping and monitoring of vast sugarcane fields, facilitating accurate yield predictions. Previous studies have utilized RS imagery to extract features for sugarcane yield estimation [6–10]. While some approaches rely on crop growth models, others employ data-driven techniques. Crop growth models offer quantitative insights into yield determinants but require extensive local data for calibration, limiting their scalability. Empirical statistical models establish linear relationships between crop yield and RS-derived indices, offering simplicity but struggling with non-linear relationships and dynamic weather effects. Overall, RS-based methods hold promise for accurate and scalable sugarcane yield predictions, crucial for ensuring food security and sustainable agricultural practices [1–13].

Machine learning (ML) techniques are increasingly utilized for crop mapping and yield estimation, particularly leveraging optical remote sensors for spectral data acquisition [7, 8]. These sensors, including MODIS, Landsat, and Sentinel-2, provide valuable information for predicting crop yield based on vegetation indexes (VIs). Studies have employed ML algorithms, such as simple linear models, to predict sugarcane yield accurately, addressing limitations like cloud occlusion and VI saturation. In India, ML algorithms, including artificial neural networks (ANNs), have been applied to predict sugarcane yield with promising results [9–12]. However, integrating crop growth processes with ML models is crucial for improving interpretability and generalizability, enhancing accuracy in yield prediction. Systematic reviews reveal the widespread use of ML methods, with neural networks and linear regression being prominent, followed by random forest and support vector machines. Deep learning approaches, although effective, require substantial data and hardware resources. Despite challenges, ML techniques offer valuable insights into crop yield prediction across various scales, facilitating informed decision-making in agriculture [11–17].

2 Literature Review

Crop mapping methodologies have evolved significantly, however, the spectral similarity among various crops poses a challenge. In the recent time, Sentinel-2A datasets were utilized for crop mapping. The study aimed to identify major crops and evaluate the effectiveness of ensemble methods for mapping purposes. Surprisingly, XGBoosT emerged as the most effective method, demonstrating impressive overall accuracy of 86.91%, outperforming traditional methods like Random Forest (RF) and Support Vector Machine (SVM) [7]. Meanwhile, in Australia, the unpredictability of dryland cropping systems due to climate variability has prompted researchers to explore machine learning methods solely using climate data for yield prediction across various crops. Among these methods, XGBoosT demonstrated superior predictive accuracy, explaining a significant portion of yield variability and outperforming other approaches. This streamlined approach simplifies pre-sowing decisions, aiding in optimal sowing dates and crop selection, making it applicable across diverse agricultural contexts [8].

Sugarcane, a vital crop for sugar and bioenergy production, necessitates precise preharvest yield estimates. Research conducted in Guangxi, China, employed LiDAR and UAV to assess sugarcane aboveground fresh weight (AFW). The study found that Random Forest Regression (RFR) was the most effective model, achieving an impressive R2 value of 0.96. These findings not only guide optimal planting density and tillage methods but also reduce human impact on sugarcane cultivation practices [9]. Another study focused on sugarcane mapping, this time exploring the use of multi-temporal orbital imagery to address challenges in on-board monitoring. By utilizing Sentinel-2 images and machine learning techniques, predictive yield models were developed for a commercial sugarcane site. The incorporation of spectral bands, particularly near-infrared, significantly enhanced prediction accuracy. Here, the Random Forest model outperformed Multiple Linear Regression (MLR) [9]. In China's South, where sugarcane cultivation is prevalent, traditional mapping methods using optical images face limitations due to cloud cover and inefficiency. However, a recent study introduced a novel approach utilizing Sentinel-1A Synthetic Aperture Radar (SAR) for early-season sugarcane mapping in Zhanjiang. The method achieved a Kappa coefficient exceeding 0.902, demonstrating the efficiency of the XGBoosT classifier in cloud-prone regions. The estimated sugarcane areas for specific regions further highlights the method's relative accuracy, promising efficient sugarcane mapping even under challenging environmental conditions [10].

Moreover, the field of sugarcane mapping has seen significant progress in integrating high-resolution remote sensing data and machine learning techniques. One notable study seamlessly integrated Sentinel-1 SAR data with Sentinel-2-derived vegetation indices, achieving accurate estimations of sugarcane yield at both country and pixel scales. The study reported a high accuracy level (R2 = 0.815) in predicting sugarcane yields in Guangxi province, demonstrating the effectiveness of this approach for precise crop management [11].

Furthermore, the importance of accurate yield prediction extends beyond sugarcane to crops like winter wheat, crucial for food security. Utilizing XGBoosT and other machine learning algorithms with satellite, climate, and atmospheric data, winter wheat yields in northern China were forecasted for the period 2005 to 2014. XGBoosT emerged as the top performer, achieving high accuracy offering valuable insights for guiding agricultural practices and policy-making [12]. Accurate forecasting of winter wheat yield remains a priority, as demonstrated by a study proposing a method using integrated Landsat 8 and Sentinel-2 data with a Bayesian optimized CatBoost regression model. This method outperformed others, with R2 values ranging from 0.63 to 0.70 and RMSE values from 0.62 to 0.73 t/ha for the years 2019–2021 [13].

In the realm of agricultural data analysis, a hybrid regression algorithm, reinforced by extreme gradient boosting, has been introduced. This method surpasses traditional algorithms, achieving 94.15% accuracy in crop yield prediction while effectively preserving the original data distribution characteristics, showcasing its potential for agricultural advancements [14]. Moreover, data mining techniques find applications in improving agricultural practices globally. A study in Nigeria leveraged historic data to predict crop yield and recommend soil nutrient enhancements. By employing the XGBoosT algorithm for yield prediction and Support Vector Machine for soil nutrient recommendations, the model achieved high accuracies of 95.28% and 97.86%, respectively, facilitating informed farming practices and improved productivity [15].

The comparison of machine learning algorithms for fruit-tree crop detection using Sentinel-2 data revealed insights into their performance. SVM achieved the highest accuracy (71%), while XGBoosT reported an accuracy of 63%. However, imbalanced training datasets significantly affected algorithm performance, emphasizing the importance of dataset quality. Sentinel-2 data proved effective for mapping fruit-tree crops, enhancing precision agriculture in heterogeneous horticultural landscapes [16].

In conclusion, the literature review highlights advancements in crop map-ping, particularly in sugarcane. improved accuracy through remote sensing and machine learning. Beyond sugarcane, these methods promise agricultural sustainability. This paper is structured into sections, with the third section focusing on the study area and dataset used. The methodology outlines the integration of remote sensing and machine learning. Results and discussion provide insights into sugarcane mapping and broader agricultural implications. Finally, major findings were listed in the conclusion section.

3 Study Area and Dataset

In this research, we employed a Sentinel-2 satellite image acquired on June 06, 2022, within the growing season. The study area, situated in the foothills of the Himalayas, plays a pivotal role in the regional economy due to its agriculture prominence. Spanning 1049.31 km^2, the area is characterized by diverse land use and land cover (LULC) classes. The sentinel-2 datasets have shown its efficacy for various applications of remote sensing domain by employing ML techniques [17–22]. In this study, we have utilized four Sentinel-2 bands (Near-Infrared, Red, Green, and Blue), each boasting a spatial resolution of 10 m. The Sentinel-2 satellite employed in this study encompasses a total of 13 spectral bands [7].

Our Study region is classified into seven LULC classes, including Orchard, Sandy area, Water, Built-up, Other crops, Sugarcane, and Fallow land. The 'Orchard' category encompasses areas with planted trees, including fruit gardens like mangoes and guavas. The 'Other crops' class includes various crops such as Fodder, Wheat, Mustard and Wheat, and vegetables like Radish, Cabbage, and Cauliflower

Special attention is given to the mapping of sugarcane, a pivotal crop in our selected region. Figure 1 illustrates the False Colour Composite (FCC) of the study area, utilizing Sentinel-2 imagery. A False Color Composite (FCC) combines near-infrared (NIR), red, and green bands, assigning them to the red, green, and blue channels, respectively [7]. This composite enhances the distinction between vegetation and non-vegetation: healthy vegetation appears bright red due to strong NIR reflection, while non-vegetated areas like water bodies appear in shades of blue or gray. FCCs are valuable for vegetation monitoring, land cover classification, and environmental assessments in remote sensing applications. This composition aids in providing a detailed overview of the study area, emphasizing the specific LULC classes of interest, particularly the mapping of sugarcane cultivation. Through this focused approach, we aim to understand and map the distribution of sugarcane cultivation, contributing valuable insights to agricultural management and sustainability in the region.

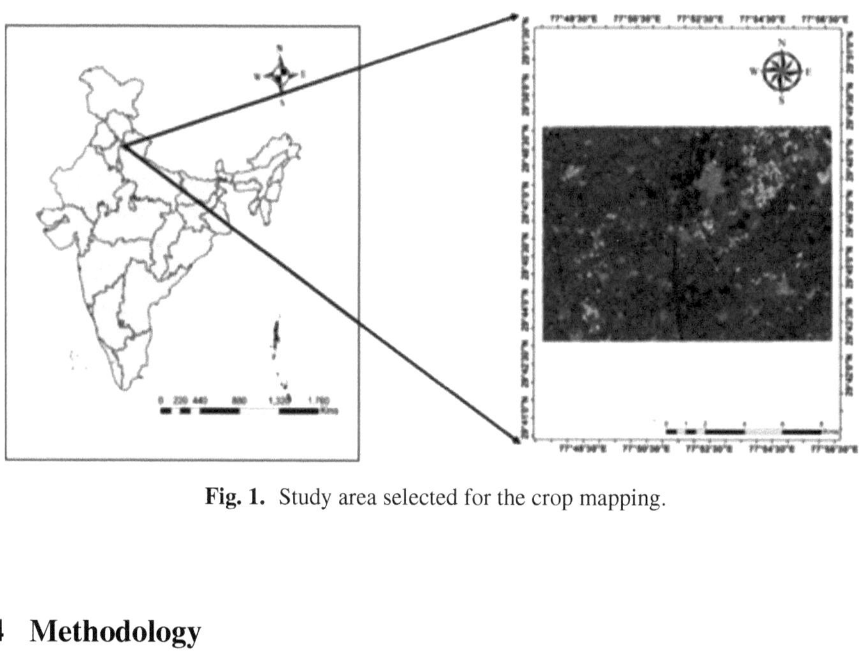

Fig. 1. Study area selected for the crop mapping.

4 Methodology

The proposed methodology for sugarcane mapping utilizes Sentinel-2 imagery and involves several key steps, as illustrated in Fig. 2. Initially, a single-date Sentinel-2 image is acquired, consisting of individual bands including Near-Infrared (NIR), Red (R), Green (G), and Blue (B), each with a spatial resolution of 10 m. These bands are stacked together to form a multispectral image cube, where each pixel contains a 4-dimensional vector representing spectral values from the considered bands. This stacked image cube provides a comprehensive representation of the study area's surface reflectance, facilitating feature extraction and classification to accurately map sugarcane and other land cover types within the area [9–14].

To establish a reference dataset for training and testing, a field survey was conducted, and ground truth values were recorded using a Global Positioning System (GPS) instrument. Additionally, some samples were selected with the aid of high-resolution Google Earth images and Indian Bhuvan ISRO data. After feature extraction and stratification of polygon samples, the total number of sample pixels amounted to 18,507. These samples underwent a process known as "mixing" or "shuffling" in machine learning terminology. Mixing involves randomizing samples to ensure a balanced representation of different classes within both the training and testing datasets, thereby enhancing the generalization capabilities of the machine learning models. Subsequently, the mixed dataset was divided into training and testing subsets, with 70% of the data allocated for training and the remaining 30% reserved for testing purposes [7]. This partitioning allowed for robust model training and evaluation. Two machine learning models Support Vector Machine (SVM) [23–25] and XGBoosT [26] and were then trained using the designated training dataset. These models serve as the foundation for the subsequent stages of the sugarcane mapping process. Through rigorous training and validation, these models are poised to provide reliable predictions, thereby facilitating precise sugarcane mapping and enhancing agricultural management strategies Fig. 2.

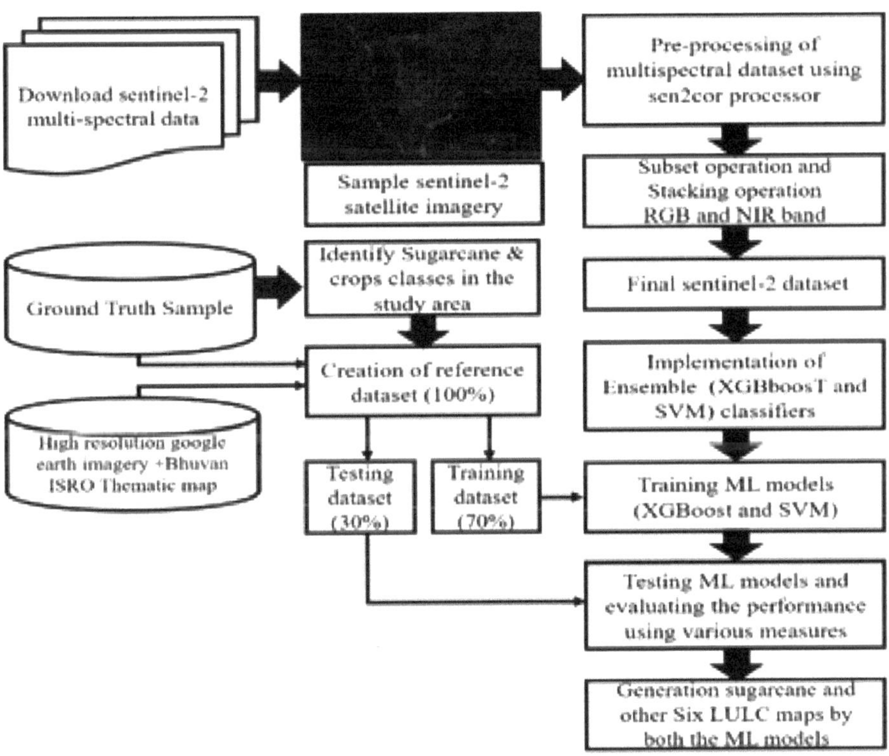

Fig. 2. Workflow of the proposed methodology.

Once the classifiers have been trained, thereafter, both machine learning models are evaluated using a testing dataset consisting of seven classes of input samples, total of 5552 randomized pixel samples. The optimum model identified after fine-tuning is then utilized to generate classification maps of the research areas. To assess the accuracy of the classifiers, precision and recall metrics are employed. Precision (p) and recall (r) are denoted for each class (i), with the F1-score serving as the metric to evaluate class-specific accuracy [7]. The F1-score is a function of the harmonic mean of precision and recall, as well as used in many studies to evaluate the accuracy of the classification models for a specific class [7, 16–22].

5 Results and Discussions

In ths study, a Sentinel-2 image acquired during the sugarcane growing season served as the primary data source. The image was constructed by combining four bands with a 10-m resolution to facilitate the classification of sugarcane crops [1–5]. The methodology involved Stratified Random Sampling and a 10-fold cross-validation scheme, ensuring the separation of training and testing pixels. Implementation of the XGBoosT, Support Vector Machine (SVM) classifiers was carried out using the R programming language. Assessing the accuracy of Land Use Land Cover (LULC) maps, especially in the context of sugarcane, is crucial for understanding map quality and suitability for specific applications. For performance evaluation in this sugarcane mapping work, overall accuracy, F1-score, and kappa coefficient were computed, with tuning parameters optimized for both classifiers.

Table 1. Overall Accuracy and Kappa coefficient value for both models.

Parameters	XgBoosT	SVM
Overall Accuracy	93.223	91.63
Kappa Cofficient	0.918	0.899

Table 1 presents the performance metrics of two classification models, XGBoosT and Support Vector Machine (SVM), applied to land cover classification using Sentinel-2 satellite imagery. XGBoosT achieved an overall accuracy of 93.223%, indicating that it correctly classified approximately 93.223% of instances, whereas SVM achieved an accuracy of 91.63%, signifying accurate classification of various LULC classes. Kappa's value, measuring agreement between predicted and true classifications, is obtained as 0.918 for XGBoosT and 0.899 for SVM. These values indicate strong agreement with the true classifications, with XGBoosT slightly outperforming SVM. Overall, both models demonstrated effectiveness in land cover classification, providing valuable insights for land use management and environmental monitoring [9].

Comparing XGBoosT and SVM classifiers across various metrics reveals distinct performance patterns. XGBoosT consistently demonstrates higher precision, recall, and F1-score for most classes compared to SVM. For example, in the sugarcane class,

XGBoosT achieves an F1-score of 94.03%, outperforming SVM's score of 92.49%. This trend continues with minor classes such as sand and fallow land, where XGBoosT exhibits higher F1-scores than SVM. Even for major classes like orchid and water, both classifiers show comparable performance. However, a detailed analysis of confusion matrices suggests that XGBoosT tends to have slightly fewer misclassifications, particularly distinguishing between sand and other classes was challenging as demonstrated in Table 2 (XGBoosT) and 3 (SVM).

In analyzing the misclassifications made by XGBoosT and SVM classifiers, it's evident that both models struggle with accurately identifying instances of the sugarcane class. Specifically, XGBoosT misclassifies 46 instances as orchid and 26 instances as other crop, while SVM misclassifies 58 instances as orchid and 32 instances as other crop. Although both classifiers exhibit misclassifications, XGBoosT demonstrates a slightly lower misclassification rate for sugarcane instances. In examining the performance of XGBoosT and SVM classifiers across individual classes, distinct trends emerge. For the orchid class, XGBoosT demonstrates higher precision (89.38% vs. 86.47%), recall (90.24% vs. 87.36%), and F1-score (89.81% vs. 86.47%) compared to SVM. For the orchid class, both classifiers tend to misclassify instances as other crop, with XGBoosT having a slightly lower misclassification rate as compared to SVM' classifier (Table 2 and 3).

Similarly, for the sand class, although both classifiers perform comparably, XGBoosT achieves a slightly better F1-score (85.53% vs. 83.69%). Conversely, for the water class, both classifiers exhibit equivalent precision, recall, but XGBoosT shows a slightly higher F1-score (94.08 vs.93.94%). A similar trend is observed in the sand class, where both classifiers frequently misclassify instances as built-up, with XGBoosT misclassifying 67 instances and SVM misclassifying 70 instances.

Table 2. Confusion matrix by produced by XGBoosT classifier.

	Reference data								
Classes		Orchid	Sand	Water	Built-up	Other crops	Sugarcane	Fallow land	Precision
Classified Data	Orchid	**564**	0	0	0	19	54	0	88.54
	Sand	0	**488**	25	67	0	0	14	82.15
	Water	0	3	**651**	3	0	0	22	95.88
	Built-up	0	35	13	**733**	0	0	17	91.85
	Other crop	15	0	0	0	**971**	17	0	96.81
	Sugarcane	46	0	0	0	26	**1127**	0	93.99
	Fallow land	0	21	16	23	0	0	**582**	90.65
	Recall	90.24	89.21	92.34	88.7	95.57	94.07	91.65	
	F1-score	89.38	85.53	94.08	90.3	96.19	94.03	91.15	

For the built-up class, XGBoosT outperforms SVM across all metrics: precision (91.85% vs. 90.27%), recall (88.74% vs. 87.65%), and F1-score (90.27% vs. 88.95%). Likewise, for the other crop class, XGBoosT outshines SVM with higher precision (96.81% vs. 95.71%), recall (95.57% vs. 94.49%), and F1-score (96.19% vs. 95.10%). In the water class, although both classifiers have a small number of misclassifications, primarily as built-up, XGBoosT misclassifies 3 instances while SVM misclassifies 4 instances. Moving to the built-up class, both classifiers tend to misclassify instances as sand, with XGBoosT misclassifying 35 instances and SVM misclassifying 47 instances (Table 2 and 3).

The trend continues with the sugarcane class, where XGBoosT surpasses SVM in precision (93.99% vs. 92.49%), recall (94.07% vs. 92.49%), and F1-score (94.03% vs. 92.49%). Both XGBoosT and SVM display similar confusion patterns for the sugarcane class, with misclassifications primarily occurring as orchid and other crop clas-ses. However, XGBoosT tends to have fewer misclassifications compared to SVM. Lastly, for the fallow land class, XGBoosT and SVM demonstrate similar perfor-mance, though XGBoosT exhibits a slightly better precision (90.65% vs. 89.64%) and F1-score (91.15% vs. 90.48%). For the fallow land class, both XGBoosT and SVM frequently misclassify instances as sand and built-up. XGBoosT misclassifies 21 instances as sand and 23 instances as built-up, while SVM misclassifies 23 instances as sand and 28 instances as built-up. In the case of the other crop class, both classifiers tend to misclassify instances as orchid, with XGBoosT misclassifying 17 instances and SVM misclassifying 21 instances. Overall, across most classes, XGBoosT consistently outperforms SVM in terms of precision, recall, and F1-score, notably excelling in distinguishing between orchid, built-up, other crop, and sugarcane classes Table 2 and 3. The resultant classification maps for XGBooT and SVM are shown in Fig. 3 (a) and (b) respectively.

Table 3. Confusion matrix by produced SVM classifier.

	Reference data								
Classes		Orchid	Sand	Water	Built-up	Other crops	Sugarcane	Fallow land	Precision
Classified Data	Orchid	**546**	0	0	0	24	68	0	85.58
	Sand	0	**473**	25	70	0	0	15	81.13
	Water	0	4	**651**	4	0	0	22	95.59
	Built-up	0	47	13	**724**	0	0	18	90.27
	Other crop	21	0	0	0	**960**	22	0	95.71
	Sugarcane	58	0	0	0	32	**1108**	0	92.49
	Fallow land	0	23	16	28	0	0	**580**	89.64
	Recall	87.36	86.47	92.34	87.65	94.49	92.48	91.34	
	F1-score	86.47	83.69	93.94	88.95	95.1	92.49	90.48	

The misclassification of sugarcane instances could have significant implications for agricultural management and planning. Accurate identification of sugarcane fields is crucial for tasks such as yield estimation, resource allocation, and decision-making. To enhance the accuracy of sugarcane classification, we implemented several strategies. First, we performed pre-processing to obtained true spectral signature of various classes. So that the classifiers better distinguish sugarcane from other classes. Moreover, we fine-tuned model parameters and explored ensemble methods to potentially improve classification performance. In summary, while both XGBoosT and SVM demonstrate reasonable performance for the sugarcane class, XGBoosT exhibits slightly better performance metrics with lower misclassification rates and higher precision, recall, and F1-score. Improving the classification of sugarcane is imperative for effective agricultural planning and management.

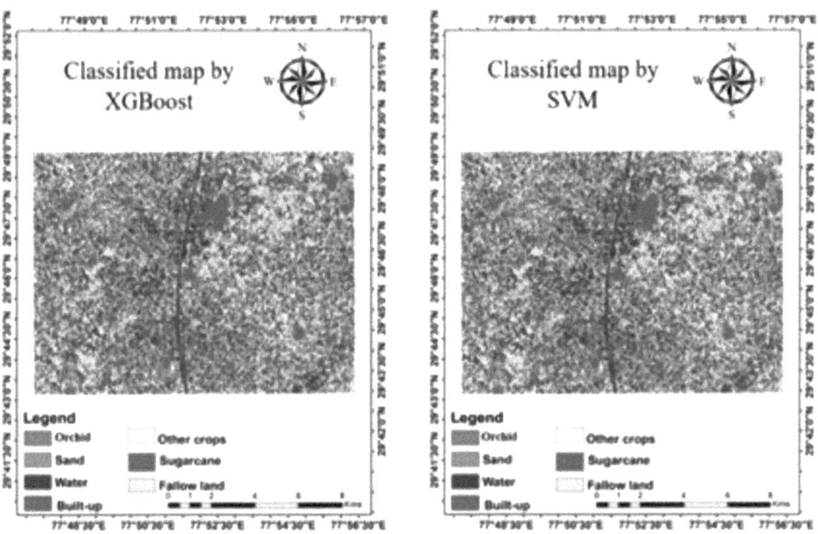

Fig. 3. Classified maps obtained by XGBoosT and SVM classifier.

6 Conclusions

In this study, we have utilized Sentinel-2 satellite data to conduct land use and land cover (LULC) mapping, with a particular focus on sugarcane and other relevant classes. The study area encompasses Roorkee, Uttarakhand, a region known for its agricultural significance. Sentinel-2 satellite imagery and advanced machine learning classifiers such as Extreme Gradient Boosting (XGBoost) and Support Vector Machine (SVM) algorithms were employed to obtain effective classification results for the sugarcane mapping. The XGBoost classifier reported the classification accuracy of 93.223%, whereas, SVM achieved the accuracy of 91.63%. Both classifiers demonstrated robust classification outcomes. These findings provide valuable insights for enhancing agricultural productivity and sustainability in the region for land use planning and management practices. Remote sensing technologies coupled with advanced machine learning algorithms play a crucial role in addressing the specific challenges when the LULC classes having similar spectral signatures. Overall, this research contributes to the broader goal of fostering economic development and environmental conservation in agricultural landscapes.

References

1. Nihar, A., Patel, N.R., Danodia, A.: Machine-learning-based regional yield forecasting for sugarcane crop in Uttar Pradesh, India. J. Indian Soc. Remote Sens. **50**(8), 1519–1530 (2022)
2. Wang, M., Liu, Z., Baig, M.H.A., Wang, Y., Li, Y., Chen, Y.: Mapping sugarcane in complex landscapes by integrating multi-temporal Sentinel-2 images and machine learning algorithms. Land Use Policy. **88**, 104190 (2019)
3. Oliveira, D.M., et al.: Is the expansion of sugarcane over pasturelands a sustainable strategy for Brazil's bioenergy industry? Renew. Sust. Energ. Rev. **102**, 346–355 (2019)
4. de Almeida, G.M., Pereira, G.T., de Souza Bahia, A.S.R., Fernandes, K., Júnior, J.M.: Machine learning in the prediction of sugarcane production environments. Comput. Electron. Agric. **190**, 106452 (2021)
5. Marcos, F.C., et al.: Drought tolerance of sugarcane is improved by previous exposure to water deficit. J. Plant Physiol. **223**, 9–18 (2018)
6. Canata, T.F., Wei, M.C.F., Maldaner, L.F., Molin, J.P.: Sugarcane yield mapping using high-resolution imagery data and machine learning technique. Remote Sens. **13**(2), 232 (2021)
7. Saini, R., Ghosh, S.K.: Crop classification in a heterogeneous agricultural environment using ensemble classifiers and single-date sentinel-2A imagery. Geocarto Int. **36**(19), 2141–2159 (2021)
8. Houshmandfar, A.: Can Machine Learning with Climate Data Alone Achieve High Yield Prediction Accuracy in Australian Dryland Cropping Systems?. Available at SSRN 4610893 (2023)
9. Xu, J.X., et al.: Estimation of sugarcane yield using a machine learning approach based on UAV-lidar data. Remote Sens. **12**(17), 2823 (2020)
10. Jiang, H., et al.: Early season mapping of sugarcane by applying machine learning algorithms to sentinel-1A/2 time series data: a case study in Zhanjiang City, China. Remote Sens. **11**(7), 861 (2019)
11. Zhu, L., Liu, X., Wang, Z., Tian, L.: High-precision sugarcane yield prediction by integrating 10-m Sentinel-1 VOD and Sentinel-2 GRVI indexes. Eur. J. Agron. **149**, 126889 (2023)
12. Cao, J., Wang, H., Li, J., Tian, Q., Niyogi, D.: Improving the forecasting of winter wheat yields in northern China with machine learning–dynamical hybrid subseasonal-to-seasonal ensemble prediction. Remote Sens. **14**(7), 1707 (2022)
13. Zhang, H., Zhang, Y., Liu, K., Lan, S., Gao, T., Li, M.: Winter wheat yield prediction using integrated Landsat 8 and Sentinel-2 vegetation index time-series data and machine learning algorithms. Comput. Electron. Agric. **213**, 108250 (2023)
14. Elavarasan, D., Vincent, D.R.: Reinforced XGBoosT machine learning model for sustainable intelligent agrarian applications. J. Intell. Fuzzy Syst. **39**(5), 7605–7620 (2020)
15. Yange, T.S., Egbunu, C.O., Rufai, M.A., Onyekwere, O., Abdulrahman, A.A., Abdulkadri, I.: Using prescriptive analytics for the determination of optimal crop yield. Int. J. Data Sci. Anal. (IJDSA). **6**(3), 72–82 (2020)
16. Chabalala, Y., Adam, E., Ali, K.A.: Exploring the effect of balanced and imbalanced multi-class distribution data and sampling techniques on fruit-tree crop classification using different machine learning classifiers. Geomatics. **3**(1), 70–92 (2023)

17. Saini, R., Singh, S.: Land use land cover mapping and snow cover detection in Himalayan region using machine learning and multispectral Sentinel-2 satellite imagery. Int. J. Inf. Technol. **16**(2), 675–686 (2024)
18. Rawat, S., Saini, R.: Cropland mapping using single date Sentinel-2 imagery using machine learning classifiers. In: 2022 International Conference on Advances in Computing, Communication and Materials (ICACCM), pp. 1–7. IEEE (2022)
19. Saini, R., Singh, S., Verma, S.K., Hatture, S.M.: Automatic mapping of deciduous and evergreen forest by using machine learning and satellite imagery. In: International Conference on Soft Computing and its Engineering Applications, pp. 197–209. Springer Nature Switzerland, Cham (2022)
20. Saini, R., Ghosh, S.K.: Analyzing the impact of red-edge band on land use land cover classification using multispectral RapidEye imagery and machine learning techniques. J. Appl. Remote. Sens. **13**(4), 044511–044511 (2019)
21. Saini, R., Ghosh, S.K.: Ensemble classifiers in remote sensing: a review. In: 2017 International Conference on Computing, Communication and Automation (ICCCA), pp. 1148–1152. IEEE (2017)
22. Rawat, S., Saini, R.: Delineation of flooded areas using a synergistic combination of optical and SAR imagery. In: 2023 1st International Conference on Innovations in High-Speed Communication and Signal Processing (IHCSP), pp. 87–92 (2023)
23. Cortes, C., Vapnik, V.: Support-vector networks. Mach. Learn. **20**(3), 273–297 (1995)
24. Vapnik Vladimir, N., Chervonenkis, A.Y.: On the uniform convergence of relative frequencies of events to their probabilities. In: Measures of Complexity. Springer (1972)
25. Chen, P.H., Lin, C.J., Schölkopf, B.: A tutorial on ν-support vector machines. Appl. Stoch. Model. Bus. Ind. **21**(2), 111–136 (2005)
26. Chen, T., Guestrin, C.: XGBoosT: a scalable tree boosting system. In: Proceedings of the 22nd ACM SIGKDD International Conference on Knowledge Discovery and Data Mining (2016)

Detecting Microservices Anti-patterns and Smells in Dynamic Environments

Shivanshu Sharma(✉) and Sangeeta Sharma

National Institute of Technology, Hamirpur 177005, Himachal Pradesh, India
shivanshusr82@gmail.com

Abstract. Microservices architecture has revolutionized the software industry by breaking monolithic applications into small, independent services. Each service focuses on specific tasks, promoting flexibility and parallel development. This approach allows for agility, scalability, and efficient development. However, managing these distributed services can be complex. This decentralization introduces a wide range complexities, including intricate service dependencies, dynamic scaling challenges, performance bottlenecks, and the need for effective monitoring. This research introduces an approach to detect different microservices anti-patterns i.e. Static anti-patterns by incorporating the code analysis in Continuous Integration/Continuous Deployment (CI/CD) pipelines and Dynamic anti-patterns by categorizing them into runtime and analysis-based anti-patterns. The runtime detection method introduces a Software Development Kit based approach to detect the anti-patterns, that intercepts the request headers of incoming and outgoing headers of a request that gets submitted to the system. And for analysis based anti-patterns and microservices smells, the research introduces an Application performance Monitoring (APM) tool to be used in the microservices system, that collect the logs from each of the service in the system. These logs can be fetched and analyzed to check for different anti-patterns. The proposed APM is a robust option for analysis based anti-patterns and catching all the runtime smells, monitoring infrastructure. It also provides various performance graphs by providing interactive dashboards.

Keywords: Microservices Anti-patterns · Microservices Smells · Distributed Logging · Network Interceptors · OpenTelemetry · Dynamic Analysis · Static Analysis

1 Introduction

Microservices architecture has become a prevalent paradigm in software engineering. It offers a modular and scalable approach to software development. As organizations increasingly adopt microservices, the challenges associated with the architecture's distributed nature requires a robust understanding of potential pitfalls, specifically the identification of anti-patterns and code smells, that can help the software developers build and debug system efficiently. As shown in

M. Paprzycki et al. (Eds.): ICACIS 2024, CCIS 2405, pp. 320–333, 2027.
https://doi.org/10.1007/978-3-032-30990-7_23

Fig. 1, there are various components involved in building a microservice system, that ensures lose coupling between different services. But this architecture poses challenges while debugging the errors, and the ideal microservice architecture violation.

The adoption of microservices brings forth a paradigm shift in system design, emphasizing decentralized and independently deployable services. Yet, this architectural style introduces a unique set of challenges that can undermine the envisioned benefits. One of the primary challenges is the presence of anti-patterns, subtle design choices that, while seemingly beneficial, can lead to system inefficiencies, increased latency, and potential service failures.

Fig. 1. Microservices System Architecture

The initial exploration, as encapsulated by the Aroma [11] tool, highlighted three notable anti-patterns: No API Gateway, Shared Persistence, and Cyclic Dependency. However, as the microservices landscape continues to evolve, it becomes important to delve deeper into the runtime behavior of these distributed systems. This research extends the Aroma framework by categorizing anti-patterns into two distinct categories: runtime anti-patterns and analysis-based anti-pattern detection.

This research aims to address the limitations of existing tools and methodologies in detecting and mitigating these issues, proposing an extended framework that categorizes dynamic anti-patterns into two types that are runtime and analysis-based anti-pattern detection.

- **Runtime anti-patterns Detection**: These anti-patterns are request specific unlike analysis based anti-patterns that are system specific.
- **Analysis based Detection**: These anti-patterns refer to the entire system i.e. when multiple requests lead to some anti-patterns affecting the entire system.

For static smells detection, which refers to the violation of defined design patterns in code. These anti-patterns are referred to the code style. These anti-patterns include Hardcoded Endpoints, Too Many Standards, Cyclic Dependency etc. For static anti-patterns detection, this research proposes the use of leveraging existing tools that are designed for that purpose, in CI/CD of a software. This is the way to keep static and dynamic smells and anti-patterns detection as coupled as possible as both of these categories can be analyzed on different stages of a Software Development Lifecycle (SDLC). One of such tools is MSANose [5], that can be integrated in the CI/CD pipeline to run an analysis on the code itself.

This research is organized into 5 sections. Section 2 defines the related work in the space that this paper is built on. Section 3 defines the background work, that provides contextual information and foundational knowledge necessary to understand the research problem. Section 4 presents the approach, methods, and techniques this research uses to detect anti-patterns. Results and findings are outlined in Sect. 5. And Sect. 6 concludes the key findings of the research.

2 Related Work

In this section, we provide a comprehensive review of existing literature relevant to Microservices architecture and anti-patterns detection. Tools to detect static anti-patterns are MSANose [5] introduced by D. Das et al., MAIG [7] by I. U. P. Gamage et al. and a tool proposed by A. Al Maruf et al. [1] that runs static code analysis for microservices reconstruction by providing centralized view of the functionality of services. This way organizations can gain insights into the dependencies, interfaces, and interactions between different services. MSANose detects code smells in different services in microservices system written in Java. The tool can detect upto 11 different code smells that can be identified and the faulty design patterns can be corrected even before the deployment. And MAIG uses the graph theory concepts and introduced one another method to detect Cyclic Dependency by applying Tarjan's strongly connected graph algorithm on the generated dependency graphs.

The configuration and architectural based approaches to make systems less vulnerable are proposed by B. Northern et al. [2] that helps to reconfigure the microservices environments by analysing the configurations of their host environments, making the system less vulnerable to cyber attacks and Roberto et al. [3] to adapt deployment strategies for better security of the architecture of systems with robust management of security keys, encryption services with robust authentication and authorization providing communication between different services through secure protocols.

The research by R. Gunawan et al. [4], authors emphasizes on using the container technologies like Docker and Kubernetes to orchestrate the Event Driven Architecture microservices systems to handle the internal communication between the services in the system. And I. Pigazzini et al. [6] extended the existing tool to detect the smells that occur due to architectural choices. This tool detected a total of three architectural smells that are Cyclic Dependency, Hard-coded endpoints and Shared Persistence.

To help developers to switch from monolith to microservices based architecture and refactor microservices R. Borges et al. [9] proposed an algorithm to detect anti-patterns that can help developers to switch from monolith to microservices based architecture seamlessly and by J. Soldani et al. [8] presents a toolchain for analyzing, mining and refactoring the microservices based architecture systems. G. Parker's [10] study suggests to detect the anti-patterns in microservices by having a logging infrastructure that is robust and decentralized. G. Parker's categorised the nature of anti-patterns and their detection in two parts in terms of the execution plan:

- **Microservices backlog**: It refers to anti-patterns detection by running analysis on the execution traces collected from different services. This category depends on the collection of data from system log files. Analyzing log files to observe the interactions among various services enables the identification of patterns.
- **Search-based antipatterns detection**: This category explores the idea of optimizing system efficiency by integrating both static & dynamic analysis methods. These papers also mentioned that static analysis doesn't contribute to detection of runtime anti-patterns.

P. Bacchiega [11] built a tool in the context of Microservices backlog that works by analysing all the logs collected by instrumenting the services with Zipkin. By analysing these traces, Aroma detected three MS smells: No API Gateway, Shared Persistence and Cyclic Dependency. The basic flow of the tool is (Fig. 2):

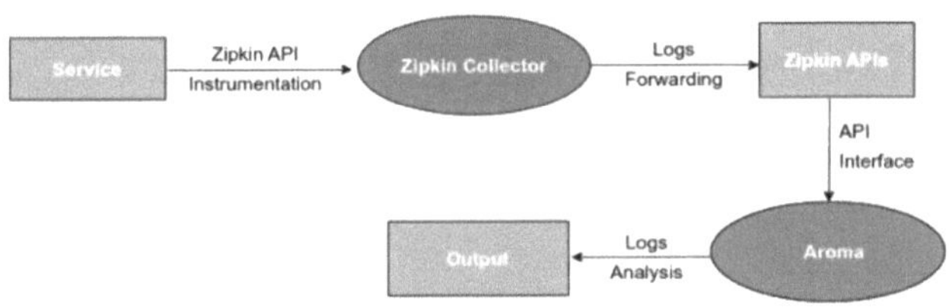

Fig. 2. Aroma Tool Workflow

Aroma [11] leverages the endpoints its instrumentation tool exposes to fetch information from Zipkin. This process yields a data stream that can be modified using the Gson library to format it into pretty JSON. The traces, now contained within a JSON file, undergo parsing to generate the microservices call graph with the help of Apache Tinkerpop. The way it works i.e. by generating the call graphs introduces the complexity to generate different call graphs for variety of anti-patterns, leads to detection of a subset of possible microservice smells. As some anti-patterns are associated to the request lifetime, and it doesn't require call graphs to detect such anti-patterns. The paper also proposes to use an APM tool that uses opentelemetry to support the wide variety of languages as the tool it uses requires Java background. There have been development of a lot of tools for anti-patterns detection but all are specific to some anti-patterns. Table 1 elaborates on the use case of each tool.

Table 1. Microservices Anti-patterns. Adapted from Parker [10]

Anti Pattern	MSANose [5]	Arcan [6]	MAIG [7]	µFRESHNER [8]	Approach from Borge et al. [9]
Ambiguous Service	X				X
API Versioning					X
Bloated Service					X
Bottleneck Service			XX		X
Cyclic Dependency	X	XX	XX		
Endpoint Based Interaction	X			XX	
Enterprise Service Bus	X				
Hard-Coded Endpoints	X	X			
Inappropriate Service Intimacy	X				
Microservice Greedy	X				
Nanoservice			XX		
No API Gateway	X			XX	
Service Chain			XX		
Shared Libraries	X				
Shared Persistency	X	X		XX	
The Knot			XX		
Ambiguous Service	X				

X = Detected, XX = Detected and Visualized

3 Background Work

This section discusses the background foundations to conduct our research. Figure 3 demonstrates the basic microservices architecture, that the systems should impose while designing microservices. All the requests/Inbound traffic gets through API Gateway before entering the system. Any patterns that are designed against this architecture can be called as anti-patterns.

3.1 Components of Microservices Systems

The building blocks of a basic microservice system are:

- API Gateway: API Gateway is a crucial component that acts as a central entry point and provides functionalities such as request routing, load balancing, authentication, and security enforcement, simplifying the interaction between clients and the distributed microservices architecture.
- Services: The different services shown in Fig. 3 are the microservices, responsible for doing independent tasks. These services are isolated from each other. The data storage, like databases are also different for each of the services in the system, making the entire system fault tolerant as failure of one service won't affect the entire system.
- Event Bus: An event bus is a communication infrastructure that enables asynchronous and decoupled communication between microservices. It allows services to publish events and subscribe to events of interest, promoting loose coupling and scalability.

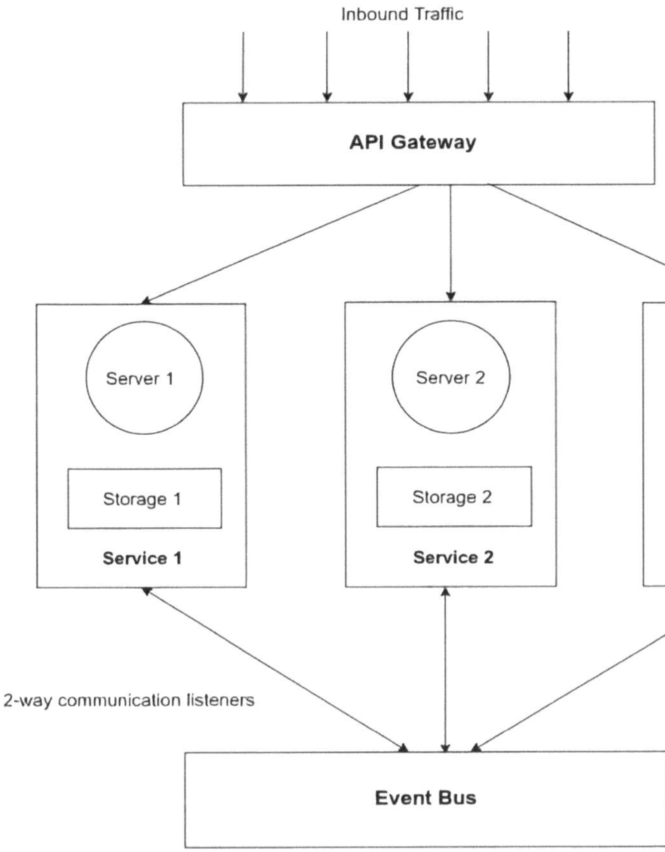

Fig. 3. Microservices System Architecture

There is one more important component in microservice architecture and that is Service Mesh: A service mesh is a dedicated infrastructure layer that manages and facilitates communication between microservices.

3.2 Overview of Different Types of Smells

Below is the overview of different anti-patterns as mentioned in Table 1:

- **Cyclic Dependency**: When two or more components or modules in a software system depend on each other in a circular manner.
- **Endpoint-based Service Interaction**: Refers to the communication and interaction between different services in a system via their endpoints or interfaces.
- **Shared Persistency**: Sharing of databases or persistent storage between two or more microservices.

- **Not Having API Gateway**: API gateway is a centralized service that manages, routes, and secures API.
- **Service Chain**: This anti-pattern occurs when microservices are connected in a sequential manner, forming a chain, and a single request has to pass through several microservices.
- **Bottleneck Service**: Refers to a service within a system that impacts the performance.
- **Nano Service**: Lightweight and minimalistic service or microservice.
- **The Knot**: Collection of disjointed services.
- **Wobbly Service Integration**: Situation where microservices integration is unstable, inconsistent, or unreliable leading to unpredictable behavior.

3.3 Application Performance Monitoring

APM refers to the practice of monitoring and managing the performance, availability, and overall health of software applications. After analysing all the available tools, we propose Signoz [16] as an APM tool. The features Signoz provides are:

- **Instrumentation**: Signoz provides instrumentation libraries or agents for popular programming languages that developers can integrate to their microservices' code.
- **Tracing**: Once the instrumentation is in place, Signoz traces requests as they flow through different microservices.
- **Data Collection**: The traces are collected and aggregated by the Signoz agent or collector.
- **Storage**: The collected trace data is stored in a backend storage system. Signoz supports various storage backends, such as Elasticsearch [17].
- **Visualization and Analysis**: Users can interact with the Signoz dashboard to visualize and analyse the trace data.
- **Alerting and Monitoring**: Signoz allows users to set up alerts based on predefined conditions or thresholds.
- **Integration with Logging and Metrics**: Signoz often integrates with logging and metrics systems to provide a comprehensive observability solution.
- **Distributed Context Propagation**: Signoz enables distributed context propagation, provides tracing a request across various services
- **OpenTelemetry Compatibility**: Signoz is designed to be compatible with OpenTelemetry.

4 Proposed Methodology

This section elaborates the strategy and tools that can be used to detect microservices anti-patterns that is scalable for anti-patterns detection in dynamic environments.

4.1 Tools Used

Below are the tools that we used to detect static and dynamic anti-patterns, where Service Mesh, Signoz [16] and NoSQL database are used for dynamic anti-patterns detection and MSANose [5] is used for the detection of static anti-patterns and JavaScript is used as a programming language for all the simulations.

- **Service Mesh** that stores the information current state i.e. services running in the microservice system. And network interceptors to attach some additional information as request traverse from one service to another.
- **Signoz** as an APM to be used that supports Open Telemetry to instrument, generate, collect, and export telemetry data (metrics, logs, and traces) to analyze the software's performance and behavior written in any language, Signoz is a great tool that offers these features.
- **NoSQL Database** as a centralized datastore to save the anti-patterns results corresponding to every trace in each of the microservice. Elasticsearch [17] and MongoDB [18] are the recommended choices as NoSQL databases to store document based data, as it provides efficient and fast reads and writes.
- **MSANose** [5] for static analysis on anti-patterns, via integrating the tool in CI/CD pipelines and detect static smells before deployments.
- **Logs Service**: This service is responsible for storing and fetching the anti-patterns logs. Each microservice in the system calls this Logs Service to register anti-patterns.

4.2 Method Breakdown

This section explains the development steps we used to detect static and dynamic anti-patterns. The steps to detect dynamic anti-patterns are:

- Divide the anti-patterns into two sub categories, below is the detailed explanation of how we categorised the dynamic anti-patterns in two clusters:
  - **Runtime anti-patterns detection**: The anti-patterns that come into this category are Cyclic Dependency, No API Gateway, Endpoint Based Interaction etc. As the name suggests we can identify these anti-patterns per request entering the system. For example: No API Gateway, this anti pattern is referred to one request per microservice and not to the entire services in the microservices architecture, similarly for Cyclic dependency, it is for the request itself and not the entire system.
  - **Analysis based anti-patterns detection**: The anti-patterns that come into this category are Shared Persistence, Microservices Chaining, Microservices Overhead, Bottleneck Services etc. Unlike runtime anti-patterns detection, these types of anti-patterns can be detected only on the entire system, using the traces of all the requests issued to the system till date. For example, Microservices Overhead, that means there's at least one service in the system that's rarely used by the requests, and system has an overhead of extra service that should be merged with some relevant service.

- For runtime anti-patterns we intercept communication calls between services, that includes two processes:
  - **Attaching headers**: In this part, we take the payload and before sending it to the other service and attach extra payload to the request data.
  - **Middleware**: It analyses all the data that is received by a service and check for the received payload, perform calculations based on the values of the parameters. If the middleware finds any potential anti-pattern, it notifies the logs service.

4.3 Architecture

This section describes the request hierarchy and the actions performed throughout the lifecycle of the request. Figure 4 shows the entire working of runtime anti-patterns detection that are, Cyclic Dependency, No API Gateway and Endpoint Based Interaction:

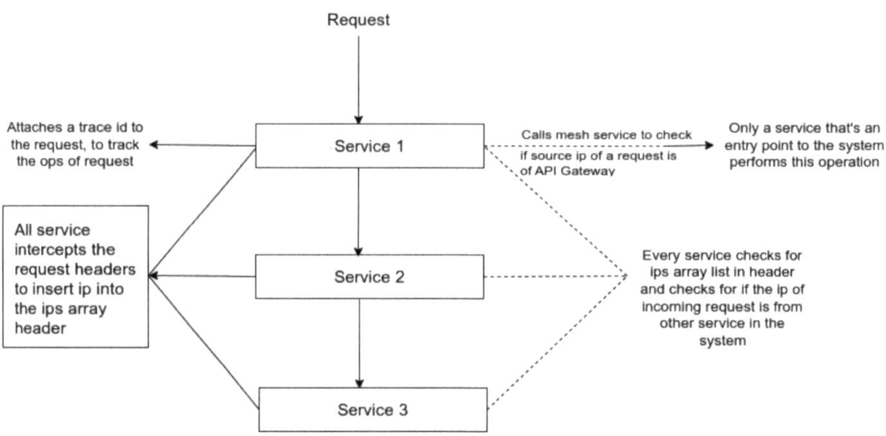

Fig. 4. Working Architecture

Below is the breakdown of the series of events a request goes through until it's resolved, when a request is issued to system:

- Entry point service checks for if a request is coming from API Gateway or not, if a request is not coming from API Gateway, then it means, the service is exposed to the pubic network, and hit the security concerns. All the requests should be routed through API Gateway. This service also attaches a trace id to request headers, so that the request can be traced all over the system. Because a request can hit a variety of anti patterns on different services and to sync the different patterns to the request, trace id is passed throughout.
- All the services intercept the incoming request and add its IP to the "ips" header, that is a list of all the particular request has been through. There is one more header in the request i.e. "ip", it contains the ip address of the source service, with this header and "Mesh" service in place we can check for No API Gateway and Endpoint Based Interaction anti-patterns.

```
{
  accept: 'application/json, text/plain, */*',
  ips: [ '192.168.211.245:3002', '192.168.211.245:3003' ],
  trace_id: '596467289',
  port: '3002',
  ip: '192.168.211.245:3002',
  'user-agent': 'axios/1.6.0',
  'accept-encoding': 'gzip, compress, deflate, br',
  host: 'localhost:3003',
  connection: 'close'
}
```


Fig. 5. Service Request Headers

- Services when they detect any anti-pattern, call the centralized log service with trace_id and the anti-pattern it detected. This "logs" service then stores, these anti-patterns as a key-value, where key is a trace id and value is an array of anti-patterns detected so far.

5 Results and Analysis

- The dynamic analysis of our microservices architecture successfully detected five key anti-patterns: No API Gateway, Endpoint-based interaction, Cyclic dependency, Microservice overhead, and Shared Persistence. This analysis has provided a clear insight into critical areas that could potentially disrupt the system's performance and operational integrity.
- Furthermore, the integration of Signoz, an OpenTelemetry supported Application Performance Monitoring (APM) tool, has broadened the dynamic analysis capabilities. This enhancement has enabled the examination of a diverse array of programming languages, which contributes to a more inclusive and versatile analysis framework.
- Lastly, incorporating MSANose into the CI/CD pipeline has significantly improved our proactive detection measures. By identifying potential code issues before deployment, MSANose ensures that structural and design-related problems are addressed early in the development cycle, enhancing the overall robustness and reliability of the system.

5.1 Dynamic Anti-patterns and Smells

With the proposed methodology, we successfully analyzed runtime and analysis based anti-patterns in dynamic environments. The anti-patterns that we detected so far are Cyclic Dependency, Endpoint Based Interaction, No API Gateway, Shared Persistence and Microservice Chaining/Microservice Overhead. Figure 5 shows the header format of a request the moment when it enters a service present in the microservice system.

Figure 6 shows the logs for each request. The key is the trace_id associated with a request when it first enters the system, and the array contains the anti-patterns that are detected in the trace of the request.

```
{
    "logs": {
        "938999279": [
            "NO_API_GATEWAY",
            "ENDPOINT_BASED_INTERACTION",
            "CYCLIC_DEPENDENCY",
            "MICROSERVICE_OVERHEAD"
        ],
        "2573669448": [
            "NO_API_GATEWAY",
            "ENDPOINT_BASED_INTERACTION"
        ],
        "9876071030": [
            "ENDPOINT_BASED_INTERACTION",
            "CYCLIC_DEPENDENCY",
            "MICROSERVICE_OVERHEAD"
        ]
    }
}
```


Fig. 6. Request Trace Logs

5.2 APM: Other Dynamic Anti-Patterns and Smells

As mentioned in the methodology, the 2nd category that is related to the entire system, are detected via APM tool that we propose i.e. Signoz [16]. The anti-patterns come under this category are Shared Persistency, Bottleneck Service, System Overwhelming. When a service is instrumented with Signoz, it detects such smells by performing health checks on the entire system. As shown in Fig. 7, it also provides traces that can be very helpful for developers to monitor their entire system running on microservices paradigm. Figure 8 shows the Call Graphs, generated by Signoz, hd and frontend are two different services Signoz detected and created the graphs for these services. Whereas the methodology of the paper [11] is creating Call Graph Models by fetching all the system logs. But we recommend using Signoz for detecting anti-patterns that requires Call Graph Models, as Signoz has in-house feature for creating efficient Call Graphs.

5.3 Combining Static Anti-Patterns Detection With the Framework

We chose MSANose [5] for static smells detection that can be integrated or combined using CI/CD i.e. Continuous Integration/Continuous Deployment pipelines. As mentioned in the Survey Section, static anti-patterns does not contribute to the runtime anti-patterns detection. So we propose MSANose to be used in CI/CD pipelines to have maximum possible coupling of static and dynamic anti-patterns detection. Figure 9 shows how using MSANose analysis in Github Workflows [19] can make detection of static anti-patterns detection coupled with dynamic anti-patterns detection. By following this pattern, now MSANose can run before deployment steps.

In our proposed solution i.e. using network interceptors approach, we were able to extend dynamic anti-patterns detection, and incorporating MSANose in CI/CD pipeline ensures tight coupling of static anti-patterns detection in dynamic environments.

Fig. 7. Traces

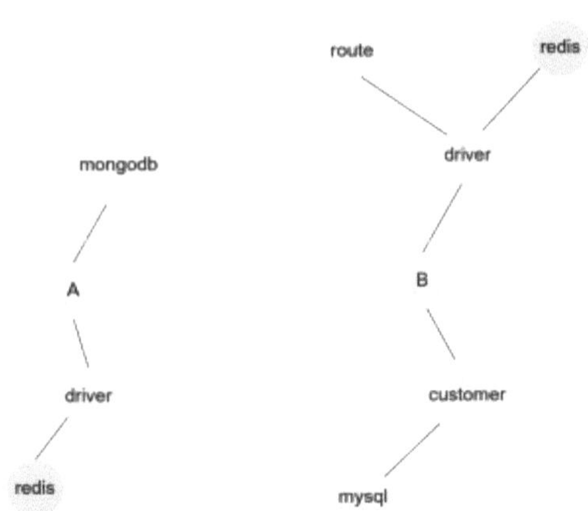

Fig. 8. Call Graph Models

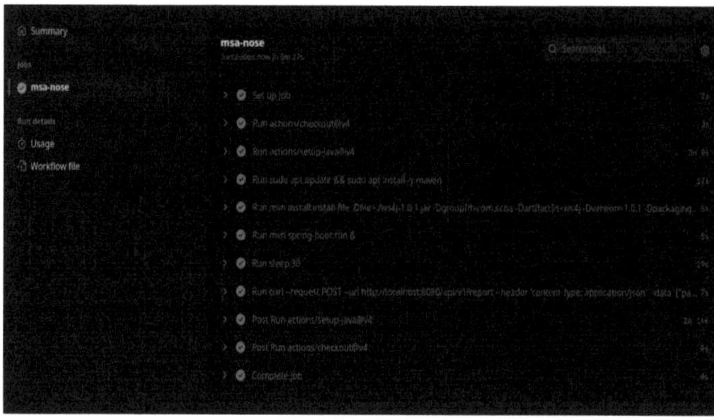

Fig. 9. MSANose Github Workflow

6 Conclusion

Due to the complex nature of microservices, it becomes important to detect & monitor systems for high availability and reliability. There should be a generic way to detect the static and dynamic anti-patterns to integrate tools to any programming background. This research has delved into the realm of microservices, focusing on the detection of smells and anti-patterns within the dynamic environments by categorizing the smells into relevant types. Our findings underscore the critical importance of proactive detection and use of a robust APM tool that can detect variety of microservices smells and anti-patterns effectively. We recommend MSANose due to its wide coverage of anti-patterns, but it restricts to Java background, and that can be improved to cover more languages either by creating tools for different languages or finding a generic solution.

References

1. A., Maruf, A., Bushong, V., Das, D., Cerny, T.: Using static analysis to address microservice architecture reconstruction. In: IEEE/ACM International Conference on Automated Software Engineering (ASE), vol. 1, pp. 1199–1201. Melbourne, Australia (2021)
2. Northern, B., Ulybyshev, D.: Building Secure Environments for Microservices. In: 2022 International Workshop on Secure and Reliable Microservices and Containers, vol. 2, pp. 27–31. SRMC, Vienna, Austria (2022)
3. da Silva, R.C.A., de Junior, R.S., Santos, M.S., Albuquerque, D.W., Almeida, H.O., Santos, D.F.S.: An Extensible and Secure Architecture based on Microservices. In: 2022 IEEE International Conference on Consumer Electronics. (ICCE), Las Vegas, NV, USA 3 (da Silva), pp. 01–02 (2022)
4. Gunawan, R., Rahmatulloh, A., Nugraha, F., Darmawan, I.: Event-driven architecture to improve performance and scalability in microservices-based systems. In: International Conference Advancement in Data Science, E-learning and Information Systems (ICADEIS), vol. 3, pp. 01–06. Bandung, Indonesia (2022)

5. Das, D., Walker, A., Cerny, T.: Automated code-smell detection in microservices through static analysis: A case study. In: Appl. Sci. **10**(3), 01–02 (2022)
6. Pigazzini, I., Fontana, F.A., Lenarduzzi, V., Taibi, D.: Towards microservice smells detection. In: Proceedings of 3rd International Conference on Tech. Debt, vol. 3, pp. 92–97 (2020)
7. Gamage, I.U.P., Perera, I.: Using dependency graph and graph theory concepts to identify anti-patterns in a microservices system: A tool-based approach. Proc. Moratuwa Eng. Res. Conf. (MERCon) **3**, 699–704 (2021)
8. Soldani, J., Muntoni, G., Neri, D., Brogi, A.; The μ TOSCA toolchain: Mining, analyzing, and refactoring microservice-based architectures. Softw. Pract. Exper. **51**(3), 1591–1621 (2021)
9. Borges, R., Khan, T.: Algorithm for Detecting Antipatterns in Microservices Projects. In: CEUR-WS, Vol. 3 (2021)
10. Parker, G.: Visualizing anti-patterns in microservices at runtime: a systematic mapping study. IEEE Access **11**(3), 4434–4442 (2023)
11. Pigazzini, I., Bacchiega, P., Fontana, F.A.: Microservices smell detection through dynamic analysis. In: 48th Euromicro Conference on Software Engineering and Advanced Applications (SEAA), vol. 3, pp. 290–293., Gran Canaria, Spain (2022)
12. Reile, C., Chadha, M., Hauner, V., Jindal, A., Hofmann, B., Gerndt, M.: Bunk8s: enabling easy integration testing of microservices in kubernetes. IEEE Int. Conf. Softw. Anal. **3**, 459–463 (2021)
13. Fink, S.J., Pistoia, M., Chandra, S., Yahav, E.: A survey of static analysis methods for identifying security vulnerabilities in software systems. In: IBM Syst. J. **46**(3), 265–288 (2007)
14. Fernando, C.: Designing Microservices Platforms with NATS: a modern approach to designing and implementing scalable microservices platforms with NATS messaging, Packt Publishing (2021)
15. Filippone, G., Autili, M., Tivoli, M.: Migrating from monoliths to microservices: enforcing correct coordination. In: 38th IEEE/ACM International Conference on Automated Software Engineering Workshops, pp. 113–118. ASEW, Luxembourg, Luxembourg (2023)
16. Signoz, Open-source Observability and Distributed Tracing. In: (2020). Retrieved from https://signoz.io/
17. Elasticsearch. In: (2010). Retrieved from https://www.elastic.co/elasticsearch
18. MongoDB. In: (2009). Retrieved from https://www.mongodb.com/
19. Github Workflows. In: (2018). Retrieved from https://github.com/features/actions

A Stacking Ensemble-Based Approach for Lung Cancer Detection

K. Suresh(✉), H. Sai Karthik V, D. Vivek Reddy, A. Suhas, and Pritam Khan

Department of Computational Intelligence, SRM Institute of Science and Technology, Kattankulathur 603203, Tamil Nadu, India
{sureshk8,hv3828,vd8837,aq7195,pritamk}@srmist.edu.in

Abstract. In this work, a framework for lung cancer classification from medical images is introduced leveraging ensemble learning approaches. We use CNNs (Convolutional Neural Networks), XG-Boost, Random Forest, and SVMs (Support Vector Machines) to increase the accuracy and confidence in diagnosing lung cancer. The deep learning-based stand-alone models are shown to perform independently. In the study, individual models are trained on a dataset of CT (Computed Tomographic) scan images, appraised, and then stacked in a novel stacking ensemble approach. The collective predictive power of the ensemble strengthens the model's accuracy, precision, and recall through a smart combination of separate models' predictions. The receiver operating characteristic-area under curve (ROC-AUC) and confusion matrix illustrate the characteristics of our proposed model to distinguish among benign, malignant, or normal situations. The proposed model finds diagnostic applications for the medical industry through the introduction of stacking ensembles for lung cancer detection.

Keywords: Lung Cancer Detection · CT Scan Images · Stacking Ensemble · Deep Learning · Machine Learning · Classification

1 Introduction

This research work focuses on a sophisticated artificial intelligence-based approach to classify lung. We conduct a comprehensive examination of various machine learning models such as Support Vector Machines (SVM), Decision Trees, Random Forest, Naïve Bayes, K-Nearest Neighbour (KNN), XG-Boost, AdaBoost as well as deep learning models such as Convolutional Neural Networks (CNN) and Restricted Boltzmann Machine (RBM). We systematically evaluate each model's unique strength and traits to determine their effectiveness in diagnosing lung cancer from complex medical imagery. The proposed model is a unified and strong ensemble that is based on stacking techniques, utilizing the collective intelligence from multiple machine learning and deep learning algorithms [12]. The ensemble method combines the various strengths of these models to create a novel solution for classifying lung cancer, which has the potential to outperform the individual models in terms of accuracy and dependability.

M. Paprzycki et al. (Eds.): ICACIS 2024, CCIS 2405, pp. 334–344, 2027.
https://doi.org/10.1007/978-3-032-30990-7_24

The intention here is to improve the survival rates of lung cancer patients who form a major fraction of cancer-related mortality world-wide, and, at the same time, the specificity of the disease, which is often diagnosed in the later stages. Leveraging machine learning, one can extract profound data-driven insights from the complex datasets phased out in medical imaging and patient records. In this way, such an approach seems to be very effective in revealing undetected markers and patterns that remain beyond the reach of conventional analysis tools, leading to the early diagnosis and most accurate prediction of the disease. Following such progress would have profound clinical implications since this could enable healthcare professionals to be armed with decision-aid tools through accurate prediction models and thus identify high-risk individuals, implement timely interventions, and improve the treatment plans for their patients. Thorough prediction models are laying the foundations for what-if scenarios of population-level screening, which can potentially provide further relief for the global epi-demic of lung cancer.

In addition to this progress, our study also examines how artificial intelligence can be combined into current clinical methods. This means doctors can make use of more sophisticated analytics while diagnosing lung cancer through embedding it with AI-driven instruments. The combination speeds up decisions and makes them more accurate at the same time as it allows for treatment protocols that are personalized according to individual patient profiles. Such a type of personalized medicine powered by AI could change cancer care forever because it ensures that treatments not only work but also do less harm and are better timed. What we propose here is an attempt on patients' lives through applying state-of-the-art technology against one of the hardest diseases in modern healthcare history.

1.1 Related Work

In recent decades, rapid advancements in pattern recognition and image processing techniques have led to an increased focus on lung cancer detection and classification. The article [1] describes current literature techniques for distinguishing various obstructive lung disorders using textural analysis of thin-section CT images. Previous studies used programs such as MATLAB to classify and process images. Steps were taken to apply artificial neural networks (ANN) and deep learning models to enhance precision. Trouble arises with the current systems because they are offline, have slow processing speeds, and have difficulties in accurately diagnosing small nodules, especially in a large population of patients [2]. Xie et al. [3] combine the application of metabolomics and AI technologies to find early-diagnosis biomarkers of lung cancer. The report demonstrates the application of LC-MSMS metabolomic methods incorporated with the Naïve Bayes machine learning method for predictive purposes, which is proven effective. However, these limits include the rather small size of the sample and the need for external validation in the studies concerning larger populations. The research by Asuntha et al. on lung cancer detection and classification includes techniques such as extracting textural features like wavelet transforms, local binary patterns (LBP), scale-invariant feature transforms (SIFT), and Zernike moments [4]. Raut et al. [5] have used digital image processing and intelligent algorithms, including C4.5 decision trees for detecting lung cancer. Strategies such as Otsu's method with thresholding and feature extraction, followed by visual image analysis with the use of CNNs, are primarily focused on, in

[5]. Challenges including the massive cloud for online software and the complexity of getting an accurate diagnosis utilizing CNN for a rapid lung cancer diagnosis, were overcome. The relevance of cancer diagnosis and the capacity of ML algorithms increased the determination rate, notwithstanding the limitations of small population datasets [5]. Singh et al. have employed image processing methods, though contrast-limited adaptive histogram equalization (CLAHE), extraction of texture features using the grey-level co-occurrence matrix (GLCM), and extraction of statistical parameters have been used alternatively. Techniques of supervised machine learning, such as image categorization, have been used. One of the challenges is that the tool may sometimes wrongly categorize cancer as benign or malignant. In addition, it can lead to overfitting a model with a relatively limited amount of data, although that can be tackled by using validation data [6]. Pawar et al. [7] have introduced a new computer-aided device (CAD) to check whether there is a tumor or not. By using this CAD, it will highlight the tumor in the circle. Radhika et al. [8] use datasets from the Machine Learning Repository on UCI and data.world to create precise classification methods for diagnosis purpose. The SVM model exhibits the highest accuracy of 96.2% as compared to other models in their study. Improving accuracy rates is a significant challenge that can be addressed through preprocessing operations [8].

1.2 Contributions

In this work, a novel method is developed for outsourcing the association of machine learning model predictions from various ML models using stacking ensemble techniques. Convolutional Neural Networks (CNNs), XGBoost, Random Forest, and Support Vector Machines (SVMs) are used to form an ensemble. This formation is able to surpass the existing limits on modeling homogeneous clusters with the new method. Given that every model among those provided gives some viewpoint on the process of recognizing complicated patterns in medical imaging, the choice of not sticking to one after another model selection was consciously made [9].

Apart from the uniqueness of longitudinal trials, which is manifested in the engraftment of a vast scope of individual models, it also portrays the strength of having aggregative proficiency through a stacking approach. This meta-model in the stacking ensemble is responsible for making a decision about whether particular stacked ensemble networks form better input for convolutional neural networks (CNNs) in spatial features or go back to traditional machine learning models for response function approximations (the decision boundaries) [10]. The multi-headed fashion and variations of a few outputs of prediction models are worked out to improve the ensemble's ability to distinguish between benign, malignant, and normal cases of lung cancer.

Another aspect that mentions the flexibility of the whole process is the choice of a model. By coming up with an integrated strategy that links old and new methods of machine learning in its approach, the method offers a hybrid structure that combines standard machine learning systems with deep learning architectures. This mix of singular stacking ensembles with single classifiers is an epitome of the field's versatility in terms of the collection of different methods and models to be tailored accordingly. Therefore, it is expected that such hybridization coupled with robustness might also be useful in the following studies.

The revolutionary part of this research is a stacking ensemble technique that gives a system long-term capacity and the ability to change by utilizing the best ways of various models for the classification of lung cancer as medical imaging is processed [11]. Here, a new opinion is formulated. Instead of choosing only the best model, different models are combined to create a powerful mechanism capable of refining clinical decision-making.

2 Methodology

2.1 Data Collection and Processing

The present study is centered on the 'Iraq-Oncology Teaching Hospital/National Center for Cancer Diseases' (IQ-OTH/NCCD) dataset that mainly consists of chest X-ray pictures, which are used for lung cancer detection in the early stages. It consists of three separate categories: 'Benign classes', 'Malignant classes', and 'Normal classes' [5]. Every class has details on various lung problems, which leads the model to produce a higher recognition rate for healthy people with lung disorders than for sick people. The data is split into training and testing sets. Thus, the process makes sure that the model will be trained by one subset, and will be tested by another, thereby enabling evaluation of the model's capability to generalize.

Performing image normalization beforehand is an important pre-processing step. Consistency of every image size to 100x100 pixel will result in uniformity, and pixel values will be meticulously adjusted so as to land within the [0, 1] range. Encoding categories into a one-hot format ensures proper compatibility of categorical labels with machine learning algorithms.

2.2 Base Models

A. **Convolutional Neural Network or CNN**

The Convolutional Neural Network (CNN) is very popular for image categorization roles. The convolutional layers extract hierarchical information from input images. The pooling and fully connected layers follow the same steps. A convolutional initial layer is followed by max-pooling, flattening, and then a dense layer. The CNN is then fine-tuned via the core process of optimizing the value of various hyper-parameters. It is necessary to consider the learning rate, optimizer, regularization, and batch size, which play a very important role in specifying the model speed, reducing overfitting, and treating vanishing gradient types.

B. **Traditional Machine Learning models**

   i. **XG-Boost:** As a gradient-boosting algorithm with strong capabilities, XGBoost has earned much appreciation for its efficiency in the field. It constructs a set of decision trees, built one by one, that aim at identifying and remedying the mistakes committed by the tree placed on top.
   ii. **Random Forest (RF):** The Random Forest is an ensemble learning algorithm that creates several decision trees (a tree-like structure of hypotheses made during training) and classifies data points according to the most common class.
   iii. **Support Vector Machine (SVM):** Support Vector Machine (SVM) is a classifier or predictive technique built upon the concept that distinct classes can be separated by the hyperplane that results in such a decision border between them.

2.3 Stacking Ensemble

The stacking ensemble fuses results from structural classification base models to generate a blended ensemble of multiple models' capabilities. Figure 1 shows the block diagram of lung cancer detection with the proposed stacking ensemble architecture.

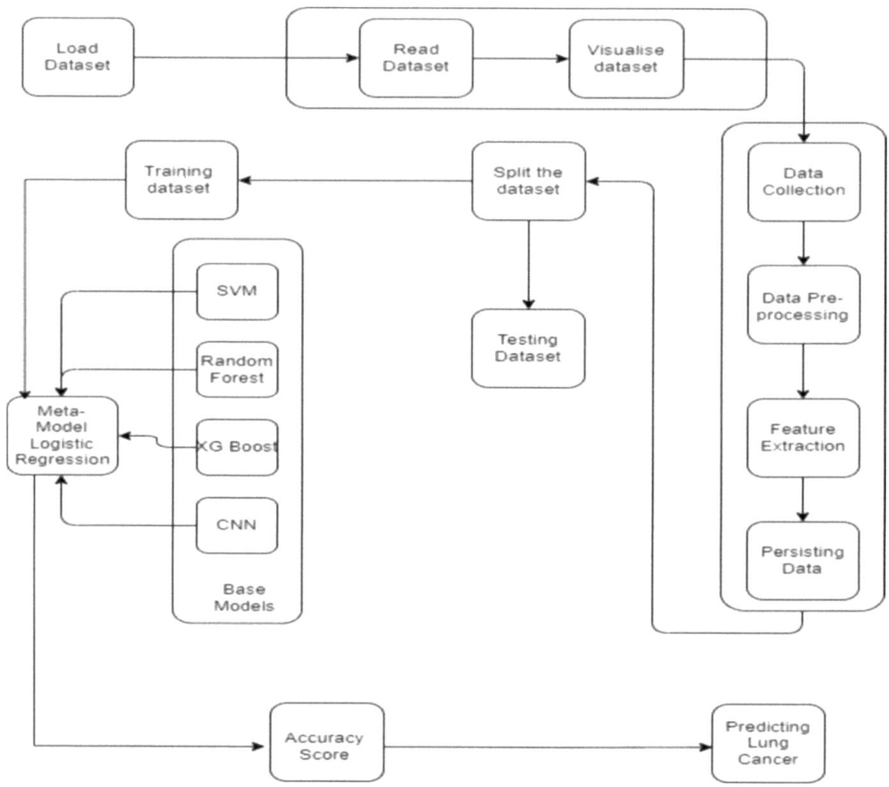

Fig. 1. Proposed stacking ensemble architecture for Detecting Lung Cancer

The central tool is a meta-package based on logistic regression. Weights are assigned to the predictions produced by the different base models using a logistic regression meta-training model. As observed from Fig. 1, the base models used in the proposed architecture are CNN, SVM, XGB, and Random Forest. Here, the sample set stacking method exchanges information, introducing a more impactful approach.

The stacking technique is based on the fact that different models specialize in one or another region of the problem space; thus, combining them with the help of stacking allows for more precise prediction of outcomes. The system proceeds with an in-depth assessment by engaging performance measurements such as accuracy, precision, and recall to implement a multidimensional evaluation of performance.

The methodical process covers data pre-processing in detail and describes the creation of each base model individually. It also explains the stacking ensemble, which leads to synergy. All the accounting is done by a set of complex math formulas that can give any advanced insight about the technical theories that are peripheral to the code.

3 Experimental Result and Discussion

The primary goal of this study was to carefully assess and classify lung cancer based on CT images. Initiating complex analysis using machine learning and deep learning models, each with unique characteristics, we explore the nuances of individual model accuracy and discuss the stacking ensemble method. In addition, the discussion extends to important aspects of the receiver operating characteristic (ROC) curve and confusion matrix analysis.

3.1 Individual Base Model Accuracies

In this work, we prudently select and test some models to ensure accuracy in lung cancer classification. From Table 1, we can observe the individual model's test performance metrics on the IQ-OTH/NCCD dataset for lung cancer detection. It is observed that the Naïve Bayes and AdaBoost algorithms do not perform well on the data. Models namely K-nearest neighbor (KNN), Decision Tree, and Restricted Boltzmann Machine (RBM) perform well individually on the test data; however, they reduce the performance of an ensemble on being a base model. Additionally, we observe the individual performances of the support vector machine (SVM), random forest, XG-Boost, and CNN, as well as the enhanced performance of the ensemble obtained by leveraging them as the base models. These examples encompass a variety of different techniques, each providing a unique insight into the complexity of CT image analysis. Notable illustrators are:

A. **Support Vector Machine (SVM):** This model shows an appreciable accuracy of 97.87%. It has a good capability in understanding complexity in a CT scan dataset.
B. **Random Forest:** In group learning, a strong random forest achieves a sufficient accuracy of 94.98%, providing a starting point when combined with other samples.
C. **XG Boost:** Taking advantage of the power of gradient boosting, XG Boost appears at an impressive accuracy of 97.35%, building on its knowledge of complex relationships with lung cancer data to emphasize the structure.
D. **Convolutional Neural Networks (CNN):** Deep learning through the mean time of CNN confirms its dominance after 100 times with an accuracy of 97.83%. The model exhibits a weak aptitude for image feature extraction and classification.

Table 1. Performance metrics of different models on the IQ-OTH/NCCD dataset for lung cancer detection

Model	Accuracy	Precision	F1 Score	Recall
SVM*	97.5904	0.94	0.96	0.98
Logistic Regression ^	96.8675	0.98	0.99	1.00

(continued)

Table 1. (*continued*)

Model	Accuracy	Precision	F1 Score	Recall
Random Forest*	93.9759	0.96	0.97	0.99
KNN	97.1084	0.99	0.99	0.99
Naive Bayes	62.0468	0.83	0.78	0.75
Decision Trees	89.8795	0.95	0.95	0.95
XG Boost*	97.3494	0.98	0.99	1.00
AdaBoost	78.5542	0.90	0.90	0.84
CNN (100 epochs)*	97.83132	1.00	0.99	0.98
RBM (100 epochs)	93.7349	0.96	0.97	0.98

^ = meta-model in stacked ensemble model
* = base model in stacked ensemble model

3.2 Stacking Ensemble Results

The Stacking Ensemble model outlines a complex ensemble technique for detecting lung cancer using CT images. Such a combination of several state-of-the-art machine learning models—which include CNNs, XG-Boost, Random Forest, and SVMs—in a synergistic way, helps to make this diagnostic tool very robust and reliable. By merging the unique strength of each model, the ensemble compensates for their individual limitations. Indeed, the ensemble achieves an incredible test data accuracy of 99.52%. Here, the ensemble demonstrates a quality of 99.11% precision, which is very crucial in medical diagnostics, where false positives' costs are highly critical. The recall rate is also at 99.07%, which helps in the detection of true cases of lung cancer, hence paving the way for effective and proper medical interventions. This approach uses logistic regression as a meta-model and finally tunes the amalgamation of predictions from the base models finely. The ROC-AUC analysis further goes ahead to prove the ability to distinguish lung condition categories with high precision. This stacking ensemble also accelerates the strategy for early detection and is thus very beneficial for effective treatment of lung cancer, thereby increasing the chances for better patient survival. Future improvements in this framework include the integration of state-of-the-art machine learning algorithms and some state-of-the-art technologies, which will improve feature extraction, interpretability, and, finally, performance of the diagnosis. This new method holds huge potential for the combination of multiple models, especially in finding hard diseases like lung cancer in medical imaging. In this sense, this will surely lead to better patient outcomes by making diagnoses that are much more accurate, reliable, and actionable (Fig. 2).

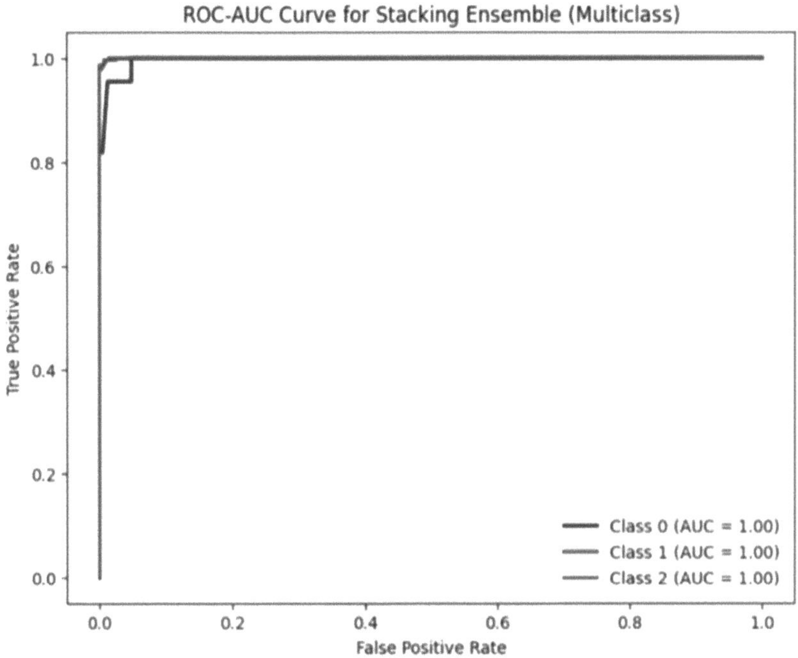

Fig. 2. ROC–AUC Curve for the proposed model

A. **ROC curve for multiple studies:**

The ROC-AUC curve that follows below is a plot showing the performance of the stacking ensemble with respect to multiclass classification for the detection of lung cancer. Each of the lines drawn in this plot represents a different class of lung conditions: Class 0, Class 1, and Class 2, that likely represent benign, malignant, and normal cases, respectively. The fact that all the classes have an AUC score of 1.00 is highly remarkable and indicates that the ensemble model can perfectly classify, without any overlap between the different classes.

Perfect performance of this kind indicates that the model can discriminate between the different classes without any false positives or false negatives and yields unequivocal diagnostic decisions. Such a clear-cut discrimination is a rarity and highly desirable in the field of medical diagnostics since, to a great extent, it indicates that the model can reliably differentiate between subtle features within the medical imagery that are specific to the various stages and varieties of lung conditions.

In the clinical domain, such high-performing models are highly desirable since they allow the physician to avail of a second opinion, which is not only highly accurate but also consistent. This may entail quicker and accurate treatment decisions and, by extension, contribute to better patient outcomes. In addition, such sharp precision in the medical imagery analysis, as achieved by the ROC-AUC curve, reduces the need for invasive diagnostic procedures, thus reducing patient discomfort and health care costs.

The perfect scores across all classes also indicate the potential of this model to act as a benchmark for future research in lung cancer detection. Researchers and medical professionals could look to this ensemble model as a gold standard against which they would compare new diagnostic algorithms. The implication is profound, both in patient care and generally across the entire field of medical imaging and diagnostics. Potential is huge in revolutionizing early cancer detection and treatment based on such a model. It is just a glimpse into the kind of groundbreaking advancements that AI and machine learning make for health care.

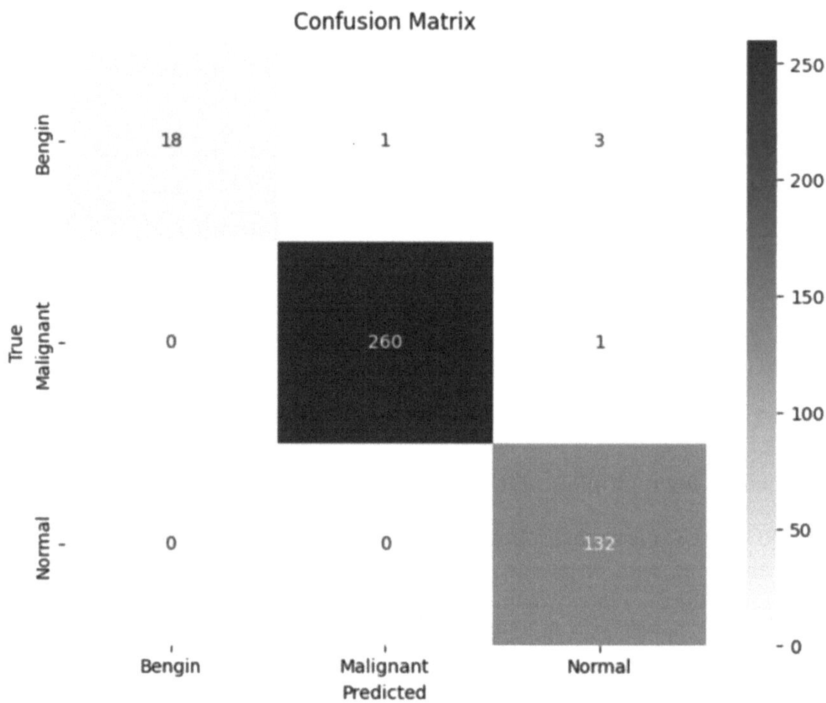

Fig. 3. Confusion Matrix for the proposed model

B. **Confusion matrix**:

The granularity test of the confusion matrix adds some depth to the classification results. Figure 3 shows the confusion matrix classifying the samples into three categories namely 'Benign', 'Malignant', and 'Normal' cases. It can be observed from the diagonal components that most of the cases of Benign and True Malignant are 18 and 260, respectively. This hints to the fact that the representation of these classes is reasonably fair across the classes. On the other hand, the count of the Normal category is around 132. This implies that there is probably an imbalance among the classes. The model shows a high degree of accuracy in the identification of malignant and benign instances. The latter was evidenced by non-zero values on the diagonal for these classifications. It is exemplary in diagnosing 18 cancer-free cases and 260 cancerous cases in particular. Significantly, it produces only a single case of miss-prediction of malignancy and three miss-predictions of normalcy which emphasizes the model's shortfalls in correctly classifying benign instances. The False Malignant predicted is a case when a benign case is marked as malignant, while only three False Normal predictions refer to the situation of misclassifying normal patients as benign. An outstanding result in the model on correctly detecting malignant entities with almost no false negatives is quite noticeable. The capability of accurately diagnosing malignant lesions helps to develop the model's skill in the diagnosis.

4 Conclusion

This research study investigates various machine learning and deep learning algorithms to classify lung cancer leveraging CT images from the IQ-OTH/NCCD data. We compare and contrast the conventional methods and the emerging deep learning systems to find out their strengths. In this work, we design a stacking-ensemble approach through an ensemble of models, including CNN, XG-Boost, Random Forest, and SVM for developing a single predictive tool. This integration not only reflects the positive features of the individual models but also amplified the model's authority in classifying cancer patients into benign, malignant, and normal cases. The designed ensemble emphasizes the usage of logistic regression as a meta-model. This unique combination exhibits high-level performance via improved precision (99.11%), recall (99.07%), and accuracy (99.52%).

Our future works focus on fine-tuning the CNN model leveraging attention mechanism for the efficient extraction of the hidden features from the medical imaging datasets with enhanced interpretability. Future research can be carried out by adopting advanced methods, such as domain adaptation and adversarial training, thereby making a positive impact on models by adapting to various medical imaging scenarios.

Author Contributions. H Sai Karthik V–Model Development and Evaluation
A Suhas–Data collection, Data Pre-processing
D Vivek Reddy–Literature Survey, Analysis of different models
Dr. K. Suresh, Dr. Pritam Khan-Supervisors

References

1. Rahane, W., Dalvi, H., Magar, Y., Kalane, A., Jondhale, S.: Lung cancer detection using image processing and machine learning healthcare. In: 2018 International Conference on Current Trends towards Converging Technologies (ICCTCT), pp. 1–5. IEEE (2018)
2. Zhang, L., et al.: Simultaneous spectral-spatial feature selection and extraction for hyperspectral images. IEEE Trans. Cybernet. **99**, 1–13 (2016)
3. Xie, Y., et al.: Early lung cancer diagnostic biomarker discovery by machine learning methods. Transl. Oncol. **14**(1), 100907 (2021)
4. Asuntha, A., Srinivasan, A.: Deep learning for lung cancer detection and classification. Multimed. Tools Appl. **79**, 7731–7762 (2020)
5. Raut, S., Patil, S., Shelke, G.: Lung cancer detection using machine learning approach. Int. J. Adv. Sci. Res. Eng.. Trends (IJASRET). (2021)

6. Singh, G.A.P., Gupta, P.K.: Performance analysis of various machine learning-based approaches for detection and classification of lung cancer in humans. Neural Comput. Appl. **31**, 6863–6877 (2019)
7. Pawar, V.J., Kharat, K.D., Pardeshi, S.R., Pathak, P.D.: Lung cancer detection system using image processing and machine learning techniques. Cancer. **3**(2020), 4 (2020)
8. Radhika, P.R., Nair, R.A., Veena, G.: A comparative study of lung cancer detection using machine learning algorithms. In: 2019 IEEE International Conference on Electrical, Computer and Communication Technologies (ICECCT), pp. 1–4. IEEE (2019)
9. Hussain, L., Rathore, S., Abbasi, A.A., Saeed, S.: Automated lung cancer detection based on multimodal features extracting strategy using machine learning techniques. In: Medical Imaging 2019: physics of medical imaging, vol. 10948, pp. 919–925. SPIE (2019, March)
10. Günaydin, Ö., Günay, M., Şengel, Ö.: Comparison of lung cancer detection algorithms. In: 2019 Scientific Meeting on Electrical-Electronics & Biomedical Engineering and Computer Science (EBBT), pp. 1–4. IEEE (2019)
11. Hazra, A., Bera, N., Mandal, A.: Predicting lung cancer survivability using SVM and logistic regression algorithms. Int. J. Comput. Appl. **174**(2), 19–24 (2017)
12. Bharathy, S., Pavithra, R., Akshaya, B.: Lung cancer detection using machine learning. In: 2022 International Conference on Applied Artificial Intelligence and Computing (ICAAIC), pp. 539–543. IEEE, Salem, India (2022). https://doi.org/10.1109/ICAAIC53929.2022.9793061

NeuroShield: Enhancing Credit Card Fraud Detection with Advanced Predictive Models

Raghav Kapoor(✉), Abhishek Singh, and R. Siva

SRM Institute of Science and Technology, Chennai, India
{rk6073,as9654,sivar}@srmist.edu.in

Abstract. To prevent customers from being wrongly charged for unauthorized purchases, credit card firms must accurately identify fraudulent credit card transactions. It is essential to make use of data science and machine learning to properly solve this problem. This research aims to emphasize the importance of machine learning by demonstrating how it can be used to detect credit card fraud. The research intends to demonstrate the potential of Data science approaches through the construction of a model utilizing historical credit card transaction data. Building a prediction model using historical credit card transactions that takes into account both valid and fraudulent situations is the issue at hand. Predicting whether new transactions are fraudulent or not is the objective; the goal is to identify fraudulent activity as thoroughly as possible while reducing the number of false positive classifications. One of the most prominent categorization issues in the context of data science and machine learning is the detection of credit card fraud. For credit card issuers, identifying and combating credit card fraud is a major task. Utilizing machine learning and data science approaches is essential for solving this problem. In this study, we highlight the value of machine learning in improving fraud detection by exhibiting its real-world use in locating fraudulent credit card transactions. Our main goal is to demonstrate how data science techniques can be used to use historical credit card transaction data to build a solid model.

Keywords: Credit Card · Machine Learning · Fraud Detection · Support Vector · Naïve Bayes · Accuracy · Random Forest · Boosting Techniques

1 Introduction

The credit card, debit card, or any other type of financial service card is a little plastic card provided to customers of that particular financial organization who have been properly identified and verified. This little piece of plastic is used to facilitate one-time or instalment payments for financial transactions. Credit card security depends on the physical security of the plastic card as well as the confidentiality of the debit/credit card account number. For online payment services, people are using the public internet. This entirely depends on the agreement between the financial institution and the cardholder. The world's e-payment purchasing has greatly improved since this approach was introduced. Fraud on credit, debit, and bank cards is an ongoing issue on a global scale. Additionally, hackers are improving their techniques and coming up with new ways to

M. Paprzycki et al. (Eds.): ICACIS 2024, CCIS 2405, pp. 345–355, 2027.
https://doi.org/10.1007/978-3-032-30990-7_25

commit financial theft, particularly with credit cards. Fraud identification systems are continually being developed to protect criminals as they adapt their phony methods. Extortion in the context of credit card interchange refers to the unauthorized and undesired use of a record by a party other than the various types of assets or properties owned by the account holder. A circumstance when a stranger uses another person's credit card for the purpose that the card is being used can be described as the crucial expected steps that can be implemented to minimize this mistreatment and then conduct fake practices that can be focused to avoid it. This is a very important problem that necessitates taking into account networks, such artificial intelligence (AI) and information science, where the solution to this problem may be automated. However, they are no longer only difficult to construct a fraud detection system in the actual world. In real-world scenarios, a large volume of payment requests is quickly examined by electronic devices to determine which transaction to approve. All of the authorized exchanges are broken down using the newest techniques of Machine Learning-specific algorithms, and any questionable ones are reported. Experts review these complaints and get in touch with the cardholders to see whether the transaction was legitimately challenging. The specialists give an input to the mechanized framework which is utilized to prepare and refresh the calculation to run the fraud recognition execution.

2 Literature Survey

To address the issue of extremely class-imbalanced datasets, a feature augmentation approach has been developed. Using under sampling methods, several sets of samples were produced and utilized as input for SMOTE [1]. This research provides a new approach for detecting credit card fraud that combines the enhanced VAEGAN oversampling method with the XGBoost classification algorithm. The enhanced VAEGAN oversampling model is trained using the minority class samples from the original training set, and a huge amount of minority class data is created as a result [2]. The hybrid SMOTE-ENN approach was used for data resampling. The suggested technique outperformed the baseline classifiers, including AdaBoost, random forest, MLP, LSTM, and GRU, with specificity, sensitivity, and area under the ROC curve values of 1, 0.997, and 1 [3]. D-AMWSPL Adaboost improved the AUC by 1.41% and the F1 score by 0.47% over previous algorithms, and it also had a faster convergence speed. In comparison to the Adaboost method, D-AMWSPL Adaboost obtained the biggest improvement in terms of AUC value and 17.01% in terms of F1 score in other datasets [4]. The model assessment findings demonstrate 521 that the model is extremely accurate and can be completely incorporated 522 in software programs to identify card fraud in the units and 523 organizations [5]. In addition to lowering memory and time required to assess algorithms, using hyper parameters to resolve data imbalance offers better outcomes than sampling approaches. We recommend adopting various hybrid models in future research and work, as well as working especially in the field of CatBoost by adjusting more hyperparameters [6]. When compared to the recently disclosed technique, the suggested LightGBM method enhanced fraud detection instances by 50% and the F1-score by 20%. They increased the algorithm's performance by using the majority voting technique [7]. The sensitivity, specificity, and AUC of the LSTM ensemble with

SMOTE-ENN data resampling was all higher than the other benchmark algorithms and state-of-the-art approaches. As a result, combining the SMOTE-ENN data resampling methodology and the boosted LSTM classifier provides an effective way for identifying credit card fraud [8]. Accuracy rates for DT-AdaBoost, RFAdaBoost, ET-AdaBoost, and XGB-AdaBoost were 99.67%, 99.95%, 99.98%, and 99.98%, respectively. In terms of classification quality, the ET-AdaBoost had an MCC of 0.99 while the XGB-AdaBoost had an MCC value of 0.99 [9]. The study examines, develops, and evaluates 15 transfer learning strategies in a variety of contexts with varying degrees of supervised tagging in the target domain. It's worth noting that for extremely few target labels and generative classifiers (like Naive Bayes) beat discriminative ones [10]. When cap Turing 91.79 percent of fraudulent cases (8.21% rate of misclassification), and optimal configuration obtained an alert reduction rate (threshold of 0.1) of 35.16 percent. and a decrease or reduction rate of 41.47 percent (threshold of 0.2) when Turing 87.75% of fraud situations (12.25% rate of misclassification) [11]. In terms of amount profiling method, both Random Forest algorithm and Multi-Layer Perceptron classifiers outperformed the master model for amounts ranging from 0 to 10 and later from 1 thousand to 1 lakh Lira of Turkey. As a result, an aware and important credit card fraud detection system may choose the best detection model and improve performance [12]. The experimental findings show that, as predicted, the samples which are comprehensive in nature generated through the model are not entirely correct data, hence injecting comprehensive examples into the training set increases the number of wrong negatives. Obviously, in a context with relatively significant wrong negative costs, this can be an issue of limitation [13]. ITrAdaBoost takes a more thorough look at the weights of incorrectly categorized cases. The determination of the distance of distribution between the target domains source and is the cornerstone of our technique, which is based on RKHS theory [14]. FCL is a specifically optimized loss function and a deep neural network. FCL may oversee the learning model with deep representation from both angle and distance, resulting in a model that improves intraclass compactness and interclass separation [15].

3 Methodology

Logistic regression is a core statistical tool for detecting credit card fraud. Using transaction data like as money, location, and time, logistic regression provides a simple and understandable framework for projecting the risk of fraud. Its capacity to set judgement boundaries based on previous data enables early identification of fraudulent activity. However, to improve the accuracy of fraud detection, logistic regression is frequently combined with other machine learning approaches. Among these strategies, the Decision Tree Classifier stands out as a popular option. Decision trees create a tree-like structure by recursively splitting information based on the most useful aspects, such as transaction amount and location, and may efficiently categories transactions as real or fraudulent. Despite their interpretability, decision trees are susceptible to overfitting, necessitating the employment of techniques such as pruning and ensemble algorithms such as Random Forests to increase their dependability and efficacy. The Random Forest Classifier, an ensemble learning technique, overcomes the constraints of individual decision trees by creating numerous trees, each trained on a unique set of attributes and data.

This ensemble method not only decreases the risk of overfitting, but it also improves accuracy and generalization in fraud detection. Random Forests analyses transaction parameters, such as amount, location, and time, to make intelligent decisions, greatly adding to financial system security. AdaBoost, or adaptive boosting, is another important ensemble learning approach in the armory of fraud detection. AdaBoost focuses on previously misclassified cases while iteratively training weak learners, such as basic decision tree classifiers, progressively increasing overall model performance. The integration of AdaBoost into fraud detection systems enables financial institutions to improve precision and efficacy in combating credit card theft, decreasing financial losses and protecting sensitive cardholder data. Extreme Gradient Boosting (XGBoost) extends the capabilities of ensemble approaches, providing a powerful solution for credit card fraud detection. XGBoost optimizes the combination of these trees by focusing on tough cases and minimizing prediction errors, resulting in a powerful ensemble of decision trees that have been independently trained to forecast the likelihood of fraudulent transactions. This results in a very precise and adaptable fraud detection system, which advances the primary goal of preventing fraudulent transactions. In addition to these ensemble approaches, Multi-Layer Perceptron Models (MLPs) offer a neural network-based approach to fraud detection. MLPs excel at understanding complicated data patterns thanks to their several layers of linked nodes. MLP models trained on past transaction data may successfully identify fraudulent trends and flag questionable transactions in real time, thereby increasing the efficacy of fraud detection systems through continuous evaluation and refining. Finally, the combination of various machine learning techniques, such as logistic regression, decision trees, ensemble methods like Random Forests and AdaBoost, and advanced approaches like XGBoost and MLP models, improves financial institutions' ability to detect and prevent credit card fraud. Organizations can use these approaches to safeguard their clients, reduce financial losses, and maintain the integrity of their financial systems. The classification report summarizes the Multi-Layer Perceptron (MLP) model's effectiveness in detecting credit card fraud. It covers important measures including accuracy, recall, F1-score, and support for both positive (fraudulent) and negative (non-fraudulent) classes. Precision reflects the proportion of properly identified fraudulent transactions out of all transactions projected to be fraudulent, whereas recall represents the proportion of correctly classified fraudulent transactions out of all actual fraudulent transactions. The F1-score, which is the harmonic mean of accuracy and recall, provides a fair assessment of the model's performance. Furthermore, the support measure indicates the number of transactions in each class, which provides context for performance evaluations. Assessing the robustness of the Multi-Layer Perceptron (MLP) model in credit card fraud detection requires not only evaluating its performance against other predictive models but also considering its scalability and computational efficiency. As financial transactions continue to increase in volume and complexity, the ability of fraud detection systems to process data swiftly and accurately becomes paramount. Therefore, researchers may delve into the scalability of MLP models, exploring their performance as transaction volumes escalate. Additionally, investigating the computational demands of MLP models in real-time applications is essential for determining their feasibility in operational settings. By addressing these aspects, researchers can provide comprehensive insights into the practical viability of MLP models and their potential to serve as foundational components of robust fraud detection systems in the financial industry. Referring to (Fig. 1), The flowchart about the architecture depicts a typical fraud detection process, emphasizing data gathering, categorization, and user alerting. It begins by retrieving transaction details from a database, which most likely include the money, time, and location. The process then divides into two halves, with transactions rated as regular or fraudulent based on established criteria or machine learning algorithms that identify anomalies. Regular transactions result in process termination, but flagged fraudulent transactions result in fraud detection and user notification, however the particular notification mechanism remains unknown. Referring to (Fig. 2), The architecture depicts a credit card fraud detection system that uses a tiered approach to identify and block unauthorized transactions. The system begins by collecting transaction data from bank servers, which may contain details such as amount, time, location, and billing information. This information is then put into a decision function and decision maker module, which serves as the system's core. This component most likely uses a combination of rule-based fraud detection and machine learning algorithms to categorize transactions as genuine or fraudulent. Rule-based detection uses thresholds and criteria to flag questionable transactions, whereas machine learning algorithms use past data to uncover trends suggestive of fraud. If a transaction is judged authentic, it is successfully processed through the system. In contrast, transactions that are marked as fraudulent send a warning to the back-end systems, indicating the possibility of fraud. The system subsequently sends a message to the bank, which can take necessary action, such as calling the cardholder to confirm the transaction or restricting the card to prevent further unauthorized usage. This flowchart provides a simple representation of a credit card fraud detection system. It emphasizes the need of data gathering, transaction categorization using rule-based and machine learning technologies, and early communication to the bank in the event of suspected fraud.

Architecture Diagram and Flow of Work

4 Results and Discussion

In our thorough investigation of credit card fraud detection, we set out to meticulously assess the effectiveness of a wide range of machine learning models. Our goal was to evaluate how well they performed the crucial duty of spotting and avoiding fraudulent transactions. The information in the Graph-1 and Table 1 provides a clear picture of the accuracy ratings each model received after thorough testing on our dataset. Referring Table 2, Logistic Regression, a model that stood out with an astounding accuracy of **94.74%,** is at the forefront of our findings. This outcome demonstrates how well it can differentiate between valid and fraudulent credit card transactions. The effectiveness of Logistic Regression in identifying the underlying patterns and attributes that define fraudulent transactions is demonstrated by its performance. Referring Table 3, The Random Forest Classifier, which scored a superb accuracy of **94.21%,** is closely behind. This demonstration demonstrates its ability to correctly categorize transactions as legitimate or fraudulent. Referring Table 4, A similar accuracy rate of **94.21%** was attained

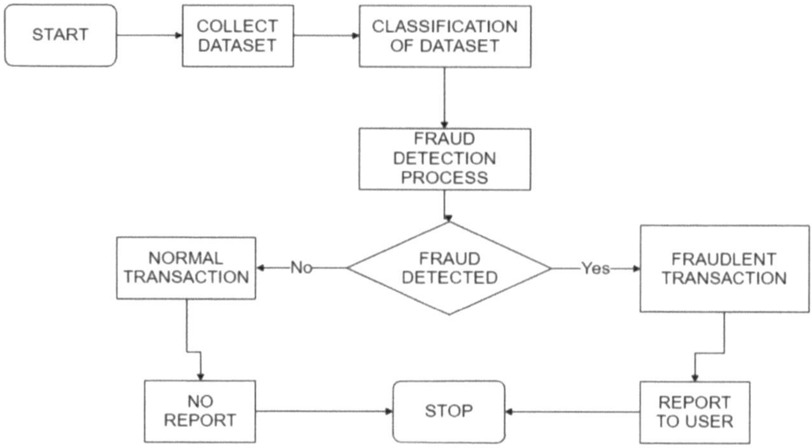

Fig. 1. Fraud Detection Process Flowchart. This flowchart outlines the steps involved in identifying fraudulent transactions. Data is collected and classified, with potential fraud reported to the user.

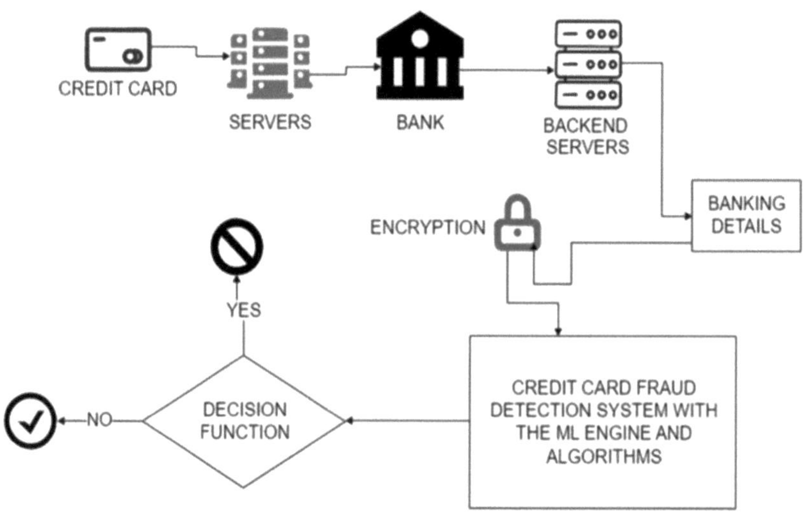

Fig. 2. Fraud Detection Process Architecture. This architecture diagram describes how the data flows through the bank servers to the end user. Data is collected and classified, with potential fraud reported to the user.

by the AdaBoost Classifier, highlighting the model's potent capacity to identify fraudulent behaviors in credit card transactions. These findings demonstrate the effectiveness of ensemble learning techniques in raising the accuracy of fraud detection. Referring Table 5, The accuracy score of **92.11%** for the Decision Tree Classifier exhibited effective performance. Although somewhat less accurate than some of its competitors, it demonstrated a strong ability to distinguish between legal and fraudulent transactions, underscoring its crucial role in offering insightful information about the categorization process. Referring Table 6, The XGBoost Classifier completes the ensemble and earned a decent accuracy score of **93.16%**. Its effectiveness as a prediction model for identifying fraudulent transactions is further supported by its performance. XGBoost's capacity to identify intricate patterns in the data assures that it will be counted among the models with high prediction accuracy. Comparing the performance of the MLP model with other predictive models, such as decision trees, support vector machines, or logistic regression, allows researchers to assess which model is most effective at accurately detecting fraudulent transactions. This comparison helps in selecting the best model for credit card fraud detection systems, aiming to minimize false positives (flagging legitimate transactions as fraudulent) and false negatives (missing actual fraudulent transactions) with the accuracy of about **99.83%**, Referring Graph-2. A comprehensive evaluation must take into account aspects like model interpretability, computational effectiveness, and adaptability to the fraud landscape's always changing trends. As a result, our research not only highlights how well these models perform at spotting fraudulent transactions, but it also emphasizes how crucial it is to strike a delicate balance between accuracy and the practical factors that are essential in the creation of efficient credit card fraud detection systems.

Table 1. Accuracy Table for all Used Models

S. No.	Model Name	Accuracy
1	Logistic Regression	**94.74%**
2	Random Forest Classifier	**94.21%**
3	Decision Tree Classifier	**92.11%**
4	AdaBoost Classifier	**94.21%**
5	XGBoost Classifier	**93.16%**
6	Multi-Layer Perceptron Model	**99.83%**

Table 2. Confusion Matrix for Logistic Regression

0	**86**	**2**
1	**8**	**94**
True/Predicted	0	1

The tables present a comprehensive evaluation of various machine learning models for credit card fraud detection. Table 1 displays the accuracy rates of each model, with the Multi-Layer Perceptron Model showcasing the highest accuracy at an impressive 99.83%. Following closely behind are the Logistic Regression and AdaBoost Classifier, both achieving accuracies above 94%. Tables 2, 3, 4, 5 and 6 provide a breakdown of the

Table 3. Confusion Matrix for Random Forest Classifier

0	**86**	**2**
1	**11**	**91**
True/Predicted	0	1

Table 4. Confusion Matrix for Decision Tree Classifier

0	**80**	**8**
1	**11**	**91**
True/Predicted	0	1

Table 5. Confusion Matrix for AdaBoost Classifier

0	**86**	**2**
1	**9**	**93**
True/Predicted	0	1

Table 6. Confusion Matrix for XGBoost Classifier

0	**85**	**73**
1	**10**	**92**
True/Predicted	0	1

confusion matrices for each model, illustrating the true positive and true negative rates alongside the false positive and false negative rates. These metrics offer insights into the performance of each model in correctly identifying fraudulent and non-fraudulent transactions. Overall, the results indicate promising performance across all models, with the Multi-Layer Perceptron Model standing out as particularly effective in accurately detecting credit card fraud.

Graphical Visualizations and Accuracies

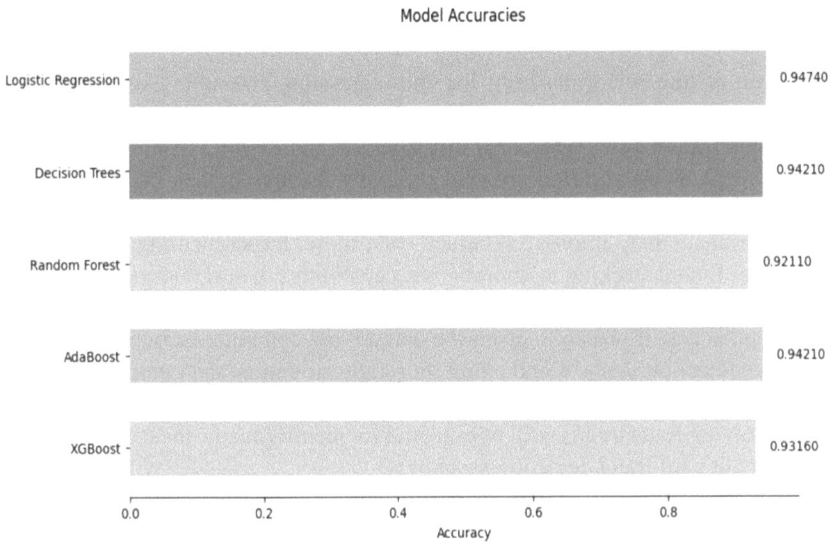

Graph 1. Model Accuracies on Credit Card Fraud Detection Task. This graph compares the accuracy of various machine learning models on a credit card fraud detection task. The x-axis represents the different models, and the y-axis represents the model accuracy.

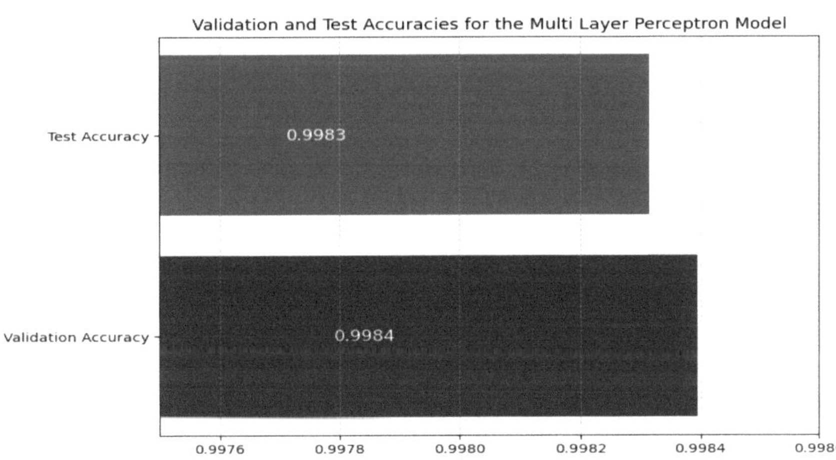

Graph 2. Validation and Test Accuracies of the Multi-Layer Perceptron Model. This graph depicts the validation and test accuracies achieved by the multi-layer perceptron model. The x-axis represents the training epochs, and the y-axis represents the model accuracy. As can be seen, both validation and test accuracy increase as the model trains, reaching a final test accuracy of 0.9983.

5 Conclusion and Future Work

Given the promising performance of logistic regression, ensemble classifiers such as Random Forest and AdaBoost, and sophisticated approaches like as XGBoost in detecting fraudulent transactions, additional investigation and refining of these models may be advantageous in the future. Furthermore, using feature engineering approaches to extract more relevant information from data and fine-tuning hyperparameters to optimise model performance may improve accuracy even more. Experimenting with ensemble approaches or model stacking to combine the capabilities of several models might also be beneficial. Furthermore, studying sophisticated anomaly detection techniques or deep learning approaches, if possible, given the dataset and computer resources, may result in increased detection skills. Conducting thorough validation and comparison studies, considering factors such as model interpretability, computational efficiency, and adaptability to evolving fraud trends, will be essential for identifying the most suitable models for future credit card fraud detection systems.

References

1. Ghaleb, F.A., Saeed, F., Al-Sarem, M., Qasem, S.N., Al-Hadhrami, T.: Ensemble synthesized minority oversampling-based generative adversarial networks and random forest algorithm for credit card fraud detection. IEEE Access. **11**, 89694–89710 (2023) (Research Partnership Program no RP-21-07-09.)
2. Ding, Y., Kang, W., Feng, J., Peng, B., Yang, A.: Credit card fraud detection based on improved variational autoencoder generative adversarial network. IEEE Access. **11**, 83680–83691 (2023) (National Natural Science Foundation of China under Grant 61901079.)
3. Mienye, I.D., Sun, Y.: A deep learning ensemble with data resampling for credit card fraud detection. IEEE Access. **11**, 30628–30638 (2023) (South African National Research Foundation under Grant 120106 and Grant 132797.)
4. Ning, W., Chen, S., Lei, S., Liao, X.: AMWSPLAdaboost credit card fraud detection method based on enhanced base classifier diversity. IEEE Access. **11**, 66488–66496 (2023)
5. Nguyen, N., et al.: A proposed model for card fraud detection based on CatBoost and deep neural network. IEEE Access. **10**, 96852–96861 (2022)
6. Hashemi, S.K., Mirtaheri, S.L., Greco, S.: Fraud detection in banking data by machine learning techniques. IEEE Access. **11**, 3034–3043 (2022)
7. Alarfaj, F.K., Malik, I., Khan, H.U., Almusallam, N., Ramzan, M., Ahmed, M.: Credit card fraud detection using state-of-the-art machine learning and deep learning algorithms. IEEE Access. **12**, 39700–39715 (2022)
8. Esenogh, E., Mienye, I.D., Swart, T.G., Aruleba, K., Obaido, G.: A neural network ensemble with feature engineering for improved credit card fraud detection. IEEE Access. **10**, 16400–16407 (2022)
9. Ileberi, E., Sun, Y., Wang, Z.: Performance evaluation of machine learning methods for credit card fraud detection using SMOTE and AdaBoost. IEEE Access. **9**, 165286–165294 (2021)
10. Rajawat, A.S., et al.: Cyber physical system fraud analysis by mobile robot, machine learning for robotics applications. In: Studies in Computational Intelligence, vol. 960. Springer, Singapore (2021). https://doi.org/10.1007/978-981-16-0598-7_4
11. Carrasco, R.S.M., Sicilia-Urbán, M.-Á.: Evaluation of deep neural for reduction of credit card fraud alerts. IEEE Access. **8**, 186421–186432 (2020)

12. Can, B., Yavuz, A.G., Karsligil, E.M., Guvensan, M.A.: A closer look into the characteristics of fraudulent card transactions. IEEE Access. **8**, 166095–166109 (2020)
13. Tingfei, H., Guangquan, C., Kuihua, H.: Using variational auto encoding in credit card fraud detection. IEEE Access. **8**, 149841–149853 (2020)
14. Zheng, L., Liu, G., Yan, C., Jiang, C., Zhou, M., Li, M.: Improved TrAdaBoost and its application to transaction fraud detection. IEEE Trans. Comput. Soc. Sci. **7**(5), 1304–1316 (2020)
15. Li, L.Z., Liu, G., Jiang, C.: Deep representation learning with full center loss for credit card fraud detection. IEEE Trans. Comput. Soc. Sci. **7**(2), 569–579 (2020)

GestoSense: A Hand Gesture Recognition System for Individuals with Auditory and Speech Impairments

Sujay Grama Suresh Kumar and Jad Abbass(✉)

School of Computer Science and Mathematics, Kingston University, Kingston-Upon-Thames KT1 2EE, London, UK
j.abbass@kingston.ac.uk

Abstract. It is estimated that over 5% of the global population experiences some degree of hearing and speech impairment. However, the scarcity of individuals proficient in sign language has created challenges in ensuring communication accessibility for deaf and hard-of-hearing individuals. In recent years, the exploration of machine learning techniques has contributed to some extent to bridge that gap. This chapter addresses the imperative need for intuitive and inclusive communication for individuals with hearing and speech challenges by creating a fully automated tool, that using the webcam, translates sign gestures into plain English. Focusing on Indian Sign Language (ISL), our work involves first, the creation of a robust imbalanced dataset comprising 80,000 images across 35 classes (Numbers 1–9 and Letters A-Z). The dataset was meticulously curated to capture diverse gestures from various angles and individuals. Then, using the dataset, we trained two convolutional neural network (CNN) models, (1) VGG-16, a pre-trained model, and (2) our custom one. Both models demonstrated proficiency in recognizing a diverse range of hand gestures, achieving F1-Score of 81 and 87 for the VGG-16 and the customized models respectively. The results showcase the superior performance of the custom model over VGG-16, establishing its efficacy for practical applications in real-world scenarios. The source code and dataset are both freely available at Codes [Click Here] and Dataset [Click Here] respectively.

Keywords: Hand Gesture Recognition · Indian Sign Language (ISL) · Convolutional Neural Network (CNN) · VGG-16 Architecture

1 Introduction

In today's interconnected world, effective communication is paramount, yet many individuals face significant barriers due to hearing and speech challenges. Approximately 460 million people worldwide experience some form of hearing impairment, with a substantial portion encountering difficulties in verbal communication [12]. Sign languages, such as American Sign Language (ASL), British Sign Language (BSL), and Indian Sign Language (ISL), serve as vital means of communication for deaf and hard of hearing individuals, each with its unique syntax and vocabulary. Despite their importance, the

M. Paprzycki et al. (Eds.): ICACIS 2024, CCIS 2405, pp. 356–368, 2027.
https://doi.org/10.1007/978-3-032-30990-7_26

accessibility of these languages remains limited, hindering interaction and comprehension for both deaf individuals and those around them. However, advancements in Artificial Intelligence (AI) and Machine Learning (ML) offer promising avenues for addressing these challenges, fostering greater understanding and inclusivity in society. There have been numerous attempts to build a machine-learning model that can accurately translate hand gestures into plain language, notably using Random Forests, decision trees, and other conventional algorithms. Convolutional Neural Networks (CNNs) have emerged as pivotal tools in computer vision, significantly impacting tasks like image recognition and pattern analysis. With their origins in artificial neural networks and their automated feature learning, thus eliminating the need for manual engineering, CNNs are adept at processing grid-like data, making them particularly suited for image-related applications. They are composed of convolutional layers, pooling layers, fully connected layers, and activation functions. The key architectural feature is the convolutional layer, where filters convolve over input data to extract hierarchical features, allowing spatial hierarchies to be captured effectively. Due to their remarkable success, CNNs have been widely used for transfer learning-a technique that involves pre-training on large datasets and then fine-tuning for specific tasks. Leveraging advanced deep learning techniques, we explore CNNs to interpret hand gestures. Our study employs two models: the pre-trained VGG-16 [6] and our custom one, focusing on ISL. Due to the large number of languages adopted in India, ISL is considered a 'unified' sign language and uses English. ISL is being used by roughly 63 million people [11] and, compared to ASL, for example, it is challenging to build an accurate model as 20 out of 35 signs include both hands. Using OpenCV [9], we have meticulously created a large imbalanced dataset of size 80,000 comprising 35 classes (A to Z and 1 to 9). Four individuals of different skin colors and hand sizes were employed to capture pictures of hand gestures from many angles and zooms.

2 Related Works

In recent years, the exploration of machine learning applications, particularly CNNs, for hand gesture recognition systems has been motivated by the imperative need to address communication challenges faced by individuals with hearing and speech impairments. This literature review aims to encapsulate key studies, focusing mainly on the recognition of ISL and advancements brought forth by various CNN architectures and other ML algorithms.

The study by Altaf and co-workers [1] utilized the DenseNet 2021 CNN architecture, achieving 100% accuracy in ISL recognition on a publicly available dataset. The dataset consisted of 1200 images per class, each standardized to 32x32 pixels. While this 'straightforward' dataset facilitated model training, it may overlook real-world challenges like class imbalances and diverse environmental conditions. Consequently, while the dataset's uniformity in image size and quality contributes to model robustness, it may limit the model's applicability to real-world settings with varying conditions, where its performance might not generalize well due to unbalanced or noisy data.

In recent studies by Ganpatye and Mane [4] and Deep [3], integration of the Media Pipe Library and Long short-term memory (LSTM) models resulted in accuracy rates of 97% and 92% respectively for ISL recognition. Ganpatye's study utilized a dataset comprising 40 commonly used ISL signs, with 30 samples per sign and 30 frames per video, while Deep's study collected a balanced dataset through OpenCV, consisting of 800 images for each of the 35 classes. Both studies utilized edge detection techniques, which may be susceptible to noise and variations in lighting conditions, leading to inaccurate boundary detection, and posing challenges in accurately identifying hand gestures.

Das [2] developed a system merging CNN and handcrafted features into a Bidirectional long short-term memory (BiLSTM) network for Indian Sign Language recognition, achieving 93.68% and 94.17% accuracy with Hu Moments and Zernike sign language, respectively, on a balanced video dataset. The dataset includes 4287 videos across 263 classes, categorized into 15 categories, with an average length of 2.57 s and a resolution of 1920 x 1080 pixels. However, video datasets pose challenges such as increased computational complexity, larger storage requirements, and the introduction of temporal dependencies, which may complicate preprocessing and require specialized techniques for feature extraction and processing.

The paper by Hatibaruah [5] introduces a system achieving a remarkable test accuracy of 99.89% using the Back Projection Histogram algorithm and CNNs. For the dataset, 1200 images were captured for each gesture, totaling 2400 images after flipping, covering 26 alphabets of ISL along with 10 digits making it a balanced dataset. However, the requirement for users to wear gloves during hand gestures and operate in well-lit backgrounds poses practical constraints in real-world deployment scenarios, significantly limiting the system's accessibility and usability in everyday settings.

Real-time sign language detectors by Pathak [8] employs Transfer Learning with a Pre-Trained Single-shot Detectors (SSD) MobileNet V2 architecture on a publicly available balanced dataset from Kaggle, achieving consistent high accuracy. The dataset consists of over 2000 images with around 400 images per class, encompassing 5 symbols crucial for real-time applications. However, reported accuracy rates of 70–80% on selected signs may indicate a lack of robustness in recognizing a broader range of gestures, suggesting potential limitations in capturing diverse sign language expressions beyond the selected signs.

The approach by Mistry [7] employs a vision-based system for translating ISL words into English equivalents using CNNs and LSTM, achieving an accuracy of 73.60%. The dataset utilized consists of video recordings corresponding to signs from Monday to Sunday, with approximately 50 sample sequences per word. Through image augmentation techniques including translation, rotation, and scaling, the dataset size was increased to around 10500 samples per word, aiming to address the initial imbalance and enhance model performance. However, while augmentation can increase the dataset size, there's a potential restriction in the system's ability to accurately interpret less frequent sign language gestures due to biases introduced during augmentation.

In the work by Khujani [10], a deep CNN-based approach was proposed for efficiently detecting 35 signs of ISL alphabet into text using hand kinematics. The custom CNN model achieved an accuracy of 92.85% on a publicly available dataset comprising 1200 images for each of the 35 classes. However, the study lacks an evaluation of the model's performance in diverse real-life scenarios, potentially limiting its reliability in varying lighting and background conditions.

This literature survey showcases significant advancements in Indian Sign Language (ISL) recognition, predominantly driven by Convolutional Neural Networks (CNNs) and various deep learning architectures. Notably, many studies achieved high accuracy rates using balanced datasets from public sources. However, this research diverges in two key aspects: Firstly, it addresses the challenge of an imbalanced dataset and diverse image size and quality, offering unique insights into model training and evaluation. Secondly, unlike previous works relying on publicly available datasets, this study utilizes a proprietary dataset captured using OpenCV, ensuring data relevance. Additionally, this project focuses on overcoming common obstacles such as background lighting conditions and the need for gloves during hand gestures, thus enhancing the system's accessibility and applicability.

3 Proposed Methodology

This section outlines the comprehensive methodology designed for the development of an effective ISL recognition system. The proposed methodology encompasses key aspects, including dataset creation, model architectures, training strategies, performance evaluation, and visual output representations.

Fig. 1. Dataset ISL Overview

Figure 1 illustrates the overview of the ISL dataset, representing all the different hand gesture classes.

3.1 Dataset Creation

Figure 2 represents the dataset creation process that plays a pivotal role in ensuring the robustness and inclusivity of the ISL recognition system. The following steps describe the approach:

1. **Tailored Data Collection Mechanism:** The dataset was meticulously crafted to enhance diversity, surpassing existing collections. It captures hand gestures from various angles and individuals, reducing the need for external augmentation.

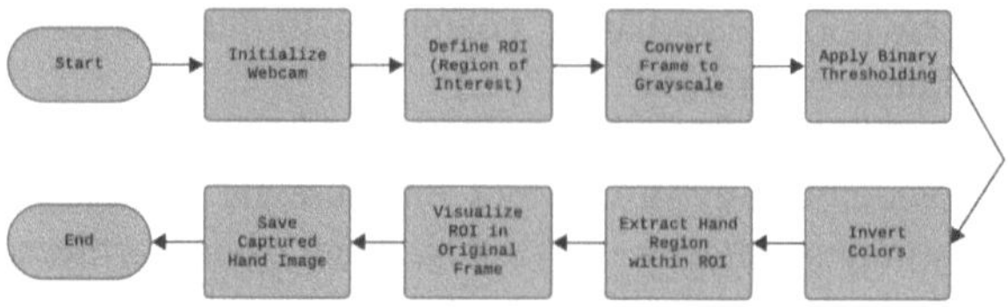

Fig. 2. Steps in Dataset Creation

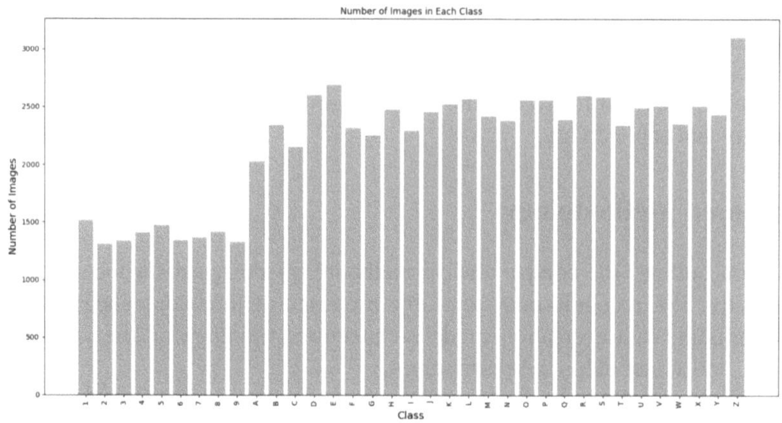

Fig. 3. Dataset Count Distribution

Figure 3 displays data distribution across 35 classes, highlighting the dataset's significant imbalance. The dataset includes images from four individuals of different skin colors and hand sizes, with approximately 400–450 images per individual encompassing all variations. During image capture using OpenCV, 30–50 images were captured within a 2-s interval for each letter/number. Each letter/number category comprises 1500–2000 images, totaling 80,000 images across 35 classes.

Figure 4 shows the augmentation techniques like rotation, shifts, flips, and brightness variation applied to enhance robustness, mimicking real-world scenarios. Image size was resized to 32 × 32, and a batch size of 32 was used during training. These measures improve the model's ability to generalize to unseen data by introducing diverse variations. The combination of augmentation and image size manipulation contributes significantly to the model's performance in real-world applications.

2. **Data Cleaning Processes:** To ensure the dataset's integrity and relevance, rigorous data cleaning processes were meticulously implemented. Initially, outlier detection techniques were employed to identify and eliminate anomalies, followed by manual inspection to remove images with artifacts or distortions. Noise elimination techniques such as median filtering and morphological operations were then applied to suppress unwanted interference, while data normalization ensured standardized pixel values across all images. These measures collectively enhanced the quality of the training data, minimizing inconsistencies and optimizing the model's performance.

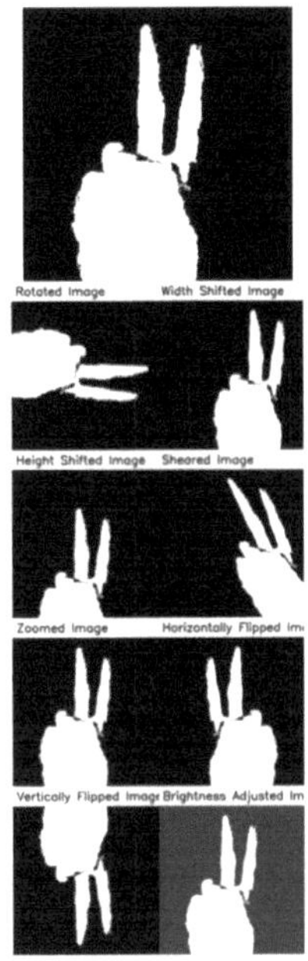

Fig. 4. Augmentation Variations Visualized

3.2 Communication Process Using Hand Gestures

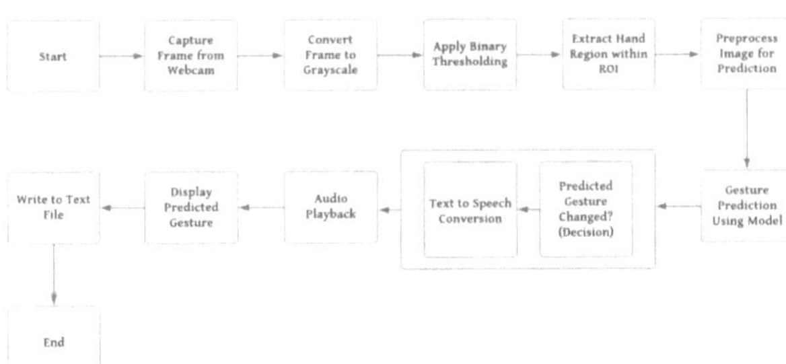

Fig. 5. Communication Process for Hard of Hearing Individuals Using Hand Gesture Recognition

Figure 5 depicts a holistic workflow for real-time hand gesture recognition, catering to the communication needs of individuals with hearing and speech impairments. The process begins with capturing dynamic hand gestures through a webcam, followed by converting the frames into grayscale. Binary thresholding enhances the foreground-background distinction, and a defined Region of Interest (ROI) isolates the key hand region. Such pre-processing step ready the image for the gesture prediction model. Simultaneously, recognized gestures are translated into text, and then converted into speech. The entire process ensures a comprehensive communication experience, addressing the unique challenges faced by individuals with hearing and speech impairments by integrating computer vision, machine learning, and audio synthesis technologies.

3.3 Model Architectures

This subsection provides an overview of the chosen model architectures, namely the VGG-16 model and a custom-designed CNN. The architectural choices and feature visualization are presented for a comprehensive understanding:

1. **VGG-16 Architecture:**

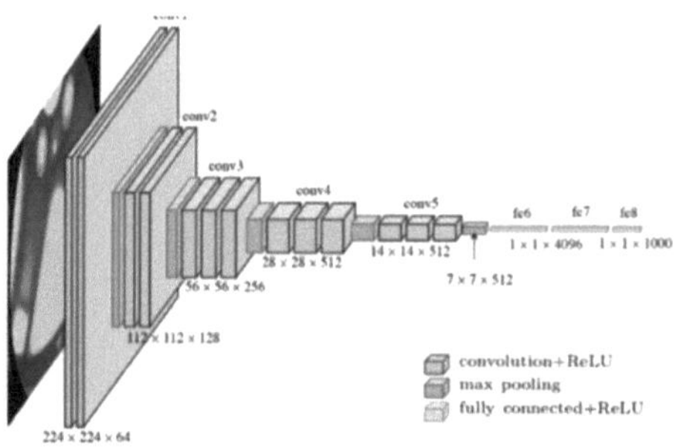

Fig. 6. VGG-16 Layer Visualization [6]

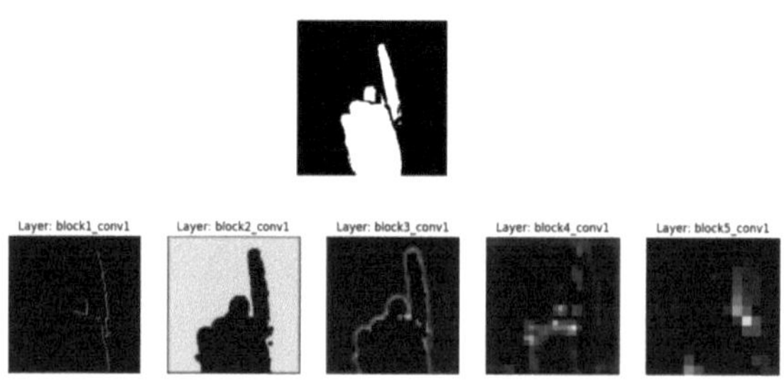

Fig. 7. Visualizing Image Evolution through VGG-16 Layers

Figure 6 displays the VGG-16-layer visualization, a renowned deep CNN architecture, consists of 16 weight layers, including 13 convolutional layers and 3 fully connected layers. Figure 7 presents the image evolution through VGG-16-layers organized into five blocks, where each block contains multiple convolutional layers followed by max-pooling layers. The fully connected layers at the end process the high-level features extracted by the convolutional layers for classification.

2. **Custom-Designed CNN Model:**

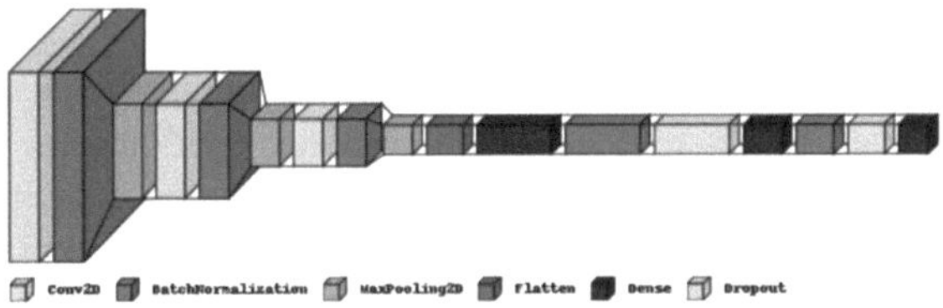

Fig. 8. Custom Model Layer Visualization

Figure 8 depicts the custom-designed CNN architecture specifically engineered for ISL gesture recognition. This model architecture intricately weaves together convolutional layers, batch normalization, and rectified linear unit (ReLU) activation functions to harness the intricate nuances of ISL gestures. Embarking with a foundational Convolutional Layer, comprising 64 filters of size (3,3) and a ReLU activation, the model swiftly transitions into a realm of feature refinement through Batch Normalization and MaxPooling.

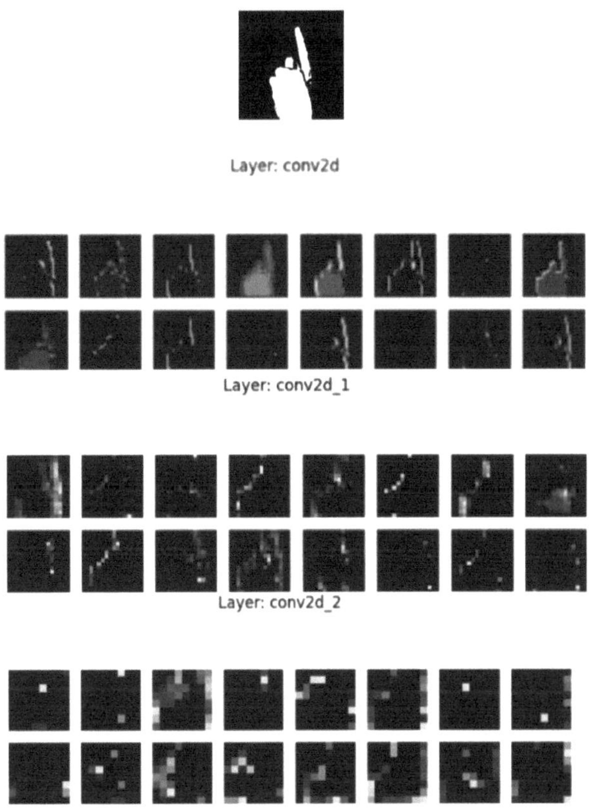

Fig. 9. Visualizing Image Evolution through Custom Model Layers

Subsequently, Fig. 9 illustrates the evolution of the image through various custom layers. The model delves deeper, progressively refining features with a sequence of Convolutional Layers, each augmented with Batch Normalization and MaxPooling to distill essential gesture characteristics.

The model architecture culminates in a flattened output, seamlessly transitioning into densely connected layers to encapsulate complex relationships within the data. Notably, these layers are fortified with regularization techniques such as Dropout and L2 regularization, ensuring robustness and generalization. The output layer, adorned with a SoftMax activation function, stands poised to discern among the diverse array of 35 ISL gestures.

Underpinning this architectural marvel is the Adam optimizer, finely tuned with a learning rate of 0.001, orchestrating the model's optimization journey. As elucidated by the model summary, this bespoke architecture embodies the fusion of meticulous design and computational prowess, poised to unravel the intricacies of ISL gesture recognition with unparalleled efficacy.

3.4 Models Training

This section details the training strategies employed for both the VGG-16 and custom-designed CNN models:

1. **Data Generators and Callbacks:** The training setup involves configuring data generators for both training and validation sets. Essential callbacks, including ModelCheckpoint and EarlyStopping, are implemented to monitor and optimize the training process. This ensures the preservation of the best-performing configurations.
2. **Epoch-Wise Progress:** Throughout the training sessions, a consistent pattern of continuous improvement is observed in both the accuracy of training and validation metrics, accompanied by a decrease in the loss of training and validation metrics. Model weights are saved at the conclusion of every epoch, ensuring the retention of the best configurations, and enabling steady progress monitoring.
3. **Colab Session Activity:** Intermittent messages are strategically incorporated to confirm the continuous activity of the Colab sessions during the training of both models, assuring uninterrupted execution.

3.5 Models Performance Evaluation

The unified performance evaluation of both VGG-16 and the custom-designed CNN model involves an in-depth analysis of metrics and visual representations:

1. **Overview of Model Performances:** A comparative analysis of the VGG-16 model and the custom-designed model reveals their commendable performance on the unbalanced ISL dataset. Metrics such as accuracy, precision, recall, F1-score, and ROC-AUC scores are systematically presented for both models. The VGG-16 model achieves an F1-Score of 81, while the custom model reaches 87.
2. **VGG-16 Model:** The evaluation of the VGG-16 model reveals a commendable F1-Score of 81%, correctly predicting class labels for 80% of the test dataset. Precision, recall, and F1-scores varied across classes, showcasing robust performance for some,

while others faced challenges, possibly due to imbalance or complexity. Notably, classes like ‘C,’ ‘J,’ ‘O,’ ‘Q,’ ‘Y,’ ‘Z,’ and almost ‘1 to 9’ exhibited high precision, recall, and F1-scores, emphasizing effective recognition for specific gestures.

3. **Custom Model:** Contrastingly, the custom-designed model outperformed VGG-16, achieving an F1-Score of 88%. Robust precision, recall, and F1-scores were observed across various classes, indicating effective generalization. Classes from ‘1 to 9’ and almost all the letters displayed excellent precision, recall, and F1-scores, highlighting the model’s efficacy. The custom model demonstrated improved performance, particularly in distinguishing similar gestures.
4. **Individual Class Metrics:**

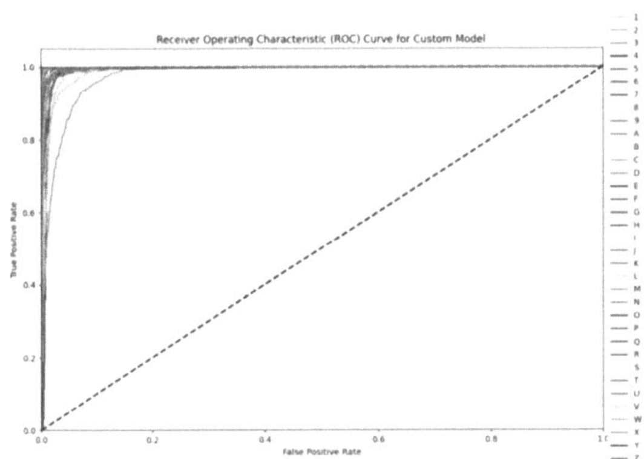

Fig. 10. Custom Model ROC Curve

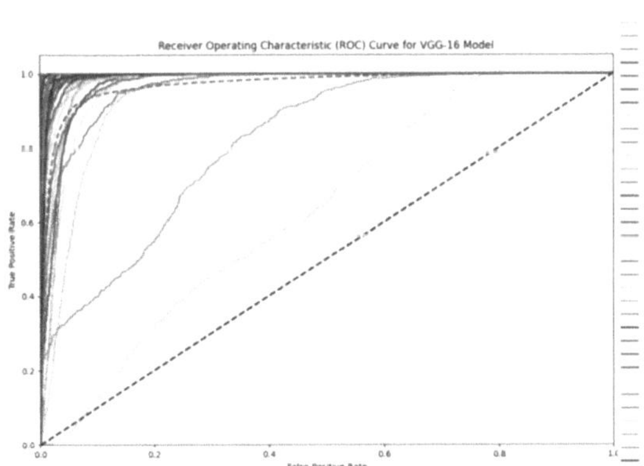

Fig. 11. VGG-16 Model ROC Curve

Figures 10 and 11 illustrate the performance of Custom and VGG-16 model assessed for individual classes, highlighting specific challenges and areas of improvement. The

ROC-AUC scores and individual class confusion matrices provide insights into the discriminative ability of each model.

5. **Summary and Comparison:** The overall comparison emphasizes the effectiveness of the custom-designed model, surpassing challenges faced by VGG-16. The ROC-AUC scores and visual representations validate the superior performance and enhanced discriminative capability of the custom model.

3.6 Models Output Snapshots

Visual representations of the models' predictions provide tangible insights into their interpretability and accuracy:

1. **VGG-16 Model Output:**

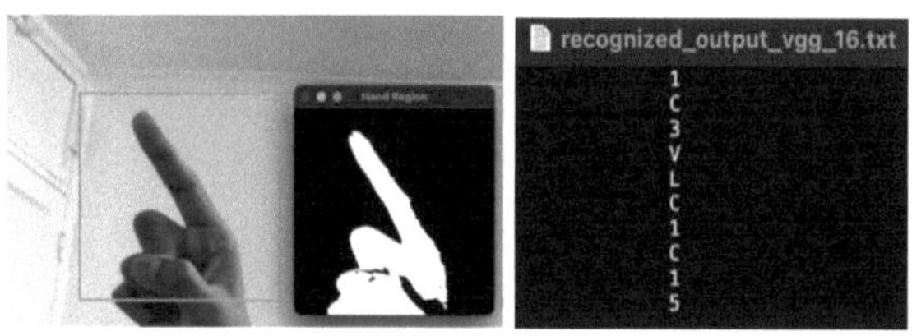

Fig. 12. Visual Representation of VGG-16 Model Predictions

Figure 12 is the visual representation highlighting the proficiency of the VGG-16 model in recognizing a diverse set of ISL symbols. Challenges, such as distinguishing between the letter "L" and the numeral "1," are acknowledged, with recommendations for targeted adjustments.

2. **Custom Model Output:**

Fig. 13. Visual Representation of Custom Model Predictions

Figure 13 illustrates the predictions of the custom-designed model which excels in accurately recognizing symbols, showcasing competence in ISL interpretation. Notably, it demonstrates significant improvement in distinguishing between the letter "I" and the numeral "1," addressing challenges observed in the VGG-16 results.

3. **Dual Communication Approach:** Both models adopt a dual communication approach, generating voice communication while concurrently saving text and voice in .txt and .mp3 formats. Real-time audio playback facilitates immediate communication, providing an interactive and user-friendly experience.

This detailed methodology provides a comprehensive overview of the proposed approach for ISL recognition, encompassing dataset creation, model architectures, training processes, performance evaluation, and visual output representations. The strategic integration of VGG-16 and a custom-designed CNN model reflects a nuanced and adaptive methodology tailored to the challenges inherent in ISL recognition.

4 Discussions and Conclusion

In conclusion, this research endeavors to address the imperative need for intuitive and inclusive communication for individuals facing hearing and speech challenges, focusing on Indian Sign Language (ISL). The development and evaluation of Convolutional Neural Network (CNN) models, including the widely recognized VGG-16 architecture and a custom-designed model, showcased commendable proficiency in recognizing a diverse range of ISL gestures. The meticulously curated dataset, captured through innovative data collection methods facilitated by OpenCV, played a pivotal role in enhancing model efficacy. The custom model, specifically tailored for the dataset, outshone the VGG-16 model, achieving an F1-Score of 87. Mitigation strategies effectively addressed challenges such as class imbalance, model complexity, and overfitting. The project's robustness is evident in its ability to handle real-world complexities, making strides toward a more inclusive and natural mode of communication for individuals with hearing and speech impairments.

Future work includes exploring various CNN model architectures to enhance accuracy and robustness, incorporating diverse representations of hands from many individuals to accommodate variations in hand sizes, shapes, and appearances.

Challenges addressed in this research encompassed class imbalance mitigation through the utilization of dual strategies involving oversampling and class weighting, which significantly enhanced model performance particularly for underrepresented classes. To counter potential overfitting, adjustments to model complexity were made by employing fine-tuning layers, thereby striking a balance between model complexity and dataset size for optimal performance. Early stopping mechanisms were implemented based on validation loss to mitigate the risk of overemphasizing training data, thereby fostering meaningful pattern learning. Additionally, regularization techniques including L1 and L2 regularization were employed to safeguard against overfitting, thereby augmenting the model's generalization capability.

Disclosure of Interests. The authors have no competing interests to declare that are relevant to the content of this article.

References

1. Altaf, Y., Wahid, A., Kirmani, M.M.: Deep learning approach for sign language recognition using DenseNet201 with transfer learning. In: Proceedings of the 2023 IEEE International Students' Conference on Electrical, Electronics and Computer Science (SCEECS) (2023) 979-8-3503-9874-8/23
2. Das, S., Biswas, S.K., Purkayastha, B.: Indian sign language recognition system for emergency words by using shape and deep features. In: Proceedings of the 2023 11th International Conference on Internet of Everything, Microwave Engineering, Communication and Networks (IEMECON) (2023) 978-1-6654-7512-9/23
3. Deep, A., et al.: Real-time sign language detection and recognition. In: Proceedings of the 2nd Asian Conference on Innovation in Technology (ASIANCON), pp. 26–28, Pune, India (2022)
4. Ganpatye, A., Mane, S.: Motion-Based Indian Sign Language Recognition using Deep Learning. In: Proceedings of the 2022 International Conference on Intelligent Technologies (CONIT) (2022) 978-1-6654-8407-7/22
5. Hatibaruah, D., Talukdar, A.K., Sarma, K.K.: A static hand gesture-based sign language recognition system using convolutional neural networks. In: Proceedings of the 2020 IEEE 17th India Council International Conference (INDICON) (2020). https://doi.org/10.1109/INDICON49873.2020.9342405
6. Kujani, T., DhilipKumar, V.: Multiple deep CNN models for Indian sign language translation for person with verbal impairment. Int. J. Intell. Syst. Appl. Eng. (IJISAE). **10**(3), 382–389 (2022). https://doi.org/10.2147/6799
7. Mistry, P., et al.: Indian sign language recognition using deep learning. In: Proceedings of the 2021 International Conference on Artificial Intelligence and Machine Vision (AIMV) (2021) 978-1-6654-4211-4/2
8. Pathak, A., et al.: Real time sign language detection. Int. J. Modern Trends Sci. Technol. **8**(01), 32–37 (2022)
9. How to capture a single photo with webcam using OpenCV in Python: Educative Explore, [Online]. Available: https://www.educative.io/answers/how-to-capture-a-single-photo-with-webcam-using-opencv-in-python
10. Mandal, M.:'Introduction to convolutional neural networks (CNN)' [online], Analytics Vidhya. (2023) Updated on November 16th, 2023
11. Regmi, Developer: "Image similarity comparison using VGG16 Deep learning model." Medium, (2023). [Online]. Available: https://medium.com/developerRegmi/image-similarity-comparison-using-vgg16-deep-learning-model-a663a411cd24
12. Garg, S., et al.: Challenges of the deaf and hearing impaired in the masked world of COVID-19. Indian J. Community Med. **46**(1), 11–14 (2021). https://doi.org/10.4103/ijcm.IJCM_581_20

Analyzing Performance of Interactive Multi-task Learning Network in Aspect Based Sentiment Analysis

Aakanksha Sharaff(✉), Ankita Pal, and Sheetal Pahadi

Department of Computer Science and Engineering, National Institute of Technology Raipur, Raipur, India
asharaff.cs@nitrr.ac.in

Abstract. Sentiment Analysis is a widely used method for analyzing the feelings expressed in words, reviews, and opinions. It assists in determining what users like and dislike. This, in turn, aids in the formulation of subsequent policies. Aspect-based sentiment analysis (ABSA) is a better approach of analyzing as it can truly find out the sentiments associated with specific features/topics/aspects. ABSA is typically performed in a pipeline fashion, with the first stage being the extraction of aspects, followed by the determination of sentiments for that specific aspect. While this strategy is simple, it does not fully exploit the availability of other data, as in a document which has its sentiment labelled. This article examines how the Interactive Multi-Task Learning Network (IMN) strategy works to help people learn many tasks at the same time, both at the token as well as in a document. The proposed method uses a message passing architecture to iteratively transfer information to various tasks through shared latent attributes. The proposed approach compared with other state-of-the-art models and finds the proposed IMN outperforms others with increase in performance of sentiment classification based on aspects.

Keywords: Multitask Learning · Concurrent Execution · Aspect Extraction · Opinion Extraction · Sentiment Classification

1 Introduction

The goal of Aspect based Sentiment Analysis (ABSA) is to understand how the users feel about certain attributes in a review. This is accomplished by extracting individual aspects which is called aspect-extraction. The subsequent step is detecting the sentiment orientation toward each withdrawn aspect which is called sentiment classification based on aspect. In the statement "Great ambiance but terrible food," the aspect terms "ambiance" and "food" are utilized, and the emotion orientations toward them are positive and negative, respectively [1].

Earlier research has focused on AE and AS separately, with the entire process being run through a pipeline, which usually doesn't fully utilize the common information between the two tasks. Integrated models, according to two recent research can generate

M. Paprzycki et al. (Eds.): ICACIS 2024, CCIS 2405, pp. 369–382, 2027.
https://doi.org/10.1007/978-3-032-30990-7_27

results which are comparable to pipeline methodologies. Li et al. [2] and Wang et al. [3] have used a tagging mechanism where, the tasks are connected by labels in their methods, and the relationship between them is not explained. Further, these methods only grab information from instances of the aspects, which are smaller in size, and do not use information from any other sources, such as documents which have their sentiments labelled and have crucial sentiment and linguistic information which are easy to access.

The proposed method uses an IMN which executes both the subtasks at the same time, allowing better exploitation. Also, IMN allows extraction and classification to be executed concurrently with associated tasks at the document level, which benefits them from the information present in big corpus. The network introduces a message transmission system which allows the sub-tasks to communicate in a way that is both instructive and useful. It does this by sending useful data from various tasks back again to the latent variables which are shared amongst the tasks. The data is then merged with the shared latent representation which is then provided to process it. With the increase in the number of iterations, the information can be modified and passed across different links.

1.1 Objectives and Importance of the Proposed Work

The objective behind the proposed work is to figure out a better mechanism to execute ABSA based on context and overall impact of the aspect/sentiment text. ABSA become a major asset in AI/ML due to its ability to deduce people's sentiment towards a particular situation [4].

ABSA is used in a variety of disciplines. It allows users to go through the reviews and gain insight into which political leaders, the public supports, as well as the users gets benefited [5]. Companies may profit from aspect-based sentiment research by gathering online consumer feedback for their product and determining which product aspects people like and dislike. This can assist them in determining which product features to include and which to exclude from their product development to increase sales. This initiative aims to uncover the enormous benefits that the IMN model may provide.

1.2 Scope

ABSA has a very broad application because of its immense capacity and usefulness. Thus, improving ABSA's findings will broaden its applicability to a wider range of disciplines, and it may soon become an essential tool for corporations, political parties, social analysts, and others. Anyone possessing such details will undoubtedly have an advantage in learning about people's interests and opinions on many subjects. Parties may develop better regulations for themselves, and businesses can determine which features to include in their goods and which to avoid. Based on a person's social media posts, their moods can be better assessed. Brand values of the specific industry can also be evaluated from the newspaper articles. Apart from these, ABSA have much more applicability.

1.3 Motivation

Users became enthralled by the marvels of AI and machine learning and what they can accomplish. Precise information can be extracted from texts and analyzed how a person thinks about something using fine-grained aspect-based analysis. ABSA makes a difference in a variety of professions. It is so important that even those who would head a government will use it to determine public policy and understand the preferences of the electorate. It also has a significant commercial impact, as businesses want to invest in the correct ABSA technologies to better understand their own operations and image among customers. These all provides the motivation to embark on this mechanism.

Major contributions of the proposed work are as follows:

- The proposed method uses an IMN allowing better exploitation.
- The concurrent executions of the data extraction and classification has been done in this current work.
- A message transmission system is enabled in this work to improve the usefulness.

The rest of the chapter is organized into different sections, where Sect. 2 represents the background studies related to ABSA. Section 3 explains the proposed approach followed by the implementation details explained in Sect. 4. Section 5 provides a clear insight of the experimental setup and the result analysis part. With a brief description of the applications of ABSA in Sect. 6, the chapter concludes in Sect. 7.

2 Literature Review

2.1 Aspect-Based Sentiment Analysis

Sirisha et al. [6] have explored the impact of internet and social media, particularly Twitter, on shaping public opinion during the Russia-Ukraine conflict. Using a novel deep-learning approach that combines Roberta with ABSA and Long Short-Term Memory, sentiments expressed in geographically tagged tweets are analyzed. The hybrid model achieves a high accuracy of 94.7%, surpassing state-of-the-art techniques, demonstrating its effectiveness in understanding people's emotions and views on the war. M.Abdelgwad et al. [7] have proposed a deep learning-based models for ABSA in Arabic, overcoming resource challenges. The models, BGRU-CNN-CRF and IAN-BGRU, outperform baselines with a 39.7% improvement in F1score for aspect target extraction and a 7.58% increase in performance for sentiment polarity evaluation, achieving notable scores of 70.67% and 83.98%, respectively.

2.2 Multi-task Learning

Zhao et al. [8] have suggested a multitask learning approach for ABSA, concurrently addressing aspect polarity classification (APC) and aspect term extraction (ATE). By emphasizing the connection between ATE and APC and employing multiheaded attention with dependency sequences, the model significantly enhances aspect polarity classification performance across benchmark datasets. Singh et al. [9] have addressed the challenge of automatically identifying customer complaints in extensive online content, emphasizing their role in shaping business strategies. Through a deep multitask framework incorporating Affective Space for commonsense knowledge, the system achieves high accuracy (83.73%) in complaint identification and demonstrates a tight correlation (69.01%) between sentiment analysis and complaint classification, showcasing their concurrent learning benefits.

2.3 Message Passing Architectures

Liang et al. [10] have proposed a model integrating affective knowledge to enhance dependency graphs, considering both contextual and aspect features' dependencies and affective information between sentiment words and aspects. Experimental analysis on public datasets showcases the superiority of the proposed Sentic GCN model over state-of-the-art methods in fine-grained sentiment analysis. Mao et al. [11] have introduced a unified end-to-end framework for ABSA, addressing opinion term extraction, aspect term extraction, and aspect-level sentiment classification. Utilizing machine reading comprehension, message passing scheme with two jointly trained BERT-MRC models, the proposed framework outperforms existing methods on benchmark datasets, demonstrating its effectiveness in solving all ABSA subtasks. The proposed method is like a recurrent neural network since each loop uses the common network to modify the associated latent attribute. The proposed mechanism is geared to solve multi-task learning challenges.

3 Proposed Methodology

In this section, the working strategy of the proposed methodology is discussed in detail.

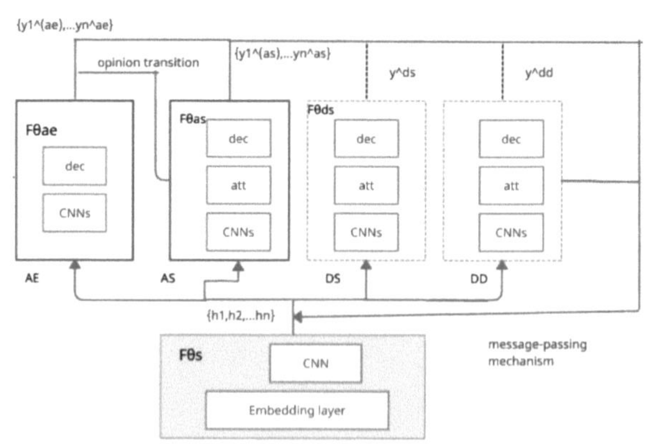

Fig. 1. Basic IMN architecture.

The proposed approach's execution is completed in multiple steps as shown in Fig. 1. As the first step, a series of credentials namely referred as $[x_1,\ldots, x_n]$ are sent to the

IMN architecture as input to a common feature withdrawing component named as fs. A word layer used for embedding is followed by a few feature extraction layers in this component. Following the word embedding layer in fs, ms layers of CNNs are used.

The feature extraction function generates a series of latent variables $h_1^s, h_2^s, \ldots, h_n^s$ that are maintained across all tasks. This series of latent vectors is then modified by merging information conveyed from multiple task components by message passing after being initialized by fs. h(t) I is defined as the value of the single layer dynamic array corresponding to x_i after t cycles of message transmission, in addition of h(0) I being the result after initial condition. A series of common latent vectors $h_1^s, h_2^s, \ldots, h_n^s$ is sent into the dissimilar task related units. Each unit with a specific task has its own set of latent and outcome variables. In extraction each token is labelled to indicate if it is related to any aspect or opinion phrase, but in finding opinion, each word is classified with its sentiment.

3.1 Aspect-Level Tasks

With the BIO tagging method, AE seeks to pick all the aspect as well as the sentiment terms that appear in a phrase, which is formulated as a sequence labelling issue. In this work, five class labels have been employed.

BA = starting of aspect term
IA = inside of aspect term
BO = starting of opinion term
IO = inside of opinion term

Here, sentiment classification is also modelled as a sequence labelling issue, with labels pos, neg, neu.

Pos = positive orientation (token scale)
Neg = negative orientation (token scale)
Neu = neutral orientation (token scale)

With gold extraction and sentiment classification tags, Table 1 depicts an example of how the aspect-level is trained. Only the aspect words are labelled with its sentiment in aspect-level datasets.

Table 1. Labelling Aspects.

Input	The	Dog	Is	Cute	But	The	Brid	Is	Ordinary	.
AE	O	BA	O	BA	O	O	BA	O	BP	O
AS	–	–	–	Pos	–	–	Neg	–	Neg	–

θ_{ae} is used to parameterized the AE component, which generates $\{y_1^{ae},\ldots, y_n^{ae}\}$. The f_{as} is an sentiment classification component that uses θ_{as} as its parameter. The shared representations are mapped to $\{h_1^{as}, h_2^{as},\ldots, h_n^{as}\}$ and $\{h_1^{ae}, h_2^{ae},\ldots, h_n^{ae}\}$ by the AS and AE encoders. These encoders are made up of CNN layers. At the top of the stacked CNNs, we use an extra self-attention layer for the AS encoder. The AS in the self-attention layer get the output of AE as the input.

A is a self-attention matrix which is A ϵ R^{nxn} and calculated using Eq. 1 and 2.

$$score_{ij}^{(i \neq j)} = \left(h_i^{as} W^{as} \left(h_j^{as}\right)^T\right) \cdot \left(\frac{1}{|i-j|}\right) . P_j^{op} \tag{1}$$

$$A(i \neq j)_{ij} = \exp\left(score_{ij}\right) / \sum_{k=1}^{n} \exp(score_{ik}) \tag{2}$$

The first item in the equation denotes the semantic significance of h_i^{as} and h_j^{as} with respect to A. P_j^{op} represents the expected likelihood that the token from j[th] is included in any opinion term, and the second term gets smaller as i and j get farther apart. By adding the anticipated probabilities on the opinion-related class labels IP and BP in y_j^{ae}, the probability $P_j^{op}j$ may be calculated. As a result, AE's forecasts have a direct impact on AS. Because context words are evaluated to infer the emotion of the target value, we set the diagonal components in A to zeros.

$h_i^{\prime as} = \sum_{j=1}^{n} A_{ij} h_j^{as}$ is the output of the self-attention layer. For the final representation of aspect extraction, the word embedding is joined, the initial shared representation $h_i^{s(0)}$ and the task specific representation h_i^{ae} in AE. Finally, $h_i^{s(0)}$ and $h_i^{\prime as}$ is joined for the sentiment classification. At the decoder side, SoftMax is used as the activation function.

3.2 Document-Level Tasks

The proposed method can use information from the documents which have their sentiments labelled to overcome the problem of inadequate aspect-scale training data. Two document-level classification tasks are introduced, which will be trained together using AE and AS. The first is classifying the document's sentiment. The alternative method is the domain categorization of the document. The task-specific operation $f\theta_0$, is made up of m_o CNN layers. This can be done using Eq. 3.

$$a_i^o = \exp\left(h_i^o W^o\right) \sum_{k=1}^{n} \exp\left(h_k^o W^o\right) \tag{3}$$

where W^o is a parameter vector $h^O = \sum_{i=1}^{n} a_i^o h_i^o$ as the decoding layer.

3.3 Message Passing Mechanism

The message passing mechanism combines predictions from various subtasks of the previous steps and utilizes this information to adjust the common latent vectors $\{h_1^s, h_2^s, \ldots, h_n^s\}$ at the ongoing stage. The message passing architecture uses information from y_i^{ae}, y_i^{as}, y_i^{ds}, a_i^{ds} and a_i^{dd} evaluated on the input $\{x_1, \ldots, x_n\}$. It then updates the vector using Eq. 4.

$$h_i^s(t) = f\theta_{re}\left(h_i^s(t-1) : \hat{y}_i^{ae}(t-1) : \hat{y}_i^{as}(t-1) : \hat{y}_i^{ds}(t-1) : a_i^{ds}(t-1) : a_i^{dd}(t-1)\right) \tag{4}$$

here t > 0, ':' is the concatenation operation and fθre is the re-encoding function.

We use a completely linked layer with ReLu activation. We combine the results of AE and AS from the previous step into the shared representations to ensure that this information is present for both jobs in the current computation step. We also consider what DS and DD have to say. y^{ds} denote the input sequence's overall emotion, which might be useful for AS. DS and DD create attention weights a_i^{ds} and a_i^{dd}.

3.4 Learning

Aspect-based problems have only aspect-based labels, whereas document-based problems have just document labels in their cases. The proposed architecture is alternatively trained on the cases based on aspect and cases based on document. While trained on aspect-based values the function of loss can be calculated using Eq. 5.

$$L_a(\theta_s, \theta_{ae}, \theta_{as}, \theta_{ds}, \theta_{dd}, \theta_{re}) = (l/N_a)\sum\nolimits_{i=1}^{N_a}(l/n_i)\sum\nolimits_{i=1}^{N_a}\left(l\left(y_i^{ae}j, \hat{y}_i^{ae}(T), j\right) + l\left(y_i^{as}j, \hat{y}_i^{as}(T), j\right)\right) \quad (5)$$

T = maximum number of messages passing mechanism repetitions
N_a = total number of training instances of aspect level
n_i = number of tokens representing ith training instance
$y_i^{ae}j, y_i^{as}j$ = gold label one hot encoding
l = entropy loss

Algorithm 1: Pseudocode for training IMN

Require: $D^a = \left\{\left(x_i^a, y_i^{ae}, y_i^{as}\right)_{i=1}^{N_a}\right\}$, $D^{ds} = \left\{\left(x_i^{ds}, y_i^{ds}\right)_{i=1}^{N_{ds}}\right\}$ $and\ D^{dd} = \left\{\left(x_i^{dd}, y_i^{dd}\right)_{i=1}^{N_{dd}}\right\}$

Require: Integer r > 0

```
for e∈[1, max_pretrain_epochs] do
    for minibatch B^ds, B^dd in D^ds, D^dd do
        compute L_d based on B^ds, B^dd
        update θ_s, θ_ds, θ_dd
    end for
end for
for e∈[1, max_epochs] do
    for b∈[1, batches_per_epoch] do
        sample B^a from D^a
        compute L_a based on B^a
        update θ_s, θ_ae, θ_as, θ_re
        if b is divisible by r then
            sample B^ds, B^dd from D^ds, D^dd
            compute L_d based on B^ds, B^dd
            update θ_s, θ_ds, θ_dd
        end if
    end for
end for
```

While trained on document-level instances the loss value is calculated using Eq. 6. The pseudocode of the training process of the proposed IMN is presented in Algorithm 1.

$$L_d(\theta_s, \theta_{ds}, \theta_{dd}) = \left(\frac{l}{N_{ds}}\right)\sum_{i=1}^{N_{ds}} l\left(y_i^{ds}, \hat{y}_i^{ds}\right) + \left(\frac{l}{N_{dd}}\right)\sum_{i=1}^{N_{dd}} l\left(y_i^{dd}, \hat{y}_i^{dd}\right) \quad (6)$$

N_{ds}= no. of training instances for DS

N_{dd}= no. of training instances for DD.
$\hat{y}_i^{ds}$ and $\hat{y}_i^{dd}$ = one of the one hot encoding of the gold label.

4 Implementation

In this section, the complete detail of the implementation is discussed.

4.1 Encoder Based on Convolutional Neural Network

As indicated in the proposed work, the first layer of CNN of the encoder that is shared consists of 128 frames of filters with kernel size three and 128 filters with kernel size five. The common encoder's additional CNN layers, as well as the stages of CNN in each task related encoder, each include filters equal to 2^6 with sizes of kernel denoted by k = 5. ReLu is used as the activation function for each CNN layer. Applying the embedding to CNN layer with dropout value p = 0.5.

4.2 Opinion Transmission

Planned sampling is employed for opinion transmission throughout the training phase to solve the issue of inaccurate opinion label predictions in the early stages of training. Gold opinion labels is sent to AS instead of the expected ones generated by AE when I is equal. The amount of training epochs considered as I for which sigmoid inversely is applied to determines the probability I.

4.3 Information of the Models under Consideration

The proposed IMN extracts aspect and opinion words simultaneously in AE, allowing for the use of extra added opinion related labels during training of model. The integrated technique INABSA, as well as the pipeline method, do not consider sentiment information into account while training in the baselines. To provide an optimal comparison, labels are appended known as BP, IP to the INABSA label sets, denoting the starting and end of each opinion term, respectively. Such models are taught on training sets with combining these two aspects and opinion word labels to conduct extraction successfully.

During pipeline approach training, additionally the gold opinion words made accessible to the AS models known as ALSTM. To get ALSTM to use the information of the label of opinion, the layer of attention is changed to assign tokens that are more similar and can be used as a part of an opinion word higher weights. This makes sense because the purpose of an AS model's attention mechanism is to identify the right context of opinion. The weight of the attention module of the given i^{th} token is modified before utilizing the SoftMax normalization in a phrase of input as described in Eq. 7.

$$a^{'}(i) = a(i) * P(\hat{}(op))(i) \tag{7}$$

In many situations, IMN still outperforms alternative baselines in this context. Furthermore, when comparing the findings, it is seen that when opinion term extraction is considered, IMN provides improved F1-I scores on datasets. When trained using opinion word labels, alternative baseline approaches do not show consistent gains. These outcomes imply that input gained via learning opinion phrase extraction is certainly valuable, but in reference to make benefit of this knowledge, a well-designed network structure is required. IMN was created to take advantage of task correlations by explicitly modelling interactions across activities, allowing it to better integrate information gained from various tasks.

5 Experimental Setup and Result Analysis

5.1 Experimental Setup

The statistics for the datasets connected to aspects are shown in Table 2. Two benchmark datasets are from SemEval-2014 dataset [12] and one from SemEval-2015 dataset [13] is used in current experiment. The opinion phrases have been given by [3]. On the document basis, two datasets are used. The first is regarding restaurant field, while the second is related to electronics domain namely Laptop dataset.

Table 2. Detail Description of the Datasets.

Dataset No.	Name	Train		Test	
		Aspect	Opinion	Aspect	Opinion
D1	Restaurant 14	3699	3484	1134	1008
D2	Laptop 14	2373	2504	654	674
D3	Restaurant 15	1199	1210	542	510

With T initialized to two, R via IMN is changed retraining via validation set on the first data set and the necessary document-related datasets. Using a batch size of 32 and a learning rate of 0.01, the ADAM optimizer is employed. Without any special adjustment for our work, the rate of learning and size of batch are initialized to standard levels.

5.2 Evaluation Metrics

Throughout testing, we identify aspect phrases and use YAE (T) and YAS to forecast emotion for each recovered aspect term (T). There are two metrics for evaluating AE execution, two for evaluating AS execution, and one for evaluating overall execution. Based on prior work for AE, F1score is used to analyze the execution of aspect term extraction and sentiment phrase extraction, that are labelled as F1score(a) and F1score(o), respectively. Based on past research, correctness, and macro level F1score is employed to assess AS efficiency [14].

They're referred to as accuracy of aspect denoted by acc[s] and the score is denoted by F1(s). For assessing overall performance, the result called F1score is calculated of the composite task, abbreviated as F1(I). Only when both the span and the emotion are accurately detected is an extracted aspect word considered correct when finding the F1(I). All phrases related to aspect have been taken while computing F1(a), but aspect words are excluded with conflict sentiment labels when calculating the other three aspects under consideration.

5.3 Overview of the Model Comparison

Pipeline Approach. DECNN is the most recent AE model. It employs a CNN structure with one or more layers that includes both generic as well as domain related embeddings. It makes use of a CNN concept of different layers with both generic and domain related characters. In the same way encoders are used in the proposed work and the Long Short-Term Memory (ALSTM) is used for AS. ALSTM is nothing but an attention-based LSTM structure.

Integrated Approach. INABSA is a newly presented technique that has attained state-of-the-art outcomes among mechanisms that are integrated. The work is modelled by tagging a sequence issue with a unified methodology in both ways. Because IMN gives the outputs of the opinion on the initial level of a withdrawn term as an aspect term during testing to avoid inconsistency in sentiment, we also execute this operation on IN-ABSA to permit fair comparison.

5.4 Evaluation and Findings

The comparative analysis is shown in Table 3. IMN conducts aspect extraction and opinion term extraction in AE simultaneously, although the baseline techniques employ extra opinion term labels during training, they do not include these details in their starting phase of models. We heavily adjusted those baselines to include co-extracting as well, with sentiments word suggests, to provide a valid comparison.

Table 3 shows that IMN improved by adding optimizers and increasing the kernel size outperforms other baselines on F1-I by a wide margin. On D1, D2, and D3, IMN improves performance even more and beats the best F1(I) findings from the baselines by 0.4%, 1.74%, and 0.96%, respectively. In most circumstances, IMN outperforms F1(a) and F1(o) for extracting feelings related terms. Also, the suggested method surpasses other approaches by a wide percentage for AS in both the acc(s) and F1(s). Using either combined training of document related tasks or domain related embeddings, the model makes use of information from bigger corpora. This shows that domain related information is extremely beneficial, and that domain related embeddings and collaborative training are both excellent methods for transferring such knowledge.

Table 3. Comparison of the Proposed Approach with the State-of-the-art Models.

	Methods	Dataset 1 (D1)	Dataset 2 (D2)	Dataset 3 (D3)
DECNN-ALSTM	F1(a)	83.94	78.38	68.32
	F1(o)	85.60	78.81	71.22

(continued)

Table 3. (*continued*)

	Methods	Dataset 1 (D1)	Dataset 2 (D2)	Dataset 3 (D3)
	Acc(s)	77.79	70.46	80.32
	F1(s)	68.50	66.78	57.25
	F1(I)	65.26	55.05	55.10
INABSA	F1(a)	83.92	77.34	69.40
	F1(o)	84.55	76.62	71.43
	Acc(s)	79.68	72.30	82.56
	F1(s)	68.38	68.24	58.81
	F1(I)	66.60	55.88	57.38
IMN	F1(a)	83.33	77.96	70.04
	F1(o)	85.61	77.51	71.94
	Acc(s)	83.89	75.36	85.64
	F1(s)	75.66	72.02	71.76
	F1(I)	69.54	58.37	59.18
IMN (Proposed)	F1(a)	83.34	76.93	**70.07**
	F1(o)	**85.72**	77.67	71.35
	Acc(s)	**84.71**	**77.01**	**85.92**
	F1(s)	**76.12**	**72.93**	**72.79**
	F1(I)	**69.94**	**60.11**	**60.14**

6 Applications

The proposed approach has a wide range of applications. Some of them are listed below.

- It can be used by businesses to better understand the customer's feelings for their products.
- Determine which aspects of the product are favored by customers and which are not. then proceed with product development considering the findings.
- Political parties can understand voters' inclination based on their online social media posts or tweets related to politics. This can help them devise better party policies.

7 Conclusion and Future Work

IMN, an interactive multitasking neural network for learning aspect extraction and opinion term identification with sentiment categorization at the aspect level is designed as the proposed work. The suggested IMN involves a different method of passing the messages which gives interactions very informative across tasks, allowing for improved utilization of correlation. Furthermore, IMN can learn from several sources of giving fine grained on the level of token tasks to benefit from the level of document labelled corpora and training the data. Similar tasks like link extraction and semantic role categorization might benefit from the proposed architecture. IMN improved by adding optimizers and increasing the kernel size outperforms other baselines. Using either combined training of document related tasks or domain related embeddings, the model makes use of information from bigger corpora. This shows that domain-specific information is extremely beneficial, and that domain-specific embeddings and collaborative training are both excellent methods for transferring such knowledge. With such a unique approach, IMN improves performance by 0.4%, 1.74%, and 0.96%, respectively as compared to the baseline models.

This work can be extended to improve the performance of the classification task. It is always a critical task to handle real-time data. So, the proposed work can be further extended to evaluate real-time data.

References

1. Zhang, W., Li, X., Deng, Y., Bing, L., Lam, W.: A survey on aspect-based sentiment analysis: tasks, methods, and challenges. IEEE Trans. Knowl. Data Eng. **35**(11), 11019–11038 (2022)
2. Li, X., Bing, L., Lam, W., Shi, B.: Transformation networks for target-oriented sentiment classification. arXiv preprint arXiv:1805.01086. (2018)
3. Wang, F., Lan, M., Wang, W.: Towards a one-stop solution to both aspect extraction and sentiment analysis tasks with neural multi-task learning. In: 2018 International Joint Conference on Neural Networks (IJCNN), pp. 1–8. IEEE (2018)
4. D'Aniello, G., Gaeta, M., La Rocca, I.: KnowMIS-ABSA: an overview and a reference model for applications of sentiment analysis and aspect-based sentiment analysis. Artif. Intell. Rev. **55**, 5543–5574 (2022)
5. Li, H., Bruce, X.B., Li, G., Gao, H.: Restaurant survival prediction using customer-generated content: an aspect-based sentiment analysis of online reviews. Tour. Manag. **96**, 104707 (2023)
6. Sirisha, U., Chandana, B.S.: Aspect based Sentiment and Emotion Analysis with ROBERTa, LSTM. (2022)
7. Abdelgwad, M.M., Soliman, T.H.A., Taloba, A.I., Farghaly, M.F.: Arabic aspect based sentiment analysis using bidirectional GRU based models. J. King Saud Univ. – Comput. Inform. Sci. **34**, 6652–6662 (2022). https://doi.org/10.1016/j.jksuci.2021.08.030
8. Zhao, G., Luo, Y., Chen, Q., Qian, X.: Aspect-based sentiment analysis via multitask learning for online reviews. Knowl. Based Syst. **264**, 110326 (2023). https://doi.org/10.1016/j.knosys.2023.110326
9. Singh, A., Saha, S., Hasanuzzaman, M., Dey, K.: Multitask learning for complaint identification and sentiment analysis. Cogn. Comput. **14**, 212–227 (2022). https://doi.org/10.1007/s12559-021-09844-7
10. Liang, B., Su, H., Gui, L., Cambria, E., Xu, R.: Aspect-based sentiment analysis via affective knowledge enhanced graph convolutional networks. Knowl. Based Syst. **235**, 107643 (2022). https://doi.org/10.1016/j.knosys.2021.107643
11. Mao, Y., Shen, Y., Yu, C., Cai, L.: A joint training dual-MRC framework for aspect based sentiment analysis. In: Proceedings of the AAAI Conference on Artificial Intelligence, pp. 13543–13551 (2021)
12. Pontiki, M., Papageorgiou, H., Galanis, D., Androutsopoulos, I., Pavlopoulos, J., Manandhar, S.: SemEval-2014 Task 4: Aspect Based Sentiment Analysis. (2014)

13. Pontiki, M., Galanis, D., Papageorgiou, H., Manandhar, S., Androutsopoulos, I.: Semeval-2015 task 12: aspect based sentiment analysis. In: Proceedings of the 9th International Workshop on Semantic Evaluation (SemEval 2015), pp. 486–495 (2015)
14. Chen, P., Sun, Z., Bing, L., Yang, W.: Recurrent attention network on memory for aspect sentiment analysis. In: Proceedings of the 2017 Conference on Empirical Methods in Natural Language Processing, pp. 452–461 (2017)

A ROUGE-Based Comparison of Text Summarization Models

Abir Chowdhury(✉), Shubh Kandpal, Nidhi Mishra, and Shuchi Mala

Amity School of Engineering and Technology, Noida, India
abir31c@gmail.com

Abstract. In the present study, a thorough comparison of three well-known transformer-based models: PEGASUS, BART, and T5 have been performed. The popular ROUGE measure has been used to evaluate the performance of these models. The ROUGE score: ROUGE-1, ROUGE-2, ROUGE-L, and ROUGE-LSUM—are used to rate the efficacy and calibre of the produced summaries. This chapter includes a detailed analysis of the models' training procedures, monitoring the models' validation, and training losses throughout several epochs. Crucial indicators of the models' learning dynamics and generalization capabilities include the training loss and validation loss. This study provides information on the convergence behaviour and overall PEGASUS, BART, and T5 training performance. Comparative analysis establishes benchmarks for evaluating future advancements in text summarization models. This study enhances our understanding of the summarization capabilities of BART, T5, and PEGASUS models. Additionally, it provides insights and suggestions for enhancing the performance of transformer-based models in future summarization tasks.

Keywords: Text summarization · PEGASUS · BART · T5 · ROUGE

1 Introduction

Text summarization uses the technique of creating a succinct and logical synopsis of a text or document while maintaining its key details and hold its significance. The evolution of automatic text summarization has had a significant impact in the field of Natural Language Processing (NLP). The objective of automatic summarization is to distill the most crucial information from its source document while maintaining its core context, the essential facts, and the concepts. In our data-driven era, where information is the lifeblood of every company, text summary gives busy individuals the advantage. For example, attorneys handle many cases at the same time in the legal industry. Large legal chapterwork and chapter works become difficult to analyse. Because they can quickly and efficiently extract the most important facts and information, automatic text summarization becomes remedial and speeds up the review process. Automatic text summarization becomes the go to solution to huge volumes of non-structured textual and unreadable data.

M. Paprzycki et al. (Eds.): ICACIS 2024, CCIS 2405, pp. 383–394, 2027.
https://doi.org/10.1007/978-3-032-30990-7_28

1.1 Background

The area of text summarization has been developing for more than 70 years, and it is continuously changing now. Rule-based methodologies were prevalent in the early years of text summarizing research. A few years later, statistical techniques began to become more and more common [1]. In order to prioritise sentences, researchers investigated methods like Term frequency-inverse document frequency (TF-IDF) [2]. The groundwork for eventual advancements in extractive summarization was established by these methods [3]. A greater emphasis was placed on machine learning techniques for text summarization in the late 1990s and early 2000s [4]. Abstractive summarization attracted interest once deep learning and transformer-based models were introduced. Over the decade, various models and algorithms have been developed to ameliorate the text summarization approaches. Many measures and benchmarks have been established to evaluate text summarizing systems and gauge how well summarization algorithms work. Early assessments in the field of text summarization were frequently impromptu and subjective. Summaries would be evaluated by researchers according to human judgements and readability. Therefore, a standardized system to evaluate the quality of summarization has failed as it varied from person to person according to the context. However, in response to this challenges, development of several standard evaluation methods, such as ROUGE (Recall-Oriented Understudy for Gisting Evaluation) metrics [5] and BLUE (Bilingual Evaluation Understudy) [6], have achieved a huge milestone.

1.2 Objective

This chapter aims to investigate and present the performance of PEGASUS, BART, and T5 models with the given dataset. It intends to compare these models based on their ROUGE score and exhibit the best performing model. This chapter also intends to study the graphical analysis of the ROUGE score against each epochs (iterations). The observations of the respective models' training loss and validation loss against each epochs are to be discussed.

2 Related Work

[7] (Jingqing Zhang, Yao Zhao, Mohammad Saleh, Peter J. Liu) assessed PEGASUS model on 12 downstream summarizations. They proposed self-supervised pre-training objective on wide range of data with the help of Transformer based models. The proposal was offered for generating gap-sentences and abstractive summarization. For evaluating the considered datasets, the optimal model settings were marked. The process of optimising PEGASUS model for better performance by fine tuning was demonstrated. After extensive research on various gap sentence approach, selecting principal sentences proved to be the best course of action. They pre-trained the model on Colossal Clean Crawled Corpus (C4) corpus. The base model was trained coupled with two objective functions: Gap Sentences Generation (GSG) and Masked Language Model (MLM). In the result section, the authors have demonstrated that the basic version of PEGASUS ($\text{PEGASUS}_{\text{BASE}}$) performed better than the transformer base ($\text{Transformer}_{\text{BASE}}$), which

clearly shows the effectiveness of the pre-training objectives, whereas, the large models, $PEGASUS_{LARGE}$ (C4) and $PEGASUS_{LARGE}$ (HugeNews), have outperformed the previous state of the art (Previous SOTA) by huge margin.

[8] (Derek Miller) proposed the use of BERT model for extractive text summarization on lectures. The output embeddings from the BERT model were further clustered with K-means. The document that is closest to the centroid in K-Means algorithm, is a represented summary for that cluster. The results were compared with used tools such as TextRank. The author depicted that using both the embeddings, GPT and BERT, the ensemble of both these architectures gave more inter clusters distance which widened the separability. But at the time, the inference time was increased even while working in a multithreaded environment. Despite, both K-Means and Gaussian Matrix Model provided similar performance, the author decided to select K-Means for clustering. Finally, the outputs of BERT and TextRank were shown. This chapter displayed the possibilities and power of the transformer models.

[9] (Colin Raffel et al) explored the limits of Transfer learning with the help of T5. On some self-supervised objectives, the main idea of transfer learning is to pre-train the model with a high quality of data. They have used the Colossal Clean Crawled Corpus (C4) dataset for their research purpose. The authors identified the flaws associated with the dataset. They found that not all the data in that collection was in natural language. Therefore, they came up with few heuristics to address these issues and have released it as a part of TensorFlow datasets. For downstream tasks, they have used abstractive summarization on news dataset from CNN/Daily Mail. They showed a hyper parameter selection process for the pre-training objective and evaluated the de-shuffling procedure. They found that the BERT-style strategy worked the best for them.

[10] (Mike Lewis et al) majorly talk about the applied pre-training scheme for the BART model. They addressed the idea of MLM in the chapter. The testing of noise reduction techniques and establishing the optimal performance by random shuffling method were done. The objective of their research is to optimise the negative log probability of the source document for pre-training. They tested various fine-tuning tasks.

3 Methodology

3.1 Dataset Description

The research was done on SAMSum dataset, which is an English-language collection of slightly more than 16000 interactions, recorded by English-speaking linguists. The Samsung R&D Institute Poland created and distributed this dataset for use in academic research. This dataset aims to support the creation of models that condense lengthy text paragraphs into short phrases.

3.2 Data Pre-processing

Preparing the dataset for analysis requires data pre-processing. The given dataset comprises of train data, validation data, and test data. The process of tokenization is performed with the help of tokenizer [11]. The input data were divided into batch size of 16 and each were passed through 100 epochs for the training purpose of each model. Upon successful data pre-processing, an accurate training and evaluation can be done.

3.3 Techniques Used

Transformer based models developed by Hugging Face community, T5 (Text-To-Text Transfer Transformer), BART (Bidirectional and Auto-Regressive Transformers), and PEGASUS (Pre-training with Extracted Gap-sentences for Abstractive Summarization), have been applied for this research chapter [12]. A set of evaluation metrics, ROUGE [5], is applied on these models to draw conclusion.

[12] BART is a sequence-to-sequence transformer model, constitute both bidirectional and auto-regressive architectures. It can be pre-trained by using denoising autoencoder. It uses encoder for processing the sequence of input and decoder for creating the output sequence. Due to its bidirectional nature, i.e. trained on activities that navigate from left to right as well as right to left, BART produces coherent sequences by gathering contextual information from both sides. It uses the concept of auto-regressive training which helps in predicting the succeeding token [12]. T5 is a Text-To-Text Transfer Transformer model having denoising autoencoder as pre-training objective. It uses the Text-To-Text framework and adheres to encoder-decoder structure. Self-Attention, which considers the dependencies of words, serves as the building block of the transformer [12]. PEGASUS is a sequence-to-sequence transformer model used to anticipate gaps within a document. It uses encoder-decoder architecture and has denoising autoencoder as pre-training objective. After pre-training, this model may be fine-tuned for certain summarizing tasks.

4 Result

4.1 Performance Measure

Let g be a generated summary by some system, and let $C = \{c1, \ldots, c_k\}$ be a set of cited summaries. Let $\delta_n(d)$ be a binary vector that represents the number of n-grams that are present in document d. If the i-th n-gram is present in document d, then its i-th component of $\delta_n^i(d)$ is 1, and if not, it is 0. The following formula may be used to calculate the metric ROUGE-N, an n-gram recall based statistic [5]:

$$ROUGE - N(g) = \frac{\sum_{c \in C} \langle \delta_n(c),\ \delta_n(g) \rangle}{\langle \delta_n(c),\ \delta_n(c) \rangle} \tag{1}$$

To put it simply, ROUGE-N can be re-written as:

$$ROUGE - N = 2 * \frac{(Precision)_n * (Recall)_n}{(Precision)_n + (Recall)_n} \tag{2}$$

where,

$$(Precision)_n = \frac{No.of\ overlapping\ n\text{--}grams\ in\ system\ summary}{Total\ no.of\ n\text{--}grams\ in\ system\ summary} \tag{3}$$

and,

$$(Recall)_n = \frac{Number\ of\ overlapping\ n\text{--}grams\ in\ system\ summary}{Total\ number\ of\ n\text{--}grams\ in\ reference\ summary} \tag{4}$$

ROUGE-L is associated with the concept of Longest Common Subsequence (LCS). The mathematical formula for ROUGE-L is given by:

$$ROUGE - L = 2 * \frac{(Precision)_L * (Recall)_L}{(Precision)_L + (Recall)_L} \quad (5)$$

where,

$$(Precision)_L = \frac{Length\ of\ Longest\ Common\ Subsequence}{Total\ number\ of\ words\ in\ system\ summary} \quad (6)$$

and,

$$(Recall)_L = \frac{Length\ of\ Longest\ Common\ Subsequence}{Total\ number\ of\ words\ in\ reference\ summary} \quad (7)$$

ROUGE-LSUM refers to the fact that this metric is computed over a whole summary, whereas ROUGE-L is computed as the average of individual sentences.

4.2 Visualisation

The two crucial metrics that are used to monitor a model's performance during training are training loss and validation loss. These factors help to demonstrate how a model is responding to new data and keep track of the learning rate from the training dataset.

[13] The training loss indicates the model's performance on the training data by displaying the difference between the target values and the model's prediction. At every epoch (iterations), adjustments to the model's parameters (weights and biases) are made to minimise the training loss. The purpose of the training loss is to provide guidance to best fit the model for the training data in an optimised way. The validation loss indicates the model's ability to generalise untested data by returning the performance of model that has not been explicitly trained on [14]. The purpose of the validation loss is to spot the overfitting condition of a model [15]. Overfitting condition for a particular model may occur when the validation loss increases while the training loss decreases.

The snapshot of both training loss and validation loss at a regular interval is shown in the Table 1. Though the training loss value for the BART model is less in comparison to other models, the validation loss value is higher than other models. This indicates the condition of overfitting for the BART model. It can be interpreted in a broader view by analysing the graph for each epoch in Figs. 1 and 2, which displays epoch-wise training loss and validation loss respectively. From Figs. 1 and 2, it is observed that models, PEGASUS and T5, have less training loss and validation loss. Therefore, these models have the tendency to perform well with the given dataset. To validate the result, the performance of the models is compared with the help of their ROUGE score.

Table 1. Training and Validation Loss for PEGASUS, BART, and T5.

Epoch Interval	PEGASUS		BART		T5	
	Training Loss	Validation Loss	Training Loss	Validation Loss	Training Loss	Validation Loss
1	1.270	2.027	0.176	1.714	1.739	2.293
10	1.270	1.544	0.176	2.260	1.739	1.954
20	1.686	1.534	0.918	2.856	2.231	1.921
30	1.231	1.538	0.187	3.153	1.919	1.911
40	1.201	1.542	0.075	3.370	1.773	1.914
50	1.198	1.541	0.043	3.536	1.672	1.926
60	1.198	1.542	0.043	3.571	1.672	1.932
70	1.199	1.542	0.029	3.646	1.599	1.939
80	1.201	1.542	0.019	3.757	1.544	1.942
90	1.197	1.542	0.014	3.808	1.510	1.947
100	1.201	1.542	0.012	3.825	1.488	1.949

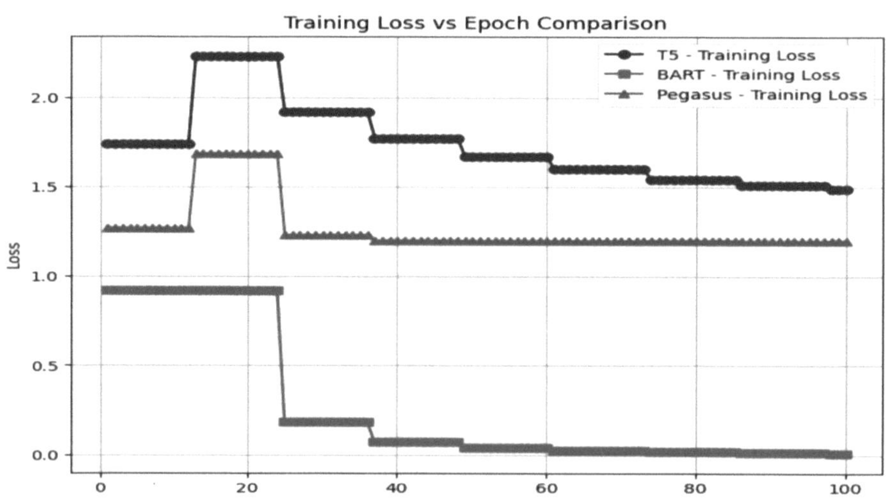

Fig. 1. Epoch-wise Training Loss Analysis.

Table 2. ROUGE score for PEGASUS.

Epoch Interval	PEGASUS			
	ROUGE-1	ROUGE-2	ROUGE-L	ROUGE-LSUM
1	0.287	0.078	0.216	0.215

(continued)

Table 2. (*continued*)

Epoch Interval	PEGASUS			
	ROUGE-1	ROUGE-2	ROUGE-L	ROUGE-LSUM
10	0.462	0.210	0.377	0.376
20	0.458	0.221	0.380	0.379
30	0.464	0.228	0.386	0.386
40	0.469	0.233	0.389	0.390
50	0.469	0.233	0.389	0.390
60	0.468	0.233	0.390	0.390
70	0.465	0.229	0.386	0.386
80	0.466	0.231	0.386	0.387
90	0.466	0.231	0.387	0.387
100	0.466	0.231	0.387	0.387

Table 3. ROUGE score for BART.

Epoch Interval	BART			
	ROUGE-1	ROUGE-2	ROUGE-L	ROUGE-LSUM
1	0.441	0.216	0.371	0.370
10	0.451	0.203	0.374	0.374
20	0.451	0.205	0.366	0.367
30	0.460	0.212	0.377	0.379
40	0.451	0.200	0.367	0.368
50	0.450	0.204	0.370	0.372
60	0.451	0.212	0.372	0.374
70	0.445	0.202	0.358	0.359
80	0.450	0.202	0.361	0.363
90	0.451	0.209	0.373	0.374
100	0.458	0.211	0.374	0.375

Table 4. ROUGE score for T5.

Epoch Interval	T5			
	ROUGE-1	ROUGE-2	ROUGE-L	ROUGE-LSUM
1	0.246	0.052	0.200	0.199

(*continued*)

Table 4. (*continued*)

Epoch Interval	T5			
	ROUGE-1	ROUGE-2	ROUGE-L	ROUGE-LSUM
10	0.370	0.142	0.303	0.303
20	0.377	0.145	0.306	0.306
30	0.384	0.147	0.309	0.309
40	0.379	0.145	0.308	0.308
50	0.387	0.153	0.312	0.312
60	0.387	0.153	0.312	0.312
70	0.387	0.151	0.314	0.314
80	0.381	0.153	0.316	0.315
90	0.388	0.158	0.321	0.321
100	0.388	0.158	0.321	0.321

4.3 Performance Comparison of Models

This research explores the comparative evaluation of three cutting-edge transformer-based models, PEGASUS, BART, and T5, when they are used to summarise text. The primary focus of the study is comparing and assessing these models' performance using the commonly used ROUGE metrics, ROUGE-1, ROUGE-2, ROUGE-L, and ROUGE-LSUM. A detailed snapshot of each model's ROUGE scores at regular intervals over its training epochs is shown. Table 2. displays ROUGE score for PEGASUS. Table 3. displays ROUGE score for BART. Table 4. displays ROUGE score for T5. Interestingly, the PEGASUS model performs better than the others on a regular basis, showing higher ROUGE scores across all metrics. This table is a useful tool that provides information about the relative advantages and disadvantages of each model at various training phases.

The descriptive analysis of ROUGE scores against each epoch is visually shown in Figs. 3, 4, 5 and 6, which helps to improve comprehension of the models' performance dynamics. Figure 3 demonstrates epoch-wise ROUGE-1 score Analysis for PEGASUS, BART, and T5. Figure 4 demonstrates epoch-wise ROUGE-2 score Analysis for each model. Figure 5 demonstrates epoch-wise ROUGE-L score Analysis for each model. Figure 6 demonstrates epoch-wise ROUGE-LSUM score Analysis for each model. The graph highlights the PEGASUS model's better performance over the others by displaying greater ROUGE values. One interesting finding is that, whereas PEGASUS's ROUGE scores are stable at comparatively smaller epochs, the BART model shows fluctuations that imply fewer epochs are needed to obtain the best outcomes. PEGASUS's stability at lower epochs suggests that the model converges to an optimal solution more quickly than BART, which exhibits fluctuation at higher epochs. This finding highlights PEGASUS's capacity to produce reliable results with the provided dataset and provides insight into the training dynamics of the models.

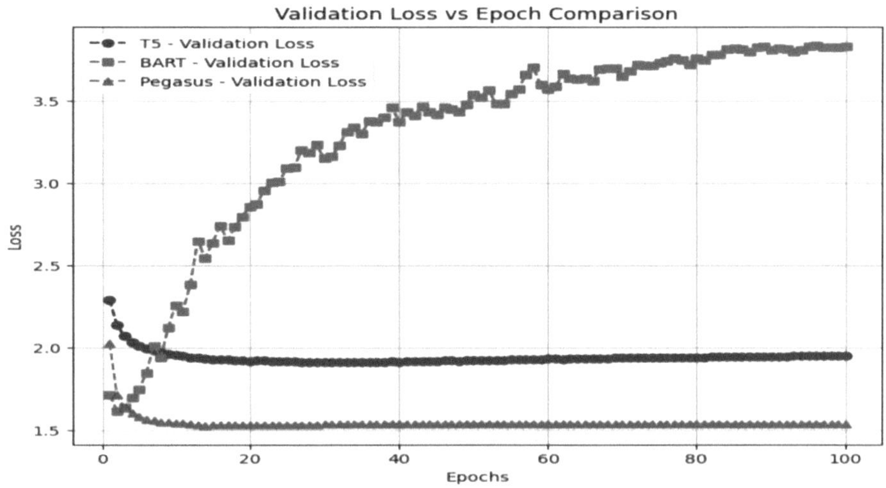

Fig. 2. Epoch-wise Validation Loss Analysis.

Ultimately, the results provide compelling evidence for the PEGASUS model's advantage in text summarization. Its efficiency and efficacy as compared to BART and T5 are demonstrated by its consistently higher ROUGE scores and sustained convergence at lower epochs. These observations add to the continuing discussion on transformer-based text summarization models and offer practitioners and academics useful pointers for optimising and choosing models.

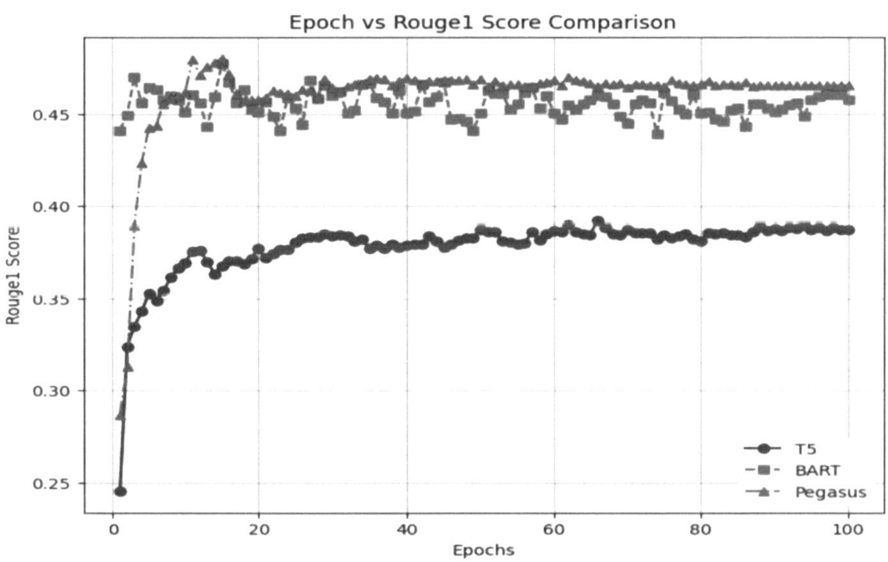

Fig. 3. Epoch-wise ROUGE-1 score Analysis for PEGASUS, BART, and T5.

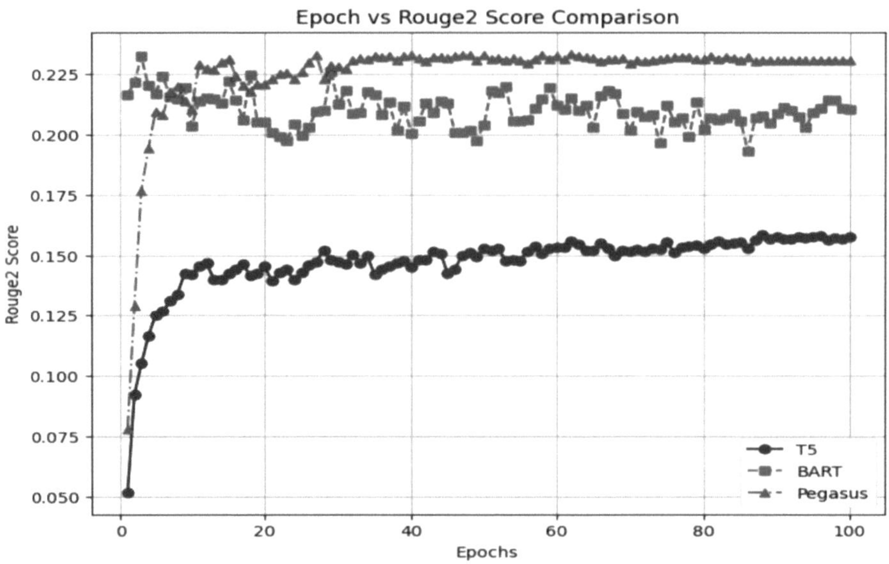

Fig. 4. Epoch-wise ROUGE-2 score Analysis for PEGASUS, BART, and T5.

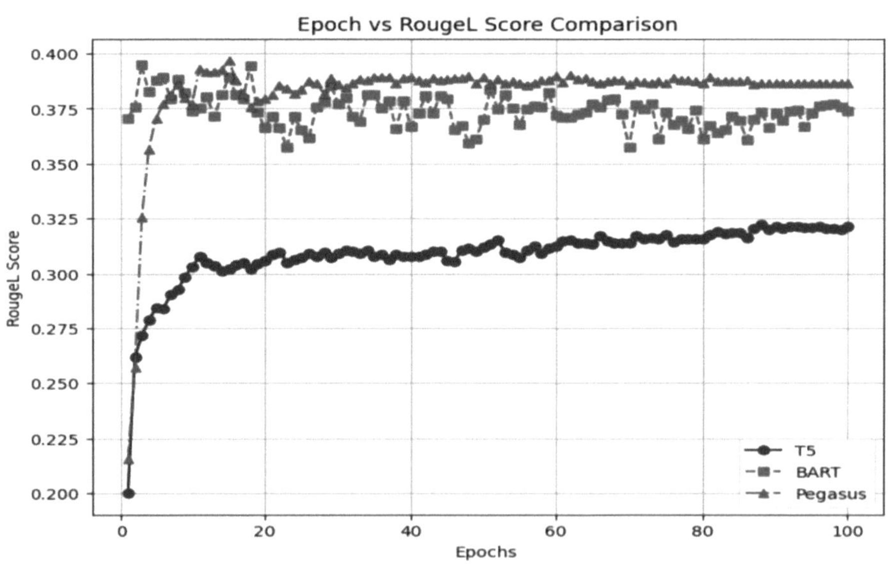

Fig. 5. Epoch-wise ROUGE-L score Analysis for PEGASUS, BART, and T5.

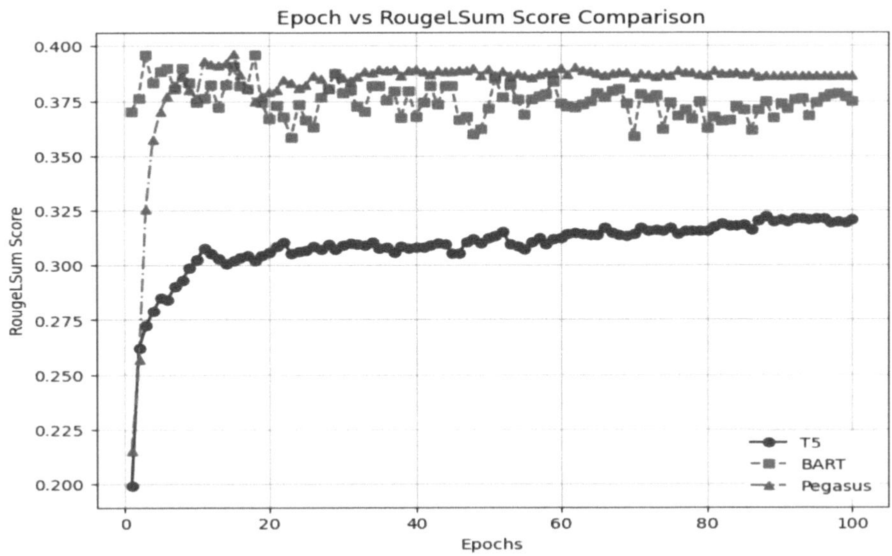

Fig. 6. Epoch-wise ROUGE-LSUM score Analysis for PEGASUS, BART, and T5.

5 Conclusion and Future Scope

The text summarising model has proven its ability to generate concise and well-organized summaries. This chapter provides the utilization techniques of text summarising models on which the SAMSum dataset has been trained. The availability of accessible dataset has made it possible to evaluate information, which has aided in the use of the applied models for text summarization. Models like, PEGASUS, BART, and T5, have been used. After a comprehensive assessment with the ROUGE measure, our algorithm was able to generate summaries.

The training and validation losses of the PEGASUS model are quite comparable. For the PEGASUS model, the average values of Training loss and Validation loss are 1.270 and 1.549, respectively. Its average ROUGE scores show that it performed well in creating summaries; in particular, ROUGE-1 and ROUGE-2 at 0.461 and 0.226, respectively, show good overlap with reference summaries. In contrast, the BART model has an average training loss of 0.176, which is noticeably less than its average validation loss of 3.291. This raises the possibility of an overfitting problem during training. Even yet, its average ROUGE scores—particularly ROUGE-1 at 0.456 and ROUGE-2 at 0.210—are competitive, demonstrating good summarising skills. On the other hand, the average validation loss for the T5 model is 1.942 and the average training loss is 1.739. With ROUGE-1 at 0.378 and ROUGE-2 at 0.147, its average ROUGE scores are lower than those of the other two models.

Therefore, in this study, the PEGASUS model has performed better than other applied models. The advancement in the NLP field has improved the quality of the result. We intend to work on several other models and respond to the limitations of the BART model in the future.

References

1. Laxmi, B., Venkata, P.: An overview of text summarization. Int. J. Comput. Appl. **171**, 1–17 (2017). https://doi.org/10.5120/ijca2017915109
2. Al-Hashemi, R.: Text summarization extraction system (TSES) using extracted keywords. Int. Arab J. e-Technol. **1**, 164–168 (2010)
3. Alguliev, R., Aliguliyev, R.: Evolutionary algorithm for extractive text summarization. Intell. Inf. Manag. **01**, 128–138 (2009). https://doi.org/10.4236/iim.2009.12019
4. Huang, D., et al.: What Have We Achieved on Text Summarization?, https://arxiv.org/pdf/2010.04529. Last accessed 30 Apr 2024
5. Das, D., Martins, A.: A Survey on Automatic Text Summarization, https://www.cs.cmu.edu/\~afm/Home_files/Das_Martins_survey_summarization.pdf. Last accessed 30 Apr 2024
6. Papineni, K., Roukos, S., Ward, T., Zhu, W.: Contribution title. In: Proceedings of the 40th Annual Meeting of the Association for Computational Linguistics (ACL), pp. 311–318, Philadelphia (2002)
7. Zhang, J., Zhao, Y., Saleh, M., Liu, P.: PEGASUS: pre-training with extracted gap-sentences for abstractive summarization, https://arxiv.org/pdf/1912.08777. Last accessed 30 Apr 2024
8. Miller, D.: Leveraging BERT for Extractive Text Summarization on Lectures, https://arxiv.org/pdf/1906.04165. Last accessed 30 Apr 2024
9. Raffel, C., et al.: Exploring the limits of transfer learning with a unified text-to-text transformer. J. Mach. Learn. Res. **21**, 1–67 (2020)
10. Lewis, M., et al.: BART: denoising sequence-to-sequence pre-training for natural language generation, Translation, and Comprehension, https://arxiv.org/abs/1910.13461. Last accessed 30 Apr 2024
11. Nallapati, R., Zhou, B., Santos, C., Gulcehre, C., Xiang, B.: Abstractive text summarization using sequence-to-sequence RNNs and beyond. In: The SIGNLL Conference on Computational Natural Language Learning (CoNLL), pp. 280–290 (2016)
12. Gupta, A., Chugh, D., Anjum Katarya, R.: Automated news summarization using transformers. In: Aurelia, S., Hiremath, S.S., Subramanian, K., Biswas, S.K. (eds.) Sustainable Advanced Computing Lecture Notes in Electrical Engineering, vol. 840. Springer, Singapore (2022). https://doi.org/10.1007/978-981-16-9012-9_21
13. Kingma, D.P., Lei Ba, J.: Adam: a method for stochastic optimization. In: 3rd International Conference for Learning Representations (2015)
14. Loshchilov, I., Hutter, F.: SGDR: stochastic gradient descent with warm restarts. In: ICLR 2017 (5th International Conference on Learning Representations) (2017)
15. Srivastava, N., Hinton, G., Krizhevsky, A., Sutskever, I., Salakhutdinov, R.: Dropout: a simple way to prevent neural networks from overfitting. J. Mach. Learn. Res. **15**, 1929–1958 (2014)

Hybrid Deep-Machine Learning Approach for Early Detection of Covid-19, Pneumonia with CBAM Integration

Waqarul Hasan[1(✉)], Nawab Shahzeb Uddin[1], Rashid Ali[1,2], and Nadeem Akhtar[1,2]

[1] Interdisciplinary Centre for Artificial Intelligence, AMU, Aligarh, India
udraenetkr1@gmail.com
[2] Department of Computer Engineering, ZHCET, AMU, Aligarh, India
{rashidali.cse,nadeemakhtar}@zhcet.ac.in

Abstract. The study offers a hybrid strategy that integrates machine learning and deep learning methods to meet the urgent need for early COVID-19 detection. The study focuses on using Contrast Limited Adaptive Histogram Equalisation (CLAHE), Gaussian blur, and X-ray imaging to improve diagnostic accuracy and speed up patient care. Furthermore, the Convolutional Block Attention Module (CBAM) is used into the process to improve the diagnostic images' feature representation. Features are extracted through the use of transfer learning models, including VGG16, VGG19, and MobileNetV2. We performed a number of experiments focusing on the classification of COVID-19 and Pneumonia using chest X-ray images into different categories: COVID-19, Pneumonia, and Normal. This included multi-class classification (COVID-19 vs. Pneumonia vs. Normal) as well as binary classification (Pneumonia vs. COVID-19). The outcomes show that the combination of MobileNetV2 with Support Vector Machine and CBAM produces the accuracy of 96.46% in the classification of Covid-19 patients against typical Pneumonia cases.

Keywords: Covid-19 · deep learning · machine learning · CBAM · pneumonia

1 Introduction

In the midst of the COVID-19 pandemic, which was officially declared by the World Health Organisation in 2020, the healthcare industry has been desperately looking for more efficient diagnostic instruments. Patients suffering from COVID-19 frequently report respiratory problems and common symptoms such as fever and cough [6]. Because of the virus's rapid spread, it is imperative to identify positive COVID-19 cases as soon as possible and expedite the diagnostic procedure [11] to better manage and comprehend the scope of the epidemic. RT-PCR, or reverse transcription polymerase chain reaction, has been the main technique for detecting COVID-19. RT-PCR has limitations despite having high sensitivity and specificity, such as the need for specialised equipment and skilled workers, as

M. Paprzycki et al. (Eds.): ICACIS 2024, CCIS 2405, pp. 395–406, 2027.
https://doi.org/10.1007/978-3-032-30990-7_29

well as the fact that it is time-consuming. Because testing for COVID-19 must be conducted frequently to assure accuracy, a quicker alternative is required. For this investigation, X-ray imaging was used since it is faster than CT scans and more accessible because X-ray machines are widely available and reasonably priced.

Artificial intelligence has advanced significantly in the last several years, especially in the field of medical diagnosis. In artificial intelligence, deep learning (DL), which uses multi-layered neural networks to learn complex data representations, is gaining popularity [3]. An essential step in the analysis of lung disease images is feature extraction. In order to achieve efficient feature extraction, our work makes use of pre-trained DL models including VGG16 [14], VGG19 [14], and MobileNetV2 [12]. It also integrates several machine learning techniques, such as Support Vector Machine (SVM) [5] and Logistic Regression (LR). This hybrid model of COVID-19 detection provides an improved analysis of Chest X-ray data by fusing the interpretability and generalisation capabilities of classical ML with the complexity of DL. The dataset used to assess the predictive value of chest X-rays in COVID-19 infection is made up of publicly available COVID-19 pictures that are hosted on GitHub. One experiment used COVID-19 vs pneumonia, while the other involved COVID-19 against pneumonia vs normal. The suggested model is displayed in Fig. 1.

Among the study's noteworthy contributions are:

1. A CNN-based model is being built to categorise patients with COVID-19 based on chest X-rays, using pre-trained DL models for feature extraction and ML classifiers to determine the most effective COVID-19 detection strategy.
2. Applying picture pre-processing techniques to the raw data, such as CLAHE and Gaussian Blur.
3. Improving the accuracy and performance of all deep learning models through the use of CBAM.

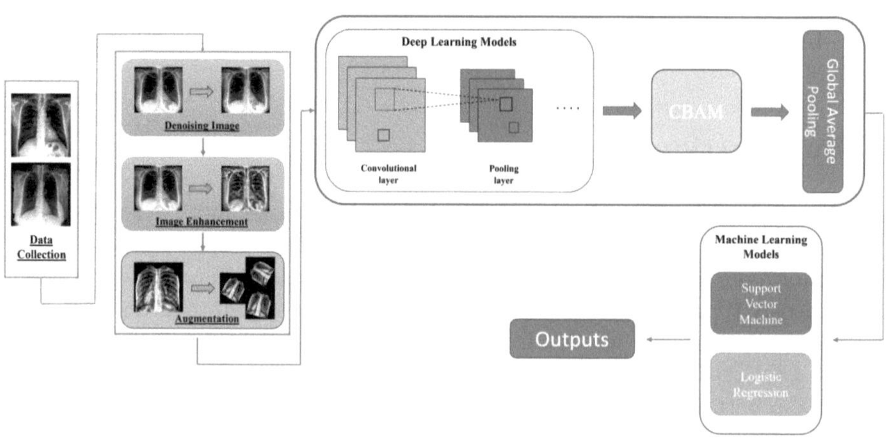

Fig. 1. The Proposed Model for Covid-19 Detection

The study is set up like this: Related work is discussed in Sect. 2. Our models and techniques are described in Sect. 3. The experimental setup and dataset are described in Sect. 4. The results are shown and discussed in Sect. 5. Section 6 concludes by summarising our contributions, shortcomings, and potential future research areas.

2 Related Work

Deep learning and machine learning techniques are widely used in COVID-19 detection. The work of Chen et al. [2] focuses on enhancing deep learning models, like VGG16, VGG19, ResNet, and AlexNet, using L2 regularisation and data augmentation through transfer learning. The Convolutional Block Attention Module (CBAM) has been employed by the author for the classification of COVID-19, pneumonia, and normal cases. This approach has been applied for both binary and multi-class classification tasks. The system achieves an accuracy of 95.21% in differentiating COVID-19 from pneumonia. Additionally, it attains an accuracy of 88.47% in the multi-class classification involving COVID-19, pneumonia, and normal cases. Hemdan et al. [7] compared the training outcomes of multiple deep learning models by utilising X-ray pictures to differentiate COVID-19 from normal. They found that with a f1 score of 0.91, DenseNet and VGG19 both attain accuracy rates of 0.89. Using raw chest X-ray images, Ozturk et al. [10] develop a novel automatic detection approach that achieves an accuracy of 98.08% in binary classification (COVID vs. No-Findings) and accuracy of 87.02% in multi-class situations (COVID vs. Pneumonia vs. No-Findings). Pre-trained CNN models such as VGG16, VGG19, ResNet18, ResNet50 and ResNet101 are used by Ismael et al. [9] to extract deep features. The recovered features are then classified using a Support Vector Machines (SVM) classifier. The dataset they use consists of 200 normal chest X-ray images and 180 COVID-19 images. The accuracy of the classifications served as a performance metric. Deep learning is useful in identifying COVID-19 from chest X-ray pictures, according to experimental data. The ResNet50 model with SVM classifier with Linear kernel achieved the greatest accuracy of 94.7%. The newly created CNN model achieved 91.6% accuracy, whereas the refined ResNet50 model demonstrated 92.6% accuracy. Abhijit Bhattacharyya et al. [1]. Three suggested an approach for categorising lung pictures into COVID-19, pneumonia, and normal categories using three steps: Using a C-GAN to segment lung images, a trained deep neural network to extract distinguishing features, and a variety of machine learning models to classify the images. The best outcome, a testing classification accuracy of 96.6%, was obtained by combining the binary robust invariant scalable key-points (BRISK) technique with the VGG-19 model.

3 Methods

3.1 Feature Extraction Using Transfer Learning

Deep learning, a rapidly advancing area in machine learning, has garnered significant interest among researchers. But the lack of readily available datasets presents a significant obstacle to medical data analysis. Large amounts of data are usually needed for deep learning models, and expert labelling this data is costly and time-consuming [13]. Here, transfer learning provides an option where models that have already been pre-trained on large datasets can be utilized. Employing these existing models can lead to substantial improvements in medical image diagnosis, resulting in increased accuracy with less data and shorter training times. This study compares the performance of several pre-trained deep learning models: VGG16 [14], VGG19 [14], MobileNetV2 [12]. The Visual Geometry Group (VGG) networks were proposed by Simonyan et al. [14]. The VGG16 architecture consists of thirteen convolutional layers, three dense layers, and a final layer with 1000 classes with softmax as the activation function. Deep convolutional neural network VGG19 is renowned for its efficiency and simplicity in picture classification. Although it uses more processing power than shallower systems like VGG16, its 19 layers and tiny 3×3 filters enable it to catch fine details in images. Convolutional neural network architecture MobileNetV2 [12] proposed by sandler et al. was created with effective mobile applications in mind. Compared to its predecessor, MobileNetV1, it has inverted residual blocks with linear bottlenecks, which improves performance and accuracy. With its cheap computing costs and state-of-the-art performance in picture classification tasks, MobileNetV2 is perfect for devices with limited resources.

3.2 Attention Module

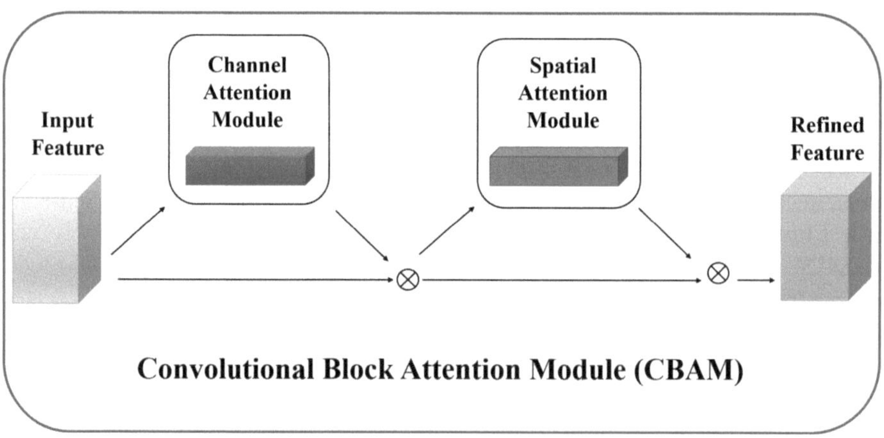

Fig. 2. Convolutional Block Attention Module (CBAM) illustration

CNNs that have been integrated with attention modules are better able to extract features. These modules let the network concentrate on the most crucial area of an image, which improves the model's efficiency and sharpness. Woo et al. proposed CBAM [16], a simple yet effective attention module that can be applied widely to boost CNN representation power. As illustrated in Fig. 2, the two subsequent submodules that comprise CBAM are the channel attention module (CAM) and the spatial attention module (SAM). Assuming that our input is an intermediate feature map A $\in \mathbb{R}^{C\times H\times W}$, CBAM can infer two maps: $M_c \in \mathbb{R}^{C\times 1\times 1}$, a 1-D channel attention map, and $M_s \in \mathbb{R}^{1\times H\times W}$, a 2-D spatial attention map. The overall attention mechanism shown in Eq. (1).

$$\begin{aligned} B &= M_c(A) \otimes A, \\ C &= M_s(B) \otimes B \end{aligned} \tag{1}$$

where $\otimes$ denotes element-wise multiplication.

Feature map from CNN-based model's is first processed by the Channel Attention Module (CAM). Two 1×1 channel attention maps are produced by applying global maximum pooling f_{mp} and global average pooling f_{ap} to the space within CAM. The ReLU activation function is then used to feed these maps into a shared-weight multi-layer perceptron (MLP) neural network with a single hidden layer. To get the weight value, the two MLP-derived features are merged and passes through a Sigmoid activation function (σ). Equation (2) illustrates how to get the channel attention weights for the feature map by multiplying this weight value by the original feature map. Figure 3 shows the CAM's structural layout.

$$\begin{aligned} \mathrm{M_c(A)} &= \sigma(\mathrm{MLP}(f_{\mathrm{ap}}(A) + \mathrm{MLP}(f_{\mathrm{mp}}(A)))) \\ &= \sigma\left(W_1\left(W_0\left(A^{c}_{\mathrm{avg}}\right) + W_1\left(W_0\left(A^{c}_{\max}\right)\right)\right)\right) \end{aligned} \tag{2}$$

$\mathrm{W}_0 \in \mathbb{R}^{C/r\times C}$, and $\mathrm{W}_1 \in \mathbb{R}^{C\times C/r}$ are MLP weights where r stand for reduction ration.

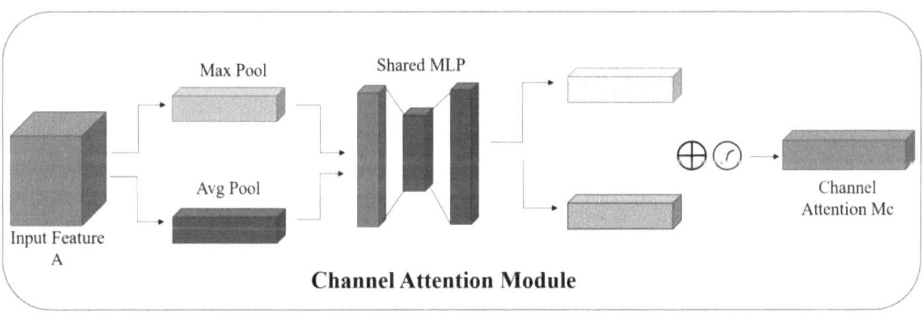

Fig. 3. Channel wise attention module

The data enters the Spatial Attention Module (SAM) after going through the Channel Attention Module (CAM). This module focuses on the characteristics of spatial information by converting the original image's spatial data into a different space while keeping important information. To process the channel-refined activation map B, average pooling f_{ap} and max pooling f_{mp} are applied, producing $B_{s_{\text{avg}}} \in \mathbb{R}^{1\times H\times W}$ and $B_{s_{\max}} \in \mathbb{R}^{1\times H\times W}$, respectively. After applying a convolutional layer, a spatial attention map, denoted as $M_s(B)$, is generated using the sigmoid function. This map resides in the space $\mathbb{R}^{H\times W}$, where H and W represent its height and width dimensions, respectively. Figure 4 shows the SAM's structural layout.

$$\begin{aligned}\text{Ms(B)} &= \sigma\left(f^{7\times 7}([f_{\text{ap}}(B); f_{\text{mp}}(B)])\right)\\ &= \sigma\left(f^{7\times 7}\left(\left[B^s_{avg}; B^s_{\max}\right]\right)\right)\end{aligned} \tag{3}$$

Here $f^{7\times 7}$ signifies a convolution operation utilizing a filter with dimensions 7×7.

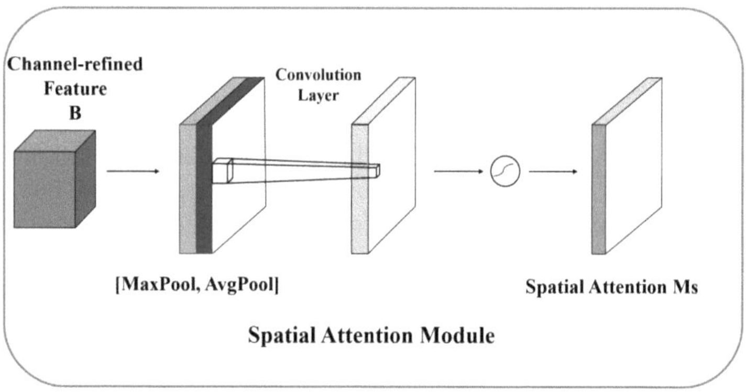

Fig. 4. Spatial Attention Module

3.3 Machine Learning Algorithms

In this study we used the machine learning algorithm as a classifier. ML algorithms identify objects by analyzing their distinctive features. Feature extracted using pre-trained CNN model used as input for ML. Several machine learning techniques, including logistic regression and support vector machines [5], are used in this work.

Table 1. Data distribution of each class before augmentation

Class	data
Covid-19	100
Pneumonia	100
Normal	100

4 Experimental Setup

4.1 Dataset

The dataset used in this research is 'SegmentedLungCXRs' [8], a public repository accessible via GitHub and Kaggle. It consists of three different kinds of X-rays: Normal Class, Pneumonia, and COVID-19. 'Covid-chestxray-dataset' [4] contains COVID-19 X-rays that are combined into the 'SegmentedLungCXRs' 'dataset' with pneumonia and normal images from the National Institute of Health dataset [15]. As indicated in Table 1, we have chosen 100 photos from each class for our investigation.

Table 2. Data distribution of each class after augmentation

Class	data
Covid-19	2400
Pneumonia	2400
Normal	2400

Table 3. Data Distribution

Case	Goal	Data Distributionl
Experiment 1	Covid-19 vs Pneumonia	Covid-19: 2400, Pneumonia: 2400
Experiment 2	Covid-19 vs Pneumonia vs Normal	Covid-19: 2400, Pneumonia: 2400, Normal: 2400

Data Pre-processing. Data preprocessing enhances model performance and robustness while preventing overfitting. In this research, Gaussian smoothing was employed to reduce image noise and detail. To improve the contrast of X-ray pictures, Contrast Limited Adaptive Histogram Equalisation (CLAHE) [17], a more advanced form of Adaptive Histogram Equalisation (AHE), is employed. Image augmentation is required to improve the model's ability to generalise to new, unseen images and to diversify the training data. We generated a new sample for every 15-degree rotation in an image. Result of image augmentation is shown in Table 2.

4.2 Experimental Setup

We've structured our work into two main experiments:

- Experiment 1: The first experiment is binary classification problem between Covid-19 and Pneumonia.

- Experiment 2: This was a multi-class classification task, differentiating among Covid-19, Normal, and Pneumonia.

The data distribution is detailed in Table 3. All experiments were conducted on a laboratory server using TensorFlow, an open-source neural network framework. Our hardware setup included an Intel® Xenon® Gold 6238R CPU @ 2.20GHz 2.19 GHz, an NVIDIA Quadro RTX 5000 GPU accelerator, and 112 GB of RAM.

For the dataset, we allocated 70% for training, 10% for validation, and 20% for testing. Each experiment had a batch size of 32, a weight decay of 0.002, a learning rate of 0.001, and was performed for 20 epochs.

4.3 Performance Evaluation Index

For this study we use 3 different evaluation metrics: -

- Accuracy: measures calculates the percentage of accurate predictions made out of all the cases that were looked at.

$$\text{Accuracy} = \frac{TP + TN}{TP + TN + FP + FN} \tag{4}$$

- Precision: how many of the predicted positive cases were actually correct.

$$\text{Precision} = \frac{TP}{TP + FP} \tag{5}$$

- Recall: how many of the actual positive cases did the model properly identify.

$$\text{Recall} = \frac{TP}{FN + TP} \tag{6}$$

Here are the definitions of some common terms used above:

- True Negative (TN): Occurs when the model accurately predicts the negative class.
- False Negative (FN): Occurs when the model incorrectly predicts the negative class, while the actual class is positive.
- True Positive (TP): Occurs when the model accurately predicts the positive class.
- False Positive (FP): Occurs when the model incorrectly predicts the positive class, while the actual class is negative.

5 Result

In order to diagnose covid-19 and pneumonia, 2 different experiments were conducted as follows (1) Covid-19 vs Pneumonia and (2) Covid-19 vs Pneumonia vs Normal.

Table 4. Experiment 1 Testing Results

Model	Accuracy	Precision	Recall
VGG16	0.9521	0.9717	0.9312
VGG19	0.9458	0.9553	0.9354
MobileNetV2	0.9604	0.9662	0.9542
VGG16 + SVM	0.9573	0.9354	0.9782
VGG19 + SVM	0.9521	0.9597	0.9437
MobileNetV2 + SVM	0.9646	0.9708	0.9588
VGG16 + LR	0.9541	0.9678	0.9396
VGG19 + LR	0.9479	0.9535	0.9417
MobileNetV2 + LR	0.9635	0.9704	0.9562

5.1 Experiment 1 (Covid-19 vs Pneumonia)

The comparative analysis reveals that MobileNetV2 outperforms VGG16 and VGG19 across a range of evaluation metrics as shown in Table 4. Due to its lightweight architecture, MobileNetV2 performs better and is therefore a good choice for environments with limited resources. The network's efficient use of parameters and faster inference speed might contribute to its enhanced accuracy, precision, and recall in the classification task.

A significant improvement in performance is shown when ensemble configurations of convolutional neural network architectures are combined with Support Vector Machines (SVM) and Logistic Regression (LR) classifiers. This supports the idea that combining the advantages of conventional machine learning classifiers with the capabilities of deep learning models might have a synergistic impact that improves classification results. The ensemble models leverage the complimentary advantages of traditional machine learning methods as well as deep learning.

The standout performer in this study is the MobileNetV2 + SVM configuration, achieving the highest accuracy (0.9646) and recall (0.9588) among all models. The usefulness of MobileNetV2 in combination with Support Vector Machines for differentiating between COVID-19 and pneumonia cases is highlighted by this remarkable outcome. The high recall shows the model's capacity to recognise a significant number of genuine positive cases, which is important in the context of medical diagnosis, while the high accuracy shows the model's proficiency in accurately classifying occurrences. Based on medical imaging, MobileNetV2 + SVM's strong performance indicates that it has the potential to be a dependable tool for identifying COVID-19 and pneumonia cases. Because false negatives in the medical field can have serious implications, the high recall is very important. This particular model configuration exhibits potential as a supplemental diagnostic tool. It could assist medical professionals in detecting conditions early and accurately, which could lead to prompt intervention and treatment.

Table 5 compares our model with the state-of-the-art model for the classification of Covid-19 against Pneumonia. Our model fared better in terms of accuracy, precision, and recall than Chen et al.'s method [2]. With an accuracy of 0.9646, precision of 0.9708, and recall of 0.9588, our model outperformed the Chen et al. reference approach in accurately identifying instances, demonstrating its usefulness in the job.

Table 5. Comparison of our model for the Covid vs. Pneumonia classification with the most recent model

Model	Accuracy	Precision	Recall
Chen et al. [2]	0.9521	0.9504	0.954
Ours	0.9646	0.9708	0.9588

5.2 Experiment 2 (Covid-19 vs Pneumonia vs Normal)

In this experiment we performed multi-class classification. The MobileNetV2 + SVM B1 combination is the best-performing model based on all analysed metrics, as demonstrated by the testing results shown in Table 6. Its ability to obtain the highest accuracy, precision, and recall of any model shows that it performs robustly in correctly identifying COVID-19, pneumonia, and normal patients. Its resilience points to its potential as a useful instrument for physicians to precisely identify and classify respiratory disorders using imaging data.

Moreover, the VGG and MobileNetV2 architectures' competitive performance with SVM and LR classifiers emphasises how adaptable and efficient they are for multi-class classification applications. When combined with conventional machine learning methods, these architectures—which are renowned for their deep learning capacities—show encouraging outcomes. By combining the best features of both deep learning and traditional classifiers, this combination demonstrates a synergistic strategy that improves classification performance.

Overall, these results highlight the possibility of merging deep learning architectures with ensemble techniques for addressing challenging multi-class classification issues in medical imaging, as well as validating the effectiveness of the MobileNetV2 + SVM B1 configuration. These models' adaptability and efficacy open the door to better diagnostic techniques, which in turn improve patient outcomes and treatment in the field of respiratory disease diagnostics.

Table 6. Experiment 2 Testing Results

Model	Accuracy	Precision	Recall
VGG16	0.8806	0.8819	0.8770
VGG19	0.8778	0.8784	0.8778
MobileNetV2	0.9028	0.9065	0.9021
VGG16 + SVM	0.8831	0.8842	0.8831
VGG19 + SVM	0.8882	0.8899	0.8882
MobileNet V2 + SVM B1	0.9042	0. 9046	0.9040
VGG16 + LR	0.8823	0.883	0.8823
VGG19 + LR	0.8868	0.8883	0.8868
MobileNet V2 + LR	0.9034	0.9044	0.9032

Table 7. Comparison of our model for the Covid vs. Pneumonia vs. Normal categorization with the most recent model

Model	Accuracy	Precision	Recall
Chen et al. [2]	0.8847	0.8939	0.9387
Ours	0.9042	0.9046	0.9040

Table 7 compares our model with the state-of-the-art model for the classification of Covid-19, Pneumonia and Normal Class. In comparison to Chen et al.'s method (0.8847), our model produced a higher accuracy (0.9042) with comparable precision and a slightly lower recall. This shows that our model did better overall in classification than theirs, proving its usefulness in correctly classifying data.

6 Conclusions

In order to prevent the spread of COVID-19, we address the vital requirement for early patient discovery in this work. We employed three advanced pre-trained deep learning models (VGG16, VGG19, and MobilenetV2) to extract features from X-ray images. These models were tasked with classifying the images into two categories: COVID-19 vs pneumonia and COVID-19 vs pneumonia vs normal. To enhance the performance of these deep learning models, we integrated the CBAM attention mechanism. This addition aimed to refine the feature extraction process, leading to more accurate classifications. Our approach also involved the use of different machine learning algorithms for the final classification phase. We conducted two experiments, encompassing both binary and multi-class classification scenarios. Among the models tested in these studies, the MobileNetV2 model performed the best. In the future, we suggest investigating different attention modules to enhance the model's effectiveness. Additionally, we suggest the inclusion of a broader range of deep learning models to further expand the scope and robustness of our approach. Future research may produce more sophisticated and precise diagnostic instruments for early COVID-19 detection.

References

1. Bhattacharyya, A., Bhaik, D., Kumar, S., Thakur, P., Sharma, R., Pachori, R.B.: A deep learning based approach for automatic detection of covid-19 cases using chest x-ray images. Biomed. Signal Process. Control **71**, 103182 (2022)
2. Chen, M.-Y., Chiang, P.-R.: Covid-19 diagnosis system based on chest x-ray images using optimized convolutional neural network. ACM Trans. Sens. Netw. **19**(3), 1–22 (2023)
3. Chhabra, P., Goyal, S.: A thorough review on deep learning neural network. In: 2023 International Conference on Artificial Intelligence and Smart Communication (AISC), pp. 220–226. IEEE (2023)
4. Cohen, J.P., Morrison, P., Dao, L., Roth, K., Duong, T.Q., Ghassemi, M.: Covid-19 image data collection: prospective predictions are the future. arXiv preprint arXiv:2006.11988 (2020)
5. Cortes, C., Vapnik, V.: Support-vector networks. Mach. Learn. **20**, 273–297 (1995)
6. Guan, W., et al.: Clinical characteristics of coronavirus disease 2019 in China. N. Engl. J. Med. **382**(18), 1708–1720 (2020)
7. Hemdan, E.E.-D., Shouman, M.A., Karar, M.E.: Covidx-net: a framework of deep learning classifiers to diagnose covid-19 in x-ray images. arXiv preprint arXiv:2003.11055 (2020)
8. Horry, M.: Segmentedlungcxrs dataset (2020). https://github.com/mhorry/SegmentedLungCXRs [Online; 15 Jan 2024]
9. Ismael, A.M., Şengür, A.: Deep learning approaches for covid-19 detection based on chest x-ray images. Expert Syst. Appl. **164**, 114054 (2021)
10. Ozturk, T., Talo, M., Yildirim, E.A., Baloglu, U.B., Yildirim, O., Rajendra Acharya, U.: Automated detection of covid-19 cases using deep neural networks with x-ray images. Comput. Biol. Med. **121**, 103792 (2020)
11. Panwar, H., Gupta, P.K., Siddiqui, M.K., Morales-Menendez, R., Singh, V.: Application of deep learning for fast detection of covid-19 in x-rays using ncovnet. Chaos, Solitons Fractals **138**, 109944 (2020)
12. Sandler, M., Howard, A., Zhu, M., Zhmoginov, A., Chen, L.-C.: Mobilenetv2: inverted residuals and linear bottlenecks. In: Proceedings of the IEEE Conference on Computer Vision and Pattern Recognition, pp. 4510–4520 (2018)
13. Shan, F., et al.: Lung infection quantification of covid-19 in CT images with deep learning. arXiv preprint arXiv:2003.04655 (2020)
14. Simonyan, K., Zisserman, A.: Very deep convolutional networks for large-scale image recognition. arXiv preprint arXiv:1409.1556 (2014)
15. Wang, X., Peng, Y., Lu, L., Lu, Z., Bagheri, M., Summers, R.M.: Chestx-ray8: hospital-scale chest x-ray database and benchmarks on weakly-supervised classification and localization of common thorax diseases. In: Proceedings of the IEEE Conference on Computer Vision and Pattern Recognition, pp. 2097–2106 (2017)
16. Woo, S., Park, J., Lee, J.-Y., Kweon, I.S.: CBAM: convolutional block attention module. In: Proceedings of the European Conference on Computer Vision (ECCV), pp. 3–19 (2018)
17. Zuiderveld, K.: Contrast limited adaptive histogram equalization. Graphics gems, pp. 474–485 (1994)

Improving Tiny Face Detection and Recognition: Augmentation, Self-attention, SSD

Yash Lokhande(✉), Ankan Deb, and Pranali Dandekar

Department of Artificial Intelligence and Machine Learning, Shri Ramdeobaba College of Engineering and Management, Nagpur, India
{lokhandeys,deba,dandekarpr}@rknec.edu

Abstract. The precise detection and recognition of tiny faces in images is an important task in computer vision presenting a significant challenge in this field, with its applications ranging from surveillance and security to personalized user experiences. In this chapter, we propose a unified approach to improve the efficiency of tiny face detection and recognition by incorporating data augmentation, self-attention mechanism, and Single Shot Multibox Detector (SSD). we used the CelebA and WiderFace datasets for our study. Firstly we implemented data preprocessing techniques, leading to an improved and optimized dataset. secondly, with the help of data augmentation techniques (mixup and Rotation), we introduced diversity in data which increased the model generalization. A face detection Algorithm based on SSD is proposed in our work which provides an accuracy of 87.1%. finally, we discussed the influence of the self-attention mechanism which resulted in an improved model accuracy of 89.9%. The model was tested on various evaluation metrics, including precision, recall, and F1-score, which are 0.8801, 0.898, and 0.8889, respectively. Our results demonstrate significant improvements in the detection and recognition of tiny faces, showcasing the potential of our approach for real-world applications.

Keywords: Tiny Face Detection · Self-Attention Mechanism · Single Shot MultiBox Detector (SSD) · Data Augmentation

1 Introduction

Digital imagery has dominated this era, The demand for more efficient and accurate systems to detect and identify faces has increased exponentially. The ability to detect faces has become important across various platforms from surveillance to social media or personalized user experiences, especially in challenging situations like crowded environments or low-resolution images. Tiny face detection is a complex task due to their small size as well as limited visual cues. Traditional face detection algorithms on the other hand mainly focus on detecting large faces thereby making them ineffective in the accurate detection of tiny ones. It is because of this that there has been an increased attentiveness toward the development of specialized techniques and algorithms tailor-made for this purpose. In this chapter, we seeks to present a unified approach towards

M. Paprzycki et al. (Eds.): ICACIS 2024, CCIS 2405, pp. 407–420, 2027.
https://doi.org/10.1007/978-3-032-30990-7_30

improving the detection and recognition of tiny faces through data augmentations, self-attention-mechanism techniques, and "Single Shot Multibox Detector (SSD)" [3]. Our study uses innovative techniques combined with the CelebA and WiderFace datasets' huge size to enhance the accuracy and efficiency of tiny face detection and recognition systems. Figure 1, illustrates the challenges faced during detecting tiny faces. As we can see some faces are occluded, low resolution, and have complex backgrounds.

Fig. 1. Image depicting the complexity of tiny face detection.

2 Background and Related Works

2.1 Tiny Face Detection

Tiny face detection is a task belonging to the area of computer vision which is meant to detect and recognize small facial features in an image. The identification and recognition of these structures is a problem because of low resolution, differences in scale, and occlusions by other objects as well as environmental factors. The recent advancements in the field of computer vision have resulted in the creation of techniques and algorithms that mainly focus on detecting and recognizing tiny faces. For example, (Hu & Ramanan, 2017) proposed a method based on multi-scale feature aggregation for detecting tiny faces, achieving promising results on benchmark datasets [1]. Additionally, (Ye et al., 2019) "introduce a Tiny Face Detection method based on deep learning techniques" [5]. Furthermore, (Zhang et al., 2019). "introduced an Aggregation Connection Network (ACN) which robustly solves these problems in tiny face detection" [2].

2.2 SSD (Single Shot Multibox Detector)

The SSD is a fast and accurate object detection [10] algorithm that is recognized widely. This contrasts with conventional two-stage detection that contains a separate regional proposal stage and classification stage, SSD performs detection in a single forward pass through a neural network. This streamlined technique helps SSD to achieve real-time performance with a very high accuracy. The major concept of SSD is to use a series of convolutional layers as shown in Fig. 2, which enables us to directly predict the bounding boxes and class probabilities from the feature map at multiple scales. SSD works by leveraging feature pyramids and smartly designed anchor boxes to be able to deal with objects of different sizes and aspect ratios in a single framework. Many researchers have examined the capabilities of SSD as well as its enhancements in different object detection tasks. Previous research by (Liu et al., 2016) "SSD model for detecting objects in images" [3]. Additionally, (Ning et al., 2017) "propose a method to improve SSD by incorporating an Inception block to replace the extra layers in SSD" [4]. Furthermore, (Unel et al., 2019) "utilized PeleeNet as a backbone in the SSD network with a tiling approach" [6]. This technique has shown promising results in improving the accuracy of detecting tiny objects.

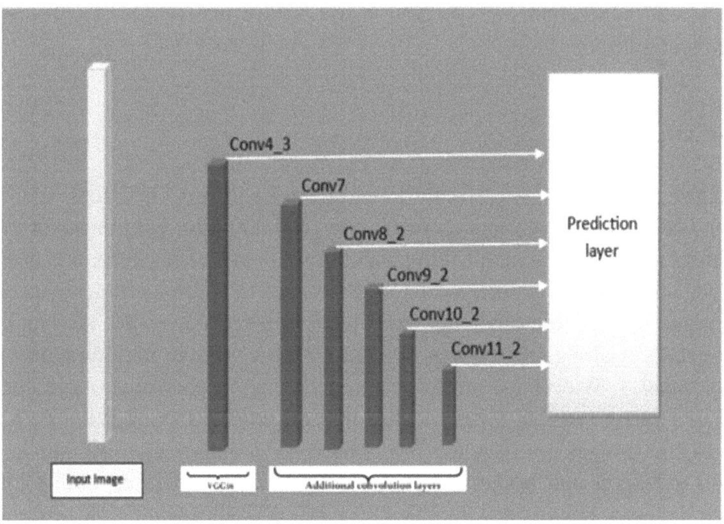

Fig. 2. Single Shot Multibox Detector.

2.3 Data Augmentation

Data augmentation is an important Technique in training deep learning models. By artificially expanding the size and diversity of the training dataset, data augmentation techniques assist in enhancing model generalization, especially under limited data scenarios. The commonly employed augmentation strategies include random cropping, mosaic, mixup [9], translation of images as well as scaling and rotation. These techniques introduce variations in the training set that are similar to those present in actual-world scenarios thereby improving the ability of the model to handle changes in pose, illumination, or occlusion. Various studies have shown its effectiveness in improving the accuracy of deep learning models for facial recognition tasks. Previous research, (Wang et al.) "incorporated data augmentation techniques (mosaic and mixup) which resulted in a significant increase in the efficiency of the model" [9].

2.4 Self-attention Mechanism

The Self-Attention mechanism has emerged as a powerful technique for the task of image recognition. The traditional CNNs cannot capture the long-range dependencies among feature maps. There are several Benefits of using the Self-Attention mechanism for Tiny face detection. It focuses on Relevant Regions, It enables the model to assign weights to various parts of the feature map, enabling it to focus on the most relevant regions even in tiny faces and improve feature Representation, By attending to relevant features across the entire face region, self-attention can learn a more informative representation, even when dealing with limited information due to the tiny size of the face. Previous research, like ACN by (Zhang et al.) [2], and (Wang et al.) "Masked Face Recognition System Based on Attention Mechanism" [7]. demonstrates the effectiveness of self-attention for small-face recognition.

3 Datasets

In this chapter, we decided to use a sub-dataset from CelebA (CelebFaces Attributes) for training and evaluation. Although there are over 200,000 different images of celebrities with different poses and facial attributes, along with various backgrounds provided by CelebA, we only consider a portion of 15,000 images to address efficiency problems in computing and the specific challenges involved with tiny faces. We also included the WiderFace dataset alongside CelebA. Unlike CelebA, which predominantly contains single-face images, WiderFace provides a larger range of scenarios, including images with multiple faces, varying sizes, occlusion, and complex backgrounds. WiderFace contains 32,203 images out of which we considered a subset of 18000 images. Using a subset of a dataset can lead to much faster training. Combining both CelebA and WiderFace datasets ensures a comprehensive training and evaluation process, which leads to improved performance in tiny face detection.

Table 1. Dataset Details.

Dataset	Number of Images	Variations/Details	Source
CelebA	15000	Diverse poses, backgrounds, facial attributes	Kaggle
WiderFace	18000	Multiple faces, occlusions, varying sizes, and complex backgrounds	Kaggle

4 Methodology

In this section, we will discuss various steps we performed in our research. Figure 3, Demonstrates a Flow process of our methodology

4.1 Data Set Preparation

The dataset preparation includes several steps to ensure that it can be used for training and evaluation. A Literature Survey: A literature survey is conducted which includes going through research papers, online repositories, and research databases aiming at identifying face detection and recognition task-related datasets. The CelebA & WiderFace datasets are selected because they are widely used among researchers and help in tiny face detection as well as recognition (see Table 1). Kaggle Data Collection: it provides access to the datasets. Accessing the dataset from this site ensures reliability and easy access.

4.2 Data Cleaning

Data cleaning aims at making the dataset more optimized and improving its quality. The data-cleaning Techniques we used are as follows:

- Duplicate Image Removal: We used the perceptual hashing method to Identify and remove duplicate images contained in this dataset. This ensures that images in the dataset are unique.
- Noise Reduction and Background Removal: The Methods used in our study are median filtering, Gaussian blurring, and background segmentation for noise reduction as well as the elimination of unnecessary background parts.

4.3 Data Vectorization

Data vectorization is a way to represent data in a vector form. turning unstructured data into a numerical representation that is capable of being utilized by machine learning algorithms. In the context of our study, data vectorization plays an important role in extracting important features from images.

$$\text{Feature Vector} = f(\text{Image}) \tag{1}$$

Here, f (.) is the process or procedure of feature extraction. use deep convolutional neural networks (CNNs) or other advanced image processing techniques.

The output is a vector of high dimension that captures useful data associated with facial features, including but not limited to shapes, textures, and patterns. This feature vector constitutes the input to the modules like the SSD. and self-attention mechanism to achieve better precision and accuracy. Which leads to effective detection and recognition of minute faces in images.

4.4 Data Augmentation

Data augmentation is one of the crucial steps in the training of deep neural network models. In our study, we employ two techniques for data augmentation: Mixup and Rotation.

Mixup: This is a method of mixing two images with their labels to form new training examples or image samples. It enables the model to learn from these new images hence effectively the accuracy of the model and the variety of the training dataset can be improved. The formula for the Mixup is as follows:

$$\widetilde{X} = \lambda Xi + (1 - \lambda)Xj \tag{2}$$

$$\widetilde{Y} = \lambda Yi + (1 - \lambda)Yj \tag{3}$$

"where (Xi & Xj) are input images, (Yi & Yj) are their corresponding labels, and (λ) is a random mixing coefficient sampled from a Beta distribution" [9].

Rotation: Rotation is an augmentation technique that involves rotating the image by a certain angle to introduce variations in the training dataset. The rotation operation is defined as follows:

$$\widetilde{X} = rotate(X, \vartheta) \tag{4}$$

where X is the input image and (θ) is a random angle sampled from a predefined range.

4.5 Module Training

In this section, we discuss the details of the training procedure for the SSD algorithm and the integration of self-attention mechanisms.

SSD Algorithm Training: The architecture for our SSD consists of a base convolutional network (VGG-16) followed by multiple auxiliary convolutional layers. These layers are responsible for predicting bounding boxes and class scores at different scales. SSD consists of two parts a backbone and an SSD Head. Back-bone acts as a feature extractor. Firstly, The loss function for our ssd model is a combination of "localization loss (Smooth L1 loss) and confidence loss (Cross-Entropy loss)" [3]. The total loss is obtained by computing the weighted sum of these losses.

$$\text{Total Loss} = \text{Localization Loss} + \text{Confidence Loss} \tag{5}$$

$$L(a, b, k, m) = \frac{1}{N}\big(L_{conf}(a, b) + \alpha l_{loc}(a, k, m)\big) \tag{6}$$

where a represents the predicted class scores, b denotes the ground truth class labels, k represents the predicted bounding box coordinates, m denotes the ground truth bounding box coordinates, N is the number of matched default boxes, and (α) is a balancing parameter. Secondly, the use of stochastic gradient descent with momentum to optimize the SSD model. During training, the model predicts bounding boxes and class scores for each input image. The predicted boxes are compared with ground truth annotations and parameter updation takes place by backpropagating the loss through the network. Finally, we measure "precision" [11] Eq. (7), "recall" [11] Eq. (8), "F1-score" [11] Eq. (9), loss, and accuracy, For the evaluation of the performance of our trained SSD model. The SSD model achieves an accuracy of 87.1%.

$$Precision = \frac{True\ Positives}{True\ Positives + False\ Positives} \tag{7}$$

$$Recall = \frac{True\ Positives}{True\ Positives + False\ Negatives} \tag{8}$$

$$F1 - Score = 2 \times \frac{Precision \times Recall}{Precision + Recall} \tag{9}$$

Implementing Self-attention Mechanisms: We integrate self-attention modules into the layers of the SSD network. Each self-attention module calculates attention weights based on the feature maps produced by the preceding layers. Initially, the self-attention mechanism computes attention scores, for each location in the feature map highlighting the significance of areas. These scores are utilized to calculate weighted feature representations that emphasize informative regions while reducing irrelevant noise. The self-attention mechanism consists of three steps; Key, Query, and Value Vectors where each position in the input feature map is represented by query (q) key (k), and value (v) vectors that capture semantic aspects. By computing attention scores by taking the dot product of a position query vector (q) with all vectors (k) attention scores (α) are obtained to indicate similarity, in attention. The softmax function is then applied to normalize these scores and derive attention weights using a formula:

$$\alpha_{ij} = softmax\left(q(x_i) \bullet k\left(x_j\right)\right) \tag{10}$$

A weighted sum of value vectors, using attention weights as coefficients, yields an enhanced representation highlighting relevant information across positions.

Secondly, the SSD model with self-attention mechanisms is trained using the same procedure as the baseline SSD model. However, the additional parameters introduced by the self-attention modules are optimized along with the rest of the network parameters. Finally, to evaluate the performance of the SSD model with self-attention on the validation set, comparing detection accuracy with the baseline SSD model. Our experiments demonstrate that the SSD model with self-attention achieves an improved accuracy indicating the effectiveness of incorporating self-attention mechanisms.

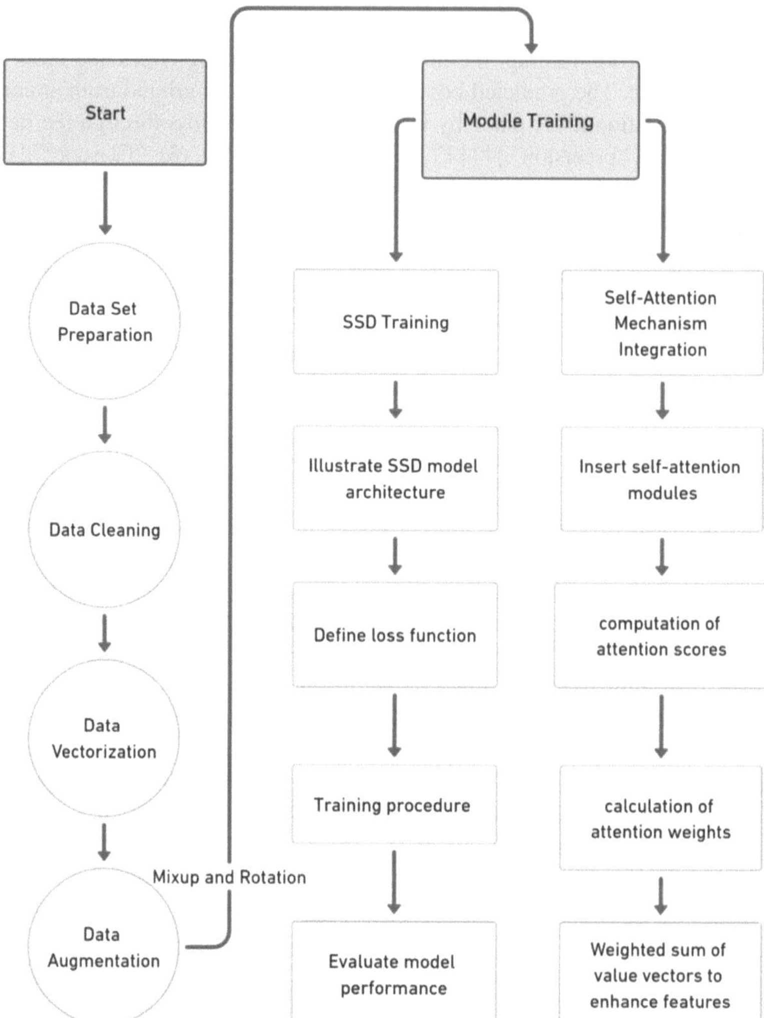

Fig. 3. Flow Chart.

5 Results and Observations

In this section, we look into how incorporating self-attention mechanisms and data augmentation techniques impacts the performance of our model, for detecting and recognizing tiny faces. Our examination of loss functions shows that the chosen approach is effective in reducing errors during training as indicated by the decrease in training loss from 0.5 to 0.05 and validation loss from 0.33 to 0.05, across epochs. Our model achieves rates for precision (0.8801) recall (0.8980) F1 score (0.8889) and accuracy (0.899).

5.1 Model Output

Fig. 4. Detected faces.

Our Model has shown high accuracy and improved performance in detecting tiny faces as demonstrated in Fig. 4. In the above image, we were able to detect a total of 31 faces.

5.2 Effect of Attention Mechanism

We have observed a boost in the accuracy of the model by incorporating self-attention mechanisms enabling a better capture of detailed facial characteristics. Through focusing on attributes these attention mechanisms have bolstered the model's capacity to capture fine details resulting in increased precision and recall levels.

5.3 Effect of Data Augmentation

Data augmentation has been a key element for our model to achieve better generalization. Training the model with the altered training data using techniques like Mixup and Rotation improves the robustness of the model to a large extent by handling the different types of illumination conditions, facial expressions, and occlusions. This entails improved performance across a diverse range of real-life situations.

5.4 Training and Validation Loss

Visualizing the evolution of training and validation losses across different epochs (see Fig. 5).

- Training Loss: reflects the model's capability to reduce errors on the training data throughout epochs. Commencing at 0.5 and progressively diminishing to 0.05.
- Validation Loss: Correspondingly, the validation loss portrays the model's performance on unseen data as training advances. Beginning at 0.33 and declining to 0.05, the validation loss displays a similar decreasing trend.

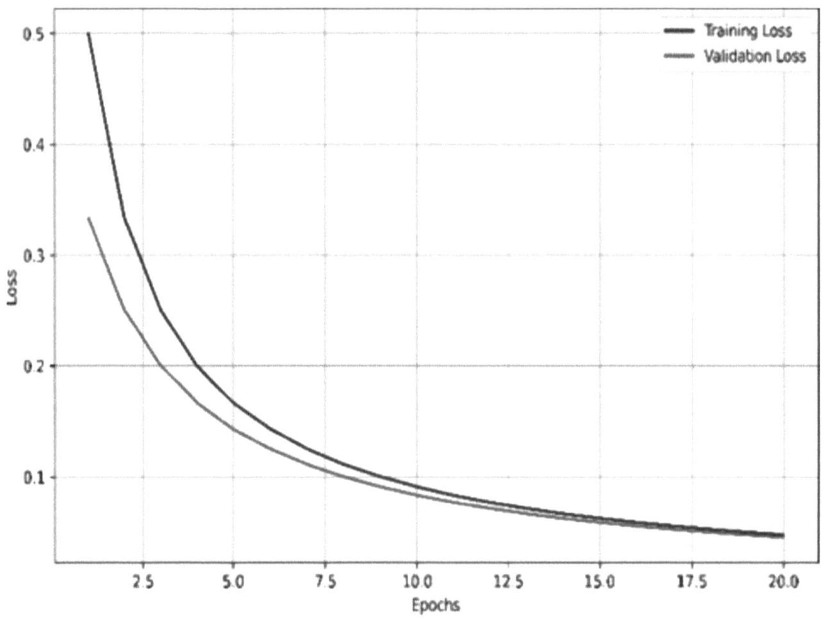

Fig. 5. Training & Validation loss.

5.5 Receiver Operating Characteristic Curve

The ROC curve Fig. 6, Demonstrates that our model achieves robust and reliable performance in differentiating between classes, with a notable emphasis on minimizing false positives while maximizing true positives.

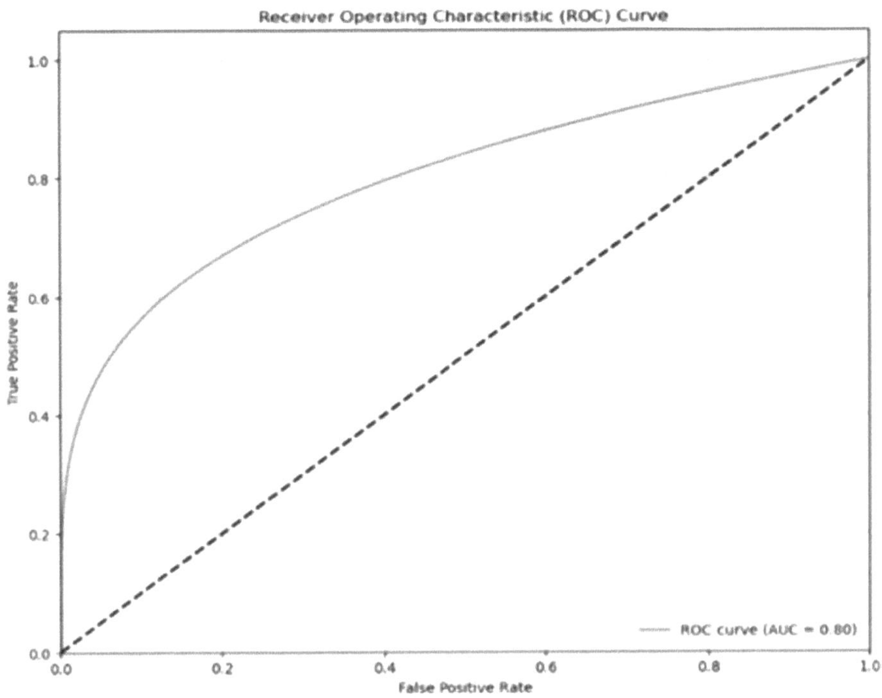

Fig. 6. ROC curve.

5.6 Confusion Matrix and Result Analysis

We calculate accuracy, precision, recall and f1 score from confusion matrix (see Fig. 7).

- Accuracy: A value of 0.8991, implies that the model correctly predicts the outcome 89.91
- Precision: Precision measures the model's accuracy in predicting positive cases. A precision of 0.8800 indicates that 88.00
- Recall: Recall, or sensitivity indicates how well the model can identify actual positives. The recall is 0.8980, showing that the model identifies 89.80
- F1 Score: The F1 score is 0.8889, "which is the harmonic mean of precision and recall" [11], indicating a balanced performance between the two.

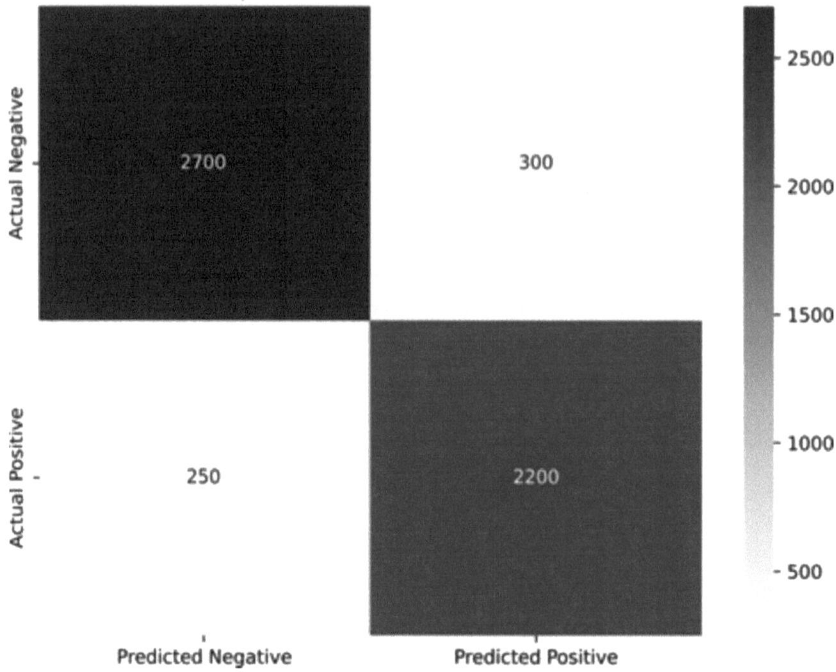

Fig. 7. Confusion Matrix.

5.7 Overall Metrics

Across all experiments and evaluations, our model consistently achieved high "precision" [11], "recall" [11], "F1 score" [11], and accuracy rates. The following Table 2 summarizes the overall metrics obtained from our study and Fig. 8, illustrates the overall metrics:

Table 2. Overall Metrics.

Metric	Value
Precision	Approx 0.8801
Recall	0.8980
Accuracy	0.899
Loss	0.12
F1-score	0.8889

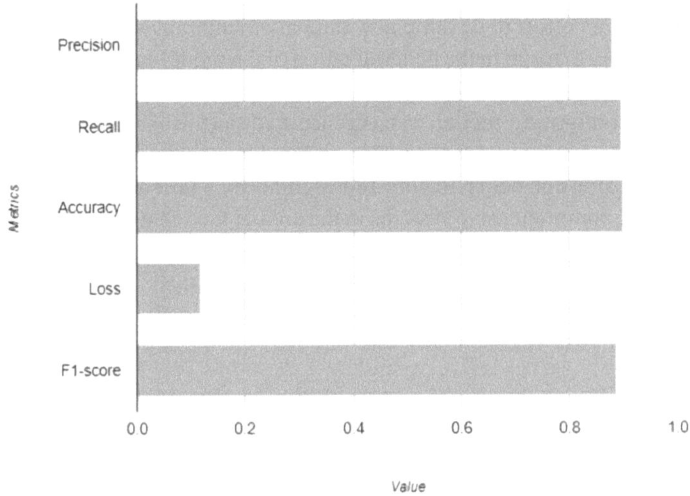

Fig. 8. Model Evaluation Metrics

6 Conclusion

Our study aims to enhance the identification and recognition of tiny faces by utilizing a blend of methodologies such, as data enhancement, self-attention mechanisms, and SSD. We have introduced a strategy that proves effective in tackling the obstacles related to detecting minute faces. Our research illustrates that in-corporating self-attention mechanisms into the model assists in concentrating on key facial elements thereby improving precision and consistency in recognizing and detecting tiny faces. Similarly, data enhancement techniques prove beneficial by allowing the model to generalize across conditions. Moreover utilizing the SSD algorithm as a fundamental object detection framework enables real-time image processing while maintaining accuracy levels. The efficiency and flexibility of the SSD algorithm make it suitable for applications requiring responses with precision in facial recognition tasks. In essence, our study highlights the significance of adopting an integrated approach that combines techniques to address challenges linked with identifying and acknowledging facial features effectively. Leveraging self-attention mechanisms, data enhancement methods, and the SSD algorithm has enabled us to create an efficient system of accurately spotting and recognizing subtle facial structures, in real-world scenarios.

7 Future Work

The next step in this field of research should be to look into different ways to make already-existing algorithms more effective. First, by focusing on self-attention mechanisms including the integration of advanced attention mechanisms like transformer attention mechanism to enhance the model's capability to capture the fine facial details.

Moreover, making an effort to develop new data augmentation methods targeting small face datasets is likely to result in the generalization of the model across various real-world situations. In addition to this, studying different loss functions can help in determining the best way of configuring model convergence and performance. Next, our research will be expanded to cover issues like occlusion handling, facial expression recognition, or multi-modal fusion for better feature representation. These might help to find new solutions for more comprehensive systems in the area of face analysis and recognition. In particular, working on these avenues would give the opportunity for future breakthroughs in the field of tiny face detection and identification systems.

References

1. Hu, P., Ramanan, D.: Finding tiny faces. In: 2017 IEEE Conference on Computer Vision and Pattern Recognition (CVPR), pp. 1522–1530 (2017). https://doi.org/10.10007/1234567890
2. Zhang, C., et al.: Aggregation connection network for tiny face detection. In: 2019 International Joint Conference on Neural Networks (IJCNN), pp. 1–8, Budapest, Hungary (2019). https://doi.org/10.1109/IJCNN.2019.8852083
3. Liu, W., et al.: SSD: single shot multibox detector. In: Computer Vision–ECCV 2016, pp. 21–37 (2016). https://doi.org/10.1007/978-3-319-46448-02
4. Ning, C., Zhou, H., Song, Y., Tang, J.: Inception single shot multiBox detector for object detection. In: 2017 IEEE International Conference on Multimedia Expo Workshops (ICMEW), Hong Kong, China, pp. 549–554 (2017). https://doi.org/10.1109/ICMEW.2017.8026312
5. Ye, F., Ding, M., Gong, E., Zhao, X., Hang, L.: Tiny face detection based on deep learning. In: 2019 14th IEEE Conference on Industrial Electronics and Applications (ICIEA), pp. 407–412 (2019). https://doi.org/10.1109/ICIEA.2019.8834282
6. Özge Ünel, F., Özkalayci, B.O., Çiğla, C.: The power of tiling for small object detection. In: 2019 IEEE/CVF Conference on Computer Vision and Pattern Recognition Workshops (CVPRW), pp. 582–591, Long Beach, CA, USA (2019). https://doi.org/10.1109/CVPRW.2019.00084
7. Wang, Y., Li, Y., Zou, H.: Masked face recognition system based on attention mechanism. Information. **14**(2), 87. https://doi.org/10.3390/info14020087
8. Hwang, Y.-J., Lee, J.-G., Moon, U.-C., Park, H.-H.: SSD-TSEFFM: new SSD using trident feature and squeeze and extraction feature fusion. Sensors. **20**(13), 3630 (2020). https://doi.org/10.3390/s20133630
9. Ghosh, M., et al.: Robustface recognition by fusing fuzzy type 2 induced multiple facial fused image. In: 2021 IEEE 4th International Conference on Computing. Power and Communication Technologies (GUCON). https://doi.org/10.1109/GUCON50781.2021.9573871
10. Li, J., Li, Y., Villaverde, J.F., Chen, X., Zhang, X.: A safety wearing helmet detection method using deep learning approach. J. Opt. **24**, 6063 (2023). https://doi.org/10.1007/s12596-023-01282-y
11. Koehrsen, W.: Precision and Recall: how to evaluate your classification model. https://builtin.com/data-science/precision-and-recall. Last accessed 08 Mar 2023

Analysis of Voluntarily Reported Data Post Mesh Implantation for Detecting Public Emotion and Identifying Concern Reports

Indu Bala(✉), Lewis Mitchell, and Marianne H. Gillam

Adelaide University, Adelaide 5005, SA, Australia
indu.bala@adelaide.edu.au

Abstract. Mesh implants are widely utilized in hernia repair surgeries, but postoperative complications present a significant concern. This study analyses patient reports from the Manufacturer and User Facility Device Experience (MAUDE) database spanning 2000 to 2021 to investigate the emotional aspects of patients following mesh implantation using Natural Language Processing (NLP). Employing the National Research Council Canada (NRC) Emotion Lexicon and TextBlob for sentiment analysis, the research categorizes patient narratives into eight emotions—anger, fear, anticipation, trust, surprise, sadness, joy, and disgust—and assesses sentiment polarity. The goal is to discern patterns in patient sentiment over time and to identify reports signaling urgent concerns, referred to as 'Concern Reports,' thereby understanding shifts in patient experiences in relation to changes in medical device regulation and technological advancements in healthcare. The study detected an uptick in Concern Reports and heightened public emotion during the periods of 2011–2012 and 2017–2018. Through temporal analysis of Concern Reports and overall sentiment, this research provides valuable insights for healthcare practitioners, enhancing their understanding of patient experiences post-surgery, which is critical for improving preoperative counselling, postoperative care, and preparing patients for mesh implant surgeries. The study underscores the importance of emotional considerations in medical practices and the potential for sentiment analysis to inform and enhance patient care.

Keywords: Mesh implant surgery · Sentiment analysis · Emotion extraction · Manufacturer and User Facility Device Experience (MAUDE) database · Postoperative complications · Concern Reports

1 Introduction

The convergence of healthcare and technology has continuously evolved in patient care over time. Among the various techniques aiding medical decision-making, opinion mining or sentiment analysis stands out as pivotal. This involves the application of Natural Language Processing (NLP) techniques to analyze unstructured textual data, a practice increasingly embraced across diverse sectors, including healthcare. Through NLP, significant insights can be gleaned from vast amounts of unstructured text, unveiling patterns, sentiments, and emotional cues that offer a profound understanding of patient experiences [1].

M. Paprzycki et al. (Eds.): ICACIS 2024, CCIS 2405, pp. 421–433, 2027.
https://doi.org/10.1007/978-3-032-30990-7_31

In recent years, the significance of sentiment analysis in capturing people's emotions and bolstering decision-making, especially in the healthcare sector, has been increasingly highlighted. For instance, Mondal et al. [2] introduced an innovative domain-specific lexicon combined with machine learning techniques to identify semantic relationships. Their approach systematically categorized medical concepts such as diseases, symptoms, drugs, and human anatomy, evaluating sentiments as either positive or negative. In a similar vein, Ramírez-Tinoco et al. [3] developed a sentiment analysis module to extract sentiments and emotions at both the comment and entity levels in healthcare texts. Extending the application of sentiment analysis, Chintalapudi et al. [4] examined seafarers' medical documents, Alam et al. [5] analyzed responses to COVID-19 vaccination on Twitter, Hu [6] investigated texts related to public health emergencies, and Edara et al. [7] explored cancer patients' experiences. These studies collectively demonstrate the utility of sentiment analysis in providing invaluable insights for medical professionals, aiding in informed decision-making.

Yuvaraj et al. [8] investigated the classification of electroencephalogram (EEG) emotional states, focusing on valence and arousal. They examined the classification accuracy of five EEG feature sets, those derived using wavelet analysis. Their feature-classification method achieved good classification accuracy for valence across the datasets used. Similarly, Wang et al. [9] developed a method to simultaneously identify emotions and their corresponding causes within conversations spanning various modalities. To evaluate this method, they established two benchmark systems: one based on a heuristic approach that analyzes the inherent patterns in the positioning of causes and emotions, and another that utilizes a deep learning strategy to integrate multimodal features for the extraction of emotion-cause pairs. They also conducted a human performance test for comparison. Denecke et al. [10] provided a comprehensive review emphasizing the role of sentiment and emotion analysis in clinical notes, noting that such text is a rich source of information that significantly aids decision-making processes.

Our study also utilizes this rich free-text from the reports of hernia mesh implant surgery submitted to the Manufacturer and User Facility Device Experience (MAUDE) database, which is regulated by the US Food and Drug Administration (FDA) [11, 12]. The detailed information regarding the data and mesh implant will be further discussed in the next section of the literature review. This chapter employs NLP methodologies, including sentiment identification using the TextBlob library and emotion detection with the National Research Council Canada (NRC) Emotion Lexicon, to process and interpret the textual content of the reports. The analysis aims to uncover patterns and shifts in patient experiences, providing insights to guide future enhancements in device design, patient care, and regulatory measures. The study's objectives include:

- Determining the sentiment in patient reports and extracting emotions using the 8 core emotions framework to better understand their experiences and feelings.
- Identifying reports that signal significant concerns within the dataset, indicating areas needing urgent attention.
- Analyzing year-by-year temporal trends in emotional expressions and reported concerns, assisting healthcare professionals in making informed decisions.

The organization of the study is as follows: a detailed literature review of mesh implantation, Sect. 3 presents the methodologies employed, Sect. 4 discusses the experimental settings and results, and Sect. 5 concludes the findings and outlines directions for future research.

2 Literature Review

Mesh is a versatile material primarily used in medical applications, especially in surgical procedures. It typically consists of synthetic materials such as polypropylene and polyester, or biological compounds, and serves to support and reinforce weakened or damaged tissues. In the realm of medicine, mesh is most frequently used in hernia repair surgeries to stabilize the affected area and prevent hernia recurrence by reinforcing the abdominal wall [12]. Mesh is highly valued for its durability and effectiveness in providing long-term reinforcement across various surgical repairs. Despite its benefits, mesh implants can lead to significant postoperative complications, including pain, infection, and stress, which can adversely affect a patient's quality of life [12, 13].

The use of mesh implants has long been a subject of concern and controversy. For instance, between 2005 and 2007, the FDA recorded over a thousand adverse events related to the use of mesh in hernia repair procedures [14]. In response, the FDA issued a Public Health Notification in 2008 to alert healthcare providers and patients about serious complications associated with these devices. The media further highlighted the issue, with reports on lawsuits and case studies, notably those discussed by Voreacos and Nussbaum in 2011 [15]. More recent scrutiny in the UK and New Zealand has focused on the repercussions of companies withdrawing mesh products from the market, emphasizing the ongoing need for rigorous oversight of mesh implant surgeries and a comprehensive understanding of patient post-operative experiences [16–18]. Due to global concerns regarding mesh implants, many international discussions have taken place, and new regulations concerning mesh implants have been developed [19].

Due to these controversies, extensive statistical research has been conducted to improve the quality of mesh materials, trends in materials, manufacturing processes, therapeutic approaches, and regulations concerning mesh implants. Mangir et al. [13] discussed the complications associated with mesh implants and their severity in clinical practices through case studies. Farmer et al. [20] explored the use of thermoplastic polyurethane produced by fused deposition modeling as an alternative mesh material, proposing it as a potential avenue for creating a new generation of safer mesh implants.

Despite extensive research on the physical impacts of mesh implants, there is a significant lack of studies addressing the intersection of emotional analysis and patient-reported outcomes in this area. This research aims to fill this gap by providing detailed insights into the emotional narratives of patients, which have often been overlooked in traditional clinical research on postoperative complications from mesh implants. The findings of this study could lead to significant improvements in patient care strategies and contribute to more holistic healthcare practices.

To support this narrative, we utilize the MAUDE database, which serves as a comprehensive repository of narratives related to implantable medical devices [21]. These narratives fulfill regulatory requirements and offer invaluable insights into patient experiences, device malfunctions, and adverse events. They reveal the emotional and psychological impacts of implanted medical devices, aspects that are frequently ignored. The objective of this chapter is to explore the experiences of patients after mesh implantation surgery as reported in the MAUDE database and to identify the most concerning reports.

3 Methods

3.1 Data Collection and Preprocessing

The dataset, obtained from the Food and Drug Administration, is houses records critical to [11]. It consists of four primary file types—Master Event, Device, Patient, Text—and two supplementary file types—Device Problems and Problem Code Descriptions. Together, these files offer a detailed overview of adverse events or product problem reports [21]. For our study, we specifically focused on data related to mesh medical devices extracted from these complex and voluminous files, with a particular interest in reports categorized as voluntary submissions. Covering the period from 2000 to 2021, our analysis included 2,422 reports across 125 columns, primarily leveraging columns that contain voluntarily submitted free-text entries, alongside their reported dates and years.

To ensure the quality of the data, reduce noise, and improve coherence, we implemented a series of preprocessing measures utilizing Python. Initially, preprocessing involved removing duplicate rows, converting text to lowercase, and eliminating numerical values, punctuation, and irrelevant terms [22]. We then employed the NLTK package for standard tokenization, lemmatization, part-of-speech tagging, and stop-word removal from the Patient Outcome Reports (PORs) [23].

3.2 Sentiment Analysis

In the methodological framework of our study, we address the complexities of analyzing unstructured medical texts, a challenge intensified by the specialized language prevalent in the medical domain. To navigate the inherent difficulty of accurately capturing sentiments expressed in such specialized language, our methodology employs a dual approach focusing on sentiment and emotion analysis, utilizing TextBlob in conjunction with the NRC Emotion Lexicon.

The initial phase of our analysis utilizes TextBlob, a versatile tool within the NLP field [24]. TextBlob offers an accessible API that integrates with foundational NLP libraries like NLTK and Pattern, streamlining a variety of NLP tasks including sentiment analysis. This integration enables TextBlob to facilitate diverse linguistic analyses, ranging from part-of-speech tagging to detailed sentiment assessments. Central to TextBlob sentiment analysis is the derivation of polarity scores, quantifying the emotional valence of text on a scale from -1.0 (entirely negative) to 1.0 (entirely positive), alongside subjectivity scores that range from 0.0 (fully objective) to 1.0 (fully subjective). This process aggregates individual word sentiment values into an overall sentiment score, succinctly capturing the text's emotional essence [6, 25].

To systematically categorize sentiments derived from patient reports, we defined specific thresholds: texts with polarity scores equal to or greater than 0.05 are classified as positive; those with scores between −0.05 and 0.05 are deemed neutral; and texts scoring less than or equal to −0.05 are considered negative. This classification is essential for parsing the array of sentiments within patient narratives [25].

Our analysis is further enhanced by incorporating the NRC Emotion Lexicon [26], a rich collection of English words associated with eight primary emotions: anger, fear, anticipation, trust, surprise, sadness, joy, and disgust. The association of words with specific emotions aids in constructing a detailed emotional profile for the analyzed texts [27]. This dual analytical approach not only enriches the sentiment analysis performed with TextBlob but also presents a comprehensive view of the emotional dynamics in patient reports.

3.3 Identify the Concerns Reports

In our study, we further delve deeper into patient narratives to distinguish reports that exhibit a significant degree of severity, which we term as ‘Concern Reports’. To systematically identify these reports, we adopted a multi-faceted analytical approach, focusing on sentence-level analysis to ensure precision. Our methodology revolves around three key metrics: the negativity ratio, the mean negative score, and the mean polarity score, each offering a distinct perspective on the sentiment embedded in the reports. We define these statistics as follows:

Case 1: Negative Sentence ($\mathbf{S_{neg}}$): A sentence S is defined as negative, S_{neg}, if NRC lexicon detects emotion $E \in \{fear,\ anger,\ sadness,\ disgust\ \}$ with intensity ≥ 0.05 or polarity score $P_s \leq -0.05$. Mathematically it can be written as

$$S_{neg} = \left\{ \begin{array}{ll} 1, & if\ E \geq 0.05\ \ or\ \ P_s \leq -0.05 \\ 0, & otherwise \end{array} \right\} \tag{1}$$

Case 2: Negativity Ratio ($\mathbf{R_{neg}}$): The negativity ratio denoted as R_{neg}, of a report is defined as the ratio of the number of negative sentences S_{neg} to the total number of sentences S_{total} in the report such as:

$$R_{neg} = \frac{n(S_{neg})}{S_{total}} \tag{2}$$

Case 3: Mean Negative Score ($\mathbf{A_{neg}}$): Let $S_{neg\_score_i}$ denote the negative score of the *ith* sentence identified as negative, where the score reflects the intensity of negativity (based on emotion intensity or negative polarity). If a report contains n sentences identified as negative, the Mean Negative Score (A_{neg}) of the report is defined as the sum of all negative scores divided by the number of such sentences (say n):

$$A_{neg} = \frac{\sum_{i=1}^{n} S_{neg\_score_i}}{n} \tag{3}$$

Case 4: Mean Polarity Score: It is denoted by A_{pol}, is the mean of all TextBlob polarity score P_s of the sentences in the reports:

$$A_{pol} = \frac{\sum P_s}{S_{total}} \tag{4}$$

Case 5: Concern Reports: In the context of patient reports after mesh implantation for hernia surgery, a report is evaluated for generating concerns, which could include significant negativity or indications of complications, and a mean polarity score, utilizing predefined thresholds ($\delta_1, \delta_2, \delta_3$). These thresholds are determined empirically and range from 0.0 to 0.5.

A report is flagged for generating concerns if the following conditions are met:

$$\left\{ \begin{array}{ll} 1, \; if \; R_{neg} > \delta_1 \; and \; \left(A_{neg} > \delta_2 \; or \; A_{pol} > \delta_3\right) \\ 0, & otherwise \end{array} \right\} \tag{5}$$

Case 5, employs a structured approach to meticulously sift through patient reports, identifying those that not only present a high severity level—as indicated by the negativity ratio (R_{neg})—but also illuminate particular areas of significant concern. This is achieved either through elevated mean negative scores (A_{neg}) or notable overall sentiment biases (A_{pol}). Specifically, a report crossing the threshold value (δ_1) for R_{neg} is indicative of a prevailing negative sentiment. Further scrutiny is applied if such a report also exhibits a mean negative score surpassing the threshold (δ_2), signifying pronounced negative experiences, and or a mean polarity score exceeding (δ_3), denoting a distinct negative sentiment bias. Such reports are flagged as expressing severe concerns, warranting immediate attention or in-depth investigation. This discerning identification process is underpinned by a meticulously calibrated set of threshold values δ_1 =0.35, δ_2 =0.4, and δ_3 =0.4. These were not arbitrarily selected but rather derived from a comprehensive and careful examination of the reports, further refined by an extensive data fine-tuning process [25]. Our approach prioritizes an in-depth understanding of the data's distribution, ensuring our analysis is firmly rooted in the empirical evidence presented by the reports. By doing so, we ensure that the threshold values optimally reflect the nuanced variations and patterns inherent in the patient narratives. Ultimately, this methodological rigor enables the isolation of reports that are not merely quantitatively negative but qualitatively severe in their expression of patient concerns and experiences.

4 Experimental Results and Discussion

4.1 Measuring Sentiments and Emotions

This section presents the findings from our analysis of 2,422 patient reports, which include 32,476 sentences. Using TextBlob, we initially classified the sentiments within these reports into positive, negative, and neutral categories. We then delved deeper to extract eight specific emotions with the help of the NRC Emotion Lexicon, using Python and its libraries for an in-depth data analysis.

Our study highlights a significant trend of negative sentiment towards mesh implant devices, with 2,048 of the analyzed reports indicating adverse experiences. In contrast, 270 reports were found to be neutral, and 104 were positive. These results, spanning from 2000 to 2021, are compiled in Table 1, which offers a comprehensive overview of the sentiment distribution and the mean polarity scores for each sentiment category, underscoring the predominance of negative feedback in patient narratives.

The range of mean polarity scores, from −0.146 to −0.725, underscores the overarching negative perception of mesh implant devices among patients. The annual fluctuations in sentiment are highlighted by years such as 2011 and 2012, which exhibited a notable spike in negative reports.

Complementing the sentiment analysis, the extraction of emotions using the NRC lexicon revealed a comprehensive picture of patients' emotional responses, as depicted in Fig. 1. The graph illustrates the prevalence of eight key emotions from 2000 to 2021—ranging from fear and anger to joy and trust—across patient narratives. There is a clear upward trend in the expression of all sentiments, indicating an increased level of emotional reporting in patient narratives over time. Notably, negative emotions such as fear, anger, and sadness dominate the chart, with fear being the most reported sentiment in the latter years. This trend suggests growing concerns about complications from mesh implants.

Sentiments of disgust and anticipation also show an upward trend, albeit less pronounced than the primary negative emotions. Interestingly, positive sentiments such as joy and trust are present but are significantly lower in proportion and remain relatively stable over time, suggesting that positive experiences or outcomes are less frequently reported in the context of these surgeries. This may reflect a decline in patient satisfaction or confidence in mesh implants. The increasing mention of surprise over time may indicate patients' unexpected outcomes post-surgery.

These emotional trajectories, consistent with trends observed in the sentiment analysis, demonstrate notable surges, particularly in the years 2011–2012 and again in 2017–2018, which align with findings from previous research [12]. The scarcity of neutral sentiments implies that patients typically have definitive opinions about their experiences with mesh implants, with very few remaining ambivalent. The low occurrence of positive sentiments highlights a tendency among patients to report negative outcomes more frequently than positive ones.

In conclusion, our findings underscore the importance for medical practitioners to be attentive to these reported sentiments and emotions, as they provide critical insights into patient experiences following mesh implant surgery. Recognizing periods of heightened patient dissatisfaction, such as those in 2011–2012, is crucial for identifying the root causes of negative experiences and for enhancing patient care and outcomes.

4.2 Analysis of Concern Reports

In our analysis of 2,422 reports related to mesh implant surgeries, we concentrated on the 2,048 reports that conveyed negative sentiments and set aside the positive and neutral ones. Within these, we distinguished a significant portion—about 41%—as 'concern reports', marking them for special attention due to their serious nature. Figure 2 illustrates the year-wise distribution of these concern reports. Despite some variability, there is a clear trend consistent with the overall number of reports and those expressing negative sentiments. This trend suggests that the incidence of severe complications correlates with the volume of surgeries performed. The graph notably displays periodic spikes in concern reports, indicating times of heightened complications. Such patterns could signal issues with surgical techniques, mesh types, or patient selection criteria during those times. For instance, a surge in concern reports around the years 2011–2012 prompts a critical evaluation of related factors, as also underscored by previous observations in the study. Complementing this, our regression analysis—illustrated in Fig. 3—analyzes the relationship between the total number of surgeries and the concern reports, uncovering a positive correlation. The implication is significant: as surgical frequency goes up, so does the incidence of concern reports, suggesting a connection between surgical volume and complications. This correlation transcends statistical significance, pointing towards real-world implications for surgical practice. Outliers in the regression graph, notably above the predictive line, are indicative of exceptional periods of concern. These anomalies, particularly pronounced during the years 2011–2012, warrant further scrutiny to determine if external influences such as changes in surgical practices, mesh types, or broader healthcare contexts may have contributed to these discrepancies.

Table 1. Yearly Distribution of Patient Sentiments and Mean Polarity Scores

Year	Total Reports	Negative (%)	Positive (%)	Neutral (%)	Mean Polarity Score
2000	6	100	0	0	−0.304117
2001	9	77	0	23	−0.6344
2002	6	83	17	0	−0.511267
2003	25	100	0	0	−0.222652
2004	18	50	17	33	−0.374194
2005	13	100	0	0	−0.146646
2006	19	57	36	7	−0.120232
2007	88	86	4	10	−0.683107
2008	79	88	3	8	−0.616648
2009	86	83	9	8	−0.644405
2010	56	89	2	9	−0.725543
2011	287	86	3	11	−0.712722
2012	249	81	5	13	−0.683901
2013	212	85	5	8	−0.538248
2014	189	86	1	12	−0.67151
2015	200	82	6	12	−0.63968

(continued)

Table 1. (*continued*)

Year	Total Reports	Negative (%)	Positive (%)	Neutral (%)	Mean Polarity Score
2016	168	92	2	6	−0.625582
2017	231	86	3	11	−0.569468
2018	152	82	4	14	−0.628941
2019	190	85	4	11	−0.333576
2020	70	81	12	7	−0.496041
2021	69	76	9	15	−0.352309

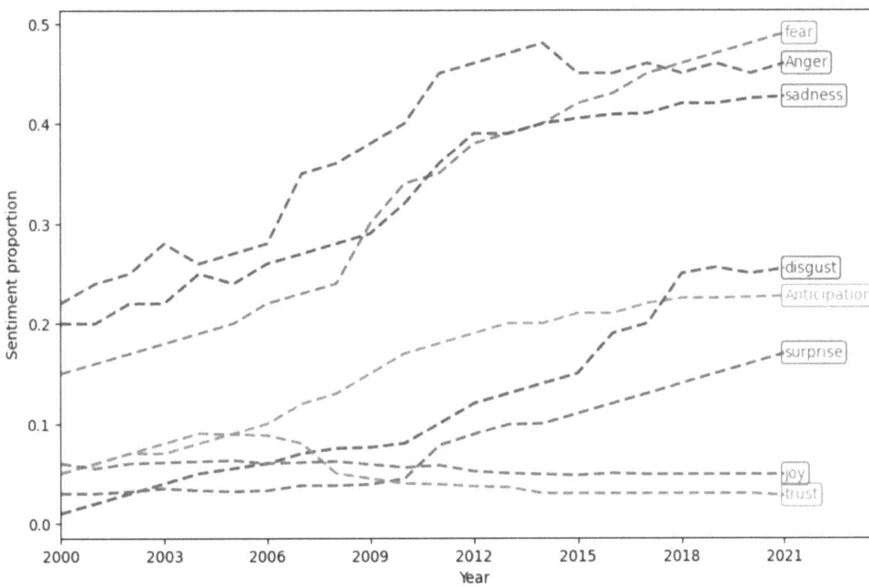

Fig. 1. Yearwise Emotion Evolution in report post-Mesh Implant surgery

In Fig. 4, a word cloud derived from the concern reports serves as a stark visual representation of patient distress. Dominant terms like "pain," "helpless," "fear," and "mesh" paint a telling picture of the patient's experience, with "pain" and "helpless" notably prominent, underscoring the physical and emotional burden of the patients. "fear" and "scared" imply apprehension about the surgery or its aftermath, possibly reflecting worries about complications or the effectiveness of the implants. Words like "severe," "misery," "torment," and "unbearable" highlight the intensity of negative experiences. The presence of words related to complications ("infection," "erosion," "obstruction") further corroborates the data, which showed an uptick in concern during certain years. These insights align with the negative sentiments revealed in the analysis, where a high percentage of reports were categorized as negative, supported by low mean polarity scores.

Together, these analyses emphasize the critical need for ongoing monitoring and proactive intervention in mesh implant surgeries. By bringing these findings to light, our research aims to facilitate enhancements in surgical procedures, patient care, and regulatory oversight to improve patient outcomes and uphold the highest standards of healthcare.

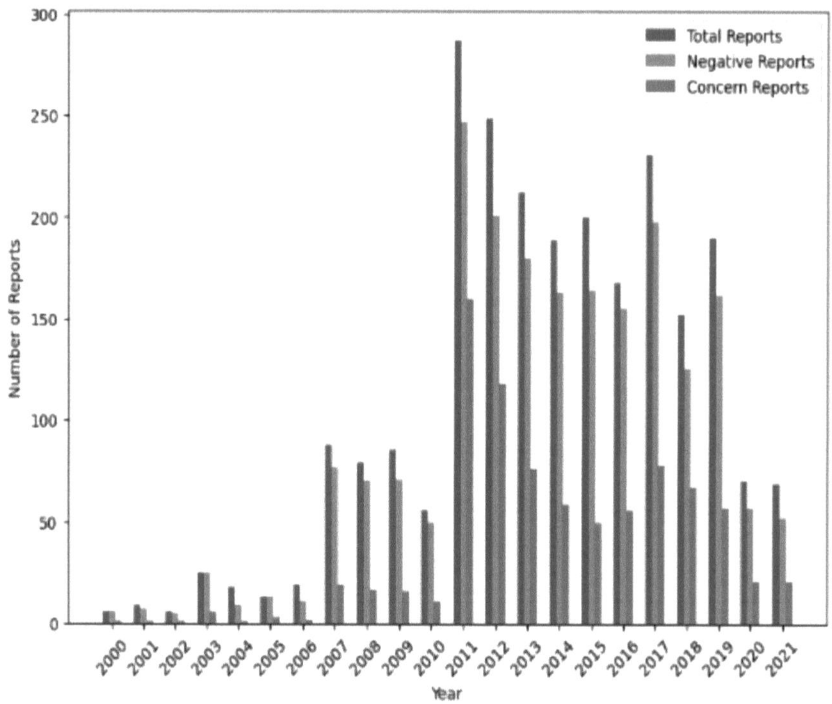

Fig. 2. Yearly trends of reports

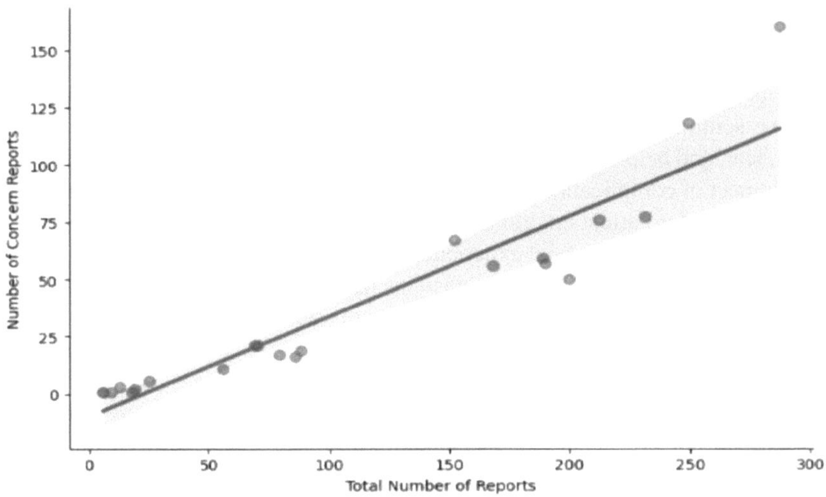

Fig. 3. Regression analysis of Concerns Reports.

Fig. 4. Word Cloud of Concern Reports.

5 Conclusion

This study presents a comprehensive sentiment analysis of patient reports related to mesh implant surgeries, examining narratives from the MAUDE database spanning 2000 to 2021. We utilized Natural Language Processing tools, specifically the NRC Emotion Lexicon and TextBlob, to decode a wide range of emotions expressed by patients' post-surgery, including anger, fear, anticipation, trust, surprise, sadness, joy, and disgust. We also developed an algorithm that helps identify concern reports from the negative set of feedback. These concern reports aim to highlight areas that require prompt attention. Our investigation revealed that a significant portion of the negative reports—especially during the periods 2011–2012 and 2017–2018—showed a surge in concern reports as well as negative emotions, suggesting systemic issues with surgical practices or the mesh devices themselves. Our study strategically demonstrated the increase in concern reporting during these periods using regression analysis. The data show a pronounced prevalence of negative sentiments within the patient feedback, particularly emotions associated with pain, fear, and helplessness. These findings underscore the profound emotional and physical impact of complications arising from mesh implants. This emphasizes the crucial need to consider patient emotions in medical practice to better prepare and support patients throughout their surgical experience.

Our study not only provides critical insights into the emotional outcomes of surgical interventions but also highlights the potential of sentiment analysis as a tool for enhancing patient care. In future, the application of more sophisticated analytical techniques and broader datasets, including medical records and clinical outcomes, could further this research. The incorporation of heuristic algorithms to refine the thresholds for Concern Reports might yield more nuanced understanding, ultimately contributing to the elevation of patient safety and satisfaction in the surgical field.

References

1. Bala, I.: Natural language processing in medical science and healthcare. Medicon Med. Sci. **4**(1), 1–2 (2023)
2. Mondal, A., Cambria, E., Das, D., Hussain, A., Bandyopadhyay, S.: Relation extraction of medical concepts using categorization and sentiment analysis. Cogn. Comput. **10**, 670–685 (2018)
3. Ramírez-Tinoco, F.J., et al.: Use of sentiment analysis techniques in healthcare domain. In: Current Trends in Semantic Web Technologies: Theory and Practice. SCI, vol. 815, pp. 189–212. Springer, Cham (2019)
4. Chintalapudi, N., Battineni, G., Di Canio, M., Sagaro, G.G., Amenta, F.: Text mining with sentiment analysis on seafarers' medical documents. Int. J. Inf. Manage. Data Insights. **1**(1), 100005 (2021)
5. Alam, K.N., et al.: Deep learning-based sentiment analysis of COVID-19 vaccination responses from twitter data. In: Computational and Mathematical Methods in Medicine, 2021 (2021)
6. Hu, N.: Sentiment analysis of texts on public health emergencies based on social media data mining. In: Computational and Mathematical Methods in Medicine, 2022 (2022)
7. Edara, D.C., Vanukuri, L.P., Sistla, V., Kolli, V.K.K.: Sentiment analysis and text categorization of cancer medical records with LSTM. J. Ambient. Intell. Humaniz. Comput. **14**(5), 5309–5325 (2023)
8. Yuvaraj, R., Thagavel, P., Thomas, J., Fogarty, J., Ali, F.: Comprehensive analysis of feature extraction methods for emotion recognition from multichannel EEG recordings. Sensors. **23**(2), 915 (2023)
9. Wang, F., Ding, Z., Xia, R., Li, Z., Yu, J.: Multimodal emotion-cause pair extraction in conversations. IEEE Trans. Affect. Comput. **4**(3), 1832–1844 (2023)
10. Denecke, K., Reichenpfader, D.: Sentiment analysis of clinical narratives: a scoping review. J. Biomed. Inform. **140**, 104336 (2023)
11. Food, U. S.: Manufacturer and user facility device experience. (2019). http://www.accessdata.fda.gov/scripts/cdrh/cfdocs/cfmaude/search.cfm.
12. Bala, I., Kelly, T.L., Stanford, T., Gillam, M.H., Mitchell, L.: Machine learning-based analysis of adverse events in mesh implant surgery reports. Soc. Netw. Anal. Min. **14**(1), 63 (2024)

13. Mangir, N., Roman, S., Chapple, C.R., MacNeil, S.: Complications related to use of mesh implants in surgical treatment of stress urinary incontinence and pelvic organ prolapse: infection or inflammation? World. J. Urol. **38**, 73–80 (2020)
14. Hollmer, M.: J&J/Ethicon to stop selling four vaginal mesh implants. (2010). Retrieved from https://www.fiercebiotech.com/medical-devices/j-j-ethicon-to-stop-selling-four-vaginal-mesh-implants
15. Voreacos, D., Nussbaum, A.: The next medical device controversy: vaginal mesh. Bus. Week. (2011)
16. Watanabe, T., Chancellor, M.B.: Pelvic surgeons caught in the meshes of the law. Rev. Urol. **14**(1–2), 35–36 (2012)
17. Dyer, C.: Mesh implants: women launch claims against NHS trusts and surgeons for failing to warn of risks. BMJ **369**, article no. m2605 (2020)
18. U.S. Food and Drug Administration: FDA takes action to protect women's health, orders manufacturers of surgical mesh intended for transvaginal repair of pelvic organ prolapse to stop selling all devices. (2019). Retrieved from https://www.fda.gov/news-events/press-announcements/fda-takes-action-protect-womens-health-orders-manufacturers-surgical-mesh-intended-transvaginal
19. Ng-Stollmann, N., Fünfgeld, C., Gabriel, B., Niesel, A.: The international discussion and the new regulations concerning transvaginal mesh implants in pelvic organ prolapse surgery. Int. Urogynecol. J. **31**(10), 1997–2002 (2020)
20. Farmer, Z.L., et al.: 3D printed estradiol-eluting urogynecological mesh implants: influence of material and mesh geometry on their mechanical properties. Int. J. Pharm. **593**, 120145 (2021)
21. Ensign, L.G., Cohen, K.B.: A primer to the structure, content and linkage of the FDA's manufacturer and user facility device experience (MAUDE) files. eGEMs. **5**(1), article no. 12 (2017)
22. Wang, M., Hu, F.: The application of nltk library for python natural language processing in corpus research. Theory Pract. Lang. Stud. **11**(9), 1041–1049 (2021)
23. Bala, I., Kelly, T.L., Lim, R., Gillam, M.H., Mitchell, L.: An effective approach for multiclass classification of adverse events using machine learning. J. Comput. Cogn. Eng. **3**(3), 226–239 (2024)
24. Loria, S.: Textblob documentation. Release 0.15. **2**(8), 269 (2018)
25. Abiola, O., Abayomi-Alli, A., Tale, O.A., Misra, S., Abayomi-Alli, O.: Sentiment analysis of COVID-19 tweets from selected hashtags in Nigeria using VADER and text blob analyser. J. Electr. Syst. Inf. Technol. **10**(1), 5 (2023)
26. Mohammad, S.M., Turney, P.D.: NRC Emotion Lexicon, vol. 2, p. 234. National Research Council, Canada (2013)
27. Khawaja, H.S., Beg, M.O., Qamar, S.: Domain specific emotion lexicon expansion. In: 2018 14th International Conference on Emerging Technologies (ICET), pp. 1–5. IEEE (2018)

KT-CIP: Distribution-Aware Knowledge Transfer-Based Uncertainty Quantification Approach Using Context-Relevant Input Pruning

Sourojt Pal[1], Sandip Roy[2], Avishek Banerjee[3(✉)], Kaushik Majumdar[4], and Sachin Shetty[2]

[1] Department of IT, Jadavpur University, Kolkata 700032, India
[2] Center for Secure and Intelligent Critical Systems, Old Dominion University, Norfolk, VA 23529, USA
{sroy,sshetty}@odu.edu
[3] Department of CSBS, Asansol Engineering College, Asansol 713305, India
avishek.csbs@aecwb.edu.in
[4] Department of CSE, Maulana Abul Kalam Azad University of Technology, Kolkata 700064, India

Abstract. Interrelationships between different forms of uncertainty have become a significant area of focus in machine learning (ML) recently. Past studies have shown factors like dataset parameters, data shifts, and noise can affect a system's performance, posing a challenge for autonomous decision-making systems. With the mission to increase the trustworthiness of ML systems, we propose a novel knowledge transfer-based context-relevant input pruning framework, KT-CIP. Based on the concepts of knowledge transfer and feature selection, this novel framework presents an amalgamation of the concepts leading to its novelty. This framework considers only context-relevant parameters during the decision-making process. The KT-CIP framework utilizes new factors like "effective influence", "damping factor", and "effective accuracy", aiding in the calibration and determination of the model's uncertainty to an actual degree of trustworthiness. The effectiveness of this framework has been studied with simple ML algorithms, their variations, and different ensemble algorithms. We tested their accuracies over the original dataset, input-pruned datasets, and noisy datasets containing data shifts. The error in the knowledge transfer process has also been considered for absolute calibration. The framework showcases a 0.44% gain in accuracy as error is reduced. This is complemented by an average gain of 0.85%, 12.99%, 2.51%, and 2.26% in accuracies, compared against the original parameter list and noisy datasets. Observed gains in effective accuracy signify enhanced reliability of the framework.

Keywords: Uncertainty quantification · Distribution uncertainty · Machine learning · Knowledge transfer · Aleatoric uncertainty · Epistemic uncertainty · Data shift

M. Paprzycki et al. (Eds.): ICACIS 2024, CCIS 2405, pp. 434–455, 2027.
https://doi.org/10.1007/978-3-032-30990-7_32

1 Introduction

Uncertainty estimation for AI driven autonomous decision making systems are critical for improving their safety. While modern machine learning (ML)-based approaches excel in predictive accuracy, they grapple to generate precise estimates for uncertainty which offers guidance on when to trust or put doubt in the output. It is important to mention the problem of predictive uncertainty arises due to epistemic (model) uncertainty, data (aleatoric) uncertainty and distribution uncertainty but the root of these uncertainties lies deeper in the concept of data shift, as [12] discussed. Context awareness of the labeled datasets plays a crucial role in determining the data dimensionality but, to our knowledge, there is not yet a method which can leverae this concept to enhance the reliability of the frameworks. In 2021, [3] undertook a detailed survey for categorizing various feature selection (FS) algorithms. In his work, [8] has shown that effective feature sets are highly correlated with the class but uncorrelated internally. This makes correlation-based approach a promising solution toward reducing data dimensionality and enhancing any system's performance.

Assessing the Actual Degree of Trustworthiness Through Context-Relevant Input Pruning: In a labeled dataset, all attributes does not hold the same level of importance for a machine learning framework. The impact of each attribute on predicting the output can differ, with certain features exerting a more substantial influence on the model's performance. For instance, in a machine learning model designed to precisely diagnose lung cancer, specific attributes, like air pollution, could serve as influential factors contributing positively to the development of lung cancer. Conversely, attributes such as snoring have no correlation with lung cancer. The presence of "negatively influential" parameters obstructs the accurate assessment of lung cancer prediction, leading to a semblance of reliability rather than an authentic reflection of the model's performance. As a result, in the context of lung cancer determination, variables such as snoring are removed through pruning, and the "effective accuracy" of predictions is computed, thereby improving the overall reliability of the model.

Motivations: While multiple techniques exist for quantifying uncertainty concerning models, data, and distributions, there is a lack of research on how the attribute of a labeled dataset shapes the level of uncertainty. In this work we aim to identify the effect of the attributes of a labeled dataset and their role on the reliability of the framework's outcome. We also try to understand whether pruning of irrelevant features can lead to better output with decreased uncertainty and improved "effective accuracy". The existence of irrelevant parameters in a labeled dataset can introduce uncertainty over the outcomes. The current equations for measuring uncertainty often present difficulties. This highlights the need for simpler equations that not only make the quantification process easier but also lead to results that are easy to understand and agree upon.

Summary of Contributions: Major contributions of this research chapter is as follows:

- Identification of the impact of parameter pruning in labeled dataset over accuracy and trustworthiness.
- Assessing lung cancer dataset to identify context relevant parameters using correlation technique.
- Inculcate this knowledge and work on further dataset to identify "damping factor", "effective influence" and shift the focus on context relevant parameters in the dataset.
- Apply the intermediate dataset with context relevant parameters to simple ML algorithms and ensemble algorithms and observe accuracy and "effective accuracy".
- Generate a gain of 0.44%, 0.85%, 12.99%, 2.51%, and 2.26% after being subjected to various types of datasets elaborated in Sect. 4.

The rest of this article is structured in the following way: Sect. 2 offers a brief literature review on various state-of-the-art approaches for uncertainty quantification. In Sect. 3, we detail our research methodology and present the proposed KT-CIP framework. Section 4 showcases the extensive work and experiments we undertook. Finally, the chapter is concluded in Sect. 5.

2 Related Works

This section briefly summarizes prior research on uncertainty quantification, offering insights into the strengths and limitations of the existing works.

The investigation of uncertainty quantification began in the 1990s, when [15] conducted groundbreaking research on the concept of uncertainty. In 2009, [17], discussed the existence of a newer concept known as *Data Shift* thereby laying a strong foundation that facilitates the need for further research in this area. This caught the interest of the [12,13] [9,14], and many more, who initiated an extensive work on uncertainty. Recently, [7] and [1] conducted an extensive review on the methods, challenges, and opportunities of uncertainty quantification approaches in deep learning and DNNs. In his research, [10] discussed the presence of data points that were significantly different from the training distribution. In 2019, Y. Ovadia *et al.* presented a thorough evaluation of the current state-of-the-art methods for predictive uncertainty, investigating the influence of dataset shifts on both accuracy and calibration, while Malinin *et al.* discussed the existence of a third form of uncertainty that coexists with epistemic and aleatoric uncertainty, known as *distribution uncertainty.* [4] demonstrated improved algorithmic capabilities for handling mixed uncertainty quantification (UQ), making analytical processes more suitable for both aleatory and epistemic propagation requirements.

Synthesis: While uncertainty quantification methods exist, there has been limited research on how the attributes of a labeled dataset affect uncertainty. This necessitates further research to measure trustworthiness based on attribute influence. It is essential to explore the potential of context-based input pruning to reduce uncertainty, improve effective accuracy, and assess its impact on the performance of both simple ML algorithms and ensemble algorithms.

3 Proposed Methodology

In this section, we discuss the proposed methodology of KT-CIP framework. All the notations used in this chapter are tabulated in Table 1.

Table 1. Brief description of key notations

Symbol	Description
ξ	Number of cases in the data set
τ	Training level
ν	Input pruned parameter set
λ	Original parameter set
α	Accuracy of first task
ϵ	Error from first task
μ	Point-estimate categorical distribution
μ_1	In-domain distribution
μ_2	Out-of-domain distribution
μ_a	Effective parameters in in-domain distribution
μ_b	Ineffective parameters in in-domain distribution
γ	Damping factor
η	Effective influence
β	Observed accuracy from machine learning algorithm
$\in$	Effective accuracy or degree of trustworthiness
$U(x)$	Uncertainty
ρ	Number of parameters in the dataset

The estimation of predictive uncertainty is important in any classification analysis. [11] in his work has stated that a classification model $P(\omega_c \mid X^*, \Psi)$ trained using a finite dataset $\Psi = \{\mathcal{X}_i, \mathcal{Y}_i\}_{i=1}^{n} \sim p(x, y)$ can experience predictive uncertainty in a bayesian framework due to data and model uncertainty. If point-estimate categorical distribution μ represents data uncertainty, then the distribution uncertainty for the distribution over predictive categorical $P(\omega_c \mid x^*, \Psi)$ is defined by [12] as:

$$P(\omega_c \mid X^*, \Psi) = \int \int P(\omega_c \mid \mu) P(\mu \mid x^*, \theta) P(\theta \mid \Psi) d\mu d\theta, \qquad (1)$$

where, $P(\omega_c \mid \mu)$ denotes data, $P(\mu \mid x^*, \theta)$ signifies the distribution of the data, and $P(\theta \mid \Psi)$ represents the model. Considering that data has in-domain components μ_1 and out-of-domain components μ_2, and μ_1 can be further subdivided into context-relevant data μ_a, and context-irrelevant data μ_b, $P(\omega_c \mid \mu)$ and $P(\mu \mid x^*, \theta)$ can be redefined to $P(\omega_c \mid (\mu_a + \mu_b + \mu_2))$ and $P((\mu_a + \mu_b + \mu_2) \mid x^*, \theta)$

respectively. However, it is crucial to recognize that making such deductions can be complex and challenging. This motivates the need to identify and develop a more straightforward approach for estimating uncertainty, accuracy, and the level of trustworthiness in the output of a task.

The proposed framework, represented in Fig. 1, comprises two independent tasks. The first task is responsible for the identification of the context and the relevant context parameters using the correlation technique in a supervised approach. The task output is then compared against the correct data. This leads to the evaluation of accuracy (α) and error (ϵ).

$$\epsilon = \frac{FP + FN}{\rho}, \tag{2}$$

$$\alpha = 1 - \epsilon, \tag{3}$$

where FP is the false positive cases; FN represents the false negative cases, and number of cases is defined by ρ. This knowledge is then transferred to the second task in the framework. Here, it is important to note that the gap in knowledge in the first task, represented by error ϵ has an implicit impact on the performance of the second task.

In an earlier discussion from Eq. 3, μ was defined as $\mu = \mu_1 + \mu_2$ where, $\mu_1 = \mu_a + \mu_b$. The presence of μ_b can affect the reliability of the outcome. This is represented by the damping factor.

$$\gamma = \frac{\mu_b}{(\mu_a + \mu_b)}, \tag{4}$$

where γ is the damping factor. As γ ranges between [0,1] it affects the reliability of the output. This means the outcome in terms of accuracy (β) generated by the second task is influenced by the presence of mu_2 or mu_b by γ%. This can get amplified further in the presence of ϵ. Thus, the reliability or degree of trust over the accuracy ($beta$) impacted by γ and ϵ. This results in the fifth equation.

$$€ = \beta.\eta, \tag{5}$$

where €: represents effective accuracy and η represents effective influence. η is defined by: $\eta = (1 - \gamma).\alpha$. As $\mu \rightarrow \mu_a$, $\gamma \rightarrow 0$, $\eta \rightarrow \alpha$ and €: $\rightarrow \beta.\alpha$. This proves that the error or gap in knowledge from the first task will always have an implicit impact on the reliability of the accuracy of the second task. Equation 5 represents the deduction of a mission-critical correlation that can help in defining the boundary conditions of uncertainty or doubt. Since €: $= \beta.\eta$, the range of uncertainty is restricted between [€, β]. This results in re-evaluation of uncertainty $P(\omega_c \mid x^*, \Psi)$ as:

$$P(\omega_c \mid x^*, \Psi) = \beta - €, \tag{6}$$

where β represents accuracy of second task and effective accuracy is defined by €.

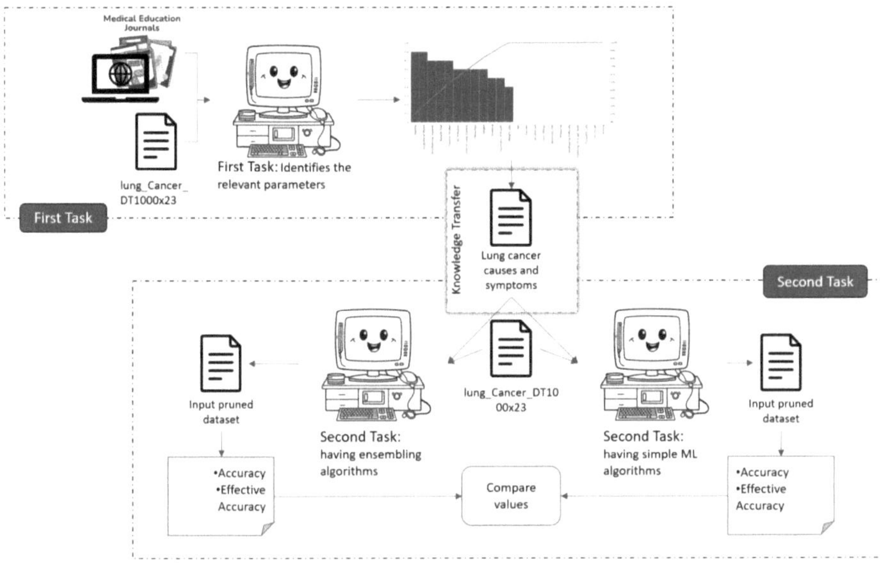

Fig. 1. KT-CIP framework

4 Performance Evaluation

4.1 Dataset Preparation

In order to conduct the experiments, 3 distinct datasets were used. These are lung cancer dataset[1], liver cirrhosis dataset[2], COPD dataset[3]. The files exclusively targeted for the experiments were comma-separated variable (.csv) files. The file on lung cancer was observed to have 23 parameters with 1000 cases histories. This file was named as "lung_Cancer_DT1000x23" and was taken as the basis for all the tests. Two more data files were created based on this file. In the first file, the symptoms from the liver cancer dataset and COPD dataset as mixed with the lung cancer to create a new dataset named "lung_Cancer_DT1000x32-Noise". In this case, the inputs from liver cancer and COPD are recognized as irrelevant noisy out-of-domain parameters. The second file was created by the introduction of outliers in relevant parameters of "lung_Cancer_DT1000x23" and was named "lung_Cancer_DT1000x23-Outliers".

In the proposed framework, the first task is responsible for detecting the causes and symptoms of lung cancer using correlation techniques from the "lung_Cancer_DT1000x23" dataset. The output of this task is preserved for reference in a file after verification against the original causes and symptoms of

[1] This file contained all the symptoms and causes which can help to predict the chances of lung cancer in a patient.

[2] This file contained the symptoms and blood parameters for a patient indicative of liver cirrhosis.

[3] This file contained the symptoms for a COPD patient.

lung cancer mentioned in different medical research journals [2,5,6,16,18]. This defines the evaluation of ϵ in the output of the initial task. Table 18 in Appendix B categorizes the symptoms related to the identification of lung cancer in a patient.

4.2 Algorithm Selection and Tuning of Hyperparameters

The experiments undertaken in this chapter were focused primarily on the simple ML algorithms existing today. The algorithms that were used include k-nearest neighbor (KNN), logistic regression (LR), simple vector machine (SVM), gaussian naive bayes (GNB), and decision tree (DTC). It is observed that simple SVM follows the radial basis function (RBF) kernel by default when few other variations like linear kernel, polynomial kernel, sigmoid and precomputed kernel are available. This led to inclusion of linear kernel and polynomial kernel in the scope to understand how the framework reacts to these SVM kernels. Additionally, naive bayes algorithms were checked and categorical naive bayes (CNB) was selected for observation along with GNB[4,5].

In order to calibrate the success rate of the simple ML algorithms, sophisticated ensemble algorithms like regression forest regressor (Ensemble: RFR), regression forecast classifier (Ensemble: RFC), bagging regressor (Ensemble: BR), gradient boosting regression (Ensemble: GBR) and extreme gradient boosting regressors (Ensemble: XGBR) were employed. GBR and XGBR under default setup were observed to return results that were not promising enough. This made us tune the hyper parameters of each of these algorithms. With alpha set to 50% with quantile loss, GBR was observed to return the best result at learning rate = 90%. XGBR, on the other hand, gave the best outcome at an eta[6] of 1.5 under the same values of alpha and objective function[7]. These values of GBR and XGBR algorithm were kept constant throughout the test.

4.3 Analysis of γ and η by Datasets

The datasets defined in Sect. 4.1 were used the experiments undertaken in this work. For each of these datasets, the number of parameters (ρ) changed. The change in the value of ρ means the change in the number of relevant and irrelevant parameters. This impacts the value of γ, which along with ϵ influences η. The value of these factors are exceptionally important for deductions used in succeeding sections. The values of γ and η are provided in Table 2. This will be used in subsequent experiments.

---

[4] When categorically distributed discrete features are used for classification, the categorical Naive Bayes classifier is selected.

[5] Assuming that feature values follow a gaussian distribution, gaussiannb is employed in classification problems.

[6] eta in XGBR algorithm is same as learning rate for GBR algorithm.

[7] Objective function in for XGBR algorithm is same as Loss function in case of GBR algorithm.

Table 2. The evaluation of damping factor γ and effective influence η for each of the datasets in scope

Context of experiment	Difference in ϵ				Presence of OOD parameters		Presence of Outlier	
Dataset	lung_Cancer_DT1000x23		lung_Cancer_DT1000x23		lung_Cancer_DT1000x32		lung_Cancer_DT1000x23	
Parameters	ν	λ	ν	λ	ν	λ	ν	λ
Total Parameter Set	14	23	12	23	12	30	12	23
Context Related Parameters	11	13	12	13	12	13	12	13
Negative influential Parameters	3	10	0	10	0	17	0	10
Damping Factor (γ)	0.2143	0.4348	0	0.4348	0	0.5667	0	0.4348
Effective Influence (ν)	0.6649	0.4783	0.9615	0.5434	0.9615	0.4166	0.9615	0.5434

4.4 Assessment of Impact of ϵ on the KT-CIP's Performance

Experiment: ϵ represents the error in the first task. This happens if the cause or symptom of lung cancer is not detected correctly. This experiment is undertaken to observe the impact of $\Delta\epsilon$ over β and €. Simple ML algorithms discussed in Sect. 4.2 are taken as candidates, with input pruned datasets taken as input.

Experiment Preparation: In this experiment, the first task was iteratively processed over two steps to generate the outcomes repeatedly. In the first step, the outcome was simply measured based on the correlation between independent variables and decision parameters. The second step involved the supervised measurement of correlation. In the first case, ϵ was observed to be 0.1538. In the second iteration, ϵ was observed to get reduced to 0.0385.

Observation: At $\epsilon = 0.1538$, average β is observed to be 96.39% and € = 64.1%. As ϵ reduces to 0.0385, β is observed to increase to 96.83% with €: increasing to 93.1% resulting in an improvement of 0.44% in β and 29% in €. This is shown in Tables 3, 4 and Fig. 7 in Appendix C.

Table 3. Change in β with change in ϵ is represented for each of the simple ML algorithms

Type of Parameter	Error (ϵ)	KNN	LR	SVM (RBF)	GNB	DTC	Mean
ν	0.1538	0.9867	0.9267	0.9989	0.9100	0.9974	0.9639
ν	0.0385	0.9733	0.9617	0.9994	0.9083	0.9989	0.9683

Inference: In a situation where multiple tasks or models are in use, the accuracy of the second task or model is implicitly influenced by the errors observed in the first task or model. In this case, the errors from the first task are observed to influence the outcome of the second task. The effectiveness increases as ϵ decreases. This shows the efficiency of a model or task can be greatly increased if the error from the first model or task can be controlled.

Table 4. Change in €: with change in ϵ is represented for each of the simple ML algorithms

Type of Parameter	Error (ϵ)	KNN	LR	SVM (RBF)	GNB	DTC	Mean
ν	0.1538	0.6561	0.6162	0.6642	0.6051	0.6632	0.641
ν	0.0385	0.9358	0.9247	0.9609	0.8733	0.9604	0.931

4.5 Review of Change in the Performance with Input Pruning

Experiment: This experiment is primarily directed toward inspecting the change in β and €: as the same dataset is iteratively tested over the original data set and input pruned dataset. For this experiment, ϵ is kept constant at 0.0385.

Experiment Preparation: We selected the dataset "lung_Cancer_DT1000x23" for the purpose of this experiment. The assumption for this experiment is that the outcome of the first task is already available, that is, the knowledge transfer on causes and symptoms of lung cancer has already happened. The second task in this case processes the dataset, and enlists the parameters that are relevant to the context. The task then iterates over this dataset and the original dataset to generate the values of β and €.

Observation: The experiment with input pruned dataset showed a gain of $\beta = 0.85\%$. This becomes significant when 40.95% gain in €: is observed over original parameter set. This is discussed in Tables 5, 6 and Fig. 8 in Appendix C.

Table 5. β is calibrated as simple ML algorithms are fed with input pruned datasets at $\epsilon = 0.0385$

Type of Parameter	KNN	LR	SVM (RBF)	GNB	DTC	Mean
ν	0.9733	0.9617	0.9994	0.9083	0.9989	0.9683
λ	0.9583	0.9800	0.9850	0.8900	0.9856	0.9598

Inference: In the case of the input-pruned dataset, the influence of irrelevant parameters is mostly absent. This helps the framework provide reliable outputs compared to the complete datasets. This helps to achieve better accuracy at improved trustworthiness.

4.6 Analysis of the Impact Caused by Out-of-Domain Parameters

Experiment: Out-of-domain parameter classification and its impact on the outcome of the decision-making framework is an interesting topic to assess. It is

Table 6. Impact on €:: with input pruning at $\epsilon = 0.0385$ is outlined for each algorithms

Type of Parameter	KNN	LR	SVM (RBF)	GNB	DTC	Mean
ν	0.9358	0.9247	0.9609	0.8733	0.9604	0.9310
λ	0.5207	0.5325	0.5352	0.4836	0.5356	0.5215

important to note that the parameters that fall under this category are neither a cause nor a symptom of lung cancer. They may be relevant to some other context. This type of parameter normally adds noise to the dataset, is categorized under imbalanced data, and can cause domain shifts. This experiment focuses on the problems that an out-of-domain parameter can pose for the framework of observations. The impact in terms of β and €: is revisited.

Experiment Preparation: "lung_Cancer_DT1000x23" and "lung_Cancer_DT 1000x32-Noise" datasets are used in this experiment. The second task in the framework is fed with individual files as input. The task prunes the datasets and extracts the parameters that are relevant to the context in each of the cases. This helps to define ρ for ν as 12. For "lung_Cancer_DT1000x23", $\rho = 23$ and for "lung_Cancer_DT1000x32-Noise", $\rho = 30$. In the next step, the evaluation of β and €: is performed.

Observation: The output from the framework showcases the variations for $\rho = 12$, $\rho = 23$, $\rho = 30$. At $\rho = 12$, $\beta = 96.83\%$ on average, which is higher compared to β for $\rho = 23$ and $\rho = 30$. β is observed to register the lowest outcome of 83.84% for $\rho = 30$. The decision tree algorithm has been observed to outperform all the other ML algorithms under this use case with an average $\beta = 98.93\%$. €: is observed to achieve maxima of 93.1% for ν even under the influence of noise. This is at least 58.17% higher compared to the €: = 34.93% for $\rho = 30$. Tables 7, 8 and Fig. 9 in Appendix C describe the observation.

Table 7. As extra parameters from other domains were introduced, the variations in β at $\epsilon = 0.0385$ is measured

Type of Parameter	ρ	KNN	LR	SVM (RBF)	GNB	DTC	Mean
ν	12	0.9733	0.9617	0.9994	0.9083	0.9989	0.9683
λ	23	0.9583	0.9800	0.9850	0.8900	0.9856	0.9598
λ	30	0.9667	0.9833	0.3683	0.8900	0.9836	0.8384

Table 8. Variation in €: corresponding to the variation of β in Table 7 has been noted

Type of Parameter	ρ	KNN	LR	SVM (RBF)	GNB	DTC	Mean
ν	12	0.9358	0.9247	0.9609	0.8733	0.9604	0.9310
λ	23	0.5207	0.5325	0.5352	0.4836	0.5356	0.5215
λ	30	0.4027	0.4096	0.1534	0.3708	0.4098	0.3493

Inference: The observation shows that the simple ML models consistently outperform their performances when subjected to ν. However, as noises are introduced into the datasets, these algorithms normally falter. As $\Delta\rho \rightarrow \nu$, β maximize. This experiment also demonstrates that our proposed framework is capable of achieving accuracy with maximum reliability even if the input dataset has noise or out-of-domain parameters.

4.7 Evaluation of the Effect of in-Domain Outliers

Experiment: Parameters relevant to the context are referred to be in-domain. The shift of the data in the in-domain parameters can result in data shifts that cause covariate shifts and prior probability shifts. This experiment is focused on the outcomes of noisy outliers and their comparison with the original dataset. Since in this experiment there is no OOD parameters, the value of ρ remains constant at 12 for ν and at 23 for λ

Experiment Preparation: The datasets "lung_Cancer_DT1000x23" and "lung_Cancer_DT1000x23-Outliers" are used for this experiment. Like Sect. 4.6, the second task in the framework is fed with individual files as input. The task prunes the datasets and extracts the parameters that are relevant to the context in each of the cases. The results are observed.

Observation: The resulting outcome from the experiment demonstrates a mild decrease in the overall β on average for both ν and λ. The presence of outliers has been observed to decrease *beta* by 2.51% and €: by 2.41% for ν. For λ, a decrease of $\beta = 1.41\%$ and €$= 0.76\%$ is observed. ML algorithms, SVM(RBF), and decision trees are observed to generate promising results with an average accuracy of $beta = 97.48\%$ and 97.69% respectively. The results are described in Tables 9, 10, and Fig. 2.

Inference: The presence of outliers in the relevant parameters eventually affects the outcome of the framework. The proposed methodology works well in recognizing the OOD parameters, but the detection of in-domain data shifts is fully dependent on the resilience of the algorithms. The observations show that the presence of outliers in relevant combinations has caused a covariate shift, due to which efficiency and reliability over the outcome have decreased to a certain extent.

Table 9. At constant $\epsilon = 0.0385$, the variations in β are listed under the presence of outliers in context-relevant parameters

Type of Parameter	ρ	KNN	LR	SVM (RBF)	GNB	DTC	Mean
ν	12	0.9733	0.9617	0.9994	0.9083	0.9989	0.9683
ν	12 Outlier	0.9733	0.9517	0.9617	0.8500	0.9795	0.9432
λ	23	0.9583	0.9800	0.9850	0.8900	0.9856	0.9598
λ	23 Outlier	0.9583	0.9750	0.9533	0.8983	0.9436	0.9457

Table 10. Change in €: corresponding to the change in β due to outliers in context-relevant parameters at $\epsilon = 0.0385$ has been tabulated for simple ML algorithms

Type of Parameter	ρ	KNN	LR	SVM (RBF)	GNB	DTC	Mean
ν	12	0.9358	0.9247	0.9609	0.8733	0.9604	0.9310
ν	12 Outlier	0.9358	0.9151	0.9247	0.8173	0.9418	0.9069
λ	23	0.5207	0.5325	0.5352	0.4836	0.5356	0.5215
λ	23 Outlier	0.5207	0.5298	0.5180	0.4881	0.5128	0.5139

4.8 Comparison of Simple ML Algorithms with ν and Ensemble Algorithms with λ

Experiment: This experiment helps to estimate the success rate of the proposed method with simple ML algorithms. Measured values of β and €: over ν for these algorithms are calibrated against the outcomes of ensemble algorithms.

Experiment Preparation: This test was carried out with "lung_Cancer_DT 1000x23", "lung_Cancer_DT1000x23-Outliers", "lung_Cancer_DT1000x32-Noise" datasets. In each of the cases, simple ML algorithms were given the pruned dataset ν as input, while complete datasets λ were given as input to ensemble algorithms.

Observation: The ensemble method was observed to reach β of 98.1% at $\epsilon = 0.1538 and \epsilon = 0.0385$ for $\rho = 23$, 97.21% and 97.79% for $\rho = 30 and \rho - 23$ with outlier at $\epsilon = 0.0385$. Simple ML algorithms with input-pruned datasets ν were able to compete against the sophisticated ensemble algorithms and achieve an accuracy β of 96.39%, 96.83% and 94.32% for $\epsilon = 0.1538$, $\epsilon = 0.0385$ and $\rho = 12$ in respective cases. With a minimum damping factor, these simple ML algorithms were able to exhibit maximum reliability. Tables 12, 13 in Appendix B and Fig. 3 showcases the outcomes.

Inference: The observations represent that the simple ML algorithms subjected to the proposed framework can achieve results close to those of ensemble algorithms.

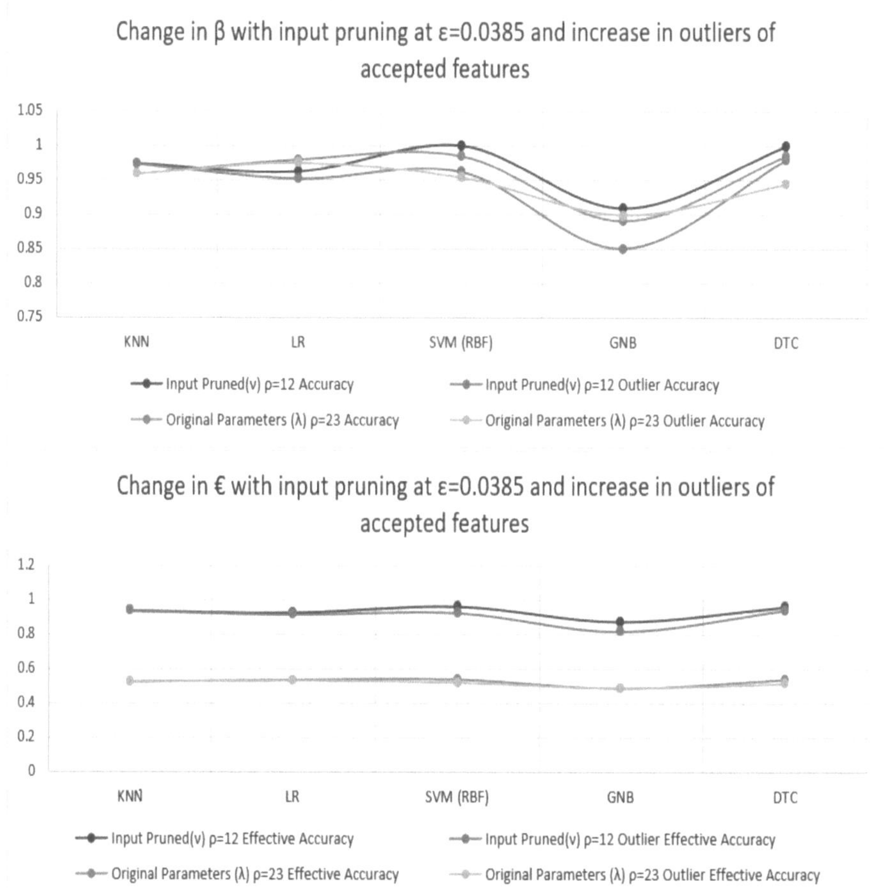

Fig. 2. The presence of outliers in the context relevant parameter creates a variation of β and €: compared to the other datasets that are free from this influence. The variation of accuracies for SVM(RBF) and DTC are also notable from the graphs

4.9 Performance Review of Simple ML Algorithms and Ensemble Algorithms with ν

Experiment: In Sect. 4.8, the experiment was undertaken to visualize the effect of the application of ν on simple ML algorithms and λ over ensemble methods. It was observed that with ν given as input, simple ML algorithms were able to achieve accuracies almost on par with ensemble methods at higher reliability. In this experiment, we perform our observations by assessing the outcome of applying ν as input for both sets of ML algorithms.

Experiment Preparation: Similar to the experiment in Sect. 4.8, datasets "lung_Cancer_DT1000x23", "lung_Cancer_DT1000x23-Outliers", "lung_Cancer_DT1000x32-Noise" are taken into consideration. However, unlike Sect. 4.8, ν is

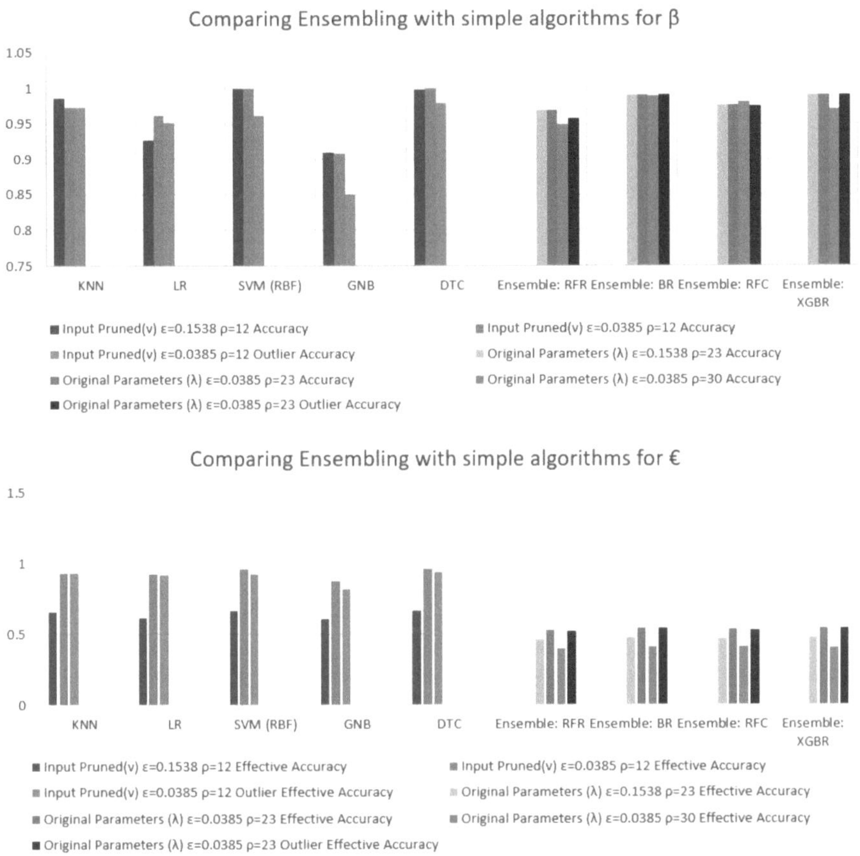

Fig. 3. ν and λ are given as input to simple ML algorithms and ensemble algorithms respectively. The variation of their performances for each of the algorithms is noted

given as input to both the simple ML algorithms and sophisticated ensemble algorithms, and the outcomes are observed.

Observation: Visual assessment of Fig. 4 demonstrates a consistent performance at high reliability for all the simple ML models close to β = 96.83% and €: = 93.10% at ϵ = 0.0385. Similar consistency is observed for RFR, BR, RFC, and GBR algorithms as well demonstrating β = 97.67%, β = 99.65%, β = 98.76, and β = 99.51% with €: = 93.91%, €: = 95.72%, €: =94.96%, and €: = 95.68% respectively at same ϵ. The evaluations are provided in Tables 14, 15 in Appendix B.

Inference: With the proposed framework, all the algorithms under observation have been seen to perform with high reliability. Ensemble methods were seen to outperform themselves when compared against the results of Sect. 4.8. A consis-

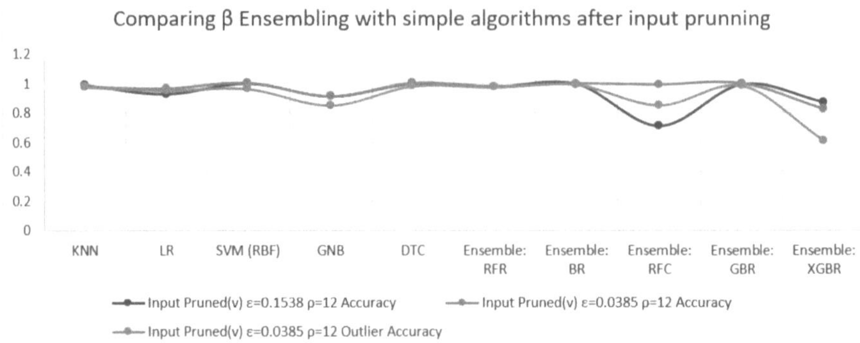

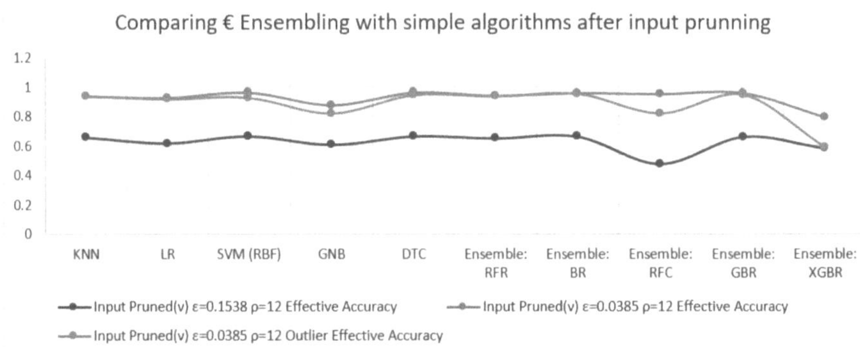

Fig. 4. As a change from the experiment in Sect. 4.8, simple ML algorithms and ensemble algorithms when subjected to ν. β and €: is noted in each of the cases

tent gain of 0.84%, 0.55%, 1.21% for β for RFR, BR, and RFC, respectively, is observed.

4.10 Understanding the Impact of Hyper-Parameter Tuning for Simple ML Algorithms

Experiment: This experiment is an evaluation of the variations of simple ML algorithms as discussed in Sect. 4.2. Variations of SVM and Naive Bayes (NB) are mostly considered for this evaluation. The impact of subjecting the algorithms to ν and λ is assessed.

Experiment Preparation: Variations in the SVM algorithm were implemented by setting the hyper-parameter "kernel" to "linear", 'RBF", and "polynomial". For NB, categorical naive bayes, or CNB, were introduced into the scope. The datasets "lung_Cancer_DT1000x23", "lung_Cancer_DT1000x23-Outliers", and "lung_Cancer_DT1000x32-Noise" were considered as input for this experiment. These datasets were set as input for each of the variations, and results were observed.

Observation: Consistent β of 94.82% is observed for all the variations for all datasets except SVM(RBF) which shows a depletion when subjected to λ for $\rho = 30$, that is a case where OOD parameters were introduced. SVM (linear) was able to achieve the highest accuracy with $\beta = 97.13\%$ under all circumstances with the highest €: of 94.87% at $\epsilon = 0.0385$ and $\rho = 12$, as represented in Fig. 5 and Tables 16, 17 in Appendix B.

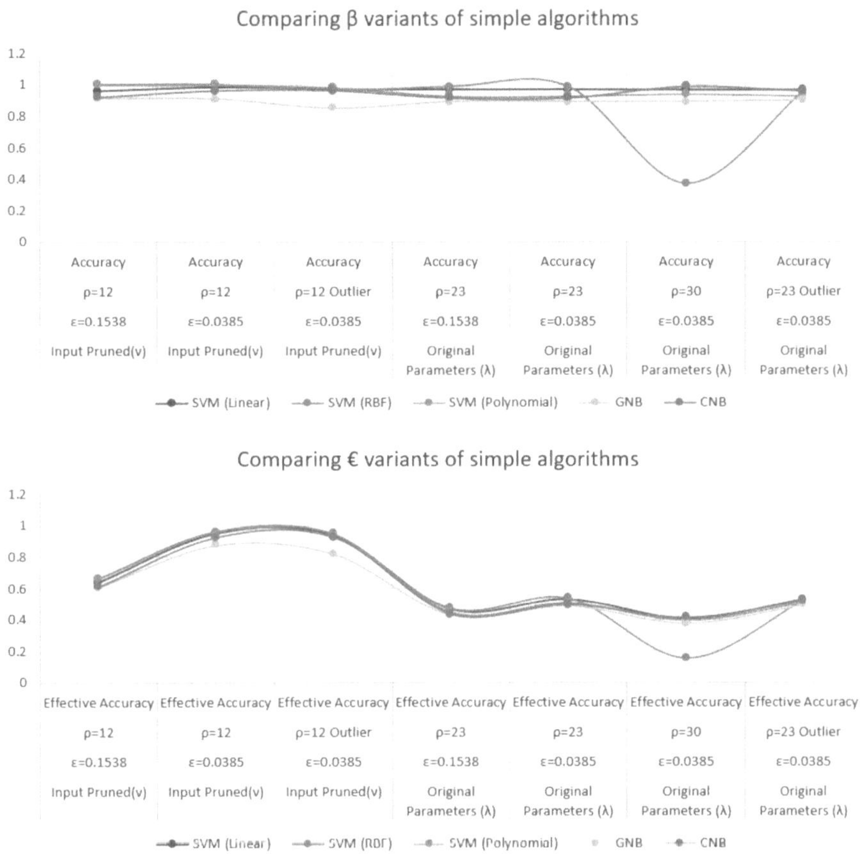

Fig. 5. The hyper-parameter of SVM were tuned to create three different variations. At the same time, a different variation of NB, CNB was placed to compete with GNB. All these variants of SVM and NB were subjected to ν and λ. The values of β and €: are noted in each of the cases

Inference: The experiment highlights the significance of fine-tuning hyperparameters of ML algorithms. The proposed framework not only delivers superior results with increased reliability but can also demonstrate further improvement in performance by fine-tuning the hyperparameters of the ML algorithms. This experiment, along with others in this section, proves the degree of trustworthiness of a model $P(\theta \mid \Psi)$ is highest when $P(\mu \mid x^*, \theta) \rightarrow P(\mu_a \mid x^*, \theta)$ and data concentration around effective parameters of in-domain component $P(\omega_c \mid \mu_a)$ increases.

5 Conclusion

This research investigates the influence of contextually relevant input pruning on both basic machine learning algorithms and ensemble algorithms. Through experiments, the study examines how dataset parameters, data shift, and noise impact the accuracy of algorithmic outputs. The findings shows the significance of limiting parameters within the study's context. It has been observed that simple machine learning algorithms employing knowledge transfer to reduce contextual analysis efforts, accompanied by proper context-based assessment and feature selection, can generate dependable outputs. Tuning of hyper-parameters can help to achieve improved outputs. The equations introduced in this research have the potential to provide a basis for performance evaluations in future researches. As a further study, the concept of this framework can be used to create hybrid models with an extension toward other fields of study to employ advanced uncertainty assessment techniques for evaluation.

A Appendix: Further Experiments

A.1 A Review of the Degree of Uncertainty

Experiment: This experiment is a continuation of Sects. 4.4, 4.5, 4.6, 4.7. In this experiment, we calibrate the maximum degree of uncertainty or doubtfulness.

Experiment Preparation: The preparation of this experiment is integral to the preceding experiments.

Observation: The assessment of the outcome shows that SVM(RBF) algorithm shows maximum reliability amongst all the simple ML algorithms with 29.91% of uncertainty. The optimum reliability is achieved for $\epsilon = 0.0385$ with ν having $\rho = 12$. The elaboration evaluation can be noted in Table 11 and Fig. 6

Table 11. The degree of uncertainty experienced by the algorithms under varying dataset and varying ϵ condition is measured and noted

Type of Parameter	Error (ϵ)	ρ	KNN	LR	SVM (RBF)	GNB	DTC
ν	0.1538	12	0.3306	0.3105	0.3347	0.3049	0.3342
λ	0.1538	23	0.4999	0.5113	0.5139	0.4643	0.5142
ν	0.0385	12	0.0375	0.0370	0.0385	0.0350	0.0385
λ	0.0385	23	0.4376	0.4475	0.4498	0.4064	0.4500
λ	0.0385	30	0.5640	0.5737	0.2149	0.5192	0.5738
ν	0.0385	12 Outlier	0.0375	0.0366	0.0370	0.0327	0.0377
λ	0.0385	23 Outlier	0.4376	0.4452	0.4353	0.4102	0.4308

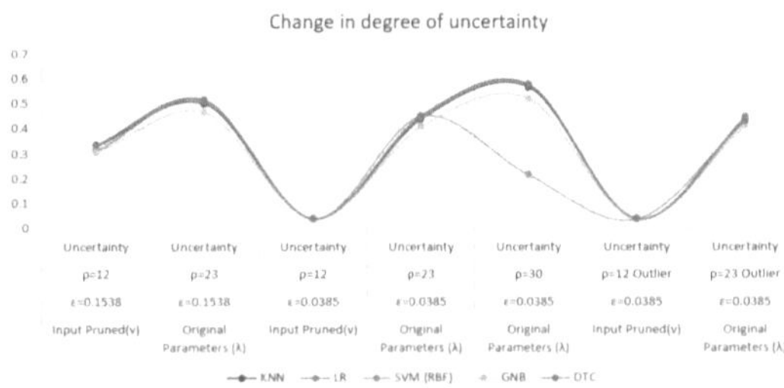

Fig. 6. Each lines represents the variation in the uncertainty experienced by each of the simple ML algorithms when subjected to different datasets under different ϵ conditions and parameter list

Inference: The results show maximum reliability on the outcome is observed when $\epsilon \rightarrow 0$, $\gamma \rightarrow 0$ and $\rho \rightarrow \nu$. This also shows that the proposed framework of distribution-aware knowledge-transfer-based context-relevant input pruning is capable of generating effective, reliable possibilities.

B Appendix: Tables

Table 12. The simple ML algorithms were subjected to ν while ensemble algorithms were given λ as input. The observed values of β for each of the algorithms under different ϵ and ρ is noted

Type of Parameter	Error (ϵ)	ρ	KNN	LR	SVM (RBF)	GNB	DTC	Ensemble: RFR	Ensemble: BR	Ensemble: RFC	Ensemble: XGBR	Mean
ν	0.1538	12	0.9867	0.9267	0.9989	0.9100	0.9974	-	-	-	-	0.963940
ν	0.0385	12	0.9733	0.9617	0.9994	0.9083	0.9989	-	-	-	-	0.968320
ν	0.0385	12 Outlier	0.9733	0.9517	0.9617	0.8500	0.9795	-	-	-	-	0.943240
λ	0.1538	23	-	-	-	-	-	0.9683	0.9900	0.9755	0.99	0.980950
λ	0.0385	23	-	-	-	-	-	0.9683	0.9900	0.9755	0.99	0.980950
λ	0.0385	30	-	-	-	-	-	0.9483	0.9897	0.9805	0.97	0.972125
λ	0.0385	23 Outlier	-	-	-	-	-	0.9567	0.9900	0.9750	0.99	0.977925

Table 13. Evaluation of €: each value of β in Table 12 is observed and noted

Type of Parameter	Error (ϵ)	ρ	KNN	LR	SVM (RBF)	GNB	DTC	Ensemble: RFR	Ensemble: BR	Ensemble: RFC	Ensemble: XGBR	Mean
ν	0.1538	12	0.6561	0.6162	0.6642	0.6051	0.6632	-	-	-	-	0.640960
ν	0.0385	12	0.9358	0.9247	0.9609	0.8733	0.9604	-	-	-	-	0.931020
ν	0.0385	12 Outlier	0.9358	0.9151	0.9247	0.8173	0.9418	-	-	-	-	0.906940
λ	0.1538	23	-	-	-	-	-	0.4631	0.4735	0.4666	0.4735	0.469175
λ	0.0385	23	-	-	-	-	-	0.5262	0.5380	0.5301	0.5380	0.533075
λ	0.0385	30	-	-	-	-	-	0.3951	0.4123	0.4085	0.4041	0.405000
λ	0.0385	23 Outlier	-	-	-	-	-	0.5199	0.5380	0.5298	0.5380	0.531425

Table 14. The simple ML algorithms as well as ensemble algorithms are subjected to ν under different ϵ and ρ. The observed values of β for each of the algorithms is noted

Type of Parameter	Error (ϵ)	ρ	KNN	LR	SVM (RBF)	GNB	DTC	Ensemble: RFR	Ensemble: BR	Ensemble: RFC	Ensemble: GBR	Ensemble: XGBR
ν	0.1538	12	0.9867	0.9267	0.9989	0.9100	0.9974	0.9767	0.9945	0.7100	0.9921	0.87
ν	0.0385	12	0.9733	0.9617	0.9994	0.9083	0.9989	0.9767	0.9955	0.9876	0.9951	0.82
ν	0.0385	12 Outlier	0.9733	0.9517	0.9617	0.8500	0.9795	0.9717	0.9900	0.8500	0.9811	0.61

Table 15. Variation in €: for each of the algorithms is measured to understand the effect of ν under varying ϵ and ρ conditions

Type of Parameter	Error (ϵ)	ρ	KNN	LR	SVM (RBF)	GNB	DTC	Ensemble: RFR	Ensemble: BR	Ensemble: RFC	Ensemble: GBR	Ensemble: XGBR
ν	0.1538	12	0.6561	0.6162	0.6642	0.6051	0.6632	0.6494	0.6612	0.4721	0.6596	0.5785
ν	0.0385	12	0.9358	0.9247	0.9609	0.8733	0.9604	0.9391	0.9572	0.9496	0.9568	0.7884
ν	0.0385	12 Outlier	0.9358	0.9151	0.9247	0.8173	0.9418	0.9343	0.9519	0.8173	0.9433	0.5865

Table 16. The tuning of hyperparameters gave rise to three distinct variants of SVM which were subjected to ν and λ. Similarly, the variant CNB and GNB related to naive bayes were also considered for the experiment and outcomes were noted over varying degree of β

Type of Parameter	Error (ϵ)	ρ	SVM (Linear)	SVM (RBF)	SVM (Polynomial)	GNB	CNB
ν	0.1538	12	0.9617	0.9989	0.9995	0.9100	0.9217
ν	0.0385	12	0.9867	0.9994	0.9995	0.9083	0.9617
ν	0.0385	12 Outlier	0.9750	0.9617	0.9823	0.8500	0.9633
λ	0.1538	23	0.9705	0.9850	0.9267	0.8900	0.9150
λ	0.0385	23	0.9705	0.9850	0.9267	0.8900	0.9150
λ	0.0385	30	0.9675	0.3683	0.9383	0.8900	0.9867
λ	0.0385	23 Outlier	0.9675	0.9533	0.9267	0.8983	0.9567

Table 17. Subjecting the variants of SVM and NB to ν and λ under varying ϵ and ρ resulted in different €

Type of Parameter	Error (ϵ)	ρ	SVM (Linear)	SVM (RBF)	SVM (Polynomial)	GNB	CNB
ν	0.1538	12	0.6394	0.6642	0.6646	0.6051	0.6128
ν	0.0385	12	0.9487	0.9609	0.9610	0.8733	0.9247
ν	0.0385	12 Outlier	0.9375	0.9247	0.9445	0.8173	0.9262
λ	0.1538	23	0.4642	0.4711	0.4432	0.4257	0.4376
λ	0.0385	23	0.5274	0.5352	0.5036	0.4836	0.4972
λ	0.0385	30	0.4031	0.1534	0.3909	0.3708	0.4111
λ	0.0385	23 Outlier	0.5257	0.5180	0.5036	0.4881	0.5199

Table 18. A tabular assessment of the symptoms of lung cancer [16]

	Symptoms														
Study (Year)	Criteria for inclusion in the final model	Cough	Haemoptysis	Weight loss	COPD	Dyspnoea	Chest pain	Appetite loss	Wheezing	Cough and Phlegm	Fatigue	Hoarseness	Heaviness in Chest	Fever/Flu	General Unwell
Hamilton et al. (2005)	P<0.01	✓	✓	✓	✓	✓	✓	✓	-	-	✓	-	-	-	-
Hippesley-Cox and Coupland (2011)	HR<0.9 or >1.2	✓	✓	✓	✓	✓	-	✓	-	-	✓	✓	-	-	-
Kubik et al. (2001)	-	✓	-	-	-	✓	-	-	✓	✓	-	-	-	-	-
Jones et al. (2007)	-	-	✓	-	-	-	-	-	-	-	-	-	-	-	-
Hoppe (1977)	-	None of the symptom diagnostic values were found to be statistically significant													

C Appendix: Figures

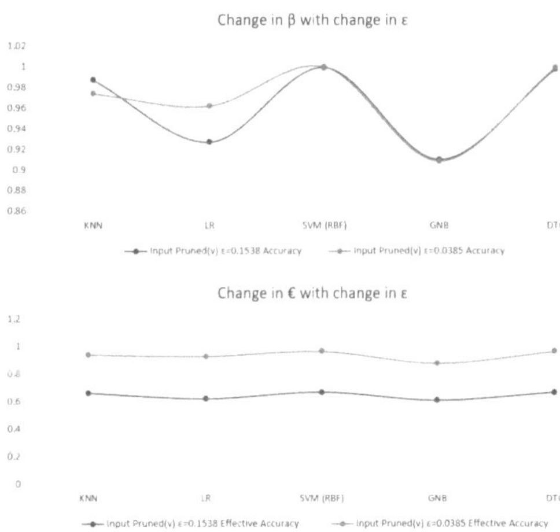

Fig. 7. The change in ϵ condition induces variation in β and €: values for the simple ML algorithms

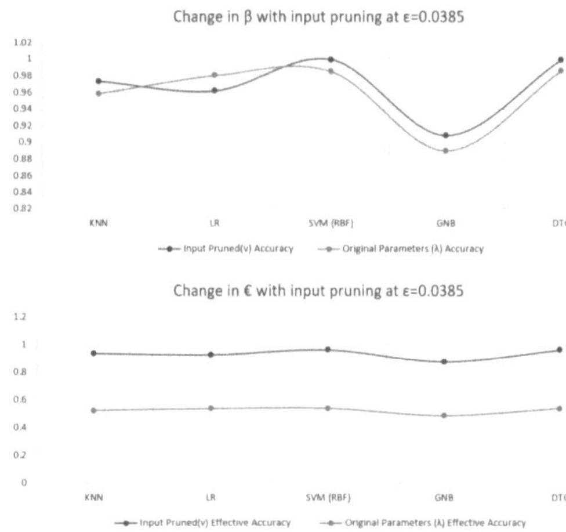

Fig. 8. The impact of ν and λ on β and €are measured and the variations are assessed. It can be observed that under the effect of ν, the ML algorithms generate improved results at higher reliability. The drastic improvement is observed in €: mainly as the impact of the irrelevant parameters are reduced in case of ν

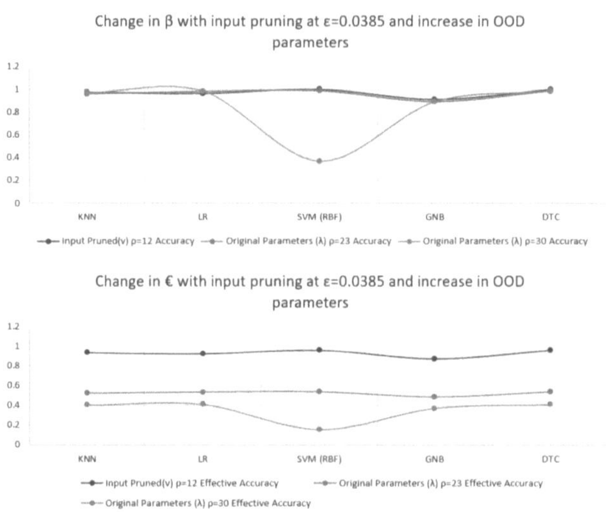

Fig. 9. The effect of noisy or out-of-domain parameters over λ and ν for each ML algorithms can be observed. In the case of ν, the simple ML algorithms show significant reliability and accuracy when even though subjected to noisy dataset

References

1. Abdar, M., et al.: A review of uncertainty quantification in deep learning: Techniques, applications and challenges. Inf. Fusion **76**, 243–297 (2021)
2. de Groot, P.M., Wu, C.C., Carter, B.W., Munden, R.F.: The epidemiology of lung cancer. Transl. Lung Cancer Res. **7**(3), 220 (2018)
3. Dhal, P., Azad, C.: A comprehensive survey on feature selection in the various fields of machine learning. Appl. Intell. 1–39 (2022)
4. Eldred, M.S., Swiler, L.P., Tang, G.: Mixed aleatory-epistemic uncertainty quantification with stochastic expansions and optimization-based interval estimation. Reliab. Eng. Syst. Saf. **96**(9), 1092–1113 (2011)
5. Fajersztajn, L., Veras, M., Barrozo, L.V., Saldiva, P.: Air pollution: a potentially modifiable risk factor for lung cancer. Nat. Rev. Cancer **13**(9), 674–678 (2013)
6. William Field, R., Withers, B.L.: Occupational and environmental causes of lung cancer. Clin. Chest Med. **33**(4), 681–703 (2012)
7. Gawlikowski, J., et al.: A survey of uncertainty in deep neural networks. arXiv preprint arXiv:2107.03342 (2021)
8. Mark, A., Hall: correlation-based feature selection for machine learning. Ph.D. thesis, The University of Waikato (1999)
9. Hüllermeier, E., Waegeman, W.: Aleatoric and epistemic uncertainty in machine learning: a tutorial introduction. arXiv preprint arXiv:1910.09457, 5 (2019)
10. Lakshminarayanan, B., Pritzel, A., Blundell, C.: Simple and scalable predictive uncertainty estimation using deep ensembles. In: Advances in Neural Information Processing Systems, vol. 30 (2017)
11. Malinin, A.: Uncertainty estimation in deep learning with application to spoken language assessment. Ph.D. thesis, University of Cambridge (2019)
12. Malinin, A., Gales, M.: Predictive uncertainty estimation via prior networks. In: Advances in Neural Information Processing Systems, vol. 31 (2018)
13. Mullins, J., Ling, Y., Mahadevan, S., Sun, L., Strachan, A.: Separation of aleatory and epistemic uncertainty in probabilistic model validation. Reliab. Eng. Syst. Saf. **147**, 49–59 (2016)
14. Ovadia, Y., et al.: Can you trust your model's uncertainty? Evaluating predictive uncertainty under dataset shift. In: Advances in Neural Information Processing Systems, vol. 32 (2019)
15. Rowe, W.D.: Understanding uncertainty. Risk Anal. **14**(5), 743–750 (1994)
16. Shim, J., Brindle, L., Simon, M., George, S.: A systematic review of symptomatic diagnosis of lung cancer. Fam. Pract. **31**(2), 137–148 (2014)
17. Storkey, A., Candela, Q.-C., Sugiyama, M., Schwaighofer, A., Lawrence, N.D.: Dataset Shift in Machine Learning. MIT Press (2009)
18. Thandra, K.C., Barsouk, A., Saginala, K., Aluru, J.S., Barsouk, A.: Epidemiology of lung cancer. Contemp. Oncol./Współczesna Onkologia **25**(1), 45–52 (2021)

WGCNA and Machine Learning Approaches to Identify Early Stage Diagnostic Biomarkers for Oral Squamous Cell Carcinoma

Pooja Singh, Pushpender Singh Chandel, and Pallavi Somvanshi(✉)

School of Computational and Integrative Sciences (SCIS), Jawaharlal Nehru University, JNU Campus, New Delhi, India
psomvanshi@jnu.ac.in

Abstract. Oral squamous cell carcinoma is the presence of tumors in mouth areas such as lips, cheeks, salivary organs, nasal depression, hard and soft palate, and pharynx. It is the sixth most common and malignant cancer globally. Bioinformatics methods facilitate the mining and analysis of large-scale oral cancer-related datasets from NCBI Gene Expression Omnibus (GSE145272), allowing the identification of differentially expressed genes and other genomic alterations associated with specific cancer types. WGCNA facilitates the prioritization of candidate biomarkers, highlighting the genes most relevant to the disease of interest. Further, machine learning-based platforms enable the validation of identified biomarkers by utilizing classification and prediction models that can be trained on cancer data to differentiate between cancerous and non-cancerous samples, leading to the identification of biomarkers that contribute to accurate diagnostic predictions. Such *in-silico* assessment aids in validating identified biomarkers by analyzing their performance across independent datasets and assessing their clinical relevance. Furthermore, this approach can guide the design of diagnostic assays or tests to measure the expression or activity of biomarkers, facilitating their translation into clinical practice for cancer diagnosis.

Keywords: Oral squamous cell carcinoma · differential gene expression analysis · WGCNA · network biology · biomarkers · machine learning approaches

1 Introduction

The eighth most prevalent cancer in the world, oral cancer has been a significant cause of illness and mortality [1–4]. Oral squamous cell carcinomas (OSCCs) are the most common type of oral cancer and typically develop in the soft and hard palate, buccal mucosa, melanomas, salivary minor glands, and lymphomas [3, 5]. Non-healing ulcers, exophytic lesions, mixed lesions, tooth discomfort, and other symptoms can be present [5]. In this concern, by identifying the genes expressed differently under specified experimental conditions, differential gene analysis may provide insights into disease mechanisms, identify biomarkers, reveal regulatory networks, direct functional studies, and advance personalized medicine strategies [6].

M. Paprzycki et al. (Eds.): ICACIS 2024, CCIS 2405, pp. 456–463, 2027.
https://doi.org/10.1007/978-3-032-30990-7_33

Researchers can find genes and pathways that are dysregulated and connected to the illness phenotype by examining gene expression patterns under various situations. This knowledge elucidates the basic mechanisms underlying the onset and progression of the illness and identifies prospective treatment targets [6, 7]. WGCNA (Weighted Gene Coexpression Network Analysis) allows for systematically exploring co-expression patterns within complex biological systems [6]. This strategy promotes the functional annotation and interpretation of identified biomarkers by associating modules and hub genes with known biological pathways and gene ontology terms. Further, ML-seq validates the potential of early diagnostic identified biomarkers by incorporating feature selection and improved classification models [8], enable it to capture complex patterns by generating classification and prediction models facilitates precise patient stratification and personalized treatment decisions [8].The current study aims to identify hub genes associated with oral cancer and validate them by including a machine-learning model to identify their respective potential in causing oral cancer. A related high throughput expression profiling dataset (GSE145272) was mined from the NCBI Gene Expression Omnibus database (GEO). The DESeq2 R package was used to identify differentially expressed genes (DEGs) using the DESeq2 normalization method. Further, genes correlated with each other were identified using WGCNA, from which the most significant gene module in oral cancer was found. In accordance with this, a machine-learning model was built using the ML-Seq technique, involving data normalization, transformation, and classification, which validates the result of WGCNA. To conclude our study, a gene enrichment analysis was performed, pathways that were mainly involved in oral cancer were identified, and hub genes were obtained, which were studied further for their function in advancing oral cancer.

2 Materials and Methodology

2.1 Data Collection and Pre-processing

Using the SRA toolkit, the data was mined from the NCBI GEO database (GSE series ID GSE145272). Among the 10 samples, 5 were metastatic tumor growth, and 5 were non-metastatic tumor growth. The downloaded data was converted into FASTQ format and classified into paired reads. Quality control was performed, and trimming was performed utilizing the Trimmomatic tool [9, 10], after which the reads were subjected to alignment using the STAR alignment tool [11]. These BAM files were then converted to the feature counts matrix by keeping the reference as Homo sapiens GRCh38 GTF file.

2.2 RNA-seq Analysis

The feature counts matrix obtained serves as input for RNA-Seq analysis. RNA-seq analysis was used to perform differential gene expression analysis on retrieved datasets [12]. This analysis was performed on R studio using packages *viz.* "*tidyverse*", "*tidyr*", "*DESeq2*", and "*dplyr*. DESeq2 analysis was assessed for normalization using negative binomial generalized linear models. After utilizing DESeq2 while keeping the design as tumor stage, a data frame was obtained to validate the up- and downregulated genes using adj-p value and logFC thresholds.

2.3 WGCNA Analysis

WGCNA was also performed on R studio [13], and the features count matrix as the input data. This analysis was performed to identify the co-expressed genes in the metastatic and non-metastatic stages of the tumor, respectively. The outliers were detected using hierarchical clustering and principal component analysis (PCA) methods. Normalization using DESeq2 was performed on the dataset, keeping the tumor stage as a design, and the gene with gene counts less than 15 in 75% of the samples was removed [14]. Further, each module's eigengenes were processed, which aids in associating modules with the phenotypic traits (tumor stages).

2.4 ML-seq Analysis

Using the RNA-seq dataset improves the classification model's and the algorithms' predictive performance. The "MLSeq" and "S4Vectors" packages in R were mainly used for this analysis. For this analysis, the results obtained from the WGCNA analysis were performed at module membership of 0.09 and the gene Significance of 0.5. The data was divided into the 70:30 ratio for the train and test datasets. To improve the model's performance, deseq-vst (deseq-Variance stabilizing transformation) and deseq-rlog (deseq-Regularized logarithmic transformation), and classification algorithms, such as Random Forest, Support Vector Machine (SVM) and NSC were trained and tested.

2.5 Network Analysis and Hub-Genes Identification

The STRING database generated a protein-protein interaction (PPI) network with a high confidence score of 0.700 as the cutoff. Cytoscape software visualizes the computational network to identify hub genes [15]. A Cytoscape plugin, StringApp, was used to import a network of driver genes obtained from the WGCNA analysis from the STRING online database into the Cytoscape software. Further, Cytohubba renders the hub genes associated with oral cancer, utilizing the MCC (Maximum Clique Centrality) algorithm. The MCC score for each node was computed, and the gene with the highest score was assigned as a hub gene in the network [15, 16].

3 Results and Discussion

3.1 Identification of DEGs

The dataset from the NCBI-GEO database was analyzed using R programming language to identify DEGs using the RNA-seq analysis approach. The Deseq2 package helps in normalizing the dataset and computing the DEGs.The results obtained for the alpha value of 0.05, gave us a total of 45,637 genes. Considering the adj-p-value of 0.05 and the logFC value>1 as a threshold for upregulated genes, we produced 27 upregulated in this study.

3.2 WGCNA Module Identification

After identifying DEGs, we sought to investigate the co-expression of genes between the metastatic and non-metastatic oral cancer cohorts. Initially, samples 'GSM4313073' and 'GSM4313082' were removed from the analysis as they were detected as outliers using HClust and PCA (Figs. 1, 2 and 3). As the outcome of this analysis, we obtained 64 modules, *i.e.*, sets of co-expressed genes, of which two contained significantly correlated genes. One module was positively correlated, while the other was negatively correlated, as represented by the heatmap (Fig. 4). The one which was positively correlated was considered for further downstream analysis. On additional filtration, keeping the Module Membership as 0.09 and Gene Significance as 0.5 as thresholds, we got 1169 that are co-expressed and highly significant in causing metastatic oral cancer.

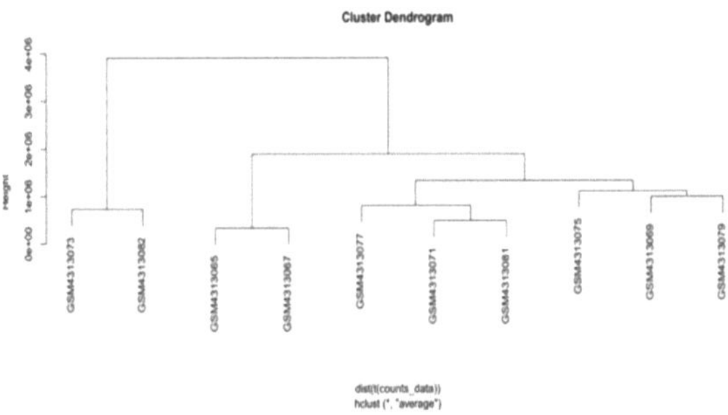

Fig. 1. Visualization of a cluster dendrogram showing identified outliers (GSM4313073, GSM4313082) using Hierarchical clustering method.

Fig. 2. Visualization of a cluster dendrogram showing identified outliers (GSM4313073, GSM4313082) using principle component Analysis method.

3.3 ML-Seq Analysis

As the driver genes were obtained from the WGCNA analysis, a Machine Learning model was built, trained on 70% of data consisting of gene expression values from 7 out

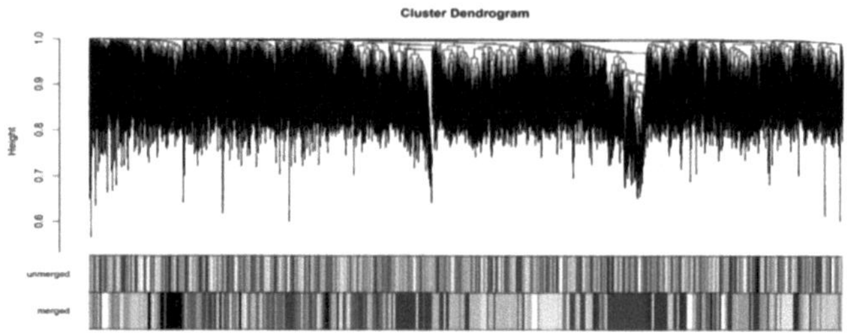

Fig. 3. Gene dendrogram obtained by hierarchical clustering analysis. The color rows underneath the dendrogram show the module assignment for merged unmerged modules. A unique color is assigned to each branch of the dendrogram signified that different genes belong to different gene co-expression modules. A total of 64 merged co-expression modules were obtained.

Fig. 4. Module trait association. Each row corresponds to a module, and the column corresponds to a single trait i.e. tumor stage. Each cell contains the corresponding correlation and p-value and shows that most significant gene module (MEantiquewhite4) with respect to metastatic oral cancer.

of 10 samples. The remaining 30% of the data of the left 3 samples was used to test the model. On building various models with various thresholds, an SVM classification, with the deseq-vst transformation-normalization technique performed the best out of all the models, with an accuracy of 100%, which indicated that the model infers true-positive predictions when kept the reference as a non-metastatic sample with a sensitivity of 97% and a specificity of 100% respectively with a p-value of 0.2963 (Fig. 5).

3.4 Network Construction and Hub-Genes Identification

The PPI (protein-protein interaction) network of the driver genes obtained from WGCNA analysis was constructed using the STRING database (Fig. 6). The network was exported to the Cytoscape software using StringApp plugins for better visualization. The generated network comprises 789 nodes and 987 edges, 2.5 average node degree, 0.343 average local clustering coefficient, and 1.2e-07 PPI enrichment p-value. In Cytoscape, the interaction scores of CytoHubba validated the top 10 genes as hub genes (Fig. 7) which included TTK protein kinase (*TTK*), Centromere protein E (*CENPE*), Cell division association cycle 5 (*CDCA5*), Centrosomal protein 55 (*CEP55*), Cell division cycle 20

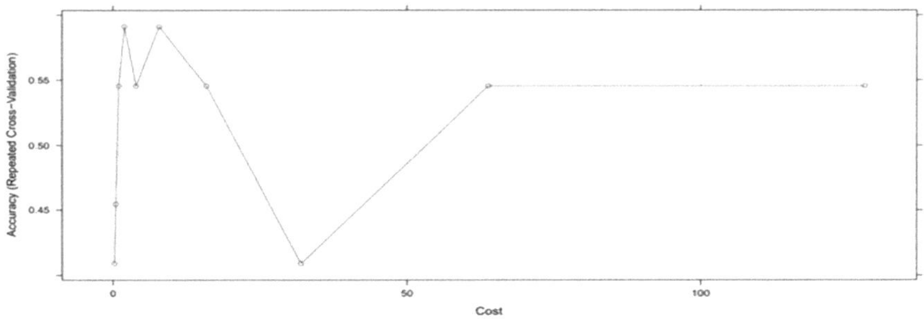

Fig. 5. Visualization of Accuracy v/s cost graph of SVM model of Machine Learning.

(*CDC20*), hyaluronan mediated motility receptor (*HMMR*), Thyroid hormone receptor interactor 13 (*TRIP13*), ZW10 interacting kinetochore protein (*ZWINT*), kinesin family member 11 (*KIF11*), Cyclin B2 (*CCNB2*).

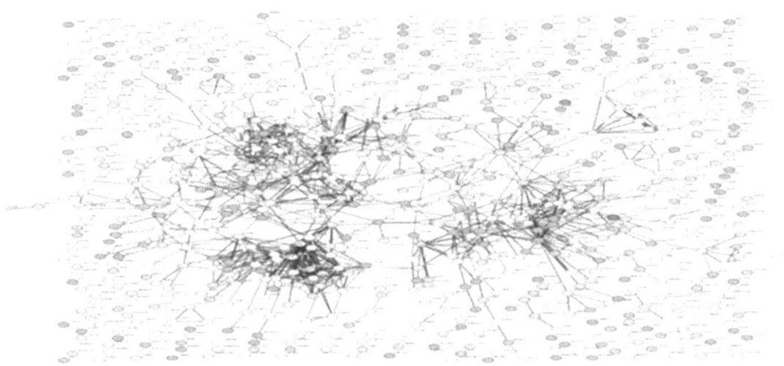

Fig. 6. PPI network constructed for the driver genes with Gene Significance > 0.5 and Module membership > 0.09 using STRING database. There were a total of 789 nodes, 987 edges, with a 2.5 average node degree and avg local clustering coefficient as 0.343, it has PPI enrichment p value as 1.2e-07.

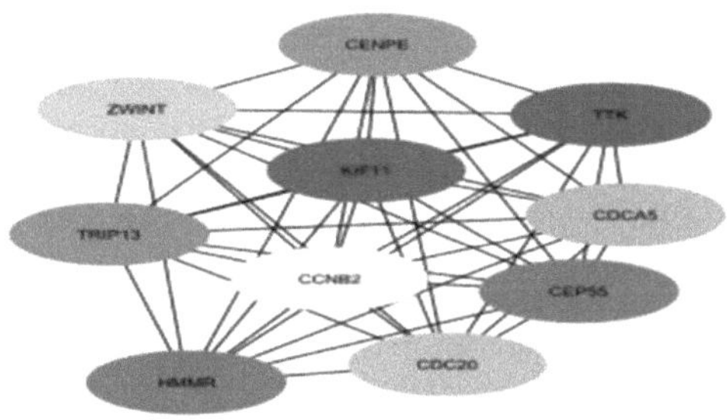

Fig. 7. Identification of the hub genes from the PPI network using maximal clique centrality (MCC) algorithm. Edges represent the protein associations.

4 Conclusion

This study employed a comprehensive methodology for analyzing oral cancer RNA-seq data obtained from the NCBI GEO database. The data curation, RNA-seq analysis, WGCNA, ML-seq analysis PPI analysis, hub gene identification, and gene-pathway enrichment provided a broad and in-depth understanding of the underlying mechanisms of metastatic and non-metastatic tumor growth. The study identified DEGs and co-expression gene modules involved in tumor progression, providing potential targets for drug design. Moreover, the ML-seq analysis delivered away to classify gene expressions in oral cancer. The STRING database and Cytoscape software helped identify hub genes crucial to oral cancer progression. Further downstream analysis could encompass identifying regulatory biomolecules, gene-set enrichment protein expression, and immune profiling for diagnostic insights. Additionally, single-gene and cumulative survival analyses can be conducted for prognostic perspectives, indicating the potential therapeutic utility of these genes and associated biomolecules.

References

1. Borse, V., Konwar, A.N., Buragohain, P.: Oral cancer diagnosis and perspectives in India. Sens Int. **1**, 100046 (2020)
2. Kavarthapu, A., Gurumoorthy, K.: Linking chronic periodontitis and oral cancer: a review. Oral Oncol. **121**, 105375 (2021)
3. Abati, S., Bramati, C., Bondi, S., Lissoni, A., Trimarchi, M.: Oral cancer and precancer: a narrative review on the relevance of early diagnosis. Int. J. Environ. Res. Public Health. **17**(24), 9160 (2020)
4. Bouaoud, J. et al.: Unmet needs and perspectives in Oral cancer prevention. Cancers (Basel). **14**(7), 1815 (2022)
5. Chattopadhyay, I., Verma, M., Panda, M.: Role of Oral microbiome signatures in diagnosis and prognosis of Oral cancer. Technol. Cancer Res. Treat. **18**, 1533033819867354 (2019)
6. Kasavi, C.: Gene co-expression network analysis revealed novel biomarkers for ovarian cancer. Front. Genet. **13**, 971845 (2022)
7. Rodriguez-Esteban, R., Jiang, X.: Differential gene expression in disease: a comparison between high-throughput studies and the literature. BMC Med. Genet. **10**(1), 59 (2017)
8. Hunter, B., Hindocha, S., Lee, R.W.: The role of artificial intelligence in early cancer diagnosis. Cancers (Basel). **14**(6), 1524 (2022)
9. Sewe, S.O., Silva, G., Sicat, P., Seal, S.E., Visendi, P.: Trimming and validation of Illumina short reads using Trimmomatic, trinity assembly, and assessment of RNA-Seq data. Methods Mol. Biol. **2443**, 211–232 (2022)
10. Corchete, L.A., Rojas, E.A., Alonso-López, D., De Las, R.J., Gutiérrez, N.C., Burguillo, F.J.: Systematic comparison and assessment of RNA-seq procedures for gene expression quantitative analysis. Sci. Rep. **10**(1), 19737 (2020)
11. Dobin, A., Gingeras, T.R.: Mapping RNA-seq reads with STAR. Curr. Protoc. Bioinformatics. **51**, 11.14.1–11.14.19 (2015)
12. Cui, W., Xue, H., Wei, L., Jin, J., Tian, X., Wang, Q.: High heterogeneity undermines generalization of differential expression results in RNA-Seq analysis. Hum. Genomics. **15**(1), 7 (2021)
13. Chen, Y., Liao, R., Yao, Y., Wang, Q., Fu, L.: Machine learning to identify immune-related biomarkers of rheumatoid arthritis based on WGCNA network. Clin. Rheumatol. **41**(4), 1057–1068 (2022)

14. Mohammad, T. et al.: Differential gene expression and weighted correlation network dynamics in high-throughput datasets of prostate cancer. Front. Oncol. **12**, 881246 (2022)
15. Wei, L.M. et al.: Identification of hub genes in triple-negative breast cancer by integrated bioinformatics analysis. Gland Surg. **10**(2), 799–806 (2021)
16. Chin, C.H., Chen, S.H., Wu, H.H., Ho, C.W., Ko, M.T., Lin, C.Y.: cytoHubba: identifying hub objects and sub-networks from complex interactome. BMC Syst. Biol. **8**(Suppl 4), S11 (2014)

Ensemble Learning and Neural Networks: Elevating Model Performance for Precise Cardiovascular Disease Detection

Kammara Jijgnas[1], K. Sai Deepak Reddy[1], Priya Gupta[2], Aarti Goel[3](✉), and Kime Sumpi[1]

[1] School of Engineering, Jawaharlal Nehru University, Delhi, India
[2] Atal Bihari Vajpayee School of Management and Entrepreneurship, Jawaharlal Nehru University, Delhi, India
priyagupta@jnu.ac.in
[3] Hansraj College, University of Delhi, Delhi, India
aarti@hrc.du.ac.in

Abstract. Cardiovascular diseases (CVDs) are the top cause of death worldwide, emphasizing the need for early detection to allow for preventive measures and effective treatment. This paper investigates the use of a dataset comprising 70,000 entries to evaluate the effectiveness of various machine learning models in predicting the presence of cardiovascular diseases (CVDs), the leading global cause of death. Such early detection is crucial for enabling prevention and treatment. Recent advances have highlighted the potential of ensemble learning techniques and neural networks in enhancing the accuracy of CVD identification. We explore and compare the performance of Logistic Regression, Random Forest, Decision Trees, XGBoost, and MLP classifiers in terms of their accuracy and precision in detecting cardiovascular diseases. This study aims to contribute to the expanding field of health research and the development of computational models that facilitate early and precise detection of cardiovascular diseases, thus promoting timely interventions and enhancing patient care.

Keywords: Cardiovascular Disease · Ensemble learning · Bagging · Neural Networks · Base Classifier · Meta Classifier

1 Introduction

Cardiovascular Diseases (CVDs) present a substantial challenge to global health, being the major contributor to global mortality. Early identification and diagnosis play a critical role in effective prevention and treatment strategies. This study aims to utilize advanced machine learning techniques in predicting CVD presence in individuals using extensive data sets with 70,000 data points. The research includes traditional statistical methods up through state-of-the-art ensemble learning practices like Neural Networks exploring how they fair when considering Decision Trees, Logistic Regression, Random Forest models XGBoost along with Multi-Layer Perceptron (MLP) classifiers on detecting CVDs strengths as well as their limitations within this context.

M. Paprzycki et al. (Eds.): ICACIS 2024, CCIS 2405, pp. 464–478, 2027.
https://doi.org/10.1007/978-3-032-30990-7_34

Recently, healthcare-related applications have been enhanced by utilizing ensemble learning methods and Neural Networks. This research paper aims to contribute to this ongoing improvement in the field of healthcare. We do this by proposing a methodology and then comparing it with other machine learning models. We aim to integrate these computational models to promote timely intervention and accurate detection of CVD hence leading to better patient care.

In the upcoming sections, we study the previous research done on CVDs on the same dataset that we use for our paper and shall examine the methodology used, features of the current dataset, and results obtained by implementing diverse machine learning models. The knowledge gained from this research is intended to guide future investigations, improve existing practices, and enhance our joint capability in identifying and resolving cardiovascular diseases with better efficiency.

2 Literature Review

Cardiovascular disease (CVD) stands out as a prominent heart disease affecting individuals across all age groups. Research has delved into comparing various Machine Learning algorithms to identify the optimal method for predicting cardiovascular disease by using a dataset with thirteen parameters and seventy thousand individual data points.. Mohan et al. [2] and T et al. [3] focused on improving the accuracy of heart disease detection through the use of diverse algorithms that determine whether an individual has heart disease. They evaluated the accuracies of machine learning models such as Decision Tree, KNN, Random Forest Classifier, and SVM, finding that the Gaussian SVM kernel achieved the highest expected accuracy of 86.2%.

Hybrid machine learning models have also been employed to predict heart diseases and optimize classification methods for such predictions. Various models, including Logistic Regression (LR) and XGBoost (XGB) hybrid algorithms, have shown high accuracy in disease prediction. Mahmud et al. [4] report that the Hybrid ensemble and XGBoost Classifier both achieve a testing accuracy of about 84%, which represents the best performance for binary classification in their studies. Similarly, Shirvaikar and Mandlik [5] advocate for the integration of Principal Component Analysis with five machine learning algorithms. Following comprehensive data preparation, the optimal model performance reached an accuracy of 73%.

A novel method was proposed by Feshki and Shijani [6] to improve the accuracy of neural networks, using a dataset of 303 samples, which represented both healthy and ill individuals. Despite the dataset containing 72 features, only 13 were selected through the PSO feature selection process. C. T. and J.P [7]. employed five machine learning models and two artificial neural networks (Logistic Regression, Decision Tree, Support Vector Machine, Random Forest and K-Nearest Neighbors), achieving an accuracy of 73.43% with the GA-ANN model.

Shorewala [8] discusses methods to increase the accuracy of coronary heart disease predictions using ensemble approaches. Further, Mohan et al. [9] sought to improve the detection precision of cardiovascular diseases. Waigi et al. [10] highlighted the importance of continuous physiological monitoring, including blood circulation rate, body temperature, and pulse rate, in their study of a machine learning model applied to the dataset.

Pasha et al. [11] focused on leveraging artificial neural networks, TensorFlow, and Keras, with a precision value specified as 0.85. Similarly, Shimaa Ouf [12] worked on assessment of the four cross-validation techniques using widely adopted mining classification techniques. The paper emphasizes the importance of utilizing data mining technologies for early detection of heart disease. These technologies can analyse extensive health data to quickly and accurately identify potential risk factors. Vanisree and Jyothi [13] developed a neural network based decision support system for diagnosing congenital heart disease using clinical signs and symptoms alone, showing that reliable automated screening is achievable even without laboratory or imaging inputs.

Data mining techniques are indispensable for optimizing healthcare delivery, empowering healthcare centres like hospitals or clinics to swiftly and accurately detect diseases in patients. This enables rapid diagnosis, ultimately leading to heightened patient satisfaction. Hazra et al. [14] summarize some research that uses data mining techniques to predict heart disease and analyzes different combinations of mining algorithms. It is completed by highlighting the significance of proper cleaning and pruning of datasets to provide better accuracy.

Palak et al. [15] evaluate different supervised learning algorithms and feature selection techniques to predict heart disease. The prediction accuracy shown by machine learning classifiers was 82.81%. The classification performance was improved by feature selection techniques to acquire an accuracy of up to 83.41%. Complementarily, Obayya et al. [16] use Honey Badger Optimization with Modified Deep Learning (ACVD-HBOMDL) Model to develop an Automated Cardiovascular Disease Diagnosis. The results of this technique were tested on a benchmark medical dataset and the results attained showed the significance of this technique over other existing techniques.

In order to predict heart disease accurately, P et al. [17] suggest a gradient boosting method that is based on RFE-GB that is- a recursive feature reduction algorithm. Similarly, Patel and Patel [18] review various types of ML algorithms and their potential to improve CVD diagnosis accuracy. It also discusses the importance of alliance between several domains like data experts, health practitioners, etc.

H et al. [19] focus on the classification of ECG heartbeat. Based on weighted XGBoost, this paper proposes a hierarchical method, the classifier consisting of two layers. Its comparison with other related works showed that their proposed method was more suitable.

Cheekati and Indraneel [20] adopts a comparative analytical approach to see if the accuracy of coronary heart disease prediction can be improved by ensemble techniques. Between conventional methods and bagged models, an increase of 1.96% was observed in its accuracy. Mohanty et al. [21] inspired the integration of advanced technologies and domain-specific knowledge in my research endeavors aimed at optimizing cardiovascular disease detection algorithms.

Among the many uses for machine learning and data mining is the ability to predict dependent variables from independent variables. These methods have great potential in the healthcare industry, as large data sets are difficult to handle manually. Globally, heart disease continues to be the leading cause of mortality, frequently as a result of delayed risk identification. Nevertheless, early risk prediction solutions are provided by machine learning. Commonly employed for this purpose are Support Vector Machines (SVM),

Neural Networks, Decision Trees, Regression, and Naïve Bayes classifiers. With 92.1% accuracy, SVM leads, followed by decision trees (89.6%) and neural networks (91%) [23]. Important contributions are played by risk factors as sex, age, smoking, diabetes, hypertension, and hypertension [22].

Analytical studies demonstrate the effectiveness of associative classification, neural networks, decision trees, and Naïve Bayes in predicting cardiac disease; associative classification is especially good at managing unstructured data [24, 25]. Decision trees are known for their ease of use and precision [26], whereas Naïve Bayes performs better than both decision trees and neural networks [24]. The Back Propagation Algorithm-trained supervised neural networks demonstrate acceptable illness prediction accuracy [28]. With remarkable success, ensemble approaches have been applied to improve the accuracy of categorization. For example, up to 99.97% accuracy was attained by combining neural networks with genetic algorithms based on fuzzy logic [27]. Similar to this, a trained recurrent fuzzy neural network based on genetic algorithms was able to diagnose heart disease with 97.78% accuracy [29]. Rough set-based categorization systems, for example, have produced accuracy levels of up to 93% [22].

Researchers have suggested feature selection techniques to increase accuracy even more [30]. Particle swarm optimization (PSO) has been used to optimize SVM-based classifiers for accurate heartbeat classification [31, 32]. Furthermore, by identifying recurring patterns linked to myocardial infarction, the K-means clustering method in conjunction with the Maximal Frequent Itemset method (MAFIA) has demonstrated potential in the prediction of heart illness [33].

Even with their successes, several categorization algorithms continue to show low accuracy. Hybrid approaches that combine many categorization algorithms have been presented as a solution to this. These methods improve prediction accuracy for cardiac disease as well as categorization efficiency. Along with feature selection, ensemble approaches including bagging, boosting, majority voting, and stacking further improve classification accuracy and provide insightful information for medical applications (Table 1).

Table 1. Analysis of Literature Review

Reference	Classifier	Accuracy	Speculation
[4]	Ensemble Hybrid voting	84.036%	Minimal Data Processing, Feature Considerations, High Correlations, Limited Hyperparameter Tuning.
[5]	LR, SVM, KNN, RF, NB with PCA	73%(RF)	used 5 ML algorithm with PCA for data selection, hyper-tuning and cross-validation not used
[7]	GA-ANN, LR, DT, RF, SVM, KNN	73.43% (GA-ANN)	given artificial neural network technique, lacks feature selection

(*continued*)

Table 1. (*continued*)

Reference	Classifier	Accuracy	Speculation
[8]	ensemble methods (Boosting and Stacking)	73.4% & 75.1%	use ensemble and cross-validation. Hyper-tuning and feature extraction are not employed
[9]	KNN, SVM, RF, DT	72.5% & 86.2% (SVM-kernel & gaussian)	used traditional learning, low accuracy
[10]	Decision Tree	73%	design a wristband for high accuracy
[11]	SVM, KNN, DT, ANN, TensorFlow	85% (ANN)	given data mining, feature extraction, and selection process not used
[12]	Data mining techniques with cross-validation	71.82% & 89.01% (NN)	ML algorithm not used for classification
[15]	Supervised learning algorithms & feature selection techniques	82.81% & 83.41% (feature selection)	Ensemble classification not employed

3 Proposed Methodology

3.1 Dataset

We use the cardiovascular disease dataset from Kaggle [1], which includes 70,000 samples encompassing 13 parameters. During model development, 70% of the dataset is assigned for training the new models, while the enduring 30% is set aside for assessing the performance of the models.

3.2 Data Exploration and Preprocessing

This paper delves into optimizing a dataset for hypertension research through meticulous preprocessing and feature engineering. The process involves standardizing age, addressing blood pressure outliers, encoding gender, and handling correlated features. Notable steps include detecting and removing outliers in blood pressure, height, and weight, as well as utilizing PyCaret for automated feature selection and hyperparameter tuning. The study culminates in a refined dataset, poised for comprehensive and insightful hypertension research.

To address high correlation, weight is removed due to its redundancy with BMI. Additionally, BMI class and pulse pressure are derived from AP_HI and AP_LO. Given the strong correlation between AP_HI and AP_LO, AP_LO is subsequently removed. The feature 'bp_cat' is eliminated due to its negligible impact, as observed during feature elimination (Table 2, Figs. 1 and 2).

Table 2. List of Features

No.	Feature	Type
1	id	Numeric
2	age	Numeric
3	gender	Categorical (0:Female, 1:Male)
4	height	Numeric
5	weight	Numeric
6	ap_hi	Numeric
7	ap_lo	Numeric
8	cholesterol	Categorical (1) Normal, (2) above normal, (3) well above normal
9	gluc	Categorical (1) Normal, (2) above normal, (3) well above normal
10	smoke	Binary (0:No, 1:Yes)
11	alco	Binary (0:No, 1:Yes)
12	active	Binary (0:No, 1:Yes)
13	cardio	Binary (0:No, 1:Yes)
14	bmi	Numeric
15	bmi_class	Categorical (0: Anorexic 1: Underweight 2: Normal weight 3: Overweight 4: Obesity Class I 5: Obesity Class II 6: Obesity Class III)
16	bp_cat	Categorical (0, 1, 2, 3, 4, 5, 6, 7)
17	pulse_press	Numeric

Algorithm 1

Data:

training data D_{train},
testing data D_{test}
validation data D_{valid},
an ensemble classifier S,
a set of classification algorithms < c1, c2, ..., cn >,
a meta-classifier M,
number of base classifiers n.

Result: ensemble classifier Z

<u>Step 1: First level classifier (Stacking)</u>

best_base_classifiers = []

Iterate through the range of base classifiers.

for i in range(n):

Perform the operation <li1, li2, ... lin>←<L1, L2, .., Ln>(si)
base_classifiers = get_base_classifiers(si)

Check accuracies <ai ai , ... ai > of <li1, li2, ...lin > on D_{valid};
accuracies = [check_accuracy(classifier, D_{valid}) for classifier in base_classifiers]

Select the best performing base classifier li from <li1, li2, ... lin > based on accuracies
best_classifier=base_classifiers[argmax(accuracies)]
best_base_classifiers.append(best_classifier)

Send the best base classifiers to meta-classifier M
send_to_M(best_base_classifiers)

Return the ensemble classifier Z, created by integrating M, for the classification of instances in Dtest
ensemble_classifier_Z = integrate_classifiers_M()
classify_instances_Dtest(ensemble_classifier_Z)

<u>Step 2: Second level classifier (Bagging)</u>

best_bagging_classifiers = []

Iterate through the range of bagging classifiers

for i in range(n):

Perform the operation li ← L(si)

classifier = get_base_classifier(si)

Check the accuracy ai of li on Dvalid
accuracy_i = check_accuracy(classifier, Dvalid)
best_bagging_classifiers.append(classifier)

Send the best bagging classifiers to meta-classifier M
send_to_M(best_bagging_classifiers)

Return the ensemble classifier Z, created by integrating M, for the classification of instances in Dtest
ensemble_classifier_Z = integrate_classifiers_M()
classify_instances_Dtest(ensemble_classifier_Z)

Step 3: Hybrid ensemble
final_predictions = []

Process input
for i in range(n):
Perform majority voting on final predictions for each iteration
final_prediction_i = majority_vote(final_prediction_i)
final_predictions.append(final_prediction_i)

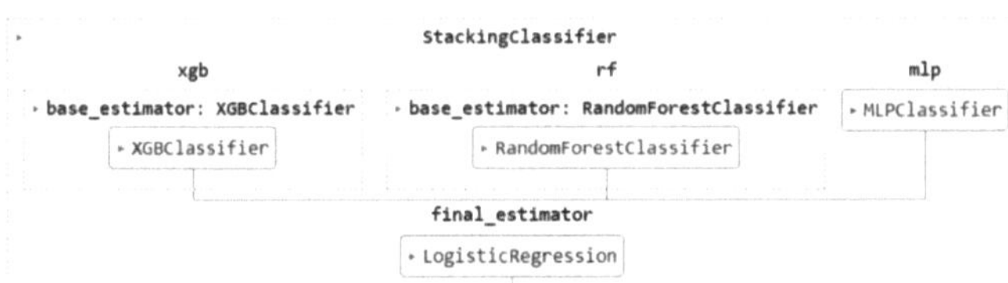

Fig. 1. Proposed Stacking Classifier

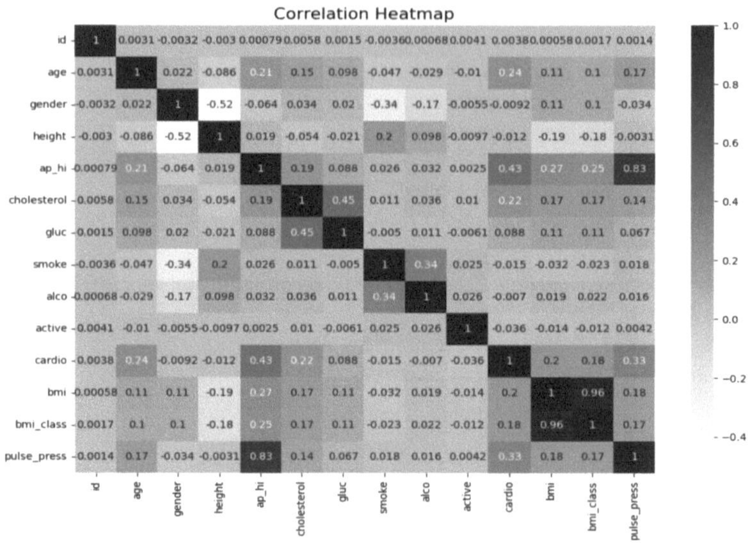

Fig. 2. Correlation Heatmap

Traditional Classifiers

Logistic Regression: The supervised Machine Learning Algorithm where we use a sigmoid function, that takes input as independent variables and output gives one of two possible values: 0 or 1.

Decision trees: It is a form of supervised learning primarily employed to address classification problems. It is structured like a branching tree, where each internal node denotes a feature of the dataset. And the branches themselves symbolize the decision rules derived from these features, guiding the flow from one node to another based on specific criteria. At the end of these branches are the leaf nodes, which signify the final outcomes or decisions of the model.

Random Forest: It is a classification model containing multiple decision trees applied to diverse dataset subsets, with subsequent averaging to enhance predictive accuracy. Greater accuracy is achieved with an increase in the number of trees. This prevents the problem of overfitting.

MLPClassifier Neural Networks: Multilayer Perceptron is a structured feedforward artificial neural network model intended for mapping input datasets to their corresponding outputs. It consists of multiple layers, each fully interconnected with the subsequent one. Neurons in these layers, excluding the input layer, utilize nonlinear activation functions.

XGBoost: XGBoost which stands for 'Extreme Gradient Boosting', is a fine-tuned distributed Gradient Boosting library created to enhance the efficiency and scalability of machine learning models. Operating as an ensemble learning strategy, it consolidates predictions from multiple weak models to generate a more robust outcome.

Ada Boost Algorithm: This ensemble learning technique is applicable to both regression and classification tasks. It is used to classify data by combining multiple weak learners by assigning the misclassified occurrences more weight to a strong learner.

Gradient Boosting Classifier: This method is known for prediction speed and accuracy for large and complex data. The core concept involves constructing models in sequence where every successive model aims to minimize the errors made by its predecessors.

SVM: The Support Vector Machine defines an optimal line or decision boundary, called hyperplane in order to linearly divide n-dimensional space into classes and to ease precise classification of incoming data points. To achieve this objective, the outermost points known as support vectors are identified by SVM for formulating the hyperplane.

KNN: KNN works on the assumption that similar data points will produce similar results. KNN is useful in classification and regression problems. The prediction is established by averaging the points in the k most similar neighbouring elements

Machine Learning Ensemble Classifier: Ensemble learning is a wide-ranging approach in machine learning which integrates multiple models for improving overall predictive performance.

The main types of ensemble learning methods are:

Bagging: This is an ensemble learning method designed to avoid overfitting by creating multiple subsets of the training dataset through bootstrapping. Here training a base model on each group, and the final prediction is made by taking the average or voting on these models.

Illustration

(a) Bagging with XGBoost: This approach helps to lessen overfitting, and to advance the model generalization, and even enhance predictive accuracy by leveraging the diversity introduced through various subsets.
(b) Bagging with Random Forest: This method enhances the model stability, even addresses overfitting, and improves overall performance by combining predictions from multiple decision trees.

Stacking: The implementation of this stacking approach involves merging predictions from different base models to build a meta-model. The predictions of these base models act as inputs for an advanced model, allowing stacking to capture intricate patterns in the data, resulting in improved predictive accuracy of the final model.

Boosting: Boosting is an ensemble learning technique designed to construct a robust classifier by combining multiple weak classifiers. This method initiates by constructing a model from the training data and subsequently generating additional models to address the errors identified in the initial model. Here this iterative process continues until the entire training dataset is accurately predicted or the maximum allowable number of models is reached.

Voting: It's like a team of models working together in this machine learning ensemble model. They get trained in a bunch, and when it comes to making a prediction, they vote on which class they think is most likely. Instead of relying on just one model, the idea is to create a strong team that considers the majority vote for each output class, making predictions together as a consolidated unit.

The Voting Classifier employs two forms of voting:

1. *Hard Voting*: It includes making predictions by taking the majority vote out of individual classifiers in an ensemble. The outcome is determined by the class that receives the majority of votes from the models within the group.
2. *Soft Voting*: Soft voting is all about figuring out the prediction for each class by thinking about the average probability assigned to that class by all the classifiers in an ensemble (Table 3)

Table 3. Models Performance Metrics

Model	Accuracy	AUC	Recall	Precision
Gradient Boosting	0.7328	**0.8030**	0.6870	0.7508
Light Gradient Boosting Classifier	0.7319	0.7988	0.6847	0.7160
CatBoost Classifier	0.7305	0.7976	0.6837	0.7487
AdaBoost Classifier	0.7276	0.7927	0.6509	**0.7626**
Extreme Gradient	0.7276	0.7906	0.6820	0.7448
Logistic Regression	0.7252	0.6657	0.7497	0.7052
Ridge Classifier	0.7231	0.0000	0.6556	0.7517
Linear Discriminant Analysis	0.7231	0.7885	0.6557	0.7517
Naive Bayes	0.7166	0.7788	0.6275	0.7568
Random Forest	0.7047	0.7623	0.6889	0.7059
Extra Trees Classifier	0.6953	0.7413	0.6830	0.6947
K Neighbors Classifier	0.6855	0.7317	0.6594	0.6898
Quadratic Discriminant Analysis	0.6846	0.7440	0.6244	0.7038
Decision Tree Classifier	0.6363	0.6360	0.6219	0.6342
SVM - Linear Kernel	0.5986	0.0000	0.8266	0.6186
Dummy Classifier	0.5063	0.5000	0.0000	0.0000
ANN	0.5000	0.5000	0.6700	0.5000
Stacking Classifier [XGB, SVM, DT, Hypertuning of RF]	0.7335	0.7982	0.7054	0.7460
Voting Classifier [SVM, DT, Hyper tuning of RF]	0.6816	0.7637	0.6829	0.6800
Bagging XGBoost	**0.7370**	**0.8029**	0.6916	0.7583
Ensemble Hybrid Voting [RF, KNN, DT, XGB, SVM, and LR]	0.7367	0.7366	**0.6916**	0.7562
Proposed Model	**0.7381**	0.7479	**0.6847**	**0.7652**

4 Results and Discussions

In this study, the Stacking Ensemble model achieved an accuracy of 0.7381, showing a good number of properly classified occurrences. This tells us that the model is pretty good at identifying the presence of cardiovascular disease. Also, with an AUC of 0.7479, our model shows strong abilities in distinguishing between different outcomes. The balance between recall (0.6847) and precision (0.7652) ensures a careful and accurate identification of people with cardiovascular disease, reducing the chances of overlooking and at the same time minimizing the chance of inaccuracies.

When we compared it to other methods like XGBoost, Random Forest, and MLP classifiers, the Stacking Ensemble performed better. Also using Artificial Neural Networks (ANN) in the analysis of the dataset yielded an initial accuracy of (0.50). This highlights that using a combination of models can really improve how accurately we can predict things. Our proposed model is like a team effort, where we bring together the strengths of XGBoost, Random Forest, and MLP classifiers in the Stacking Ensemble framework. This way, we use each model's special skills to make a more robust and accurate predictive model (Figs. 3 and 4).

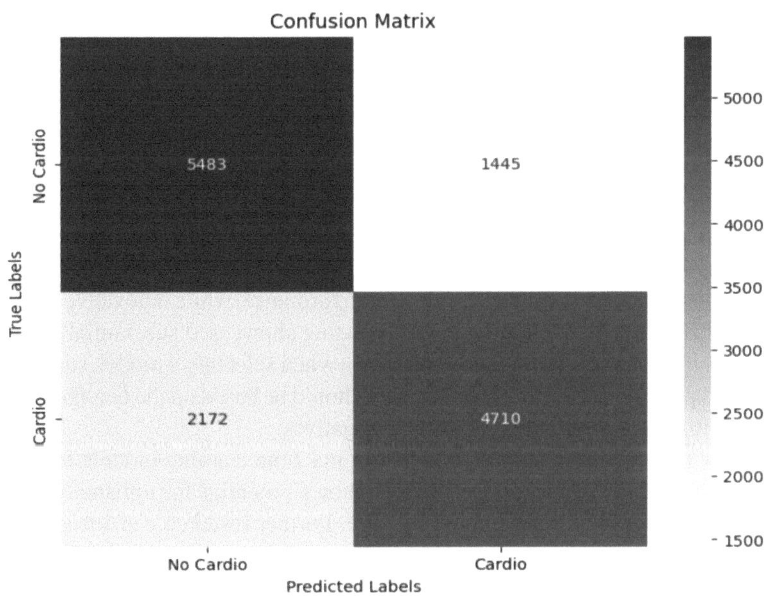

Fig. 3. Confusion Matrix

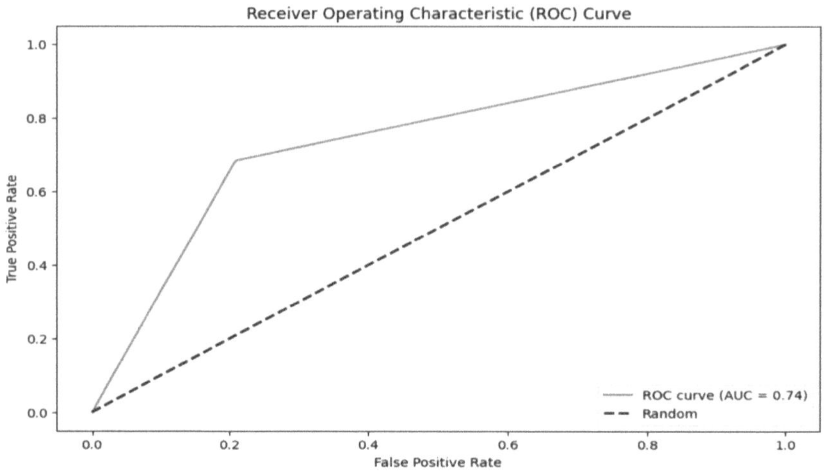

Fig. 4. ROC Curve of Proposed Model

5 Conclusion

We have studied and utilized different machine learning algorithms, each of which shows diverse outcomes. A notable result was displayed by our proposed model which also achieved the highest accuracy and precision. Through the analysis of our literature review on other research papers and the results of our proposed method, we highlight the significance of considering ensemble learning techniques like Bagging XGBoost and Ensemble Hybrid Voting for competitive results. Decision Tree classifiers and Logistic Regression, being traditional classifiers, showed moderate performance, while innovative approaches like Gradient Boosting and Light Gradient Boosting showcased substantial accuracy.

However, it is important to consider priorities when selecting a model, such as giving importance to precision or recall. This decision should be based on the healthcare context and the potential costs of positives and false negatives.

Our study provides insights into comparing machine learning models for detecting cardiovascular disease. The proposed model shows potential for enhancing detection and timely intervention thereby improving care. Further research can focus on feature engineering, refining models. Implementing them in real world scenarios to advance healthcare practices.

References

1. Sulianova, S.: Cardiovascular Disease Dataset. Kaggle (2019). https://www.kaggle.com/datasets/sulianova/cardiovascular-disease-dataset/data
2. Jagan Mohan, S., Kancharla, S., Illa, M., Arigela, S.: Effective detection of cardiovascular disease using machine learning. Int. J. Comput. Sci. Commun. (2021) https://csjournals.com/IJCSC/PDF12-2/12.%20Jagan.pdf

3. Chidambaram, T., Logesh Kannan, N., Gowsalya, M., et al.: Heart Disease Detection Using Machine Learning, 27 October 2020, PREPRINT (Version 1) available at Research Square https://doi.org/10.21203/rs.3.rs-97004/v1
4. Mahmud, T., Barua, A., Begum, M., Chakma, E., Das, S., Sharmen, N.: An improved framework for reliable cardiovascular disease prediction using hybrid ensemble learning. In: 2023 International Conference on Electrical, Computer and Communication Engineering (ECCE), pp. 1–6, Chittagong, Bangladesh (2023). https://doi.org/10.1109/ECCE57851.2023.10101564
5. Advait Shirvaikar, P.S.P.R., Mandlik, A.: Prediction of cardiovascular disease by applying a combination of principal component analysis with machine learning techniques. Int. Res. J. Eng. Technol. **8**(9) (2021)
6. Feshki, M.G., Shijani, O.S.: Improving the heart disease diagnosis by evolutionary algorithm of pso and feed forward neural network. In: 2016 Artificial Intelligence and Robotics (IRANOPEN), pp. 48–53. IEEE (2016)
7. Arroyo, J.C.T., Delima, A.J.P.: An optimized neural network using genetic algorithm for cardiovascular disease prediction. J. Adv. Info. Technol. **13**(1) (2022)
8. Shorewala, V. "Early detection of coronary heart disease using ensemble techniques." Informatics in Medicine Unlocked, vol. 26, 2021, p. 100655.
9. Mohan, S.J., et al.: Effective detection of cardiovascular disease using machine learning
10. Waigi, D., et al.: Predicting the risk of heart disease using advanced machine learning approach. Eur. J. Mol. Clin. Med. **7**(7), 1638–1645 (2020)
11. Pasha, S.N., et al.: Cardiovascular disease prediction using deep learning techniques. IOP Conf. Series Mater. Sci. Eng. **981**(2), 022006 (2020)
12. Shimaa Ouf, A.I.: A proposed paradigm for intelligent heart disease prediction system using data mining techniques. J. Southwest Jiaotong Univ. **56**(4) (2021)
13. Vanisree, K., Jyothi, S.: Decision support system for congenital heart disease diagnosis based on signs and symptoms using neural networks. Int. J. Comput. Appl. **19**(6), 6–12 (2011)
14. Hazra, A., et al.: Heart disease diagnosis and prediction using machine learning and data mining techniques. Adv. Comput. Sci. Technol. **10**(7), 2137–2159 (2017)
15. Khurana, P., Sharma, S., Goyal, A.: Heart Disease Diagnosis: Performance Evaluation of Supervised Machine Learning and Feature Selection Techniques (2021). https://doi.org/10.1109/SPIN52536.2021.9565963
16. Obayya, M., Alsamri, J., Al-Hagery, M., Mohammed, A., Hamza, M.: Automated Cardiovascular Disease Diagnosis Using Honey Badger Optimization with Modified Deep Learning Model, p. 1 (2023). https://doi.org/10.1109/ACCESS.2023.3286661
17. P Theerthagiri, et al. "Cardiovascular disease prediction using recursive feature elimination and gradient boosting classification techniques." arXiv preprint arXiv:2106.08889 (2021)
18. Patel, D.U., Patel, S.: A review, synthesizing frameworks, and future research agenda: use of AI & ML models in cardiovascular diseases diagnosis. Int. J. Innov. Technol. Explor. Eng. **12**(11), 12–19
19. Shi, H., Wang, H., Huang, Y., Zhao, L., Qin, C., Liu, C.: A hierarchical method based on weighted extreme gradient boosting in ecg heartbeat classification. Comput. Methods Prog. Biomed. **171**, 1–10 (2019)
20. Cheekati, D.D.N., Rao, V., Indraneel, S.: Ensemble approaches can aid in the early detection of coronary heart disease. In: NVEO-Natural Volatiles & Essential Oils Journal-NVEO, pp. 12224–12239 (2021)
21. Mohanty, S.N., Chatterjee, J.M., Jain, S., Elngar, A.A., Gupta, P.: Recommender System with Machine Learning and Artificial Intelligence. John Wiley & Sons (2020)
22. Nahar, J., Imam, T., Tickle, K.S., Chen, Y.-P.P.: Association rule mining to detect factors which contribute to heart disease in males and females. Expert Syst. Appl. **40**(4), 1086–1093 (2013). https://doi.org/10.1016/j.eswa.2012.08.028

23. Rao, S.N., Shenoy M, P., Gopalakrishnan, M., Anitha Kiran, B.: Applicability of the Cleveland clinic scoring system for the risk prediction of acute kidney injury after cardiac surgery in a south Asian cohort. Indian Heart J. **70**(4), 533–537 (2018). https://doi.org/10.1016/j.ihj.2017.11.022
24. Cheng, C.-A., Chiu, H.-W.: An artificial neural network model for the evaluation of carotid artery stenting prognosis using a national-wide database. In: Proc. 39th Annu. Int. Conf. IEEE Eng. Med. Biol. Soc, pp. 2566–2569. EMBC (2017)
25. Esfahani, H.A., Ghazanfari, M.: Cardiovascular disease detection using a new ensemble classifier. In: Proceedings IEEE 4th International Conference Knowledge Based Engineering and Innovation, pp. 1011–1014. KBEI (Dec. 2017)
26. Dammak, F., Baccour, L., Alimi, A.M.: The impact of criterion weights techniques in TOPSIS method of multi-criteria decision making in crisp and intuitionistic fuzzy domains. In: Proceedings IEEE International Conference Fuzzy Syst. (FUZZ-IEEE), vol. 9, pp. 1–8 (2015)
27. Baccour, L.: Amended fused TOPSIS-VIKOR for classification (ATOVIC) applied to some UCI data sets. Expert Syst. Appl. **99**, 115–125 (2018). https://doi.org/10.1016/j.eswa.2018.01.025
28. Kelwade, J.P., Salankar, S.S.: Radial basis function neural network for prediction of cardiac arrhythmias based on heart rate time series. In: Proceeding IEEE 1st International Conference Control, Measurement Instrument (CMI), pp. 454–458 (2016)
29. Das, R., Turkoglu, I., Sengur, A.: Effective diagnosis of heart disease through neural networks ensembles. Expert Syst. Appl. **36**(4), 7675–7680 (2009). https://doi.org/10.1016/j.eswa.2008.09.013
30. Liberatore, M.J., Nydick, R.L.: The analytic hierarchy process in medical and health care decision making: a literature review. Eur. J. Oper. Res. **189**(1), 194–207 (2008)
31. Abdullah, A.S., Rajalaxmi, R.R.: A data mining model for predicting the coronary heart disease using random forest classifier. In: Proceedings of the International Conference Recent Trends Computing Methods, Communication and Controls, pp. 22–25, Apr (2012)
32. Nahar, J., Imam, T., Tickle, K.S., Chen, Y.-P.P.: Computational intelligence for heart disease diagnosis: a medical knowledge driven approach. Expert Syst. Appl. **40**(1), 96–104 (2013). https://doi.org/10.1016/j.eswa.2012.07.032
33. Kumar, P.S., Anand, D., Kumar, V.U., Bhattacharyya, D., Kim, T.-H.: A computational intelligence method for effective diagnosis of heart disease using genetic algorithm. Int. J. Bio-Sci. Bio-Technol. **8**(2), 363–372 (2016)

Breast Invasive Ductal Carcinoma Tumor Detection and Classification Across Different Magnification Levels Using Transfer Learning

Muniraj Gupta[1], Naveen Kumar Singh[1], Mankirat Kaur[1], Nidhi Verma[2(✉)], and Saurabh Kumar Sharma[1(✉)]

[1] School of Computer & Systems Sciences, Jawaharlal Nehru University, New Delhi 110067, India
saurabhsharma@mail.jnu.ac.in

[2] Department of Microbiology, Ramlal Anand College, University of Delhi, New Delhi 110021, India
nidhiverma5@gmail.com

Abstract. Breast cancer most commonly diagnosed in women is called invasive ductal carcinoma (IDC), and it is the leading cause of cancer-related mortality for women globally. The detection and classification of breast cancer pose substantial challenges for the researcher's community. The artificial network of neurons has emerged as a formidable tool for extracting features for classifying cancer data. This paper addresses the challenges of precise detection and classification of breast cancer at multi-level magnifications using transfer learning that employs the pre-trained EfficientNet (ENet) and MobileNetV2 (MNet) with low computational cost. The modified via transfer learning ENet and MNet tailored the capture intricate patterns within histopath breast cancer images at multi-level magnifications with prior knowledge of pre-trained model weights. Our experimental methodology utilizes a breast histopath image dataset, partitioned into training (80%), validation (10%), and testing (10%) segments at different magnifications.

Keywords: Benign and Malignant Tumors · Histopathology Images · Deep Learning · Transfer Learning · Breast Cancer

1 Introduction

In 2022, approximately 20 million new cancer cases were reported globally, and 9.7 million fatalities were recorded. Among these fatalities, 11.6% were attributed to breast cancer, making it the second most common cause of mortality globally [1]. Notably, the incidence of cancer is rising annually in developing countries, such as India. According to the 2024 report from Apollo Hospitals on Indian national health, cancer is occurring at younger ages in India compared to Western countries, with the number expected to rise from 1.39 million cases in 2020 to around 1.57 million cases by 2025 [2].

Authors Muniraj Gupta and Naveen Kumar Singh have equally contributed to this chapter.

M. Paprzycki et al. (Eds.): ICACIS 2024, CCIS 2405, pp. 479–488, 2027.
https://doi.org/10.1007/978-3-032-30990-7_35

Cancer can develop in any organ when cells proliferate uncontrollably beyond normal limits human cells regularly divide and develop to create new cells as required, replacing cells that are dead or damaged. However, when this regulated process fails, damaged or abnormal cells accumulate, leading to what is known as a tumor [3]. This could be triggered by lifestyle changes, dietary habits, and genetic factors. Tumors can be benign or malignant. Benign tumors are often not life-threatening and do not infiltrate tissue adjacent to them; they generally do not return once removed. Malignant tumors, on the other hand, spread swiftly via the lymphatic and circulatory systems into the surrounding tissues, making timely detection and treatment crucial [4]. Early recognition might reduce the severity of cancers by involving both screening along with early-stage diagnosis [5].

Early detection is feasible through screening methods that identify abnormalities, including breast MRI, mammography, ultrasound, and biopsy. Mammography is particularly effective in developed countries with robust healthcare systems. However, in developing countries like In India, where resources are scarce mammography could not be as widely available or reasonably priced [6].

Usually, the lobules (the glands that produce milk) or ducts (the tubes that transport milk to the nipple) are where breast cancer begins. These regions are susceptible to the development of two primary cancer types: ductal carcinoma in situ and invasive lobular carcinoma in the ducts, and lobular carcinoma in situ and invasive lobular carcinoma in the lobules [7, 8]. As per research, IDC accounts for 80% of all breast cancer cases [9]. This kind of cancer can spread to other body areas and goes beyond the typical duct borders. Axillary dissection, Lumpectomy, Sentinel Lymph Node Biopsy, Contralateral Prophylactic Mastectomy, and Mastectomy are some of the main surgical treatments for treating breast cancer. While histopathological images are invaluable for diagnosing breast cancer, they pose challenges in terms of processing time, magnification level and image quality. In the medical sector, breast cancer detection and classification are essential for early, life-saving medications. Computer Based Diagnostic Systems (CBDS) are progressively used to interpret these images, as physical interpretation can be tedious and prone to errors. Significant potential has been demonstrated in CBDS by recent developments in deep learning (DL) models, analyzing data from various sources, including text, sound, and images. However, challenges remain, such as high error rates in large datasets, computational expense, and inadequate training. Our research aims to address these issues in comparison to existing methods. The primary contributions of this study are as follows:

- In this paper a novel approach utilizing transfer learning with low computational overhead; propose MNet and ENet models with pre-trained weights from the MobileNetV2 and EfficientNetB0 architectures.
- We investigate the impact of image at different magnification levels on the detection and classification of benign and malignant tissue. Differentiation, highlighting their significance in capturing complex patterns within the images.
- In contrast to existing models, our proposed approach demonstrates exceptional performance in the form of precision, recall, F1 score, and accuracy across various magnification levels.

- Furthermore, our model excels in classification tasks even at low magnification level (100X), offering potential cost savings in image capture setups and Computer Based Diagnostic Systems (CBDS).

The remainder of the paper's structure is arranged as follows: Sect. 2 examines relevant research. Section 3 delves dataset. In Sect. 4 proposed methodology. In Sect. 5 experimental framework. Section 6 presents the results and discussion. The conclusion is finally outlined in Sect. 6.

2 Related Work

When using computational technologies to detect abnormalities, such as those used in cancer-screening algorithms, learning processes primarily, utilize pre-processed data instead of relying on separate feature extraction techniques [10]. Each system within a CBDS framework performs a specific function, sequentially passing results to subsequent processes [11].

The adoption of automatic methods for the classification and prediction of breast cancer is on the rise, proving to be more effective and accurate than traditional human assessments [12]. A Convolutional Neural Network (CNN) model designed to predict Invasive Ductal Carcinoma (IDC) has been developed and tested across two datasets featuring distinct image divisions, where datasets are segmented into validation and testing phases [13]. In [14] have employed a transfer learning strategy utilizing the VGG19 model to address histopathological and imbalance classification challenges with each network layer within VGG19 designated for feature extraction. In [15] introduced a classifier based on Quaternion Discrete Radial Tchebichef Moments (QRTM) for robust color image representation in biomedical applications.

Significant progress has been made in the field of artificial intelligence in a variety of fields. DL models excel in discerning intricate patterns and relationships within data, enabling accurate predictions and decision-making across multiple applications. This has led to practical implementations in autonomous driving, medical diagnostics, and many more. DL models frequently utilize the ImageNet dataset for classification; however, in scenarios with limited data, transfer learning strategies are adopted [16]. In [17], a dual-path feature map extraction trained at different magnification levels is used to power a hybrid deep neural network that incorporates residual and initiation blocks for cancer diagnosis. In [19], a model explicitly designed for detecting IDC in women. To accomplish this, they employed the Resnet model for both feature extraction and classification using a pre-trained Resnet 50 network and the stochastic gradient descent optimizer using histopathology images.

In our study, we apply transfer learning on multi-level magnification histopath images and, achieving improved precision, recall, F1-score, and accuracy.

3 Dataset

Breast cancer histology (BCH) images dataset obtained from a clinical investigation conducted in 2014 [18], comprising 82 patients and 9,109 microscopic images of breast cancer tissue overall, divided into two groups: malignant and benign. Multiple magnification levels, including 40X, 100X, 200X, and 400X, are used to obtain these images. Fig. 1 show distribution of BCH images for both benign and malignant classes.

4 Proposed Model

Initially, the base models of EfficientNet and MobileNetV2 are acquired without including the ImageNet classifier at the top. These models are tailored for classification tasks leveraging their prior training on ImageNet datasets. The output from the second-to-last dense layer is retrieved once the base model is acquired, and then a global average pooling 2D layer is used. Moreover, several new dense layers are introduced, incorporating Relu, Dropout layers, and Dense. A network architecture, illustrated in Fig. 2, comprises three layers: First, there is a fully connected (FC) layer with 256 neurons. This is followed by another FC layer with 64 neurons. Lastly, there is a layer for binary classification that uses a softmax function. The initial layers' dropout rates are fixed at 0.2. By using input from the base model and producing output as specified in the final dense layer for classification. The model is compiled using the adam optimizer with a learning rate of 0.001. In our proposed model, the Mnet and Enet CNN architectures encompass multiple parameters and hyper parameters, such as loss function selection, early stopping criteria, number of epochs, historical tracking of accuracy and loss aimed at enhancing the model's efficiency.

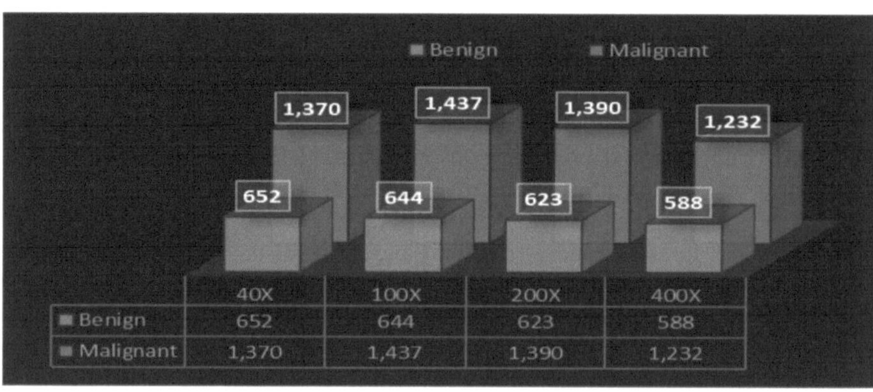

Fig. 1. Dataset counting for benign and malignant at different magnification levels.

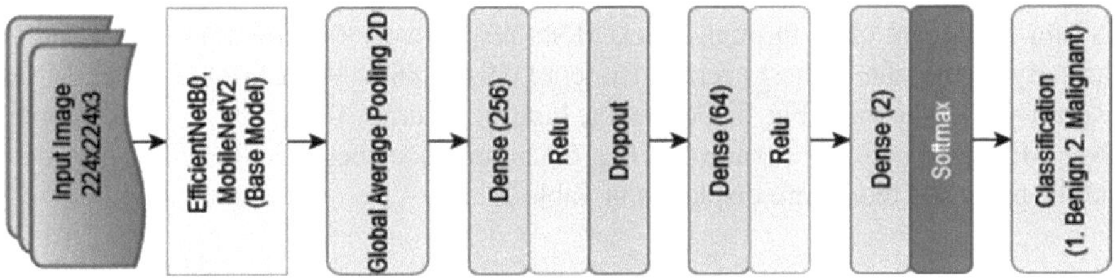

Fig. 2. Proposed model flow chart.

5 Experimental Framework and Evaluation Measures

The experiment is performed on Dell Power Edge R750 server having Nvidia A2 GPU, and used the python 3.1 with Tensorflow, Keras, Scikit learn libraries and its parameters. Take 32 batches and 0.001 learning rate for Adam optimizer. To test model performance, different evaluation matrics are used for classification task. Through the analysis of this input data, the model acquires the necessary information. The model then classifies the test data according to its training and forecasts the results based on model performance.

Different metrics, including precision (Pd), which represents the proportion of correct positive predictions, is defined in Eq. 1. Recall that, as described in Eq. 2, quantifies the percentage of real positives that are accurately recognized. F1 score, which serves as a metric for evaluating the effectiveness of a classification scheme by assessing the accuracy of its predictions for the positive class demonstrated in Eq. 3. Accuracy utilized to evaluate the effectiveness of our proposed moded defined in Eq. 4.

$$Pd = \left\{ \frac{\mathrm{TP}}{(\mathrm{TP} + \mathrm{FP})} \right\} \tag{1}$$

$$Recall = \left\{ \frac{\mathrm{TP}}{(\mathrm{TP}+\mathrm{FN})} \right\} \tag{2}$$

$$F1 = \left\{ 2 \times \frac{(\mathrm{Pd} \times Recall)}{(\mathrm{Pd} + Recall)} \right\} \tag{3}$$

$$Accuracy = \left\{ \frac{\mathrm{TP}+\mathrm{TN}}{(\mathrm{TP}+\mathrm{FP}+\mathrm{TN}+\mathrm{FN})} \right\} \tag{4}$$

6 Results and Discussion

In this work, we classified the histopathological cancer images as benign or malignant at multilevel magnification using a transfer learning strategy in conjunction with the Relu activation function. The last dense layer of the proposed model uses the Softmax function as a classifier. the proposed architectrue divided the dataset into 3 form. The model was trained using 80% of the training data, verified over the validation data 10%, and then tested using the test data 10%. Tables 1, 3, 4 and 5 presents the model's post-test differential performance matrices. We get the highest F1-score at 100X magnification level in both the classs from both the propose model. 0.94, 0.88 for benign and 0.94,

0.87 for malignant class through ENet, MNet respectively as shown in Figs. 3 and 4. Similarly getting the highest average F1-score 0.94, 0.88 at 100X through ENet, MNet respectively as shown in Fig. 5. Getting the highest accuracy 0.94, 0.88 at 100X through ENet, MNet respectively as shown in Fig. 6. Comparisons between the existing models and the proposed model are displayed in Table 2.

Table 1. The proposed model's accuracy at various magnification levels.

	Accuracy			
Model	40X	100X	200X	400X
MNet	0.84	0.88	0.81	0.81
ENet	0.90	0.94	0.89	0.83

Table 2. Compared to existing models.

Reference	Model	Dataset	Accuracy
[17]	Hybrid DL model	Histopath images	0.86
[19]	ResNet50	Histopath images	0.79
Proposed	**Mnet**	Histopath images	0.88
	Enet	Histopath images	0.94

Table 3. Proposed model precision and recall at different magnification levels.

Model	Class	Precision	Recall	Precision	Recall	Precision	Recall	Precision	Recall
		40X		100X		200X		400X	
MNet	Benign	0.87	0.80	0.87	0.88	0.82	0.81	0.77	0.88
	Malignant	0.82	0.88	0.88	0.87	0.81	0.82	0.86	0.74
ENet	Benign	0.96	0.84	0.96	0.92	0.91	0.86	0.77	0.95
	Malignant	0.85	0.96	0.92	0.96	0.87	0.91	0.94	0.71

Table 4. Proposed model F1-Score at different magnification levels of benign class.

	F1-Score Benign class			
Model	40X	100X	200X	400X
MNet	0.84	0.88	0.81	0.82
ENet	0.89	0.94	0.89	0.85

Table 5. Proposed model F1-Score at different magnification levels of malignant class.

	F1-Score Malignant class			
Model	40X	100X	200X	400X
MNet	0.85	0.87	0.81	0.79
ENet	0.90	0.94	0.89	0.81

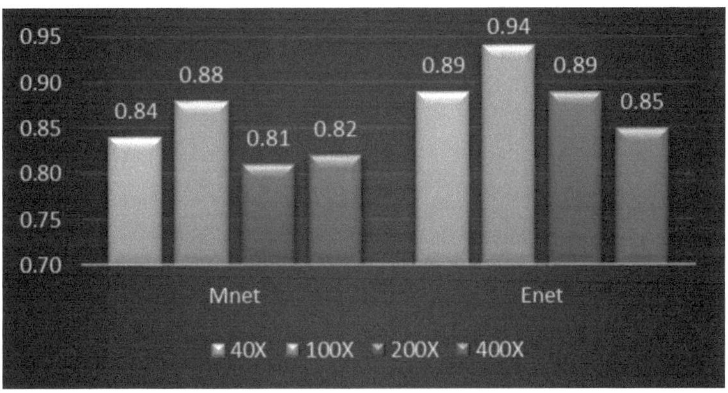

Fig. 3. Cross-magnification analysis of F1-scores in benign class.

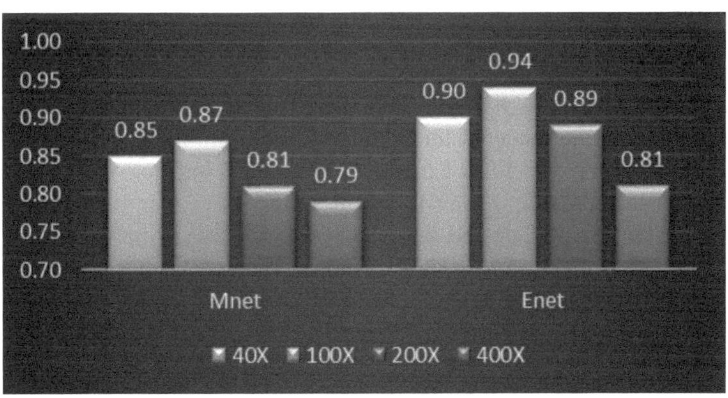

Fig. 4. Cross-magnification analysis of F1-scores in malignant class.

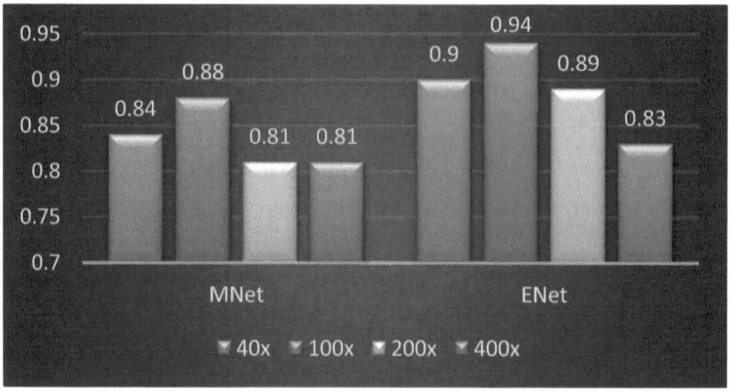

Fig. 5. Cross-magnification analysis of average F1-scores in both class

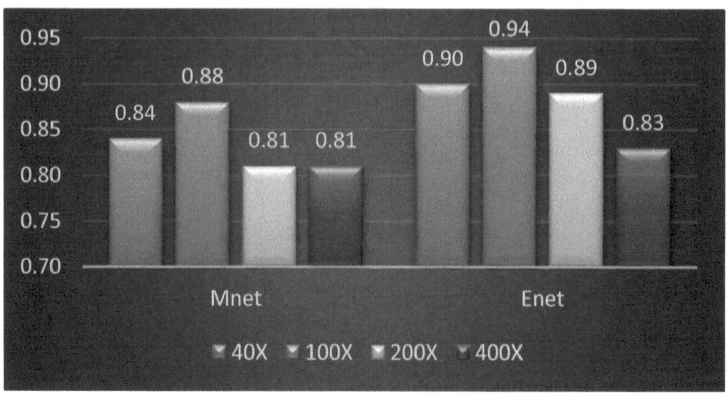

Fig. 6. Cross-magnification analysis of accuracy.

7 Conclusion

The classification of breast cancer holds significant importance within the medical domain. In this study, we introduce our model, MNet, and ENet, which leverage transfer learning techniques, confirming encouraging improvements in classification using the assessment criteria accuracy, F1 score, precision, and recall. With application of these methodologies holds the potential for enhancing breast cancer diagnosis and medical interventions, ultimately benefiting patients. However, it is imperative to conduct further research on transfer learning models to enhance their efficacy in breast cancer classification. Moreover, the privacy and safety concerns of patients must be meticu-lously addressed when implementing deep learning models for medical diagnostic applications.

Funding Statement This research work is financially supported by DHR, ICMR, New Delhi.

References

1. Jacques Ferlay, M.E., Siegel, R.L., Isabelle Soerjomataram, M.D., Ahmedin Jemal, D.V.M.. Global Cancer Statistics 2022: GLOBOCAN Estimates of Incidence and Mortality Worldwide for 36 Cancers in 185 Countries (2024)
2. https://www.cnbctv18.com/healthcare/apollo-hospitals-health-of-the-nation-2024-report-sounds-alarm-on-rising-cancer-rates-19393478.htm. Last accessed 8 Apr 2024
3. Saini, A., Kumar, M., Bhatt, S., Saini, V., Malik, A.: Cancer causes and treatments. Int. J. Pharm. Sci. Res. **11**, 3121–3134 (2020)
4. Boutry, J. et al.: The evolution and ecology of benign tumors. Biochimica et Biophysica Acta (BBA)-Reviews on Cancer. **1877**(1), 188643 (2022)
5. Crosby, D., et al.: Early detection of cancer. Science. **375, no. 6586**, eaay9040 (2022)
6. Lee, C.H., et al.: Breast cancer screening with imaging: recommendations from the Society of Breast Imaging and the ACR on the use of mammography, breast MRI, breast ultrasound, and other technologies for the detection of clinically occult breast cancer. J. Am. Coll. Radiol. **7**(1), 18–27 (2010)
7. Reed, M.C., Amy, E., Kalinowski, L., Simpson, P.T., Lakhani, S.R.: Invasive lobular carcinoma of the breast: the increasing importance of this special subtype. Breast Cancer Res. **23**, 1–16 (2021)
8. Hussain, M., Cunnick, G.H.: Management of lobular carcinoma in-situ and atypical lobular hyperplasia of the breast–a review. Eur. J. Surg. Oncol. **37**(4), 279–289 (2011)
9. The American Cancer Society. www.cancer.org/cancer/types/breast-cancer/about/types-of-breastcancer/invasive-breast-cancer. Last accessed 8 Mar 2024
10. Kumar, G., Alqahtani, H.: Deep learning-based cancer detection-recent developments, trend and challenges. CMES-Comput. Model. Eng. Sci. **130**(3) (2022)
11. Sharma, S., Mehra, R.: Conventional machine learning and deep learning approach for multi-classification of breast cancer histopathology images—a comparative insight. J. Digit. Imaging. **33**(3), 632–654 (2020)
12. Zahoor, S., Lali, I.U., Khan, M.A., Javed, K., Mehmood, W.: Breast cancer detection and classification using traditional computer vision techniques: a comprehensive review. Curr. Med. Imag. **16**(10), 1187–1200 (2020)
13. Deepa, B.G., Senthil, S.: Predicting invasive ductal carcinoma tissues in whole slide images of breast cancer by using convolutional neural network model and multiple classifiers. Multimed. Tools Appl. **81**(6), 8575–8596 (2022)
14. Singh, R., Ahmed, T., Kumar, A., Singh, A.K., Pandey, A.K., Singh, S.K.: Imbalanced breast cancer classification using transfer learning. IEEE/ACM Trans. Comput. Biol. Bioinform. **18**(1), 83–93 (2020)
15. Amakdouf, H., Zouhri, A., El Mallahi, M., Tahiri, A., Chenouni, D., Qjidaa, H.: Artificial intelligent classification of biomedical color image using quaternion discrete radial Tchebichef moments. Multimed. Tools Appl. **80**, 3173–3192 (2021)
16. Alruwaili, M., Gouda, W.: Automated breast cancer detection models based on transfer learning. Sensors. **22**(3), 876 (2022)
17. Singh, S., Kumar, R.: Breast cancer detection from histopathology images with deep inception and residual blocks. Multimed. Tools Appl. **81**(4), 5849–5865 (2022)

18. P&D Laboratory – Pathological Anatomy and Cytopathology, P., Brazil Breast Cancer Histopathological Database (BreakHis). https://web.inf.ufpr.br/vri/databases/breast-cancer-histopathological-database-breakhis/. Last accessed 15 Feb 2024
19. Chapala, H.R., Sujatha, B.: ResNet: detection of invasive ductal carcinoma in breast histopathology images using deep learning. In: In 2020 International Conference on Electronics and Sustainable Communication Systems (ICESC), pp. 60–67. IEEE (2020)

Author Index

M. Paprzycki et al. (Eds.): ICACIS 2024, CCIS 2405, pp. 489–490, 2027.
https://doi.org/10.1007/978-3-032-30990-7

MIX
Papier aus verantwortungsvollen Quellen
Paper from responsible sources
FSC® C105338

If you have any concerns about our products,
you can contact us on
ProductSafety@springernature.com

In case Publisher is established outside the EU,
the EU authorized representative is:
Springer Nature Customer Service Center GmbH
Europaplatz 3, 69115 Heidelberg, Germany

Printed by Libri Plureos GmbH
in Hamburg, Germany